Circle of Friends

ALSO BY SWĀMĪ B. V. TRIPURĀRI

Aesthetic Vedanta
Ancient Wisdom for Modern Ignorance
Bhagavad-gītā: Its Feeling and Philosophy
Form of Beauty
Gopāla-tāpanī Upaniṣad
Joy of Self
Rasa: Love Relationships in Transcendence
Sacred Preface
Śikṣāṣṭakam of Śrī Caitanya
Śrī Guru-paramparā
Tattva-sandarbha

Circle of Friends

SWĀMĪ B. V. TRIPURĀRI

DARSHAN
darshanpress.com
PHILO, CALIFORNIA

Darshan Press
Philo, California
darshanpress.com
info@darshanpress.com

Cover artwork: Mahaveer Swami
Cover design: Gurunisṭhā
Copyediting: Haridāsa and Lalitā-sakhī
Indexing: Gauravāṇī and Madana Gopāla
Interior book design and substantive editing: Vṛndāraṇya
Proofreading and Sanskrit editing: Lalitā-sakhī

ISBN: 978-0-9973773-3-0
Library of Congress Control Number: 2024936303

Printed by Imaging Hawaii in CN

vande 'haṁ śrī rāma kṛṣṇau
abhaya caraṇau sakhau
sukhadau paramānandau
sundarau subala priyau

I offer my *ātmā* to Rāma and Kṛṣṇa,
friends at whose feet one becomes fearless. These beautiful *sakhās*, so dear to Subala, bestow *sukha* and *paramānanda*.

To my Prabhupāda,
who is *abhaya caraṇāravinda*.

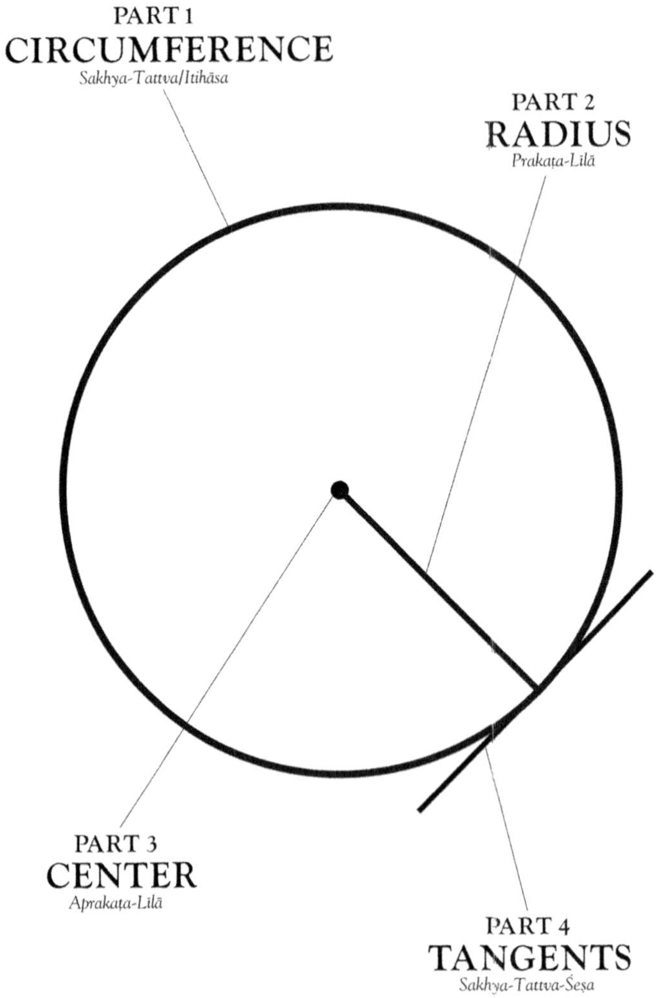
PART 1
CIRCUMFERENCE
Sakhya-Tattva/Itihāsa
PART 2
RADIUS
Prakaṭa-Līlā
PART 3
CENTER
Aprakaṭa-Līlā
PART 4
TANGENTS
Sakhya-Tattva-Śeṣa

CONTENTS

Preface

A sacred preface should include a prayer—*namaskāra*—in praise of the deity that presides over the pages of a *smṛti* text. In this text, that deity is a duad, the *yugala* Kṛṣṇa-Balarāma, and this is its *namaskāra* verse:

> I serve the shelter-giving, youthful Śrī Śrī Rāma-Kṛṣṇa. Of white and black complexion, both beautiful and benevolent, they are constituted of condensed *prema-rasa*. Masters of great masters, these two brothers live in cow pastures! They are the very life therein of both the cowherds and the cows and as such they are absorbed in astounding *līlās* with their *gopas*, each of whose person is composed of *praṇaya*.

What then in essence does the text concern? This too is revealed at the text's outset in a *vastu-nirdeśa* verse.

> What can be said about the gift of Gaura—Śyāma's Vraja *līlā*—about which the Upaniṣads are stunned into near silence and left to mumble barely coherent phrases such as "*śyāmāc chavalaṁ prapadye śavalāc chyāmaṁ prapadye*"?[1] What then to speak of the giver of this gift, Gaura himself, his *nāma, rūpa, guṇa, pārṣadas*, and *līlā*? And of the *avadhūta*, Nitāi, who gave us Gaura, his gift, and more? Nityānanda Rāma personifies the *sakhya-rasa* explained in depth by Śrī Rūpa, and his pupils shared it near and far, serving

1. *Chāndogya Upaniṣad* 8.13.1: "By the help of black (*śyāma*/Kṛṣṇa), we shall be introduced to the service of white (*śavala*/Rādhā); by the help of white (*śavala*/Rādhā), we shall be introduced to the service of black (*śyāma*/Kṛṣṇa)."

> Kṛṣṇa-Balarāma. Surely that is what friends are for, but more, that friend is best who with sympathy reminds Śyāma of the girl that he adores. *Jaya* Rādhe! *Jaya* Śyāma!—*gāḍhopakārī smṛti-daḥ priyāṇām.*[2]

And last but far from the least, such a bold undertaking should offer a blessing to its sympathetic reader—its *adhikārin*—in an *āśīrvāda* verse.

> By the grace of Nitāi, may the ardent readers of this book attain the *prema* they idealize, be it *sakhya* or *mādhurya*. For, *heno nitāi vine bhāi, rādhā-kṛṣṇa paite nāi!*[3] But to those disposed toward *sakhya-prema* as a result of having received through *sādhu-saṅga* such impressions, as did Brahmā of yore[4]—and, more, the mercantile community of Bengal and beyond—may this book serve to assist them in their journey of *sādhana* to their *sakhya-rasa sādhya.*

The parallels between the *seva* of my *gurudeva* in the twentieth century and the divine campaign of Śrī Nityānanda Rāma during the budding stages of the Caitanya *sampradāya* are many and striking. As do many other Vaiṣṇavas, I see the broad outreach of my *gurudeva* to be *seva* that was especially empowered by Nitāi. A.C. Bhaktivedanta Swami Prabhupāda appeared in the world in the extended Saptagrāma community that was personally blessed by Nitāi, and in his adulthood he petitioned Kṛṣṇa for a blessing of *śakti*, the likes of which we see in Nitāi.

In his heartfelt petition in poetry and prayer, he artfully secured in no uncertain terms Kṛṣṇa's blessing to do the bidding of his *guru*. Speaking to Kṛṣṇa as he did with regard to his friend's dependence upon Rādhā and reminding him of such, he placed before his comrade a request for the *śakti* to deliver *gaura-vānī* to the West in service to his *guru*, a member of the group of Rādhā's *sakhīs*. How could his good friend refuse a request to please a maidservant of his dearmost?[5] Thus Śrī Kṛṣṇa-candra sent the *śakti* of Nityānanda Rāma to my *gurudeva* and in doing so inadvertently also released a tidal wave of *sakhya-rati* in our times just as Nitāi himself released in the course of directing all eyes to Gaura-candra and Gaura's

2. *Bṛhad-bhāgavatāmṛta* 1.7.128.

3. "Without the grace of Nitāi, no one can attain the service of Rādhā-Kṛṣṇa." Narottama dāsa Ṭhākura, *Manaḥ-śikṣā*.

4. See chapters 8, 29, and 30 of this book.

5. See his "*Bhagavān Kṛṣṇera Pāda-padme Prārthanā*" penned aboard the *Jaladuta*. Also see chapter 2 of this book for further details.

quest for Rādhā *dāsyam* that made this highest ideal of *prema* accessible to anyone and everyone.

Nitāi gave Gaura to the world, but in doing so he also effortlessly attracted a following of his own. And so, *sakhya-rasa* plays a supportive role in the Caitanya *sampradāya*, even as this aesthetic rapture of fraternal love is itself contagious. From time to time it will surface and remind us of itself and also of its camaraderie with *mādhurya-rasa*, and in its highest reach of its capacity to mix with a drop of *mādhurya*'s sweetness.[6]

Here I write in the service of my *gurudeva* about such inexhaustible topics, of which by his grace I never tire. Should others find this interesting, in me they have a friend. However, not everyone will see as I do herein, despite the rigorous effort I have undertaken to support the thrust of this book with *śāstra-yukti*. No harm. There is more than one way to gaze at the sapphire-like gem of Śyāmasundara and his associates. If other opinions are equally well supported—*tathāstu*, I welcome them. Best not to have any enemies, if not only friends.

And to the friends that repeatedly urged me to write this book, I bow. I was at first shy to embrace their encouragement, but having proceeded to publish I have found that expressing myself has humbled me and also served to nurture my faith and conviction. From spiritual conviction comes taste and then attachment to the object of one's love, which in turn grows into longing to attain that love. Then in the pursuit of fraternal love for Gopāla Kṛṣṇa, *sakhya-prema*'s primary characteristic of confidence, *viśrambha*, and also intimacy in friendship, *praṇaya*, with Gopāla Kṛṣṇa, free from hesitation, is born. To put it another way, ultimately this is not something to be shy about.

Of course *bhāva* is like a candle in one's heart that one must protect lest the wind of drawing undue attention to oneself blows it out. But in order that this candle may be lit to begin with, the candle itself must be in place. To love Kṛṣṇa with *viśrambha* in *sakhya-praṇaya*, one will be well served by first understanding the theology and philosophy that underlies this love. Add to this an acquaintance with the playful *līlās* of Bhagavān, both *prakaṭa* and *aprakaṭa*, in which this love is showcased, and one has at least put that candle in place. May this book serve that purpose, and may that candle be lit through a concerted effort to accrue grace. And may its flame be protected with humility and the spiritual confidence that is the polar opposite of *pratiṣṭhā*.

6. Here I refer to *narma-sakhā-bhāva*, discussed in detail in chapter 5.

Introduction

The virtues of fraternal love are many. Among them is its semblance of spirituality, in which friendship fosters a healthy sense of independence and a rising above nature and emotion in ways that parental and erotic love do not. Anglican theologian C. S. Lewis suggests that in the "luminous, tranquil, rational" world of friendship—"a relationship freely chosen" rather than biologically mandated—one rises above the biology driving eros and parental love; thus, among all these loves, friendship alone seems to "raise you to the level of gods or angels."[1] True friendship is also brutally honest. Furthermore, only when eros turns into friendship does the relationship meaningfully endure. If parental affection is to endure, it must also turn into friendship between parents and their adult children, and the love of the student for his or her teacher is best when it borders on friendship.

And while amorous love is ultimately for two alone and three is a crowd, fraternal love is enhanced as the number of true friends increases:

> Two friends delight to be joined by a third, and three by a fourth, if only the newcomer is qualified to become a real friend. They can then say, as the blessed souls say in Dante, "Here comes one who will augment our loves." For in this love "to divide is not to take away." . . . We possess each friend not less but more as the number of those with whom we share him increases. In this, friendship exhibits a glorious "nearness by resemblance" to Heaven itself where the very

1. C. S. Lewis, *The Four Loves* (Beijing: Foreign Language Teaching and Research Press, 2011), loc. 1463, Kindle.

multitude of the blessed (which no man can number) increases the fruition which each has of God.[2]

But if worldly friendship represents a semblance of divine love more than any other type of love in the here and now, is there the possibility of divine friendship itself? Is there any scope for fraternal love of God? If so, where shall we turn to learn about it? Eastward, to be sure, where the faces of God are countless and the ways of divine love manyfold.

In this pursuit, let us for good reason be guided by the brightest star among the sacred texts of the eastern sky—the *Bhāgavata*. The *Bhāgavata* is a Purāṇa—the *Bhāgavata Purāṇa*—and while the Veda speaks to us as a king would to his subjects and the flowery *kāvya* (drama/poetry) speaks to us as a lover, the Purāṇas speak to us as one friend would to another. Yes, the *Bhāgavata* speaks to us as a friend. However, it also speaks to us in the other two voices as well, and this is but one example of why it is considered the brightest star of revelation. It is *śruti-sāram*, *amalaṁ purāṇam*, and above all it is *rasam ālayam*.[3]

While different Purāṇas focus on one face of God or another, the *Bhāgavata* is a tour de force on the many faces of God and the face from which all other faces follow in response to the measure of love they correspond with. Nowhere in the Purāṇas is the central Hindu theological notion of *avatāra-tattva* so thoroughly explored as it is in the *Bhāgavata*. Therein we find a condensed, concise discourse on both the countless manifestations of God and the love that corresponds with them evaluated objectively.

And with regard to feelings of fraternal love, the *Bhāgavata* echoes the *Muṇḍaka Upaniṣad*'s faint *śruti* reference to friendship, wherein the *ātmā* and Paramātmā are compared to two birds in the tree of the body who share a relationship as intimate, friendly companions (*dvā suparṇā sayujā sakhāyā*).[4] The endearing humanlike, metropolitan-based friendship between warrior Arjuna and Godhead Kṛṣṇa that is central to the *Gītopaniṣad* is also showcased in the *Bhāgavata*, as is Kṛṣṇa's fraternal love for Arjuna's wife, Draupadī, his brother Bhīmasena, and others. We also find the Purāṇic face of God who presides over the *rasa* of friendship—Vāmana—and his fraternity with celestial Indra. But above all we find the intimate friendship

2. Lewis, loc. 1531–1533.

3. *Śrīmad Bhāgavatam* 1.2.3 (the essence—cream—of the Veda); 12.13.18 (the purest Purāṇa); 1.1.3 (the reservoir of *rasa*, which is the soul of poetry). Thus, the text contains all three voices.

4. *Muṇḍaka Upaniṣad* 3.1.1; *Śrīmad Bhāgavatam* 10.2.27, 11.11.6.

between Gopāla Kṛṣṇa and his cowherd friends in the poetry of the text's tenth book that causes its primary speaker, Śukadeva, to pass out in ecstasy, rendering him temporarily unable to continue his *līlā* narrative of *sakhya-rasa*.[5] And here we find another meaning of the text's "*rasam ālayam*."[6]

While Kṛṣṇa and his pastoral friends are described in other Purāṇas, the *Bhāgavata* alone showcases the emotional life of intimate fraternal love of God such that the attentive reader can feel the text inviting one to enter into this sacred realm of *sakhya-rasa*, as it also invites its readers alternatively to embrace either *dāsya-rasa*, *vātsalya-rasa*, or more so, paramour love in *mādhurya-rasa*. While the *Bhāgavata* is centered on the possibility of romantic love of God, *sakhya-rasa*, unlike *dāsya-rasa* and *vātsalya-rasa*, is compatible with and in many respects an assistant to divine eroticism. Thus, it holds a special place in the text. However, should one feel the call of fraternal love and its attraction to cowherd Kṛṣṇa, how shall one proceed to get dressed for the occasion?

The answer to this question is addressed only in the Caitanya *sampradāya*. However, it is overshadowed by the lineage's attention to the call of paramour love of God. *Sakhya-rasa* itself stands in the shadow of *mādhurya-rasa*, even as *sakhya-rasa*'s influence is unprecedented in its effort to deliver the *Bhāgavata*'s invitation into *mādhurya-rasa*. Here of course I refer to Nityānanda Rāma in his *sakhya-praṇaya*, who gave *gopī-bhāva* to the world by giving us Gaura Kṛṣṇa.[7]

Thus, we have to look deeply within the Caitanya *sampradāya* to find the means to enter into intimate fraternal love of Kṛṣṇa, and this book seeks to assist interested devotees in doing so. Its success will be realized to the extent that it uncovers that which is hiding itself in plain sight: the fact that along with *mādhurya-rasa*, the dramatic stage in the theater of the Caitanya *sampradāya* alternatively offers its actors a supporting role in *sakhya-rasa*, and all the assistance one needs is there to be taken advantage of. One simply has to look for it.

5. *Śrīmad Bhāgavatam* 10.12.44.

6. As noted above, *rasam ālayam* means "abode of *rasa*." However, *ālaya* also means, "including (*a*) the bliss of liberation (*laya*)." And the highest form of liberation is *prema* constituted of great attachment to Kṛṣṇa, which includes *pralaya*—passing out—the eighth involuntary ecstasy (*sāttvika-bhāva*). Thus, the text tells us that one should drink the *rasa* of the *Bhāgavata* until one experiences the *sāttvika-bhāva pralaya*. And upon regaining external consciousness one should continue to drink the *Bhāgavata*'s *rasa*, repeating this cycle again and again. See the commentaries of Jīva Goswāmī and Viśvanātha Cakravartī Ṭhākura.

7. *Caitanya-bhāgavata* 3.5.303.

Circle of Friends is divided into four sections. Parts one and four focus on the philosophical and theological underpinnings of *sakhya-rasa*. Sections two and three focus on the *prakaṭa* and *aprakaṭa-līlās*, respectively, from the vantage point of *sakhya-rati*. Notably, the latter section explores *sakhya-rasa* influenced by *mādhurya-rasa*, specifically focusing on the distinctive role of the *priya-narma-sakhā*, a unique insight found exclusively within the lineage of Śrī Caitanya.[8] Each of the first three sections of the text is preceded by its own introduction as well. The fourth section—Tangents—explores in greater detail philosophical/theological points raised in the main body of the book.

All of the Bengali and Sanskrit translations in *Circle of Friends* are mine unless otherwise stated. In this regard a number of the translations are not literal. Often, literal translations leave much to be desired in terms of conveying the spirit and intention of the prose or poetry. Thus, they require commentaries to bring home the author's intention and feeling for the subject. Literal translations can also be awkward and fail to convey the captivating beauty and eloquence of the original language. Furthermore, fluency in the language does not necessarily equate with cultural fluency and thus linguistic fluency alone may still keep the reader outside looking in, while the intention of the text is to bring the reader inside the circle of the text's concern. This is especially so when the text is concerned with the *bhakti-rasa* of Kṛṣṇa *līlā*.

While poetry gives rise to worldly *rasa*, it is not the cause of *bhakti-rasa*. However, poetry through which *bhakti-rasa* expresses itself can serve as an aid to attaining *rati* oneself. Such is the poetry of the *Bhāgavata* and the Goswāmī *līlā-granthas* that elaborate upon it. May the sympathetic hearts of my English readers with affinity for *sakhya-rasa* experience this book as an elaboration on what the *Bhāgavata* and the Goswāmī *granthas* have shared with regard to the *sakhya-rasa* of Kṛṣṇa's Vraja *līlā*. The text's translations are perhaps better described as "renderings," and as stated in some sections, "adaptations," in which commentary is woven into the rendering. English poetic license and modern cultural sensibilities are also invoked at

8. In *Sāhitya-darpaṇa*, which Rūpa Goswāmī draws upon to erect his theater of *bhakti-rasa*, Viśvanātha Kavirāja (3.39–40) lists only four typical companions of the romantic lover: the *pīṭhamarda* (principal companion of the drama's hero), the *ceṭa* (servant-friend), *viṭa* (cunning rogue companion), and *vidūṣaka* (buffoon), to which Rūpa Goswāmī adds the *priya-narma-sakhā* (*Ujjvala-nīlamaṇi* 2.1). But here I include Caṇḍīdāsa within the lineage, even as he precedes it historically, for Śrī Caitanya drew considerable inspiration from his poetry. According to *Subala Maṅgala*, Caṇḍīdāsa himself is considered to be an incarnation of Subala-sakhā, and in Śrī Rūpa's texts Subala is the foremost *narma-sakhā*.

times—all for the purpose of displacing the reader from the outside looking in to place him or her squarely within the circle of Kṛṣṇa's friends.

But literary considerations and their limitations aside, it should be underscored that the very purpose of the *Bhāgavata* is to foster one's own feelings that arise from following, not fabricating. God knows I have followed. Whatever I have felt is but his grace and that of my *guru*. And in the service of *śrī guru* I have also shared those fraternal feelings in these pages.

If an author can say, as Mitchell sings,[9] "Part of you [the original person] pours out of me in these lines from time to time," one can say that in writing about it one has understood the *Bhāgavata* and that two souls—Kṛṣṇa as the holy wine of *rasa*[10] and oneself as *ātmā*—have touched and thus loved. This is the perfection of *Bhāgavata kīrtana*.

Still, no book is perfect and, indeed, the *Bhāgavata* says this about itself![11] However, can an author actually err if his or her only intention is to praise Kṛṣṇa and his friends? May the learned devotees decide with regard to this book. That said, learning is one thing, while loving is something more. It is the end of learning, without which nothing has been learned. *Circle of Friends* is about loving, and there is no person more loveable than Kṛṣṇa. Encircled by his friends, he is only that much more so. Indeed, to see the young herdsmen, Śyāma and Rāma, surrounded by their friends as they herd their cows on Mount Govardhana is the perfection of the eyes, for Kṛṣṇa shines more brightly in their company. May readers come to this conclusion. It is certainly Rādhā's conviction,[12] and she herself is the highest reach of love for Kṛṣṇa—*mahābhāva-svarūpiṇī*. He as a herdsman is her hero. She will not have him any other way—not as a princely knight in shining armor riding upon an elephant, but only as a so-called prince among cowherds running behind his bovines.

Within your meditation, imagine this: A *cowherd prince*. And how among his constituent cowherd friends he shines more brightly, he who is himself the light of lights. What then must be their love? And especially the friendship of those privy to his love for Rādhā. Indeed, the mere sight of Subala is an excitant for Rādhā's *rasa-mādhurī*.[13] Surely, we should follow her lead, if not in one way, why not another? *Jaya* Rāma! *Jaya* Kṛṣṇa! *Jaya* Rādhe!

9. Mitchell, Joni, "A Case of You," *Blue, The Reprise Albums (1968–1971)*.

10. *Taittirīya Upaniṣad* 2.7.1—*raso vai saḥ*—identifies Brahman/Kṛṣṇa himself as "*rasa*."

11. *Śrīmad Bhāgavatam* 1.5.11.

12. *Śrīmad Bhāgavatam* 10.21.7.

13. *Bhakti-rasāmṛta-sindhu* 3.3.49 and *Ujjvala-nīlamaṇi* 10.85.

PART I

Circumference

Sakhya-Tattva/Itihāsa

1

Śrī Rūpa and Nityānanda Rāma

A circle consists of the center point, which is the locus equidistant from all the points along the edge of the circle; the circumference, which forms the outer edge of the circle; and the radius, which connects the circumference to the center point in a straight line. In the circle of Kṛṣṇa and his friends in Vraja, we can consider the center point to be Kṛṣṇa. The *tattva* of Kṛṣṇa *bhakti* from the vantage point of fraternal love can be considered the circumference or boundary between that which is included in the circle and that which is not. The radius of the circle consists of the innumerable cowherd boyfriends of Kṛṣṇa, who are inseparable from him, just as a radius cannot exist without a connection to the center.

Approaching from the outside of any given circle, the most direct way to access the center is to enter through the circumference and then travel inward along the radius. In the same way, one has to approach the circle of Kṛṣṇa and his friends first through *tattva*, which will lead to taking shelter of the eternal associates of Kṛṣṇa, who form the radius and thus link the circumference to the brightly radiating nucleus of Kṛṣṇa.

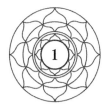

To continue the circle metaphor in relation to the contents of this book, in the first part we will examine the circle's circumference, or *tattva*: what *sakhya-rasa* consists of (*sambandha*), the means to attain it (*abhidheya*), and the nature of *priya-narma-sakhā-bhāva* in particular (*prayojana*). In this part, we will also briefly explore the history of *sakhya-rasa* as it has manifested in this world through the Gauḍīya *sampradāya*. In the second part, we will move along the radius of Kṛṣṇa's pastimes with his friends in the manifest (*prakaṭa*) *līlā* recorded in the *Śrīmad Bhāgavatam*, which serves as a portal to the unmanifest *līlā*. In the third part of this book, we will enter the center, consisting of the eternally occurring daily eightfold pastimes of Kṛṣṇa and his *sakhās* in the unmanifest (*aprakaṭa*) *līlā* viewed through the lens of *narma-sakhā-bhāva*. After passing through the radius and center of the circle, we will find ourselves in the circumference again in the form of tangents, the final part of this book, which reflects further on the *tattva* underlying *sakhya-rasa* and the means to attain it.

But before we begin to penetrate the circle through the circumference of *tattva*, let us express our indebtedness to Rūpa Goswāmī for his unique insights into *sakhya-rasa*. Those who follow his lead in this regard are his *anugas*—*rūpānugas*—in the broadest sense of the term.[1] Although such devotees do not follow the same internal mood of Rūpa Goswāmī, appearing as he does in the Vraja *līlā* as Śrī Rūpa-mañjarī,[2] they have made the understanding of *sakhya-rasa* articulated by Rūpa Goswāmī in his *Bhakti-rasāmṛta-sindhu* their ideal. How can we possibly proceed without underscoring his overall contribution to the religious world and our allegiance to him?

The name Rūpa means "beauty" and the word *mañjarī* refers to a "bud or blossom." Thus, from an internal perspective, Rūpa Goswāmī is the budding beauty of Rādhā manifest as a maidservant of Śrī Rādhikā—Śrī Rūpa-mañjarī—whose body is formed out of *ujjvala-rasa*: *ujjvalamaya tanu.*[3] Given his internal reality, Rūpa Goswāmī is thus uniquely qualified to teach us about the inner world of *bhakti-rasa*. Furthermore, in our world Rūpa Goswāmī was well versed in classical Indian aesthetic theory. Accordingly, from both an internal and external perspective, Śrī Caitanya chose him as his principal exponent of a novel aesthetic form of Vedānta discourse that extols the virtue of *bhakti* as an end unto itself.

From the vantage point of Indian aesthetics, Rūpa Goswāmī sheds a very bright warm light on the Absolute. He convincingly concludes that when the omniscient, omnipresent Absolute is fully experienced, he is the

1. The term *rūpānuga* first appears in the writing of Śrī Rūpa's follower Raghunātha dāsa Goswāmī. In the final stanza of his *Manaḥ-śikṣā*, Dāsa Goswāmījī invokes this term, identifying himself as a follower (*anuga*) of Rūpa Goswāmī and his group (*yūtha*). Raghunātha dāsa arguably refers to following Rūpa Goswāmī in terms of his teaching as well as his inner life as the leader among Śrī Rādhā's *mañjarīs*.

2. Rūpa-mañjarī is the foremost handmaiden of Śrī Rādhikā.

3. *Prema-bhakti-candrikā* 8. *Ujjvala* is Rūpa Goswāmī's chosen word for Bharata Muni's *śṛṅgāra-rasa* of romanticism. *Ujjvala* and *mādhurya* are most commonly invoked by Gauḍīya *ācāryas* with reference to this classical *rasa*. Both terms have also been used by earlier *rasa* theorists.

lovestruck dancing cowherd God of the *Bhāgavata Purāṇa*—Śrī Kṛṣṇa, the perfect object of love experienced in the meditative mind. And one who rises above the demands of the mind and senses—the call of the wild that knows no reason—as Śrī Rūpa has, is a *goswāmī*. Thus, in Rūpa we have a *goswāmī* who is well reasoned yet wild about Kṛṣṇa.

Śrī Rūpa's transcendent romantic feelings for Kṛṣṇa are unique in the realm of spiritual eroticism in that they are decidedly platonic.[4] Rūpa-mañjarī considers Kṛṣṇa the perfect object of selfless romantic love but also understands that only Rādhā's love for Kṛṣṇa can fully satisfy Kṛṣṇa. Śrī Rūpa strives only to bring about the union of Rādhā and Kṛṣṇa, positioning herself as a maidservant of Rādhā and, arguably, a female romantic friend of Kṛṣṇa in the land of *līlā*. In other words, Rūpa-mañjarī's romantic feelings for Kṛṣṇa are subjugated by her attitude of service to Rādhā, which in turn affords her the most intimate access to the romanticism of Rādhā and Kṛṣṇa in that she is able to vicariously experience Rādhā's love for Kṛṣṇa. Thus, Rūpa-mañjarī is also the servant/friend of Rādhā, who favors her friend Rādhā slightly more than she does Kṛṣṇa.[5]

As a female friend of Kṛṣṇa, Rūpa-mañjarī is well acquainted with his male friends, especially those who are also sympathetic to the romantic plight of her combined object of romantic love, Rādhā and Kṛṣṇa. And as we shall see, it is these sympathetic male friends of Kṛṣṇa—their fraternal love for him—that we have highlighted within the circle of his friends.

There are, of course, other mystics born in Bhārata who have poeticized about fraternal love of God in the form of Gopāla Kṛṣṇa, and some of them have, arguably, attained it. But more than anyone else, Śrī Rūpa has opened the lotus of this form of divine love with his illuminating sunlike discourse. In doing so, he has enabled *sādhakas* to examine the petals of fraternal love of God and equipped them to systematically pursue it.

4. See *Caitanya-caritāmṛta* 2.8.207. This verse applies to the *mañjarīs*' love: they never personally desire union with Kṛṣṇa, who takes more pleasure in their resistance to his occasional advances because it underscores their dedication to Rādhā. However, some modern devotees believe that *mañjarīs* do on rare occasions give in to Kṛṣṇa's advances, at least partially. *Kṛṣṇa-bhāvanāmṛta* 13.34–37, *Muktā-carita* 152, and *Vṛndāvana-mahimāmṛta* 16.94 have been interpreted by such devotees as evidence. However, I do not believe that any of these sections provide definitive support for this notion.

5. In his *Vilāpa-kusumāñjali* 16, Raghunātha dāsa Goswāmī famously prays not for *sakhya* with his mistress, but rather for *dāsya*. This *dāsya* borders on *sakhya*, and thus the *mañjarī*'s love for Rādhā is considered an exalted form of *suhṛt-rati* (love of the friend) known as *bhāvollāsa*. See *Bhakti-rasāmṛta-sindhu* 2.5.128 for an explanation of *bhāvollāsa*.

Śrī Rūpa tells us that the way to attain *sakhya-rasa* is *rāgānugā-bhakti* and within that *sambandhānugā-bhakti*, leading to *sakhya*'s *praṇaya*, *prema*, *sneha*, and *rāga*, as well as even to the possibility of *anurāga* and *mahābhāva*, all of which are discussed in detail in our circle's circumference.[6]

Śrī Rūpa reveals four basic divisions of devotees within *sakhya-rasa* and explains the transpsychological makeup of the members of each of the four divisions, his descriptions replete with examples from the greater body of the Hindu scriptural canon. He sheds light on the nature of *sakhya-rasa* in union and in separation. He also reveals which *rasas* are compatible with *sakhya-rasa* and which are incompatible with it. And last but far from least, he reveals how Gopāla Kṛṣṇa is experienced by those who approach him in friendship. Thus, Śrī Rūpa's insight into the nature of fraternal love of God is considerable and his contribution immense.

Rūpa Goswāmī refers to the divine *rasa* of fraternal love with the Sanskrit word *preyān* (friendly affection)—*preyo-bhakti-rasa*. This term is not seen in classical Indian aesthetic theory until the middle of the ninth century CE in the contribution of Rudraṭa.[7] Among *rasa* theorists, only Rudraṭa considers worldly friendship a *rasa*. However, Rūpa's *rasa* is otherworldly—*bhakti-rasa*—and includes fraternal love of God. Notably, friendship as an expression of *bhakti-rasa* requires an object of love that is more friendly than godly for such intimacy to take place: Kṛṣṇa rather than Nārāyaṇa. Thus, not only is Śrī Rūpa's *preyo-bhakti-rasa* otherworldly, as is the majesty of Vaikuṇṭha-loka, it corresponds with a realm that lies beyond Vaikuṇṭha—Goloka. Consequently, Śrī Rūpa's contribution is also unique.

However, there is someone even more important than Rūpa Goswāmī for Gauḍīya *sādhakas* pursuing the ideal of *sakhya-rasa*, someone he himself pays tribute to. Indeed, within the Gauḍīya *sampradāya*, no *rasa* can be attained without the blessing of Nityānanda Rāma, Śrī Caitanya's other self. Because Śrī Nitāicāṅda is the personification of *sakhya-rasa*, his fraternal love plays a significant yet subordinate role in the lineage. He gives *sakhya-bhāva* almost inadvertently while broadcasting the gift of Gaura Kṛṣṇa's Rādhā *dāsyam*.

From Nitāi and his immediate followers, the history of *sakhya-rasa* in the Gauḍīya *sampradāya* unfolds, as does the *sampradāya* itself. Nityānanda Rāma is Balarāma appearing in historical time, and through him and his followers we learn of the timeless origin of fraternal love of God. Nitāi

6. These terms are explained in chapters 4 and 5 of this book.

7. Maya Chattopadhyay, "Devotional Friendship (*Sakhya*) in the Vaiṣṇavism of the Early Caitanya Tradition" (master's thesis, Concordia University, 1995), 88.

saves us from thinking that Kṛṣṇa and Balarāma, the divine *yugala* of *sakhya-rasa*, are merely mythological figures. He does so by exhibiting the full measure of Balarāma's fraternal love for Kṛṣṇa. As a by-product, this love completely harnesses the human passions, a supernatural feat in and of itself. The divine fraternal love that Nitāi shares with us is real enough to retire the many myths of our minds. His *sakhya-bhāva* uncovers the *ātmā* and places before it the prospect of *prema—prema-prayojana*. Nityānanda Rāma appears in human society as the embodiment of fraternal love for Kṛṣṇa, and his history of disseminating fraternal love is thus important for those who cherish this ideal.

Therefore, we will turn our attention to this history of *sakhya-rasa* and Nityānanda Rāma as we begin to explore the circumference of the circle of Kṛṣṇa's friends in the chapter ahead. Then, at the conclusion of the book, we will return to Nityānanda Rāma once more by way of discussing Balarāma *tattva* and the necessity of *sakhya-rasa* in fulfilling Kṛṣṇa's desire for friendship. May Nityānanda Rāma allow us to enter this sacred circle and may Balarāma keep us eternally within its circumference.

2

A Brief History

While our focus in this book is to enter the circle of Kṛṣṇa's friends in his eternal Vraja *līlā*, the path to this *sakhya-prema* runs through the *līlā* of Gaura and Nityānanda Rāma as it expresses itself on earth in Śrī Navadvīpa-dhāma. It is from within the depths of Kṛṣṇa's Vraja *līlā* amid his *mahā-rāsa* with Śrī Rādhā and the other milkmaidens of Vraja that the seed of Gaura *līlā* sprouts, and as it blossoms on earth, it bears the fruit of Vraja *prema*, offering this *prema* to the world.

From Kṛṣṇa *līlā*, Gaura *līlā* emerges, as Kṛṣṇa expresses his indebtedness to the *gopikās* for their love, seeks to repay them, and desires to experience himself from Rādhikā's vantage point. But how will he repay the *gopīs* in kind for their love, which is its own reward? The best he can do to repay them for their saintliness is to become a saint himself and sing of their virtues, recruiting for their ranks. And in this effort, no one assists him more than Nityānanda Rāma. Although Balarāma does not directly participate in Kṛṣṇa's romantic life, he fervently engages in promoting Gaura and distributing *gopī-bhāva* when he descends in Gaura *līlā* as Nityānanda Rāma. As mentioned in the previous chapter, this in turn brings attention to himself and the *sakhya-prema* he personifies. Let us thus turn to Gaura *līlā* along with its sacred geography—Gauḍa-maṇḍala-bhūmi—and locate Balarāma therein in the form of Nityānanda Rāma along with his associates as we consider the history of *sakhya-rasa* in the Gauḍīya *sampradāya* in greater detail.

The sacred geography of Gaura-dhāma—*sādhaka-siddha-bhūmi*—is populated by many *siddhas* playing the role of *sādhakas*. Narottama Ṭhākura sings, *gaurāṅgera saṅgi-gaṇe nitya-siddha kori māne*: "The associates of Gaurāṅga are all eternally liberated."[1] Arguably, the most influential among them was Nityānanda Rāma, Balarāma appearing in Gaura *līlā*. Śrī Nityānanda appeared in Ekacakrā and entered the circle of Gaura's associates just after Śrī Caitanya began his school of *prema-saṅkīrtana* upon returning from Gayā in December of 1508.[2]

The Bengali poetry of Narottama dāsa informs us that the treasure of Goloka is its *prema* and that this *prema* was exported to this world, packaged in *nāma-saṅkīrtana—golokera prema-dhana harināma-saṅkīrtana*.[3] The principal bearers of this gift are Śrī Caitanya and Prabhu Nityānanda, whom Narottama identifies with Kṛṣṇa and Balarāma—*vrajendra-nandana yei śacī-suta haila sei, balarāma haila nitāi*.[4] This *saṅkīrtana* is very special. It is *saṅkīrtana* woven together with Vraja *prema* into a garland worn by Gaura and given to the world by Nitāi *bhāi*, without whose touch such *prema* is impossible to attain—*hena nitāi bine bhāi rādhā-kṛṣṇa pāite nāi*.[5] That which Gaura is all about Nitāi knows very well. Śrī Vṛndāvana dāsa writes that the *gopī-bhakti* described in *Śrīmad Bhāgavatam* was given to the world by Nitāicāṅda.[6] He gave it out of love for Gaura Kṛṣṇa and for the joy of participating openly in *mādhurya-rasa* by way of its dissemination, which he could not do as Balarāma in the Vraja *līlā*. Although Nityānanda Rāma did not articulate who Gaura-candra was in Vedāntic detail and locate him on the scriptural map, his conviction in Gaura's divinity and the treasure of Gaura's gift to the world was contagious. Thus, even before the founding *ācāryas* of the Gauḍīya *sampradāya* gathered and turned the waterfall of Gaura's ecstasy into an approachable lake of teachings, Nityānanda Rāma amassed a large following of devotees dedicated to Gaura-candra.

After arriving in Nadīyā, it was Nitāi who started the Gauḍīya *sampradāya* along the Gaṅgā delta. He did so with the help of his twelve eternal associates—the *dvādaśa-gopālas*. While Gaura had begun his nocturnal school of Kṛṣṇa *saṅkīrtana* in the courtyard of Śrīvāsa Ṭhākura, Nityānanda Rāma turned the focus from Kṛṣṇa to Gaura—Gaura Kṛṣṇa.

1. *Prārthanā*, "*Sāvaraṇa-śrī-gaura-mahimā*."

2. Gaura *līlā* dates mentioned in this chapter are derived from Janmajit Roy's *Theory of Avatāra and Divinity of Chaitanya* (New Delhi: Atlantic Publishers and Distributors, 2002).

3. *Prārthanā*, "*Iṣṭa-deve Vijñapti*."

4. *Prārthanā*, "*Iṣṭa-deve Vijñapti*."

5. *Prārthanā*, "*Manaḥ-śikṣā*."

6. *Caitanya-bhāgavata* 3.5.303.

Instead of repeating the teaching of Gaura to worship Kṛṣṇa, teach about Kṛṣṇa, and chant Kṛṣṇa *nāma*, Nitāi boldly declared, *bhaja gaurāṅga kaha gaurāṅga laha gaurāṅgera nāma re*: "Worship Gaurāṅga, speak of Gaurāṅga, chant Gaurāṅga's name." He assured everyone that he himself could be purchased by those who followed his advice—*ye jana gaurāṅga bhaje sei āmāra prāṇa re*, "Those who worship Gaurāṅga are my life breath." Again, to date there were no theological/philosophical texts that constituted a Gauḍīya scriptural canon, books which later promoted Nitāi's outspoken insight into not only the divinity of Gaura but also the sense that he was Kṛṣṇa himself in golden hue. Given Nitāi's own spirituality, the idea that he could be purchased by focusing on Gaura was a compelling prospect.

Śrī Vṛndāvana dāsa describes Nitāi's appearing for the first time in Nadīyā:

> Dressed as a great *avadhūta*, towering in stature, and with a boundless gravity, he had immeasurable depth. Day and night he chanted Kṛṣṇa *nāma*. He was Caitanya-dhāma itself, incomparable within the worldly realms *bhūr bhuvaḥ svaḥ*. Roaring in his own *ānanda*, he appeared intoxicated, as if he were the Balarāma *avatāra*. His heartwarming countenance conquered millions of moons. The enchanting smile on his lips was the life of the universe. His teeth shone like pearls, while his reddish eyes beautified his face. His two hands reached his knees; his chest was raised high; his pair of soft lotus feet were tender yet deft at dancing. He spoke to all with great compassion. On hearing the words from his lotus mouth, one's *karma* was destroyed.[7]

Nitāi arrived on the eve of Guru-pūrṇimā—July of 1509. But on the night before his arrival, he appeared to Gaura in a dream in the dress of Balarāma, riding a vehicle marked by a flag bearing the insignia of a palm tree—the mark of Balarāma's chariot.[8] With a loud voice he repeatedly called out for Nimāi Paṇḍita, and as morning broke, Gaura informed the assembled devotees that a great person had arrived in Nadīyā. However, when Gaura sent his associates to find this *mahā-puruṣa* they could not do

7. *Caitanya-bhāgavata* 2.3.125–131.

8. Balarāma's palm insignia is that of the *tāla* palm, or palmyra, which is associated with the *nāgas* and which plays a significant role in Balarāma's slaying of Dhenukāsura. See chapter 12 for further details.

so. Perhaps they were looking for a respectable gentleman and overlooked the *avadhūta*. When they returned somewhat bewildered, Gaura brought them to Nandana Ācārya's door, where Nitāi sat waiting, more effulgent than millions of moons and smiling in contentment. Seeing his elongated lotus eyes, the lotus itself would wilt.

Here in Nadīyā, the elder brother who previously oversaw Kṛṣṇa's behavior in Vraja now exhibited a childlike disposition. And it was Gaura who repeatedly protected Nitāi's reputation—a reversal of roles—making sure that the assembly of devotees did not misunderstand him. Nitāi carried his heart in his hand extended to Gaura in spiritual madness. Thus, his behavior often breached social norms, and on such occasions, it was Gaura who taught his devotees to always show Nitāi the greatest respect despite his unorthodox behavior. Vṛndāvana dāsa describes Nitāi as "dressed as an *avadhūta*." The Sanskrit word *avadhūta* refers to one who fails to adorn his body, being practically unaware of it. Śrīdhara Swāmī defines the word *avadhūta* accordingly as *asaṁskṛta-deha*, "one whose body is unadorned." Inner spiritual absorption leading to forgetfulness of bodily necessities can result in uncommon behavior. On the occasion of Gaura's first meeting with Nitāi, Gaura took Nitāi on *his* lap—Viṣṇu supporting Śeṣa!—in order to assure the assembled devotees of Nitāi's spiritual standing.

Nityānanda Rāma was thirty-five years old when he met Śrī Caitanya, while Śrī Caitanya was only twenty-three and just beginning to manifest his *saṅkīrtana-līlā*. Nitāi appeared in the world a dozen years before Gaura and departed a decade after his departure. In January of 1510, less than one year after the two first met, Mahāprabhu accepted the renounced order and left Nadīyā for Jagannātha Purī accompanied by Nitāi. It was within this short period in Nadīyā before Gaura's departure to Purī that Nityānanda began to gather his band of twelve principal associates—*dvādaśa-gopālas*—who shortly thereafter widely initiated disciples along with him in Bengal, thus giving the initial shape to what would become the Gauḍīya *sampradāya*.

In *Gaura-gaṇoddeśa-dīpikā*, Kavi-karṇapūra divides the early leaders of the *sampradāya* between the *mahāntas* and the *gopālas*. The *gopālas* were a more close-knit group that included what came to be referred to as the initial *dvādaśa-gopālas* and the extended *upa-gopālas*. In contrast, the *mahāntas* were a more loosely connected group—if they could be considered a group at all—consisting of the balance of Gaura's associates. Their defining characteristic was that they were different from the *gopālas*, who shared the common ideal of *sakhya-rati*.

Like Nityānanda himself, his closest associates had no qualms about associating with and initiating people from lower castes or in other ways breaking with worldly social norms as dictated by their *bhakti* sensibilities, appropriately placing the spiritual experiential path of *bhakti* above the socioreligious path of *varṇāśrama*. They initiated many disciples, especially from the socially disenfranchised mercantile class. Indeed, *Caitanya-bhāgavata* informs us that Nitāi appeared in the world to deliver this mercantile community.[9]

Although the Gauḍīya community's keen insight into the *dvādaśa-gopālas* is a unique contribution, the term itself is rooted in the *Brahma-vaivarta Purāṇa*. In this Purāṇa, twelve cowherds are named and the group is dubbed the *dvādaśa-gopālas*.[10] In Gauḍīya texts, the term *dvādaśa-gopāla* first appears in Locana dāsa Ṭhākura's sixteenth-century *Caitanya-maṅgala*, where he mentions eight of the twelve *nitya-siddha-gopas* but only in terms of their Gaura *līlā* names. From the same century, *Ananta Saṁhitā* also mentions this term and lists twelve *gopas* along with their Gaura *līlā* identities. Surprisingly, Kavi-karṇapūra's *Gaura-gaṇoddeśa-dīpikā*, also from the sixteenth century, does not invoke the term, while identifying more than a dozen Gaura *līlā* *nitya-siddhas* with principal *gopas* in Kṛṣṇa *līlā*. A host of later texts also mention the *dvādaśa-gopālas*, the most significant of which is *Gaura-gaṇa-svarūpa-tattva-candrikā*, written in the mid-to-late seventeenth century by the universally revered Gauḍīya *ācārya* Viśvanātha Cakravartī Ṭhākura. None of the texts from the sixteenth century onward entirely agree on who these twelve *gopas* are in Kṛṣṇa *līlā* or in Gaura *līlā*. However, every book I have researched includes the following nine *gopas* in its list, with most of them also agreeing on the corresponding Gaura *līlā* identities listed below.

Śrīdāmā: Abhirāma
Sudāmā: Sundarānanda
Vasudāmā: Dhanañjaya
Subala: Gaurīdāsa
Mahābala: Kamalākara Pippalāi
Subāhu: Uddhāraṇa Datta
Mahābāhu: Maheśa

9. *Caitanya-bhāgavata* 3.5.454.

10. The names of the *dvādaśa-gopālas* in the *Brahma-vaivarta Purāṇa* are Śrīdāmā, Sudāmā, Vasudāmā, Subala, Supārśva, Śubhāṅga, Sundara, Candrabhānu, Vīrabhānu, Sūryabhānu, Vasubhānu, and Ratnabhānu. It is not uncommon for a *gopa* to be known by more than one name (*Brahma-vaivarta Purāṇa, Kṛṣṇa-janma-khaṇḍa* 27.58–59).

Stokakṛṣṇa: Puruṣottama
Arjuna: Parameśvara

Although the texts mentioning the *dvādaśa-gopālas* differ on exactly who the three remaining *gopālas* are, they agree on the essential *bhāva* of the *dvādaśa-gopālas*, identifying them with either *priya-sakhās* of unmixed *sakhya-rati* or *priya-narma-sakhās*, whose *sakhya-rasa* is influenced by *mādhurya-rasa*. Furthermore, the texts introduce us to other prominent *sakhās* of Kṛṣṇa *līlā*, such as Lavaṅga, Dāmā, and Kiṅkiṇi, as well as listing numerous *upa-gopālas* and corresponding *nitya-siddhas* from Gaura *līlā*, all intimate associates of Nityānanda Rāma.

Descriptions of Nityānanda Rāma's intimate associates in both *Caitanya-bhāgavata* and the early-seventeenth-century *Caitanya-caritāmṛta* are colorful. Unlike the Vṛndāvana Goswāmīs, who exhibited a standard of dress and decorum in their perfected *sādhaka-dehas* of Gaura *līlā* that was distinct from that of their meditative *siddha-dehas* as *mañjarīs* of Kṛṣṇa *līlā*, the *dvādaśa-gopālas* of Gaura *līlā*, much like Nityānanda himself, wore their *sakhya-rati* on their *sādhaka-dehas* in some measure. Kṛṣṇadāsa Kavirāja describes them as bearing buffalo horns and herding sticks, adorned in cowherd dress, and crowned with the plumes of peacocks.[11] Similarly, Vṛndāvana dāsa describes them as decorated with armlets, bracelets, ankle bangles, ankle bells, and garlands, and bearing in their hands sticks, flutes, horns, and ropes.[12] However, it appears from artistic depictions from their time that such dress was only occasional. The worshipable painting of *parama-patita-pāvana* Uddhāraṇa Datta that adorns his altar in Saptagrāma, West Bengal, depicts him in a more traditional *sādhaka-deha*: head shaved; adorned with *ūrdhva-puṇḍra-tilaka* and a necklace of *tulasī* beads; his limbs, torso, and forehead marked with impressions of Kṛṣṇa's name and lotus feet; and dressed in white cloth with a *japa-mālā* of *tulasī* in hand.

Furthermore, despite descriptions of the *gopālas*' eccentric dress and decorum, Vṛndāvana dāsa also makes clear their accompanying saintliness: "They had no engagement other than *nāma-saṅkīrtana*. . . . Symptoms of Kṛṣṇa *prema*—tears, trembling, and horripilation—were constantly visible on their bodies."[13] Typically the *sāttvika-bhāvas* of tears and horripilation can be observed from time to time in the *sādhaka-dehas* of intermediate and superlative *bhaktas*, whereas other *sāttvika-bhāvas* more typically manifest in

11. *Caitanya-caritāmṛta* 1.11.21.
12. *Caitanya-bhāgavata* 3.5.352–353.
13. *Caitanya-bhāgavata* 3.5.713–715.

their internal, meditative *siddha-dehas*. Indeed, all of Śrī Rūpa's examples of the manifestation of *sāttvika-bhāvas* in his *Bhakti-rasāmṛta-sindhu* involve *siddha-dehas* in Kṛṣṇa *līlā*. The multiple and intensified ecstatic transformations of Śrī Caitanya—Kṛṣṇa in *sādhaka-deha*—are thus all the rarer and more extraordinary. The same is true to a lesser extent with the ecstasy of the *dvādaśa-gopālas*—simultaneous trembling, weeping, horripilation, immobilization, and so on.[14] Furthermore, much of the *gopālas*' unconventional behavior was not possible for ordinary persons or developing *sādhakas*—chasing and riding on the backs of Bengal tigers, playing with cobras, remaining submerged in water for more than twenty-four hours, and so on.[15]

Despite their ecstasy-induced eccentricity, the *dvādaśa-gopālas* appearing in Gaura *līlā* were also learned men who exemplified high standards of ritualistic worship within their lineages. Gaurīdāsa Paṇḍita is an excellent example of this.[16] It was through Gaurīdāsa Paṇḍita that the now widespread ritual worship—*arcana*—of the images of Gaura and Nityānanda was first instituted in the Gauḍīya *sampradāya*. Gaurīdāsa Paṇḍita was the vehicle through whom Gaura-Nitāi made themselves accessible to their devotees as *arca-avatāras*. Śrī Caitanya told Paṇḍitjī to gather *nīma* wood from Nadīyā and carve images of himself and Nitāi out of it. Doing so, Gaurīdāsa and his associates established the images through the *prāṇa-pratiṣṭhā* ritual. Gaurīdāsa then served the images, cooking for them and decorating them daily, often conversing with them as well. *Bhakti-ratnākara* relates how the deities spoke to Gaurīdāsa:

> "O friend, Subala, do you remember your previous life? Can you remember the immense joy we had herding cows on the bank of the Yamunā?" Saying this, the deities showed themselves as Kṛṣṇa and Balarāma with black and fair complexions. In those forms they

14. Descriptions of multiple *sāttvika-bhāvas* manifesting simultaneously in the perfected *sādhaka-dehas* of Śrī Caitanya's eternal associates are not exclusive to the *dvādaśa-gopālas*.

15. *Caitanya-bhāgavata* 3.5.425–432. This passage describes Murāri Caitanya dāsa, who is not listed as one of the *dvādaśa-gopālas* but is nonetheless one of Nityānanda Rāma's *sakhya-rati* associates.

16. Who is Gaurīdāsa? From Bijoy Krishna Goswami's *A Walk Through History*, we learn that one day when Gaurīdāsa was drenched in ecstatic tears of love for Nimāi, the young Paṇḍita took Gaurīdāsa to the bank of the Ganges and showed him his own reflection, thereby reminding him of his previous life. Reflected on the water, Gaurīdāsa saw the face of Subala "as if a second image of Rādhā." Then gradually he remembered his cowherd life and his Rādhā-like appearance.

> held horns, flutes, and canes, and they were adorned with peacock plumes and other ornaments. How beautiful they looked in the dress of *gopas*! Beholding their beauty, Gaurīdāsa was overwhelmed with *ānanda*.[17]

Furthermore, the divine images expressed distress at seeing Gaurīdāsa labor so in love, especially with regard to his elaborate cooking, and thus suggested that they would be happy if he offered whatever could be prepared without much effort. When he desired to decorate them with valuable jewels, they told him that they preferred the simplicity of flowers. Such intimate and extraordinary interactions between Gaurīdāsa and the sacred images of Gaura-Nitāi were the norm in his worship, and his *sevā-pūjā* had a significant influence on the outreach of Nityānanda Rāma despite Gaurīdāsa's otherwise reclusive nature.

Unlike Gaurīdāsa, Uddhāraṇa Datta Ṭhākura, another prominent member of the *dvādaśa-gopālas*, was very outgoing in nature. He hailed from Saptagrāma, an area within West Bengal consisting of seven villages, which had an extensive mercantile community—*suvarṇa-vaṇik*—primarily involved in trading gold. Centuries later, with the help of this community, the British were able to establish Calcutta as the center of their influence in India. By that time, more than half of Calcutta was populated by members of the *suvarṇa-vaṇik* community.[18]

During the fifteenth century, the *suvarṇa-vaṇik* community's social standing was questionable. The community's *vaiśya* status had been sullied by Hindu ruler Ballālla Sena, making day-to-day living more difficult for them, and it was Nityānanda Rāma who came to their rescue. Nityānanda elevated them above caste status altogether, replacing their sacred threads, symbolic of their status within the three higher castes, with strands of *tulasī* beads decorating their necks and marking them as Vaiṣṇavas. During this transformative period, Nitāi met Uddhāraṇa Datta Ṭhākura in Saptagrāma.

Like the other *gopālas*, Uddhāraṇa Datta had extraordinary character. When Nitāi visited Saptagrāma with his associates amid *nagara-nāma-saṅkīrtana*, Uddhāraṇa Ṭhākura immediately came forward and fell at Nitāi's lotus feet, bathing them with tears flowing from the restless river of his heart's *ānanda*. At that very moment, Nitāi blessed Uddhāraṇa. Placing his hand over Uddhāraṇa's head, Nitāi told his eternal *gopāla*—Subāhu—now

17. Adapted from *Bhakti-ratnākara*, chapter 7.

18. See A.C. Bhaktivedanta Swami's purport to *Caitanya-caritāmṛta* 1.11.41. Prabhupāda himself was a member of this community.

appearing in another *līlā*, "Arise. Do not cry anymore. From today you are my beloved servant." Then Nitāi changed his name from Divākara to Uddhāraṇa.[19]

Together they visited Śrī Caitanya in Purī and on that occasion Mahāprabhu kept Uddhāraṇa Datta with him for six months and ate whatever he cooked. However, in 1516 Gaurasundara ordered Nityānanda not to return to Purī the following year but instead to focus his attention entirely on delivering the mercantile community of West Bengal, acknowledging Uddhāraṇa Datta as Nitāi's principal assistant. And eventually the entire community followed Uddhāraṇa Datta's lead by accepting Nitāi as their guide. Thus, the community's social status was taken above and beyond caste designation, as it embraced the singular ritual of Śrī Kṛṣṇa *saṅkīrtana* and as its Vaiṣṇavism became centered on *sakhya-rati*.

Śrī Uddhāraṇa Datta preoccupied himself with only the very essence of *dharma*—*jīva-dayā* (kindness to others) and Kṛṣṇa *nāma*. His kindness to others made him famous not only in Saptagrāma but throughout all of Bengal, where together with the other *gopālas* he propagated the all-inclusive *saṅkīrtana* ritual. This propagation resulted in the formation of numerous *śrīpāṭas*, centers of Gauḍīya Vaiṣṇavism, pursuing *sakhya-rati* in the service of Gaura and Nityānanda Rāma.[20]

Perhaps the best example of his *jīva-dayā* is his famous *anna-chatra*—a kitchen and food-storage arrangement that covered ten acres of land from which he fed thousands upon thousands of poor villagers suffering from the great drought of West Bengal in the first quarter of the sixteenth century. Along with feeding the multitudes, he also constructed housing for thousands of poor and suffering villagers in the Bhadravana forest along the banks of the Saraswatī.

His dedication to and taste for Kṛṣṇa *nāma* was such that after the departure of Nitāi from Saptagrāma, the Ṭhākura chanted throughout the day and night in solitary *bhajana*, sleeping for only thirty minutes a day and subsisting on milk. Although a Sanskrit scholar and deeply acquainted with *Śrīmad Bhāgavatam*, he could not find the time to write anything himself.

19. *Divākara* refers to the sun, "the day-maker," extending its rays everywhere and illuminating the world. *Uddhāraṇa* refers to someone who can deliver others from material existence and thus extend sunlike rays of mercy far and wide.

20. *Pāṭa* means "village," and *śrī* denotes "sacred village." A *śrīpāṭa* is so designated because of being the residence of an eternal associate of Gaura-Nityānanda. The *dvādaśa-gopālas* and *upa-gopālas* turned a number of these *śrīpāṭas* into centers from which the teachings of Gaura-Nityānanda were disseminated.

In this regard, he has been compared to Raghunātha Bhaṭṭa Goswāmī, who alone among the Six Goswāmīs made no literary contribution for the same reason. The poet Vāsu Ghoṣa describes Datta Ṭhākura thus:

> In Kaicara he built a *kuṭīra* and lived there, his head shaved, wearing only *kaupīna* and outer cloth, his forehead adorned with beautiful *tilaka*. Around his neck were three strands of *tulasī* and the straps of a bag for his *japa-mālā*.

Then, from his *nirjana-bhajana*, Uddhāraṇa Ṭhākura again became a public figure. Empowered by the *śakti* of Nityānanda within his heart, he preached extensively, especially in Katwa, where he is said to have visited every village and every home bearing the good tidings of Gaura and Nityānanda Rāma. In Uddhāraṇa-pura he established a deity of *ṣaḍ-bhuja* Gaura—Gaura with six arms (two of Rāma, two of Kṛṣṇa, and two of Gaura himself)—to teach the public that Gaura was *svayaṁ* Bhagavān, the *avatārī* of all *avatāras*. On one side of *ṣaḍ-bhuja* Gaura, he placed the *mūrti* of Nitāi, and on the other side, a *mūrti* of Gadādhara. Thus, the Ṭhākura was an indispensable instrument in Nityānanda Rāma's outreach, which resulted in a flood of *sakhya-rati* throughout Bengal.

The last devotee to be personally initiated by Nityānanda Rāma was the famed Vṛndāvana dāsa Ṭhākura, whom Kavi-karṇapūra identified with the cowherd in Kṛṣṇa *līlā* named Kusumāpīḍa.[21] In the highly regarded *Caitanya-bhāgavata*, Vṛndāvana dāsa—the Vyāsa of Gaura *līlā*—expresses his personal *sakhya-rati* aspiration in relation to Gaura *līlā* thus:

> Surrounded by his *śiṣyas*, Śrī Śacī-nandana sat on the bank of the Ganges. If I had a million mouths, I could not do justice to this beautiful sight! Nothing in the three worlds compares. Not the moon surrounded by stars, for the moon bears spots and waxes and wanes, while Prabhu is always full and spotless. Not Bṛhaspati, who is partial to the gods, for Prabhu is partial to everyone. Not Cupid, who enters one's heart, causing agitation, for when Prabhu enters one's heart, *saṁsāra* is destroyed and one's heart becomes happy. Thus, all these comparisons are faulty. But there is one fitting comparison that comes to mind. Just as Śrī Nanda-kumāra sat amid the *gopas* on the bank of the Yamunā reveling in his cowherd *līlā*, that same Śrī Kṛṣṇa-candra in the form of a *brāhmaṇa* enjoyed

21. *Gaura-gaṇoddeśa-dīpikā* 109.

> himself sitting amid those same cowherd boys on the bank of the Gaṅgā.... Who can calculate the fortune of the lucky souls who saw this bliss? Merely seeing one who has witnessed this bliss, one is freed from *saṁsāra*. Because of my impiety, I did not take birth at that time, and hence I was cheated out of the joy of that *darśana*. O Śrī Gaura-candra! Show me your mercy that I may remember this *līlā* birth after birth. Wherever you and Nityānanda perform pastimes with your cowherd companions, may I be present there in service.[22]

A generation later, in the *Śrī Caitanya-caritāmṛta*, which served to establish the orthodox Gauḍīya theology, Kṛṣṇadāsa Kavirāja Goswāmī followed Vṛndāvana dāsa in terms of respect for Nityānanda Rāma. Both authors go to great lengths to emphasize the role of Nityānanda Rāma from their own spiritual perspectives, *sakhya-rati* in the case of Vṛndāvana dāsa and *mādhurya-rati* in the case of Kṛṣṇadāsa Kavirāja. Both authors also owe their texts to Nityānanda Rāma, and both glorify his *gopālas*. Vṛndāvana dāsa identifies Nitāi as the soul of his soul—his *antaryāmī*. He informs us that it was Nitāi who told him from within his heart to write the *Caitanya-bhāgavata*.[23] Similarly, it was Nitāi, mystically appearing with his *gopālas* before the young Kṛṣṇadāsa, who gave Kṛṣṇadāsa the blessing that led to his writing the *Caitanya-caritāmṛta* later in his life.[24]

In the context of relating how he was mystically visited and blessed by Nitāi and his associates, Kṛṣṇadāsa describes his earlier encounter with Mīnaketana Rāmadāsa, another prominent associate of Nityānanda Rāma. Kavirāja Goswāmī's description of Rāmadāsa is breathtaking:

> Brimming with *mahā-prema*, he sat in my courtyard. All the Vaiṣṇavas bowed at his feet. In the ecstasy of *prema*, he sometimes climbed on top of a devotee bowing before him. Sometimes he struck others with his flute or mildly slapped them. When others looked into his eyes, tears fell from their eyes, for an uninterrupted shower of tears flowed forth from the eyes of Rāmadāsa. Sometimes I saw him stunned in ecstasy with horripilation erupting like *kadamba* flowers

22. *Caitanya-bhāgavata* 1.12.255–266 and 1.12.282–286.
23. *Caitanya-bhāgavata* 1.1.80.
24. *Caitanya-caritāmṛta* 1.5.182–196.

> on one limb, his other limb trembling. Whenever he loudly shouted the name of Nityānanda, everyone was awestruck.[25]

The above history informs us that despite the effort of Nitāi to focus people's attention on Gaura and his gift of *gopī-bhāva* and even though no one has done more to distribute this gift of Gaura than Nitāi, some devotees were nonetheless influenced by Nityānanda's own *sakhya-rati*. As we shall see, that influence continues to this day. However, in the later part of the sixteenth century, this *sakhya-rati* current gradually receded to the background of the *sampradāya*, giving way to its more prominent wave of *mādhurya-rati*. Although Nityānanda Rāma played a significant role in the authoring of both *Caitanya-caritāmṛta* and *Caitanya-bhāgavata*, the two texts speak to us of a sublime divide in the early years of the *sampradāya*.

The outreach of Nitāi and his associates represented in *Caitanya-bhāgavata* depicts the early *saṅkīrtana* of Nityānanda Rāma as a revolt against complex brahminical ritual and its religious monopoly. Their outreach was also a means of communicating and disseminating a new socioreligious standard and providing the community with a unifying congregational form of spiritual practice—*nāma-saṅkīrtana*. The philosopher Brajendranatha Seal refers to Śrī Nityānanda as Bengal's first "true democrat."[26] In his outreach, Nitāi disregarded both caste and gender distinctions, and the well-known Vaiṣṇava anthology *Gauḍa-pada-taraṅgiṇī* in a verse attributed to Locana dāsa speaks of Nityānanda as the savior of women.[27]

Although deeply spiritual, Nityānanda's outreach was also notably a wave of compassionate social activism. While Śrī Caitanya ordained such activism, he turned his own attention more toward the brahminical community itself in an effort to bring this community into the fold of his *prema-dharma*. For this he empowered the Six Goswāmīs, commissioning them to write and theologize in Sanskrit as to the significance of his descent. Their works were synthesized and interwoven with a description of the *līlā* of Śrī Caitanya in Kṛṣṇadāsa Kavirāja's *Caitanya-caritāmṛta*, which was written in the more accessible language of Bengali. Therein, we find an emphasis on the internal reason for Śrī Caitanya's advent, which highlights the ideal of *mādhurya-rati* and Gaura's pursuit of its limits. In contrast, Vṛndāvana

25. *Caitanya-caritāmṛta* 1.5.163–167. *Gaura-gaṇoddeśa-dīpikā* 68 describes Mīnaketana Rāmadāsa as an incarnation of Saṅkarṣaṇa.

26. Amiya P. Sen, *Chaitanya: A Life and Legacy* (New Delhi: Oxford University Press, 2019), 1911–96, Kindle.

27. Sen, *Chaitanya*, 100.

dāsa Ṭhākura's *Caitanya-bhāgavata* emphasizes the compassionate nature of the *avatāra*'s outreach. However, this distinction is not sharp, and there is considerable overlapping between the two books. The authors intended to bring the lower and higher classes, as well as the classless, together in spiritual passion while emphasizing two closely related aspects of the same precept. Nonetheless, *Caitanya-caritāmṛta*'s emphasis on *mādhurya-rati* was compelling.

After the passing of Nitāi, his consort Jāhnavā-devī became a prominent spiritual figure in the Gauḍīya community of devotees with close ties to Nityānanda Rāma. Kavi-karṇapūra partially identifies Jāhnavā with Anaṅga-mañjarī of Vraja, whom others identify as Balarāma's *śakti* expansion and the younger sister of Rādhā.[28] Thus, she and her stepson and foremost disciple, Vīrabhadra Goswāmī, were bearers of *mādhurya-rati* rather than *sakhya-rati*, and their efforts to share their inner wealth also received philosophical and theological backing from the Goswāmī *granthas*, texts that primarily emphasized the ideal of *mādhurya-rati*. As a result, the current of *sakhya-rati* assumed low tide as the high tide of *mādhurya-rati* corresponding with Gaurasundara's inner aspiration inundated the Gauḍīya landscape.

However, under scrutiny the Goswāmī *granthas* clearly showcase *sakhya-rati* as an ideal worthy of attainment, and they reveal that *sakhya-rati* devotees are essential allies for those in *mādhurya-rati*. The seminal text of Sanātana Goswāmī, *Bṛhad-bhāgavatāmṛta*, does so through two separate Purāṇic-like narratives in which *sakhya-rati* plays a significant role.[29] In *Bṛhad-bhāgavatāmṛta*'s first narrative, sage Nārada, who is situated in *sakhya-rasa*,[30] interviews various paradigmatic figures, who represent a gradation of spiritual ideals culminating in *gopī-bhāva*. In the final chapter, we find

28. *Gaura-gaṇoddeśa-dīpikā* 65–66 identifies her as a partial incarnation of Anaṅga-mañjarī and Balarāma's consort in Dvārakā, Revatī. See chapter 28 for details concerning her role and influence.

29. Sanātana Goswāmī describes his text as a supplement to an alternative account of the *Mahābhārata* spoken by sage Jaimini to Mahārāja Janamejaya. However, although alternative accounts of the *Mahābhārata* are mentioned in the original text, no other versions are available today, nor is Sanātana Goswāmī's *Bṛhad-bhāgavatāmṛta* known other than through Sanātana Goswāmī himself. The book's narrative is also supplemented by an extensive commentary that the Goswāmī attributes to himself.

30. *Bhakti-rasāmṛta-sindhu* 3.4.83 places Nārada primarily in *sakhya-rasa* bundled together with *dāsya-rasa*. Aside from this, some Purāṇas inform us that Nārada also temporarily experienced *gopī-bhāva*. However, this is intended, both here and in a similar story concerning Pāṇḍava Arjuna, only to showcase *gopī-bhāva* as the highest ideal within Vraja and not to teach that Nārada and Arjuna eternally serve in *gopī-bhāva* in addition to *sakhya-rasa*.

Nārada in Dvārakā, where he inadvertently reminds Kṛṣṇa of his Vraja *līlā*, and this in turn plunges Kṛṣṇa into separation for his Vraja *līlā* milkmaidens. Taking note of Nārada's remorse, Kṛṣṇa informs the sage that one who reminds him of his *gopīs'* love for him is his best friend—*gāḍhopakārī smṛti-daḥ priyāṇām*—for the *gopīs'* ideal of devotion is supreme.[31] In response, Nārada invokes names of Kṛṣṇa such as *gopa-gopījana-priya* in the ecstasy of *saṅkīrtana*.

Nārada serves Kṛṣṇa in *sakhya-rasa* outside of Vraja. He is a partial manifestation of Kṛṣṇa's *brāhmaṇa* friend Madhumaṅgala, a *priya-narma-sakhā* mindful of Kṛṣṇa's love for Rādhā.[32] Thus, Kṛṣṇa, in his assurance to Nārada at the apex of this concluding section of the *Bṛhad-bhāgavatāmṛta*'s first canto, subtly pays respect to the supporting role of *sakhya-rati* influenced by *mādhurya-rati*—*priya-narma-sakhā-rati*—in pointing to the zenith of spiritual intimacy realized in *mādhurya-rati*. In other words, it is Nārada, a partial manifestation of the *priya-narma-sakhā* Madhumaṅgala, who reminds Kṛṣṇa of the measure of the Vraja *gopīs'* love for him.

The emphasis on *sakhya-rati* is more direct in the much longer narrative of *Bṛhad-bhāgavatāmṛta*'s second canto. The protagonist of this narrative is the *priya-narma-sakhā* Gopa-kumāra, also known as Sarūpa after he attained his ideal in *līlā-sevā*. Gopa-kumāra seeks to determine the abode that corresponds with the zenith of spiritual intimacy. Both Gopa-kumāra and his disciple, Janaśarmā, attain the ideal of *sakhya-rati* as cowherd friends of Kṛṣṇa who are privy to his romantic life and who assist him in his rendezvous with Rādhā. Thus, Sarūpa is depicted as a male servitor of Rādhā from her extended family as well as a *sakhā* of Kṛṣṇa and Balarāma. It is Rādhā herself who empowers Sarūpa to recruit Janaśarmā and teach him how to enter into the same ideal of *līlā-sevā*. Again, while Sanātana Goswāmīpāda's book teaches that *mādhurya-rati* affords the greatest intimacy with the Godhead, it does so in its second canto through the voice of *sakhya-rati* influenced by *mādhurya-rati*—*narma-sakhā-bhāva*. Therefore,

31. *Bṛhad-bhāgavatāmṛta* 1.7.128. This phrase is the *mahā-vākya* of the canto.

32. *Gopāla-campū* 2.36.42 states, "Madhumaṅgala is Nārada's counter-image with a joking nature." Also see *Gopāla-campū* 1.2.29 and 1.3.71–72. In *Caitanya-caritāmṛta* 2.14.229, we also find Śrīvāsa acting like Madhumaṅgala. Just as *svayaṁ* Bhagavān manifests expansions of himself for *līlās* outside of Vraja, so too do his associates, such as Madhumaṅgala in the form of Nārada. In *līlā* and *bhāva*, Madhumaṅgala is the disciple of Nārada, while from the *tattva* perspective he is the source of Nārada. Hence, there is considerable support for identifying Śrīvāsa Ṭhākura of Gaura *līlā* with Madhumaṅgala of the Vraja *līlā*. And while some texts identify Madhumaṅgala as one of the *dvādaśa-gopālas*, this notion ignores that fact that although he is a *narma-sakhā*, he is a *brāhmaṇa* and not a *gopāla*.

while sharpening the lineage's focus on *mādhurya-rati* in Rādhā *dāsyam*, Sanātana Goswāmī also shows deference to the early efforts of Nitāicāṅda and his *sakhya-rasa* associates.

With such texts in hand, Jāhnavā and Vīrabhadra's *mādhurya-rati* outreach was sure to succeed. Vīrabhadra's influence was widespread, and earlier predictions of a great *saṅkīrtana* general—a *senā-pati* Vaiṣṇava—who would travel to foreign lands and preach the *prema-dharma* of Mahāprabhu were thought to have been realized in the person of Vīrabhadra Goswāmī.[33] With the focus on *gopī-bhāva* coming from other Gauḍīya lineages and now prominently from Nitāi's sector as well, and with the passing of Nitāi and his *gopālas*, the earlier widespread influence of *sakhya-rati* was largely overshadowed.

However, despite *sakhya-rati*'s decline in terms of circulation, Nayanānanda Ṭhākura's *Śrī Śrī Preyo-bhakti-rasārṇava* serves as evidence of its ongoing vitality extending into the middle of the eighteenth century. Nayanānanda Ṭhākura's lineage stems from Sundarānanda Ṭhākura, one of the *dvādaśa-gopālas*, who is identified with Sudāmā-gopa of Kṛṣṇa *līlā*. Sundarānanda's extraordinary abilities are described in the book *Vaiṣṇava-vandana*. It is written therein that, among other amazing feats, he caused *kadamba* flowers to bloom out of the branches of a lime tree and played in the Ganges with alligators. He was a lifelong celibate, and he established his *śrīpāṭa* at Maṅgala-dihi in the Birbhum district of West Bengal. Nayanānanda Ṭhākura is a fifth-generation disciple in the line of Sundarānanda.

Nayanānanda Ṭhākura's *Śrī Śrī Preyo-bhakti-rasārṇava* is a fairly comprehensive guide to the ideal of *sakhya-rati* centered on the *priya-sakhā* Sudāmā/Sundarānanda. Nayanānanda repeatedly defers to "the Goswāmī" throughout his text, a respectful reference to Śrī Rūpa Goswāmī and his seminal work, *Bhakti-rasāmṛta-sindhu*. Nayanānanda's work is well grounded in the *bhakti-rasa-siddhānta* of Rūpa Goswāmī's text while diving deeply from that shore of *tattva* into a wave of fraternal love of God—*preyo-bhakti-rasa*—found in the tome's third wave of its southern ocean. At the same time, Nayanānanda's text contains undercurrents of its own, in particular its suggested meditation on a typical day in the life of Rāma and Kṛṣṇa from the perspective of a *priya-sakhā*. Although this section also follows

33. This prediction is found in *Caitanya-maṅgala, sūtra-khaṇḍa* 564–565. Over the centuries, devotees have identified other saints with this prediction. For example, in the twentieth century the disciples of A. C. Bhaktivedanta Swami Prabhupāda have identified him with it.

the lead of Rūpa Goswāmī, as does Kavirāja Goswāmī's *Govinda-līlāmṛta* and Viśvanātha Cakravartī Ṭhākura's *Kṛṣṇa-bhāvanāmṛta*, its *priya-sakhā* perspective is notably distinct. That said, it is clear that Nayanānanda follows a particular approach to the pursuit of *sakhya-rati* that parallels what appears to have been the dominant approach to *rāgānuga-sādhana* of that time. This approach has often been attributed to Dhyānacandra Goswāmī, which we will explore in a subsequent chapter.

Two generations of disciples after Śrī Nayanānanda, the Sanskrit drama *Śrī Govinda-vallabha-nāṭakam* was composed by Dvārakānātha Ṭhākura. It is a classical drama celebrating the eighth lunar day of the bright fortnight of the month of Kārtika—Gopāṣṭamī—the day Kṛṣṇa officially became a cow-herder. This text was most likely written in the first half of the nineteenth century. Thus, we find examples of *sakhya-rasa*'s current extending well into that century, and it is likely that an effort to mine the other principal *śrīpāṭas* (centers of Gauḍīya Vaiṣṇavism) of the *dvādaśa-gopālas* and the *upa-gopālas* would uncover further gems of evidence as to its vitality before the *sampradāya*'s interface with modernity. Of course, *sakhya-rasa* is a secondary current that provides a supporting role, but that in itself is beautiful—the beauty of differentiation in ecstatic emotion that decorates the singular tree of Gauḍīya *tattva*.

However, the entire current of Gauḍīya Vedānta's *bhakti-rasa* also began to stagnate sometime in the nineteenth century. At least its stagnation was noted at this time. Just how long before this period its current began to recede and cease to influence the intelligentsia of Bhārata—flourishing only within its own midst—is difficult to say. At the outset of the reign of the British, Śrī Caitanya's precepts—his *rasa* revolution—spoke softly, if at all, even to the educated men and women of Bengal.

Of course, it is not uncommon for a spiritual current to go underground for some period before resurfacing. Śrī Kṛṣṇa mentions this in the *Gītā* to *pura-sambandhi* Pāṇḍava Arjuna.[34] In doing so, Kṛṣṇa also states the remedy for renewal: the revitalizing of the *guru-śiṣya-paramparā*. In the case of the Gauḍīya *paramparā*, this included the extra task of interfacing with modernity. This is not to say that Gauḍīya lineages were without life altogether—surely saints of the *sampradāya* existed at the time—but

34. *Bhagavad-gītā* 4.2. *Pura-sambandha* is a form of *sakhya-rati* outside of rural Vraja and in the metropolitan (*pura*) areas of Kṛṣṇa's later *līlās*. Unlike the *sakhya-rati* of bucolic Vraja, it can recede to the background when confronted with Kṛṣṇa's *aiśvarya*, as seen in the *Gītā*'s eleventh chapter.

rather that the extent to which the *sampradāya* was misrepresented was considerable. The actual saints were, for the most part, unto themselves, preoccupied with their *bhajana* and thus having little or no thought about the rapidly changing world around them and its implications for the community. Centuries earlier, the Vṛndāvana Goswāmīs virtually ignored the Copernican revolution, even as some traditionalists of other Hindu spiritual lineages did not.[35] However, in the latter half of the nineteenth century, European influence and modernity could no longer be ignored, and the Bengal community of Gauḍīya Vaiṣṇavism rose to the occasion in the person of Kedarnātha Bhaktivinoda, who proved to be fit for the task at hand.

Ṭhākura Bhaktivinoda observed stagnation of the overall current of Caitanya *bhakti*, which gave way to considerable misrepresentation of the precepts. In his estimation, several previously prominent and spiritually vital lineages had become more formal than spiritually substantial. Competition in the spiritually compromised marketplace appears to have led some of the once prominent *sakhya-rati* lineages that lacked spiritual vitality at the time to unceremoniously claim that their lineages also offered the ideal of *mādhurya-rati*. Indeed, suddenly some of the *dvādaśa-gopālas* were purported to have *mañjarī-svarūpas* as well as *gopa-svarūpas*. In some sectors, Nityānanda himself was turned into Rādhā! The philosophical problems with these notions attest to the loss of philosophical acumen in some sectors of the community, with sentiment ungrounded in *tattva* leading the day.

Ṭhākura Bhaktivinoda himself was initiated in the line of Nityānanda Rāma stemming from his consort Jāhnavā-devī. Dubbed "the Seventh Goswāmī" by the Calcutta media, Ṭhākura Bhaktivinoda wrestled Gauḍīya authority out of the hands of those misrepresenting it. In doing so, he turned to the world stage to find common ground with the existing world religions. Placing Gauḍīya Vaiṣṇavism on that stage, he then pointed to its unique contribution to the world of spiritual insight—*mādhurya-rati*'s *mañjarī-bhāva*—a previously unknown expression of romantic love of God. However, he also made clear that there was a place for *sakhya-rati* in Gauḍīya Vaiṣṇavism. *Sakhya-* and *mādhurya-ratis* are the two windows of opportunity offered by the Gauḍīya *sampradāya* given that the lineage is presided over by Gaura and Nityānanda Rāma, and thus *bhakti-saṁskāras* for both of these *bhāvas* run through it.

35. See Christopher Z. Minkowski, "The Pandit as Public Intellectual: The Controversy over *Virodha* or Inconsistency in the Astronomical Sciences," in *The Pandit: Traditional Scholarship in India*, ed. Axel Michaels (New Delhi: Manohar Publishers, 2001).

Ṭhākura Bhaktivinoda's seminal work, *Jaiva Dharma*, is centered around two characters, Vrajanātha and Vijaya-kumāra. Both are depicted as learned in Gauḍīya *tattva*, religious by nature, humble, and spiritually resolute. The book charts their spiritual progress prior to the moment they are blessed with *mantra-dīkṣā*, as well as their ongoing development to *prema* thereafter. Their *mantra-dīkṣā* was momentous, and in due course they experienced a profound spiritual epiphany: *antara-darśana* of Mahāprabhu and his associates. Following this, they met with their *dīkṣā-guru*, who asked them about the particulars of their spiritual affinity resulting from the *ruci* of their practice. They responded by citing the effect the *līlās* recorded in the tenth book of the *Bhāgavata Purāṇa* had on them. While Vijaya-kumāra related his affinity for *mādhurya-rati* arising from his practice, Vrajanātha disclosed his affinity for *sakhya-rati*: "When the calves wander far off to graze, I would very much like to bring them back in the company of Subala. When Kṛṣṇa sits in a place to play upon his flute, I will take the permission of Subala to let the cows drink water, and then I will bring them to Kṛṣṇa *bhāi*. This is my heart's desire."[36] Vrajanātha idealized *sakhya-rati*. In response, the *guru* of these two disciples helped them to fix their resolve to attain their ideals: Vijaya-kumāra in pursuit of *mādhurya-rati* and Vrajanātha in pursuit of *sakhya-rati*.

It should be noted that while Bhaktivinoda dutifully explained all the five primary and seven secondary *rasas* in his philosophical works, his treatment of *sakhya* and *mādhurya* in *Jaiva Dharma* makes clear that these are the two principal spiritual portals of the Gauḍīya *sampradāya* through which it affords passage into Śrī Kṛṣṇa's Vraja *līlā*. While there are examples of associates of Mahāprabhu in other *rasas* and from other *līlās*, the support that the *sampradāya* systematically offers to *sādhakas* that consistently manifests in its initiating *gurus* is either for *sakhya-rati* or *mādhurya-rati*. And the latter, which is more prominent, is the principal focus of the Goswāmīs' *bhakti-śāstras*.

Other than his philosophical works, the Ṭhākura also writes in other genres in ways that can be helpful for *sādhakas* pursuing *sakhya-rati*. A good example is his nine-verse visualization of Godruma found in his text *Navadvīpa-bhāva-taraṅga*. Bhaktivinoda Ṭhākura conceived of himself as Kamala-mañjarī. He reveals this information in *Navadvīpa-bhāva-taraṅga* along with details about his *līlā-sevā-svarūpa*. His confession comes at the end of *Navadvīpa-bhāva-taraṅga*, following an overview of the spiritual

36. *Jaiva Dharma*, chapter 21.

wonders of Nadīyā's nine islands and what one may encounter there in terms of its emotional ecstasies. However, on the island of Godruma, the Ṭhākura speaks of Gaura relishing *sakhya-rati* and paints a picture relevant to *sādhakas* pursuing this ideal.

Godruma represents the *bhakti-aṅga* of *kīrtana* and corresponds with Vṛndāvana's area of Nandagrāma, which is saturated with *sakhya-rati*. Contemplating Godruma, Bhaktivinoda recalls Gaura's *pūrvāhna* (mid-morning) *līlā*, which typically involves visiting the houses of devotees while performing *saṅkīrtana*. At this time, in Bhaktivinoda's visualization, Gaura, Nityānanda Rāma, and their entourage encounter Godruma's cowherds herding their cows, preparing to cross the sacred Gaṅgā. As these local cows and cowherds come into view, Gaura and his associates remember Kṛṣṇa's cowherding *līlās*. Bhaktivinoda envisions Gaura and his devotees in *sādhaka* dress eating milk products from the hands of the cowherds they encounter and conversing with them. The cowherds themselves see through Gaura's guise as a *brāhmaṇa*, and one of them cries out,

> Brother, you are Gopāla. The form of a *brāhmaṇa* does not suit you. Come! We will carry you on our shoulders, herd cows, and bring you to your mother in Māyāpura. . . . O brother! Come to my house every day. You may be the God of the *brāhmaṇas*, but you are the life of the *gopas*. . . . Look there! Seeing you, all the cows moo and leave aside their grass and calves. . . . Since it is now getting late, you should go home to your father's house, and tomorrow we'll meet again at this place. I'll save some yogurt, cheese, and condensed milk for you—but if you come late, I'll be very upset![37]

Typically, as such encounters play out, all of Gaura's devotees in *sādhaka-veśa* who have *sakhya-rati* for Kṛṣṇa see themselves in *gopa-veśa* and relish *sakhya-rasa*, blessed with the *darśana* of Gaura and Nityānanda as Kṛṣṇa and Balarāma. Bhaktivinoda concludes his description of Godruma expressing appropriate spiritual longing:

> *hena dina āmāra ki haibe udaya*
> *heriba godruma-līlā śuddha-premamaya*
> *gopa-saṅge gopa-bhāve prabhu-sevā-āśe*
> *ekamane vasiba se godruma-āvāse*

37. *Navadvīpa-bhāva-taraṅga* 45–48.

> When will that day be mine that I will see the pure *prema*-filled *līlā* in Godruma performed by Prabhu amid the *gopas* in *gopa-bhāva*? Then, with a mind fixed in the longing to serve, I will reside in Godruma.[38]

Here the word *prabhu* is modified by the words *gopa-saṅge gopa-bhāve* (amid the *gopas* in *gopa-bhāva*). This is the meaning appropriate for one speaking about this *līlā* from a *mādhurya-rati* perspective. Such a devotee desires to see Gaura enter the mood of a cowherd at this time in Godruma, but the devotee aspiring for *mādhurya-rati* does not want to enter into the eternal pastimes in the mood that Gaura is expressing at this time.

Bhaktivinoda Ṭhākura's aspiration here is not to attain *sakhya-rati* himself. Again, he is writing from a *mādhurya-rati* vantage point, and he desires to see Gaura at this time and place when he typically enters into *gopa-bhāva*. Nonetheless, his description serves as a beautiful visualization appropriate for those who do desire to attain *sakhya-rati* and appropriately approach this ideal through the medium of Gaura *līlā*.

Indeed, his concluding verse of this section cited above can also be translated as an aspiration to attain *gopa-bhāva*. And unless one tries to understand the verse in light of *mādhurya-rasa*, as I have above, the verse more overtly speaks of a longing for fraternal love. In this case the translation would be as follows:

> When will that day be mine that I will see the pure *prema*-filled *līlā* in Godruma? When will I reside in Godruma amid the *gopas* in *gopa-bhāva*, one-minded in my desire to serve Prabhu?[39]

Understood in this way, the Bengali poetry of Bhaktivinoda constitutes an aspiration to attain *gopa-bhāva* in the context of a meditative visualization of Gaura *līlā* in Godruma—in other words, rather than desiring only to see Gaura as he enters this *bhāva*, desiring to enter into *gopa-bhāva* oneself. Thus, while writing from his *mādhurya-rati* perspective, Bhaktivinoda at the same time mercifully provides a meditative visualization for those pursuing *sakhya-rati*.

38. *Navadvīpa-bhāva-taraṅga* 50.

39. *vasiba*—[When] will I reside; *se godruma-āvāse*—in the abode of Godruma; *gopa-saṅge*—with the cowherd boys; *prabhu-sevā-āśe ekamane*—with single-minded desire to serve Prabhu; *gopa-bhāve*—in the *bhāva* of a *gopa*. Here, of course, serving in *gopa-bhāva* refers to serving Kṛṣṇa in the mood of a cowherd boy (because Gaura in this *līlā* is in the mood of Kṛṣṇa). In one's perfected *sādhaka-deha* in Gaura *līlā* itself, one serves Gaura in *dāsya-bhāva*.

As explained earlier, the Ṭhākura's own *mādhurya-rati* flows through the line of Jāhnavā-devī, whose respect for the *dvādaśa-gopālas* is well documented. Hence the lineage has respect for *sakhya-rati* despite its otherwise exclusive focus on *mañjarī-bhāva-upāsanā*. As Bhaktivinoda shares his meditative reflections on Godruma in the pages of his *Śrī Navadvīpa-bhāva-taraṅga*, he highlights the ideal of *sakhya-rati*. Perhaps he is also thinking of those before him who brought this *bhāva* to the world, as well as those who will be blessed by it in the future. Such thinking is consistent with what the Ṭhākura teaches elsewhere: in the Gauḍīya *sampradāya* one can attain *līlā-sevā* in Nadīyā in *dāsya-rati* for Gaura along with the ideal of either *mādhurya-rati* or *sakhya-rati* for Kṛṣṇa in Vraja.

During the time of Ṭhākura Bhaktivinoda yet outside of the Nityānanda *parivāra*, we also find *sakhya-rasa* idealized in the family lineage of Advaita Ācārya. In the Advaita *vaṁśa*, Bijoy Krishna Goswami's birth is thought to have fulfilled an early prophecy stating that Śrī Caitanya would prominently bless Śrī Advaita's tenth generation with his empowerment for the sake of further disseminating Śrī Caitanya's teachings. A contemporary of Bhaktivinoda and a spiritually renowned reformer, Prabhupāda Bijoy Krishna Goswami identified with *sakhya-rasa* from his early childhood, and this ideal served as his lifelong pursuit. In his childhood, Goswami conversed with the family deity of Śyāmasundara, who appeared before him by Goswami's own account, accepting Bijoy as his playmate.[40]

The heir to Bhaktivinoda's own dissemination of Gauḍīya Vaiṣṇavism on the world stage was his son and *harināma* initiate Bhaktisiddhānta Saraswatī Ṭhākura, who at the suggestion of Ṭhākura Bhaktivinoda accepted Gaura-kiśora dāsa Bābājī as his *mantra-dīkṣā-guru*. Before he passed from the world, Bhaktivinoda Ṭhākura wrote to Bhaktisiddhānta Saraswatī Ṭhākura, encouraging him to carry on with what he had already started in terms of outreach. This outreach developed into the institution known as the Gauḍīya Maṭha. In the presence of and with the blessing of both Bhaktivinoda Ṭhākura and Gaura-kiśora dāsa Bābājī,[41] Saraswatī Ṭhākura

40. In *Advaita-maṅgala*, Advaita is identified with Ujjvala-sakhā (Rebecca J. Manring, *The Fading Light of Advaita Ācārya: Three Hagiographies* [New York: Oxford University Press, 2011], 90). And in *Gaura-gaṇoddeśa-dīpikā*, Kavi-karṇapūra identifies Advaita as a cowherd boy in Vraja (verses 76–80), stating further that Advaita displayed symptoms of both *dāsya-* and *sakhya-bhāva* (verse 24).

41. He initiated his first disciple, Rohiṇī Kumāra Ghosh, in 1906. Ṭhākura Bhaktivinoda passed away in 1914 and Gaura-kiśora dāsa Bābājī passed in 1915. Thus, Bhaktisiddhānta Saraswatī Ṭhākura was initiating in their presence and with their blessings for almost a decade.

began initiating disciples. Before he passed away, he had opened sixty-four Gauḍīya monasteries throughout India and sent Gauḍīya missionaries to Europe.

Among Saraswatī Ṭhākura's disciples, the prolific author O. B. L. Kapoor (Ādi Keśava dāsa) recounts the history of a *sakhya-rasa-upāsikā* named Śrīmatī-devī from the middle of the twentieth century:

> Śrīmatī-devī was a disciple of Kṛṣṇānanda Swāmī, a student of Prāṇa Gopāla Goswāmī who hailed from the Nityānanda *vaṁśa*. Differing in *bhāva* from Prāṇa Gopāla's *mañjarī-bhāva* ideal, Kṛṣṇānanda Swāmī idealized *sakhya-rati*. Nonetheless, Prāṇa Gopāla Goswāmī acknowledged Kṛṣṇānanda Swāmī's significant spiritual standing and requested him to initiate others himself. But Kṛṣṇānanda Swāmī was reluctant to do so until he met Śrīmatī-devī, who at the time was only eleven years old.
>
> Śrīmatī-devī lived in the village of Nagla Lakshmanpur within the Vraja-maṇḍala. Widowed at the age of eleven, she devoted herself entirely to the worship of her Kṛṣṇa deity. She had a tendency toward the friendly mood of devotion and had heard of Kṛṣṇānanda Swāmī and became attached to the idea of becoming his disciple. Eventually, at the insistence of some of her relatives, Kṛṣṇānanda Swāmī wrote the *mahā-mantra* on a piece of paper and some instructions on how to worship Kṛṣṇa.
>
> Śrīmatī-devī still wished to see her *guru* and vowed that until she saw him, she would not go outside in the light of day. She would rise at four in the morning and bathe, then sit indoors, chanting the holy names until sunset. She kept this up for three years, but still she was not allowed to see her *guru*. Finally, she began fasting, and after nine days, Kṛṣṇānanda Swāmī had a vision in which Balarāma told him that for Śrīmatī-devī's sake he could break his vow of avoiding the opposite sex.
>
> After making this breakthrough and receiving personal contact with her *guru*, Śrīmatī-devī quickly attained perfection in the friendly mood. Indeed, her *sakhya-bhāva* manifested even in her *sādhaka-deha*. Her behavior, her language, and so on all took on the characteristics of a cowherd boyfriend of Kṛṣṇa, and people even began to call her *bhaiyā* (brother).

> Her health was poor, and she did not live much longer after this. One day, when her *guru* came to visit her, he took her head in his lap and she said, "Buddy, let's go. Look, Balarāma and Kṛṣṇa are calling their friends to come." Kṛṣṇānanda Swāmī replied, overcome with emotion, "Go ahead, buddy. I'll be right along." Having received this permission from her *guru*, she entered the eternal world of Vraja.[42]

Like Bhaktivinoda, Saraswatī Ṭhākura also internally conceived of himself in *mañjarī-bhāva*—as Nayana-maṇi-mañjarī—steeped in Rādhā *dāsyam*. However, among his many disciples, at least two of them—Akiñcana Kṛṣṇadāsa Bābājī and A.C. Bhaktivedanta Swami Prabhupāda—longed for *sakhya-rati*, and both of them also became prominent in the later part of the twentieth century. Akiñcana Kṛṣṇadāsa is well known for his absorption in *saṅkīrtana* and his nonsectarian posture. A.C. Bhaktivedanta Swami Prabhupāda is famous for his miraculous dissemination of Gauḍīya Vaiṣṇavism throughout the world. I am blessed to have had their personal association and to have received three initiations from the latter.

Akiñcana Kṛṣṇadāsa Bābājī was well loved by all and was especially close with my *śikṣā-guru*, B.R. Śrīdhara Deva Goswāmī. The two met in 1926. Śrīdhara Deva Goswāmī remembers Kṛṣṇadāsa Bābājī as "young and smart, beautiful, jolly, and very firm in his spiritual practice, especially towards *nāma-bhajana*...and satisfied under any circumstances." In the words of Śrīdhara Mahārāja, a natural and intimate bond between himself and Bābājī formed owing to their similarities in "social rank, and similar education, similar simplicity, and earnestness for Kṛṣṇa consciousness."[43]

After the breakup of the Gauḍīya Maṭha, Bābājī retired from missionary activities and settled in Nandagrāma in Vraja-maṇḍala. From there, he wrote a letter to Śrīdhara Mahārāja in which he related that he had attained his ideal in *sakhya-rati* as a follower of Subala:

> He wrote a letter to me from there. I found in his language *śuddha-sattva*—that he had attained complete satisfaction in his present life....So many years had passed, so many nights of Ekādaśī he kept awake and went on with his *nāma-bhajana*. He deeply engaged himself and remarked, "I felt the highest bliss in my life in Nandagrāma." He was fond of *sakhya-rati*, and from the visible world to the

42. Here I have paraphrased Kapoor's account related in *Braja ke bhakta*, vol. 3, 132–133.

43. B.R. Śrīdhara Deva Goswāmī, recorded conversation, April 29–30, 1982.

> invisible he entered—the invisible aspect of Vṛndāvana. He told plainly that he had much attraction for *sakhya-rasa*—to Subala, who has some connection with *mādhurya-rasa*. Among all the friends of Kṛṣṇa, Subala is considered to be the highest for his intimate connection with *mādhurya-rasa*.[44]

These two saints, B.R. Śrīdhara Deva Goswāmī and Akiñcana Kṛṣṇadāsa Bābājī, were also close with Bhaktivedanta Swami Prabhupāda. Named from birth Abhaya Caraṇa De, A.C. Bhaktivedanta Swami was born in the previously mentioned *suvarṇa-vaṇik* community. As a child he would annually visit the *śrīpāṭa* of Uddhāraṇa Datta Ṭhākura along with his family to pay homage to the Ṭhākura. About his experience as a member of the *suvarṇa-vaṇik* community, he writes that "all the members of the *suvarṇa-vaṇik* community enthusiastically take interest in this temple of Uddhāraṇa Datta Ṭhākura."[45] Prabhupāda considered his birth in a Vaiṣṇava family in light of the *Gītā*'s statement that one who takes birth in a family of transcendentalists is rare in this world.[46] Therein, Śrī Kṛṣṇa tells Arjuna that such practitioners who take birth in the family of transcendentalists on the strength of impressions—*saṁskāras*—from their previous life's association and subsequent practice are very rare. Driven by such spiritual impressions, they continue their practice with spontaneity in their next birth.

When blessing Abhaya Caraṇa with *mantra-dīkṣā*, Bhaktisiddhānta Saraswatī Ṭhākura preserved his given name at birth, adjusting it slightly to Abhaya Caraṇāravinda dāsa. It is Kṛṣṇa at whose lotus feet (*caraṇāravinda*) one attains fearlessness (*abhaya*) in service to them (*dāsa*), and Prabhupāda exhibited such fearlessness. Upon receiving the blessing of *sannyāsa-dīkṣā* from his *guru-bhai* Pūjyapāda Bhakti Prajñāna Keśava Mahārāja and being given the *sannyāsa* name Bhaktivedanta Swami, Prabhupāda, as his disciples later respectfully referred to him, always retained the initials A.C. from his birth and *mantra-dīkṣā* epithets, referring to himself as A.C. Bhaktivedanta Swami. The name Abhaya Caraṇa/Caraṇāravinda was significant to him, fearless as he was in his *viśrambha*—his confidence in Kṛṣṇa's friendship and absence of restraint in that fraternal love—which is central to *sakhya-rati*.

44. B.R. Śrīdhara Deva Goswāmī, recorded conversation, April 30, 1982. Edited for clarity.

45. See A.C. Bhaktivedanta Swami's purport to *Caitanya-caritāmṛta* 1.11.41.

46. *Bhagavad-gītā* 6.42.

This name roughly corresponds with the *pradhāna*, or primary characteristic, of *preyo-bhakti*: *viśrambha* (confidence in intimacy).[47]

The story of Prabhupāda's global *saṅkīrtana* is one of the most inspiring and touching narratives of Gauḍīya saints in the history of its lineage. Unlike narratives of Śrī Caitanya and his associates from centuries past, it is well documented in terms of its historicity, leaving no room for the kind of exaggeration about miracles often assumed by historians. Historically well documented, it is at the same time nothing less than miraculous. The *śakti* driving Prabhupāda's *saṅkīrtana* that makes for such a magical narrative is also closely tied to his inner life of *sakhya-rati*.

Penniless, he managed to secure passage on a freight liner from Bombay to Boston by the strength of his commitment to fulfilling the expectations of his *guru*. He departed on the auspicious evening of Baladeva's *pūrṇimā*, his baggage consisting primarily of his chest of books—copies of his translation of the first canto of *Śrīmad Bhāgavatam*—and a personal copy of *Śrī Caitanya-caritāmṛta*. Aboard the boat, despite experiencing severe seasickness and a heart attack, he penned a personal prayer—"*Bhagavān Kṛṣṇera Pāda-padme Prārthanā*" (Prayer to the Lotus Feet of Kṛṣṇa)—to his intimate friend, Kṛṣṇa *bhāi*.

Prabhupāda's prayer was not written for publication. It serves as a glimpse into his private life of *bhajana* and *guru-sevā*. However, the depth of his inner life in *sakhya-rasa* also propelled his public life, serving as the *śakti* behind his miraculous *saṅkīrtana* campaign, which took the world by surprise and fulfilled Śrī Caitanya's five-century-old prophecy that his name would be heard around the world.[48] The prayer consists of an intimate appeal in the context of offering moral advice to Kṛṣṇa in a manner characteristic of a cowherd friend privy to his romantic life. Prabhupāda advises his friend Kṛṣṇa that if Rādhā is pleased with him, Kṛṣṇa's life will be successful. He explains that it is therefore in Kṛṣṇa's interest to bestow upon him the necessary *śakti* required to disseminate *bhakti* in the Western world and thus enable him to fulfill his *guru*'s order in the service of Rādhā. The body of the prayer is divided into verses characterizing submission (*śaraṇāgati*) in pursuit of doing the bidding of one's *guru* in this world, followed by verses of appropriate longing (*laulyam*) for the spiritual attainment in the next. The attainment Prabhupāda longs for is *sakhya-rasa*. And the words

47. *Caitanya-caritāmṛta* 2.19.224. *Viśrambha* will be discussed in greater detail in chapter 4.

48. *Caitanya-bhāgavata* 3.4.126.

he uses speak of the *sādhāraṇa anubhāvas* of *sakhya-rati* (those common to all types of *sakhās*), and their very sound—*kata bane chuṭāchuṭi bane khāi luṭāpuṭi*—carries the spirit of intimacy in *preyo-bhakti-rasa*:

> *tomāra milane bhāi ābār se sukha pāi*
> *gocārane ghuri din bhor*
> *kata bane chuṭāchuṭi bane khāi luṭāpuṭi*
> *sei dina kabe habe mor*
>
> O brother, when will that day be mine when I will meet you again and attain the happiness of herding cows, wandering through the pastures from early morn throughout the entire day, running and frolicking through the many forests of Vraja, tumbling on the ground in playful sport?[49]

Prabhupāda's close friend and at times mentor, B.R. Śrīdhara Deva Goswāmī, reflects upon his beloved godbrother's poem thus:

> He expressed his own position in eternal *līlā* in his poem. I conjecture like that. Hare Kṛṣṇa! In his diary in Bengali he wrote, "Today I cooked some *bāṭi-khichaṛi*. It was quite delicious. So I ate something. Today I expressed my inner feelings to my friend and wrote a poem about that."
>
> And that friend came to his aid. He was so earnest in his prayer to Kṛṣṇa that he might be able to discharge the duty that had been given to him by his Guru Mahārāja that Kṛṣṇa came down to help him. His friend helped him in this propaganda work. So *śaktyāveśa-avatāra* I take him. I cannot but take him to be so.
>
> Addressing Kṛṣṇa he wrote, "You are my eternal friend. Forgetting you, I have come to this world and I have been suffering the kicking of *māyā*, the goddess of misconception. If you come to help me in this campaign, then after finishing this I can again join you. When I shall be united with you again, I shall wander along with you the whole day in keeping the cows in the forest, running this side and that side in the jungle, in the forest. And then, *luṭāpuṭi*, to fall on the ground in different shows of play. I aspire after that day. I have got this good chance to serve my *gurudeva*. For that reason, my heartfelt

49. "*Bhagavān Kṛṣṇera Pāda-padme Prārthanā.*"

appeal to you is that you please come to help me. I am your eternal servitor; therefore, so much aspiration I have got for you. You, no other, are my only resort."

> So after performing this service, he aspires after a life in the cow-keeping *līlā* of Kṛṣṇa, and he is appreciating that sort of friendly service of Kṛṣṇa very much from the core of his heart, his aspiration after finishing his worldly preaching campaign. I take it that Nityānanda Prabhu has given some special recognition to the section of the *suvarṇa-vaṇik* community from which Swami Mahārāja has come. He has special grace for that particular section and the preaching about Gaurāṅga, and this is mentioned in the scriptures. The *suvarṇa-vaṇik* are the most favorite section of Nityānanda Prabhu. It is mentioned in the *śāstra*, *Caitanya-bhāgavata.* I thought that Nityānanda Prabhu is also in charge of preaching about Mahāprabhu's glory. So I took it that Nityānanda Prabhu must have awakened some special dedication in him in his last days which helped him to inundate with such an inconceivable magnitude the whole of the world.[50]

Thus, just as Gaura Kṛṣṇa sent Nityānanda Rāma, Uddhāraṇa Datta, and others to distribute his blessings in Bengal among the outcastes more than five centuries ago, in the middle of the twentieth century Kṛṣṇa empowered A.C. Bhaktivedanta Swami Prabhupāda—Nityānanda *āveśa*—to do the bidding of Rādhā (*gaura-vānī pracāriṇe*) to those outside of the *varṇāśrama* socioreligious framework. He did this in response to the sincere and spiritually insightful request of Swami Prabhupāda, who like Uddhāraṇa Datta was a member of the *suvarṇa-vaṇik* community. Thus, a great wave of *sakhya-rati* once again surfaced in the *sampradāya* and simultaneously pointed to the ideal of Gaura's Rādhā *dāsyam*. As we have seen above, one of the *dvādaśa-gopālas*, Gaurīdāsa (Subala-sakhā in Kṛṣṇa *līlā*), manifested the very first worshipable images of Gaura and Nityānanda Rāma in West Bengal. And these same holy images emerged from the heart of A.C. Bhaktivedanta Swami and accepted *sevā* from his *śiṣyas* all over the world, even as he instructed his students in the *arcana* of Rādhā and Kṛṣṇa *vigrahas* as well, worship that is also common for *priya-narma-sakhās*.

He shared with us that Māyāpura is his place of worship—the Gauḍa-maṇḍala of Gaura and Nityānanda Rāma—while his home is Vṛndāvana. There, he placed his heart on the central altar of his well-named Krishna

50. B.R. Śrīdhara Deva Goswāmī, conversation, February 26 and 28, 1981.

Balaram Mandir: This temple has three altars—Gaura-Nityānanda to the left, Rādhā-Śyāmasundara to the right, and Kṛṣṇa-Balarāma in the center. Of the three flags extending from the domes above, the central flag flies highest in the sky of his heart. In this way, the ideal of *sakhya-rati* is subtly and tastefully heralded, signaling the grace of Nityānanda Rāma, who is the way to Rādhā-Śyāma.

In this regard a poem has been written:

> Youthful, confident, wrapped in *aruṇa*,
> rising like the sun at dawn—a new day
> darkness gone away.
> Ahead two brothers lead the way—
> white pearl, blue sapphire shining—calling.
> Herding in a sea of black, white, yellow, red,
> and spotted cows, who are lowing softly.
> Following at the brothers' feet, soft and lotus-like,
> fearless is his name, frolicking, tumbling
> in sportive play from morn to midday.
> Oh, the strength of Rāma, his arms extended!
> Trees bend and flowers bloom in *bhāva*
> all out of season in a land beyond reason,
> as love calls and Kṛṣṇa conjures
> an excuse to proceed with a select few:
> that fearless one with Subāhu,
> Subala, Ujjvala, and Madhumaṅgala too,
> to one who has a way with words may they call,
> "Don't hesitate. Come serve with friends forever."

The book *O My Friend! O My Friend!* extensively documents my Guru Mahārāja's affinity for *sakhya-rati*.[51] The present text follows that work, and both bear testament to the renewed current of *sakhya-rati* in the Gauḍīya *sampradāya*. May they please the Vaiṣṇavas.

51. Swāmī B. A. Āśrama, *O My Friend! O My Friend! Exploring the Inner Life of His Divine Grace A.C. Bhaktivedanta Swami Prabhupāda* (Philo, CA: Darshan Press, 2020).

3

Sambandhānugā-bhakti

In the previous chapter, we presented a brief historical overview of *sakhya-rati*'s influence within the Gauḍīya *sampradāya*, replete with compelling examples of both *nitya-* and *sādhana-siddhas*. The prospect of attaining this ideal oneself will no doubt resonate with readers who are sympathetic—*sa hṛdayaṁ*—to this ideal. But what is the means to attain this sublime expression of divine love? To answer this question, we turn to Rūpa Goswāmī, who informs us that the path to this form of *prema* is *sambandhānugā-sādhana-bhakti*, a division of *rāgānugā-sādhana-bhakti*. Therefore, let us discuss it within the context of exploring Rūpa Goswāmī's overall understanding of *rāgānugā-bhakti*.[1]

Rāgānuga-sādhana is the spiritual practice by which Vraja *prema*—the gift of Gaura and Nityānanda Rāma—is attained. In his *Bhakti-rasāmṛta-sindhu*, Śrī Rūpa dedicates thirty-eight verses to explaining this esoteric path (1.2.271–309). The Sanskrit word *rāga* refers to passion for something, and *anuga* implies following. *Rāgānuga-sādhana* thus essentially consists of following the inborn passion or rapture for Kṛṣṇa observed in the intimate associates of his Vraja *līlā*—making that passion one's ideal.

Viśvanātha Cakravartī Ṭhākura explains in his commentary to Śrī Rūpa's *Bhakti-rasāmṛta-sindhu* that Kṛṣṇa's eternal associates have *anādi-siddha-saṁskāras* (beginningless perfect loving propensities for Kṛṣṇa) that

1. Śrī Rūpa's two divisions of *rāgānugā-bhakti* are *sambandhānugā* and *kāmānugā*. The two are essentially the same except that *kāmānugā-sādhana-bhakti* is focused on attaining *mādhurya-rasa*. Thus, in *kāmānugā-bhakti* one will follow the example of Kṛṣṇa's cowherd maidens rather than his male friends.

drive their love for Kṛṣṇa.[2] Rūpa Goswāmī refers to these associates as *rāgātmikas*, *ātmās* who are constituted of sacred rapture for Kṛṣṇa.[3] Through association with devotees who have the *bhāva* of such *rāgātmikas*, as well as through *smaraṇam* on the *rāgātmikas* themselves, those *jīvas* within *saṁsāra* can acquire similar *bhakti-saṁskāras*, which also dissipate the bound *jīvas*' infinite material *saṁskāras* arising from their *anādi karma*.

In Vedānta, the *antaḥ-karaṇa* (inner apparatus of thought and feeling) has four constituents: *manas*, *buddhi*, *citta*, and *ahaṅkāra*. *Ahaṅkāra* gives each of us a sense of false individuality and makes us think of our material experiences as our own. *Manas* is the cognitive faculty that receives information from our various senses, combines these impressions into a sense of the object as a whole, and makes a preliminary judgment of whether we like or dislike the object. *Buddhi* (intelligence) categorizes the object and determines how to respond to it. This process may involve such functions as reason, judgment, and comprehension. *Citta* is the storehouse of all the mental impressions from this life as well as from previous lives. The constant flow of information from our senses to *manas* and *buddhi* is compared to waves or ripples (*vṛttis*) that empty into the sea of the *citta* and thereby disturb its tranquility. As *vṛttis* continue to flow into the *citta*, our intelligence perceives patterns in our experiences and forms impressions about the world. These thought patterns or psychological impressions are the material *saṁskāras* stored in the *citta*. Once these *saṁskāras* form, we filter new information through them. The scholar Stephen Phillips describes the *saṁskāra* theory as "broadly empiricist,"[4] likening it to David Hume's notion of "impressions," in which everything we believe is ultimately traceable to our experience.

In his *Śikṣāṣṭakam*, Śrī Caitanya compares the *citta* to a dirty mirror because the stored impressions (*saṁskāras*) in our *citta* reflect back to us a biased perception of reality. We can clean the mirror of the *citta* and thus remove material *saṁskāras* by spiritual practice. Although the *antaḥ-karaṇa* is constituted of material influences gathered by the functions of *manas*, *buddhi*, and *citta*, *bhakti-sādhana* is able to reverse the identity-making

2. *Bhakti-rasāmṛta-sindhu* 3.2.77.

3. Kṛṣṇa is God intertwined with his *svarūpa-śakti*. This internal *śakti* is located within himself and in this sense *is* himself (*svarūpa*), while it is also manifest outwardly as his splendor (*tad-rūpa-vaibhava*). The latter includes his associates, who are further described as "parts of his own self" (*tad-aṅga-bhūta*) and "part of his essential nature" (*svarūpa-bhūta*). See *Bhagavat Sandarbha* 75–76.

4. Stephen Phillips, *Yoga, Karma, and Rebirth: A Brief History and Philosophy* (New York: Columbia University Press, 2009), 82.

process by awakening one's spiritually informed ego, spiritualizing one's intellect, and cleansing the mirror of the *citta*. Spiritual practice involves imprinting *bhakti-saṁskāras* on the *citta* such that as it is cleansed, it begins forming a spiritual ego by reflecting the image of the *ātmā* and its spiritual prospect as a follower of one of the Vraja *līlā-rāgātmikas*, such as Śrīdāmā or Subala, eternal friends of Rāma and Gopāla Kṛṣṇa. Thus, the *sādhaka*'s subtle body is spiritualized upon attaining *bhāva-bhakti*.[5] As that *bhāva* is churned into *prema*, the gross physical body is fully spiritualized as well. Along with attaining a spiritualized subtle and gross *sādhaka-deha*, one also experiences an internal meditative spiritual body suitable for *līlā-sevā* in the super-subjective meditative world of Kṛṣṇa *līlā*.

However, the cleansing takes some time. It must remove innumerable material *saṁskāras* arising from one's thoughts and sense experiences that have been stored in the *citta* for countless material lifetimes. We should note that stored *saṁskāras* are destroyed only by spiritual practice. Hence, the joy of building and ornamenting a temple within our hearts first involves clearing the heart of a jungle of material *saṁskāras*, a formidable task. However, it is a task that *bhakti* is well equipped for, especially *rāgānugā-bhakti*.

The power of *rāga-bhakti* lies essentially in this: people approach Kṛṣṇa for things, attachment for which is the womb from which suffering is born. This does nothing for him. Others approach him with an appeal to get away from things and thereby live in eternity. They are wiser, but they have little love for him. Others love him but in a formal way, in which the distance between the worshiper and the object of worship is kept in place. About such reverential love, Kṛṣṇa, through the pen of Kṛṣṇadāsa Kavirāja, says, "Love weakened by majesty does little for me," *aiśvarya-śithila-preme nāhi mora prīta*.[6] The *rāgātmikas* of Vraja, on the other hand, want nothing from him, nor do they want to worship him. They want to love him as their son, friend, or lover. About them, Kṛṣṇa says:

> To one who in *śuddha-bhakti* thinks of me as their son, friend, or lover—thinking oneself superior and me an equal or subordinate—I become subservient. Mother sometimes binds me as her son. She

5. *Sādhana-bhakti* constitutes limbs of *bhakti* such as hearing and chanting performed with the senses (*Bhakti-rasāmṛta-sindhu* 1.2.2), while *bhāva-bhakti* constitutes the same activities driven by spiritual emotion (*Bhakti-rasāmṛta-sindhu* 1.3.1), attaining such emotion being the goal of *sādhana-bhakti*. *Prema-bhakti* is characterized by the condensation of that *bhāva*, or spiritual emotion, the goal of *bhāva-bhakti* (*Bhakti-rasāmṛta-sindhu* 1.4.1).

6. *Caitanya-caritāmṛta* 1.4.17.

> nourishes and protects me, thinking me utterly helpless. My friends climb on my shoulders in pure friendship, saying, "What kind of big man are you? You and I are equal!" If my beloved consort rebukes me in a sulky mood—*māna*—she steals my mind from the reverent hymns of the Vedas.[7]

This is love, not worship. It is not bound by any formalities. And those who desire to love Kṛṣṇa in this way, as *rāgātmikas* like his friends Śrīdāmā and Subala do, get his attention like no one else does. Indeed, Kṛṣṇa is eternally indebted to his intimate friends beyond his capacity to reciprocate in kind.[8] This is the power of *rāga-bhakti*. It involves a keen interest in Kṛṣṇa "as he is" in the hands of his most intimate devotees, which in turn draws his attention to the *sādhaka* to an extent that no other appeal can compete with.

But who are we—fallen souls in the degraded age of Kali—to approach in this most intimate way? We are those blessed by the mercy of *sādhus*—*mahat-kṛpā*—and who have thus embraced this ideal. Śrī Rūpa Goswāmī concludes his discussion of *rāgānugā-bhakti* underscoring this point, *kṛṣṇa-tad-bhakta-kāruṇya-mātra-lābhaika-hetukā*.[9] The mercy of Kṛṣṇa and his devotees is the *only* reason this ideal appears in the hearts and minds (*citta*) of others. From *sādhus*, who are agents of Kṛṣṇa, we receive our initial *bhakti-saṁskāras*, transmitted by their very presence, thoughts, and actions, as well as through the *aṅgas* of *bhakti* they engage us in. Thanks to the well-wishing of their *rāga*-driven *bhakti* that gives birth to the *sādhaka*'s *bhakti*, in due course through continued *sādhu-saṅga* the *sādhaka* will attain *rāga* as well.[10]

Sādhu-saṅga is, of course, generally also the cause of *rati* within *vaidhī-bhakti*. I say generally because some devotees reason that *vaidhī-bhakti* can arise without *sādhu-saṅga* from merely following *varṇāśrama-dharma*, which includes the worship of Viṣṇu.[11] While this approach will possibly be effective in producing *rati* for Viṣṇu, it can never give rise to

7. *Caitanya-caritāmṛta* 1.4.21–22, 24–26.

8. Brahmā declares that while Kṛṣṇa has given himself—which is everything—to his *sakhās* in return for their love, he also gave himself to Pūtanā, who merely dressed like a Vraja *vāsī*. What then does he have left to give to his *sakhās*? Thus, Brahmā accurately depicts Kṛṣṇa as their eternal debtor. See *Śrīmad Bhāgavatam* 10.14.35.

9. *Bhakti-rasāmṛta-sindhu* 1.2.309.

10. *Caitanya-caritāmṛta* 2.22.83.

11. The idea here is that *bhakti* can arise from following the rules of *varṇāśrama*, given that in the context of doing so one worships Viṣṇu along with other gods or offers the results of prescribed *karmic* duties to Viṣṇu. See Jīva Goswāmī's comments on *Bhakti-rasāmṛta-sindhu* 1.2.309.

rāgānugā-bhakti and *rati* for Vṛndāvana Kṛṣṇa. Thus, again, the *only* way in which the ideal of *rāga-bhakti* can be transmitted is through *sādhu-saṅga* with *rāga-mārga-bhaktas*.

If we associate with *mādhurya-rati-sādhus*, this ideal will imprint itself on our *citta*, and if we associate with *sakhya-rati-sādhus*, *bhakti-saṁskāras* for *sakhya-rati* will be imprinted on our *citta*. Rūpa Goswāmī makes this point while answering a question that might arise: If *mādhurya-rati* is the highest ideal, why do all *sādhakas* not embrace it? He answers: "Because of *vāsanās*."[12]

As we have seen earlier, the flow of sense experiences and our thoughts in relation to them are termed *vṛttis*. The patterns we see in similar *vṛttis* and our judgments about them are imprinted in our *citta* as psychological impressions (*saṁskāras*), and *saṁskāras* in turn form into *vāsanās* (psychological dispositions). While the words *saṁskāra* and *vāsanā* are synonyms for one another, *vāsanās* refer more precisely to latent *saṁskāras* stored from previous lives, whereas *saṁskāras* are those impressions that are actively forming in this life. As such, *vāsanās* operate in the subconscious and serve to mold one's disposition and personality. Rūpa Goswāmī is saying that one develops *ruci* for one *rati* rather than another because of *vāsanās*, here referring to clusters of *bhakti-saṁskāras* that have formed into *vāsanās* and not to material *saṁskāras* or the *vāsanās* subliminally involved in forming one's individual material disposition. Indeed, as we have learned earlier, such material *saṁskāras* and *vāsanās* must be cleared from the mirror of one's *citta* for *rati* to appear.

The emphasis here is that one's *ruci* for *sakhya* or *mādhurya* derives in part from one's association with *sādhus*, often extending over lifetimes, and culminates in attaining one's spiritual destiny—one's own inherent *ānanda*.[13]

Finally, in four succinct verses Rūpa Goswāmī sums up the assisting factors (*bhakti-saṁskāras*), the role of *sādhana*, and how *bhakti-rasa* appears:

> Only those devotees who possess latent impressions of *bhakti* acquired in both the present life and previous lives are eligible to taste *bhakti-rasa*. First *sādhana-bhakti* cleanses all sins from the soul and makes it

12. *Bhakti-rasāmṛta-sindhu* 2.5.38.

13. In his *Prameya-ratnāvalī*, Baladeva Vidyābhūṣaṇa states that *mukti* involves attaining one's own inherent *ānanda*, and the means to do so is unalloyed *bhakti*—*muktir naija-sukhānubhūtir amalā bhaktiś ca tat-sādhanam*. The *Kāntimālā-ṭīkā* to the text explains that the *jīva* has its own form, *jīvasya naija rūpam*, as servant of Hari endowed with happiness and knowledge in minute quantity—*aṇuvijñāna sukhaṁ*. And its inherent form of servitude manifests upon attaining Hari's feet. Thus *bhakti* is paradoxically inherent yet at the same time must be bestowed to give rise to *ruci*.

> bright and blissful, and then a strong inclination arises for studying the *Bhāgavata* in the association of those whose life and soul is the joy of devotion at the feet of Govinda. Next a devotee becomes fully absorbed in devotional practices and is thereby blessed with God's grace. Then present and past *bhakti-saṁskāras* strengthen the devotee's *rati* and transform it into *rasa*, the apex of *ānanda*.[14]

In this way, a *jīva* is often not aware of the beginning of *rāgānugā-bhakti*—the blessing of *sādhu-saṅga* within a *rāga-mārga* lineage, such as the Gauḍīya *sampradāya*. As a result of this *sādhu-saṅga*, a longing to attain the selfless service ideal of Vraja *bhakti* manifests in the *sādhaka* in due course. Rūpa Goswāmī refers to this longing by the word *lobha*,[15] which literally means "greed"—sacred greed. Such longing is an obsession that constitutes the eligibility to systematically tread the *rāga-mārga*.

Notably, *rāga-bhakti*'s ideal is more attractive to Kṛṣṇa than the ideal of reverential love in *vaidhī-bhakti*, and the sacred greed that drives *rāgānuga-sādhana* also serves as a more compelling motivation for the *sādhaka* than the motivation that drives *vaidhī-bhakti*. Due to this difference in motivation, perfection of love in intimacy is easier to attain through *rāgānugā-bhakti* than the perfection of love in majesty is to attain through *vaidhī-bhakti*. Nonetheless, the limbs of *vaidhī-bhakti* are for the most part applicable to *rāgānuga-sādhana*. Scriptural mandates are not to be disregarded in *rāgānuga-sādhana*, but at the same time their purpose is fulfilled when one's practice is driven by *lobha*. The *Bhāgavata* teaches that adherence to scriptural law—*dharma*—that does not result in a taste for descriptions of Kṛṣṇa and his associates is a waste of time.[16] Furthermore, one who has attained such a taste need not be concerned with scriptural law, in that it is not required to motivate the *rāga-bhakta*'s practice. However, neither is it necessarily ignored other than when such scriptural mandates conflict with the pursuit or ideal of *rāga-bhakti*. Simply put, when our actions are driven by a natural liking for our ideal, the *sādhana* to attain that ideal is more easily performed than when we are driven by dutifulness. God *should* be worshiped. Kṛṣṇa in Vraja, on the other hand, is lovable in all respects.

14. *Bhakti-rasāmṛta-sindhu* 2.1.6–10. Here my translation includes the import of the commentaries.

15. In *Bhakti Sandarbha*, Jīva Goswāmī uses the word *ruci* (taste) instead of *lobha*.

16. *Śrīmad Bhāgavatam* 1.2.8. Here, the verse is also saying that *varṇāśrama* is a waste of time because it does not lead to such a taste. See also Sanātana Goswāmī's commentary on *Bṛhad-bhāgavatāmṛta* 2.7.147.

Rūpa Goswāmī informs us that the symptom of this sacred greed is that a *sādhaka*'s practice is driven by a taste for the sweetness of the *rāgātmikas*' love, which the practitioner has come to realize in some measure through the process of hearing from the scriptures and reasoning about their conclusions. Realization of the sweetness of the *rāgātmikas*' love involves understanding the theological and philosophical implications that underlie it, and this is in itself no small task. Here, scriptural study refers primarily to the study of *Śrīmad Bhāgavatam*, which is a *rasa-śāstra* and not a particularly easy text to understand. The very purpose of this text is to highlight the feelings of the *rāgātmikas* described in the text's tenth canto and to showcase their meditation—*satyaṁ paraṁ dhīmahi*—through a comprehensive philosophical and theologically grounded *līlā* narrative. The *Śrīmad Bhāgavatam* seeks to attract its readers to one of the types of love that the *rāgātmikas* embody, inspiring the reader to follow in that *rāgātmika*'s footsteps. In the *līlā* narrative of the tenth canto, this emphasis reaches its peak. Thus, the *Bhāgavata*'s sacred narrative of Kṛṣṇa *līlā* differs dramatically from the *līlā* narratives in other texts such as the *Viṣṇu Purāṇa*, *Padma Purāṇa*, and *Hari-vaṁśa Purāṇa*. In brief, the *Bhāgavata* tells the story with depth of feeling. It is a history of the *rāgātmikas*' feelings for Kṛṣṇa, as opposed to an informative surface narration of the *līlā*'s sequence of events and listing of its primary participants.

Furthermore, it is also necessary to study the scriptures after *lobha* has appeared in order to understand the proper *sādhana* of *rāgānugā-bhakti*.[17] Thus, in the initial stages of one's budding *lobha*, it will take the shape of interest in understanding exactly what *rāgānugā-bhakti* consists of. Śrī Viśvanātha Cakravartī Ṭhākura gives the example of one who desires to regularly consume milk and its by-products. Such a person will become very interested in learning how to acquire and care for a cow. Similarly, the *rāgānuga-sādhaka* in whom *lobha* has sprouted will be very interested in learning all about the philosophy and theology underlying *rāgānugā-bhakti* and the corresponding *sādhana* required to attain the desired *rāga*. The Ṭhākura comments that "it is only through reasoning as to the implications of the *śāstric* injunctions—*śāstra-yukti*—that the way to attain this *rāga* is ascertained, not by any other means."[18]

Given the above, it is understandable that *lobha* may not appear for some time even after one is initiated into the Gauḍīya *sampradāya* and has

17. See Viśvanātha Cakravartī Ṭhākura's commentary on *Bhakti-rasāmṛta-sindhu* 1.2.293.

18. *Rāga-vartma-candrikā* 1.7.

studied the *Bhāgavatam*.[19] We saw this in the reference to the two disciples of Ṭhākura Bhaktivinoda's *Jaiva Dharma* cited in the previous chapter. Indeed, in the *Bhakti Sandarbha*, Śrī Jīva Goswāmī offers the following explanation of *lobha*: "When a person develops a taste [*lobha*] for *rāga*, even while the *rāga* itself is yet to manifest, his or her heart [*citta*] becomes clear like a crystal, shining as it reflects the rays of the moon of that *rāga*." In other words, mature *lobha* purifies one's *citta*. Similarly, Mukunda Goswāmī comments that attaining *lobha* is rarer than attaining *bhāva* on the path of *vaidhī-bhakti*, and Rūpa Goswāmī characterizes such *bhāva* as *sudurlabhā*, very difficult to attain.[20] Here such authors are speaking of mature *lobha*. However, budding *lobha* is also often spoken of, as is *rāgānugā-bhakti* in which no *lobha* has manifested.

Thus, one may ask exactly what kind of practice one is qualified to engage in if one's *lobha* is not mature or if, despite one's being initiated into a *rāga-mārga-sampradāya*, one has yet to attain any *lobha* at all. Jīva Goswāmī answers this question, invoking the term *ajāta-ruci-rāgānugā-bhakti*, *rāgānugā-bhakti* lacking *lobha*.[21] He explains that in the Gauḍīya *sampradāya* a *sādhaka* in whom *lobha* has not yet sprouted will adopt those practices of *rāga-bhakti* that he or she is capable of adopting, which for the most part consists of engaging in the *aṅgas* of *vaidhī-bhakti* with the ideal in mind. For example, one pursuing *sakhya-rasa* might listen to *sakhya-rasa līlā-kathā* from the lips of like-minded, spiritually advanced devotees, which in turn will result in the sprouting of *lobha* leading to *rāga*.

Just as eligibility for *vaidhī-bhakti* constitutes faith—*śraddhā*—in its efficacy and this *śraddhā* informed by *śāstra* is either pliable, firm, or well informed, similarly the *lobha* that grants eligibility for *rāga-bhakti* also arguably appears on a scale from immature to mature. Thus, Bhaktivinoda Ṭhākura describes eligibility for *rāgānuga-sādhana* as *lobha-mayī-śraddhā*, faith infused with *lobha*. Furthermore, he writes that "according to the degree of greed possessed by the rightful candidates for *rāgānugā-bhakti*, they can also be divided into the three categories of *uttama*, *madhyama*,

19. This is the case when *lobha* is attained in the present life due to *sādhu-saṅga* and so forth. On the other hand, if *lobha* already appeared in a previous life, then it will appear again in the present life, and it will then guide one to the appropriate *guru*.

20. *Bhakti-rasāmṛta-sindhu* 1.2.309.

21. *Bhakti Sandarbha* 312. In the Sandarbha, the word *ruci* is synonymous with *lobha*. *Ajāta-ruci-rāgānuga-sādhana* is also sometimes referred to as *vaidhī-bhakti* practiced not with a view to attain reverential *prema* but rather to attain greater qualification for the practices of *rāga-bhakti* and ultimately to attain Vraja *prema*.

and *kaniṣṭha*.[22] Such an understanding includes within it both the budding and the mature definitions of *lobha* we find in the Gauḍīya community and places each initiated member of the *sampradāya* on the *rāga-mārga*. And as we have seen, this eligibility extends further to also include those yet to experience *lobha*—*ajāta-ruci-sādhakas*. Hence as *lobha* manifests and matures, the *sādhaka*'s heart is cleansed and he or she is able to gradually adopt all the practices of *rāgānugā-bhakti*.

Let us now explore Rūpa Goswāmī's verses about the nature of *rāgānugā-sādhana*. He begins with the following verse:

> One should engage in *smaraṇam* on the dearmost form of Kṛṣṇa and on those of his dear associates who have a similar serving disposition to one's own. Absorbing oneself in hearing topics related to them, one should always reside in Vraja.[23]

Śrī Rūpa first highlights the *bhakti-aṅga* of *smaraṇam*, which is central to *rāgānuga-sādhana*. He points out that it is to be aided by *śravaṇam*, or hearing, which should be done in a systematic manner. Aside from learning the *tattva* that underlies the *līlā*, Śrī Rūpa posits a focused sense of *bhajana*. One should hear about and remember Vraja Kṛṣṇa—his form, his attributes, and his *līlās*. One should also hear about and remember how his Vraja *līlā* devotees—*rāgātmikas*—who personify one's ideal serve him. The spirit of this *sādhana* is to absorb the mind in thoughts of one's cherished ideal of divine love and the object of love it corresponds with.

With regard to the kind of hearing that promotes the *smaraṇam* that Rūpa Goswāmī speaks of, Bhaktivinoda Ṭhākura invokes the term *krama-śuddha-śravaṇam*, hearing methodically about Kṛṣṇa and his associates from advanced devotees in a manner that gives one a sense of how Kṛṣṇa's *līlās* connect with one another. Thus, he recommends hearing the descriptions of Kṛṣṇa's *līlās* as they manifest sequentially throughout the eight divisions of the day. This type of hearing from the lips of advanced devotees nourishes the *sādhaka*'s budding *lobha*. Although such hearing applies to whichever *rasa* one pursues, to give an example of the result of such *krama-śuddha-śravaṇam*, Bhaktivinoda writes, "At that time one thinks within oneself, 'Oh! Subala has such wonderful *sakhya-bhāva*, I will also render loving *sevā* to Kṛṣṇa like him in *sakhya-rasa*.' "[24]

22. *Bhakti-tattva-viveka*, chapter 4.
23. *Bhakti-rasāmṛta-sindhu* 1.2.294.
24. *Jaiva Dharma*, chapter 40. *Krama-śuddha-śravaṇam* is also discussed in this chapter.

As an aid to this *sādhana*, Śrī Rūpa teaches that one should reside in Vṛndāvana. There are two ways to reside in this sacred domain. One can reside there physically and mentally, or just mentally. It is not to be thought of as a limited geographical area of the world, even as it has its earthly manifestation that one can reside in. Thus, in essence, this aspect of *rāgānuga-sādhana*—living in Vṛndāvana—also constitutes *smaraṇam*.

In his *Bhakti Sandarbha*, Jīva Goswāmī begins his discussion on *smaraṇam* with the following statement: "If one's heart has become pure by surrender, service to devotees who embody the truth, and hearing and singing the names, forms, attributes, and pastimes of the Lord, one can perform *smaraṇam*, or remembrance of the Lord. The practice of remembrance, however, should be undertaken without giving up *nāma-kīrtanam*."[25] Here, *nāma-kīrtanam* is stressed in relation to the *aṅga* of *smaraṇam*. *Smaraṇam* should be preceded and followed by *kīrtanam*. Although *smaraṇam* is central to *rāgānuga-sādhana*, *kīrtana* nonetheless takes precedence. Indeed, Jīva Goswāmī informs us that even *nāma-smaraṇam* is not as effective as *nāma-kīrtanam* and that it requires a pure heart as a prerequisite![26] Thus, those practicing *ajāta-ruci-rāgānugā-bhakti* should embrace *nāma-kīrtanam* in particular as the means by which further qualification is attained.

In his instruction on *kīrtanam*, Jīva Goswāmī explains that *nāma-kīrtanam* should generally precede other forms of *kīrtanam*. *Nāma-kīrtanam* can then more effectively be followed by *rūpa-*, *guṇa-*, and *līlā-kīrtanam*, in this order. Similarly, in his instruction on *smaraṇam*, Śrī Jīva cites the same sequence. Thus, *smaraṇam* is best approached by first becoming proficient in *nāma-smaraṇam*. One can then best proceed to meditate on the form, qualities, and, finally, *līlās* of Kṛṣṇa, all of which are said to be contained within his holy name.

Furthermore, Jīva Goswāmī explains five stages of intensity in *smaraṇam*:[27]

1. *Smaraṇam*: thinking of Kṛṣṇa in any manner and to any extent.

2. *Dhāraṇā*: withdrawing the mind (*pratyāhāra*) and concentrating it (*dhāraṇā*) on Kṛṣṇa in general.

3. *Dhyāna*: specifically meditating on Kṛṣṇa's name, form, attributes, and *līlās*.

25. *Bhakti Sandarbha* 275. Śrīla Jīva Gosvāmī, *Śrī Bhakti Sandarbha*, trans. by Dr. Satya Nārāyaṇa Dāsa and Bruce Martin, vol. 3 (Vrindavana, India: Jiva Institute, 2006), 901.

26. *Bhakti Sandarbha* 276.

27. *Bhakti Sandarbha* 278.

4. *Dhruvānusmṛti*: constantly remembering Kṛṣṇa without interruption.

5. *Samādhi*: being completely immersed in meditative trance.

Despite the fact that *smaraṇam* requires a pure heart, it is also said throughout the *śāstra* that remembering Kṛṣṇa purifies one's heart. Thus, it is the intensified sense of *smaraṇam*—*dhruvānusmṛti* and *samādhi*—that is not possible without a pure heart, whereas even the neophyte *rāga-mārga-sādhaka* will endeavor to remember Kṛṣṇa and his associates in the focused sense described above and endeavor to withdraw his or her mind from other objects. *Ajāta-ruci-rāgānuga-sādhakas* will also engage in *dhyāna*. For example, Śrī Jīva Goswāmī suggests the following meditation/visualization—*dhyāna*—to accompany the *japa* of the principal *dīkṣā-mantra* of the *sampradāya*, the *aṣṭādaśākṣara* (eighteen-syllable) Kṛṣṇa/Gopāla *mantra*:

> I chant this *mantra* that my *guru* has given me so that I may attain my desire and become one of the people of Vraja. Then I will directly serve Kṛṣṇa, the son of the king of Vraja.[28]

In his *Kṛṣṇa Sandarbha*, Jīva Goswāmī also points to the eighteen-syllable Gopāla *mantra* as an example of a *mantra* that can be employed in *mantra-mayī upāsanā*, or meditative worship on a still frame of the motion picture of Kṛṣṇa *līlā*—focusing the mind on a vision of one frame of the *līlā* described in a particular verse. This type of *dhyāna* is intended to help the *sādhaka* enter into the *līlā* with the help of a *mantra* or verse, and when one is accomplished in this type of meditation, spontaneous meditation—*svārasikī upāsanā*—on the flow of the *līlā* becomes possible. Jīva Goswāmī gives an example to illustrate these two types of meditation. He compares *mantra-mayī upāsanā* to a virtual lake within a river that has formed as a result of the banks of the river widening.[29] It is much easier to enter the river at such a lake, where the current is practically nil. However, because the current is still flowing in such a lake, as one enters into it one eventually finds oneself moving with the meditative flow of the river and into the current where the banks have narrowed. Thus, from *mantra*-assisted meditation on one phase of the *līlā*, spontaneous meditation on the flow of the *līlā* arises, which is further assisted by scriptural descriptions of the typical eightfold divisions of the daily *līlā*.

28. *Bhakti Sandarbha* 312.
29. *Kṛṣṇa Sandarbha* 153.

Śrī Jīva cites three verses from the *Gopāla-tāpanī śruti* (1.9–11) that serve as a *mantra-mayī* visualization to accompany the Gopāla *mantra*:

> Śrī Kṛṣṇa's eyes are like perfect lotus petals, his bodily color that of a monsoon cloud, and his garments are the color of lightning. He has two arms, with his hand held in the *jñāna-mudrā*. Wearing a garland of forest flowers, he is surrounded by *gopas*, *gopīs*, and cows, and sits decorated with divine ornaments on a jeweled lotus at the foot of a divine desire tree. He is fanned by pleasant breezes moistened by spray from the waters of the Yamunā.[30]

While *dhyāna* and the other two less intense forms of *smaraṇam* are practiced, *dhruvānusmṛti* and *samādhi* are more a result of practice. *Dhruvānusmṛti* and *samādhi* are spontaneous forms of *smaraṇam* and will arise only out of a pure heart, whereas *smaraṇam*, *dhāraṇā*, and *dhyāṇa* have some capacity to purify the heart but not as much power unto themselves to do so as *nāma* and other forms of *kīrtanam*. Aided by *kīrtanam*, their efficacy is enhanced and useful for those *sādhakas* whose hearts remain cluttered by desires other than for *bhakti*, desires that a *sādhaka* consistently endeavors to retire.

> Following after the inhabitants of Vraja, one should perform service in one's *sādhaka-rūpa* and in one's *siddha-rūpa* with a desire for a particular *bhāva*.[31]

Here in his second verse, Śrī Rūpa introduces the two forms mentioned above, a *sādhaka-* and *siddha-rūpa*. Unlike in Advaita Vedānta, which advocates formless *mukti*, here in the Gauḍīya tradition we learn of two bodies, neither of which is material. And while Śaṅkara has no enduring use for the material body, Śrī Caitanya spiritualizes it. Such is the power of *bhakti*! Kavirāja Goswāmī relates the instruction of Mahāprabhu to Sanātana Goswāmī in this connection:

> At the time of *dīkṣā*, the *bhakta* consigns his *ātmā*, and as he does so, Kṛṣṇa makes him one with himself. Thus, the *bhakta*'s *sādhaka-deha* becomes *cit-ānanda-maya*, an *aprākṛta-deha* suitable for engaging in *bhajana* at the feet of Kṛṣṇa.[32]

30. *Kṛṣṇa Sandarbha* 153. *Gopāla-tāpanī* considers these verses to represent the *dhyāna* that corresponds with the eighteen-syllable Gopāla *mantra*.

31. *Bhakti-rasāmṛta-sindhu* 1.2.295.

32. *Caitanya-caritāmṛta* 3.4.192–193.

The *sādhaka-deha* is not a material body, nor is it a *siddha-rūpa*, at least not immediately. It is a spiritual work in progress. The more the *sādhaka*'s senses are in touch with sense objects only for the purpose of pleasing the transcendental senses of Kṛṣṇa, the more it is spiritualized. Adorned with *tilaka* and *kaṇṭhī-mālā*, in this world but not of it, the *sādhaka-deha* is no longer moving under the influence of the *māyā-śakti*, but rather that of the *svarūpa-śakti*, which *bhakti* is constituted of. Śrī Kṛṣṇa describes such devotees in his divine song to Pāṇḍava Arjuna:

> O cousin brother, son of Pṛthā, those who engage in one-minded *bhajana* to me are *mahātmās* moving under the influence of my *svarūpa-śakti*—*daivīṁ prakṛtim*.... They are always engaged in *kīrtana* of my names, forms, qualities, and *līlās*—*satataṁ kīrtayanto māṁ*.[33]

The *Sārārtha-darśinī* comments of Viśvanātha Cakravartī in this regard are insightful:

> One's *sādhaka-deha* is considered to be *nirguṇa* because, on the order of one's spiritual master, all of one's senses are engaged in the transcendental service of Kṛṣṇa, one's ears in hearing about Kṛṣṇa, one's tongue in chanting Kṛṣṇa's names and glories, one's mind in remembering Kṛṣṇa, one's entire body in prostrating oneself in supplication to the deity, and one's hands in various types of service. Thus, because the objects of the devotee's senses are Bhagavān's qualities, the devotee also becomes *nirguṇa*. However, at the same time, because the *sādhaka* also makes material things the objects of his or her senses now and again, the *sādhaka*'s body is also *guṇa-maya*, or constituted of material qualities. Therefore, the *sādhaka-deha* is partly *nirguṇa* and partly *guṇa-maya*. According to the indications of the *Bhāgavata* verse (11.2.42) that compares advancement in devotional service to the satisfaction felt by a hungry person while eating, the gaining of strength, and the relief from the discomforts of hunger, one can understand that these three things are attained gradually, for as much as one has eaten, to that extent one will feel these beneficial effects. Similarly, as one progresses spiritually through *sādhana*, the spiritualized portion of one's body increases, and the material portion is gradually reduced. When one reaches

33. *Bhagavad-gītā* 9.13–14.

> the stage of *prema*, one's body is completely spiritualized, and no mundane portion remains.[34]

To better understand the spiritualization of the material body and the spiritual personality that arises from it, it will be helpful to consider that one's present material personality is largely a result of the way in which one's senses interact with sense objects, resulting in mental impressions, likes, and dislikes. If, on the other hand, one interacts with sense objects through one's senses only for the pleasure of Kṛṣṇa, will this not result in very different impressions, all of which are instrumental in forming a relationship with him?

Thus, the mature *sādhaka-rūpa* is a spiritually infused body such that despite the inevitable demise of the *sādhu*'s *sādhaka-deha*, his or her form is entombed, venerated, and meditated upon, resulting at times in meditative visitations and dreams wherein *mantras* and counsel are sometimes imparted.[35]

Śrī Rūpa prescribes service in one's *sādhaka-rūpa—sevā sādhaka-rūpeṇa*. Indeed, the *sādhaka-rūpa* is an embodiment of *sevā*. However, the service rendered is different than that rendered in one's *siddha-rūpa*. Although in each form one follows the lead of the *rāgātmika*'s *sevā*, in one's *sādhaka-rūpa* one follows the service example of the *rāgātmikas* such as the Vṛndāvana Goswāmīs and *dvādaśa-gopālas* as they appear in Gaura *līlā* in the role of *sādhakas*, and not the service of the *rāgātmikas* as they manifest in Kṛṣṇa *līlā* in the forms of *gopīs* and *gopas*. This latter form of service manifests as one's internal *siddha-rūpa*. This *sādhaka-rūpa* is the gift of *śrī guru*. Using it wisely gives rise to the second spiritual form mentioned in Śrī Rūpa's verse—the *siddha-rūpa*. Indeed, the *siddha-rūpa* arises out of the *sādhaka-rūpa*'s *antaḥkaraṇa* absorbed in meditation.

It is only in a purified *citta*, and beyond that after attaining *bhāva*, that the *siddha-deha* Rūpa Goswāmī speaks of in his second verse will fully manifest. Serving in this internal meditative body is a form of *līlā-smaraṇam* particularly suitable for liberated contemplatives, or *bhāva-bhaktas*. In the opinion of Jīva Goswāmī, cited earlier, *līlā-smaraṇam* is the most spiritually advanced form of *smaraṇam*. The *siddha-rūpa* suitable for internal *līlā-sevā* "appears through inner contemplation with a desire for a particular *rati*" and "is developed by internal meditation."[36] The desire to attain a

34. *Śrīmad Bhāgavatam* 10.29.11.

35. Regarding the imparting of *mantras* through dreams, see *Govinda-bhāṣya* 3.2.4.

36. *Bhakti-rasāmṛta-sindhu* 1.2.295, commentaries of Viśvanātha Cakravartī and Jīva

bhāva-deha is the seed of the spiritual body, which is imparted through spiritual impressions. In the early stages of *sādhana-bhakti* it is cultivated for the most part by preparing the field and doing away with weeds. It sprouts in *bhāva-bhakti*, where it is cultivated further, and it fructifies in *prema*. And while there are different approaches to this overall cultivation, deference to the instructions of one's own *guru* is the best course, while respect for the approach of other *gurus* is also called for.

The earliest support for a *siddha-rūpa*, or spiritual body, is found in the Upaniṣads. Here we shall view this support through the lens of *Vedānta-sūtra* and Śrī Baladeva Vidyābhūṣaṇa's *Govinda-bhāṣya* commentary. The fourth *adhyāya* of the Sūtras concerns attainment, the *prayojana-tattva*, and 4.4.1 deals with the "manifestation of *jīvātmā*'s *svarūpa*"—*sampady-āvirbhāvādhikaraṇam*. As such, its first *sūtra* seeks to explain *Chāndogya Upaniṣad* 8.12.3, which states that upon attaining one's own form and nature (*svena rūpeṇābhini padyate*) resulting from approaching the highest light (*paraṁ jyotir*) one laughs, moves about, and plays, etc. (*jakṣat krīḍan ramamāṇaḥ*). However, the doubt raised by the *pūrvapakṣa* is, "This form must be similar to the celestial forms that *jīvas* attain in heaven as a result of their pious acts, forms that are different from one's *ātmā*. How so? Because if this form were inherent in the *jīva*, it would not be something to be attained, since it would already be there." Baladeva Vidyābhūṣaṇa answers this doubt for Gauḍīya Vedānta in agreement with all schools of Vaiṣṇava Vedānta: This spiritual form that facilitates moving about and playing with the Godhead is inherent in the *ātmā*. It manifests through the medium of *sādhana-bhakti* served by *jñāna* and *vairāgya* and is one with the *ātmā*. Previously it was present but unmanifest, and thus despite its being inherent, it is nonetheless attained (*abhiniṣpadyate*) when it manifests. And Śrī Baladeva in Gauḍīya fashion goes on to say that upon attaining the highest light (*raso vai saḥ*), the *ātmā*'s attributes are fully manifest and one tastes *rasa*—*rasaṁ hy evāyaṁ labdhvānandī bhavati* (*Taittirīya Upaniṣad* 2.7.1).

In *sūtra* 4.4.12 Śrī Baladeva explains further that one attains a spiritual body by the power of one's liberated will.[37] As such, the liberated *jīva*'s desire

---

Goswāmī, respectively.

37. The Sūtras explain that formless *mukti* is also attainable, should one so desire. However, Sanātana Goswāmī comments in *Bṛhad-bhāgavatāmṛta* 2.2.197 that it is still possible for *muktas* merged in *brahma-sāyujya* to attain a *siddha-rūpa*. He cites *Vedānta-sūtra* 1.3.2, rendering it thus: Brahman is "approached for shelter by persons who are liberated." Also see *Bṛhad-bhāgavatāmṛta* 2.2.186, 207. Similarly, in his *Dāsa Mūla* 8 Ṭhākura Bhaktivinoda explains, "When the knowledge of one's original identity is indistinct, it leads to

for a spiritual body arises under the influence of Bhagavān's *svarūpa-śakti*, which *bhakti* is constituted of. This *śakti* exists only for giving pleasure to Bhagavān. As such, the *mukta*'s yearning for a spiritual body signifies an ardent desire to wholeheartedly serve the form of Bhagavān in every aspect. However, while this liberated and spiritual longing gives rise to the devotee's spiritual body during *bhāva-bhakti*, Baladeva Vidyābhūṣaṇa explains that the cultivation of the spiritual body begins during the stage of *sādhana-bhakti*.[38] Jīva Goswāmī suggests that this cultivation is the *dhyāna* that should accompany the *japa* of the principal *dīkṣā-mantra* of the *sampradāya*.

The idea here is that one should harbor the ideal of attaining a *siddha-rūpa* for *līlā-sevā* from the outset of one's *sādhana*. It will be either a *gopa-* or a *gopī-siddha-rūpa* relative to one's practice. Through *sādhu-saṅga* the *sādhaka* attains both the grace of opportunity and the ingredients required to take advantage of that opportunity. Then, through his or her effort and sincere desire, the *sādhaka* prepares these ingredients and offers them in the form of his or her spiritual personality.

As the *citta* is cleansed of material *saṁskāras*, the further ingress of Kṛṣṇa's *svarūpa-śakti* affords the advanced *sādhaka* the opportunity to desire spiritually in greater detail under the influence of that *śakti*, which exists only to please Kṛṣṇa. With a crystal-like cleansed *citta*, the *sādhaka*'s *rāga* colors his or her *citta*. And the purified seat of the *sādhaka*'s desire and emotion—*manas*—gives rise to the details of one's *siddha-rūpa*, which, while one in kind—*sakhya* or *mādhurya*, and so forth—is unique in detail from every other *mukta*'s, even as it follows a particular personified ideal such as that of Subala-sakhā. The *sādhaka*'s will manifests as spiritualized *buddhi*, or resolve, and causes that *siddha-rūpa* to manifest. In other words, as one progresses from the higher stages of *sādhana-bhakti*—*ruci* and *āsakti*—to *bhāva-bhakti*, the details of one's *siddha-rūpa* are determined, and then they sprout. The *sādhana* stage of *ruci* is characterized by spiritual longing for *bhakti* and absence of material desire. This longing is specific, and thus focused on a particular spiritual emotion that corresponds with a specific object of love that the *sādhaka* develops attachment for in the stage of *āsakti*. If the longing is for *sakhya-rati*, the object of that love is Gopāla Kṛṣṇa replete with qualities that are excitants for *sakhya-rati*. Then, as the sprout of one's

---

sāyujya-mukti. However, when the original identity is clearly understood, the *jīva* attains eternal and pure servitorship to Śrī Kṛṣṇa."

38. We have seen that realizing one's *siddha-rūpa* requires *sadhu-saṅga*, from which one acquires *bhakti-saṁskāras* and engagement in *sādhana-bhakti*. And *sādhana-bhakti* in turn involves the will/desire of the *sādhaka*. This desire matures in the stage of *ruci*.

sthāyi-bhāva appears in *bhāva-bhakti*, it is further cultivated and gradually it flowers and fructifies into *prema*—the form of the *mukta*'s love.

Here it must be stressed that the *siddha-rūpa* is at the same time eternal in that the *bhāva* it is constituted of is eternally existing. This *bhāva*, be it *sakhya* or *mādhurya*, and so on, is embodied in the *rāgātmikas* of Vraja, and it expresses itself in limitless forms—from unmanifest to manifest—for the pleasure of Śrī Kṛṣṇa. The *sādhana-siddha*'s attainment of such a form is thus merely that particular *bhāva* manifesting out of its grace in yet another eternal form for the service of Kṛṣṇa, just as the *svarūpa-śakti* eternally manifests newer and newer *līlās* for his pleasure. *Prema*, after all, is full yet ever-expanding, and *bhakti* is both an eternal being and an eternal becoming, even as it is a discovery of that which already exists. The mystery of Rādhā's love, for example, is that despite the fact that it is full and all-pervading with no room to grow, it expands at every moment throughout eternity.[39]

Here it is important to note the unique nature of eternity in Gauḍīya Vedānta. This dynamic eternity involves two contradictory features: It has no past, present, or future and at the same time it is dynamic, and thus it constantly moves and enriches itself. It has no past, present, or future not because it does not move but rather *because it is full and complete*. And it moves not because of any unrealized possibility but because of its perfection.[40] Accordingly, Ṭhākura Bhaktivinoda describes Kṛṣṇa as the *su-nitya-nūtana-murti*, "the form of eternal newness."[41] Indeed, "Brahman" is derived from the Sanskrit root *bṛh*—to grow or expand—and as such means "that which grows and causes other things to grow." And such is the *līlā* of Para-brahman Gopala Kṛṣṇa—eternally new and ever-fresh—leaving room for newcomers to enter and be all that they can be eternally. Such *sādhana-siddhas* are part of the celebratory movement of Kṛṣṇa's own perfection orchestrated by his *svarūpa-śakti*, an unfolding of transcendental variety that is both eternal and ever-expanding—*sā sā viśeṣa-vaicitrī sadā sampadyate yataḥ*.[42]

39. Citing Śrī Rūpa's *Dāna-keli-kaumudī* 2, Kṛṣṇadāsa Kavirāja also describes the *prema* of Rādhā as all-pervading and thus leaving no room for expansion while simultaneously ever-increasing (*Caitanya-caritāmṛta* 1.4.127–128). Thus, Kṛṣṇa is omnipresent yet moving, driven to dance by his devotees' love.

40. Brahmachari, Mahanamabrata, *Vaisnava Vedanta*, Das Gupta & Company (P) LTD 1974, p 216.

41. *Śrī Gītā-mālā* 4.2.

42. See *Bṛhad-bhāgavatāmṛta* 2.4.176. Sanātana Goswāmī comments that here the word *sadā* indicates that variety manifest by Kṛṣṇa's *svarūpa-śakti* is both eternal and ever expanding.

It is also important and of great interest to note that the *mukta* who attains its form of eternal service attains an entire spiritual personality. In other words, the *mukta*'s form includes both a spiritual body of working and perceiving senses as well as an ego, mind, intelligence, and awareness. The spiritual body is *krīḍana-deha*, "paraphernalia suitable for Kṛṣṇa's recreational pursuit."[43] The *mukta* desires and enjoys only in relation to pleasing Kṛṣṇa. And it is for this reason that the Sūtras conclude that *mukti* with form is more fulfilling than formless *mukti*.[44] In formless *mukti*, one ends the ongoing attempt to *become*, which drives us in material life, and the formless *mukta*'s being far exceeds anything one can become materially. However, on the *bhakti-mārga*, while the attempt to become in a material sense also comes to an end, the *siddha-bhakta* does not rest with merely being but pursues all that the *ātmā* can become as a result of the ingress of *bhakti* into one's life. Such transcendental becoming does not constitute a transformation of the *ātmā*, but rather an eternal becoming of the more that we are when we love.

To borrow a term from Charles Hartshorne, Kṛṣṇa is dipolar in nature. He personifies the admirable aspects of both contrasting metaphysical poles; that is, he embodies that which is admirable in immanence as well as that in transcendence—permanence as well as change, and so on. He is full and also ever-increasing. This makes for a dynamic Absolute. It is said that at one point Lakṣmī had never experienced Narasiṁha. Yet Narasiṁha is eternal. In the same sense, our *siddha-rūpa* lies within the depths of God's being, as do we, and manifests when *prema* appears. The *siddha-svarūpa* is an extension of God's own form, and thus the devotee in his or her manifest *siddha-rūpa* experiences, through what is really an extension of God's senses, a dynamic union with God in love. In the *siddha-rūpa*, the *mukta* sees, hears, tastes, and so forth only for God's pleasure, just as God's senses function for his own pleasure.[45]

Just as Śrī Rūpa prescribes *sevā* in one's *sādhaka-rūpa*, he also prescribes *sevā* in one's *siddha-rūpa*. As mentioned earlier, this meditative internal *sevā* emulates the *prema-sevā* of the *rāgātmika* of Kṛṣṇa *līlā* that one follows. In his *Rāga-vartma-candrikā* Viśvanātha Cakravartī Ṭhākura cites two means by which knowledge required for meditative *līlā-sevā* is acquired. In this regard, he paraphrases Uddhava's words to Kṛṣṇa:

43. This term is found in *Śrīmad Bhāgavatam* 10.33.35 in reference to Kṛṣṇa's body, but the same applies to the spiritual bodies of his devotees.

44. *Vedānta-sūtra* 4.4.14.

45. In his *Govinda-bhāṣya* (4.4.12), Baladeva Vidyābhūṣaṇa cites *Bṛhad-āraṇyaka Upaniṣad* 4.5.15 and an unspecified verse from *Bṛhad Tantra*.

> Śrī Bhagavān inspires the *sādhaka* by manifesting himself in two ways: Externally he gives instructions in the form of the *ācārya*. Alternately, he provides this same instruction internally as the *caitya-guru*—God himself within—inspiring a *sādhaka* from within the heart concerning the means to achieve the desired goal.[46]

In his commentary on the above verse, Viśvanātha Cakravartī cites and paraphrases the essence of *Bhagavad-gītā* 10.10, which further substantiates his latter claim that the *caitya-guru* in some instances provides all one needs to know through gradual internal realization: "Inspiring them with intelligence to attain you, and making them worship you, you reveal to them the goal of becoming an associate with *prema*." In his *Rāga-vartma-candrikā*, Ṭhākura Viśvanātha also cites *Bhāgavatam* 11.14.26:

> To the degree that the *ātmā* becomes purified by hearing and chanting my glories, a person is able to perceive my real form and qualities, just as the eye when smeared with special ointment is able to see finer objects.

This verse supports the idea that all that one needs to know—the details of one's *siddha-rūpa* and how to engage in meditative *līlā-sevā* with it—will arise naturally through gradual realization derived from one's appropriately *rāga-mārga*-oriented *sādhana*. Perceiving Kṛṣṇa's form in meditation on the path of *rāga-bhakti* also includes perceiving one's *siddha-rūpa* because Kṛṣṇa is perceived relative to how he is approached. If we approach him influenced by *sakhya-rati*, we will experience him as he appears to his cowherd friends of Vraja. In other words, the beauty of Gopāla Kṛṣṇa is not separate from or independent of the eye of its beholder.[47] *Śrīmad Bhāgavatam* explains that Kṛṣṇa enters his devotee's heart in a particular form and in doing so simultaneously bestows upon his devotee a spiritual form that corresponds with this particular form as well as with the nature of the devotee's worship—*tat-tad-vapuḥ praṇayase sad-anugrahāya*.[48] The implication of *Bhāgavatam* 11.14.26 cited by Viśvanātha Cakravartī is that this is

46. *Śrīmad Bhāgavatam* 11.29.6. See *Rāga-vartma-candrikā* 1.9.

47. See *Śrīmad Bhāgavatam* 10.43.17 for an example of how different persons see Kṛṣṇa differently.

48. *Śrīmad Bhāgavatam* 3.9.11. In *Bhagavat Sandarbha* 40, Jīva Goswāmī comments that the significance of the phrase *śrutekṣita-pathaḥ* (seen through the ear) in this verse is that Bhagavān appears in the forms mentioned in the scriptures. He is not bound to appear in whatever form someone imagines. Accordingly, a *sādhaka* will meditate on God as he is described in the scriptures. Śrī Jīva also references *Śrīmad Bhāgavatam* 3.24.31 in this regard.

a gradual development and one approach to acquiring all that is required for meditative *līlā-sevā*.

Thus, with spiritual progress and the purification of one's *citta*, just how to serve internally in a *siddha-rūpa* manifests in proportion to the manifestation of the *siddha-rūpa* itself. Notably, the exemplars cited from the sacred lore of those who rendered this service and attained their ideal through *kāmānuga-sādhana*—the sages of Daṇḍakāraṇya and the personified *śrutis*—learned how to render *siddha-rūpa-sevā* in this way. The same holds true in the case of *Bṛhad-bhāgavatāmṛta*'s Gopa-kumāra/Sarūpa in his *sambandhānuga-sādhana*. None of these devotees received any esoteric instruction on *siddha-rūpa-sevā* aside from what they received through internal realization. Indeed, Gopa-kumāra's *guru* instructed him on how to chant the Kṛṣṇa *mantra* and then told him that by the power of that *mantra* alone "all other secrets will be automatically revealed to you."[49] Subsequently, Gopa-kumāra attained a form suitable for liberated life.[50]

However, following Uddhava Mahāśaya's words to Kṛṣṇa above, Ṭhākura Viśvanātha also posits that while some learn this esoteric service internally in the context of their *sādhana*, others are instructed in this *sevā* externally by their *dīkṣā-* or *śikṣā-guru* prior to such realization. A prominent text supportive of this approach is *Gaura-govindārcana-smaraṇa-paddhati* of Dhyānacandra Goswāmī. Although Viśvanātha Cakravartī Ṭhākura does not mention the contribution of Dhyānacandra Goswāmī, the Goswāmī's mid-seventeenth-century work is a virtual *arcana-paddhati* for *mānasī-sevā* in pursuit of *gopī-bhāva*—a handbook or manual for absorbing the mind in meditative service much like a manual for physical *arcana-sevā* that contains, for example, a prototype of the *mañjarī-svarūpa* that *sādhakas* of this ideal will attain.[51] Accordingly, it is drawn largely from the Pāñcarātrika and Tāntrika texts, where *mantras*, *yantras*, visualizations, and procedures for worship are found and *śakti-tattva* is emphasized. Notably, in describing

49. *Bṛhad-bhāgavatāmṛta* 2.3.6.

50. *Bṛhad-bhāgavatāmṛta* 2.3.9. In his commentary on this verse, Sanātana Goswāmī states that Gopa-kumāra experienced the transubstantiation of his material body, which turned into a spiritual body.

51. This prototype is drawn from the *Sanat-kumāra Saṁhitā*. It highlights eleven aspects of the *mañjarī-svarūpa*. This prototype is imparted to the disciple, who is to think of it as the spiritual body he or she will attain. However, it is a matter of controversy as to whether the *guru* imparts such a prototype or a unique *mañjarī-svarūpa* revealed to him or her in meditation. Often the latter is said to be the case, perhaps to instill faith that in turn will fuel relevant practice short of having attained *ruci*, but Dhyānacandra's text itself speaks only of the former—imparting of the prototype.

the Kali *yuga-avatāra*, the *Bhāgavatam* teaches that worship of him is drawn principally from the Tāntrika texts, *nānā-tantra-vidhānena*.[52] As mentioned in the previous chapter, Nayanānanda Ṭhākura appears to have followed this approach in his *Preyo-bhakti-rasārṇava*, which serves to a limited extent as a corresponding *sambandhānugā-mānasī-sevā sādhana* handbook.

Arguably, when budding realization—the flowering of the seed of *rati* derived from *sādhu-saṅga* and corresponding *sādhana*—is met with appropriate instruction combining the two approaches, one is best equipped to proceed with the desired *siddha-rūpa-sevā*. One is typically better off with good spiritual instruction, but good spiritual instruction is only so when it corresponds with the appropriate stage of spiritual realization that enables the *sādhaka* to take advantage of it. Successful *sādhana* requires a measure of skill, as does a great work of art.

Bhaktivinoda Ṭhākura himself advocated a combination of these two approaches in that he emphasized the imparting of specific instruction on *līlā-sevā* only to those who had attained higher stages of *sādhana-bhakti*—*ruci* and *āsakti*.[53] His wise insight here is that *līlā-sevā-smaraṇam* will not be consistent and fruitful unless driven by taste. He stressed that such instruction imparted to qualified *sādhakas* follows and supports one's budding *lobha*, leading to higher realization. Thus, he taught that the *krama-śuddha-śravaṇa* mentioned earlier is the central practice for one in the stage of hearing (*śravaṇa-daśā*), which leads naturally to the stage of acceptance (*varaṇa-daśā*), or the embrace of a particular spiritual identity and corresponding *sevā*. At this stage, *śrī gurudeva* assists the *sādhaka* in determining the details of his or her *siddha-rūpa* and its *līlā-sevā*. Thus, the *siddha-rūpa* ideal that one embraces involves, among other things, a desired *sevā*, such as the desire to placate the mind of Kṛṣṇa in his separation from Rādhā and/or to placate the mind of Rādhā in her separation from Kṛṣṇa, resulting in their union—a service akin to that of Subala, who exceeds every other *rāgātmika* in his ability to render this particular service. The following stage of *līlā-sevā* in meditation (*smaraṇa-daśā*) is done without actual *bhāva*. One

52. *Śrīmad Bhāgavatam* 11.5.31.

53. In his commentary on *Manaḥ-śikṣā*, Bhaktivinoda also refers to Raghunātha dāsa Goswāmī's body of work as an example of the esoteric path—*antaḥ-panthāḥ*—concerning *siddha-rūpa-sevā*. In doing so, Bhaktivinoda arguably identified this path with the approach in which the *caitya-guru*'s role is predominant. He further identifies Dhyānacandra Goswāmī's *Śrī Gaura-govindārcana-smaraṇa-paddhati* as an example of the exoteric course—*bahiḥ-panthāḥ*—in which external instruction is predominant. He reasons that both paths originate in a work of Svarūpa Dāmodara that is no longer available.

idealizes the desired *bhāva* as one hears about and contemplates Kṛṣṇa's daily *līlā*, following the *bhāva* of Subala in the example cited. This is the gist of *siddha-rūpa-sevā* that in practice leads to the stage of *bhāva* (*bhāvāpanna-daśā*) and finally to the stage of *prema* (*sampatti-daśā*).

In *Jaiva Dharma* and *Harināma-cintāmaṇī*, Bhaktivinoda forged a confluence between realization of and instruction on *siddha-rūpa-sevā*, and his depth of insight overflowed onto the world stage in the teaching of his successor Bhaktisiddhānta Saraswatī Ṭhākura. The following excerpt from a letter to Bhaktisiddhānta Saraswatī Ṭhākura's British disciple serves as an example:

> All those esoteric truths that are revealed solely through one's advancing practice of chanting the Holy Names are to be considered the introduction to one's *svarūpa*, one's true spiritual identity.... The revelations one has while submerged in chanting the Holy Names with a sincere heart should be humbly presented to *sādhu* and *guru* so that one's conception may be refined and approved. . . . Those who attain *svarūpa-siddhi*, or realization of their eternal spiritual form and identity, come to realize their eternal identity of their own accord (*svataḥ-siddha*) [through *sādhana*]; *śrī gurudeva* merely assists them in making progress in realizing these topics on the path of *bhajana*.[54]

We see an example of this in the life history of Narottama dāsa Ṭhākura. In his *Narottama-carita*, Ananta dāsa Paṇḍita relates the history of how Narottama dāsa, having accepted *harināma* and the Gopāla *mantra*, received a revelation during his practice of *nāma-sevā* that his eternal service was to stir milk for Kṛṣṇa at midday under the direction of Rādhā and that his *mañjarī* name in this *līlā-sevā* would be Campaka-mañjarī. Narottama dāsa then related this revelation to his *guru* Lokanātha Goswāmī, who confirmed it.

Thus, some Gauḍīya lineages emphasize spiritual practice and *nāma-kīrtana* in particular with a specific *rāga-mārga* ideal in mind as the means to bring about *siddha-rūpa-sevā*. Among them, Bhaktisiddhānta Saraswatī Ṭhākura wrote the following in his compelling poem *Vaiṣṇava Ke*, which arose out of many years of solitary *nāma-bhajana*: "By the power of *kīrtanam*, *smaraṇam* naturally arises, and at that time solitary *bhajana* [*siddha-rūpa-sevā*] becomes possible." Thus, he embarked on a compassionate campaign of *kīrtana* that manifested sixty-four Gauḍīya monasteries in India and

54. Bhaktisiddhānta Sarasvatī, *Śrīla Prabhupādera Patrāvalī*, vol. 1 (Calcutta: Kalikata Gaudiya Math, 1931) Letter to "Best of Virtuous Women," November 17, 1930.

exported the teaching to the West while also nourishing his own internal *siddha-rūpa-sevā*.

Such compassionate outreach leading to *siddha-rūpa-sevā* is also found in the example of Śrī Caitanya. Upon accepting the renounced order of *sannyāsa*, he travelled throughout India promoting and taking part in *nāma-saṅkīrtana*. He also instructed his followers to do the same—not only Nityānanda Rāma and his associates but the Vṛndāvana Goswāmīs, who were also deeply compassionate and thus busy in their *sādhaka-dehas* writing books, building temples, and engaging in *nāma-saṅkīrtana*. Śrīnivāsa Ācārya describes them thus:

> Ardently engaged in Kṛṣṇa *kīrtana* and dancing, dipped in the ocean of the deathless nectar of *prema*, they are dear to both the righteous and the rogues. Devoid of envy and thus indiscriminate in their dispensation, they are worthy of everyone's worship. Having received the mercy of Śrī Caitanya in this world, here on earth they relieved others of the burden of material life.... Scriptural geniuses, brimming with compassion, they deliberated on the essence of the Eastern revelation with a view to establish its conclusion of *prema-dharma* and deliver the people of the world.[55]

Śrī Caitanya taught principally by example. After leaving Nadīyā as a *sannyāsī*, he showed the way to enter his *rasa-kīrtana* in the literal and figurative courtyard of Śrīvāsa Ṭhākura's heart, which corresponds with Vṛndāvana. Therein he had previously revealed to his associates their Kṛṣṇa *līlā siddha-rūpa-sevā* in the context of *kīrtana-rasa*, and it is this courtyard of Gaura *līlā saṅkīrtana* that *rāga-mārga-sādhakas* desire to enter and thereby experience Kṛṣṇa *līlā siddha-rūpa-sevā* through the medium of Gaura *līlā*. Worship Gaura and live in Vraja. This is the teaching.

After living a life of *nāma-saṅkīrtana* and compassionate outreach, Gaura became incapable of public life due to the intensity of his *kīrtana*. Thus, he taught by his example how cleansing one's *citta* in *nāma-saṅkīrtana* with the ideal of *rāga-bhakti* in mind first gives rise to universal compassion and then draws one uncontrollably inward to *siddha-rūpa-sevā*. Although establishing the *yuga-dharma* is an incidental aspect of Gaura *līlā*, one should not think that Gaura's *saṅkīrtana* is separate from and external to his internal pursuit of *siddha-rūpa-sevā* in Rādhā *bhāva*. He established the *yuga-dharma* as a by-product of his garlanding the world with *prema-saṅkīrtana*. He wove

55. *Ṣaḍ-goswāmy-aṣṭakam* 1–2.

together *prema* and *saṅkīrtana* and thereby gave *rāga-mārga-bhakti* to the world and tasted it himself.[56]

Notably, Kṛṣṇadāsa Kavirāja states that his *Caitanya-caritāmṛta* is centered—*mukhya*—on Gaura's *madhya-līlā*, wherein he shows the way.[57] Thus, Gaura's *madhya-līlā* occupies more of the text than discussion of the *antya-* and *ādi-līlā* combined. Kavirāja Goswāmī defers to Vṛndāvana dāsa's *Caitanya-bhāgavata* and Murāri Gupta's *Śrī-kṛṣṇa-caitanya-caraṇāmṛta* with regard to more details on Gaura's *ādi-līlā* in Nadīyā, and his treatment of Gaura's internal life in his *antya-līlā* is brief in comparison to his treatment of the *ādi-* and *madhya-līlās*. Internal life is not something that can be easily taught. Nonetheless, Gaura did have teachers in this stage of his spiritual pursuit.

In the arms of Svarūpa Dāmodara and Rāya Rāmānanda and with their assistance, Gaura turned inward to Rādhā-Kṛṣṇa *līlā-smaraṇam* throughout the day and night. Kṛṣṇadāsa Kavirāja compares these two *rāga-mārga-gurus* of Gaura to Lalitā-sakhī and Subala-sakhā, respectively, in terms of how they assisted Rādhā and Kṛṣṇa in their love for one another. Just as Lalitā and Subala assisted Rādhā and Kṛṣṇa, similarly Svarūpa and Rāmānanda assisted Gaura Kṛṣṇa in his effort to experience the *siddha-rūpa-sevā* of Rādhā.[58] What we find in the text itself in terms of their assistance is how they could determine Gaura's inner spiritual emotional struggle through his external symptoms and thus cite esoteric verses to pacify and enhance his emotional pursuit of Rādhā *bhāva*.

Having discussed *sevā* in both the *sādhaka* and *siddha-dehas*, Śrī Rūpa next turns his attention to the *aṅgas* of *vaidhī-bhakti* and the role they play in *sambandhānugā-bhakti*.

> Discriminating practitioners should accept the *aṅgas* that were described in relation to *vaidhī-sādhana-bhakti* such as hearing and chanting as *aṅgas* of *rāgānugā-bhakti* also.[59]

Prior to his teaching on *rāgānuga-sādhana*, Rūpa Goswāmī teaches about *vaidhī-sādhana-bhakti*, the path to reverential love of God. He describes the characteristics of this form of *bhakti* and explains that faith alone constitutes eligibility to tread this path. Then he lists and explains the limbs (*aṅgas*) of

56. *Caitanya-caritāmṛta* 1.4.15–16.
57. *Caitanya-caritāmṛta* 1.13.37.
58. *Caitanya-caritāmṛta* 3.6.9–10.
59. *Bhakti-rasāmṛta-sindhu* 1.2.296.

the body (*aṅgī*) of *vaidhī-bhakti*, consisting of sixty-four methods of worship involving both physical and psychological dimensions of the *sādhaka-deha*.[60] Thus, there are *aṅgas* of *uttama-bhakti* that pertain to the body as a whole as well as to speech, taste, smell, touch, sight, sound, and the mind individually. Also included among the *aṅgas* are ten preliminary items that are to be embraced, beginning with taking shelter of the *guru*, and ten items that are to be shunned, such as association with those opposed to God. These twenty *aṅgas* constitute the doorway to *uttama-bhakti*. Among these preliminary *aṅgas*, taking shelter of the *guru*, accepting initiation from the *guru*, and taking instruction from the *guru* are considered the most important.

Śrī Rūpa defines an *aṅga* of *bhakti* thus:

> The learned define an *aṅga* of *bhakti* as either a complex of devotional actions with internal divisions or only one action of *bhakti* that does not have clearly defined divisions within it.[61]

Kīrtanam is an example of an *aṅga* that is a complex of devotional actions with internal divisions, such as *nāma-kīrtana*, *guṇa-kīrtana*, and *līlā-kīrtana*, whereas the *aṅga* of *sakhyam* (as an *aṅga* and not as a *rati*) is an example of an *aṅga* without internal divisions. Furthermore, among the various *aṅgas*, some are prominent and others secondary.

As mentioned, Rūpa Goswāmī begins his enumeration of the sixty-four *aṅgas* of *vaidhī-sādhana-bhakti* with *gurupādāśraya*, taking shelter of the *guru*. Although his description of *rāgānuga-sādhana* does not mention the sixty-four *aṅgas* individually, Śrī Rūpa says in his third verse about how to perform *rāgānuga-sādhana* that the *aṅgas* of *vaidhī-sādhana-bhakti* are also to be considered *aṅgas* of *rāgānugā-bhakti*. Thus, for example, *rāgānuga-sādhakas* must also come under the shelter of the *guru*, and so on. In other words, the *aṅgas* apply to both types of *sādhana*, while the two types of *sādhana* differ in terms of the motivation behind their execution.

However, it should be noted that even in *vaidhī-bhakti* one is not required to follow all sixty-four limbs. Rūpa Goswāmī says, "*Bhakti*, taking shelter of one principal *aṅga* or many *aṅgas* according to one's desire, and practiced with steadiness, brings about the desired result (*bhāva* and *prema*)."[62] In regard to *rāga-bhakti*, Jīva Goswāmī comments that one should follow those

60. In *Bhakti-rasāmṛta-sindhu* 1.2.72, Rūpa Goswāmī states that the *aṅgas* of *bhakti* are not limited to the sixty-four he lists and explains. He refers the reader to *Hari-bhakti-vilāsa*, where "innumerable *aṅgas* of *bhakti* are mentioned."

61. *Bhakti-rasāmṛta-sindhu* 1.2.73.

62. *Bhakti-rasāmṛta-sindhu* 1.2.264.

aṅgas of *bhakti* that are favorable to one's particular *rāgānuga* cultivation. Viśvanātha Cakravartī adds that some items related to the *aṅga* of *arcana*—ritual worship of the deity—are unfavorable to *rāga-bhakti*. Specifically, "Although prescribed in *śāstra*, procedures related to *arcana* such as worshiping Rukmiṇī, meditating on Dvārakā, performing *mudrās* and *nyāsas*, or identifying oneself with God through self-worship (*ahaṅgrahopāsanam*) should be rejected."[63]

Mudrās are gestures using one's hands and are typically applied to purify items used in *arcana*. *Nyāsa* involves touching various parts of the body with the fingers while uttering *mantras*. These procedures, along with worship of Kṛṣṇa's queens in Dvārakā, are detailed in the Tantra *śāstras* as aspects of *arcana*. Thus, they are not in and of themselves *aṅgas* but are aspects of the *aṅga* of *arcana* that are not favorable for *rāgānuga-sādhana*. The self-worship of thinking, "I am Brahman, as is the deity," is likewise unfavorable, and the *rāgānuga-sādhaka* is also cautioned against thinking oneself to be the *rāgātmika* one meditates on.

One may question how it is possible to neglect *aṅgas* of *bhakti* that the *bhakti-mārga* is constituted of. After all, on the paths of *karma*, *jñāna*, and *yoga*, one cannot neglect aspects of these paths and expect to attain the desired goal. However, this is not the case on the *bhakti-mārga*, which, unlike *karma*, *jñāna*, and *yoga*, is not a process constituted of the *guṇas*. *Bhakti* is *nirguṇa* and is thus not subject to the defects of a materially influenced process. Thus, it is so spiritually powerful that it is not necessary to engage in all of the *bhakti-aṅgas* to attain the goal of *sādhana-bhakti*. In this regard, Viśvanātha Cakravartī Ṭhākura cites *Śrīmad Bhāgavatam* 11.2.35 and 11.29.20 in his *Rāga-vartma-candrikā* 1.12. The Ṭhākura paraphrases the import of both verses thus:

> If one engages in one *aṅga* of *bhakti* for a short period or engages in it for a long period, there is no loss as there is in *karma*. One will not lose the result by performing only one *aṅga* for a short period. Though one is ignorant at present, if one performs *bhakti* without awareness, it is not a fault. What to speak then of performing *bhakti* with awareness?[64]
>
> In following other processes, if one starts and performs the actions until completion of the process without interruption, observing all

63. *Bhakti-rasāmṛta-sindhu* 1.2.296, commentary.
64. *Śrīmad Bhāgavatam* 11.2.35.

> the principles and secondary parts of the process, one will attain the result. If one does not complete the process, if the process is interrupted, or if one does not follow all the parts of the process, the desired result will not be attained. However, this does not apply to *bhakti*. Even if one starts and does not complete the process, or if one does not perform all the parts (*aṅgas*), such incomplete practice is not useless. O Uddhava, if one starts *bhakti-yoga* or if one performs one *aṅga* and does not complete it, the results are not destroyed because of such irregularity, since *bhakti* is beyond the *guṇas*. It is impossible for results derived from *nirguṇa* actions to be destroyed.[65]

The idea is that *bhakti* is a path of the heart, and where there is love, rules do not predominate. In contrast, where there are rules, love does not predominate. On the *karma-mārga* there is practically no love. On this path, the practitioner is more akin to a merchant than a lover, as one practices only with a view to get something in return. It is the path of material acquisition and attachment within piety, and the desired result involves perfect execution of all the prescribed rules. *Jñāna* and *yoga* are practiced in pursuit of freedom from the ignorance and attachment that bear the fruit of suffering, and all of the *aṅgas* of these paths must be practiced to attain the desired goal of *mukti*, which also requires God's grace. *Bhakti*, on the other hand, is the effort to love the deity, who fulfills the ambitions of *karmīs* and ends the suffering of *jñānīs* and *yogīs* while giving himself to his devotees. Rather than freedom, *bhakti* is a contract for a labor of love. Thus, it is hard to go wrong on the path of *bhakti*, where one's heart is in the right place. And this is especially so on the path of *rāgānugā-bhakti* that so endears Śrī Kṛṣṇa.

However, despite her generosity, *bhakti* is at the same time a precise path, and *sādhakas* earnestly seek to embrace all of the *aṅgas* relative to their path of *vaidhī-* or *rāgānugā-bhakti*. If a *sādhaka* fails to engage in the *aṅgas* of *bhakti* properly while trying to execute them correctly, there is no fault, for the desire to properly execute the *aṅgas* is in place. But if one fails to embrace the relevant *aṅgas* of *bhakti* as a consuming lifestyle, to that extent one is not even on the path of *bhakti*.

It is not that *sādhakas* of *uttama-bhakti* must follow every scriptural injunction of the *śruti*, *smṛti*, Purāṇas, and Pañcarātra texts.[66] While proper

65. *Śrīmad Bhāgavatam* 11.29.20.

66. Although the *Brahma-yamāla* verse cited in *Bhakti-rasāmṛta-sindhu* 1.2.101 states that *bhakti* that is not in accordance with scriptural texts is a disturbance to the society of

execution of *bhakti* necessitates scriptural conformity, *bhakti* does not require adherence to every scriptural injunction. "Following the rules according to the scriptures as approved by the *ācāryas*"—*sādhu-vartmānuvartanam*, an *aṅga* of *bhakti*—is a mandate for executing *bhakti* in accordance with the *bhakti-śāstras*. It is not a prescription for following the mandates of each and every sacred text, such as those pertaining to *varṇāśrama-dharma*.

The point here is that *rāgānugā-bhakti* is not an excuse for not following *śāstra*, as it is sometimes thought to be, and as a form of *bhakti* in practice it is constituted of executing the *aṅgas* of *bhakti* suitable to attaining one's particular ideal. Rūpa Goswāmī is stressing *śravaṇam* and *kīrtanam* in relation to nourishing one's capacity to engage in *smaraṇam*. *Śravaṇam*, *kīrtanam*, and *smaraṇam* are the three *aṅgas* most emphasized in the *Bhāgavatam* and those most relative to the *sādhana* of *rāgānugā-bhakti*.[67] These *aṅgas* are not only the way; when their execution is perfected, they become one with the goal.

With regard to the various *aṅgas*, in his *Rāga-vartma-candrikā* Viśvanātha Cakravartī Ṭhākura posits a fivefold division:

> *svābhīṣṭa-bhāva-maya*: the practice of absorbing oneself in thoughts of one's desired *rati*.
>
> *svābhīṣṭa-bhāva-sambandhi*: the practices related to one's desired *rati*.
>
> *svābhīṣṭa-bhāva-anukūla*: the practices favorable to one's desired *rati*.
>
> *svābhīṣṭa-bhāva-aviruddha*: the practices that are neutral, or not opposed, to one's desired *rati*.
>
> *svābhīṣṭa-bhāva-viruddha*: the practices that are detrimental to one's desired *rati*.

We have already discussed *aṅgas* detrimental to one's desired *rati*—*svābhīṣṭa-bhāva-viruddha*—and in his *Rāga-vartma-candrikā* Viśvanātha Cakravartī

---

devotees, Jīva Goswāmī explains that this verse means that one should follow the Vaiṣṇava scriptures pertaining to one's path and not that one should follow other texts that do not pertain to the *bhakti-mārga*.

67. *Sakhyam*—thinking and acting as if Kṛṣṇa is one's friend—is also an *aṅga* of *sādhana-bhakti*, but it is reserved for advanced *sādhakas*. Rūpa Goswāmī cites an example of *rāgānuga-sādhana* of *sakhyam* from *Agastya Saṁhitā*: "A person who is dedicated to serving the Lord, and out of friendship sees and treats him as a human, lies down in the Lord's temple." Viśvanātha Cakravartī comments on *Bhakti-rasāmṛta-sindhu* 1.2.190: "It should be understood that only some rare persons performing *sādhana* who are almost *siddhas* are qualified for these *aṅgas* (*sakhyam* and *ātmā-nivedanam*), and not all *sādhakas*."

does not add any further insight to this division. Thus, we shall proceed to discuss the other four divisions.

To be filled with feelings for *sakhya-rati* is an example of *svābhīṣṭa-bhāva-maya*. In this regard, it should be noted that *rāgānuga-sādhana* is an active spiritual culture performed with one's senses. Its purpose is to manifest the inner emotive component of *bhakti*—to attain the sprout of *rati* in the form of one's budding *sthāyi-bhāva*. This *bhāvāṅkura*, or sprout of defining spiritual emotion and personhood, is then further cultivated through the course of *bhāva-bhakti*, until it flowers and finally fruits in *prema*. Thus, to be filled with the desired feelings of *sakhya-rati* is both the means and the goal.

Practices that are related to the desired *rati*—*svābhīṣṭa-bhāva-sambandhi*—are many. Viśvanātha Cakravartī includes the first forty-six of the sixty-four *aṅgas* enumerated by Rūpa Goswāmī—from taking shelter of the *guru* to *mantra-japa* and meditation. Also included are hearing, chanting, and so on in a manner suitable for attaining one's desired *rati*. They are related to the desired *rati* because they are the direct causes of attaining it, and when as a result of such practice *bhāva* is attained, they transform from being classified as related to the desired *bhāva* to being one with that *bhāva*.

Viśvanātha Cakravartī emphasizes two particular *aṅgas*: meditating or doing *japa* of the Gopāla *mantra* and *nāma-kīrtana*, with the latter taking precedence over *smaraṇam* despite *smaraṇam*'s prominence in *rāgānuga-sādhana*. With regard to *kīrtana*, the Ṭhākura states what we have underscored earlier:

> Previously it was mentioned that *smaraṇam* is the primary limb of *rāgānugā-bhakti*. However, one should understand that *smaraṇam* is dependent on *kīrtanam*. In the present age of Kali, everyone can attain eligibility for *bhajana* through *kīrtanam*. All of the scriptures proclaim *kīrtanam* to be the best *aṅga* of *bhakti*.[68]

The Gopāla *mantra* has also been mentioned earlier with regard to meditation. This is the best of all Kṛṣṇa *mantras* used in meditation, as distinguished from the thirty-two-syllable *nāma-mahā-mantra* typically employed in *kīrtana*. The eighteen-syllable Gopāla *mantra* is also often abbreviated into a ten-syllable *mantra*, and this ten-syllable *mantra* was the *mantra* of *Bṛhad-bhāgavatāmṛta*'s Gopa-kumāra. Gopa-kumāra attained *sakhya-rati* by regularly engaging in the *dhyāna* of this *mantra* along with *kīrtana* of his favorite names of Kṛṣṇa and the *līlā-smaraṇam* these practices gave rise to. Viśvanātha Cakravartī Ṭhākura mentions both the eighteen-syllable and

68. *Rāga-vartma-candrikā* 1.14.

the ten-syllable Gopāla *mantra*, referring to employing them in meditation as the best example of a *bhakti-aṅga* that is related to the feelings of one's desired *rati*—*svābhīṣṭa-bhāva-sambandhi*. Other examples of *svābhīṣṭa-bhāva-sambandhi* he mentions are the wearing of *tulasī* garlands, scents, garments, and flower garlands that have been offered to the deity. He also underscores the *aṅga* of hearing *Śrīmad Bhāgavatam*'s tenth canto, referring to this as a perpetual duty.

Observing Vaiṣṇava Ekādaśī is a prime example of a vow taken for the pleasure of Kṛṣṇa, and such vows constitute penance within *uttama-bhakti*. Ekādaśī is an event that warrants observance each time it arises. It is said that Ekādaśī is "Hari's day"—*hari-vāsara*—and thus its observance directly causes *smaraṇam*, or remembrance of Kṛṣṇa. *Aṅgas* such as observance of Janmāṣṭamī and Kārtika are similar. Observance of these vows consists of two basic aspects. On the one hand, they call for various austerities, such as fasting from food and drink, including Kṛṣṇa *prasādam*. On the other hand, they call for increased hearing, chanting, and participation in other *aṅgas* of *bhakti* that are directly related to the attainment of *rati*. Thus, Viśvanātha Cakravartī considers them both indirectly and directly related to attaining one's desired *rati*.

Aṅgas classified by Viśvanātha Cakravartī as favorable to one's desired *rati*—*svābhīṣṭa-bhāva-anukūla*—include wearing a necklace of *tulasī* beads and ornamenting the body with Vaiṣṇava *tilaka*. Adopting these external markings are favorable, and they serve in the least as a code of Vaiṣṇava dress. Moreover, these external markings are more than a mere dress code to be adopted during the practice of other *aṅgas*. According to the Vaiṣṇava *śāstras*, such bodily ornamentation has inherent spiritual power. *Tulasī* is the external manifestation of Bhagavān's *śakti* in the material world, and she represents the forest of Vṛndāvana. Adorning oneself with a *guru*-given *tulasī-mālā* promotes identification with the sacred geography—the *dhāma*—of Kṛṣṇa *līlā*. Similarly, adorning the body with *tilaka* in twelve places accompanied by invoking the corresponding twelve names of Viṣṇu serves to facilitate the transformation of the *sādhaka-deha* from a material substance to one of *cit-ānanda-maya*.[69] Abandoning such *aṅgas* with the idea that they are merely formal and external to the essential substance of *rāgānugā-bhakti*, which is an internal culture, ignores the importance of

69. Roman Catholics and Eastern Orthodox Christians also believe that material elements can transform into spiritual ones: transubstantiation is the miraculous change by which bread and wine can become the body and blood of Christ through consecration.

identifying one's *sādhaka-deha* as such. Furthermore, such external *aṅgas* serve to promote the internal *aṅga* of *smaraṇam*. Adding to these *aṅgas* of ornamentation that are *svābhīṣṭa-bhāva-anukūla*, Viśvanātha Cakravartī mentions serving *tulasī*, circumambulating the *dhāma* or the deity, and offering *praṇāma* to the deity.

Aṅgas such as honoring *brāhmaṇas*, cows, and sacred trees are also noteworthy, and thus Viśvanātha Cakravartī labels these *aṅgas* as *svābhīṣṭa-bhāva-aviruddha*, neutral/not unfavorable but nonetheless helpful. It is said that Kṛṣṇa himself gives pleasure to cows by composing cowherd songs.[70] Furthermore, in his commentary on this verse Śrī Jīva Goswāmī cites the *Gautamīya Tantra*:

> One should scratch the necks of the cows, feed them, and circumambulate them. Gopāla is pleased when the cows are happy.[71]

Appropriately, this chapter comes to a close praising *go-sevā*, which in the *siddha-rūpa-sevā* of *sakhya-rati* plays a significant role. Having discussed the genesis and practice of *rāgānugā-bhakti* in some detail in the present chapter, we can now turn in the following chapter to the ideal of *sambandha-rūpa-bhakti* in *sakhya-rati*, that which is attained through the *sambandhānugā-bhakti* division of *rāgānuga-sādhana*.

70. *Bhakti-rasāmṛta-sindhu* 2.1.87.
71. *Bhakti-rasāmṛta-sindhu* 1.2.110.

4

Preyo-bhakti-rasa

In the previous chapter, we discussed *sambandhānugā-bhakti*, a division of *rāgānugā-bhakti*, as the means for attaining the ideal of *sakhya-rasa* in Vraja. We learned that the *sādhaka* pursues his or her cherished type of *rati* for Kṛṣṇa by watering the seed of *rāga-bhakti* implanted through *sādhu-saṅga*. In this chapter, we will focus on the ecstatic ingredients of *sakhya-rasa* itself. As the sprout of *sakhya-rati* manifests and one enters the domain of *bhāva-bhakti*, this sprout—*bhāvāṅkura*—is then further cultivated in *bhāva-bhakti* such that it buds, blossoms, and fructifies in the form of *sakhya-rasa*, or *preyo-bhakti-rasa*.

The central ingredient of *sakhya-rasa*, in both its budding and its mature stages, is its *sthāyi-bhāva*. A *sthāyi-bhāva* is an ecstatic transpsychological emotion that defines a devotee. In the case of *sakhya-rasa*, the *sthāyi-bhāva* defines a devotee not only as a friend of Kṛṣṇa, but as a particular friend with unique emotional sensibilities that fall within the parameters of *rasa-tattva*.[1] Thus, the *sthāyi-bhāva* of *sakhya-rati* determines one's fraternal role in the drama of Kṛṣṇa *līlā*. It forever retires one's material identity—the false personhood that was a material construct—and acquaints one personally with what was previously only the theological personhood of Kṛṣṇa.

As the practitioner's *sthāyi-bhāva* sprouts in *bhāva-bhakti*, the *antaḥ-karaṇa*, or subtle body, is spiritualized. Some Gauḍīya theologians from previous centuries have given the example of sulfur mixing with mercury. In times gone by, alchemists thought that by rubbing mercury with sulfur, one could produce gold, although we now know this is not the case. However,

1. Each of the Vraja *rasas*—*dāsya*, *sakhya*, *vātsalya*, and *mādhurya*—has a corresponding *sthāyi-bhāva*.

continued contact with *bhakti* with one's subtle body *does* transform it from material to spiritual. Perhaps a better analogy is that of Bhaktivedanta Swami Prabhupāda: As one pours milk into a bottle of ink, ink mixed with milk is expelled until there is no ink left and only milk remains in the bottle. Similarly, as one pours the nectar of *bhakti* into one's subtle body, its material properties are expelled, and in due course only spiritual properties remain. An analogy employing milk as an example of a transformative agent also seems most appropriate in a discussion concerning fraternal love for the cowherd Kṛṣṇa.

The primary characteristic, or *pradhāna*, of *sakhya-rati* is *viśrambha*—confidence imbued with familiarity and unfettered by restraint. With friends, one can be oneself. This *viśrambha* arises out of the young cowherds' sense of equality with Kṛṣṇa—not an absolute equality but an equality of kind: "We are all cowherds of Vraja, nothing more." Such a sense of equality expresses itself and is characterized by actions such as joking and loud laughing.[2]

Rūpa Goswāmī describes *viśrambha* as "deep familiar trust without restriction," and Jīva Goswāmī adds "freedom from fear or excessive reverence, a particular kind of deep faith in the other, in which friends have a sense of being in no way different from each other."[3] Thus, in *sakhya-rati* there is a sense of equality between Kṛṣṇa and his friends. Sometimes they serve him, and sometimes he serves them—*kṛṣṇe seve, kṛṣṇe karāya āpana-sevana*![4] His cowherd friends think of him as their closest friend. Each boy feels that Kṛṣṇa loves him the most, and each and every one of them is correct in his assessment. As opposed to *dāsya-* and *vātsalya-rasas*, where the master/servant and parent/child are not equals and thus have a different emotional experience from one another, in *sakhya-rasa* the devotee and Kṛṣṇa experience the same emotions.[5] And for this reason, *sakhya-rasa* is

2. In *Bhakti Sandarbha* 306, Jīva Goswāmī writes, "It is said, '*nādevo devam arcayet*: if one is not identical with God, one cannot worship him.' But unalloyed devotees do not embrace absolute identity, because it rules out service (instead they accept equality in *bhāva*)."

3. *Bhakti-rasāmṛta-sindhu* 3.3.9, 3.3.106.

4. *Caitanya-caritāmṛta* 2.19.223.

5. *Bhakti-rasāmṛta-sindhu* 3.3.136. Here Rūpa Goswāmī acknowledges that because Kṛṣṇa and his friends experience the same emotions, some devotees consider *sakhya* the best expression of divine love within *sambandha-rūpa*. Nonetheless, he places *vātsalya* above *sakhya* in his ascending order of *rasas*—*śānta*, *dāsya*, *sakhya*, *vātsalya*, and *mādhurya*. However, Jīva Goswāmī in his *Prīti Sandarbha* places *sakhya* above *vātsalya* in his ascending order. Thus, in his opinion, *sakhya* exceeds *vātsalya* in excellence.

considered the best within *sambandha-rūpa-bhakti*, which expresses itself as either *dāsya-rasa*, *vātsalya-rasa*, or *sakhya-rasa*.

Thus far we have discussed the *sthāyi-bhāva* of *sakhya-rati*, explaining that it sprouts in *bhāva-bhakti* from the seed planted at the outset of *sādhana-bhakti*. However, we have not discussed how the seed of *sthāyi-bhāva* matures. Śrīla Rūpa Goswāmī has compared the *sthāyi-bhāva* to an ocean that during the monsoon rises into a tidal wave of *bhakti-rasa*. Just as the ocean is the source of clouds, which then shower rain on the ocean and increase its tide, so the budding of one's *sthāyi-bhāva* gives rise to the other emotional ingredients that shower down on the ocean of one's *sthāyi-bhāva*, increasing its depth and issuing forth a tidal wave of *rasānanda*.

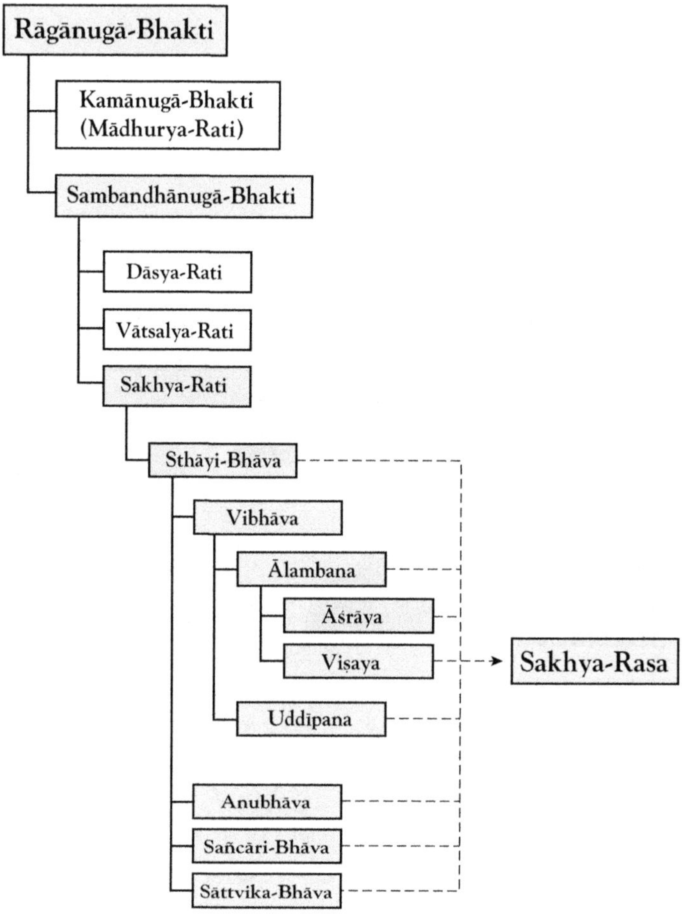

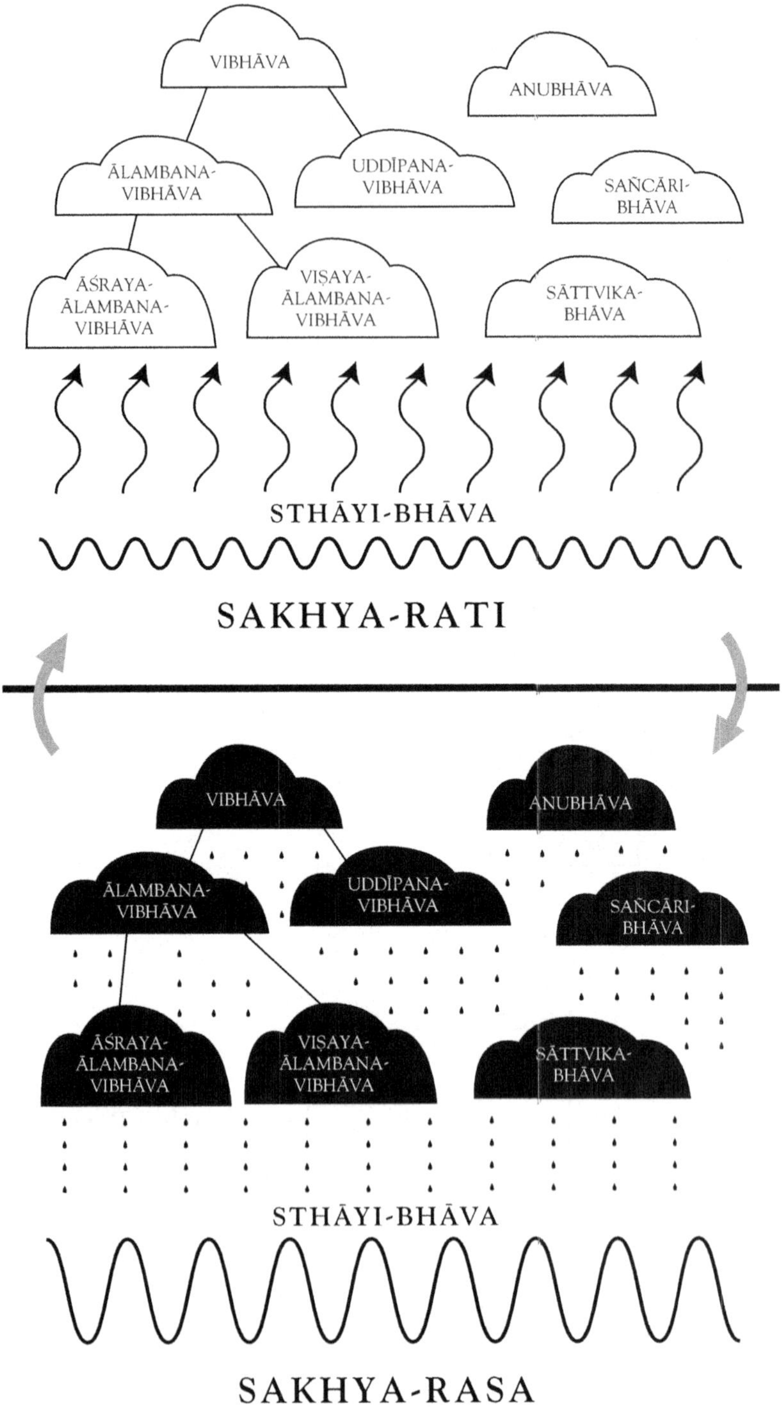
VIBHĀVA
ANUBHĀVA
ĀLAMBANA-VIBHĀVA
UDDĪPANA-VIBHĀVA
SAÑCĀRI-BHĀVA
ĀŚRAYA-ĀLAMBANA-VIBHĀVA
VIṢAYA-ĀLAMBANA-VIBHĀVA
SĀTTVIKA-BHĀVA
STHĀYI-BHĀVA
SAKHYA-RATI
VIBHĀVA
ANUBHĀVA
ĀLAMBANA-VIBHĀVA
UDDĪPANA-VIBHĀVA
SAÑCĀRI-BHĀVA
ĀŚRAYA-ĀLAMBANA-VIBHĀVA
VIṢAYA-ĀLAMBANA-VIBHĀVA
SĀTTVIKA-BHĀVA
STHĀYI-BHĀVA
SAKHYA-RASA

The *sthāyi-bhāva* appears, or is sheltered, in a particular devotee (*āśraya-ālambana-vibhāva*) and has a corresponding object of love (*viṣaya-ālambana-vibhāva*) in Kṛṣṇa. There are also things associated with the object of love that excite the *sthāyi-bhāva* (*uddīpana-vibhāvas*). As an internal transpsychological emotion, *sthāyi-bhāva* also gives rise to external bodily movements, some voluntary (*anubhāvas*) and some involuntary (*sāttvika-bhāvas*). It is also nourished by other, lesser emotions that come and go (*sañcāri-bhāvas*). Together with these four attendant *bhāvas*, or ecstatic ingredients, the *sthāyi-bhāva* of *sakhya-rati* matures into *sakhya-rasa.*

As mentioned above, the first of the four attendant *bhāvas*, or ecstatic ingredients of *rasa*, is termed *vibhāva.* It has two divisions: *ālambana-vibhāva* and *uddīpana-vibhāva.* There are two *ālambana-vibhāvas*: the object of fraternal love in which that love is reposed (Gopāla Kṛṣṇa) and the embodiment of fraternal love (the devotee). *Uddīpana-vibhāvas* act as excitants of the *sthāyi-bhāva.* Among the four ingredients, *vibhāvas* in particular are thought to be causal, making the *sthāyi-bhāva* flourish and assisting it in maturing from *sakhya-rati* into *sakhya-rasa.*

It will be helpful to invoke the image of a drama to better understand these terms. In doing so, let us begin by discussing *ālambana-vibhāvas.* In a drama in which friendship is the dominant emotion, there must be at least two roles: the role of the friend who embodies friendship and the role of the friend who serves as the object of that friend's fraternal love. These two roles together make up the *ālambana-vibhāva*: the embodiment (*āśraya-ālambana*) of fraternal love and the object (*viṣaya-ālambana*) of fraternal love. The dominant emotion of divine friendship is thus exchanged between the embodiment and the object of fraternal love. Hearing about them both nourishes one's budding *sthāyi-bhāva.*

In his explanation of *sakhya-rasa* drawn from the tenth canto of *Śrīmad Bhāgavatam*, Rūpa Goswāmī begins by describing the perfect object of fraternal love. Of course, that perfect object of love is Kṛṣṇa. However, it is a particular Kṛṣṇa as well—Gopāla Kṛṣṇa. Just as it is popular in postmodern films to explore a singular event through the experience of different people associated with the event, the drama of Kṛṣṇa *līlā* can be viewed through the lens of *dāsya-*, *vātsalya-*, *mādhurya-*, or *sakhya-rati.* Therefore, each *rasika* lens is focused differently. Thus, to proceed in discussing *vibhāvas* arising out of *sakhya-rati* that in turn nourish it, we shall first explore in some detail the perfect object of fraternal love, the young cowherd Kṛṣṇa as he is experienced by his comrades. In this context, we will also discuss particular qualities of Kṛṣṇa that fall within the *viṣaya-ālambana* and *uddīpana* divisions of *vibhāva*. Then we shall proceed to discuss the friends of Kṛṣṇa themselves—the paradigmatic figures that embody fraternal love.

The Object of Fraternal Love (viṣaya-ālambana)

Rūpa Goswāmī describes the object of the Vraja *sakhās*' love experienced through their divine eyes:

> As the slayer of Agha returns from the cow pen playing a flute, his complexion charming like that of a blue sapphire, his broad white smile like a *kunda* flower, his cloth beautiful like the brilliant, golden *ketakī* flower, a forest garland decorating his chest, he steals our—his friends'—minds.[6]

Kṛṣṇa also appears outside of Vraja in his metropolitan *līlās* as the object of *sakhya-rasa* to *sakhās* such as Arjuna and Draupadī-devī. However, this form of Kṛṣṇa—sometimes two- and sometimes four-handed—is not our focus. In the verse above, Śrī Rūpa describes Kṛṣṇa in relation to the rural environment of Vraja as "Aghahara"—the slayer of Agha. Kṛṣṇa slays Aghāsura amid the *Bhāgavatam*'s *brahma-vimohana-līlā* during the last stage of his childhood, and it is at this age that Kṛṣṇa begins herding calves with his young friends and his *sakhya-rati-līlās* commence. Thus, Śrī Rūpa has invoked a very fitting epithet to introduce the object of the Vraja *sakhās*' fraternal love.

This cowherd form of Kṛṣṇa is constituted of physical, mental, and verbal qualities. Rūpa Goswāmī cites sixty-four prominent qualities of Kṛṣṇa overall, and among them he highlights seventeen that correspond with *sakhya-rati*—qualities included in *sakhya-rati*'s object of love:

> (1) Well dressed (*suveśaḥ*), (2) adorned with auspicious bodily markings (*sarva-sal-lakṣaṇānvitaḥ*), (3) strong (*balināṁ varaḥ*), (4) an astonishing linguist (*vividhādbhuta-bhāṣā-vit*), (5) eloquent (*vāvadūkaḥ*), (6) learned (*supaṇḍitaḥ*), (7) ingenious (*vipula-pratibho*), (8) expert (*dakṣaḥ*), (9) compassionate (*karuṇaḥ*), (10) very heroic (*vīra-śekharaḥ*), (11) artistic (*vidagdhaḥ*), (12) intelligent (*buddhimān*), (13) tolerant (*kṣānta*), (14) the cynosure of everyone

6. *Bhakti-rasāmṛta-sindhu* 3.3.4.

(*rakta-lokaḥ*), (15) prosperous (*samṛddhimān*), (16) joyful (*sukhī*), (17) a very important person (*varīyān*), and more.[7]

Here, Śrī Rūpa looks at these qualities as intrinsic to the person Kṛṣṇa, and thus they are included in his depiction of the object of love, the *viṣaya-ālambana-vibhāva*. Kṛṣṇa's qualities can also be *uddīpana-vibhāvas*. Commenting on *Bhakti-rasāmṛta-sindhu* 2.1.23, Jīva Goswāmī explains that Kṛṣṇa's qualities can be looked at as either *ālambana-* or *uddīpana-vibhāvas*:

> Qualities function in two ways: as primary indicators and as secondary indicators. If we talk about the beautiful limbs of Kṛṣṇa, the emphasis is placed on the quality of Kṛṣṇa, the beautiful limbs. In this case, acting in a primary way, the quality acts as *uddīpana*. If we talk about beautiful-limbed Kṛṣṇa, the emphasis is on Kṛṣṇa, and the quality is secondary (intrinsic to his very self). The quality in this case acts as the *ālambana*.

Hence, the seventeen qualities that correspond with *sakhya-rati* are taken in a secondary sense: "Gopāla Kṛṣṇa—the object of fraternal love—has these qualities."

The qualities of Kṛṣṇa astonish others because of their majesty or their sweetness. These qualities are either physical, mental, or verbal in nature. Among his physical qualities, Kṛṣṇa is prosperous, well dressed, adorned with auspicious bodily markings, strong, and the center of attention wherever he goes. Among his mental qualities, Kṛṣṇa is learned, tolerant, joyful, intelligent, and ingenious. Among his verbal qualities, Kṛṣṇa is both an astonishing linguist and eloquent. Among his qualities that straddle the mental and physical realms, Kṛṣṇa is most important among very important people, artistic, heroic, and expert. The qualities of Kṛṣṇa that stand out to those in *sakhya-rati* are not limited to these seventeen, but these qualities in particular should be contemplated by *sakhya-rati-upāsakas*, and thus they merit further discussion.

Rūpa Goswāmī does not elaborate on these qualities from the vantage point of *sakhya-rati*, but he does give examples and further explanations of most of them in his overall discussion of Kṛṣṇa as the perfect object of love. Let us discuss those that most readily lend themselves to being part of the composite of Gopāla Kṛṣṇa as the object of fraternal love.

7. *Bhakti-rasāmṛta-sindhu* 3.3.6–7. The first quality among the seventeen—*suveśaḥ* (well dressed)—is not listed among the other sixty-four prominent qualities and appears to be an addition that Rūpa Goswāmī finds relative only to fraternal love.

Suveśaḥ

Kṛṣṇa is a meticulous dresser, and his concern for dressing himself and how he appears to others begins with his boyhood, his *paugaṇḍa-līlā*, which is central to *sakhya-rati*. At this age, he refuses to allow his mother to continue dressing him. Befitting any particular occasion, he typically dresses in (1) a two-piece lower garment and shawl; (2) a four-piece shirt, turban, sash, and lower garment; or (3) a multipiece outfit suitable for a performing artist, all of which come in a variety of colors with emphasis on different shades of saffron—orange, red, and yellow.[8] In his cowherding *līlās*, Kṛṣṇa typically dresses in a two-piece outfit, while for more formal occasions he dresses in his four-piece or multipiece outfits. In either case, in his boyhood and adolescence he shows concern for his attire even amid trying circumstances. Before leaping from the branch of a *kadamba* tree onto the heads of Kāliya-nāga, he took the time to straighten his attire and tighten his belt, as he did in preparing to deal with Ariṣṭāsura,[9] a trait that does not go unnoticed and is much appreciated by his friends. His friends, too, were impressed and delighted by Kṛṣṇa's and Balarāma's multipiece outfits—clothing befitting princes—that were initially intended for Kaṁsa but taken by the two brothers for themselves as they proceeded to the wrestling match arranged by the evil king of Mathurā. While in Vraja, Kṛṣṇa and his friends pretend to be kings in play, but in this instance Rāma and Kṛṣṇa actually wore the king's clothing, delighting their accompanying comrades. This is expressed as follows:

> The enemy of Kaṁsa, smiling and wearing a beautiful pink *dhotī*, an orange turban, an excellent vest of shining gold, and a multicolor belt, is himself a festival and thus gives us joy.[10]

Having dressed themselves in the king's apparel, Rāma and Kṛṣṇa distributed the king's remaining garments among their friends—their equals.

Sarva-sal-lakṣaṇānvitaḥ

Gopāla Kṛṣṇa is adorned with the bodily characteristics thought to be indicative of a morally and spiritually elevated person.[11] These characteristics are

8. *Bhakti-rasāmṛta-sindhu* 2.1.347–350.

9. *Śrīmad Bhāgavatam* 10.16.6 (Kāliya) and *The Nectar of Devotion*, chapter 24 (Ariṣṭāsura).

10. *Bhakti-rasāmṛta-sindhu* 2.1.351.

11. Physiognomy is thought to be nothing but folk science, but some aspects of it have

of two types: bodily characteristics and markings on one's hands and feet. As they appear on Kṛṣṇa, the auspicious bodily characteristics refer to the length, elevation, breadth, depth, and texture of his various bodily features, as well as to the redness appearing on the edge of his eyes, the soles of his feet, the palms of his hands, the roof of his mouth, his upper and lower lips, his tongue, and his nails. Auspicious markings on his hands and feet include the lotus, flag, thunderbolt, parasol, and many others.

The markings on the soles of Kṛṣṇa's lotus-like feet are particularly prominent in connection with *sakhya-rati*. Although Kṛṣṇa walked barefoot in his childhood, his body did not weigh enough for the markings on the soles of his feet to make an impression on the bare ground. And when he grew older, his mother insisted he wear shoes. However, he refused to wear shoes while herding. Thus, the soles of his feet made impressions on the forest floor for all his friends to witness daily and discuss. Again, the numerous marks on his feet, which are inexhaustibly described in the sacred texts, leave impressions on the ground that become an ongoing source of discussion and delight. Sanātana Goswāmī comments that the already beautiful Vṛndāvana became beautified by such marks.[12]

Such markings and bodily characteristics are described in a number of sacred Hindu texts.[13] Carried over into Buddhism, it is thought that each auspicious characteristic corresponds with one hundred meritorious acts that in turn correspond with one hundred virtuous thoughts. Buddhist commentators have offered explanations as to why such characteristics and markings are admirable in their own right. But the overriding point relative to our discussion is that it is astonishing that the markings of an *avatāra* would appear on the body of a mere cowherd! Moreover, with regard to *sakhya-rati*, such markings and characteristics are nothing more than a source of amusement and conversation. Kṛṣṇa's cowherd friends conjecture as to their implications and compare them to their own bodily features.

---

proven to be credible in recent experiments. For example, a 2017 study at the University of Toronto concluded that emotions mask lifelong habits of expression that become etched on a person's face. R. Thora Bjornsdottir and Nicholas O. Rule, "The Visibility of Social Class from Facial Cues," *Journal of Personality and Social Psychology* 113, no. 4 (May 2017): 530–546, https://doi.org/10.1037/pspa0000091.

12. *Śrīmad Bhāgavatam* 10.15.1.

13. Buddhism and Hinduism both draw from the Vedic tradition of *Sāmudrika-śāstra*, which connects a person's physical markings with his or her psychology. This tradition is also represented in the *Garuḍa Purāṇa*. Twentieth-century Western insights into this correlation, such as psychologist William Sheldon's somatotype taxonomy, unfortunately arose out of Francis Galton's sense of eugenics and was ultimately dismissed as quackery.

The boys are also very familiar with the various markings on Kṛṣṇa's body, given that they massage him on a daily basis.

Balināṁ Varaḥ

There are many examples of Kṛṣṇa's extraordinary strength. Śrī Rūpa cites this strength as one of Kṛṣṇa's sixty-four qualities—*balīyān*. However, when writing about *sakhya-rati*, he describes Kṛṣṇa as the *balināṁ varaḥ*, "best of the strong."

In *sakhya-rati*, Kṛṣṇa's extraordinary strength is a preoccupation of his friends because of its being experienced daily in the forests of Vraja. Thus, they observe and appreciate this quality more than any of the other residents of Vraja do. However, despite their experience of Kṛṣṇa's strength, they also challenge it and bring it into question. This is especially so in conjunction with *yuddha-vīra-rasa*, or the mock fighting so compatible with *sakhya-rati*. For example, speaking of his own strength and prowess in mock battle as he assesses the opposition, Śrīdāmā says about himself, "The extremely powerful Śrīdāmā does not consider even a hundred Balarāmas."[14] We should note that Jīva Goswāmī considers Balarāma "somewhat stronger" than Kṛṣṇa.[15] That may be, but cowherds may feel otherwise: "Balarāma's team thinks itself strong and able to defeat our team with Kṛṣṇa on our side, but is there anyone weaker than Balarāma's team in this world?"[16] And, speaking to Kṛṣṇa, Śrīdāmā says, "Your pride has become impoverished in being defeated by the strength of my arms."[17] Śrīdāmā is known to defeat Kṛṣṇa in wrestling, pinning Kṛṣṇa to the ground, even as Kṛṣṇa nonetheless claims victory because it is *his* nose that is pointing upward. Thus, in *sakhya-rati*, Kṛṣṇa is "the best of the strong"; that is, all his companions are "the strong," and Kṛṣṇa is the best cowherd among such equally strong comrades.

Jīva Goswāmī comments that Kṛṣṇa sometimes appears weak and fatigued after wrestling with his friends, and beads of perspiration are visible on his brow.

> This indicates the strength of the other boys. It is said, "The boys had similar qualities, character, age, actions, and dress." But we see that they had no inclination to kill demons themselves because

14. *Bhakti-rasāmṛta-sindhu* 4.8.38.
15. *Bhakti-rasāmṛta-sindhu* 4.1.17. See Śrī Jīva's commentary.
16. *Bhakti-rasāmṛta-sindhu* 2.4.167.
17. *Bhakti-rasāmṛta-sindhu* 2.5.32.

Kṛṣṇa's *līlā-śakti*, whose only purpose is to please him, prevented such inclination in the boys.[18]

Vividhādbhuta-bhāṣā-vit

An astonishing linguist is one who can speak fluently the language of many countries. In the case of Kṛṣṇa, this includes both the language of the gods and the language of the nonhuman species. The common language of Mathurā and Vṛndāvana in Kṛṣṇa *līlā* is Śurasenī.[19] In this language, Kṛṣṇa spoke with the *maṇḍala*'s human residents. However, his cowherd friends also witnessed him speaking to the gods at the close of the Govardhana *līlā*. Although Kṛṣṇa kept himself at a distance from his friends to provide a more comfortable environment for Indra to apologize, his friends nonetheless saw him speaking with a four-headed being, a five-headed being, a being covered with eyes, and other *devas*, all of whom offered gifts to Kṛṣṇa as they crowned him "Govinda," the God of the gods. Kṛṣṇa's friends also witnessed him speaking to the nonhuman forest residents on a daily basis.

Vāvadūkaḥ

There are two types of eloquence in speech: speech that is pleasing to the ear and speech that is clever.[20] Eloquence involves the sweetness of diction, composition, and tone. Such speech is clear in its intention even as it can be layered with meaning. Kṛṣṇa himself expresses his affinity for layered, esoteric speech—*parokṣaṁ mama ca priyam*.[21] Some also say that eloquence is calm, measured, authoritative, colorful, and creative. Uddhava, whose *dāsya-rati* is tinged with *sakhya*, describes Kṛṣṇa's eloquence thus:

> The words of Kṛṣṇa, skillful at changing the hearts of his adversaries, superior to all in extinguishing all doubts in the universe, authoritative and economical, endowed with many meanings, have today made all my mental functions blissful.[22]

Both Kṛṣṇa's eloquence and his overall linguistic ability are not fully manifest until he attains boyhood—*paugaṇḍa*—and this age is particularly attractive to those in *sakhya-rati*. Upon attaining boyhood, Kṛṣṇa's speech is

18. *Śrīmad Bhāgavatam* 10.15.16.
19. *Bhakti-rasāmṛta-sindhu* 2.1.66. See Jīva Goswāmī's commentary.
20. *Caitanya-caritāmṛta* 1.1.106 cites the adage *mitaṁ ca sāraṁ ca vaco hi vāgmitā*, "Essential truth spoken concisely is true eloquence."
21. *Śrīmad Bhāgavatam* 11.21.35.
22. *Bhakti-rasāmṛta-sindhu* 2.1.74.

precise and his pronunciation is perfect. And as Kṛṣṇa attains adolescence, his speech becomes even more perfect. Jīva Goswāmī comments thus on Hari's welcoming words expressed to the *gopīs* as they met with him under the autumn moon:

> Such words are charming to all beings and tender, as they are steeped in *prema*. They are sweet and proper with regard to their placement of syllables and intonation. Thus, they are attractive, filled with longing, qualification, attachment, and beauty. The words are attractive to the intelligent, pleasing them by their depth of meaning, ornamentation, emotion, *rasa*, and essence expressed through direct and indirect meaning.[23]

Viśvanātha Cakravartī informs us in his comments on *Ujjvala-nīlamaṇi* 1.5 that merely with the movement of the edge of his eyes, Kṛṣṇa explains everything about *rasa*. What, then, must his speaking be like?

Supaṇḍitaḥ

A learned person is one acquainted with the fourteen divisions of scriptural knowledge, which correspond with the fourteen qualities of a bride.[24] Thus, knowledge itself is sometimes referred to as a bride.[25] To be learned also involves knowing how to properly conduct oneself in different circumstances.

Vipula-pratibho

Kṛṣṇa's genius is especially exhibited in his ability to offer quick-witted replies. One who is *pratibhānvitaḥ* is possessed of creativity and thus is able to effortlessly express novel ideas. Rūpa Goswāmī gives the following example from *Padyāvalī* 283 of Kṛṣṇa's genius, demonstrating his ability to respond in a novel way to Rādhā's inquiry with a play on words:

23. *Śrīmad Bhāgavatam* 10.31.8.

24. The fourteen branches of knowledge are the four Vedas, the six *aṅgas*, the Mīmāṁsā, scriptures based on logic, the *dharma-śāstras*, and the Purāṇas. They can be interpreted in relation to a bride/wife: "The bride of knowledge with fourteen branches, whose lineage is distributed by the four Vedas, and which includes the *smṛtis*, is made brilliant by the six *aṅgas*, is followed by the *ṣaḍ-darśanas*, is assisted by the Purāṇas, and is decorated with the *karma-* and *jñāna-kāṇḍas*." See *Bhakti-rasāmṛta-sindhu* 2.1.77.

25. In *Śikṣāṣṭakam* 1, Caitanya Mahāprabhu describes his Śrī Kṛṣṇa *saṅkīrtana* as the "life of the bride of knowledge," implying that Śrī Kṛṣṇa *saṅkīrtana* is the end of all knowledge that corresponds with Śrī Kṛṣṇa's Vraja *līlā*.

Rādhā: O Kṛṣṇa, where do you stay [*vāsa*] now?

Kṛṣṇa: O Rādhā, with bewitching eyes! Can you not see that I am wearing my cloth [*vāsa*]?

Rādhā: How crafty you are! I am talking about your residence, not your cloth!

Kṛṣṇa: O Rādhā, with natural sweet aroma! I am fragrant [*vāsa*] by touching your limbs.

Rādhā: O cheater! Where did you stay during the night [*yāminyām uṣitaḥ*]?

Kṛṣṇa: How could I be stolen by the night, which does not even have a body [*yāminyā muṣitaḥ*]?

May Kṛṣṇa, who joked with Rādhā using tricky words, protect you!

Dakṣaḥ

A skillful person is one who can accomplish difficult tasks quickly and easily. An example of such skillfulness is Kṛṣṇa's ability to manifest himself in as many forms as there were cowherd friends assembled for a picnic lunch along the banks of the Yamunā, giving the impression to each cowherd that he had chosen to sit next to him alone, as was the desire of every cowherd.

Karuṇaḥ

A person who cannot tolerate the suffering of others is called compassionate. Kṛṣṇa's compassion for his cowherd friends manifests primarily in his response to their hearts' pain of separation from him.

Vīra-śekharaḥ

Rūpa Goswāmī comments that Kṛṣṇa gives bliss to all the cows by composing cowherd songs and brings joy to his friends by his heroic actions.[26] Kṛṣṇa's heroism in Vraja during his *prakaṭa-līlā* was observed daily by his friends alone, having saved them as he did from the plight of Kaṁsa's henchmen, such as Agha, Baka, Ariṣṭa, and so forth, and from events such as forest

26. *Pārāvatī*, referred to here, is a form of song peculiar to cowherds, a type of folk song. See Jīva Goswāmī's comments to *Bhakti-rasāmṛta-sindhu* 2.1.87.

fires. Others witnessed his heroism less frequently, such as when he defeated Indra and chastised Kāliya.

In his *Gopāla-campū*, Śrī Jīva Goswāmī explains that friends of Kṛṣṇa such as Śrīdāmā, Subala, and Stokakṛṣṇa have strength similar to that of Kṛṣṇa and Balarāma and, like them, understand the hidden meaning of things and follow the principles of *dharma*. Thus, they are firm friends, and because they have powers equal to those of Kṛṣṇa and Balarāma, they are always thinking of the two brothers' heroic acts.[27]

Vidagdhaḥ

One whose mind is absorbed in the sixty-four arts, such as dancing and singing, and in various amusements is called *vidagdha*—artistic/an aesthete. These sixty-four arts (*kalās*) come under fourteen subheadings (*vidyās*). In the context of the *līlā*, Kṛṣṇa learned these arts in the *gurukula* of Sāndīpani Muni in only sixty-four days. This training occurred after Kṛṣṇa killed Kaṁsa, and thus it was outside of Vṛndāvana but along with Balarāma and in the company of his dear classmate friend Sudāmā *vipra*. However, Kṛṣṇa is more completely manifest in Vṛndāvana than he is elsewhere, owing to the measure of the *prema* found there that he is the object of. Thus, in the *līlā-granthas* of the Goswāmīs, we find him to be accomplished in these arts in Vraja even without any training, as are his *gopas* and *gopīs*.

Buddhimān

One who is intelligent has the capacity to absorb knowledge. Furthermore, Jīva Goswāmī compares Kṛṣṇa's intelligence to one's eyes: just as the eyes have the ability to see fine detail, Kṛṣṇa's intelligence is capable of discerning things very minutely. His intelligence is such that it immediately enters into the heart of a situation with correct judgment. His sharp intelligence in determining how to deal with adversity in his cowherd *līlās* and in his romantic life is notable.

Kṣānta

In the *Gītā*, Kṛṣṇa teaches that the fruit of tolerance is liberation, and this not necessarily in relation to tolerating other persons but rather in tolerating the perceived dualities of hot/cold and so forth, which material identities arise out of. Persons themselves, and particularly those who offend, are arguably more difficult to tolerate. The best example of Kṛṣṇa's tolerance

27. *Gopāla-campū* 1.14.10.

is in the face of the numerous offenses committed by Śiśupāla in Kṛṣṇa's metropolitan *līlā* surrounded by Pāṇḍava Arjuna and his brothers.

Rakta-lokaḥ

Kṛṣṇa's appearance in the public wrestling arena, which was arranged and promoted by King Kaṁsa in Mathurā, illustrates the fact that all types of people find him attractive. Rūpa Goswāmī cites a statement attributed to a member of the audience: "When Kṛṣṇa entered the arena of Kaṁsa, the sages uttered blessings of 'Victory! Victory! Victory!' The *devatās* uttered sweet songs of praise. Out of joy, the women shouted loudly all around. Who did not develop attraction for Kṛṣṇa at the sports arena?"[28]

Samṛddhimān

The prosperity of Kṛṣṇa is evident in his abode, which is nondifferent from him, with its *kalpa-vṛkṣas* (wish-fulfilling trees), *kāma-dhenus* (wish-fulfilling cows), and *cintāmaṇi* (wish-fulfilling stones). Indeed, it is the place of pastimes for the Supreme Goddess of fortune, Śrī Rādhā. While Lakṣmī is served by everyone in Vaikuṇṭha, she serves incessantly in Vraja.[29]

Sukhī

One who is untouched by sorrow and takes pleasure in life is considered *sukhī*—a joyful person. Rūpa Goswāmī cites the statement of a messenger that mediated between Kṛṣṇa and the wives of the *brāhmaṇas* of Mathurā:

> O wives of the *brāhmaṇas*! Not even a trace of sorrow can touch Kṛṣṇa, for in him there is no destruction, no decrease, no suffering in household affairs, no cause of fear, and no worry. He does not experience any of the suffering of this world. He is eternally engaged in amusing himself in Vṛndāvana with beautiful women who are perfect, the best of friends, and possessed of the highest love.[30]

Varīyān

He who is the chief of all people is considered the most important among VIPs. The name Indra means "the Chief," chief of the gods, what to speak of his importance in human society. After the Govardhana *līlā*, Indra

28. *Bhakti-rasāmṛta-sindhu* 2.1.163.
29. *Śrīmad Bhāgavatam* 10.5.18 and 10.31.1.
30. *Bhakti-rasāmṛta-sindhu* 2.1.147.

apologized to Kṛṣṇa for his offense. In doing so, he was accompanied by Brahmā, Śiva, and other divine personalities, all of whom offered gifts to Kṛṣṇa and participated in the impromptu coronation of Kṛṣṇa headed by Indra. At that time, Kṛṣṇa was given the name Upendra/Govinda, "the God of the gods." All of this was observed by Kṛṣṇa's friends, who stood at a distance witnessing Kṛṣṇa's importance among those considered important and worshipable from the human perspective—personifications of the powers of nature that humans are dependent upon. When the cowherds reunited with Kṛṣṇa, they shared the gifts of the gods among themselves and joked about the ceremony and its participants, to the amazement of the gods.

The Excitants of Fraternal Love (uddīpana-vibhāva)

As mentioned earlier, the qualities of Kṛṣṇa can be included as part of a composite description of Kṛṣṇa's form and person as the object of *sakhya-rati*, or they may be considered individually as excitants of fraternal love. Other than Kṛṣṇa's qualities that may be viewed as excitants, Rūpa Goswāmī also cites other principal excitants of *sakhya-rati*: Kṛṣṇa's ages, form/beauty,[31] horn, flute, conch, sports, joking, his intimate devotees, and his imitating the actions of kings and gods. Śrī Rūpa also cites Kṛṣṇa's quality of heroism cited above as a principal excitant of *sakhya-rati*.

Kṛṣṇa is said to be endowed with the quality of ideal age—*vayasānvitaḥ*. His age in all three of its phases—*kumāra* (childhood), *paugaṇḍa* (boyhood), and *kiśora* (adolescence)—serves as an excitant for *sakhya-rati*. In each of these ages, Kṛṣṇa attains a distinct identity: as the son of Nanda and Yaśodā (*kumāra*), as a cowherd companion (*paugaṇḍa*), and as a lover of the *gopīs* (*kiśora*). Although his *paugaṇḍa* age is central to *sakhya-rati*, the final section of his childhood—*śesa-kumāra*—and the entirety of his adolescence also serve as *uddīpanas* for fraternal love. In the final portion of his childhood, Kṛṣṇa becomes a calf-herder whose exploits are described in the *Bhāgavatam* narrative of the *brahma-vimohana-līlā*. His boyhood, at the outset of which he officially becomes a cow-herder, is depicted in detail in the *Bhāgavata*'s *dhenukāsura-vadha-līlā*, as is the beginning of his adolescence relative to *sakhya-rati*.

31. Earlier in *Bhakti-rasāmṛta-sindhu* (2.1.306–307), Rūpa Goswāmī states that Kṛṣṇa's *svarūpa* (form) is not an *uddīpana* but rather is to be included in the description of him as the *viṣaya-ālambana-vibhāva*, unlike his qualities, which can be viewed from either perspective. However, in *Bhakti-rasāmṛta-sindhu* 3.3.81, Śrī Rūpa cites Kṛṣṇa's *rūpa* in his list of *uddīpanas* for *sakhya-rati*, citing the beauty of Kṛṣṇa's bodily luster in his example. Thus, here the word *rūpa* may refer to Kṛṣṇa's beauty more than his form.

It should be noted that Kṛṣṇa's *kiśora* age is the most perfect, and it is in this age that he appears in Vraja as well as in Mathurā and Dvārakā. Thus, his *kumāra* and *paugaṇḍa* ages are found only in his Vraja *līlā*.[32] At the same time, all of these ages are eternal. As the *kumāra* body of Kṛṣṇa ages during the *prakaṭa-līlā* from childhood to the boyhood of *paugaṇḍa*, it becomes sweeter while at the same time retaining the excellences of his childhood body. His *paugaṇḍa* body then attains more excellence and becomes his *kiśora* body without giving up the previous excellences of *kumāra* and *paugaṇḍa*. Again, among these ages, boyhood is most suitable for *sakhya-rati*,[33] and thus we shall discuss his childhood and adolescence in brief and explore his boyhood in some detail.

The *mantra-mayī* visualization of the calf-herder Kṛṣṇa, steeped in *sakhya-rati* during his late childhood, is beautifully depicted in a central *śloka* of the *Bhāgavata*'s prelude to the *brahma-vimohana-līlā*:

> As the denizens of heaven looked on, he who is otherwise the enjoyer of their sacrifices, *yajña-bhuk*, took pleasure instead in childish play, *bāla-keli*. He bore a flute in his belt along with a buffalo horn and herding staff. He held yogurt rice with pieces of fruit between the fingers of his left hand. Standing amid his friends, he made them laugh as he joked and played with them.[34]

Kṛṣṇa carried his flute between his cloth and waist. On his left hip he carried a horn and stick. In his left hand, he held a ball of rice mixed with condensed yogurt, which he then placed a morsel of into his right hand to place in his mouth without touching his fingers to it. In this way, he amused his friends, who surrounded him and laughed at his jokes. While the inhabitants of heaven looked on in amazement, the enjoyer of sacrifice, the *parama-puruṣa*, played as a small child. They could see him with their own eyes—he who is the enjoyer of sacrifices was enjoying himself and frolicking

32. In his *Bhāgavatāmṛta-kaṇā*, Viśvanātha Cakravartī Ṭhākura explains that in Kṛṣṇa's unmanifest (*aprakaṭa*) *līlā*, his ages of *kumāra* and *paugaṇḍa* are also manifest. Rūpa says the same in *Laghu-bhāgavatāmṛta* 1.5.451. In *Kṛṣṇa Sandarbha* 174, Jīva Goswāmī explains that "although Kṛṣṇa's ages of childhood and so on are also present in the *aprakaṭa-līlā* of the *mantra-mayī-upāsanā* variety, because of the primacy of his adolescent form (*kiśorākāra*), which is grounded in the *svārasikī-līlā*, all *līlās* proceed only on the basis of that form." That said, in *Ānanda-vṛndāvana-campū* 1.117–118, Kavi-karṇapūra appears to differ, stating that Kṛṣṇa's *kumāra-līlās* do not appear in the *aprakaṭa* realm.

33. *Bhakti-rasāmṛta-sindhu* 2.1.310.

34. *Śrīmad Bhāgavatam* 10.13.11.

as a young boy. The obvious question here is, What was the status of those boys who surrounded him, those in *sakhya-rati* engaged in the *yajña* of *prema*!

Boyhood typically begins at age five and ends at ten. However, Kṛṣṇa is said to be mature for his age, and thus his *paugaṇḍa-līlā* begins and ends earlier than normal. It is divided into three subsections.

Rūpa Goswāmī cites the words of bards who, having returned to Vṛndāvana after being absent for some time, more readily noticed the development in Kṛṣṇa's age:

> O Kṛṣṇa! Your abdomen is as beautiful as an *aśvattha* leaf. O lotus-eyed one! Your throat appears like a conch beautified by three lines. O moon on earth! Your lips conquer the red effulgence of rubies. What can be said? This new, indescribable beauty gives bliss to the eyes of your friends.[35]

In the first part of Kṛṣṇa's *paugaṇḍa* age, his lips are very red, his waist is thin, and three lines appear on his throat like a conch. He is decorated with a variety of flower ornaments, and his body is marked with minerals from the soil and wrapped in yellow silk. He wears a *guñjā*-berry necklace. He is crowned with the feather of a peacock. His activities include herding, playing various games, and learning hand-to-hand combat. Dancing, playing, and protecting cows, he showers his friends with bliss.

In the middle of his *paugaṇḍa* age, Kṛṣṇa begins to appear handsome. Because he is mature for his age, in his middle *paugaṇḍa* years he begins to manifest an early sense of adolescence—*kiśora*—in both disposition and appearance. His nose and chest are raised, and his cheeks are round. Overall, he appears more graceful. At this age, he begins to wear a turban tied with silk cords, and he carries a black staff that is four and a half feet long and crowned with a golden tip. His play becomes more adventurous, exploring the forests of Vraja and the wonders of Mount Govardhana.

The final division of Kṛṣṇa's *paugaṇḍa-līlā* finds him with his hair braided and extending down to his waist, and his shoulders noticeably strong and broad. His dear friend Subala describes him thus:

> O Keśava! Your attractive clothing, the tilted turban, the play lotus in your hand, the golden *tilaka* and musk dot on your forehead are

35. *Bhakti-rasāmṛta-sindhu* 3.3.63.

> making me, courageous Subala, completely dizzy! How much, then, will your appearance affect the softhearted *gopīs*![36]

During this age, Kṛṣṇa takes pleasure in wordplay, enjoying intimate conversations with his *priya-narma-sakhās*, and praising the forms of the young girls of Gokula in front of his friends. Śrī Rūpa characterizes the content of such intimate conversations thus:

> Kṛṣṇa! You are clever, evidenced by the fact that you have understood my heart. Thus, I whisper into your ear the fact that the young *gopīs* are now exhibiting enhanced power to bewilder. Among them, five or six young girls have become most beautiful, august, and attractive. O friend! It seems that Cupid has become mad with bliss, passing his own duty of conquering the world onto them.[37]

The following *Bhāgavata* verse spoken by the *gopīs* illustrates *kiśora* Kṛṣṇa's dress and ornaments:

> Crowned with a peacock feather, adorned with a *karṇikāra* flower behind his ear, wrapped in a reddish-gold garment, and garlanded with a wreath of five different forest flowers stretching down to his knees, Kṛṣṇa, his form that of the best of dancers, filled the holes of his flute with the nectar of his lips as he entered the forest of Vṛndāvana in the midst of his cowherd friends singing his praise. Leaving a path to follow, his footprints beautified the forest.[38]

And in *Muktā-carita*, we find Madhumaṅgala praising Kṛṣṇa's *kiśora* form and age:

> Subala! Why are you praising Kṛṣṇa's *paugaṇḍa* prowess so highly? Now that he, the wish-fulfilling tree of love, has been sprinkled with the nectar of youthful maturity, he has extended his branches and creepers in all directions, thus far surpassing his previous virtues.[39]

In any of Kṛṣṇa's ages, his form and beauty stand out to those in *sakhya-rati*. Unlike a material form, which loses its beauty with age, the beauty of

36. *Bhakti-rasāmṛta-sindhu* 3.3.75.
37. *Bhakti-rasāmṛta-sindhu* 3.3.77.
38. *Śrīmad Bhāgavatam* 10.21.5.
39. Raghunātha dāsa Goswāmī, *Muktā-carita*, verse 89.

Kṛṣṇa's form is not diminished with age. Its beauty is such that it beautifies his bodily ornaments.

Kṛṣṇa's principal horn is named Mandraghoṣa due to its sound, which resembles rumbling thunder. It is the horn of a spotted antelope embossed with gold on both ends and inlaid with jewels. Like his flute, it has an intoxicating effect. He has several different types of flutes—*veṇu*, *muralī*, and *vaṁśī*. A particular type of *vaṁśī*—the *ānandinī* or *bhuvana-mohinī*—is especially dear to the Vraja *vāsīs*. No other form of the Godhead bears the flute, not even Kṛṣṇa in Mathurā or Dvārakā.[40] During his stay in Mathurā and Dvārakā, Kṛṣṇa gave his horn to Stokakṛṣṇa and his flute to Subala for safekeeping. Otherwise, his flute is his constant companion in Vraja. It is considered to be a male friend of Kṛṣṇa and the best friend of everyone in Vraja because it informs them of his whereabouts when he is not nearby.[41] Like him, Kṛṣṇa's cowherd friends also carry flutes, horns, and sticks.

Kṛṣṇa's conch, named Pāñcajanya, serves as an excitant of *sakhya-rati* outside of Vraja in relation to his *pura-sambandhi* friends such as Pāṇḍava Arjuna and his wife Draupadī-devī. Kṛṣṇa does not carry his conch within his Vraja *līlā*. Nonetheless, when he sounds his conch in his Mathurā and Dvārakā *līlās*, it reminds him of Vraja such that his eyes fill with tears and his heart swells with compassion for his Vraja *vāsīs*.[42] Thus, arguably Kṛṣṇa derives his strength in battle outside of Vraja from bugling his conch and remembering the Vraja devotees and the strength of his *sakhās* therein.

Rūpa Goswāmī cites an instance of Kṛṣṇa's dressing as Rādhā as an example of his sportive diversions that serve as an excitant for *sakhya-rati*:

> Dear friend! When Subala saw Kṛṣṇa dressed in Rādhā's clothing, appearing with bright pink cloth, his body smeared with saffron and thus golden, his hair bound up beautifully, and wearing jeweled earrings, he was astonished, and he smiled.[43]

Kṛṣṇa's joking and overall jovial, carefree nature as well as his heroism, described as one of his qualities above, are central to his identity as a cowherd, a *gopa*. The word *gopa* can also mean "protector of the earth." Go

40. Although Balarāma also bears a flute at times, he cannot play it like Kṛṣṇa does. Thus, Kṛṣṇa's quality of *veṇu-mādhurya*—sweet flute—pertains to him alone.

41. The word *veṇu* is masculine, but the words *muralī* and *vaṁśī* are feminine. Nonetheless, these feminine words refer to the masculine flute, just as the masculine word *dāra* refers to one's wife.

42. *Gopāla-campū* 1.33.71–72.

43. *Bhakti-rasāmṛta-sindhu* 3.3.85.

means "earth," and *pa* means "protector." Kṛṣṇa is "Gopendra," the best of the protectors of the earth, or the best of kings. The *Amara-kośa* thesaurus also says, *gopo bhūpa*: "*Gopa* means 'king.' " Thus, Kṛṣṇa's imitation of kings and gods is a natural extension of his cowherd identity, and such imitation serves as an excitant of *sakhya-rati*. Kṛṣṇa's intimate devotees in moods other than fraternal love whose *sthāyi-bhāva* is nonetheless compatible with *sakhya-rati* serve as *uddīpanas* of fraternal love as well.

Other than the excitants listed by Rūpa Goswāmī, Śrī Jīva Goswāmī cites a number of qualities manifest in the cowherd friends of Kṛṣṇa themselves that also serve as excitants for *sakhya-rati*: friendliness, straightforwardness, gratitude, intelligence, learning, genius, skill, bravery, strength, tolerance, compassion, red eyes, and the beauty of their ages and bodily limbs. Furthermore, in *Prīti Sandarbha* 246–252, Śrī Jīva also lists various activities of Kṛṣṇa and his varieties of dress cited in the *Bhāgavatam* as excitants.[44] One may ask, "What time is an excitant for *sakhya-rati*?" Śrī Jīva answers, "That time suitable for playing."

Having discussed Kṛṣṇa as the object of *sakhya-rati* and also its excitants to some extent, we shall now turn to Kṛṣṇa's intimate friends, who are examples of the embodiment (*āśraya-ālambana-vibhāva*) of various types of Vraja's *sakhya-rati*. In so doing, we will complete our overall discussion of *sakhya-rati*'s *vibhāvas*—its object of love, its excitants, and its embodiments.

The Embodiments of Fraternal Love (āśraya-ālambana-vibhāva)

Rūpa Goswāmī explains that both perfected devotees (*siddhas*) and intermediate devotees who have attained *rati* serve as embodiments of sacred aesthetic rapture—devotees whose "hearts are full of attraction for Kṛṣṇa."[45] The latter have attained *rati* through either *sādhana* or grace, but in either case they follow the example of those who are eternally perfect (*nitya-siddha*). All such devotees serve as embodiments of *bhakti-rasa* because love of God has overtaken their hearts, and this love of God corresponds with God as the object of that love. However, in this section we will discuss only the *rāgātmikas* of Kṛṣṇa's Vraja *līlā* who serve as embodiments of *sakhya-rati*, devotees constituted of *svarūpa-śakti*.

In his prayers following the *brahma-vimohana-līlā*, Brahmā reflects upon the good fortune of the residents of Vraja with a verse that also represents

44. Activities: *Śrīmad Bhāgavatam* 10.35.20–21, 10.13.11, 10.15.9–10, 10.15.12–13, 10.18.19, and 10.14.47; Dress: 10.21.19, 10.35.6, 10.23.22, and 10.15.45.

45. *Bhakti-rasāmṛta-sindhu* 2.1.273 and 2.1.276–277.

his own ideal of fraternal love imbibed at the dawn of creation.[46] Rūpa Goswāmī cites this verse in a broad sense as support for the idea that Kṛṣṇa is surrounded in Vraja by eternally liberated devotees.

> Oh, how fortunate! O how fortunate are Nanda and the cowherds of Vraja! He who is the highest bliss, the most complete expression of Brahman, is their eternal friend.[47]

Jīva Goswāmī explains that the word *mitram* (friend) in this verse is qualified by the word *sanātanam* (eternal). What type of friend is he who is the *paramānanda* and *pūrṇaṁ brahma*, a possessor of qualities that distinguish and promote him above the indeterminate, all-pervading manifestation of Godhead known as *nirviśeṣa* Brahman? Kṛṣṇa, who is the determinate manifestation of the Godhead, in relation to whom one can taste not merely *brahmānanda* but moreover *paramānanda* or *bhaktyānanda* in its fullest expression, is a friend extending over all three phases of time—*mitraṁ sanātanam*. Just as Kṛṣṇa is eternally perfect, so his friends are as well.

The word *mitram* in this verse speaks of friends in both a broad sense—in that it speaks of all the residents of Vraja, some of whom are embodiments of *dāsya*, *vātsalya*, or *mādhurya*—and the specific sense of referring to those in *sakhya-rati*. Viśvanātha Cakravartī Ṭhākura comments that Brahmā is primarily praising those who have *sakhya-rati* and by extension those in other *rasas* as well. Furthermore, this verse also speaks to us as to the pervasive nature of *sakhya-rati* in Vraja, in that it touches all the other *rasas* and serves as the baseline of aesthetic rapture in Kṛṣṇa's pastoral *līlās*. The *dāsya-rati* of Vraja is for the most part combined with *sakhya*;[48] *vātsalya* is also in some instances combined with *sakhya*; and although Rūpa Goswāmī does not speak about *sakhya* and *mādhurya* combining or mixing together as a *sthāyi-bhāva*, Jīva Goswāmī does in his *Prīti Sandarbha*.

Since *sakhya-rati* itself is of four varieties, there are four divisions of devotees who are the shelter of such love. Before elaborating on these four divisions, Rūpa Goswāmī describes the intimate nature of the *sakhās*'

46. See *Śrīmad Bhāgavatam* 2.9.30—*yāvat sakhā sakhyuṛ*—and the commentaries of Bhaktivedanta Swami Prabhupāda and Viśvanātha Cakravartī Ṭhākura for insight into the *sakhya-rasa* ideal Brahmā identified with.

47. *Śrīmad Bhāgavatam* 10.14.32. See chapter 30 for a deeper explanation of this verse.

48. *Bhakti-rasāmṛta-sindhu* 3.2.90–91. Jīva Goswāmī comments that generally in the *dāsya-rasa* of Vraja, *rāga* is experienced with the influence of *sakhya*. Rūpa Goswāmī cites Raktaka as an example.

relationship with Kṛṣṇa—their feelings for Kṛṣṇa and his feelings for them—with reference to the Govardhana *līlā* and *aghāsura-vadha-līlā*:

> The cowherds speak to Kṛṣṇa: You have endured seven nights on your feet without sleep holding the hill. Surely you are tired. Our minds are disturbed seeing you in this condition. Dear friend, toss the mountain to Śrīdāmā, or in the least place it in your right hand. Then we can massage your left hand.
>
> Kṛṣṇa speaks to an older cowherd boy: O brother! O respected one! On seeing all my friends enter the stomach of the Agha demon without hesitation, hot tears began to flow from my eyes, and my cheeks became thin. Despondent, for some time my mind became vacant.[49]

In the mood of a *sādhaka* who has attained *mādhurya-rati*, Śukamuni describes the *siddha-sakhās* and their good fortune thus:

> Sometimes Kṛṣṇa would go to a somewhat distant place to see the beauty of the forest. Then all the other boys would run to accompany him, each one saying, "I shall be the first to run and touch Kṛṣṇa! I shall touch Kṛṣṇa first!" In this way they enjoyed life by repeatedly touching Kṛṣṇa, blowing flutes, bugling on buffalo horns, singing along with bumblebees, imitating the sounds of the cuckoos and other birds, running with arms stretched following the shadows on the ground of birds flying above, imitating the graceful movements of the swans, sitting silently with ducks, dancing with peacocks, attracting young monkeys and jumping into the trees with them, and imitating the monkeys' facial expressions as they jumped from one branch to another. Some boys went to the waterfall and crossed the river, jumping with the frogs, laughing at their own reflections, and criticizing their echoes. The cowherd boys of Vraja must have engaged in *bhakti* for many, many lives to now be able to play intimately with Kṛṣṇa. After all, *jñānīs* realize a mere impersonal form of Kṛṣṇa (the bliss of Brahman), *vaidhī-bhaktas* realize him at some distance as their venerable deity, and ordinary persons see him as but a mundane child.[50]

49. *Bhakti-rasāmṛta-sindhu* 3.3.18 and 3.3.20.

50. *Śrīmad Bhāgavatam* 10.12.6–11. The words *kṛta-puṇya-puñjāḥ* in 10.12.11 refer to *bhakti*, not *puṇya-karma*.

Later in the text of the *Bhāgavatam*, the *gopīs* also marvel at the fortune of the Vraja *gopas* and those who witness their *līlās* with Rāma and Kṛṣṇa:

> O friends! We know of no vision more perfect than that of beholding the beautiful faces of the sons of Vraja *rāja* Nanda's sons—Rāma and Kṛṣṇa—as these two sons surrounded by their friends enter the forest herding their cows ahead of them. They hold their flutes to their mouths and glance back lovingly upon the Vraja *vāsīs* as they depart for the forest. Those who experience this scene are truly blessed.[51]

This *Bhāgavata* verse, spoken in Śukadeva's developing *gopī-bhāva*, is particularly heartening to *sakhya-rati-upāsakas*. From their perspective, it constitutes a glorification of *sakhya-rati* and the fortune of Kṛṣṇa's cowherd friends sung by the beloved Vraja *sundarīs*. It is this vision of the *gopīs* that such *sakhya-rasa-sādhakas* aspire to participate in. And in doing so, any prior reverence on their part transforms into unhesitating eagerness to join the circle of cowherds as they enter the forest with Rāma, Kṛṣṇa, and their cows. When understood in budding *sakhya-rati*, this scene is all one requires in the form of an invitation to enter into *sakhya-rati* proper. Those with a sympathetic heart—*sa hṛdayam*—for *sakhya-rati*, having cultivated it appropriately, will experience Kṛṣṇa's glancing back upon those witnessing his entrance into the forest as an invitation to enter his cowherd *līlā* forever. When Kṛṣṇa beholds his friends' eyes fixed upon his face and that of Rāma, even as those friends are themselves part of the portrait, that vision causes Rāma's and Kṛṣṇa's hearts full of fraternal love to flow outward through their own lotus eyes in search of anyone whose heart also resonates with this scene in *sakhya-rati*. Blessed is this window to the world of Kṛṣṇa and his cowherd friends, and most blessed are his friends!

But how can a *sādhaka* accept Kṛṣṇa's invitation and enter the *līlā* through such a window and serve him as he so desires? The answer lies in his or her purified will. While one's inherent nature is aroused through *sādhu-saṅga*, the subsequent *sādhana* involves one's exercise of will in response to grace and informs the details of one's attainment. Baladeva Vidyābhūṣaṇa explains in his *Govinda-bhāṣya* that it is the will of the *sādhaka* that determines the details of his or her status in transcendence.[52] As one is freed from *anarthas*

51. *Śrīmad Bhāgavatam* 10.21.7.

52. *Vedānta-sūtra* 4.4.12. Baladeva Vidyābhūṣaṇa comments that the will (*saṅkalpa*) of the *sādhaka* blooms into fruition when one attains *mukti*. This *saṅkalpa* is to be cultivated from the earliest stages of one's *sādhana*, because the *śruti* says, *yathā kratuḥ*: "As a person wills in this life, so he or she gets in the next." Long before the *mukta* attains *mukti*, he

and one's conceptual orientation is refined, one's will to serve is influenced by Kṛṣṇa's *svarūpa-śakti*, which expresses itself only for the pleasure of Kṛṣṇa. Kṛṣṇa's *svarūpa-śakti* exists only for this purpose, anticipating and fulfilling his every desire. Thus, willing or making strong resolutions (*saṅkalpa*) under its influence is tantamount to uniting one's own will with Kṛṣṇa's will in pursuit of sacred aesthetic rapture, from which Kṛṣṇa derives the greatest *ānanda*. Therefore, the influence of Kṛṣṇa's *svarūpa-śakti* assures the fructification of the spiritually advanced *sādhaka*'s desire. Influenced by this spiritual environment and in consultation with *śrī guru*, the advanced *sādhaka* wills the details of his or her *sakhya-rati* that, among other things, place the *sādhaka* in one of the divisions of fraternal love. The *guru* may suggest details, or in some lineages he or she is thought to "reveal" these details. But in any event, they are willed into manifestation through the effort of the spiritually advanced *sādhaka*.

Thus, each and every cowherd, *nitya-siddha* and *sādhana-siddha* alike, is unique and constitutes a particular embodiment of desire to serve Kṛṣṇa in *sakhya-rati* in accordance with his will. Some prefer mangoes over bananas and so on, and Kṛṣṇa knows precisely what most pleases the palate of each of his dear friends. Through them he expresses and experiences the fulfillment of his own desires. Some cowherds dress in golden cloth, others in sapphire blue, ruby red, shades of saffron, and so on. They have different colored complexions and different preferences with regard to dress as well as different residences, names, ages, *sevā*, and behavior. They belong to different groups with different ambitions and moods. They follow different orders and are in different relationships with Kṛṣṇa. Such differences that define their individual personalities are as much expressions of their own *sakhya-rasa* as they are manifestations of Kṛṣṇa's desires expressed and fulfilled through the senses of his friends; that is, Kṛṣṇa's *sakhās* are both one with Kṛṣṇa and different from him at the same time.[53]

---

or she has been constantly willing, "I am walking through the feet of Viṣṇu; I am seeing through the eyes of Viṣṇu," and so forth. See also *Vedānta-sūtra* 4.4.14. The argument that the *mukta* has no desire does not hold, because *rasa*, which is to be relished, is desired by the *mukta*, who knows it to be Bhagavān's mercy. Kṛṣṇa desires to enjoy *rasa* despite being self-satisfied, because his devotees desire to please him in this way.

53. From the perspective of nondifference (*abheda*), the cowherds' bodies are manifestations of Kṛṣṇa's own form through which he expresses himself and experiences variety, whereas from the perspective of difference (*bheda*), the cowherds are individual persons with desires pleasing to Kṛṣṇa. The perspective of non-difference is discussed in *Govinda-bhāṣya* 4.4.12 with reference to the *śruti*.

About these cowherds, Śrī Rūpa Goswāmīpāda cites the following verses:

> The cowherd friends of Kṛṣṇa are more or less the same age as Kṛṣṇa, with similar qualities, activities, clothing, and beauty. They are equipped with pleasing flutes, horns, and *vallakī* leaves (for making instruments), and they have complexions of dark blue, gold, crystal, and ruby. Always filled with love for Kṛṣṇa, may they protect you! By possessing various natures, the sweet friends increase the wonder and pleasure of pure friendship with Kṛṣṇa.[54]

The Four Divisions of the Embodiments of Fraternal Love (āśraya-ālambana-vibhāva)

To penetrate the *tattva* of fraternal love for Kṛṣṇa more deeply, we shall now proceed to discuss the four divisions of Kṛṣṇa's friends—*sakhā*, *suhṛt-sakhā*, *priya-sakhā*, and *priya-narma-sakhā*—in some detail, as they represent the embodiments of perfected *sakhya-rati* (*rāgātmikas* in *sakhya-rasa*) referred to at the outset of this chapter.

Among the four divisions of Kṛṣṇa's intimate friends, the *sakhās*' and *suhṛt-sakhās*' *rati* is termed *saṅkula*; their dominant fraternal love is bundled together (*saṅkula*) with other *rasas* that are either neutral to *sakhya* (*dāsya*) or incompatible with it (*vātsalya*).[55] The *priya-sakhās*' fraternal love, on the other hand, is *kevala*, or exclusively fraternal. And the fourth variety of *sakhya-rati* is found in the *priya-narma-sakhās*, whose fraternal love is influenced by *mādhurya-rati*, the two being compatible.[56]

Friends can be younger and to some extent inclined toward service. They can also be older and to some extent protective. Younger and older brothers come to mind. Thus, although *dāsya* and *vātsalya* are incompatible with one another and are respectively neutral to or incompatible with *sakhya-rasa*, they can be bundled together with *sakhya* to form *saṅkula-rati*, in which Kṛṣṇa's younger and older friends sometimes experience *dāsya* or *vātsalya*, respectively, independently of their fraternal sentiments. In Balarāma, we find *sakhya* bundled with both *dāsya* and *vātsalya*. Thus, he experiences *sakhya* primarily and is thereby defined by fraternal love, but at times he

54. *Bhakti-rasāmṛta-sindhu* 3.3.17.

55. The incompatibility here refers to the effect that the other *rasa* has on the primary *rasa* and does not imply that devotees in *sakhya-rati* and *vātsalya-rati*, for example, are incompatible with each other.

56. This influence of *mādhurya-rati* on fraternal love will be discussed in the next chapter.

also relishes either *dāsya* or *vātsalya*.[57] In discussing such *saṅkula-rati*, Rūpa Goswāmī explains that combinations of these three *mukhya-rasas*—*dāsya*, *sakhya*, and *vātsalya*—can appear bundled together as *saṅkula-rati*. He also notes that the most dominant *rati* determines the particular devotee's *sthāyi-bhāva*.[58]

There is no form of *saṅkula-bhāva* that includes *mādhurya-rati*. However, unlike *dāsya* and *vātsalya*, *mādhurya* is very compatible with *sakhya*. Thus, there is a place for some special friends of Kṛṣṇa to be involved in his romantic life out of both sympathy for Rādhā and Kṛṣṇa's romantic life and the desire to assist them. But this is the subject of the following chapter. Herein, we shall cite examples of the four varieties of *sakhya-rati* and describe *sakhās* of each variety, following the lead of Rūpa Goswāmī.

Suhṛt-sakhās

Suhṛt-sakhās are a little older than Kṛṣṇa. Among them, Balarāma stands out. However, as we have seen, his *sakhya-rati* is tinged with both *dāsya* and *vātsalya*, unlike that of the other *suhṛt-sakhās*, whose fraternal love is bundled only with *vātsalya-rati*. Although Balarāma himself is Bhagavān and also the object of *sakhya-rati* for his devotees, Rūpa Goswāmī places more emphasis on Rāma's role as the prime exemplar of *sakhya-rati*. Thus, Śrī Rūpa includes him among those exemplifying the embodiment of fraternal love.

Along with Baladeva, Rūpa Goswāmī cites Maṇḍalībhadra as a prime example of a *suhṛt-sakhā*. These two are "the best" of Kṛṣṇa's well-wishing friends, while the leader of the *suhṛt-sakhās* is Vijayākṣa, the son of Kṛṣṇa's wet nurse Ambikā. Maṇḍalībhadra is described thus:

> Maṇḍalībhadra decorates his shining limbs with pink cloth. He carries a club in his hand, wears a peacock feather on his head, and has a complexion like that of a shining, brilliant black bumblebee.[59]

Rūpa Goswāmī cites the following *suhṛt-sakhās*. Read their names out loud, hear these sacred sounds, and be blessed: Bhadravardhana, Gobhaṭa,

57. Jīva Goswāmī precludes *vātsalya*'s mixing with *dāsya* or either of them being compatible with *sakhya* in his commentary on *Bhakti-rasāmṛta-sindhu* 4.8.81. Therein, he explains this point about the nature of Balarāma's *saṅkula-rati* experience, which holds true for others as well. In 3.3.22 and 3.3.30, Rūpa Goswāmī describes the influences of *dāsya* and *vātsalya* in *saṅkula-sakhya-rati* as "scents" (*gandha*) of the loving moods of servant and parent, respectively.

58. *Bhakti-rasāmṛta-sindhu* 3.4.80 and 2.5.26.

59. *Bhakti-rasāmṛta-sindhu* 3.3.26.

Yakṣa, Indrabhaṭa, Bhadrāṅga, Vīrabhadra, Vijaya, Subhada, Kulavīra, Mahābhīma, Divyaśakti, Suraprabha, and Raṇasthira. Śrī Rūpa also adds Kṛṣṇa's paternal cousins Subhadra, Kuṇḍala, Daṇḍī, and Maṇḍala to this list, as well as Sunanda, Nandī, and Ānandī.[60]

Kṛṣṇadāsa Kavirāja describes Yaśodā's parental love as she projects it onto the *suhṛt-sakhās* at the outset of the midmorning *līlā*, just as Kṛṣṇa sets out to enter the forest with his friends and cows:

> O Subhadra, Maṇḍalībhadra, and Balabhadra! O boys, I hand my tender child over to you! He should always be controlled, instructed, and protected. And when he misbehaves, you must inform me! O boys headed by Vijaya! Stay close to Kṛṣṇa with your swords, bows, and arrows and protect him![61]

Viśvanātha Cakravartī envisions the same scene thus:

> Although Hari is very tender, he is still the leader of all the rowdy cowherds. While he is very bright, he does not know his own limits.[62] Although he is weak, he is also very dashing and thus captivating. Therefore, you boys should surround him to protect him. His father cannot control him, nor can his mother, nor can any of his elders. However, he may listen to you older boys. I pray that my request of you will not be in vain. If you see Kaṁsa's cruel, demonic henchmen, you should run, leaving even the cows, and quickly take shelter of us![63]

Sakhās

Sakhās, the second group of Kṛṣṇa's friends, are a little younger than Kṛṣṇa, and their *sakhya-rati* is bundled with *dāsya-rati*. Foremost among them is Devaprastha:

> He is very strong, a ready scholar, and is very expert in playing ball. He wears a white dress, and he ties his hair into a bunch with a rope. Whenever there is a fight between Kṛṣṇa and the demons, Devaprastha is the first to help, and he fights just like an elephant.

60. *Bhakti-rasāmṛta-sindhu* 3.3.23 and *Rādhā-kṛṣṇa-gaṇoddeśa-dīpikā* 2.22–25.
61. *Govinda-līlāmṛta* 5.31–33.
62. This is because he has no limits.
63. *Kṛṣṇa-bhāvanāmṛta* 7.52–54.

> One of the *gopīs* once said to her friend, "My dear beautiful friend, when Kṛṣṇa, the son of Mahārāja Nanda, was taking rest within the cave of a hill, he was keeping his head on the arms of Śrīdāmā, and he was putting his left hand on Dāmā's chest. Taking this opportunity, Devaprastha, out of his strong affection for Kṛṣṇa, immediately began to massage his legs.[64]

Along with Devaprastha, *Śrīmad Bhāgavatam* also mentions Varūthapa, Viśāla, Vṛṣabha, and Ojasvī.[65] Rūpa Goswāmī identifies them as *sakhās* and adds the holy names of Maranda, Kusumāpīḍa, Maṇibandha, Karandhama, Candana, Kunda, Kalinda, and Kulika to his list of Kṛṣṇa's prominent younger friends.[66]

Bhaktivedanta Swami Prabhupāda describes these *sakhās* thus:

> All of these *sakhā* friends of Kṛṣṇa seek only to serve him. Sometimes some of them would rise early in the morning and immediately go to Kṛṣṇa's place and wait at the door to see Kṛṣṇa and to accompany him to the pasturing grounds. In the meantime, Kṛṣṇa would be dressed by Mother Yaśodā, and when she would see a boy standing at the door, she would call him: "Well, Viśāla, why are you standing there? Come here!" So with the permission of Mother Yaśodā, he would immediately enter the house. And while Mother Yaśodā was dressing Kṛṣṇa, he would try to help put on Kṛṣṇa's ankle bells, and Kṛṣṇa would jokingly strike him with his flute. Then Mother Yaśodā would call, "Kṛṣṇa, what is this? Why are you teasing your friend?" And Kṛṣṇa would laugh, and the friend would also laugh.... Sometimes the *sakhās* would take care of the cows who were going hither and thither. They would tell Kṛṣṇa, "Your cows were going off here and there," and Kṛṣṇa would thank them.
>
> Sometimes when Kṛṣṇa and his *sakhās* went to the pasturing ground, Kaṁsa would send a demon to kill Kṛṣṇa. Therefore, almost every day there was a fight with some different kind of demon. After fighting with a demon, Kṛṣṇa would feel fatigued, the hairs on his head would be scattered, and the *sakhās* would immediately come and try to relieve him in different ways. Some friends would say, "My dear

64. Bhaktivedanta Swami Prabhupāda, *The Nectar of Devotion*, chapter 41. See also *Bhakti-rasāmṛta-sindhu* 3.3.34–35.

65. *Śrīmad Bhāgavatam* 10.22.31.

66. *Bhakti-rasāmṛta-sindhu* 3.3.31 and *Rādhā-kṛṣṇa-gaṇoddeśa-dīpikā* 2.29–30.

> Viśāla, please take this fan of lotus leaves and fan Kṛṣṇa so that he may feel some comfort. Varūthapa, you just brush the scattered hairs on Kṛṣṇa's head which have fallen upon his face. Vṛṣabha, don't talk unnecessarily! Immediately massage Kṛṣṇa's body. His arms have become tired from fighting and wrestling with that demon. Oh, just see how our friend Kṛṣṇa has become tired!"[67]

Priya-sakhās

Kṛṣṇa's friends whose *sakhya-rati* is not mixed with *vātsalya* or *dāsya* are closest in age to him. Rūpa Goswāmī refers to them as *priya-sakhās*, dear friends, indicating that they share a greater level of intimacy with Kṛṣṇa than do his *sakhās* and *suhṛt-sakhās*, in whom the influence of *dāsya* and *vātsalya*, respectively, inhibit the equality central to fraternal love's intimacy. Notably, Nayanānanda Ṭhākura, identifying himself as a *priya-sakhā*, proclaims, "*Saṅkula-rati* is compared to the desire-fulfilling gem called *cintāmaṇi*. . . . But *kevala-rati* is compared to the transcendentally superior Kaustubha-maṇi. Indeed, I do not see any mood other than pure eternal friendship."[68]

Most prominent among the *priya-sakhās* is Śrīdāmā, the older brother of Rādhā. Rūpa Goswāmī also mentions Sudāmā, Dāmā, Vasudāmā, Kiṅkiṇi, Stokakṛṣṇa, Aṁśu, Bhadrasena, Vilāsi, Puṇḍarīka, Viṭaṅka, and Kalaviṅka.[69] Śrī Rūpa offers the following description of Śrīdāmā:

> I worship dark-complexioned Śrīdāmā, who competes with Kṛṣṇa out of friendship. He wears yellow-greenish cloth, holds a horn in his hand, sports a copper-colored turban, and is adorned with a flower garland.[70]

Within the group of *priya-sakhās*, Bhadrasena is the commander of what Rūpa Goswāmī refers to as "the army of Kṛṣṇa's friends."[71]

With reference to *Krama-dīpikā* and *Gautamīya Tantra*, Nayanānanda Ṭhākura underscores the special position of four of these *priya-sakhās*:

> In the four directions stand the all-worshipable Dāmā, Sudāmā, Vasudāmā, and Kiṅkiṇi, who have forms of effulgent

67. *The Nectar of Devotion*, chapter 41.

68. Nayanānanda Ṭhākura, *Śrī Śrī Preyo-Bhakti-Rasārṇava, trans.* Daśaratha-Suta Dāsa (Charlottesville, VA: Bookwrights Press, 2018), 105–106.

69. *Bhakti-rasāmṛta-sindhu* 3.3.36–37.

70. *Bhakti-rasāmṛta-sindhu* 3.3.41.

71. *Rādhā-kṛṣṇa-gaṇoddeśa-dīpikā* 2.33.

> splendor—*tejo-rūpa*. One should worship Keśava along with these who are his external limbs.[72]

> Famous are Dāmā, Sudāmā, Vasudāmā, and Kiṅkiṇi, personifications of Kṛṣṇa's *antaḥ-karaṇa*. Nondifferent from his very self, they should be worshiped like Kṛṣṇa with flowers and sandalwood.[73]

The above citation from *Gautamīya Tantra* is also cited by Jīva Goswāmī in his *Laghu-toṣaṇī* commentary on *Śrīmad Bhāgavatam* 10.22.8 and his commentary on *Bhakti-rasāmṛta-sindhu* 3.3.36–37, which Nayanānanda Ṭhākura refers to and elaborates on:

> These four *sakhās* are nondifferent from Kṛṣṇa himself. Their dress and ornaments are impossible to do justice to within the limits of the written word. The personification of Kṛṣṇa's *buddhi* is the *gopa* named Śrīdāmā; and the personification of Kṛṣṇa's *ahaṅkāra* is Sudāmā; the personification of Kṛṣṇa's *citta* is Vasudāmā; the personification of Kṛṣṇa's *manas* is Kiṅkiṇi. There is not a single confidential *līlā* that Kṛṣṇa-candra secretly performs in Vraja that these four *gopas* are not witnesses to. Surely one is never abandoned by one's own intelligence, ego, heart, and mind. In all of one's actions, these accompany one while always remaining in the background. All of Kṛṣṇa's *līlās* performed in Vraja throughout his three different ages are never enacted without these particular boys. There is not a single thing about Kṛṣṇa that they are unaware of, from his parental relationships up to and including his amorous affairs.[74]

The above scriptural citations concerning the special position of these four cowherds all appear to exclude the foremost of the *priya-sakhās*, Śrīdāmā. In his place we find the cowherd Dāmā. However, Nayanānanda Ṭhākura takes the position that in these citations from the Tantras, the name Dāmā actually refers to Śrīdāmā, rather than the cowherd Dāmā, and that Śrīdāmā is referred to as such in consideration of metrical sensibilities: taking into account meter, the syllable *śrī* in Śrīdāmā is left out, and thus "Dāmā" is

72. *Krama-dīpikā* 4.28.

73. *Gautamīya Tantra* 10.82–83.

74. *Śrī Śrī Preyo-bhakti-rasārṇava*, chapter 2. Also note that it is because of their special position as Kṛṣṇa's *antaḥ-karaṇa* personified that Jīva Goswāmī describes them as *priya-narma-sakhās* in his commentary to *Bhakti-rasāmṛta-sindhu* 3.3.37. That is to say, they are privy to the romantic life of Kṛṣṇa as otherwise only the *priya-narma-sakhās* are. But unlike the *priya-narma-sakhās*, they play no active role in it.

an abbreviation of "Śrīdāmā." This appears to be a significant insight, for throughout *śāstra* and the commentaries of the Goswāmīs, Śrīdāmā is considered the preeminent *priya-sakhā*.

Priya-narma-sakhās

Again, the fourth and final division of *sakhya-rati* involves those embodiments of fraternal love who assist Kṛṣṇa in his romantic life in addition to fully participating in Kṛṣṇa's fraternal dealings with the other three groups of his friends. Śrī Rūpa describes these *priya-narma-sakhās* as superior to the other three groups, possessed of a special *bhāva* (*bhāva-viśeṣiṇaḥ*), and participating in the highest and most confidential affairs of Rādhā and Kṛṣṇa (*ātyantika-rahasyeṣu yuktāḥ*). Śrī Goswāmījī mentions Subala, Arjuna, Gandharva, Vasanta, and Ujjvala,[75] with Subala and Ujjvala being the most prominent *priya-narma-sakhās*. Given the complexity of their *bhāva* and their prominence in the Gauḍīya *sampradāya*'s *sakhya-rati*, we shall discuss them in detail in the following chapter.

Thus far we have been discussing the four types of Kṛṣṇa's friends in the context of an overview of the divisions of *vibhāva*. *Vibhāva* is only one of the four ecstatic ingredients that assist the *sthāyi-bhāva* of fraternal love in maturing from its budding stage and flowering into *sakhya-rasa*. To summarize, *vibhāva* has two divisions. The first division—*ālambana-vibhāva*—is that which constitutes a locus for the *bhāva* to express itself in loving reciprocation: a personified object of love (*viṣaya-ālambana-vibhāva*) and the personification of that love (*āśraya-ālambana-vibhāva*), in which the love is sheltered.

The second division of *vibhāva*—*uddīpana-vibhāva*—is that which excites or stimulates the *sthāyi-bhāva*. It consists of any number of things related to Kṛṣṇa and his transcendental drama of divine love: dramatic props such as a particular setting, Kṛṣṇa's age, his flute, his herding stick, the sound of his horn, and so on.

Next, we will discuss *anubhāvas*, or intentional ecstatic expressions that manifest as a natural consequence after the *vibhāvas* have nourished the *sthāyi-bhāva* by defining its roles and exciting it.

Intentional Ecstatic Expressions (anubhāvas)

Unlike the more causal nature of *vibhāva* that allows the *sthāyi-bhāva* to be tasted by giving it shape and exciting it, *anubhāvas* are conscious gestures

75. *Bhakti-rasāmṛta-sindhu* 3.3.43.

through which spiritual emotion is externally expressed as an effect. They are activities that manifest in the body after the different causes of love—*vibhāvas*—have nourished the dominant emotion of fraternal love. *Anubhāvas* serve as charming expressions of inner spiritual emotion, adding yet another dimension to fraternal love. In *sakhya-rati*, some *anubhāvas* are common to all four groups of *sakhās*, while others are relative to a particular group.[76] Rūpa Goswāmī defines them as follows:

> *Anubhāvas* common to all of Kṛṣṇa's comrades include delighting him in combat; playing ball; gambling; riding atop one another's shoulders; stick fighting; sleeping and sitting with Kṛṣṇa on his bedstead, seat, or swing; entertaining him with jokes; engaging in water sports; and singing and dancing together with him.[77]
>
> Activities particular to the *sakhās* include placing betel nut in Kṛṣṇa's mouth, adorning his forehead with *tilaka*, smearing sandalwood on his body, and painting designs of leaves and vines on his body.[78]
>
> The activities particular to the *suhṛts* include giving advice on what should and should not be done, engaging in beneficial acts, and assuming leadership in whatever act is performed.[79]
>
> Activities particular to the *priya-sakhās* include conquering Kṛṣṇa in mock fighting, grabbing his clothes and pulling him, snatching flowers from his hands and making *him* adorn *them*, and engaging in hand-to-hand combat.[80]
>
> Activities particular to the *priya-narma-sakhās* include serving as messengers for the Vraja *kiśorīs*, sympathizing with their love for Kṛṣṇa, taking his side in the *gopīs'* love quarrels with him when only they are present and in their absence cleverly supporting the particular *gopī* group leader they have taken shelter of; and whispering secret messages in each other's ears.[81]

76. Note that the list of *anubhāvas* here pertains to one's internal *siddha-deha* and not one's *sādhaka-deha*. *Anubhāvas* of the *sādhaka-deha* will be the same for devotees regardless of their internal relationship with Kṛṣṇa. They will be *anubhāvas* that correspond with *dāsya-rati* for Gaura Kṛṣṇa and his *līlā* as a *sādhaka*, such as chanting and dancing.
77. *Bhakti-rasāmṛta-sindhu* 3.3.86–88.
78. *Bhakti-rasāmṛta-sindhu* 3.3.91.
79. *Bhakti-rasāmṛta-sindhu* 3.3.90.
80. *Bhakti-rasāmṛta-sindhu* 3.3.92.
81. *Bhakti-rasāmṛta-sindhu* 3.3.93–94.

Concluding his brief discussion of the *anubhāvas* of *sakhya-rati*, Rūpa Goswāmī cites some of the *anubhāvas* that Kṛṣṇa's friends also share with those in *dāsya-rati*. He also states that from his list of *anubhāvas* in general found in *Bhakti-rasāmṛta-sindhu* 2.2, some may also be relevant to *sakhya-rati*:

> Adorning Kṛṣṇa with forest flowers and jewels, singing, dancing before him, caring for his cows, massaging his body, stringing garlands for him, and fanning him are activities that the friends share in common with those in *dāsya-rati*. Furthermore, the wise consider that in addition to all the previously mentioned *anubhāvas*, there are others not mentioned here that also apply to the *sakhās*.[82]

Unintentional Ecstatic Expressions (sāttvika-bhāvas)

While *anubhāvas* are expressed consciously, as are ordinary bodily activities, *sāttvika-bhāvas* by contrast are abnormal, involuntary expressions of ecstasy. *Anubhāvas* reveal or shed light on one's internal emotional reality, and thus they are driven by one's *antaḥ-karaṇa* being infused with *bhāva*. They enhance one's love for Kṛṣṇa by way of rendering it observable. However, the conscious manner in which *anubhāvas* are expressed and the involuntary way in which *sāttvika-bhāvas* express themselves underscore the difference between these two. Both are manifestations of a *bhāva*-infused heart, but *anubhāvas* are an external expression of this *śuddha-sattva* (not to be confused with *sattva-guṇa*) combined with intellect or intention,[83] whereas *sāttvika-bhāvas* are derived from an internal flow of *śuddha-sattva* throughout the body and constitute an expression of *śuddha-sattva* alone. The latter appear of their own accord with no intention to express them on the part of the devotee. And in contrast to the more charming *anubhāvas*, they are uncommon bodily transformations of ecstasy that underscore the extraordinary nature of *sakhya-rati*. Furthermore, unlike *anubhāvas*, *sāttvika-bhāvas* express themselves both physically and as internal states of mind.

Rūpa Goswāmī gives the following example, in which tears pour like fountains from the cowherds' eyes out of concern for Kṛṣṇa's safety:

82. *Bhakti-rasāmṛta-sindhu* 3.3.95–96.

83. *Sattva* is "beingness." *Sattva-guṇa* is the influence of material nature that gives rise to intelligibility. It brings clarity, purity, knowledge, and happiness. In the optimum, this influence reveals the *ātmā*. *Śuddha-sattva*, on the other hand, refers to transcendental existence and the ground of being on which the drama of *bhakti-rasa* is performed.

> Seeing the forest fire spread around through the dry cotton reeds, Kṛṣṇa's friends, not considering their own bodies, surrounded Kṛṣṇa on all sides, appearing to extinguish the fire with the tears from their eyes.[84]

In *sakhya-rati*, the *sāttvika-bhāvas* are eight in number: paralysis, perspiration, hair standing on end, choking of the voice, trembling, changing color, tears, and fainting.[85] The vital air, or *yogic prāṇa*, circulates throughout the body, sometimes resting in earth, water, fire, or ether and sometimes resting unto itself. Its connection with these elements or its keeping to itself is the mechanism through which the eight *sāttvika-bhāvas* manifest. When the *prāṇa* connects with earth, *sattva* carried on the vital air generates the *sāttvika-bhāva* of paralysis. When *prāṇa* connects with water, *sattva* generates the *sāttvika-bhāva* of tears. When *prāṇa* connects with fire, *sattva* generates the *sāttvika-bhāvas* of perspiration and change of color/complexion. When *prāṇa* connects with ether, *sattva* generates the *sāttvika-bhāva* of fainting. When *prāṇa* remains unto itself slightly, moderately, or extremely, *sattva* generates the *sāttvika-bhāvas* of horripilation, trembling, and choking of the voice, respectively.[86] Furthermore, these *sāttvika-bhāvas* also manifest in different degrees of intensity as the *sthāyi-bhāva* intensifies from *praṇaya* onward.[87]

84. *Bhakti-rasāmṛta-sindhu* 3.3.101.

85. *Sāttvika-bhāvas* may also arise in Kṛṣṇa's *sakhās* driven by a secondary *rasa* rather than by their primary *rasa* of fraternal love. Prominent examples of secondary *rasas* are when *rasas* such as *hāsya-* or *yuddha-vīra-rasa* temporarily take precedence over *sakhya-rasa*. *Sañcāri-bhāvas*, yet to be discussed, can also play a role. *Sāttvika-bhāvas* may also arise out of an overall accumulation of love but not related to a primary or secondary *rasa* centered on Kṛṣṇa himself. For example, a *sakhā* may dream of a demon, causing his body to tremble or perspire.

86. Just as the physical body is made of the gross elements and the psychological body is made of the subtle elements, the spiritual body of Kṛṣṇa and those of his friends also have an appearance of being similarly constituted.

87. *Sāttvika-bhāvas* manifest in four ascending degrees of intensity—*dhūmāyita* (smoky), *jvalita* (luminous), *dīpta* (flaming), and *uddīpta* (blazing)—relative to the duration of their manifestation, the extent to which they pervade the various parts of the body, and the excellence of *sattva* involved or the number of *sāttvika-bhāvas* manifested. The exceptions here are tears and choking of voice, which cannot appear in more than one bodily part. Thus, rather than their pervasiveness being a consideration, swelling of the eyes, whiteness, and the condition of the pupils are the considerations with regard to tears, and distortion of the voice, inaudibility, and agitation are the considerations with regard to choking of the voice. See *Bhakti-rasāmṛta-sindhu* 2.3.62–81.

Transitory Emotions (sañcāri-bhāvas)

Like *anubhāvas*, *sāttvika-bhāvas* involve observable external expressions, but unlike *anubhāvas*, they are involuntary and are also constituted of internal mental/emotional states. This latter aspect of *sāttvika-bhāvas* is what makes them similar to the final ingredient of *bhakti-rasa*, *sañcāri-bhāvas*.[88] Thus, Rūpa Goswāmī considers *sāttvika-bhāvas* to be similar to *anubhāvas* in terms of their physical ingredient and similar to *sañcāri-bhāvas* in terms of their transitory emotive ingredient.[89]

That which is *sañcārin* is transitory. Thus, the term *sañcāri-bhāva* refers to transitory emotions that come and go and in doing so augment the *sthāyi-bhāva* of *sakhya-rati*. Unlike *vibhāvas*, which are causes, and *anubhāvas*, which are effects, *sañcāri-bhāvas* are companions of the *sthāyi-bhāva*. Just as waves arise out of and merge back into the ocean, so the *sakhās*' *sañcāri-bhāvas* arise out of their *sthāyi-bhāva* and eventually merge back into it. Thus, they enhance and nuance the *sthāyi-bhāva* of *sakhya-rati* temporarily.

Rūpa Goswāmī lists thirty-three *sañcāri-bhāvas*:

> (1) self-disparagement (*nirveda*), (2) despondency (*viṣāda*), (3) depression (*dainyam/dīnatā*), (4) debility (*glāni* or *mlāni*), (5) fatigue (*śrama*), (6) intoxication (*mada*), (7) pride (*garva*), (8) apprehension (*śaṅkā*), (9) alarm (*trāsa*), (10) agitation (*āvega*), (11) madness (*unmāda*), (12) loss of memory (*apasmṛti*), (13) sickness (*vyādhi*), (14) bewilderment (*moha*), (15) death-like symptoms (*mṛti*), (16) indolence (*ālasyam*), (17) stupefaction (*jāḍyam*), (18) shame (*vrīḍā*), (19) concealment of one's feelings (*avahitthā*), (20) remembrance (*smṛti*), (21) doubt (*vitarka*), (22) pondering (*cintā*), (23) resolve (*mati*), (24) steadiness (*dhṛti*), (25) joy (*harṣa*), (26) eagerness (*autsukyam*), (27) wrath (*augrya*), (28) intolerance (*amarṣa*), (29) envy (*asūyā*), (30) carelessness (*cāpalya*), (31) drowsiness (*nidrā*), (32) dreaming (*supti*), and (33) insight/awakening (*bodha*).

88. *Sañcāri-bhāvas* are also referred to as *vyabhicārī-bhāvas*. The syllable *vi* implies that these *bhāvas* enhance (*viśeṣa*); the syllables *ab hi* imply that these *bhāvas* act in relation to the foundational, or *mukhya*, emotion—the *sthāyi-bhāva*—(*ābhimukhya*); the syllables *cā ra* imply that these *bhāvas* move (*caranti*) to and from the *sthāyi-bhāva*. See Viśvanātha Cakravartī's comments on *Bhakti-rasāmṛta-sindhu* 2.4.2.

89. *Bhakti-rasāmṛta-sindhu* 2.3.20. But as we have seen, the inner emotion can also be the *sthāyi-bhāva* of the dominant *rasa* itself or a secondary *rasa*. However, in relation to *sāttvika-bhāvas*, even these dominant emotions generate a temporary effect, and thus their influence, like *sañcāri-bhāvas*, comes and goes.

Among them, only thirty are experienced in *sakhya-rati*. The *sañcāri-bhāvas* of wrath, alarm, and indolence do not arise in *sakhya-rati*. Jīva Goswāmī explains that Kṛṣṇa's friends never express wrath directed at Kṛṣṇa, nor do they ever experience sudden alarm or fear of him, and indolence does not arise in them unless it is favorable for serving Kṛṣṇa. Furthermore, in *sakhya-rati*, intoxication, joyfulness, pride, drowsiness, and steadiness do not appear in separation from Kṛṣṇa, and death-like symptoms, fatigue, sickness, loss of memory, and depression do not appear in union with Kṛṣṇa. Śrī Rūpa Goswāmī defines each of the thirty-three *sañcāri-bhāvas* in greater detail and describes different circumstances in which they arise along with examples.[90] Let us close this section with two examples of a *sañcāri-bhāva* in fraternal love. Śrī Rūpa refers to the joy—*harṣa*—experienced by Kṛṣṇa's cowherd friends when he arose from the Yamunā after successfully chastising the serpent Kāliya.[91] Prior to this, the young cowherds had passed out after seeing Kṛṣṇa wrapped in Kāliya's coils. *Śrīmad Bhāgavatam* describes this event:

> Seeing Kṛṣṇa, the young *gopas* all immediately arose, as if coming back to life. Filled with immense joy, they affectionately embraced him.[92]

Rūpa Goswāmī has also penned his own verse describing the *gopas*' joy and how it overtook their speech and bodily functions:

> When Kṛṣṇa returned after dispelling Kāliya, his friends lost control of their bodies in great joy. They could not stand on their feet, and their speech was incoherent.[93]

The second example that Śrī Rūpa cites is that of envy arising in the cowherds. Here, envy refers to turning good qualities into faults. In this example, the cowherds on Kṛṣṇa's team find fault in the strength of those on Balarāma's team, while in reality Rāma's team is quite strong:

90. See *Bhakti-rasāmṛta-sindhu* 2.4.

91. Here the joy—*harṣa*—is experienced separately from the *ānanda* that underlies the entire experience of *sakhya-rasa*. Thus, there is joy and sorrow and so forth within the overriding *ānanda* of *sakhya-rasa*, just as there is joy and sorrow with the overall feeling of incompleteness in material life.

92. *Śrīmad Bhāgavatam* 10.17.14.

93. *Bhakti-rasāmṛta-sindhu* 3.3.104.

> Balarāma's team thinks itself strong and able to defeat our team with Kṛṣṇa on our side, but is there anyone weaker than Balarāma's team in this world?[94]

Thus, we have learned that mature *sakhya-rati*, also known as *sakhya-rasa*, includes five ecstatic ingredients: (1) the dominant self-defining emotion (*sthāyi-bhāva*), (2) the object and embodiment of *sakhya-rati* along with its excitants (*vibhāvas*), (3) intentional bodily expressions (*anubhāvas*), (4) unintentional mental and bodily expressions (*sāttvika-bhāvas*), and (5) transitory, enhancing emotions (*sañcāri-bhāvas*). Together these ingredients constitute *sakhya-rasa*, the very soul of fraternal love.

From Rati to Rasa

One may wonder how exactly one puts these ecstatic ingredients together. To answer this question, we must remember that they arise out of the ocean of one's budding *sthāyi-bhāva*, and like clouds of rain drawn from that ocean, they rain down upon the *sthāyi-bhāva* to embellish it. In other words, through honing one's hearing, chanting, and meditating in the context of culturing the self-defining emotion of fraternal love, separate ingredients arise and gradually merge into the unified experience of *sakhya-rasa*, just as through properly preparing separate ingredients, one particular entrée becomes suitable to serve. However, even within the composite of *sakhya-rasa*, the individual taste of the ingredients is not entirely lost. And we should carefully note that the same ingredients mixed differently will result in a different tasteful end product, such as *mādhurya-rasa* rather than *sakhya-rasa*. Thus, it is important to be acquainted with the different ingredients of the *rasa* one idealizes in one's *sādhana*. To further distinguish *rati* from *rasa*, Śrī Jīva Goswāmī compares budding *sakhya-rati* to meditation (*dhyāna*) and its maturation into *sakhya-rasa* to realization (*samādhi*).[95]

Here we are discussing very deep spiritual realization—*bhakti-rasa*—that causes realization of the indeterminate feature of the Godhead (Brahman) to pale in comparison. Following Rūpa Goswāmī in this discussion, we have employed technical terms from Indian aesthetic theory, such as Bharata Muni's contribution. But does one need to become a poet to taste *sakhya-rasa*? Is poetry the cause of *rasa*? No. Although poetry, often in

94. *Bhakti-rasāmṛta-sindhu* 2.4.167.
95. *Bhakti-rasāmṛta-sindhu* 2.5.132.

combination with the arts, is the cause of worldly *rasa*, it is not the cause of transcendent *bhakti-rasa*.

It is *rati*, a ray of the sun of *prema-rasa*—not poetry—that gives rise to *bhakti-rasa*. However, this same *rati* has the effect of transforming *bhakti-rasa* into poetic expressions—into theistic *rasa-śāstras* such as *Śrīmad Bhāgavatam* and extensions of Vyāsa's *samādhi-bhāṣya* such as the *līlā-granthas* of the Vṛndāvana Goswāmīs. And these theistic poetic works arising out of *rati* and *rasa* in turn are then secondary causes of *bhakti-rasa* when heard by sincere *sādhakas*.

What can one filled with *bhakti-rasa*—*bhaktyānanda*—say about it, when words fail to do justice even to *ātmānanda*? One cannot say enough about it. Indeed, the fact that we cannot say enough about *bhakti-rasa* only underscores the limit of language, while indicating that *bhakti-rasa* is at the same time the best utilization of speech. As much as in poetry the moon can sprout wings and fly across the night sky, that which is inconceivable and whose possibilities know no bounds—Kṛṣṇa *rati*—is best expressed with poetic license. Furthermore, the theoretical knowledge of Śrī Rūpa's terms assists the *sādhaka* in developing more feeling for all that the *līlā* narrative contains and thus enhances his or her ability to identify with it, much as knowledge of drama theory enhances one's ability to draw more out of any particular performance—to relish its heart and soul.

That said, it is not only poetry that *rati* can spiritualize. Indeed, it has the capacity to turn the entire world into a *vibhāva* of *bhakti-rasa*. For Śrī Caitanya, steeped in *bhakti-rasa*, all bodies of water became the Yamunā, all hills became Govardhana, and rain clouds and accompanying lightning excited his *rati* for Rādhā-Kṛṣṇa.

Rasa is said to be the soul of poetry and dramatic experience in Indian aesthetic theory. But in worldly *rasa* theory, the various poetic ingredients themselves are thought to create the emotional experience of *rasa*. Although Śrī Rūpa has borrowed terms and dramatic theory from Bharata to express *bhakti-rasa* in this world, *bhakti-rasa* differs from Bharata's rasa in that it is not of this world. As we have seen, it is transmitted in seed through *sādhu-saṅga*—*bhakti-saṁskāras*—and then further cultivated by the *sādhaka*, whose focus in the practice of hearing, chanting, and so on narrows as the object of the *sādhaka*'s developing *rati* and its personification as one of the paradigmatic members of Kṛṣṇa *līlā* come into view. With the honing of one's *sādhana*, *rati* sprouts, and its outer effects begin to manifest along with accompanying emotions that nuance the self-defining internal *sthāyi-bhāva*.

And gradually a whole meditative spiritual personality is formed, one suitable to participate in the *līlā* one meditates on. First, the initial ingress of *rati*, or spiritual love, purifies the *sādhaka*'s heart, dissolving one's illusory material identity. And as it does so, it also gives rise to an inner spiritual identity (composed directly and indirectly of the above five ingredients) that buds, blossoms, and bears the sweet fruit of *sakhya-rasa*.

Thus far we have discussed how the seed of *sakhya-rati* is planted, how it sprouts into budding spiritual emotion, and how it flowers and fruits into *sakhya-rasa*. However, it should be noted that for the sprout of *sakhya-rati* to mature into *sakhya-rasa*, considerable intensification of this *rati*, or *bhāva*, is required. As we have seen in the previous chapter, Rūpa Goswāmī explains that having attained *vāsanās* for *bhakti* in one life, one must still take another birth and intensify one's *bhakti* for it to rise to the level of *rati* and from there bear the fruit of *sakhya-rasa*.[96] But spiritual progress in *bhakti-rasa* does not end there. What remains in terms of further spiritual development is how *sakhya-rasa* intensifies into different stages termed *praṇaya*, *prema*, *sneha*, and *rāga*, as well as into *anurāga* and *mahābhāva* in the case of the *priya-narma-sakhās*, who participate in Kṛṣṇa's romantic life.[97]

These stages are intensifications of *sakhya-rati*, much like stages of intensification involved in turning sugarcane into molasses and other successively sweeter forms of itself. This intensification involves one object changing its state and acquiring different names in accordance with its level of spiritual excellence. As Viśvanātha Cakravartī Ṭhākura explains in his commentary on *Ujjvala-nīlamaṇi*, these stages of intensification typically develop in one's internal *bhāva-deha* after one appears in a spiritual body within the *prakaṭa-līlā*. Therein, association with *nitya-siddhas* participating in the drama of Kṛṣṇa *līlā* is the cause of these stages of intensification, which ultimately qualify one to enter Kṛṣṇa's *aprakaṭa-līlā*.[98] There is simply no substitute for participating in the *līlā*, wherein association with the *nitya-siddha* associates of Kṛṣṇa is afforded. For college draftees into professional sports, there is no substitute for actual playing time, wherein athletes can learn through direct experience that which they cannot possibly learn regardless of how

96. *Bhakti-rasāmṛta-sindhu* 2.1.6–10.

97. Other than *anurāga* and *mahābhāva*, this represents the development of these stages in *sakhya-rasa* described in *Bhakti-rasāmṛta-sindhu*. Among Kṛṣṇa's friends, the stages of *anurāga* and *mahābhāva* pertain only to the *narma-sakhās*, and Rūpa Goswāmī discusses these stages in *Ujjvala-nīlamaṇi* in the context of *mādhurya-rasa*. Śrī Jīva also lists *māna* (angry or jealous love) as a possibility within *sakhya-rasa* in *Prīti Sandarbha* 89.

98. *Ujjvala-nīlamaṇi* 3.49–51. See Viśvanātha Cakravartī's commentary.

much film they review or how much coaching they receive. Similarly, intensification of one's mature *sthāyi-bhāva* requires direct experience.

As *sakhya-rati* intensifies, the intimacy of its confident familiarity (*viśrambha*) gives way to *praṇaya*, the *svarūpa-lakṣaṇa* of which is a further intensification of intimacy.[99] Its marginal characteristic is absence of respect even in circumstances that warrant it.[100] In circumstances that warrant respect for Kṛṣṇa and in this sense distance one from him, not a trace of such respect appears in the cowherds' *praṇaya*.

Understandably, this *praṇaya*, which also literally means "friendship," does not manifest in the *sthāyi-bhāvas* of *vātsalya* and *dāsya*, as these two *ratis* place one above or below Kṛṣṇa, respectively, rather than on the same level as him. And *praṇaya* is more central to *sakhya-rati* than it is to *mādhurya-rati*, even while *praṇaya* plays a significant role in the *mādhurya* of Vraja. Furthermore, in Rūpa Goswāmī's opinion, in *sakhya-rasa* alone *praṇaya* develops before *prema*, and in this sense it is also unlike the *praṇaya* of *mādhurya-rasa*, which follows *prema*. Because it manifests after *rati* and before *prema*, it also develops to some extent in the *sādhaka-deha*,[101] rather than being entirely contingent on direct participation in the manifest *prakaṭa-līlā*, and also like *prema* it pervades *sakhya-rasa* at all times. Rāma and Kṛṣṇa are *gopālas* absorbed in astounding *līlās* with their *gopa* friends, each of whose entire person is composed of *praṇaya*.

In *praṇaya*, Kṛṣṇa and his friends consider each other's life, mind, intellect, body, and belongings to be one another's. Whatever belongs to Kṛṣṇa is also his friends', and whatever belongs to Kṛṣṇa's friends is also Kṛṣṇa's. This is the feeling of *praṇaya*. Thus, Kṛṣṇa's friends have no reservations about touching him with their feet any more than they do about touching their own bodies. If a friend of Kṛṣṇa finds something particularly delightful to his palate, he will not hesitate to take a portion from his own mouth as soon as he discovers its delight and place it in Kṛṣṇa's mouth to share the experience, as if he wanted his other tongue to experience the taste as well.

To illustrate the *sakhās*' *praṇaya* as it manifests in perfection, Rūpa Goswāmī cites an instance in which the *devas* headed by Śiva suddenly appear from the heavens and show respect to Kṛṣṇa, proclaiming him to be the Supreme God—an extraordinary and earth-shaking event

99. *Ujjvala-nīlamaṇi* 14.110. See Jīva Goswāmī's commentary.

100. *Bhakti-rasāmṛta-sindhu* 3.3.108.

101. When stating that *praṇaya* precedes *prema* in *sakhya-rasa*, Rūpa Goswāmī refers only to *praṇaya*'s *taṭastha-lakṣaṇa*.

demonstrating that Kṛṣṇa is worthy of the highest regard. Meanwhile, the *priya-narma-sakhā* Arjuna of Vraja, exhibiting *praṇaya*'s marginal characteristic—absence of respect—pays no heed to the gods' appearance or their proclamation and merely places his arm on Kṛṣṇa's shoulder and proceeds to remove the dust from his peacock feather. Jīva Goswāmī cites the example of Kṛṣṇa's carrying Śrīdāmā on his shoulders after losing to him in mock battle,[102] which seems to exemplify both *praṇaya*'s intimacy and its absence of respect.

In the progression of developing *sakhya-rati*, *praṇaya* resulting in complete absorption gradually gives rise to *sakhya*'s *prema*. Rūpa Goswāmī defines this sense of *prema* as love that does not suffer from any fear or doubt that it may decrease due to circumstances. It expresses itself in complete attachment to Kṛṣṇa.[103] When this *prema* thickens, it turns into *sneha*, or heart-melting affection, a state in which a *sakhā* cannot tolerate even a moment's separation from Kṛṣṇa. Then from *sneha* comes *rāga*, which turns what otherwise might cause sorrow into happiness, because that sorrow results in Kṛṣṇa's pleasure. This is the fourth and final development and highest reach of *sakhya-rasa*, other than the *anurāga* and *mahābhāva* of the *priya-narma-sakhās*, which we shall discuss separately in the following chapter.

The above terms identifying states of intensification of fraternal love are subtle and difficult to explain and understand short of experience. Suffice it to say here that *sakhya-rasa* is full of subtle transpsychological emotional nuance that can be fully understood only through direct experience.

Having discussed the basic ingredients of *sakhya-rasa*, we will conclude this chapter with a brief discussion of the two phases of the experience of *sakhya-rasa* itself—the low and high tide of the ocean of *bhakti-rasa*. Like the moon, which controls the ocean's tide, Śrī Kṛṣṇa-candra waxes and wanes in the life of his devotees—appearing and disappearing—causing feelings of both union (*yoga-rasa*) in his presence and separation (*ayoga-rasa*) in his absence.

Separation from Kṛṣṇa—*ayoga*—appears in the life of Kṛṣṇa's friends in two forms: *utkaṇṭha* and *viyoga*. *Utkaṇṭha* expresses itself as intense longing to meet Kṛṣṇa for the first time. Before Kṛṣṇa's friends meet him for the first time in the context of his *līlā* as it manifests on earth, they experience a sense of separation from him arising from things they have heard about him. Then, after having met him and having entered into a relationship

102. *Prīti Sandarbha* 86.

103. *Bhakti-rasāmṛta-sindhu* 3.2.81. See also 3.2.169 and 1.4.1.

with him, when he then departs, his friends experience the second kind of separation, termed *viyoga*.

Viyoga in its most intense form expresses itself through ten conditions collectively termed *daśa-daśā*:

> (1) intense heat (*tāpa*), (2) emaciation (*kṛśatā*), (3) insomnia (*jāgarya*), (4) helplessness (*ālambana-śūnyatā*), (5) irresolution (*adhṛti*), (6) inertness (*jaḍatā*), (7) apparent disease (*vyādhi*), (8) madness (*unmāda*), (9) unconsciousness (*mūrcchita*), and (10) apparent death (*mṛti*).

Corresponding with the separation of *utkaṇṭha* and *viyoga* are three types of union—*siddhi*, *tuṣṭi*, and *sthiti*. The union of meeting Kṛṣṇa for the first time after *utkaṇṭha* is termed *siddhi* (perfection). The union that occurs after incidental periods of *viyoga*, such as the separation from Kṛṣṇa experienced by his friends at night during their sleep, is termed *tuṣṭi* (satisfaction). The union that corresponds with the full face of separation that occurs when Kṛṣṇa remains in Mathurā and in which the ten conditions mentioned above manifest is termed *sthiti* (sustained union).

Hearing about the separation of Kṛṣṇa's friends in the context of a *prakaṭa-līlā* narrative assists the *sādhaka* in entering that fire of separation, which in turn affords the desired union with Kṛṣṇa in *sakhya-rasa*. Kṛṣṇa's *nitya-siddha* associates appear along with him when his *līlā* manifests in the world. In this *līlā*, time plays a role facilitating the sequence of events. However, each event simultaneously has no beginning or end and thus serves as an appropriate object of meditation. Even Kṛṣṇa's occasional *līlās* that appear only in this world live eternally in the hearts of his devotees and appear elsewhere in the world—in another universe—as soon as they complete themselves in this universe. Although his *prakaṭa* and *aprakaṭa-līlās* are constituted of the same *bhāvas*, in the *prakaṭa-līlā* intense separation is predominant. And it is this *līlā* through which *sādhakas* can enter his eternal drama of *bhakti-rasa*.

In Mathurā, Kṛṣṇa relied upon his friends to assist him in pacifying his parents and lovers—sending letters with them and giving them instructions on how to console his mother, his servants, his cows, and his lovers. In this *līlā* we see how his friends rose to the occasion in a manner characteristic of fraternal love.[104] In an extended sense, this is what friends are

104. Kṛṣṇa also sent Uddhava and then Balarāma to pacify the residents of Vraja. Balarāma is of course situated in *sakhya-rasa*. Uddhava is situated in *dāsya-rasa* coupled with

for. However, while embracing the task temporarily mitigated their own feelings of impending separation, upon completing it they themselves fell prey to all ten psychophysiological conditions of transcendental love in separation corresponding with the full measure of *viyoga*.

After the *sakhās* returned to their village from metropolitan Mathurā, their *viraha-bhāva* peaked, and they sometimes experienced conditions such as extreme bodily heat (*tāpa*). Following the lead of Subala, the *sakhās* took shelter of the shade of the great banyan tree or the cooling waters of the Yamunā. However, in either case their *viraha-jvālā*—fever of separation—only increased in intensity, warming the shade and the water even in the winter months.

At times, the *sakhās* of Vraja became slight and fragile, experiencing emaciation (*kṛśatā*). At such times the spiritual earth, fire, water, and ether elements of their *aprākṛta* bodies diminished, while their bodily air intensified in the form of deep breaths. Emaciated like *yogīs* in trance, they lived practically on air alone.

Sometimes the *sakhās* were unable to keep their composure in bouts of insomnia (*jāgarya*). At such times, they could not tell the difference between day or night, nor could they tell the difference between one place or another. They simply remained wherever they were, scattered about here and there. The lotus-like eyes of these *sakhās* welled with tears in separation from the sun of Śyāmasundara, and thus the bee of sleep avoided them altogether.

Sometimes they experienced mental instability (*ālambana-śūnyatā*) and their minds could not focus on any particular task. Thus, their hearts became restless, and they felt as if they had entered a void and were somehow living but without any support. "Where should I stay? Where should I go? I can't see any way to attain Kṛṣṇa's company!" Such were the cries of Śrīdāmā, Sudāmā, Dāmā, Subala, Ujjvala, Lavaṅga, Arjuna, and *sakhā* Mahābala. Rising and falling again and again, they ran here and there in confusion. The boys, light-headed and lost, their minds drifting like cotton in the wind, were unable to concentrate.

From the sorrow of separation, at times irresolution (*adhṛti*) arose, at which time Kṛṣṇa's *sakhās* lost interest even in herding cows, their source of livelihood. They found no impetus to sing, dance, or play musical instruments. They derived no pleasure from any activity. Indeed, the very idea

---

sakhya-rasa, and when in Vraja, this *sakhya-rasa* takes precedence. Thus, *sakhya-rasa* carries the extra burden of separation in the form of attempting to tend to the separation of those in other *rasas* amid one's own separation.

of remaining alive held no promise for them. They stopped adorning their limbs with ornaments, stopped weaving and wearing flower garlands, and even stopped tying their hair in topknots. With no concern to maintain their lives without Kṛṣṇa, they became divested of the requisite resolve to act in any way at all.

Afflicted by inertness (*jaḍatā*), Kṛṣṇa's *sakhās* lacked luster like trees without leaves, and they were silent like trees in which no birds sat to sing. Like trees with no fruit, they were unproductive. And like trees they became unmoving. They lost any sense of identification with their bodies, and as a result their limbs and torsos diminished in stature. Indeed, at such times they appeared to be made of dull matter. Their limbs did not twitch, and their only movement was the tears that trickled from their eyes.

Sometimes they appeared overcome by disease (*vyādhi*) caused by their psychology in separation rather than infirmity caused by biological conditions.[105] At other times they appeared to be insane (*unmāda*), laughing loudly like madmen, babbling and delirious. Sometimes calling out "Kṛṣṇa! Kṛṣṇa!" in loud voices, they wailed, "Where has our *prāṇa-sakhā* gone, leaving us behind?" Mistaking a *tamāla* tree to be Kṛṣṇa, they would embrace it. Then, after understanding that they had not attained Kṛṣṇa, they would fall unconscious to the ground. Shouting "*bhāi*! *bhāi*!" they suddenly dashed off running in any direction and then rolled in the dust, covering themselves with it.

At other times, they appeared unconscious (*mūrcchita*), fainting for some time. Their limbs did not move, their eyes did not blink, and foam oozed from their mouths as their throats gurgled. Fainting and falling unconscious, they lay here and there upon the ground. And in the height of their separation, Kṛṣṇa's *sakhās* experienced a death-like state (*mṛti*), symptoms of which include incoherence, changing of bodily color, diminished breathing, and so on. Some cowherd boys collapsed, while others lay by the banks of the river as if paralyzed, barely breathing, their complexions turned pale.[106]

We have heard how Kṛṣṇa employs his *sakhās* in mitigating the separation his servants, elders, and lovers feel for him in his absence, and now we have also heard of the Vraja *sakhās*' own separation. But how does Kṛṣṇa feel for them, and how does he seek to mitigate that separation other than

105. *Bhakti-rasāmṛta-sindhu* 2.4.90.

106. See *Bhakti-rasāmṛta-sindhu* 3.3.116–127 and 3.2.118–128 as well as *Śrī Śrī Preyo-bhakti-rasārṇava* 4.109–118.

through his *sphūrtis*?[107] We glimpse this in his instructions to Uddhava, when Kṛṣṇa sends this dearest *dāsya-bhakta* of Mathurā, whose *dāsya* is bundled with *sakhya-rati*, to Vraja. Remembering his *sakhya-rasa-līlās* of Vraja, Kṛṣṇa implores Uddhava,

> My dear companions, Śrīdāmā and others, brought me great joy when they competed with one another, trying to touch me—each shouting, "I will touch him first"—as I wandered off to look at the flowering beauty of a distant part of the forest. In my name, O expert one, affectionately embrace each one of them again and again. [108]

Again, the enduring separation of *viyoga*, in which the above ten apparently undesirable conditions are most likely to occur, predominates in the *prakaṭa-līlā*. Kṛṣṇa departs for Mathurā at the age of eleven and remains between there and Dvārakā for thirty-three years in his princely *līlā* before finally returning to rural Vraja and entering his *deva-līlā* with his Vraja associates.[109] Mature *sakhya-rati-upāsakas*, upon attaining *praṇaya* and *prema*, take birth in Kṛṣṇa's manifest *līlā* of Vraja and thus pass through this fire of love in separation. However, as undesirable as such love in separation seems, *viraha-bhāva* is a deep and sublime aspect of the ecstasy of *līlā-sevā* that has its own reward and also culminates in the most complete form of union—*sthiti*—that characterizes the *aprakaṭa-līlā*.

Thus, the river of Kṛṣṇa's fraternal *līlā* flows between the banks of union and separation, its resolute current forming inner whirlpools, rising and falling in waves of spiritual wonder. *Sādhakas* follow its flow by hearing, reciting, and remembering its narration pouring from the hearts of *rasika* Vaiṣṇavas and thus in due course attain mature *sakhya-rati* themselves.

107. Here a *sphūrti* is something like an apparent hallucination of Kṛṣṇa that in fact is an actual manifestation of himself intended to mitigate his devotees' feelings of separation.
108. *Uddhava-sandeśa* 95.
109. In *Gopāla-campū* 2.29, Paurṇamāsī explains that Kṛṣṇa departed for Mathurā at the age of eleven and returned at the age of forty-four after slaying Dantavakra and Śālva. Shortly thereafter he returned to his *aprakaṭa-līlā* with his associates, while in another form he resided in Dvārakā for protecting the earth.

5

Priya-narma-sakhā-bhāva

"Your mind is constantly flickering nervously, and your colorful, sacred flute songs have fled far away. O my heart's friend! You are concealing that which you hold in your heart! When I see your face, my heart melts! The emerald-like glow of your body is now overshadowed but nonetheless shines beautifully like the night-blooming lotus. Who knows how my heart feels when I see your flawless eyes crying all these tears?" Ghanaśyāma dāsa says: "Hearing these words from his dear friend [Subala], Kṛṣṇa sighed deeply and turned his hands upside down, realizing [and indicating] that his friend had dipped into the depth of his heart's most treasured desire."

—*Ghanaśyāma dāsa, Gauḍīya Vaiṣṇava Padāvali*

Such is Kṛṣṇa's *pūrva-rāga* for Rādhā and the empathetic role of his *priya-narma-sakhās*.

In the previous chapter, four basic types of *sakhya-rati* were described in brief. In this chapter, we will explore the nature of Kṛṣṇa's *priya-narma-sakhās* in greater detail. When our Gauḍīya *ācāryas* describe the romantic pastimes of Rādhā and Kṛṣṇa, these *sakhās* play a more prominent role than the other three types of *sakhās*. Within the Gauḍīya *līlā-granthas* that view the *līlā* through the lens of *mādhurya-rati*'s Rādhā *dāsyam*, we repeatedly encounter the role of prominent *priya-narma-sakhās* such as Subala, Madhumaṅgala, Ujjvala, and others.

Among Kṛṣṇa's friends, the *priya-narma-sakhās* are far and away his most intimate companions. This is so because not only do these bosom buddies know him in terms of his cowherd sensibilities, they also know his heart in terms of its romantic stirrings, which are extremely strong and which so define his personality that at times they cause him to lose interest in cowherding altogether. These friends know his heart so well that they can read it through his body language and reply to it perfectly through their own body language or through poetic words laden with hidden meaning, speaking privately to him alone while in public. What, then, is the precise nature of the *rati* they personify, from which they derive their ability not only to tend to Kṛṣṇa's romantic heart in ways that no one else can in the hour of his greatest necessity but also to serve as instruments that bring about solutions to his ongoing romantic crises? Whatever the composition of their *rati* is, which we will explore ahead, one thing we know for sure: these *narma-sakhās* are well aware that the road to Kṛṣṇa's heart runs through Rādhā, and thus it is through her heart that they have skillfully entered his and, in doing so, conquered both Rādhā and Kṛṣṇa in the sacred realm of *rasa*![1]

In an effort to understand the *rasa-tattva* underlying the *rati* of the *priya-narma-sakhās*, we shall turn to the literary contributions of the *ācāryas*. We have much to learn from all of their works. Let us invoke their blessing in this effort. May we accurately represent them and, drawing from their experiential insight, present a definitive explanation of the emotional ecstasy of Kṛṣṇa's dearmost friends and the transpsychological composition of this ecstasy.

From the previous chapter, we learned that the *priya-narma-sakhās' rati* is not a form of *saṅkula-rati*, in which devotees are situated permanently in various combinations of *dāsya*, *sakhya*, and *vātsalya*. We discussed two types of *saṅkula-rati* as it pertains to *sakhya-rasa* in Vraja: the *sakhya-rati* of Kṛṣṇa's younger and older friends. We also learned of a third type of *sakhya-rati* that is *kevala* and thus exclusively composed of fraternal feelings. Rūpa Goswāmī distinguishes the *rati* of the *priya-narma-sakhās* from both the *saṅkula-* and *kevala-rati* of Kṛṣṇa's other comrades and simply states that the *priya-narma-sakhās* are possessed of a very special *rati* (*bhāva-viśeṣiṇaḥ*) that enables them to participate in Kṛṣṇa's most confidential *līlās* (*ātyantika-rahasyeṣu*).[2] In other words, their *rati* is unique—*viśeṣiṇaḥ*. Śrī Jīva explains that the special *rati* that Rūpapāda refers to derives from the *priya-narma-sakhās'* desire to please Kṛṣṇa by way of assisting him and his girlfriends in

1. *Rādhā-rasa-sudhā-nidhi* 98 says as much: "By taking shelter of Rādhā you can easily become a friend of Govinda (like Subala)."

2. *Bhakti-rasāmṛta-sindhu* 3.3.43.

their romantic exploits, which in turn are the most confidential of Kṛṣṇa's *līlās*. In *Bhakti-rasāmṛta-sindhu-bindu* 20, Śrī Viśvanātha Cakravartī writes that the *priya-narma-sakhās* desire to experience the *bhāva* of the *gopīs*—*ye tu preyasī-rahasya-sahāyāḥ śṛṅgāra-bhāva-spṛhās*. However, they do so only out of friendship in order to be acquainted with the nature of the *gopīs*' love. Thus, *priya-narma-sakhās* long for this *rasa* with the express purpose of employing the experience they gain from it in Kṛṣṇa's service, rendering services such as assisting him in uniting with the *gopīs*, bearing messages to and from the *gopīs*,[3] adding to the intrigue of Kṛṣṇa's romantic affairs, and lending a sympathetic heart to Kṛṣṇa and the *gopīs* in their romantic exploits.

Śrī Rūpa cites two *gopīs* speaking to one another about the participation of the *priya-narma-sakhās* in Kṛṣṇa's romantic life as an example of such *sakhās*' intimate *sevā*:

> Just see, Subala is relating the messages of Rādhā into Kṛṣṇa's ear; Ujjvala is secretly placing the love letter of Śyāmā into Kṛṣṇa's hand; Catura is putting the *pān* prepared by Pāli in Kṛṣṇa's mouth; Kokila is placing the wreath made by Tārā on Kṛṣṇa's head. In this way, O slender one, the sportive, intimate friends of Kṛṣṇa are thus expanding the *sevā*![4]

In the above verse, we find each *priya-narma-sakhā* associated with a *yūtheśvarī*, or *gopī* group leader, each of whom has a direct relationship with Kṛṣṇa. Thus, the *priya-narma-sakhā*, even if he is a male group leader himself (*yūtheśvara*) also serves under the influence of a *gopī* group leader (*yūtheśvarī*): Subala/Rādhā, Ujjvala/Śyāmā, Catura/Pāli, and Kokila/Tārā.[5]

3. *Sāhitya-darpaṇa* 3.47 describes three types of messengers, *nisṛṣṭārtha*, *mitārtha*, and *sandeśa-hāraka*. The *nisṛṣṭārtha* messenger understands the body language of Rādhā and Kṛṣṇa and anticipates their moods in advance, to which he responds accordingly, surprising and endearing himself to them that much more. The *mitārtha* is one who speaks concisely to achieve the desired result of uniting Rādhā and Kṛṣṇa after he learns of their desire for union. And the *sandeśa-hāraka* messenger is one who speaks only in the way he is told to speak. *Priya-narma-sakhās* tend to be *nisṛṣṭārtha* messengers, while they can also function as *mitārtha* and *sandeśa-hāraka* messengers.

4. *Bhakti-rasāmṛta-sindhu* 3.3.44.

5. Our direct concern is only with *priya-narma-sakhās* whose *yūtheśvarī* is either Rādhā herself, as in the case of Subala, or a friend of Rādhā, whereas in the above verse, cowherds associated with other *yūtheśvarīs* are also mentioned. In this verse, Ujjvala is associated with Śyāmā, who is neutral rather than favorable or unfavorable toward Rādhā; but in *Kṛṣṇa-bhāvanāmṛta*, he is more clearly associated with Viśākhā, one of Rādhā's closest friends.

Rūpa Goswāmī further explains the nature of the *narma-sakhās'* dealings with Kṛṣṇa and the *gopīs*:

> Activities particular to the *priya-narma-sakhās* include serving as messengers for the Vraja *kiśorīs*, sympathizing with their love for Kṛṣṇa, taking Kṛṣṇa's side in the *gopīs'* love quarrels with him when only they are present and in their absence cleverly supporting the particular *gopī* group leader they have taken shelter of, and whispering secret messages in each other's ears.[6]

From the above, it is clear that the *sakhya-rati* of the *priya-narma-sakhās* is influenced by *mādhurya-rasa*, and this influence is what differentiates it—*viśeṣa*—from the *sakhya-rati* of Kṛṣṇa's other cowherd friends. However, Rūpa Goswāmī has not classified the *narma-sakhās'* fraternal love as *saṅkula-rati*. What, then, is the precise way that the *priya-narma-sakhās' sakhya-rati* is influenced by *mādhurya-rati*? Is there a way in which *rasas* mix with one another other than that which we find in *saṅkula-rati*?

This question was answered affirmatively but only briefly in the previous chapter. Rūpa Goswāmī has dedicated an entire chapter to the mixing of *rasas* in his *Bhakti-rasāmṛta-sindhu* (4.8). Therein we find an outline of primary (*mukhya*) and secondary (*gauṇa*) *rasas* in terms of their compatibility/incompatibility with one another based upon logical inference derived from our common human experience of the way in which some emotions enhance others while other emotions cause the same emotion to diminish in influence.[7] Among the *mukhya-rasas*, only *mādhurya-rasa* is compatible with *sakhya-rasa*,[8] in as much as friends can be supportive of the romantic life of their friends, which in turn endears them to such friends that much more.

When *sakhya* and *mādhurya-rasas* mix (*miśra*) with one another in the *priya-narma-sakhās*, *mādhurya-rasa* takes the role of further nourishing their *sakhya-rasa*. In Śrī Rūpa's terms, *mādhurya* becomes the *aṅga-rasa*, the limb (*aṅga*) that nourishes the body (*aṅgī*) of *sakhya*, the *aṅgī-rasa*. In other words,

6. *Bhakti-rasāmṛta-sindhu* 3.3.93–94. In their commentaries on this verse, Jīva Goswāmī, Viśvanātha Cakravartī, and Mukunda Goswāmī all emphasize that the *narma-sakhās* cleverly establish only the side of their own respective *yūtheśvarīs*. Mukunda Goswāmī emphasizes that they do not establish the side of any other *yūtheśvarī*.

7. This is the overall implication of *Bhakti-rasāmṛta-sindhu* 4.8.15, wherein logical inference is suggested as a means of determining the status of neutral *rasas*.

8. The *gauṇa-ratis* friendly to *sakhya* are *yuddha-vīra* (mock fighting) and *hāsya* (joking). Those inimical are *bhayānaka* (fear) directed toward Kṛṣṇa and *raudra* (anger) directed toward Kṛṣṇa. *Raudra* and *bhayānaka* directed toward others are neutral. Among *mukhya-rasas*, *vātsalya* (parental) is incompatible and *dāsya* is neutral.

priya-narma-sakhās do not sometimes experience *sakhya-rasa* and at other times *mādhurya-rasa*; rather, *mādhurya* acts as a nourishing influence on their own *sakhya-rati* as it blends with *sakhya*. Śrī Rūpa explains that the sole purpose of an *aṅga-rasa* in such instances is to nourish the *aṅgī-rasa*.[9]

This mixing is different from *saṅkula-rati* in that in the *saṅkula-rati* of Kṛṣṇa's *suhṛt-sakhās*, the *vātsalya* aspect of their *sakhya-rati* diminishes the sense of equality between Kṛṣṇa and his friends that is central to *sakhya-rati*, and thus it diminishes the intimacy central to fraternal love. The same holds true to a lesser extent in the *sakhās* whose *rati* is combined with *dāsya*. After all, *dāsya* and *vātsalya* unto themselves are not compatible with *sakhya-rasa*, the former being neutral and the latter incompatible. Thus, comparatively speaking, the *kevala-rati* of Kṛṣṇa's *priya-sakhās* is considered more desirable than *saṅkula-rati*. However, in the case of the *priya-narma-sakhās*, the way in which their *sakhya-rati* mixes with *mādhurya-rati* sweetens the cowherds' *sakhya-rati*, much as sugar added to yogurt sweetens the curd. Regarding the desired sense of equality in *sakhya-rati*, there are no secrets Kṛṣṇa and his *narma-sakhās* keep from one another. *Saṅkula-rati* also differs from the *rati* of the *narma-sakhās* in that in the *saṅkula-rati* of Kṛṣṇa's older and younger friends, we find two permanent *rasas* with one (*sakhya*) more powerful than the other yet giving way at times to the less powerful *rasa* (*dāsya* or *vātsalya*). Thus, sometimes *sakhās* with *saṅkula-rati* experience *dāsya* or *vātsalya* separate from their fraternal feelings, and neither their *dāsya* nor their *vātsalya* nourishes their fraternal love.[10] In contrast, in the *priya-narma-sakhās*, we find one *rasa* nourished by another compatible *rasa*, much like a *sañcāri-bhāva* that nourishes a *sthāyi-bhāva*, rising at times and receding at others.

The *priya-narma-sakhās* are touched by Kṛṣṇa's love for the *gopīs* that they observe in him,[11] and they desire to be associated in fraternal *līlā-sevā* with this aspect of his life in addition to everything about him that captivates the *priya-sakhās*. Thus, these most intimate friends of Kṛṣṇa, above

9. *Bhakti-rasāmṛta-sindhu* 4.8.51. See also Jīva Goswāmī's commentary.

10. *Bhakti-rasāmṛta-sindhu* 4.8.81. See also Jīva Goswāmī's commentary, where he includes the *saṅkula-rati* of Baladeva as an example.

11. In his commentary to *Bhakti-rasāmṛta-sindhu* 4.8.2, Jīva Goswāmī cites five ways in which *bhāvas* are present: (1) in Kṛṣṇa's devotee who is experiencing the *aṅgī-rasa*, (2) in Śrī Kṛṣṇa, (3) in another devotee of Kṛṣṇa, (4) in a person neutral to Kṛṣṇa, and (5) in a person inimical toward Kṛṣṇa. In *Bhakti-rasāmṛta-sindhu* 4.8.5, Jīva Goswāmī explains that *mādhurya-rasa* appearing in Kṛṣṇa as his love for the *gopīs* (2) is favorable for *sakhya-rasa*. His *narma-sakhās* see this love's influence on Kṛṣṇa, and they desire to support it.

and beyond their normal unmixed *sakhya-rati*, seek the service of those who are embodiments of *mādhurya-rasa*—the *gopīs*—by which they gain appreciation for and partial experience of the *mādhurya-rasa* of a particular type of *gopī-bhāva*, described ahead. Again, their experience of this form of *mādhurya-rasa* with Kṛṣṇa is from a sympathetic perspective and only partial in that they are males and situated in another *rasa*—*sakhya-rati*. Nonetheless, it is substantial.

Rūpa Goswāmī cites the following example of the mixing of *sakhya* and *mādhurya*, wherein *sakhya* is the *aṅgī-rasa* and *mādhurya* is the *aṅga-rasa*:

> O Subala! The young women of Vraja, who drink the nectar of Kṛṣṇa's lips, are the topmost of all fortunate people.[12]

Here, a *sakhā* is speaking to Subala, and the two friends are marveling at the fortune of the *gopīs*: two devotees in *sakhya-rasa* observing and appreciating *mādhurya-rasa* and thus Kṛṣṇa's lips. These two companions are not desiring to personally taste Kṛṣṇa's lips. However, they are capable of identifying with the fortune of the *gopīs* and approve of their desire, while they themselves are content to exchange cheek kisses with Kṛṣṇa.[13] But again, not only do they admire the *gopīs*' fortune; they also actively engage in assisting the *gopīs* in their desire to taste Kṛṣṇa's lips, which in the context of the *parakīya-līlā* of Vraja is easier said than done.

While the above example is one of the mixing of two compatible *rasas*—*sakhya* and *mādhurya*, with *sakhya* as primary and *mādhurya* as subservient—Śrī Rūpa's chapter on the mixing of compatible *rasas* includes many other examples of such mixing. For example, we find the mixing of *mādhurya* with *sakhya* where *mādhurya* is primary and *sakhya* is subservient; we find *dāsya* and *śānta* mixed, wherein *dāsya* is primary and *śānta* subservient and vice versa. However, this mixing between the principal five *rasas* and other compatible *mukhya-rasas* does not give rise to a special *bhāva* characterizing a particular class of devotees whose *bhāva* requires its own separate explanation.[14] While there are instances of *dāsya* mixing with *śānta* and so on, such mixing in and of itself is incidental and does not serve to characterize the *dāsya-bhakta* and place him or her in a special *bhāva* of its own, and certainly not one that is *ātyantika-rahasya-jñaḥ*, or such that it

12. *Bhakti-rasāmṛta-sindhu* 4.8.26.

13. See *Bṛhad-bhāgavatāmṛta* 2.4.114, the commentary on 2.4.269, and 2.6.75 for references to such kissing in *sakhya-rasa*.

14. The mixing of compatible *rasas* also includes the mixing between *gauṇa-rasas* and *mukhya-rasas* as well as between *gauṇa-rasas* themselves.

affords one knowledge of and participation in the most intimate secrets of *parakīya-rasa*. However, this is what we find in the case of the *priya-narma-sakhās*, and thus their *bhāva* begs further explanation. Indeed, it is unique in the kingdom of *rasa*. The *narma-sakhās* are tuned in to Kṛṣṇa's romanticism, and as much as his romantic heart manifests, they are affected by it. And to what extent is Kṛṣṇa's heart beating for Rādhā?

Raghunātha dāsa Goswāmī describes *priya-narma-sakhās' bhāva* as "the transformation of the most indescribable love combined with the purest and most pleasing, intimate friendship personified."[15] Thus, the *priya-narma-sakhās'* longing for *mādhurya-rasa* enhances their *sakhya-rasa*, enabling it to intensify into the stages of *anurāga* and *mahābhāva*, stages of intensification that are otherwise exclusive to *mādhurya-rasa*. Their *sakhya-rasa* is also enhanced by the influence of *mādhurya-rasa*, in that in this enhanced form of *sakhya-rasa* such friends are afforded the capacity to extend their friendship into direct participation in Kṛṣṇa's romantic life.

The two basic types of *mādhurya-rasa* are romantic love in which the devotee desires direct union in intimacy with Kṛṣṇa for his pleasure—*sambhoga-rasa*—and romantic love in which the devotee does not desire such union with Kṛṣṇa but rather desires to assist Kṛṣṇa and his lover in their romantic love and thus relish *mādhurya-rasa* through a sympathetic heart. This latter type of *mādhurya-rasa* is termed *tad-bhāva*, referring to the fact that it is focused on serving and vicariously experiencing the *bhāva* of one serving in *sambhoga-rasa*—Rādhā, that is, in the Gauḍīya tradition. Within *mādhurya-rasa* itself, this sympathetic *bhāva* is considered preferable.[16] In other words, to assist Rādhā in her desire for union with Kṛṣṇa is superior to desiring direct union with him oneself. The reason for this, or the logic underlying this *bhāva*, is that no one can satisfy Kṛṣṇa more comprehensively through direct union with him than Rādhā, whom other *gopīs* are but partial manifestations of for serving Kṛṣṇa in different instances. Thus, by assisting her and experiencing her *bhāva* through a sympathetic heart, such *gopīs* can experience greater intimacy with Kṛṣṇa than they could

15. Like Jīva Goswāmī in his *Ujjvala-nīlamaṇi* 9.43 commentary, in *Muktā-carita* 412, Dāsa Goswāmī poeticizes that *mādhurya-rasa* personified is itself a *priya-narma-sakhā* and then goes on to describe this *narma-sakhā's bhāva* in this way. The translation cited above is that of Jagadānanda Dāsa: Gaudiya Discussions Archive; Pastimes; "The Great Pearl Dispute—Mukta-carita of Raghunath Das Goswami," trans. Jagadānanda Dāsa, March 24, 2004, https://gaudiyadiscussions.gaudiya.com/topic_1396.html.

16. *Bhakti-rasāmṛta-sindhu* 1.2.299. Jīva Goswāmī describes *tad-bhāva* as the principal variety of *mādhurya-rasa*.

through direct union with him in competition with Rādhā. Thus, this *tad-bhāva mādhurya-rasa* involves the desire to experience the *bhāva* of Rādhā herself through service to her—Rādhā *dāsyam*. As we know, this is the *bhāva* of Rūpa Goswāmī, who appears in Kṛṣṇa *līlā* as Rūpa-mañjarī. His is one particular form—the most extreme—of *tad-bhāva mādhurya-rasa* that is often referred to as *mañjarī-bhāva*. Notably, such *mañjarīs* are also referred to as *priya-narma-sakhīs*,[17] the feminine form of the word *priya-narma-sakhās*.

Śrī Jīva Goswāmī refers to this *tad-bhāva-rasa* by the term *tad-anumodana* (sympathetic joy). Such joy is unadulterated by self-interest: one finds happiness in the joy experienced by others. In the case of the *priya-narma-sakhās*, we see that they share in Kṛṣṇa's romantic joy in a manner that is supportive of it, and this support also gives rise to empathy. The difference between the English words "sympathy" and "empathy" is that empathy also involves listening to another, sharing their sorrow and spending time with them to help them cope and feel better. We find this empathy in Kṛṣṇa's *narma-sakhās*. Thus, *anumodana* includes not only empathy for the plight of others, but also sharing in and celebrating their happiness. In his comments on the nature of the *priya-narma-sakhās' bhāva*, Jīva Goswāmī explains that its *mādhurya-rasa* component is of the *anumodana* variety.[18] The *priya-narma-sakhā* desires to tend to the heart of Kṛṣṇa in terms of his love for Rādhā. To do so, he must know something about the nature of Rādhā's love, and thus longs for acquaintance with it, which he acquires through service to his *yūtheśvarī*.

In his *Prīti Sandarbha*, Jīva Goswāmī further distinguishes between two types of sympathetic joy (*anumodana-bhāva*): partial and direct. Those situated in *mādhurya-rasa* of the *anumodana* variety experience it more directly, whereas those situated in another *rasa* such as the fraternal love of the *narma-sakhās* experience it partially. Jīva Goswāmī describes such devotees as *prema-kalā-baddhā*, possessed of a small portion (*kalā*) of *kānta-bhāva* (romantic love).[19] Among those who experience it partially, no

17. In *Govinda-līlāmṛta* 1.86, Rūpa-mañjarī has been referred to as a *priya-narma-sakhī*. However, the term is also used in reference to other types of Rādhā's *sakhīs*, such as the *parama-preṣṭha-sakhīs*—Lalitā, Viśākhā, and so on. See the *Ujjvala-nīlamaṇi* 8.137 commentary of Śrī Viśvanātha.

18. *Anumodana* (sympathetic joy) is one of the *brahma-vihāras* (sublime attitudes) to be cultivated in Buddhism, one of that tradition's four "immeasurables."

19. See *Prīti Sandarbha* 353–354 for an explanation of partial and direct *tad-anumodana-bhāva*. Aside from what Jīva Goswāmī writes, in the *gopīs'* direct (*sākṣād*) *tad-anumodana-bhāva*, Rādhā's handmaidens will vicariously experience Rādhā and Kṛṣṇa's separations and union. For example, in Rādhā and Kṛṣṇa's union, the love bites that Kṛṣṇa inflicts upon

other *rasika* experiences it more than a *priya-narma-sakhā*, who through its influence gains access to serve Rādhā and Kṛṣṇa in their intimate moments.

Thus, the *priya-narma-sakhā* desires to experience *mādhurya-rasa* so that he can have enough familiarity with it to be able to assist Kṛṣṇa in his romantic life, and in doing so, he also develops empathetic feelings for Rādhā by way of partially experiencing her *bhāva*. Thus, he is not only a devotee in fraternal love for Kṛṣṇa—he is also a *kiṅkara*, or servitor, of Rādhā in male form; his normal male sensibilities toward women recede to the background when serving Rādhā and the *gopīs* as a result of the influence of *tad-anumodana mādhurya-rati*. Although the *priya-narma-sakhās* are males, who like Kṛṣṇa are more mature than their ages suggest, they experience no romantic attraction for the *gopīs*. Thus, Rūpa Goswāmī also refers to their *bhāva* as a type of *sakhī-bhāva* that covers their adolescent male sensibilities in relation to the *gopīs*.[20]

The *priya-narma-sakhās* are skillful at joking, always endowed with deep attachment for Kṛṣṇa, knowledgeable of time and place, skillful at pacifying angry *gopīs*, and able to give intimate counsel.[21] In modern psychological terms, the *priya-narma-sakhā* is perhaps the perfect alpha-beta male, resolving the contradictions between the alpha and beta poles and transforming romantic attraction for women into service to romantic attraction as it appears in Kṛṣṇa and the *gopīs* for one another. While they are cowherd friends of Kṛṣṇa in all respects like the other three types of Kṛṣṇa's *sakhās*, their *bhāva* exceeds that of the other cowherds in that it includes the capacity to fully participate in the romantic affairs of Rādhā and Kṛṣṇa. And their service in this latter extended sense is so integral to Rādhā and Kṛṣṇa's romantic *līlās* that they cannot fully blossom without the *narma-sakhās*' participation.

In this regard, Kṛṣṇadāsa Kavirāja Goswāmī asserts that without the involvement of the *sakhīs*, the intimate *līlās* of Rādhā and Kṛṣṇa cannot be nourished to reach their fullest expression and that it is the *sakhīs* who

---

Rādhā may also manifest on the neck of her handmaidens in a manner perhaps similar to Catholic stigmata. After all, such handmaidens do have *kāma* for Kṛṣṇa, which is suppressed by their service to Rādhā, and thus in such instances they can experience this *kāma*. However, partial (*leśa*) *tad-anumodana-bhāva*, while also affording the *narma-sakhās* partial experience of Rādhā and Kṛṣṇa's union and separation, does not result in such direct erotic experience, nor is *narma-sakhā-bhāva* homoerotic in nature, and as such there is no underlying *kāma* in their *sakhya-bhava*.

20. *Ujjvala-nīlamaṇi* 2.13.

21. *Ujjvala-nīlamaṇi* 2.1–2. See the commentaries of Śrī Jīva and Viśvanātha Cakravartī.

expand these *līlās* and make them relishable. His assertion arguably extends to include the *sakhī-bhāva* of the *priya-narma-sakhās*.[22] Also, as stated earlier, Śrī Jīva and Raghunātha dāsa Goswāmī assign the personality of a *narma-sakhā* to *mādhurya-rasa*, a poetic personality who is thought to be indispensable to the sweetness-producing intrigue of the *līlā*.

Through their service to the *gopīs*, the *priya-narma-sakhās* can at times see Kṛṣṇa with the same intensity as the *gopīs* see him. Thus, they understand the *gopīs'* feelings very well, and their *rati* is extremely pleasing to Rādhā.[23] Viśvanātha Cakravartī comments thus on *Śrīmad Bhāgavatam* 9.24.65, wherein both the *sakhīs* and the *sakhās*, while experiencing *rūḍha-mahābhāva*, curse Brahmā for creating eyes that blink, because during the momentary period of blinking they cannot see Kṛṣṇa:

> Among the inhabitants of Vraja, the *gopīs* and the *priya-narma-sakhās*, such as Subala, are the best among all for drinking Kṛṣṇa's sweetness.... Among the women, only the *gopīs* exhibited *rūḍha-mahābhāva*, in which they could not tolerate the blinking of their eyes. Among the men, only Kṛṣṇa's *priya-narma-sakhās*, such as Subala, had such experiences, since it is possible only for the *gopīs* and the *priya-narma-sakhās* to experience this *mahābhāva*.

In the above verse, Subala in particular is highlighted. As we have seen earlier, he is the most prominent among the *narma-sakhās*. Rūpa Goswāmī describes Subala thus:

> I offer my respects to Subala, who has a complexion that conquers gold, who is dear to Hari, who wears a pearl necklace and green cloth, whose eyes are like blue lotuses, and who gives joy to his friends by his conduct.
>
> With Subala, Mādhava discussed topics full of allusions that were difficult for others to understand, since Subala was most expert among all the friends in grasping Kṛṣṇa's hints and communicating with him through sign language.[24]

To help us further understand the intimate nature of Subala-sakhā's *sevā*, Rūpa Goswāmī cites words spoken by himself in his Vraja *līlā-svarūpa* as

22. *Caitanya-caritāmṛta* 2.8.203.

23. *Ujjvala-nīlamaṇi* 14.233. Jīva Goswāmī comments that the *narma-sakhās' rati* is extremely pleasing to Rādhā's *rati*.

24. *Bhakti-rasāmṛta-sindhu* 3.3.46–47.

Rūpa-mañjarī, words originally spoken to awaken love for Subala in the heart of one of her friends—*kva śrīmān adhikāritāṁ na subalaḥ sevā-vidhau vindati*:

> What *sevā* is Śrīmān Subala not eligible for! When a lover's quarrel arises between the enemy of Agha and his beloved, Subala pacifies the heart of Kṛṣṇa's darling with endearing words, thus convincing her to return to her lover. He prepares a bed fit for their erotic exploits, and when Kṛṣṇa perspires in his lovemaking and lies fatigued on his beloved's breast, Subala fans him intensely.[25]

In his commentary on this verse, Jīva Goswāmī explains that hyperbole (*udātta-alaṅkāra*) has been invoked with regard to the description of Kṛṣṇa's physical condition, and in doing so he dismisses an alternate reading in which the description of Kṛṣṇa's condition is toned down.[26] Thus, he notes that Śrī Rūpa uses hyperbole for the express purpose of underscoring the eligibility of Subala-sakhā to serve the divine couple during their most intimate affairs.

In his *Rādhā-kṛṣṇa-gaṇoddeśa-dīpikā*, Śrī Rūpa describes Subala as, among other things, a servant of Rādhā. Cowherd friends of Kṛṣṇa who serve Rādhā take greater pleasure in her *sevā* than they do in direct service to Kṛṣṇa because they know that service to her is more pleasing to him. Gopa-kumāra/Sarūpa, a *sādhana-siddha narma-sakhā* and the protagonist of Sanātana Goswāmī's *Bṛhad-bhāgavatāmṛta*,[27] explains this to his student. His student, Janaśarmā, was a sincere *sādhaka* of *priya-narma sakhya-rati* whom Rādhā asked Sarūpa to bring to her, so that Janaśarmā might quickly attain Kṛṣṇa's grace. Upon receiving her order, Sarūpa explains, "On her request I swiftly

25. *Ujjvala-nīlamaṇi* 2.14.

26. An example of hyperbole is "She cried a river of tears." This is said just to emphasize how sad this lady is. In Śrī Rūpa's verse the emphasis is placed on the measure of Kṛṣṇa's intimacy with Rādhā that Subala has service access to, which in Śrī Jīva's mind has no limits. The alternate reading that Jīva Goswāmī rejects says, "He continuously fans him (Kṛṣṇa), whose body is perspiring being in the company of his beloved."

27. Sarūpa resides in the family of Śrīdāmā, who is a *priya-sakhā*. Nonetheless, Sarūpa is a *narma-sakhā*, and for that matter, Śrīdāmā's family is also the family of Rādhā. There are a number of examples of Sarūpa's *narma-sakhā* status in *Bṛhad-bhāgavatāmṛta*. For example, see 2.6.369 in relation to *Śrīmad Bhāgavatam* 10.83.43 and Śrī Viśvanātha's commentary on this verse. Sarūpa's desire to massage the lotus feet of Kṛṣṇa smeared with *kuṅkuma* from the breasts of the women of Vraja is an example of his *sakhya-rasa* being mixed with *mādhurya-rasa* and an example of the *priya-narma-sakhā*'s *rūḍha-mahābhāva*. In *Bṛhad-bhāgavatāmṛta* 2.5.233, Nārada instructs Gopa-kumāra to learn about *prema* directly from Rādhā.

came here, overjoyed, without even a thought about missing the happiness of Kṛṣṇa's company."[28] Sanātana Goswāmī comments that Sarūpa left early in the morning and knew that in doing so he would miss an entire day of cowherding with Kṛṣṇa, a daily occurrence he lived for. But Sarūpa did not mind missing the company of Kṛṣṇa, because his happiness is derived from his desire to please Kṛṣṇa and he knew that there was no better way to do so than through service to Rādhā.

Notably, when Gopa-kumāra attained perfection as Sarūpa-gopa, he learned the details of his residence through the direct *śikṣā* of Kṛṣṇa—the *ādi guru*—albeit imparted in a *rasika* manner. For example, when Sarūpa sat for his first meal at Nandagrāma, Kṛṣṇa suddenly frowned upon tasting one of Rādhā's *laḍḍus*, spitting it out in disgust. Causing quite a commotion, he then cast the balance of the sweet onto Sarūpa's plate. Sarūpa tasted it in turn only to find that it was delicious, and he realized thereby that Kṛṣṇa's apparent displeasure was a ruse, an instance of humor, or *hāsya-rasa*, through which Kṛṣṇa implicitly instructed him that his residence was in Vṛṣabhānu-pura and that in the *līlā* he was related to Rādhā.[29] In other words, pretending not to like the *laḍḍu* prepared by Rādhā, he threw it to Sarūpa's plate since he was part of her extended family.

Through the oral tradition of Vraja, we are told that all of the eight principal *gopīs* along with the twelve principal cowherd friends of Kṛṣṇa are members of the extended family of Rādhā, her cousins fathered by the three brothers of Vṛṣabhānu Mahārāja—Ratnabhānu, Subhānu, and Śrī Bhānu.[30] Nayanānanda Ṭhākura, for example, identifies the *sakhā* Sudāmā as the brother of Rūpa-mañjarī and son of Ratnabhānu:

> To the east of Sudāmā-candra's residence is an enchantingly ornate villa. It has four nicely designed gateways all around, and the breeze blows very gently there. At that place, Sudāmā-candra's sister Śrī Rūpa-mañjarī plays along with her girlfriends. In front of these four gates shine four magnificent trees of different species—namely, *santāna, pārijāta, campaka*, and *kiṁśuka*.[31]

28. *Bṛhad-bhāgavatāmṛta* 2.7.11.

29. Kṛṣṇa also exclaimed to Śrīdāmā upon meeting Sarūpa, "Look, Śrīdāmā! Here is my dear friend Sarūpa, the sun who shines on the lotus of your family!" *Bṛhad-bhāgavatāmṛta* 2.6.55.

30. The *Guṭikā* of Siddha Kṛṣṇadāsa includes a fourth brother, Svarbhānu.

31. *Preyo-bhakti-rasārṇava*, chapter 6.

Although we find differing opinions among *sādhus* on this subject,[32] *narma-sakhā-sādhakas* would be well advised to follow the lead of the paradigmatic *sādhana-siddha* and *priya-narma-sakhā* Gopa-kumāra/Sarūpa with regard to one's own residence in Vraja. In this case, such *sādhakas* will long to enter the *līlā* at the time of "cow dust," waiting patiently but enthusiastically—until the cows come home—for Kṛṣṇa to return to the village.[33] Thereafter they will find their place of residence in Śrī Vṛṣabhānu-pura as cowherd relatives of Rādhā and followers of Subala. Alternatively, and in a general sense, they may accept Yaśodā as their mother, even as they have their own mother and father, and reside in Nandagrāma. Kṛṣṇa will introduce such *sādhana-siddhas* to Yaśodā, and she will take them on her lap and shower them with motherly affection.[34]

The prominence of Subala-sakhā among Kṛṣṇa's *narma-sakhās* cannot be overemphasized. Rūpa Goswāmī, in his *Dāna-keli-kaumudī*, reveals Rādhā's thoughts regarding the fortune of Subala as Kṛṣṇa embraces him:

> O Subala, there is no one as fortunate as you! Even in the presence of elders, Hari freely embraces you while placing you on his broad lap, causing you to horripilate in ecstasy as he also places his arm

32. In *Rādhā-kṛṣṇa-gaṇoddeśa-dīpikā*, Rūpa Goswāmī does not follow this oral tradition. It is apparent that in this work, at least some of the names of the *gopālas'* parents (not all of which are listed) have been taken from the Purāṇas. An example is that of Sudāmā's parents. *Rādhā-kṛṣṇa-gaṇoddeśa-dīpikā* cites the Purāṇic parental names of Sudāmā Vipra, Kṛṣṇa's friend and classmate from Mathurā, as the names of the parents of the cowherd Sudāmā of Vraja. Furthermore, in *Rādhā-kṛṣṇa-gaṇoddeśa-dīpikā*, Rūpa-mañjarī is not described as the younger sister of Sudāmā, whereas in the lineage of Sudāmā stemming from Sundarānanda Ṭhākura, she has been. Therein, Sudāmā is also identified as the son of Ratnabhānu. Siddha Kṛṣṇadāsa Bābājī's *Guṭikā* also identifies Rūpa-mañjarī's father as Ratnabhānu, as does the *Śikṣa-tattva-dīpikā*. However, there are many editions of *Rādhā-kṛṣṇa-gaṇoddeśa-dīpikā* that differ with regard to verses omitted or added/edited. Furthermore, there are other differences between *Rādhā-kṛṣṇa-gaṇoddeśa-dīpikā* and *Bhakti-rasāmṛta-sindhu*. See note 50 of this chapter for an example of such differences.

33. However, Gopa Kumara did not first take birth in the *prakaṭa-līlā* before entering the *aprakaṭa-līlā*. He is arguably an exception to the norm in this regard. Nonetheless, his example is noteworthy and speaks to us of the principle involved: attaining the *aprakaṭa-līlā—vastu-siddhi*—requires deep absorption in *līlā-smaraṇam*. We see this deep absorption in his example, despite his not experiencing the *nitya siddhas'* association in the *prakaṭa-līlā* that serves to foster such absorption. Thus, birth in the *prakaṭa-līlā* is no doubt helpful, to say the least, to attaining the *aprakaṭa-līlā*, but arguably it is not absolutely essential, while deep absorption in *līlā-smaraṇam* is required.

34. *Bṛhad-bhāgavatāmṛta* 2.6.82.

> on your shoulder. Tell me, at which pure perfected place—*siddha-kṣetra*—and in what measure did you perform *tapas* to attain this fortune?[35]

In the above verse, we find the mindset and desire of Rādhā that corresponds with Raghunātha dāsa Goswāmī's epithet for her: *subala-nyasta-sārūpyā*—"she who dons the form of Subala" or "she who gives her form to Subala." Arguably, when Rādhā herself timelessly considers the advantages of *sakhya-rasa*, Subala manifests as the embodiment of her contemplation.[36] Thus, the two, Subala and Rādhā, are look-alikes, not only facially but in terms of their hands and feet as well. Furthermore, Śrī Raghunātha dāsa informs us through another name for Rādhā—*subala-prīti-toṣitā*—that "when Subala is pleased, Rādhā is pleased," indicating that internally, or mentally, Rādhā and Subala *also* share striking similarities.[37] No such claim concerning Rādhā's form and mind is made about any other devotee. Thus, we find the two exchanging clothes at times—sometimes in the joy of *hāsya-rasa*, at other times so that Rādhā can meet secretly with Kṛṣṇa while Subala-sakhā in Rādhā's attire pretends to be her and remains at her unsuspecting mother-in-law's home.[38] Śrī Rūpa cites a verse in Rādhā's voice:

> Look, slender-waisted woman! Placing his hand on the attractive shoulder of Subala, who is dressed in my clothes and whose hairs are standing on end, Kṛṣṇa whispers a message in his ear that is intended for me.[39]

And another:

> Subala, disguised in Rādhā's attire, came to the beautiful bank of the Yamunā beneath the blossoming *aśoka* trees. Watching Kṛṣṇa rise up with great joy [thinking Subala was Rādhā], he covered his face to hide his cheeks, which were breaking into a smile.[40]

35. *Dāna-keli-kaumudī* 38.

36. The principal Vraja *gopīs* are all *kāya-vyūha*, or expansions of the body of Rādhā, and as such they embody an aspect of her love. In Subala we arguably find a male form of such an expansion.

37. *Śrī Rādhikā-aṣṭottara-śata-nāma-stotram* 34–35.

38. Baladeva Vidyābhūṣaṇa comments on *Utkalikā-vallarī* 59 in the voice of a Vraja *vāsī*, "It seems that Śrī Kṛṣṇa has learned this art of dressing up as a woman from Subala, who deceives our elders thus." For an example of this art of dressing on Subala's part, see chapter 21.

39. *Bhakti-rasāmṛta-sindhu* 4.8.33.

40. *Bhakti-rasāmṛta-sindhu* 4.8.28.

Offering respect to Subala in the mood of a *jāta-rati-rāga-mārga-upāsaka*, Raghunātha dāsa Goswāmī also underscores Rādhā's affection for Subala-sakhā:

To him, Subala, whose body is overwhelmed with *prema*, whose *anurāga* for the moon of Gokula—Kṛṣṇa—is so deep that even in dreams Subala will not let go of Kṛṣṇa's hand for fear that he will be separated from Śyāma, and whose heart is showered by the stream of Rādhā *praṇaya*, to that Subala-sakhā I offer my respects.[41]

In this verse, the words *yo rādhikā-praṇaya-nirjhara-sikta-cetā*, "showered by the stream of Rādhā *praṇaya*," are significant. Rādhā loves Subala more than her own life because Subala is more expert than anyone else among those who assist her in her hour of need—in her plight to meet with Kṛṣṇa. And Subala's heart is overwhelmed with *prema* as he remembers how his friend relishes the highest happiness in union with Rādhikā. Thus, he also bathes in the cascade of her love for Kṛṣṇa. Indeed, Subala lives for this *praṇaya*.[42] In this regard, Subala is active not only during the daylight hours. When he is not at home dreaming of Kṛṣṇa, he is active in the *līlā-sevā* of Rādhā-Govinda by moonlight!

In his *Prema-pūrābhidha-stotram* 1, Raghunātha dāsa Goswāmī hints at the moonlight *sevā* of Subala:

> O Rādhe! On a sweet moonlit spring night, dressed in a white flower garment and anointed with ground camphor, you place your hand on the shoulder of one of your messenger girls as you follow Subala-sakhā. For just one moment may my eyes delight in this sight!

Accompanied by Subala, Śyāma beholds the stunning moonlit spring night, and his feelings of separation from Rādhā swell in anticipation. Subala readily understands and empathizes with Śyāma's sense of urgency,[43] and later that evening upon Śyāma's request, he seeks a solution to his friend's love pangs and sets out to find Rādhā by the light of the moon. Meanwhile, with the help of her *sakhīs*, Rādhā has dressed herself in white and colored her complexion moonlike with powdered camphor. Although this effort has

41. *Vraja-vilāsa-stava* 22.

42. Here *praṇaya* refers to the love within *mādhurya-rāsa* that follows the separation arising from *māna*. Subala lives for this love, but as Raghunātha dāsa Goswāmī's verse says, Subala also bathes in Rādhā's *praṇaya*, referring simply to her love for him.

43. This short period of separation between Rādhā and Kṛṣṇa is called *pravāsa*, of which there is a short and long version, as discussed ahead. Here Subala experiences Kṛṣṇa's feeling of separation after a short period of time and empathizes with it.

caused delay, her moonlight attire makes her more likely to go undetected by her elders as she sets out, following the lead of Vṛndā-devī and trailed close behind by Dāsa Goswāmī in his *mañjarī-svarūpa*. Subala meets the three halfway and then leads them to Śyāma.[44]

Here we find another example of Subala's extraordinary love. In Dāsa Goswāmī's verse from his *Vraja-vilāsa-stava*, he addresses Kṛṣṇa as the moon of Gokula in terms of his ability to cool the fire of Subala's fear of separation, just as the moon has a cooling and consoling effect upon the fire of the mind. Subala's own separation from Kṛṣṇa is considerable in and of itself. Thus, Dāsa Goswāmī describes him as *gāḍhānurāgī*—possessed of very deep *anurāga*. Subala cannot bear the thought of Kṛṣṇa's separation, and thus he grips the lotus hand of his friend Gokula-vidhu ever so tightly. However, as we learn from Dāsa Goswāmī's *Prema-pūrābhidha-stotram*, Subala also experiences Rādhā and Kṛṣṇa's feelings of separation for one another in some measure, which in turn enables him to empathize with their plight.

Rūpa Goswāmī understands the above very well. Thus, steeped in *jāta-rati-rāga-bhakti* with the ideal of *mañjarī-bhāva* in mind, Śrī Rūpa petitions Subala-sakhā for a solution to his own sorrow in separation:

> O Subala, in Vraja-maṇḍala you are a *priya-narma-sakhā*, a bosom friend of Śrī Nanda's son and Vṛṣabhānu Mahārāja's daughter. On this day, have mercy on me and relate my sad story to your two friends.[45]

Baladeva Vidyābhūṣaṇa comments that because Subala is so close with the divine couple, he has the capacity to petition them with great empathy on behalf of their aspiring maidservant who is suffering in separation. Here, Śrī Rūpa speaks in the voice of longing that characterizes *bhāva-bhakti* and, in doing so, of the intimacy that Subala shares with Rādhā and Kṛṣṇa and his empathetic love for them. Śrī Rūpa knows that no one in Vraja is more

44. The early Sanskrit commentary of Baṅgavihārī Vidyālaṅkāra, later Gauḍīya *padāvalī*, and the recent commentary of the late Ananta dāsa Paṇḍita all understand Dāsa Goswāmī's verse in this way, in which the words *subala-sakhām upetā* refer to Subala-sakhā guiding Rādhā on her way to meet Kṛṣṇa. However, it can be argued that it is grammatically more correct to translate the words *subala-sakhām upetā* as "the friend of Subala"—a reference to Kṛṣṇa, with whom Rādhā meets—rather than to Subala, who meets her halfway and who then helps her to meet with Kṛṣṇa. This translation also arguably fits better in relation to the second verse of the text. However, if translated in this way, the epithet *subala-sakhām* denoting Kṛṣṇa nonetheless serves as a veiled reference to Subala's participation in this *līlā*, participation that has been consistently envisioned over centuries of Gauḍīya commentary.

45. *Utkalikā-vallarī* 24.

capable of mitigating the *māna* of Rādhā—of uniting Rādhā and Kṛṣṇa by breaking her indignation that constitutes a type of love in separation. Because no one can equal Subala in accomplishing this daunting assignment, he can surely mitigate the longing of the *jāta-rati-sādhaka* to meet with the divine couple in *sevā* by turning their attention to such a budding *sakhī*.

Rādhā's displeasure with Kṛṣṇa, which arises either for good reason or for no reason at all, is one of the four types of love in separation experienced in *mādhurya-rasa*. While the union and separation of *yoga* and *ayoga* discussed in the previous chapter also apply to *mañjarī-bhāva*, the *mañjarī* also vicariously or empathetically experiences the divine couple's romantic love in separation, which takes the forms of *pūrva-rāga*, *māna*, short and long *pravāsa*, and *prema-vaicittya*, collectively referred to as *vipralambha*—the ecstatic pain of unrequited longing.

Pūrva-rāga refers to the feelings of separation experienced between young lovers before they express their love to one another, as well as to the shyness in the earliest stages of romantic love. *Māna* is jealous love but also love that for whatever reason appears to be otherwise and is expressed as displeasure with one's lover. Short *pravāsa* refers to the separation by time and location for a short period. Long *pravāsa* refers to the separation of lovers who were previously intimately associated but are at present separated by a long period of time and distant locations; it also implies separation derived from great obstacles over such a period and distance. *Prema-vaicittya* is love that brings about a sense of imminent separation while still in the presence of one's lover. The terms from Sanskrit drama that refer to the types of union corresponding with these experiences of separation are *saṅkṣipta* (brief), *saṅkīrṇa* (confused), *sampanna* (accomplished), and *samṛddhimān* (complete), respectively.[46] They are collectively referred to as *sambhoga*—complete joy of romantic intimacy.

At the beginning of this chapter, we have seen an example of how Subala-sakhā empathizes with Kṛṣṇa during Kṛṣṇa's experience of *pūrva-rāga*, how Subala's own heart is pained by the pain of Kṛṣṇa's heart in separation from Rādhā. It is during such *pūrva-rāga* that the strong hand of Kṛṣṇa, capable of lifting Mount Govardhana, trembles tenderly at the thought of touching the body of Rādhā. Śyāma ponders, "From my birth I have never done such a thing. How should one enjoy with a woman?" And it is Subala who steadies his hand. Drawing further from the poetry of Rūpa Goswāmī and the *padāvalī kīrtana* tradition, let us now examine

46. *Ujjvala-nīlamaṇi* 15.190–191.

how Subala also experiences the *māna* of Rādhā enough to empathize with it and ultimately cause it to break, thus facilitating the confused type of union that corresponds with it.[47]

Māna is confusing at its outset and its middle phase but not so as it ends, leading back to the intimacy of renewed *praṇaya*. At the beginning and onward through its middle phase, unpleasant thoughts of that which brought about the *māna* in the first place linger even as it begins to dissipate. *Māna* is thus somewhat contradictory—love expressed as displeasure. It is like hot sugarcane juice: too hot to drink yet too sweet to refuse. At times, it is extreme. Indeed, occasionally Rādhā's *māna* causes her to become very haughty. In his *Śrī Gāndharvā-samprārthanāṣṭakam* 8, we find Śrī Rūpa pining to experience such extraordinary pride in its full measure:

> When will I see Rādhā, ecstatic after defeating the son of Vraja's cowherd king in an exciting playful war of words and thus boasting among her *sakhīs*, while they shower her with hymns of praise—"*Jaya* Rādhe! *Jaya* Rādhe!"

Here, Rādhā proudly recalls her ability to defeat Kṛṣṇa in wordplay, openly displaying this pride before her handmaidens. Desperate because no *sakhī* bearing his message has been able to pacify her, Kṛṣṇa resorts to sending Subala, who in his own *sakhī-bhāva* is the most expert within the entire circle of Rādhā and Kṛṣṇa's intimate *sakhīs* and *sakhās* in reuniting the youthful couple. His message is in the form of a *mahā-mantra*:

> *Rādhe!* You should know that you have stolen the heart of my dear friend *Śyāma*. *Rādhe!* Don't think that because I am his close friend you cannot trust me. I am your friend as well, and I know *Śyāma* better than any of your *sakhīs*. Therefore, please listen to me. *Śyāma* attracts the hearts of all the Vraja *vāsīs*. Without *Śyāma* the world will become dark, but without you his world becomes dark. *Rādhe!* I have come to tell you this. I am not praying to you, proud girl, nor shall I beg you to go to him, but given our mutual and long-standing

47. In the previous chapter, we cited Jīva Goswāmī's *Prīti-sandarbha* 89, in which he states that Kṛṣṇa's friends can experience *māna*. In this treatise, Śrī Jīva defines *māna* as anger in love on the part of his friend or lover that causes fear in Kṛṣṇa's heart. Otherwise, Kṛṣṇa's *sakhās* have no reason to be jealous of one another or anyone else, as their *sthāyi-bhāva* is rooted in the confidence—*viśrambha*—that Kṛṣṇa loves them the most, and each of them is correct. It is more in romantic love that the beloved may doubt her lover's commitment and experience *māna* as jealousy. However, Kṛṣṇa's *narma-sakhās* partially experience Rādhā's jealous *māna* through empathetic, vicarious experience.

friendship, you should at least hear me out and consider my message carefully. *Rādhe!* The gist of it is this: Hari is lost without you, and just now, at the thought of not gaining your company, he is about to take his own life, drowning himself in your *kuṇḍa*!

Rādhe! Śyāma is so strong that even Balarāma, who could support the whole world on his head, rests on his shoulder. *Rādhe!* How will his brother and the rest of his family, who are dearer to you than your own life, continue to live if *Śyāma* commits suicide? Balarāma may be his older brother with arms as strong as an elephant's trunk, but he will become weak and incapable of consoling Yaśodā, as he did when your *Śyāma* was wrapped in the coils of Kāliya. What will become of her? Although Balarāma knew then that no one could destroy your *Śyāma*, he also knows that without your love Kṛṣṇa will destroy himself! *Rādhe!* Go to him without delay and take away his suffering for the sake of all his family members, who love him so dearly. Although you may be justified in not loving him yourself, considering his questionable behavior, please do this for their sake before he takes his life, unable to bear the pain of separation from you. *Rādhe!*[48]

Thus, we have seen examples of Subala's empathetic participation in *mādhurya-rasa*'s *pūrva-rāga*, *māna*, and *pravāsa* after a short period of time. Śrī Rūpa does not cite any examples of the *narma-sakhā*'s empathetic participation in *mādhurya-rasa*'s extended form of *pravāsa* or its *prema-vaicittya*, experienced in the stages of *anurāga* and *mahābhāva*. However, we do know that these stages of intensification of one's *sthāyi-bhāva* are included in *narma-sakhya-rati*. As we recall from the previous chapter of this book, the *sthāyi-bhāva* of *sakhya-rati* intensifies in stages termed *praṇaya*, *prema*, *sneha*, and *rāga*, which were explained in that chapter. But again, in the *narma-sakhās*, it intensifies further such that these *sakhās* experience ecstasy typical of, if not exclusive to, *mādhurya-rasa*: *māna*, *anurāga*, and *mahābhāva*.

48. Because Mahāprabhu has taken the *prema* of Vraja and woven it together with the *mahā-mantra*, he has given *nāma-śreṣṭham*, or the highest conception of the holy name, to the world. This implies that all of the *prema-līlās* of Vraja are present in his conception of the *mahā-mantra*. Thus, we often find "translations" and "commentaries" on the *mahā-mantra* that depict a particular pastime or a part of one. This commentary is inspired from the pride of Rādhā in *māna*, which was indirectly experienced by Subala. It is in his voice and adapted from the early *padāvalī* tradition of Gauḍīya Vaiṣṇava poetry.

Subala's experience of *māna* has been discussed. *Anurāga* and *mahābhāva* are yet to be explained. *Anurāga* is the extension of *rāga* that causes the devotee to experience Kṛṣṇa during an encounter as if the devotee is experiencing him for the first time. Kṛṣṇa thus appears particularly ever fresh in *anurāga*. Śrī Rūpa cites no particular example of the *narma-sakhās*' *anurāga*; however, he does cite an example of their *mahābhāva*, which develops from *anurāga* and in which all the qualities of the previous stages exist. Just as all the qualities of all the *avatāras* exist in *svayaṁ* Bhagavān, all the qualities of *praṇaya*, *prema*, *sneha*, *māna*, *rāga*, and *anurāga* exist in *mahābhāva*. At the same time, there are varieties of *mahābhāva*, and thus it has its own qualities. And among the varieties of *mahābhāva*, it is only the *gopīs*, Subala, and other *narma-sakhās* who experience *rūḍha-mahābhāva*.[49]

Rūpa Goswāmī cites *Śrīmad Bhāgavatam* 10.82.38, in which a quality of *rūḍha-mahābhāva* shared by the *gopīs* and *narma-sakhās* is exhibited. It is similar to *Śrīmad Bhāgavatam* 9.24.65, cited earlier, in that in both verses Brahmā is cursed for creating defective eyes—eyes that blink. The quality of *rūḍha-mahābhāva* found in these verses is the inability of the *gopīs* and *narma-sakhās* to tolerate a very short period of time—the blink of an eye—in which the vision of Kṛṣṇa is lost. In everyday life, no one can fathom the duration of the blinking of one's eyes, much less feel that it is taking forever! Such is the experience not only of the *gopīs* but of Kṛṣṇa's *narma-sakhās* such as Subala as well.

We have discussed Subala's involvement with *mādhurya-rasa* as an example of *mādhurya-rasa*'s influence on the *narma-sakhā*'s *rati*. Subala is the *pārṣada* among Kṛṣṇa's *narma-sakhās* that those pursuing this ideal should internally emulate. However, we would be remiss not to mention Ujjvala-sakhā as well. His name—Ujjvala—while literally meaning "brilliant," is often used as an alternate epithet for romantic love, or *śṛṅgāra-rasa*, itself, just as *mādhurya*, meaning "sweet," is also used to refer to *śṛṅgāra-rasa*. Indeed, Rūpa Goswāmī named his text on *śṛṅgāra-rasa* *Ujjvala-nīlamaṇi*, which means "Brilliant Blue Sapphire." This name is a reference to Śyāmasundara, who is often compared to a blue sapphire (*nīlamaṇi*) in terms of his complexion, shining in the brilliance (*ujjvala*) of *śṛṅgāra-rasa* that is also identified with the color—*śyāma* (indigo)—of the dark blue sapphire. As we learned from the previous chapter, Rūpa Goswāmī considers Ujjvala-sakhā

49. *Sārārtha-darśinī* 9.24.65 and *Ujjvala-nīlamaṇi* 14.232–233.

and Subala to be the two most prominent *narma-sakhās*. He cites the following description of Ujjvala-sakhā:[50]

> I worship Ujjvala, dear to Kṛṣṇa, with his orange cloth, restless eyes, and complexion dark blue like Kṛṣṇa's. He is decorated with spring flowers, and he wears a jewel necklace.
>
> O friend! Not far off, Kṛṣṇa's messenger Ujjvala is approaching. How will I protect my honor? Is there any chaste, shy, respectable woman here who, as Ujjvala approaches, would remain without desiring the best of cowherd boys—Kṛṣṇa?[51]

Let us explore the implications of Śrī Rūpa's cryptic description of Ujjvala's relationship with Kṛṣṇa, a description in which one *gopī* speaks to another about the two cowherds' friendship. Earlier in this chapter, we cited both Śrī Jīva and Raghunātha dāsa Goswāmīs suggesting that the personification of *mādhurya-rasa* is a *priya-narma-sakhā*. In this they follow the lead of Rūpa Goswāmī, who informs us,

> *Śṛṅgāra-rasa* personified resides in Vraja as a *priya-narma-sakhā* of the slayer of Agha, Kṛṣṇa, who is more charming than a multitude of Cupids.[52]

Viśvanātha Cakravartī Ṭhākura comments, "The words *agha-vidviṣaḥ* indicate that Kṛṣṇa destroys all the sins (*agha*) of those who taste this *rasa*, whereas material Cupid increases sin. The *śṛṅgāra-rasa* of Kṛṣṇa is personified in Vraja as *ujjvala-śṛṅgāra*."

The point these *ācāryas* are making is that in the *śṛṅgāra-rasa* of Vraja, we find jealousy and other petty or undesirable qualities among rival parties of *gopīkās*, qualities the *sādhaka* strives to overcome. However, these qualities are nonetheless very much part of human romantic love. Thus, for the *śṛṅgāra-rasa* of Vraja to be humanlike, these qualities and the various rivalries among the *gopīs* must also be present in the *līlā*. Indeed, their presence and the intrigue that accompanies it add sweetness to the divine drama of romantic love for Kṛṣṇa, the slayer of sin. Unlike material faults, in this drama they

50. Here I have cited Śrī Rūpa's verses in *Bhakti-rasāmṛta-sindhu*. In *Rādhā-kṛṣṇa-gaṇoddeśa-dīpikā*, also attributed to Rūpa Goswāmī, the descriptions of both Subala and Ujjvala contradict the descriptions in *Bhakti-rasāmṛta-sindhu*. Therein, Subala is dressed in blue (*nīla-vastra*) and Ujjvala's complexion is red (*rakta-varṇa*).

51. *Bhakti-rasāmṛta-sindhu* 3.3.48–49.

52. *Ujjvala-nīlamaṇi* 9.42.

are divine ornaments. Cakravartī Ṭhākura asks, "How can the *śṛṅgāra-rasa* of Kṛṣṇa, who is more attractive than millions of Cupids, be maintained and nourished without spiritual anger and aversion?"[53] In Kṛṣṇa's Vraja *līlā*, even such qualities are found in their original spiritual form! However, they manifest only as expressions of transcendental competition, the goal of which for all concerned is to please Kṛṣṇa the most. Once it is determined that he has been pleased the most by one party, rival parties share affection for one another among themselves. The classic example of this is in the *Bhāgavata* when Rādhā's rivals realize that she has pleased Kṛṣṇa more because he left them to be with her alone. At this point, their competitive mood transforms at first into appreciation of Rādhā's devotion and later into sympathy for her when they find that she has also been left behind by Kṛṣṇa.

Thus, while Kṛṣṇa himself is the transcendental Cupid and his *rāsa-līlā* is ever victorious over lust—*kāma-vijaya*—the *śṛṅgāra-rasa* that he shines brilliantly under the influence of is itself a transcendental Cupid as well, poetically personified as a *narma-sakhā*. It is thus notable that among Kṛṣṇa's *narma-sakhās*, Ujjvala-sakhā has been identified with the Cupid of Vraja's *śṛṅgāra-rasa*. In his commentary on *Utkalikā-vallarī* 41, Baladeva Vidyābhūṣaṇa comments that Kṛṣṇa's *sakhā* Ujjvala is in fact Cupid,[54] the god of love—*smaro deva*—in Kṛṣṇa *līlā*. Thus, he nourishes Rādhā and Kṛṣṇa's *līlā* as a seen and unseen force, a form of divine intervention. It is only by his desire to please Kṛṣṇa in this way that the *līlā* of love between Kṛṣṇa and the *gopīs* is seen to take various twists and turns, giving rise to all the nuances of romantic love.

Baladeva Vidyābhūṣaṇa comments on Śrī Rūpa's use of the word *daivād*, which means "divine intervention" or "transcendental fate." It is the influence of Kṛṣṇa's *līlā-śakti/yogamāyā* that is personified in various forms, such as Paurṇamāsī and Vṛndā-devī. Śrī Baladeva includes Ujjvala-sakhā among these forms. However, in doing so, he does not posit the physical presence of Ujjvala in the *līlā* that Śrī Rūpa is envisioning. Rather, he refers to the very nature of *ujjvala-rasa* that, for example, causes Kṛṣṇa on his way to meet

53. *Ujjvala-nīlamaṇi* 9.43, commentary.

54. Despite his prominence, Ujjvala is not typically listed among the *dvādaśa-gopālas*. However, he is listed as one of them in the later *Caitanya-saṅgītā* (1866 CE). In other texts, he is listed as an *upa-gopāla*. In *Gaura-gaṇoddeśa-dīpikā* 70, he is arguably the *narma-sakhā* mentioned by Kavi-karṇapūra who is identified in Gaura *līlā* with Raghunandana Ṭhākura and in Kṛṣṇa's Dvārakā *līlā* with Pradyumna, whom the *Bhāgavatam* identifies as a reflection of Cupid (*Śrīmad Bhāgavatam* 10.55.40). Locana dāsa Ṭhākura also identifies Raghunandana Ṭhākura as a Gaura *līlā* incarnation of Cupid (*Caitanya-maṅgala* 2.193).

Rādhā to run into Padmā, a *sakhī* of Candrāvalī. Padmā then leads Kṛṣṇa to Candrāvalī rather than to Rādhā, which in turn sets up the opportunity for Kṛṣṇa to experience Rādhā's jealousy. The idea is that such chance or destiny that lies outside of any plan of Kṛṣṇa himself is the arrangement of *ujjvala-rasa* itself, which as we have seen is identified with the nature of a *priya-narma-sakhā* in general and the *narma-sakhā* named Ujjvala—the transcendental Kāmadeva—in particular.[55] The broader idea here is that these *priya-narma-sakhās* are indispensable to the intrigue of Rādhā and Kṛṣṇa's *ujjvala-rasa*, which makes it as tasteful as it is.

Other than Subala and Ujjvala, the most prominently portrayed *priya-narma-sakhā* within the *līlā-granthas* of the Gauḍīya *ācāryas* is Madhumaṅgala. Although he is not a *pārṣada* to follow in pursuit of *sakhya-rati* for reasons explained ahead, any book dealing with *sakhya-rati* or Kṛṣṇa's Vraja *līlā* would be incomplete without mentioning him.

Neither in his *Bhakti-rasāmṛta-sindhu* nor in his *Ujjvala-nīlamaṇi* does Rūpa Goswāmī describe Madhumaṅgala as a *narma-sakhā*. In *Ujjvala-nīlamaṇi*, he is identified as a *vidūṣaka*, a jester. However, Śrī Raghunātha dāsa elaborates on this identity, hinting also at his *narma-sakhā* sensibilities when stressing his love for Rādhā and Kṛṣṇa:

> Praise to Madhumaṅgala, Vṛndāvana-candra's *narma* companion, the embodiment of *hāsya-rasa*, always happy yet always hungry. He sparkles with festivity, making his *prāṇa-preṣṭha* friends Rādhā and Kṛṣṇa laugh daily at his clever jokes and gestures.[56]

And Śrī Rūpa's *Rādhā-kṛṣṇa-gaṇoddeśa-dīpikā* does identify the *dvija-rāja* of Vraja not only as a *vidūṣaka* but also as a *priya-narma-sakhā*.[57] Therein, Rūpa Goswāmī further describes this farcical *brāhmaṇa* thus:

55. *Rādhā-kṛṣṇa-gaṇoddeśa-dīpikā* 2.43 describes Ujjvala as "Rasarāja personified." *Gaura-gaṇoddeśa-dīpikā* 70 identifies Raghunandana with an unnamed *narma-sakhā* and also with Pradyumna of Kṛṣṇa's Dvārakā *līlā*, who is commonly identified with Cupid. Arguably this *narma-sakhā* is Ujjvala. However, *Caitanya-saṅgītā* (1866 CE) identifies Ujjvala with Kānu Ṭhākura (also known as Nidu Kṛṣṇadāsa) and lists him among the *dvādaśa-gopālas*.

56. *Vraja-vilāsa-stava* 24.

57. *Priya-narma-sakhā matāḥ... madhumaṅgala* (*Rādhā-kṛṣṇa-gaṇoddeśa-dīpikā* 2.41–42). However, it should be noted that the *vidūṣakas* are "skillful at pacifying angry *gopīs* and able to give intimate counsel," which fits the person of Madhumaṅgala well even without classifying him as a *priya-narma-sakhā* (*Ujjvala-nīlamaṇi* 2.1–2). And Śrī Jīva comments on the same verse that one should consider the *vidūṣakas* to be devoid of male attraction for females in their service to Kṛṣṇa during his affairs with the *gopīs*. The same is said to be the case with the *narma-sakhās*.

> Madhumaṅgala's complexion is slightly *śyāma*, his clothes golden in hue, and he wears a wreath of forest flowers. He is forever Kṛṣṇa's friend and a *vidūṣaka*.[58]

Among the friends of Kṛṣṇa, Madhumaṅgala stands out, not only as a *vidūṣaka* like Vasanta-sakhā and other *vidūṣakas* but also because, unlike all of Kṛṣṇa's other friends, some of whom serve as examples of *sakhya-rati* to emulate, Madhumaṅgala is a *brāhmaṇa* and not a *vaiśya* or cowherd by nature. Although a resident of Vraja, he hails from Ujjain as the son of Sāndīpani Muni.[59] He arrives in Vraja with Paurṇamāsī just before Kṛṣṇa's birth, but the two are not introduced until early in Kṛṣṇa's *kiśora-līlā*,[60] and previously in chapter 4 we learned from Raghunātha dāsa Goswāmī of Madhumaṅgala's preference for Kṛṣṇa's adolescent form—*kiśora*—and its corresponding *līlās*. At Nandagrāma, where Madhumaṅgala lives as an adopted family member, Yaśodā-māyī engages him in the *sevā-pūjā* of Narasiṁha-deva, the household deity. For the price of room and board, he blesses the household, even while it appears as if he eats more than the entire household combined. And while it is said that a *brāhmaṇa* should not eat more than the knowledge he shares, the purpose of sharing knowledge is to make others happy, which Madhumaṅgala does through his joking nature in even greater measure than the amount that he eats. May this *brāhmaṇa* bless me with *preyo-bhakti*.

In this chapter, we have learned about the nature of the *narma-sakhās*' love, and we have also learned something about Subala, Ujjvala, Madhumaṅgala, and Sarūpa. There are, of course, an infinite number of *narma-sakhās* and room for an infinite number more, all of whom can fit into the extended family of either Rādhā or Kṛṣṇa as it appears in the *nitya-līlā*. In that realm, these boys are either the same age as Kṛṣṇa or slightly younger yet mature enough in age that, even if they are younger, this age difference has no bearing on their intimacy with *kiśora* Kṛṣṇa. The opportunity to follow their example, making it one's ideal—the goal of one's *sādhana*—is

58. *Rādhā-kṛṣṇa-gaṇoddeśa-dīpikā* 2.64–65.

59. *Rādhā-kṛṣṇa-gaṇoddeśa-dīpikā* 2.65.

60. In *Gopāla-campū*, Madhumaṅgala enters Kṛṣṇa's life just after Dhenukāsura is slain, which marks the beginning of Kṛṣṇa's *kiśora-līlā*. In Śrī Rūpa's *Lalita-mādhava*, Kṛṣṇa meets Madhumaṅgala in Avantī-pura, or Ujjain, as the lost son of Sāndīpani Muni, whom Kṛṣṇa and Balarāma brought back to life. Madhumaṅgala figures prominently into Kṛṣṇa's Dvārakā *līlā*, showcased in that work. However, Viśvanātha Cakravartī asserts that that work describes Kṛṣṇa *līlā* as it manifests in a different *kalpa* from that of the *līlā* narrative found in *Śrīmad Bhāgavatam*. See the *Ujjvala-nīlamaṇi* 15.207 commentary of Śrī Viśvanātha.

the blessing of Nitāicāṅda and his twelve principal associates, all of whom, again, are either *priya-sakhās* or *priya-narma-sakhās*, the latter being preferable for reasons explained in this chapter.

With the end of this chapter, we come to the end of our initial exploration of the *tattva* underlying *sakhya-rasa*, including its descent into the world and the history of its dissemination. We have also discussed the way of following the *rāgātmikas*—*rāgānugā-bhakti* and its subdivision of *sambandhānugā-bhakti*—and we have explored the nature of *sakhya-rasa*, which reaches its zenith in the *narma-sakhās' rasa*.

As we have learned, the knowledge of the nature of *rāgānugā-bhakti*, and in this case its subdivision of *sambandhānugā-bhakti*, is essential to its practice. Again, if one desires milk, one must learn how to milk and care for cows. With such knowledge underpinning one's practice, the practice itself is relatively easy. Some sections of the first division of this book should be helpful to that practice—for example, one can incorporate any number of the verses, visualizations, and *līlā* remembrances cited into one's daily *sādhana*. As we have learned thus far, overall the practice consists of hearing about and reciting Kṛṣṇa's *sakhya-rasa-līlās*, chanting Kṛṣṇa *nāma* and one's favorite names of Kṛṣṇa related to this *rasa*, remembering and ultimately meditating on these *līlās*, and in this way fully engaging one's *sādhaka-deha* in such focused acts of devotion that they give rise to an internal meditative form of a *priya-narma-sakhā*. Therefore, to further assist the reader in such practice, the second part of this book consists of an extended *prakaṭa-līlā* narrative interspersed with *tattva*. That section follows a *sakhya-rasa* perspective on Kṛṣṇa's *līlās* as described in the tenth canto of the *Bhāgavata Purāṇa*.

O sympathetic readers! Fix your resolve! As Śrī Nārada instructed Gopa-kumāra:

> Overcoming obstacles born of fear, attain that *prema* in which one conceives of Kṛṣṇa as one does a friend in this world by way of desiring to serve the *gopas* and *gopīs*. That *prema* can be achieved through the principal *aṅgas* of *bhakti*—meditating on and singing about the Vraja *līlās* of Kṛṣṇa and *saṅkīrtana* of the beloved names of Kṛṣṇa.[61]

Relative to your ability to actually absorb your mind in this *bhajana* of *sakhya-rati*, practice with all your heart. With the balance of your energy, share the teachings of Gaura and Nityānanda, engaging in and assisting others in Śrī Kṛṣṇa *saṅkīrtana*. These two—*kīrtana* and internal

61. *Bṛhad-bhāgavatāmṛta* 2.5.217–218.

bhajana—should complement one another, as we have learned from the example of Mahāprabhu. *Kīrtana* goes outward and takes one inward, wherein one discovers something worthy of sharing in celebration. Do this until Rādhā and Kṛṣṇa can no longer bear—in separation—to share you with others and want you all to themselves.

> O *priya-sakhās* and *priya-narma-sakhās*! You are dearer than life itself to the ever-youthful couple of Vraja, and your wealth of *prema* is incomparable. Only by personally bathing in the dust of your lotus feet will my resolve attain perfection.[62]

62. *Saṅkalpa-kalpa-druma* 98.

PART 2
Radius

Prakaṭa-Līlā

6

The Prakaṭa-līlā

As we learned from the circumference of this circle of friends, our ideal is to enter the Vraja *līlā* ourselves.[1] But what exactly is *līlā*? In the works of Sanskrit poetry, *kāvya*, we find that the verbal root *lī*, "to melt" or "to absorb," is thought to be that from which the word *līlā*—"play"—derives. When the mind becomes absorbed as it can only in *samādhi* and when its constructs melt, then, having also been invited by *bhakti*, one is in a position to enter the play of Kṛṣṇa.

The word *līlā* also implies the freedom of possibility found in drama and poetry that extends beyond the limits of everyday life. It is a feminine noun meaning "drama, play, or pastime." It is arguably related to the Latin word *lūdus*, and from there to the English word "ludic"—spontaneous and undirected playfulness. In his *Bhāvārtha-dīpikā* commentary on the *Śrīmad Bhāgavatam*'s *brahma-vimohana-līlā*, Śrīdhara Swāmī describes *līlā* as "the play of consciousness rendered into a theatrical performance."

What to speak of Kṛṣṇa *līlā* as it appears in our world of time and space in one universe after another, the entire world of time/space itself originates from the *līlā* of Kṛṣṇa's *avatāra*, arising out of his own *ānanda*—*loka-vat tu līlā kaivalyam*. This is his *sṛṣṭi-līlā*, or drama of creation set in motion by his descent in the form of Mahāviṣṇu.

Reality is God's play, circles of *līlā* within *līlā*, all of which have no purpose other than play itself. They rhyme but do not answer to any reason of our limited conjecture. Still, we may reason about them to understand reason's own limits and then through wise, committed spiritual practice know in

1. See also *Śrīmad Bhāgavatam* 10.47.58, wherein the learned Uddhava informs us that entering the Vraja *līlā* is the highest goal one can attain.

ways we could not otherwise, with a knowing that is comprehensive in that it satiates the self. Such is the *paro dharma* of the *Bhāgavatam*'s *bhakti*, through which we can learn the script and play the role of *bhakti-rasa* with Līlā Puruṣottama—Kṛṣṇa.

Although we find exceptions, the general rule is that Kṛṣṇa's *prakaṭa* (manifest) *līlā* in this world serves as the principal entry point into his eternal *aprakaṭa* (unmanifest) *līlā*.[2] The sages of Daṇḍakāraṇya and the personified *śrutis* serve as examples of those who entered the Vraja *līlā* through its manifestation on earth. They each entered collectively as a group, whereas alternately one can enter unaccompanied.[3]

Thus this earthly manifest *līlā* is arguably the most important expression of Kṛṣṇa's play for the practitioner. While the word *prakaṭa* means "manifest" or "visible," it also means "best." This *prakaṭa-līlā* serves as an invitation for humanity to enter into an intimate relationship with "Reality the Beautiful," the heart of divinity. It appears on earth at a specific time while transcending time altogether.

Ṭhākura Bhaktivinoda refers to descriptions of the *prakaṭa-līlā* by the term *nidarśana*. They are an approximation of its nature that employs language, thought, and things of this world, all of which cannot do justice to the reality of the *līlā* but nonetheless render such descriptions an entry point into the *līlā* itself for those who lend their hearts and minds to them. The manifest *līlā* appears at the junction of time and eternity. It is not a limited expression of human culture. Reality does not transcend itself to become a formless abyss of eternal bliss; rather, it is ultimate reality itself. Those who experience it describe it as best they can, drawing on our humanity, which itself is a reflection of that reality. And being humanlike, the Vraja *līlā* sets a standard for human culture: that if humanity is to be differentiated from the

2. For the general rule, see *Ujjvala-nīlamaṇi* 3.49–51. For an example of the exception, the second canto of Sanātana Goswāmī's *Bṛhad-bhāgavatāmṛta* describes the course of *krama-mukti*, attaining transcendence step by step (passing through realm after realm of spiritual possibilities). However, the text's protagonist, Gopa-kumāra/Sarūpa, attains Kṛṣṇa's *aprakaṭa-līlā* without passing through the *prakaṭa-līlā*. He does so through the vehicle of *nāma-saṅkīrtana* and *līlā-smaraṇam* while residing in the Vraja region on earth at a time when the *prakaṭa-līlā* is not occurring.

3. In *Bhakti-rasāmṛta-sindhu* 1.2.307, Śrī Rūpa gives the example of a carpenter from Hastināpura who worshipped the deity of Kṛṣṇa as his son. Jīva Goswāmī comments that this carpenter is referenced in the *Skanda Purāṇa* and that he took his next birth in the *prakaṭa-līlā*, where he perfected his Kṛṣṇa consciousness within the *brahma-vimohana-līlā*, during which Kṛṣṇa became the sons of all the cowherd men. This carpenter is thus an example of an individual entering Kṛṣṇa's eternal drama through the portal of his *prakaṭa-līlā*.

less-complex species, it must be in pursuit of transcendence extending beyond human boundaries and the limitations they place on our capacity to love.

As much as love is about giving, we are constrained from loving as a result of our over-identification with the biological and psychological embodiment, which leaves the *ātmā* feeling as if something is missing in its life. Thus we seek, but for the most part only to acquire, and as a result we cover the gem that we are with a mountain of emptiness in the form of things and endless thoughts about them. Such are only the very basic philosophical implications one can draw from Kṛṣṇa *līlā*, while within the *līlā*'s details we find complex theological lessons for *sādhakas* in the art of love.

Because the *prakaṭa-līlā* appears at the junction of time and eternity, it is similar to one's *sādhaka-deha*, or practitioner's body, in that it constitutes the juncture of matter and spirit. Viśvanātha Cakravartī Ṭhākura explains that one of its purposes is to illustrate "the methodical nature of the culture of *bhakti*" through instances in the *līlā*.[4] For example, Devakī's childbearing and her fear of Kaṁsa serve as a metaphor for the healthy sense of fear that a *sādhaka* must have toward being distracted by sense indulgence.

In his *Kṛṣṇa Sandarbha*, Śrī Jīva Goswāmī compares this *prakaṭa-līlā* to the *arcā-vigraha*. Like the deity, it is free from the limits of time and space but nonetheless, under the influence of the *svarūpa-śakti*, has an apparent beginning and an end and consists of both phenomenal and transcendental elements.[5] Thus, just as the *arcā-vigraha* form of Kṛṣṇa is an extension of himself that serves to assist practitioners in conceptualizing and serving their *iṣṭa-devatā*, similarly Kṛṣṇa's *prakaṭa-līlā* is an extension of himself and his *śakti* that serves as an introduction to his eternal play, inviting us to participate in it.

In literature, the *prakaṭa-līlā* is best represented in the *Śrīmad Bhāgavatam*. Thus, in the radius of our circle, we shall proceed with an extensive *sakhya-rati līlā* narrative following the lead of *Śrīmad Bhāgavatam*, which *sakhya-rati-sādhakas* can use to their advantage in pursuit of their ideal. The *Bhāgavata* is by far the most theologically complex text known to the world. As the essence of Vedānta—*śruti-sāram ekam*[6]—it dams the tide of material emotion and is at the same time rich with *rasa*, thus bathing its

4. *Śrīmad Bhāgavatam* 10.2.8.

5. *Kṛṣṇa Sandarbha* 153.

6. *Śrīmad Bhāgavatam* 1.2.3. Here the *Bhāgavatam* describes itself as the essence/cream of the *śruti* texts, even while in form it is identified with the *smṛti* texts. *Garuḍa Purāṇa* considers it the natural commentary on the *Brahma-sūtra*, penned by the same author in an effort to demonstrate the consistency of the body of *śruti* texts.

readers in an ocean of transpsychological emotion. The *Bhāgavata* undresses the *ātmā*, which in its nakedness is more beautiful in its resemblance to Brahman than in any role it plays in the dress and drama of *saṁsāra*, while simultaneously re-dressing that *ātmā* beautifully and suitably for the dance of Bhagavān's *līlā-sevā*. It does so, unlike other Purāṇas, by retelling the *līlā* drama of Kṛṣṇa such that the transpsychological emotions animating its players are shared with its readers, who are encouraged at the outset of the text to drink its intoxicating beverage of *bhakti-rasa* to the point of passing out, *rasam ālayam*, and then get up and do it again—*Amen*.

The *Bhāgavata*'s *līlā* narrative arises out of the spiritually intoxicated *samādhi* of the legendary Vyāsa. The text of the *Bhāgavata* explains that Vyāsa sat in *samādhi*, meditating on the manifest *līlā* as instructed by Nārada—*samādhinānusmara tad-viceṣṭitam*.[7] He then poeticized his philosophical and theological insights. Regardless of how Kṛṣṇa may have appeared to mundane eyes, when seen with eyes of devotion his *līlā* carries far-reaching implications. Vyāsa's devotional vision arose out of a fully concentrated meditative mind undistracted in pure *yogic* objectivity—free from any bias arising out of material attachment. And Vyāsa sketched out the implications of his vision in the text of the *Bhāgavatam*, implications that are further explored by its ongoing Gauḍīya commentators.

Thus, the modern mind's doubts concerning the historicity of the *Bhāgavatam*'s *līlā* narrative are dismissed by the fact that Kṛṣṇa *līlā* explains itself to be a *yogic* vision of the historical Kṛṣṇa—Kṛṣṇa seen by wise eyes tinged with the salve of love. Indeed, the *Bhāgavata* repeatedly declares *itself* to be a manifestation of the *prakaṭa-līlā*. The text of the *Bhāgavata* is more than a record of sacred history, it is another form of the *prakaṭa-līlā* manifest in word—the literary incarnation of Kṛṣṇa. And the book claims at its conclusion that those who are born after Kṛṣṇa returns to his abode can reach that abode—*vimucyet*—simply by absorbing themselves in the *līlā* narrative of the text.[8]

The *Bhāgavata*'s Kṛṣṇa *līlā* narrative spans the breadth of three centers of population—metropolitan Mathurā, celestial seaside Dvārakā, and bucolic Vraja. As we know, we are concerned with Vraja, and so too is the *Bhāgavata* itself. It is there that Kṛṣṇa is born of Nanda and Yaśodā, there that he makes his closest friendships, there that he comes of age and falls

7. *Śrīmad Bhāgavatam* 1.5.13.

8. See Edwin Bryant's *Krishna: A Sourcebook*. Kindle edition 1691–1696, which references *Śrīmad Bhāgavatam* 1.3.40, 10.90.49–50, 11.31.28, and 12.13.18.

in love. He lives in Mathurā for the sake of Vraja and its protection, and it is out of his longing for Vraja in Dvārakā that he returns to village life. The attentive reader will note that Prince Kṛṣṇa's various adult duties and relationships outside of Vraja are contrasted in the subtext with Kṛṣṇa's one-mindedness in play with his earlier cowherd community friends. For these special friends, life for all intents and purposes ends with his apparent departure, even as they continue breathing for the balance of thirty-three years,[9] their hearts beating only for his return. As acknowledged by his devotees outside of Vraja, the Vraja *vāsīs*' love for him is more intense than the *prema* found elsewhere, and so he who is the object of the Vraja devotees' love is mystically more present in their community even in his apparent absence than he is present in Mathurā or Dvārakā during his princely *līlā*. Wherever we go, we are only wherever our heart lies, and Kṛṣṇa's heart is grounded in the cow dust of Vraja.

Within the *Bhāgavata*'s Vraja *līlā* narrative, there are three centers of focused spiritual emotion corresponding with the three identities of Vraja Kṛṣṇa. In Vraja, Kṛṣṇa is the son of Yaśodā, the cowherd friend of Śrīdāmā and other *gopas*, and the lover of the *gopīs* and Rādhā in particular. Chapters 8–10 of the tenth canto focus on parental love for Kṛṣṇa and thus his childhood; chapters 11–18 focus on fraternal love for Kṛṣṇa and thus his boyhood; chapters 29–33 focus on romantic love for Kṛṣṇa and thus his adolescence. To put it another way, these sections are focused on Kṛṣṇa's elders, equals, and lovers, respectively.

Within the Vraja region today, parental love is showcased in the lineage of Vallabhācārya, as is a form of *mādhurya-rasa*. Yet another form of *mādhurya-rasa* is the focus of the Nimbārka *sampradāya*. And as we know, the Gauḍīya lineage showcases a particular form of *mādhurya-rasa*, extreme Rādhā *dāsyam*, and to a lesser extent two forms of *sakhya-rasa*—*priya-sakhā-bhāva* and *priya-narma-sakhā-bhāva*.

Our purpose in focusing first on the *sakhya-rati* expressed in the *prakaṭa-līlā* of the *Bhāgavatam* is to afford *sādhakas* a general acquaintance with the nature of the *līlā*, and more so to draw them into this particular *bhāva* through compelling examples of fraternal love. To achieve this purpose,

9. In *Gopāla-campū* 2.29.60, Jīva Goswāmī explains that Kṛṣṇa returned to Vraja at the age of forty-four. He left at the age of eleven. Thus, after slaying Dantavakra and returning to Vraja, Kṛṣṇa enfolds the Vraja portion of his *līlā* into his unmanifest (*aprakaṭa*) *līlā*. Then, in his princely expansion, he winds up the balance of his *līlā*, including his Kurukṣetra discourse—*Bhagavad-gītā*—and the demise of the residents of Dvārakā, which takes another seventy-five-plus years.

we shall examine the *līlā* narrative of the *Bhāgavata*'s *sakhya-rasa* center by way of retelling its story, drawing upon relevant commentaries, other texts, and personal insight to bring out its deep feeling and thus generate impressions—*bhakti-saṁskāras*—of fraternal love to affect the hearts of our readers. Thus, we move from precept—the *tattva* constituting the circumference of this circle—to an extended example here in its radius, which should speak louder and more compellingly to the reader.

7

Herding Calves

The daylight hours in the life of Rāma and Kṛṣṇa's cowherd friends begin with the sound of Balarāma's buffalo horn. Rāma, glowing like a confident full moon that never fades even as the night ends, stands on a raised platform against the copper sky just before the sun peeks above the horizon. Sūrya, that is, waits for Rāma to herald the new day while the sound of Rāma's horn calls the cowherds to assemble,[1] and thus their nighttime dreams longing for cowherding throughout the forests of Vraja come true.[2]

In the Vraja *līlā*, there is waking (*jāgrat*) and dreaming consciousness (*svapna*) but no dreamless sleep (*suṣupti*), and there the fourth and transcendent state of consciousness, *turīya*, pales in comparison to the fifth—*turyātīto gopālaḥ*. Therein the waking and dreaming states of consciousness both

1. In Kṛṣṇa's later *līlās*, he is of course secretly out at night meeting with Rādhā. Thus, Sūrya waits before rising for Rāma's horn to sound and signal that all is clear and that Rādhā and Kṛṣṇa have safely and secretly returned home. Therefore, Rāma's bugling is an example of his indirect assistance in Kṛṣṇa's romantic life. After all, the gods move only with the sanction of the Godhead.

2. Regarding such dreams, the present-day descendants of Ṭhākura Nayanānanda related to me the following anecdote from the Ṭhākura's life: Śrī Nayanānanda traveled widely and spoke often and with great feeling for Rāma and Kṛṣṇa's *sakhya-rasa-līlās*, but he never spoke of such *līlās* at night. His feeling was that in Vraja, *sakhya-rasa* sleeps at night. However, one night he was requested by the king of the area he had been traveling in to speak on these *līlās* the following night. Śrī Nayanānanda knew that, practically speaking, he could not refuse the king, yet his developing *sakhya-rati* sensibilities would not allow him to comply, placing him in an awkward situation. Understanding the plight of his devotee, Śrī Gopāla-deva appeared to him in a dream and told him that at night he and his friends are active in their *sakhya-rasa-līlās* in the form of their dreams, and thus it was not inappropriate to speak of such pastimes in one's *sādhaka-deha* throughout the night.

occur in *prema* beyond mere *mukti*. So says the *Gopāla-tāpanī śruti*.[3] Vraja is that land where the sky reflects Śyāma's brilliant complexion—sapphire blue—the *śruti* originates from his flute, and "the dreams that one dares to dream really do come true." We learn about Vraja from *Śrīmad Bhāgavatam*'s description of that realm and its *līlā* manifesting on earth, where the unborn takes birth and grows up to become a cowherd along with his friends.

The merciful *Śrīmad Bhāgavatam*, which is the essence of the *śruti*—*śruti-sāram ekam*[4]—opens the lotus of its *sakhya-rasa* center in the tenth canto's twelfth chapter. This chapter describes daybreak on a special day during the final sequence of the cowherds' childhood—*śeṣa-kumāra*—when the sense of friendship begins to take precedence over parental love. Although Rāma characteristically signals the start of the cowherds' day with his horn, on this day Kṛṣṇa rose early and blew his own buffalo horn at dawn.

In this section of the *Bhāgavata*, *sakhya-rati* takes center stage beneath the text's bright lights, sharing the *sakhās*' excitement with its sympathetic readers and inviting them to enter the drama of *preyo-bhakti* with the same enthusiasm themselves.[5] Plans were made with great excitement the night before to rise and depart early for the forest. Kṛṣṇa and his friends planned a picnic. Thus, it is a wonder that on this night they slept at all! Indeed, Kṛṣṇa rose uncharacteristically early without being called by his mother, who was busy preparing the picnic brunch. Instead of waiting for Balarāma

3. *Gopāla-tāpanī* 2.95. Our everyday waking dimension of consciousness (*jāgrat*) affords us the most impoverished experience of reality. Thus, it finds us largely at odds with one another and the natural world. The dream dimension (*svapna*) finds us within a subtle-body perspective of greater possibility and symbolic meaning. The dimension of dreamless sleep hints that we exist beyond the limits of physical and psychic matter and that such an existence is peaceful. However, the fourth dimension (*turīya*)—erroneously thought to be a pathological condition by those identifying entirely with the waking dimension—affords us the richest experience of all: the noetic bliss of self and God realization, in which the interconnectedness of all things is apparent, giving rise to universal compassion and reverential love of God. Beyond this lies the fifth (*turyātīta*) dimension of love of God in the *prema* of Vraja's *sakhya-rasa-sevā*.

4. *Śrīmad Bhāgavatam* 1.2.3.

5. The description of Rāma and Kṛṣṇa's calf-herding actually begins in chapter 11, but at this early beginning of their herding they remain close to home and their herding is limited. Nonetheless, in chapter 11 Kṛṣṇa gives his young friends something special to talk about by slaying Vatsāsura and Bakāsura. The chapter ends on the note of Kṛṣṇa's *kumāra-līlā* nearing its end. The last verse of chapter 11 is repeated as the last verse of chapter 14, framing the entire *brahma-vimohana-līlā*.

to blow his horn, Kṛṣṇa blew his own horn and with its sweet sound, which caused ripples to flow in undifferentiated Brahman, he accomplished two tasks at once: he personally woke the calves and signaled for his friends to come to Nanda's courtyard.[6]

That Kṛṣṇa woke without the call of his mother's parental affection underscores his immersion in *sakhya-rasa*. It was the anticipation of realizing the cowherd dreams he shared with his *sakhās* and the plans they had laid out the night before that made him wake early. That he personally woke the calves underscores just how thrilled he was to begin his herdsman's life, his love for cows being boundless. Rāma's absence on this day implies that Kṛṣṇa's play would not be burdened even slightly by parental constraints, and this in turn gave rise to wonder in the heart of Rāma as to the measure of the sportive mischief destined to occur.

That Balarāma was not involved on this day was primarily due to his being forcibly held hostage by parental love on the auspicious day of the month in which the constellation ruling over his birthday made its appearance, and thus Rohiṇī held him back from herding to observe the otherwise auspicious occasion. And as we shall see, this arrangement of *līlā-śakti* by which Rāma was left behind serves the *tattva* of this *līlā* well. Sanātana Goswāmī suggests that the three wonders of Kṛṣṇa's waking without his mother's call, Kṛṣṇa's personally waking the calves and calling his friends, and Rāma's absence at the outset of this *līlā* are one after another progressively more astonishing. Śrī Jīva Goswāmī comments that each word, sentence, verse, and topic in this pastime from beginning to end is filled with more wonder than anything described previously in the text of the *Bhāgavatam*. Here we cannot help but notice Śrī Jīva's preference for *sakhya* over the *vātsalya-līlās* that precede this chapter.

Rāma and Kṛṣṇa's cowherding and sporting throughout the forests and pasturelands of Vraja in fraternal love create considerable tension between fraternal and parental love, which are often at odds with one another. The desire for herding brings with it worrisome separation for those in parental love, as Rāma and Kṛṣṇa begin to lead unchaperoned lives in the forest with their friends. But at least their friends are pious and, as much as can

6. In the final year of Kṛṣṇa's childhood, the cowherd community relocates from Gokula to Vṛndāvana, crossing the Yamunā. From the last year of his childhood through his entire boyhood, the community nomadically roams between Vṛndāvana and Nandīśvara. During Kṛṣṇa's adolescence, the community establishes permanent residences throughout the area, with Nanda residing in Nandīśvara.

be expected at this age, well behaved despite their unbridled enthusiasm. And they arrive in Nanda Bābā's courtyard at sunrise like never-ending waves of the milk ocean, their calves before them, both boys and calves uncountable—*asaṅkhya*—in number. Can one ever have too many cowherd friends? Can cowherd friends ever have too many cows?

But how can Nanda's courtyard accommodate an infinite number of comrades struggling to contain themselves? At dawn this courtyard becomes the very space of fraternal affection itself that knows no bounds. Although Yaśodā is about to lose Kṛṣṇa for the better part of the day, at the same time she gains the company—at least for the morning—of so many affectionate lads, who love her like their own mothers. Just as these extremely beautiful boys bear bugles, sticks, and flutes, they also have parents that are integral to their spiritual identity, whose love for them is the *sañcāri-bhāva* of *suhṛt-rati*.[7] Thus, in Nanda Bābā's house, they are as much or more at home than they are in their own homes. At Nanda's home they are typically nourished with a hearty breakfast prepared by the hands of Śrī Rādhā under Yaśodā and Rohiṇī's direction—a festive setting, to say the least, although tame in comparison to the planned picnic lunch.[8]

On a typical day, eating in earnest begins after milking; and after eating, herding begins. Thus, however much Yaśodā's parental affection swells in the company of Kṛṣṇa and his *sakhās*, she finds it much more difficult to let the boys go when the herding commences. Thus, the learned *rasikas* have labored hard to express this scene that weighs so heavily on their hearts:

> When their beloved Kṛṣṇa departed on this day with his friends and his herd, all the residents of Vraja who were destined to remain behind became silent and motionless. Like a young lady whose lover has left for a foreign land, they stood stunned, covered by the dust upraised by the hooves of the herd. As Gopāla-deva and his friends reached the line demarking the forest from the pasture, Gopāla turned to look back and saw his parents and the entire village

7. Rūpa Goswāmī mentions *suhṛt-rati* (love of the friend) in *Bhakti-rasāmṛta-sindhu* 2.5.128. Here I have used the term broadly to refer to the love between different devotees—the *gopas* and their mothers and the *gopas* and Yaśodā—which acts as a *sañcāri-bhāva*, augmenting the *gopas*' *sthāyi-bhāva* for Kṛṣṇa. The *sakhās*' sticks, flutes, and bugles, as well as their parents, are aspects of the *sakhās*' *sthāyi-bhāva*. Each *sakhā*'s *sthāyi-bhāva* arises out of the *satya-saṅkalpa* quality of his spiritual perfection under the influence of the *svarūpa-śakti*.

8. This picnic lunch represents the first day the boys will stay out herding rather than returning home for lunch. This schedule becomes the norm going forward as Kṛṣṇa ages.

following him. Thus, he stopped his herd and fellow herdsmen and stood still.

Clutching Gopāla's shoes and a parasol, Yaśomatī took the opportunity to again approach Kṛṣṇa, "You are a delicate young boy. If you wander all day long in the forest barefoot and without an umbrella to block the sun, how will we, who worry about your well-being, survive?" Kṛṣṇa replied, "My *dharma* is to herd. Thus, there is no turning back. In this *dharma*, the cows and I are intertwined. While herding, I should not accept more luxury than the herd has, and as they do not have shoes or an umbrella, neither should I."

Pleased to see the virtue of her son, she nonetheless called upon the older cowherds headed by Maṇḍalībhadra, appealing to their parental sensibilities: "I am placing this delicate, restive boy in your charge. He will no longer listen to me. Please always teach and protect him, and if he becomes restless and refuses to obey your order, then report it to me at once. My dear cowherd boys, please arm yourselves with swords, bows, and arrows. Surround my boy and always protect him." She then touched Kṛṣṇa's body while chanting various *mantras*, invoking the names of Bhagavān in order to protect him, and then she tied a protective Narasiṁha *kavaca* around his wrist.

Kṛṣṇa then fell at the feet of his parents, who lifted him up and embraced him, bathing him with their tears and the milk from Yaśodā's breasts. They kissed his lotus face and stroked it with their hands. They smelled his head while choking with tears, unable to speak. Then at last they gave their blessing, acknowledging the undeniable, immutable *dharma* of it all—Kṛṣṇa, after all, is a cowherd![9]

The above pastime happens every single day, beginning with Kṛṣṇa's *śeṣa-kumāra-līlā* as he begins herding calves and continuing throughout his boyhood after he begins herding full-grown cows. That is to say, day after eternal day, as Kṛṣṇa sets out in the morning to herd, it is affirmed that his *dharma* is cowherding. As wetness is the *dharma* of water—its intrinsic, incontrovertible characteristic—Kṛṣṇa's incontrovertible nature is that of a cowherd. Acts that are intrinsically connected to an entity's essential being—their *svarūpānubandhinī* function—cannot be altered. As burning is the *svarūpānubandhinī* function of fire, cowherding is the *svarūpānubandhinī*

9. See *Govinda-līlāmṛta* 5.14–36.

function of *svayaṁ* Bhagavān Śrī Kṛṣṇa. How can I say it more clearly? Śrī Gopāla-deva has been, is, and always will be a cowherd boy. While the stars will fall from the sky and the sun will one day go dark, mountains will turn into valleys, rivers will turn into oceans, and the entire universe will enfold back into Viṣṇu, Kṛṣṇa in his abode—Vraja—will always be a cowherd boy.

Thus, the boys entered the forest, their calves before them, marching to the sound of millions of horns and flutes intermingled with cowherds shouting joyously and calves mooing loudly, sounds that made Balarāma's heart tremble. While the villagers wept piteously in separation, the forest, full of flora, showcased her capacity to nourish the calves and cater to their curiosity, since the calves, being *Bos indicus*, were not only grazers but also browsers. Thus the forest assisted Kṛṣṇa in his *dharma*, indicating that his labor of herding would be no more than play in her suitable setting. Vṛndāvana also began to seductively reveal her prospect of mystery and adventure for the cowherds, all the while delighting in her ensuing union with Mādhava. During the spring season—*mādhava*—the forest enlivens the senses with new beginnings full of hope, making the heart happy. But Mādhava—spring himself and much more—enlivened the forest with the prospect of *prema* as he entered her loving and longing embrace that in concert with her flora and fauna played to all of his senses.

The bees, birds, insects, and animals all played sweet sounds pleasing to Gopāla's ears. The wind playfully blew ever so gently, bearing the cooling moisture of the clear ponds, pleasing Gopāla's sense of touch, and also playing to his sense of smell by carrying the sweet fragrance of the lotus. The composite beauty of the entire forest played itself out as an offering to Gopāla's eyes. Its many ponds provided the sweetest refreshing water for Gopāla's tongue to taste, and these placid and clear pools settled silently and peacefully in his mind. And the boys played.

First the cowherds played at decorating themselves with different colored clays from the forest floor, with *guñjā* berries, fruits, flowers, flower buds, leaves of different shapes and shades, different colored grasses of varying lengths, and other natural ornaments—all this despite the fact that their mothers had already dressed and decorated them before they left their homes with what the worldly would consider expensive jewelry. These *gopas* were more at home in the forest with Kṛṣṇa than they were in their own homes, and daily in their mirthful youth they solemnly swore to one another (ignoring their inability to uphold such vows) never to return to the village again. So absorbed were they in play, they saw no difference between their expensive pearls from home and the common *guñjā* berries from the forest. They did not consider that one thing was better than another by any standard other than their own fancy, and by this rubric, whatever they did feel was more valuable they brought to Kṛṣṇa's attention for his pleasure. Carefree and thus without concern for expense, they reveled only in the wealth of *sakhya-prema*.

The boys carried their picnic lunches in sacks tied on the end of sticks held over their shoulders, but instead of thinking about lunch, their minds and senses were captivated by the enchanted forest, which turned down the fire of each boy's digestion. When these fires did burn, they burned as much for appeasing Kṛṣṇa's hunger as for their own. After all, he is himself the fire of digestion, and he lives only for the nourishment of his friends.[10] If they are pleased, he is pleased. If he is pleased, they are pleased. Sometimes they serve him, and sometimes he serves them. In either case, he is satisfied, the two being one in fraternal love. In this spirit, they sported as equals. Enchanted by the prospect of play that the forest held, they tied their lunches onto tree branches to free both hands for collectively stealing and concealing the lunch of one of their comrades. They tossed it above their heads to one another, keeping it out of the tearful owner's reach before returning it to him in a drama directed by the movements of Kṛṣṇa's lotus eyes. When Kṛṣṇa's love-laden glance then fixed itself on the clouded face of his tearful friend, that friend's heart thundered, calling back its tears, causing that *sakhā*'s lips to part the clouds with the brightness of his smile surrounded by the boundless sky of playful, loving friends. Sometimes Kṛṣṇa's friends stole his lunch, tossing it among themselves, playing keep-away with it. On such occasions, one boy from a poorer family would throw his lunch to Kṛṣṇa and then sit down with Kṛṣṇa's more opulent lunch and eat the rich *purī*, *halavā*, *kacaurī*, and *laḍḍus*, while Kṛṣṇa sat with him and happily ate the friend's simple rice, *capātī*, and *sabjī*.

Such was their playful love in union that gave way to love in separation when Kṛṣṇa was drawn by the beauty and mystery of the forest to venture unaccompanied, having sent his *sakhās* to search for their calves. The boys' hearts, grown fonder by the fuel of such separation, drove the vehicles of their bodies in a race to catch up to Kṛṣṇa, each exclaiming, "I will touch him first! No, I will touch him first!" And together they all touched him, each first in his own mind, each proudly and appropriately claiming

10. In *Bhagavad-gītā* 15.14, Kṛṣṇa identifies himself with everyone's fire of digestion—*ahaṁ vaiśvānaro*.

victory—proud to give pleasure to Kṛṣṇa—as their union triumphed over separation. Such is *sakhya-prema*, proud yet pure.

They played their flutes to indicate one thing and then suddenly another, the wisdom of cowherds alone capable of grasping their intentions. Some blew their horns such that the sounds made Kṛṣṇa laugh, while others considered their horns and flute inharmonious with the natural sounds of the forest, the sounds of birds, bees, and crickets. Thus, the boys imitated these natural sounds themselves. In this way, with all of their sounds together, both natural and unnatural, they created a supernatural concert not only pleasing to the ear but profound, resolving all philosophical conundrums.

Some boys reasoned that it is speed first and foremost for which cowherds are praised, and thus they chased and magically appeared to catch their own shadows. Others imitated the gracefulness of the swans, the songs of the cranes, and the dancing of peacocks, thinking themselves high-minded and their games superior to the shadow-chasing antics of their friends. Seeking to outdo everyone else, others climbed high in the trees and imitated the monkeys, declaring themselves to be the best of *yogīs*, moving about dexterously without ever touching the ground. However, others made similar claims of levitation while chanting *oṁkāra* in imitation of the croaking of frogs and leaping along with them. Joining the competition, others chanted "Nārāyaṇa" into the hollow of caves in reciprocation with their own echoes, while others upon Kṛṣṇa's suggestion simply looked at their own reflections in the water in mockery of self-worship—*ahaṅgrahopāsanā*. In the midst of such amusement, the youngest boys served Kṛṣṇa personally as he relished these astonishing antics of the other skillful and playful cowherds. Indeed, Śukadeva was not exaggerating when he exclaimed in awe that the magic of *māyā*, the gnosis of *jñānīs*, the *yoga* of *yogīs*, and the *bhakti* of *bhaktas* such as Nārada are all surpassed by such *sakhās' prema*.[11] Thus, he was puzzled as to how these boys attained a measure of love that turns God into a cowherd—an equal![12] It is to sages such as Śuka that I offer such a bold book as an answer, seeking their approval and blessing. If not by *karma*, *jñāna*,

11. *Śrīmad Bhāgavatam* 10.12.11.

12. In *Bhakti-rasāmṛta-sindhu* 3.3.133, Rūpa Goswāmī cites this verse (*Śrīmad Bhāgavatam* 10.12.11) as an example of *sthiti*, permanent attainment of union (*yoga*) in *sakhya-rasa*. This status cannot be attained by *puṇya-karma*. Thus, the word *puṇya* in this verse refers to the "sacred" path of *rāga-bhakti*, the path that corresponds with the goal the boys attained. Jīva Goswāmī also comments that, "Amara-kosa (3.3.159) states: '*puṇyaṁ tu cārv api*. *Puṇya* also means beautiful.' " A beautiful means is required to attain such a beautiful end result.

yoga, or *vaidhī-bhakti*, it must be by mercy alone—*mahat-kṛpā*—that these cowherds attained such good fortune. So says Śrī Rūpa.[13]

Among these blessed *gopas*, there were three groups. One group consisted of *rāgātmikas*—*nitya-siddha* associates of Rāma and Kṛṣṇa. The two other groups were *sambandhānuga-sādhana-siddhas*—one group that entered Kṛṣṇa's *nitya-līlā* from the celestial realm of the *devas* and one that entered this intimate circle of friends from earth. The celestial group also started their sojourn on earth, but having only partially perfected their practice, they took birth among the gods. In other words, this group's incomplete practice of *sambandhānugā-bhakti* resulted in attaining that which those in pursuit of heavenly delight can attain only by perfecting the practice of *varṇāśrama-dharma*. These *gopas* attained heaven and more because they ascended to heaven with something else in mind—a much higher ideal.[14] Thus, their ideal ultimately defined them, and because they were in heaven when Kṛṣṇa manifested his *līlā* on earth, they were blessed to join it rather than return to earth and continue their practice from there—the normal course. With their blessing, let us now allow the *līlā* itself to illustrate their good fortune.

The play of the *gopas* described by Śukadeva was so absorbing and so pleasing to Kṛṣṇa that he and his *sakhās* forgot about the picnic they had planned the night before, for which special individual lunches for each and every *gopa* had been prepared. Thus, Kṛṣṇa's *līlā-śakti* intervened to distract the *gopas* from their play. She did so by allowing the very personification of impiety—Agha—to assume the form of a gigantic python and lie on the forest path, his mouth gaping open. The all-devouring mouth of sin thus opened before the cowherds, causing the pious *devas* to shudder in fear, knowing that despite their heavenly attainment, they remained within serpent-like sin's striking distance.

However, while the gods shuddered in fear and doubt as to the fate of the cowherds, Kṛṣṇa and the *gopas* were fearless. Indeed, their *bhāva* turned the gaping mouth of sin into a playground begging exploration. Gazing upon this forest phenomenon, the majority of the *gopas* concluded that the serpent's mouth was the opening to a vast cave. And while they considered the possibility that it might not be a cave but rather a giant

13. *Bhakti-rasāmṛta-sindhu* 1.2.309. *Rāgānugā-bhakti* begins only by *mahat-kṛpā*.

14. See *Bhagavad-gītā* 6.41. Bhaktivedanta Swami Prabhupāda applies this verse to practitioners not only of *aṣṭāṅga-yoga* but of *bhakti-yoga* as well. In the commentary on *Bhakti-rasāmṛta-sindhu* 3.3.53–55, Jīva Goswāmī considers both those who descended from heaven—*suracaras*—and those coming from earth to be *sādhana-siddhas*.

serpent seeking to devour them, they nonetheless did not hesitate to enter into Aghāsura's mouth. Indeed, pretending in childhood play that it was a serpent of gigantic proportion lying before them, they marched within the cave of Agha's mouth, confident of Kṛṣṇa's protection.

The arrival of Aghāsura in the pages of the *Bhāgavata* is well placed. This *asura*'s intriguing appearance and the curious challenge of entering the cave of his mouth serve the purpose of showcasing the central feature of *sakhya-rasa*, the *sakhās*' confidence in their friendship with Kṛṣṇa. As *śaraṇāgatas*, they were confident of Kṛṣṇa's protection; and as *siddhas*, they were confident of the mutual *prema* they shared with Kṛṣṇa. Thus, throwing caution to the wind, they all marched fearlessly into the jaws of sin, even as Kṛṣṇa, understanding the situation, desired to protect them and prevent them from entering. Here we find that the power of the *gopas*' liberated will prevailed in its competition with Kṛṣṇa's will, as they entered Agha's mouth despite Kṛṣṇa's desiring otherwise. What, then, is the power of his friends—the power of *sakhya-rasa*? It deftly dispels impiety, dismisses material sanctity, grants salvation, and overwhelms Kṛṣṇa!

There is of course a backstory to the sudden appearance of Aghāsura along the forest path. Thus far, we have only discussed the primary causal factor of the pastime—*līlā-śakti*'s intervention in the interest of keeping the *līlā* on course for its preplanned picnic lunch. However, the backstory is Agha's connection to Kaṁsa and his atrocities, which included sending Pūtanā and Baka to Vraja to kill Kṛṣṇa, both of whom failed miserably and instead met with their own demise. These two were Agha's sister and brother, respectively. Thus, it was not difficult for Kaṁsa to inspire Agha to pursue Kaṁsa's agenda and in the course of doing so avenge Agha's sister and brother. Agha's approach to the task was to swallow Kṛṣṇa's friends and calves. This in turn would surely cause Kṛṣṇa to follow after them and be devoured as well. Thus Agha would avenge his siblings and assist Kaṁsa in his desire to kill Kṛṣṇa. However, although Kṛṣṇa followed his friends, neither he nor his friends and calves met with disaster. For that matter, neither did Agha, who, to the surprise of the gods, attained *bhagavat-sāyujya* and ultimately *sārūpya-mukti*.[15]

As the cowherds followed by their calves entered Agha's mouth like straws proceeding into the fire of Aghāsura's belly, Kṛṣṇa became overwhelmed by

15. Agha merged into the body of Kṛṣṇa (*bhagavat-sāyujya*) and also attained a form like that of Nārāyaṇa (*sārūpya-mukti*).

karuṇa-rasa, the aesthetic rapture of transcendental compassion.[16] Under the influence of *bhakti-rasa*, Kṛṣṇa was overwhelmed with concern for his very life in the form of his friends, whom he could not live without and who also felt the same for him. Although his heart melted with compassion for them, knowing that they had no shelter other than him as they playfully marched toward their apparent demise, his compassion turned to astonishment. Thus, *adbhuta-bhakti-rasa* entered the drama. Kṛṣṇa's discrimination was then momentarily lost, but then *adbhuta* gave way again to *karuṇa*. His heart was filled with compassion for his friends, and he skillfully determined how he could save his friends and calves and at the same time slay Aghāsura. Such transpsychological emotions, followed by his full powers of discrimination, drove Kṛṣṇa to enter the serpent's mouth as his own life was unraveling before his eyes with the prospect of his friends' demise.

This is Kṛṣṇa's primary preoccupation—loving, and thus protecting, his devotees—in comparison to which establishing *dharma* is only secondary.[17] This secondary purpose was accomplished in this case as a by-product of Kṛṣṇa's experiencing astonishment at the working of his *līlā-śakti* and expressing compassion for his friends and acting on it. Aghāsura resisted swallowing, waiting in anticipation for Kṛṣṇa to enter his mouth. However, upon entering, Kṛṣṇa kept the serpent from swallowing, despite the fact that Aghāsura's mouth had closed, by expanding himself within Agha's mouth to save his friends. Thus, Agha suffocated and *dharma* prevailed, while Kṛṣṇa, his friends, and their calves all walked out of the serpent's mouth unharmed. Therefore, the sinful Aghāsura met with his demise, and as we shall see, he met with *mokṣa* as well.

This secondary purpose, however, took precedence in the minds of the *devas* over Kṛṣṇa's primary purpose involving the unseen arrangement of Kṛṣṇa's *līlā-śakti*. Indeed, the gods were not privy to such insights into the intricacies of Kṛṣṇa's primary, internal *śakti*, which *bhakti* is constituted of. However, among the *devas* stood four-headed Brahmā, the intellectual giant above them all. This particular Brahmā was fortunate to have been blessed with *bhakti-saṁskāras* for *sakhya-rasa* at the dawn of the *sṛṣṭi-līlā*. At that time, his *guru* Śrī Gopāla-deva manifested before him—*antara-darśana*—and

16. This *gauṇa-rasa* is different from compassion for the world, which, while desirable, in and of itself does not constitute *bhakti-rasa*. *Karuṇa-rasa* is compassion *within bhakti-rasa*. In this instance, Kṛṣṇa tastes it as the *āśraya*, and his *sakhās* are the *viṣaya*. More typically, Kṛṣṇa is the object of *karuṇa-rasa*, and his elders are its shelter. See *Bhakti-rasāmṛta-sindhu* 4.8.85 for Śrī Rūpa's explanation of Kṛṣṇa as the *āśraya* and his devotees as the *viṣaya*.

17. *Bhagavad-gītā* 4.8.

dressed in *gopa-veśa* and posing in the *jñāna-mudrā*, he imparted the Gopāla *mantra* and impressions of *sakhya-rasa*.[18] Thus, while the other gods were concerned only with *dharma*, Brahmā alone had a natural attraction to Kṛṣṇa's early cowherd life and a budding curiosity as to its nature. But what happened next astounded all the *devas*, including Brahmā.

Just prior to Kṛṣṇa's emerging from Aghāsura's mouth, Agha's *ātmā* burst through the *brahmarandhra* at the top of his head. This is the objective of *siddha-yogīs* seeking to enter into the world of the Paramātmā. However, that world of transcendental majesty was within Kṛṣṇa.[19] Thus, Agha's *ātmā* hovered above, waiting for Kṛṣṇa to emerge from Aghāsura's now-deceased body. Then Kṛṣṇa awarded *sārūpya-mukti* to the *ātmā* of Agha.[20] Attaining an effulgent spiritual body like that of Nārāyaṇa/Paramātmā, this *mukta* respectfully awaited Kṛṣṇa's emergence from his previous sinful serpent's body. Then, in his newly acquired spiritual body, brilliant and blinding in its effulgence, he appeared to merge into the body of Kṛṣṇa as Kṛṣṇa himself had emerged from Agha's previous body! The *ātmā* itself cannot be seen, even with celestial eyes. Thus, it was the effulgence of Agha's spiritual body that the gods glimpsed as it entered into Gopāla Kṛṣṇa, in whom even Nārāyaṇa is contained. Here we find the beginning of the lesson in *tattva* that this *līlā* underscores—*kṛṣṇas tu bhagavān svayam*. Knowing Kṛṣṇa to be the source of all forms of divinity is the key to understanding the essential *tattva* of *Śrīmad Bhāgavatam*, which revolves around this central truth of

18. *Gopāla-tāpanī Upaniṣad*, *Brahma Saṁhitā*, and *Śrīmad Bhāgavatam* all describe Brahmā's *darśana* of Kṛṣṇa, from whom Brahmā received initiation and spiritual instruction. In *Śrīmad Bhāgavatam* 2.9.19, Kṛṣṇa, smiling, extends his hand to Brahmā. As he clasps Brahmā's hand, Kṛṣṇa showers Brahmā with impressions of *sakhya-rasa*. In *Śrīmad Bhāgavatam* 2.9.30, Brahmā says, *yāvat sakhā sakhyur iveśa te kṛtaḥ*, which Bhaktivedanta Swami Prabhupāda translates, "You have shaken hands with me just as a friend does with a friend [as if equal in position]." Prabhupāda comments that the implication here is that Brahmā will attain *sakhya-rasa*. Similarly, paraphrasing Brahmā, Viśvanātha Cakravartī writes, "Brahmā reveals his desire, praying, 'O Lord! You have treated me as a friend treats a friend, by touching me with your hand! May I attain *bhakti* with a feeling of friendship!' " Notably, in his comments on 10.86.50, wherein Kṛṣṇa, smiling, also clasps the hand of the *brāhmaṇa* Śrutadeva, Viśvanātha Cakravartī comments, "He took Śrutadeva's hand in his, indicating that he would drown Śrutadeva in *sakhya-rasa*."

19. Majesty is only one aspect of Kṛṣṇa.

20. Opinions as to Agha's final destination differ, ranging from *sāyujya* to *sārūpya*. The word *ātma-sāmyam* in 10.12.38 is supportive of *sārūpya*, which is typically granted only to devotees. Thus, for Kṛṣṇa to bestow this upon a non-devotee underscores his magnanimous disposition. Then again, *Bhakti-rasāmṛta-sindhu* 1.2.279 explains that the enemies that Kṛṣṇa liberates generally attain *sāyujya*, but some of them attain a semblance of a form similar to God's form (*sārūpyābhāsam*) and remain absorbed in the happiness of Brahman.

the *brahma-vimohana-līlā*. Knowing this, Kṛṣṇa asserts in his song to Arjuna, one can engage in the kind of worship by which one can enter the *rāga-mārga*—*budhā bhāva-samanvitāḥ*.[21] The way to *sakhya-rati* involves locating and recognizing that person who can accept such love—Rasarāja Kṛṣṇa.[22]

Aghāsura did not attain *sakhya-rati*, which as we know involves the specific culture of *sambandhānugā-bhakti*. Instead, he attained the more general *sārūpya-mukti*. However, Agha's attainment *was* a by-product of Kṛṣṇa's own absorption in *sakhya-rasa*. Kṛṣṇa's compassion for his *sakhās* resulted in an overflow of his kindness, by which Agha became a *kṛpā-siddha*, one whose spiritual perfection is a result of mercy—*kṛpā*—rather than a result of spiritual practice. There is no instance of such attainment on the part of an *asura* in relation to any other form of God. Only Śrī Kṛṣṇa grants *mokṣa* to those who approach him with inimical feelings! Thus, no form of God is more merciful.[23]

Furthermore, while Agha's *ātmā* became a *mukta*, its identity as Agha having dissolved, his serpent body left behind was purified and preserved, serving as an ongoing place of pastimes for Kṛṣṇa and his friends—a cave with a gaping opening that extended inward a great distance. In the pages of the *Bhāgavatam* itself, Śukamuni describes this as follows:

> O Rāja, the body of the boa dried [but did not decay] and became a cave-like place of amusement for the cowherds for a long, long time to come. This deed—Hari and his dear friends' dance with near death and the deliverance of Agha—occurred during the final period of the cowherds' *kumāra* age. However, the boys who witnessed it disclosed it to others in Vraja a year later, during the beginning of their *paugaṇḍa* age [as if it had just occurred].[24]

21. *Bhagavad-gītā* 10.8.

22. The importance of establishing that Kṛṣṇa is the source of Nārāyaṇa, rather than one of Nārāyaṇa's *avatāras*, also lies in the fact that if Kṛṣṇa were an *avatāra* of Nārāyaṇa, he would not have a realm of his own (Goloka), in which *sakhya*, *vātsalya*, and *mādhurya rasas* were ideals that *sādhakas* could embrace, for in all of Vaikuṇṭha only *dāsya* and *śānta rasas* serve as goals one can attain.

23. *Kṛṣṇa Sandarbha* 29.

24. *Śrīmad Bhāgavatam* 10.12.36–37. Owing to the influence of *bhakti*, it is not uncommon for a *mukta*'s material body to exhibit no signs of decay for an extended period of time after he or she passes on. This is true even for *yogīs* who factor some *bhakti* into their *sādhana*. A famous example is that of Paramahansa Yogananda. Mortuary Director Mr. Harry T. Rowe reported, "No physical disintegration was visible in his body even twenty days after death. . . . No indication of mold was visible on his skin, and no visible drying up took place in the bodily tissues. . . . No odor of decay emanated from his body at any time."

Curiously, this fantastic story was not shared with the elders of Vraja until one year after it occurred, and then as if it had just happened. Of course, when it was shared with the elders of Vraja, it was in their elderly estimation barely believable, for young boys are known to exaggerate. But *sakhya-rati-sādhakas* believe it, as did Rāja Parīkṣit![25] And the mystery of why it took one year for the story to be told is something attentive practitioners should be keen to understand. Indeed, the *rāja*, sincere and serious in his budding *rati*, rightfully reasoned that there should be no secrets between *guru* and *śiṣya*. To the sincere, spiritually advanced student, the teacher reveals all the esoteric truths required for attaining the goal of *sakhya-rasa*. Understanding the king's keen interest and how it had enabled him to catch and further inquire about this detail of the narrative, Bādarāyaṇi lost external consciousness,[26] exhibiting the *sāttvika-bhāva* of *pralaya* as he had done previously. Knowing that Śukadeva was prone to such bouts of ecstasy, Rāja Parīkṣit had asked his son Janamejaya to assemble various instruments for *kīrtana*. Thus, to revive sagely Śukadeva, Nārada Ṛṣi with great effort led the *kīrtana* of Rādhikā-ramaṇa *nāma* as others responded. Then, coming to his senses from the depths of his *samādhi*, the sage Śuka related to the *rāja* the balance of the *līlā* involving the stunning nature of *sakhya-rasa* witnessed by Brahmā, his subsequent bewilderment, and his prayerful petition.

25. In *Bhakti-rasāmṛta-sindhu* 3.2.90, Rūpa Goswāmī places Rāja Parīkṣit in *dāsya-rasa* as a *pāriṣada* of Kṛṣṇa in Dvārakā.

26. Upon hearing the *rāja*'s question, the sage was reminded of the unparalleled sweetness and grandeur of the *līlā* described in the subsequent chapter, leading him into a deep trance.

8

Brahmā Bewildered

What caused Śukadeva to lose external consciousness and fall into a swoon of ecstasy at the thought of answering Rāja Parīkṣit's question? To answer his question, the sage would have to proceed with the description of Kṛṣṇa's forest luncheon with his friends and how such intimacy, which exceeds that of earlier descriptions of their play, led to an even greater display of *aiśvarya* than the salvation of Aghāsura. Vaiyāsaki, the *śiṣya* of Vyāsa, would also have to speak about both the bewilderment and the progress in *sambandhānugā-bhakti* of Brahmā, the *parama-guru* of his *guru*! How could the *guru* of Nārada—Brahmā—become bewildered? As we shall see, a glimpse into the implications of his heart's desire for *sakhya-rasa* precipitates Brahmā's *vimohana*, through which Kṛṣṇa drives home the *tattva* of his own position as *svayaṁ* Bhagavān.

As we have seen, typically the cowherds consume a hearty breakfast in the presence of Nanda Bābā prior to their day of herding. But Nanda and Yaśodā were not present to oversee the cowherds' picnic luncheon on their first of many extended days in the forest. And this further facilitated the cowherd *sakhās*' intimate dealings with one another.

While the *sakhās* celebrated the prowess of Kṛṣṇa in dealing with Aghāsura, comparing it to their own abilities, Hari suggested they all sit and picnic together along the banks of a placid pool within the Yamunā that was pleasing to the mind.

> O friends! This place is possessed of a wealth of all things suitable for the occasion. Here we find plenty of room for sitting in rows on soft, clean sand, and the setting is filled with fragrance from the Yamunā's blossoming lotuses, while the celebrated bees hum

> as if singing to us, and the clear, cool water and the shade of trees provide relief from the heat of the sun. Come, gather lotus leaves to use as plates, and let the calves drink and graze freely![1]

Thus, the *gopas* watered their calves and pastured them on green grasses, feeling confident that the grasses would keep them in reach while the boys themselves lunched. Then, exercising their extraordinary creative sensibilities, some gathered leaves, others flowers, fruits, tree bark, or rocks, and made them into an artistic variety of plates suitable for assorted dishes. They did this after first retrieving their lunch baskets from the trees they had hung them on to facilitate their previous play, ensuring that it would in no way be impeded. Lunches in hand and plates arranged, they sat in rows of concentric circles around Gopāla-deva, appearing much like the many petals of a lotus, the whorl of which was wonderful Kṛṣṇa. Then, by the force of overwhelming *sakhya-prema* for each and every *gopa*, Kṛṣṇa expanded into unlimited, identical forms of himself such that each *gopa* experienced Gopāla-deva sitting directly in front of him alone, drawing his undivided attention! Each boy felt that Kṛṣṇa loved him the most, and each boy was correct.[2]

As they unpacked their lunches, they began to taste each and every item like accomplished connoisseurs and determine relative to their own palate which of the innumerable preparations were most tasteful. Upon arriving at such a conclusion concerning any particular dish, each boy immediately removed that preparation from his own mouth before swallowing and placed it instead in Kṛṣṇa's mouth. Those preparations that were considered second best were immediately passed on to one of their friends, and those taking third place in each individual cowherd's mind they ate themselves. Because each cowherd boy arrived at a different opinion in his grading of the delicious items, each boy ended up eating every dish. Furthermore, items that any *gopa* previously considered suitable only for his own consumption—being less tasty than others—when passed on to him from a friend of different opinion, tasted best, as did and more so

1. Based on *Śrīmad Bhāgavatam* 10.13.5–6.

2. In *Caitanya-caritāmṛta* 2.11.233, Kṛṣṇadāsa Kavirāja makes a comparison between this scene and Śrī Caitanya's appearing simultaneously in four different *saṅkīrtana* groups during his *madhya-līlā* in Purī, at which time each group thought that Mahāprabhu was present only in their group and each member of each group experienced his undivided attention.

the items Kṛṣṇa took from his mouth and pressed into theirs. Thus, every preparation was best!

Although all of this feasting among very hungry boys left little time for joking, they nonetheless laughed heartily at their own eating antics and the various faces they made at one another in pretense. They joked and made merry mischief in ways that would never have been tolerated at Nanda's breakfast table. Thus, they also tasted *hāsya-rasa*, the whole affair intensely pleasing to the center of this scene, Kānāi Kṛṣṇa, who in other circles is seen as the enjoyer of all sacrifice, the stomach of the body of Vedic ritual. Oh! How different he appears as the object of fraternal love to the vision perfected by lifetimes of service and sacrifice—*kṛta-puṇya-puñjāḥ*! And this is precisely how the scene struck the spiritually curious four-headed Brahmā.

This is the form that Brahmā saw:

> He who is otherwise the enjoyer of the gods' sacrifices, *yajña-bhuk*, took pleasure instead in childish play, *bāla-keli*. He bore a flute in his belt along with a buffalo horn and herding staff. He held yogurt rice with pieces of fruit between the fingers of his left hand. Standing in the midst of his friends, he made them laugh as he joked and played with them.[3]

These were his thoughts:

> How could this be? This same Nārāyaṇa appeared before me in my meditation—*antara-darśana*—at the dawn of creation in the form of a *gopa*, his right hand configured in the *jñāna-mudrā*. This *gopa* form aroused fraternal feelings of love in my heart, and that same Gopāla-deva instructed me in a very broad sense about the secrets of *śāstra*, its *sambandha*, *abhidheya*, and *prayojana*, his instruction rich with far-reaching esoteric implications that I have not yet fully understood. Subsequently, in my abode I have been worshiping that same Nārāyaṇa in the form of the *mahā-puruṣa*, who lies comfortably on the bed of Ananta Śeṣa. He is the Lord of sacrifice—*yajña-bhuk*—to whom I offer sacrifice during his waking hours by which he appears to eat,[4] and then I experience separation

3. *Śrīmad Bhāgavatam* 10.13.11.

4. Here Brahmā is also questioning whether the *mahā-puruṣa* actually eats, whereas there is no doubt that Kṛṣṇa does. Indeed, by comparison, the *mahā-puruṣa* can be considered

from him during his mystic sleep. He appears to be in one place yet at the same time appears all-pervasive, as if he has innumerable heads, arms, and legs. He teaches the *aṅgas* of *vaidhī-bhakti*, to which I adhere so strictly that others often refer to me as Vidhi. Yet I have been permanently affected by the faint feelings of fraternal love that I felt in the presence of Gopāla Kṛṣṇa—sentiments that the *mahā-puruṣa* does not entertain.

Then, one day the *devas* approached me with concern for the well-being of the earth, and thus I relayed their concerns to Nārāyaṇa, who informed me that he would soon appear on earth. In doing so, he also fulfilled his promise to the residents of Vraja that he would appear in their cowherd lineage to make up for my abrupt and somewhat inappropriate marriage to the Vraja *gopī* Gāyatrī-devī. He did so in the form of Gopāla Kṛṣṇa, who is again stirring feelings of fraternal love in my heart that, as of yet, I do not know how to systematically cultivate.

This is confusing enough, but moreover now it appears to me that perhaps the Nārāyaṇa conception of Bhagavān is contained within this form of Gopāla Kṛṣṇa, who merged Aghāsura into his *gopa-svarūpa* and awarded Agha a form like Nārāyaṇa's. Why did he do so? Simply because despite the *asura*'s evil intentions, Agha inadvertently afforded Kṛṣṇa's friends a fantasy playground in the form of his serpent body, thereby pleasing Kṛṣṇa. Such is Kṛṣṇa's love for his friends, and that attracts me. But the conduct of this cowherd Kṛṣṇa during his picnic lunch bewilders me. Can the *mahā-puruṣa* and Nārāyaṇa himself be but partial manifestations of this cowherd boy bearing yogurt rice mixed with fruit in his left hand and about to press it into the mouth of one of his friends? Who are these friends? Can this very intimate setting and the exchange between Kṛṣṇa and his friends constitute a form of worship and service? Is it possible that this is what the culture of fraternal love comes to in due course, or is my *guru* in *jñāna-mudrā* being misrepresented by an imposter?

---

yajña-bhuk, or one who does not literally eat. He may accept sacrifices from everywhere in the form of the *mahā-puruṣa*, but for eating he remains in Vraja. That said, the *yajña-bhuk* form of Viṣṇu is said to preside over the human function of eating.

Unbeknown to Brahmā, Kṛṣṇa's *līlā-śakti* arranged for Brahmā to witness Kṛṣṇa's picnic, thus fulfilling Kṛṣṇa's desire to answer the prayers of his *rāga-mārga-sādhaka* even while fully absorbed in *prema-rasa* with his liberated *sakhās*. Indeed, Brahmā needed to become acquainted not only with Vraja Kṛṣṇa himself as the *viṣaya-ālambana* of *sakhya-rasa* but also with *sakhya-rasa*'s *āśraya-ālambana* in the form of the Vraja *gopas*. Of course, this *sakhya-rasa* setting also included the relative *uddīpana-vibhāvas*, *sañcāri-bhāvas*, *anubhāvas*, and *sāttvika-bhāvas* of *sakhya-rasa*. Although it was Kṛṣṇa's desire to bring Brahmā into this *prakāśa* of his pastimes, his *līlā-śakti* arranged that his desire remained unknown to others, so as not to disturb his *līlā*. In other words, Brahmā arrived by Bhagavān's desire, but Gopāla-deva himself remained almost unaware of his own role in bringing him there in order that the sweetness of his *sakhya-rasa-līlā* would not be interrupted by a display of majesty.

As we shall see ahead, however, Brahmā's truly teachable moment appeared only after his doubts had been cleared as to the Godhood of Gopāla—after he fully understood the theological implications of *kṛṣṇas tu bhagavān svayam*.[5] Thus Kṛṣṇa's *aiśvarya* eventually came into play and in no uncertain terms, but only after his calves and cowherd friends were temporarily removed from the picture. How did this happen, and where did they go? Oh! The very thought of this, beginning with the disappearance of the calves, gave rise to fear in the heart of Śukadeva, who at this point so identified with the cowherds in the drama that he experienced their fear for the calves' safety, a fear that threatened to dampen their hunger and disturb their play.[6] How can a cowherd think of or do anything else if his calves' safety is in question?

By *līlā-śakti*'s arrangement the calves wandered out of sight, providing an entry point for Kṛṣṇa's *aiśvarya-śakti* to manifest itself and educate Brahmā. Kṛṣṇa then rose to the occasion of the boys' concern and assured them no harm would come to the calves. He also informed them that he would be saddened if they stopped eating and assured them that fear itself was afraid

5. It is in this chapter of the *Bhāgavatam* that this foundational and singularly most important point of *siddhānta*—that Kṛṣṇa is the source of all forms of the Godhead—is taught in *līlā* narrative form. This point first appears in the text's first section on *avatāra-tattva* in 1.3.28.

6. Here the cowherds are not fearful of Kṛṣṇa, which would be an instance of *bhayānaka-rasa* being incompatible with *sakhya-rasa*, but rather the cowherds' fear is for circumstances that may endanger Kṛṣṇa's calves, which renders *bhayānaka-rasa* neutral in relation to *sakhya-rasa*.

of him. He then went alone to find the calves himself, eating as he went. Thus, his gradual transition in mood from *mādhurya* to *aiśvarya* began.

Meanwhile, Brahmā had exerted his own power in an effort to steal the calves as part of his plan to test the powers of Kṛṣṇa, unaware that Brahmā's power had no efficacy in this realm governed by Kṛṣṇa's *svarūpa-śakti*. Then, as Kṛṣṇa searched everywhere and did not find the calves, now separated from them and his cowherds, his *aiśvarya* took precedence, and he understood that his *līlā-śakti* had hidden the calves from sight by confining them to an individual *līlā-prakāśa*, making them otherwise invisible. He also understood that at the same time, Brahmā was attempting to test his prowess. Returning to the setting of the picnic, he saw that his *līlā-śakti* had also placed his friends in the same condition, allowing Brahmā for the moment to think that he had kidnapped both the calves and cowherds on the strength of his own power. Kṛṣṇa's *līlā-śakti* accomplished this by manifesting *māyic* representations of the boys and calves that Brahmā kidnapped and rendered unconscious in a nearby cave. Understanding all of this in his now fully manifest omniscience, Śrī Bhagavān Gopāla-deva began to demonstrate his prowess to Brahmā. He did so first by pretending to be bewildered as to where to the calves and cowherds had gone.[7]

Seeing Kṛṣṇa, who appeared to be confused about the whereabouts of his calves and friends, Brahmā thought the exercise of his power was successful. He is, after all, quite powerful in his own right, or so it would seem. The post of Brahmā is that of the presiding deity of *buddhi-tattva*—*vijñāna-śakti*.[8] *Buddhi*—or intellect—is, according to *Bhāgavata* Sāṅkhya, a result of *ahaṅkāra* mixing with *raja-guṇa*. It is active—*rajas*—but in the form of creating, discriminating, learning, and making wise decisions. It is thus constituted of that which *manas* (the cognitive faculty) lacks and without which *manas* is simply the chattering seat of endless thoughts and emotions that toss and turn in relation to impressions recorded on the *citta*, which we identify with through *ahaṅkāra*.

In this way, *buddhi* is the key to unravelling *ahaṅkāra*. It enables us to discriminate, learn, and make wise decisions as to the nature of the overarching discontent in our lives that arises from *ahaṅkāra* itself. But without *buddhi*, this discontent will never be overcome, and *ahaṅkāra* will

7. In his *Siddhānta-ratna*, Baladeva Vidyābhūṣaṇa cites *āśaṅkā* (apparent doubt) and *moha* (apparent confusion) on Kṛṣṇa's part as to where the calves and boys went as examples of apparent character flaws in the omniscient Godhead, which endear his devotees to him and are thus necessary aspects of the *viṣaya-ālambana* of Vraja *prema*.

8. *Śrīmad Bhāgavatam* 3.9.24. See Viśvanātha Cakravartī's commentary.

never be understood to be the very source of it. However, when through *buddhi* this is understood, our attention—*citta*—can be turned inward to the actual self and its source, giving rise to permanent spiritual impressions and subsequent spiritual thoughts and emotions. *Buddhi* can function in this way when it is spiritualized by revelation—by the directives of *śāstra* that shed light on our material predicament and the transrational solution to it, *sādhana*. As Kṛṣṇa states in the *Gītā*, "I give *buddhi* by which one can come to me."[9] Accordingly, it is Kṛṣṇa who gives us Brahmā. Formal sectarian considerations aside, he is the original member of the Gauḍīya *sampradāya*, in that he is the first to receive and pass on its principal *dīkṣā-mantra*—the eighteen-syllable Gopāla *mantra*. And since Brahmā is the presiding deity of *buddhi*, it is he who manifests the Veda—Eastern revelation. He does so in the context of Viṣṇu's drama of creation—*sṛṣṭi-līlā*.

Although Brahmā is also associated with creation, he does not have the power to create unto himself. He derives that power from Viṣṇu and prays not to get carried away with his intellect but to keep it tied to revelation instead and to the pursuit of its stated goal rather than letting it get to his four heads. It would appear from this *līlā* that he failed in this regard. However, under closer examination, we find that this is not the case. He is, after all, one of our *gurus*—indeed, the founder of our *sampradāya*.[10]

Remembering the early history of Brahmā cited above, we know that he, unlike some Brahmās, is a *bhakta*.[11] We also know that he was initiated with the Gopāla *mantra* and instructed in its efficacy. At that time, he also received impressions of *sakhya-rati* from *gopaveśa* Kṛṣṇa. However, it was only much later—at this time—that Kṛṣṇa saw fit to acquaint him more fully with the implications of that fraternal love, to acquaint him with its *ālambana-vibhāva* and other related ecstatic components of *sakhya-rasa*. Thus, even before Brahmā thought to test the powers of Kṛṣṇa, he himself was under the power of Kṛṣṇa, whose *līlā-śakti* brought him there for Kṛṣṇa's own purpose! Goodness, how can Kṛṣṇa do so many things at once?

9. *Bhagavad-gītā* 10.10. In this verse, *buddhi-yoga* can also be construed to refer to *bhakti-yoga*. Baladeva Vidyābhūṣaṇa comments that Kṛṣṇa elevates one's intelligence (*buddhi*) and destroys the ignorance within.

10. This notion—the Brahmā-Madhva-Gauḍīya *sampradāya*—is supported by the early writing of Kavi-karṇapūra and is also acknowledged by Viśvanātha Cakravartī, Baladeva Vidyābhūṣaṇa, Ṭhākura Bhaktivinoda, and many other Gauḍīya *ācāryas*.

11. Typically, *jīvas* attain this post through perfect execution of the *karma-mārga*—*varṇāśrama*—for one hundred lifetimes. However, a *jñānī* or a devotee can also attain the post of Brahmā, and sometimes Viṣṇu himself assumes this post. An example of attaining this post through *bhakti* is *Bṛhad-bhāgavatāmṛta*'s cowherd Gopa-kumāra.

Such is his *acintya-śakti*! Thus, we can find no fault in Brahmā. Although it appears that his intellect went to his heads, this was all part of Kṛṣṇa's arrangement to teach him the core principle of *tattva—kṛṣṇas tu bhagavān svayam*—central to attaining the ideal of *sakhya-rasa* and acquaint him with the ingredients of *sakhya-rasa*. Furthermore, through Brahmā, Kṛṣṇa also teaches all *sādhakas* that intellect unto itself, unhinged from revelation, is spiritually bankrupt: it has no power to capture Kṛṣṇa or his friends.

Of course, Brahmā thought he had outsmarted Kṛṣṇa. Then he tried to hide himself to see what would happen next. By the calculation of his own celestial time, he left the scene of his apparent crime for but a moment, and in that moment Kṛṣṇa manifested forms of himself that were exact replicas of all the *gopas* and their calves. While in Brahmā's time he left the scene for a very short time, in earthly time this span constituted one year. Thus, for one year on earth, Kṛṣṇa continued his pastimes with exact replicas of his friends and calves.

The original calves and cowherds were manifestations of Kṛṣṇa's internal *śakti*, which Brahmā does not have the power to delude. By *līlā-śakti*'s arrangement, these *śakti-tattva* cowherds and their calves remained invisible, blissfully absorbed in an eternal moment of Kṛṣṇa *līlā*. The replica forms that Kṛṣṇa manifested, however, were not *śakti-tattva*. They were Kṛṣṇa himself—*śaktimān*. This manifestation is remarkable, in terms of both its *aiśvarya* and its *mādhurya*. First we will consider its *mādhurya*, its sweetness—and that from both the *sakhya-* and *vātsalya-rasa* perspectives.

Kṛṣṇa's self-manifested duplicates of all his cowherd friends and their calves were identical to the original boys in every respect down to the minutest detail, including their moods, mannerisms, and memories. The sweet implication of this from the *sakhya-rasa* perspective is the extent to which Kṛṣṇa understood his friends' physical details, hearts, and minds and, by extension, their calves. After all, he had examined the heart of each and every one of them and confirmed his friendship with them while sitting simultaneously before each and every boy during their picnic, much as Kṛṣṇa confirmed his romantic love for each and every *gopī* during their *rāsa* dance.

There was nothing that he did not know about his *sakhās*; such was his fraternal love for them. And how could it be otherwise, when they themselves were each unique varieties of fraternal love of Kṛṣṇa personified? If you love someone, they will tell you all of their secrets. Thus, there were no secrets between each cowherd boy and his object of love, Gopāla

Kṛṣṇa—experienced as he was through the lens of each of the four basic types of *sakhya-rati.*

Sage Śukadeva explains this manifestation of Kṛṣṇa's love for his friends thus:

> Kṛṣṇa assumed the forms—hands, feet, and bodily features—of as many calves and calf-herders as there were. He also took on the shape of their many staffs, horns, flutes, lunch bags, ornaments, and garments and adopted their individual behaviors, qualities, names, ages, appearances, and playful personalities.[12]

However, the fact that the newly manifested *gopas* were all manifestations of Kṛṣṇa himself, who is the object of fraternal love (*viṣaya-ālambana-vibhāva*) presented a problem, given the overriding difference between them and the original *gopas*, who were vessels of fraternal love personified (*āśraya-ālambana-vibhāva*). For Kṛṣṇa to taste *sakhya-rasa*, both of these *ālambana-vibhāvas* must be present. Thus despite the extent to which Kṛṣṇa replicated the *gopas*, he could not experience *sakhya-rasa* with them. This fact of the manifest *līlā* serves to underscore just how irreplaceable and perfect the original *gopas* are, a point implied by Śrī Jīva Goswāmī in his *Prīti Sandarbha* discourse on *sakhya-rasa.*[13]

But this problem does not arise with regard to *vātsalya-rasa.* In this case the newly manifested *gopas* were in fact the *viṣaya-ālambana* of *vātsalya-rasa,* albeit in disguise. And the elders and the cows were the *āśraya-ālambana.* Kṛṣṇa carefully considered how they would feel if they were able to detect that the cowherd boys or calves were missing and therefore replicated them in minute detail. Readers will recall the heartrending tension between these two sentiments—*sakhya* and *vātsalya*—that we felt at the beginning of this narrative. And here we come full circle, as Kṛṣṇa sets off to return to the village after a day of herding. How could he go home alone without his friends and calves? What would their mothers say? How would the cows feel?

The intense parental love that Nanda and Yaśodā experienced for Kṛṣṇa as he set out for the day was shared by all of the adult *gopas* and *gopīs* of Vraja. Although they had their own sons who were Kṛṣṇa's playmates, they desired to have Kṛṣṇa as their son as well. They loved Kṛṣṇa in parental love, and their *suhṛt-rati* for their sons acted as a *sañcāri-bhāva* augmenting

12. *Śrīmad Bhāgavatam* 10.13.19.
13. *Prīti Sandarbha* 100. See Prāṇa Gopāla Goswāmī's commentary.

their *vātsalya-rati* for him. In other words, their love for their own sons was an aspect of their love for Kṛṣṇa.

Earlier in his *kumāra-līlā*, Kṛṣṇa would go to the neighboring houses and behave mischievously, stealing yogurt and corrupting their sons. This then gave the neighboring mothers of Kṛṣṇa's playmates the excuse to complain to Yaśodā. Then in the evening they would relate Kṛṣṇa's misbehavior and their discussions about it with Yaśodā to their husbands, and in this way their day was filled with *hari-kathā* saturated with *vātsalya-rasa*. Thus, when Kṛṣṇa went to the forest with his friends and calves, these neighboring mothers' hearts went with him. As he now returned himself and in the forms of all the boys, their longing to directly experience Kṛṣṇa as their own son was fulfilled. Furthermore, their longing, which Kṛṣṇa could not ignore, being bound by *prema*, created an opening for *vātsalya-rati-sādhakas* to enter the *prakaṭa-līlā* and also attain Kṛṣṇa as their son.[14]

Thus, here we find how the difference between Kṛṣṇa and the otherwise identical expansions of himself in the form of the boys and calves played out in relation to *vātsalya-rasa*. From the description above, it would seem that Kṛṣṇa in the form of his friends should have expressed the same love for the elders that their actual sons did. But here, Kṛṣṇa's power to replicate the boys failed when confronted with the power of *vātsalya-prema* that he was controlled by. In terms of the measure and nature of their love, the parents' love for their sons now constituted their *sthāyi-bhāva* for Kṛṣṇa, and Kṛṣṇa could not respond in any way other than to return such love. However, while the love of the parents for their sons who were now Kṛṣṇa increased day by day—a characteristic of their *prema*—their love for Kṛṣṇa himself in his own charming form as the son of Yaśodā also increased and exceeded their love for their own sons, his expansions.[15] What, then, can be said about Yaśodā's *vātsalya-rasa*?

14. In *Bhakti-rasāmṛta-sindhu* 1.2.307, Rūpa Goswāmī cites the example of a carpenter living in Hastināpura in ancient times who desired to have Kṛṣṇa as his son and worshipped the deity form of Kṛṣṇa with this in mind, serving him in his *sādhaka-deha* alone. In his commentary, Viśvanātha Cakravartī emphasizes that the carpenter did not also engage in meditative *siddha-rūpa-sevā* but was successful nonetheless. Jīva Goswāmī comments that the carpenter attained his ideal during this *prakaṭa-brahma-vimohana-līlā*. This means that during this pastime the intensity of his parental love reached the level required to enter the unmanifest *līlā*.

15. Jīva Goswāmī explains that affection is of three types: because of beauty in the object, because of possessiveness, and because of natural bodily relationship. Aside from the fact that their sons were Kṛṣṇa himself, the parents of the boys had affection for them on the basis of the latter two types, whereas the personal beauty of Kṛṣṇa was lacking in

What has been said above about the parents of the boys also held true for the cows who were the mothers of the calves that Kṛṣṇa had replicated. Although by this time the calves were already weaned yearlings eating pasture grass, their mothers desired to give their milk to them, and this for an entire year, even if it meant not giving milk to their newborn calves. While the adult cowherd men tried to separate the mothers from these calves, they were mostly unsuccessful.[16]

Five or six days before the year ended, Rāma, whose name indicates that he gives pleasure to Kṛṣṇa and his friends, observed the cows' extraordinary affection for these particular calves, as well as the adult cowherds' extraordinary love for their sons. This was clearly Kṛṣṇa's arrangement, for out of great affection he could not keep this secret from Balarāma any longer without constraining his own *ānanda*. Thus, by Kṛṣṇa's arrangement, this is what Balarāma observed:

> The cows grazing on grass atop of Mount Govardhana saw their calves foraging at a distance close to the village and were overcome with affection for them. Self-forgetful, they hastened downhill over terrain difficult for even experienced herdsmen to traverse. Driven by their affection, they ran with their two front and two back feet so close together that it appeared as if they were adeptly running on only two legs instead of four. Heads and tails raised, their necks stretching, humps swaying, they made lowing sounds as milk gushed from their udders. Then, upon catching up to their calves, they made them drink their milk while licking their limbs as if about to swallow them, despite the fact that they had already been weaned.
>
> Seeing this, the herdsmen were frustrated and embarrassed by their inability to prevent it. But when they followed the difficult downhill course of the cows and saw their sons there with the calves, their hearts surged with *rasa*. Thus, their frustration and embarrassment

---

their sons. That beauty was found in Yaśodā's son.

16. In the text of the *Bhāgavata*, the *rāja* asks Śukadeva how the cowherd women could have developed more love for Kṛṣṇa than they felt for their own children. His question comes at the close of the chapter. Śukadeva answers that love in this world is for the body only if one identifies oneself with it, and such self-love when extended into others is the cause of loving them. However, if one understands that one is not the body, one's love is then based on the *ātmā*. It is the *ātmā* that is the actual object of love in this world, and one loves one's body only because one is identified with it. But love of the *ātmā* is based on the fact that the *ātmā* is part and parcel of Kṛṣṇa, who is the perfect object of love.

> were mitigated, and they hoisted their sons up, embraced them, smelled their heads, and attained *anurāga*, the furthest reach of their *sthāyi-bhāva*. Then in due course, the adult *gopas* slowly departed, leaving their sons with great difficulty, their minds happy from embracing their boys, and tears welled up in their eyes remembering them.[17]

Although Rāma witnessed increased affection of the parents for their sons and of the cows for their calves over the course of the passing year, it did not register with him as something out of the ordinary. Nor did his own increased affection for the *gopas* strike him as something out of the ordinary. There were two reasons for this. First of all, although his affection for the *gopas* increased, just as the parents' love for their sons increased, their love for Kṛṣṇa himself also increased. Similarly, Rāma's increased love for his friends was coupled with his increased love for Kṛṣṇa. Thus, in one sense everything seemed normal. Then again, Rāma is the Godhead himself, unlike the parents and cows. Did he not have the power to understand what had taken place? This brings us to the second reason, and the simple answer is that he did not have such power in the face of Kṛṣṇa's power. Surely Kṛṣṇa found it difficult to keep this secret from Rāma, and in the end he could not continue to do so. But he held out from revealing everything to his brother for as long as he could because he felt that had Rāma known what had occurred, Rāma might have felt separation from his friends. Such separation, however, was not experienced by Kṛṣṇa himself, because in his original form he had remained within the now invisible *līlā-prakāśa* along with the calves and cowherds. Thus Kṛṣṇa waited until the year had almost passed before he allowed his *yogamāyā* to lift her influence over Balarāma. This happened gradually so that Kṛṣṇa could taste the *dāsya* aspect of Balarāma's *saṅkula-bhāva*, as Kṛṣṇa's *aiśvarya-śakti* took precedence over his *mādhurya-śakti* and underscored in no uncertain terms his position as *svayaṁ* Bhagavān.

17. *Śrīmad Bhāgavatam* 10.13.30–34. In 10.33, the text invokes the word *jātānurāgā*, while Rūpa Goswāmī describes the *sthāyi-bhāva* of *vātsalya* as reaching only to the stage which precedes *anurāga* (*Bhakti-rasāmṛta-sindhu* 3.4.53). Here the idea is that on this special occasion, in which Kṛṣṇa became the boys and calves, the increased affection in *vātsalya* reached this pitch, while otherwise it does not. This applies also to Yaśodā, who was experiencing increased affection for all of the boys as well as for her own son. Thus, the overall increase was from *rāga* to *anurāga*.

As Rāma gradually began to puzzle over this uncommon display of affection and as his thinking progressed with the lifting of the veil of *yogamāyā*, he arrived at a reverential conclusion and began to taste *dāsya-rasa*. At first, Balarāma, thinking himself and the Vraja residents to be ordinary cowherd people, considered that perhaps his and the Vraja community's increased affection for the *gopas* and calves may have been caused by the power of a celestial god or goddess, for at times their influence had been witnessed in Vraja. Alternately, he considered that perhaps foul play was somehow at hand by the likes of one of Kaṁsa's agents, as the community had experienced earlier when Pūtanā assumed the form of a nursemaid. But these assessments did not account for the spiritual nature of the increased attraction he and others felt for the *gopas* and calves, a spirituality that came to the foreground of his thinking as his *bhāva* gradually shifted from his humanlike fraternal love to a reverential *dāsya-bhāva* similar to his mood as Ananta, the bedstead of Vāsudeva Kṛṣṇa. Thus he began to consider that perhaps sages had merged with the forms of the *gopas* and calves, having engaged in *ahaṅgrahopāsanā*,[18] or that devotees such as Nārada and Garuḍa had entered their forms. But as his *dāsya-bhāva* consumed him and then his omniscience also surfaced, he rejected these considerations and concluded that only Kṛṣṇa and his *yogamāyā-śakti* could have such an influence over him and that this power alone was at play.

It should be noted, however, that Balarāma's bewilderment under the influence of Kṛṣṇa's *yogamāyā* is not a defect, for Kṛṣṇa himself, despite his omniscience, does not know the limits of *yogamāyā*'s power.[19] He does not know her limits, that is, because she does not have any. Not knowing something that does not exist does not cancel one's omniscience.

Then as quickly as Rāma's omniscience surfaced to serve him, it submerged itself in the sea of another wave of his fraternal love, and he asked Kṛṣṇa with an element of embarrassment why he had assumed the forms of his cowherd friends and calves. Although Rāma understood what Kṛṣṇa had done, he felt somewhat embarrassed that he remained unable to ascertain why Kṛṣṇa had done it. After all, Rāma was Kṛṣṇa's closest companion. How could he have missed such a significant event?

18. In his *Ujjvala-nīlamaṇi* commentary on 3.52–53, Viśvanātha Cakravartī Ṭhākura explains that there are those who follow the eternal Vraja devotees by identifying themselves in meditation with the associates, a form of meditation found in the *śruti* termed *ahaṅgrahopāsanā* (self-worship). As a result of their worship, they merge into those that they follow.

19. *Śrīmad Bhāgavatam* 10.13.36.

Kṛṣṇa then explained everything to his brother in confidence, leaving Rāma with mixed feelings—feelings of concern for the actual *gopas*, frustration that he had been kept at home the day that the event occurred and thus had missed out on seeing the huge python, disappointment with Kṛṣṇa for keeping him out of the loop amid deep and abiding affection for him, and so on. Thus, he stayed home from herding for the days of the year that remained and, as a result, also missed the return of Brahmā, who revisited Vraja momentarily by celestial time, eager to see what Kṛṣṇa would do now that he had kidnapped Śyāma's *sakhās* and heifers. A year within a moment is possible: earthly time within celestial time within transcendental time, which has no beginning or end, serving as it does only for the sake of sequence.[20]

To say that when Brahmā returned he was bewildered as to what had happened does not do justice to the measure of his confusion. He checked the cave where he had placed the calves and cowherds and saw that they were still there. He did not realize that these were only *māyic* representations of Kṛṣṇa's playmates and herd. Seeing them there, he looked again at Kṛṣṇa apparently continuing his pastimes with his friends and calves as if nothing had changed. Kṛṣṇa, he saw, had found his friends and calves and reunited with them. Then Brahmā returned to the cave, running back and forth in an effort to understand Kṛṣṇa's power in relation to his own power. Was Kṛṣṇa somehow moving the boys and calves every time Brahmā went to the cave and then moving them again to the forest? He soon realized that this was not the case, and although he analyzed the situation with his four heads, each head merely began to spin.

Thus far, Brahmā had been bewildered by Kṛṣṇa's display of majesty in liberating Agha. Then he saw Kṛṣṇa's sweetness in his intimate interactions with his friends. This was also bewildering. How could a person of such power act in this apparently contradictory way, overwhelmed by the love of his friends? Thus, he tested Kṛṣṇa's power. But his test also proved bewildering. He had kidnapped Kṛṣṇa's friends and calves, but Kṛṣṇa's *līlā* with them continued for an entire year as if the kidnapping had not taken

20. In modern thought, there are two theories as to what time amounts to. Tensed/dynamic time, or A time, consists of ordered, objective aspects of reality—past, present, and future. The present exists, the past no longer exists, and the future exists only as a potentiality. Tenseless/static time, or B time, on the other hand, considers time a subjective perception—an illusion. In this theory, time does not actually pass and what is referred to as past, present, and future is in fact always existing. In Gauḍīya Vedānta, roughly speaking, our space-time continuum involves tensed time, and the land of *līlā* involves tenseless time.

place. At the same time, it appeared as if the same boys and calves remained kidnapped and asleep under Brahmā's spell in a distant cave.

Buddhi is no match for Vraja *bhakti* and its object, *svayaṁ* Bhagavān. While it is debatable whether or not one can attain self-realization—*jīvan-mukti*—by the exercise of *buddhi* alone,[21] one cannot attain any form of final *mukti* without *bhakti*. *Jīvan-mukti* for the *jñānī* is the penultimate stage of spiritual culture that leads to *videha-mukti*, the final stage of actual liberation. *Jīvan-mukti* may appear praiseworthy, but if one's journey stops there because of absence of or offense to *bhakti* and Bhagavān, what value does such *mukti* hold?

Of course, Brahmā was a *bhakta*. His bewilderment, while also teaching us the limits of the intellect, was arranged by Kṛṣṇa to humble him and help him better understand *sambandha-jñāna*—that is, the nature of his relationship with the object of his *bhakti*. And that bewilderment only increased with what Kṛṣṇa did next. Suddenly Kṛṣṇa turned all of the expansions of himself in the form of *gopas* and calves into four-armed Viṣṇu *mūrtis*, from each of whom manifested a complete universe. He showed Brahmā that the multiverse—not just the one universe in which four-headed Brahmā appeared as a secondary creator—issued from himself. He demonstrated that the totality of existence is a person in whose dream we appear and participate. Perhaps we can conceptualize this with the help of chemist James Lovelock's popular Gaia principle, which in its original form was teleological and in which he suggests that the earth itself is an organism that we merely participate in. In doing so, Lovelock invoked the name of the Greek goddess Gaia, who personified the earth. Similarly, in Gauḍīya Vedānta, reality is a person—Kṛṣṇa—in whose mind we exist. This concept of reality represents a panentheistic, "everything in God," perspective.[22]

This display of Kṛṣṇa's majesty forms the background for the intimacy he shares with his friends. Kṛṣṇa is the source of everything, but his power of *bhakti* subjugates his majesty and makes him accessible to his friends on the most intimate terms, the two being one in fraternal love—*ekajātīya*. Were he not who he is in *tattva*, his intimate dealings with his friends would lack their ambience of sweetness—their charm.

The vision Brahmā experienced was not derived from the power of his eyesight or *yogic* ability, but rather it was revealed to him. It was descending

21. See *Bṛhad-bhāgavatāmṛta* 2.2.208–212 with Sanātana Goswāmī's commentary, and Viśvanātha Cakravartī's commentary on *Śrīmad Bhāgavatam* 10.2.32.

22. We find this teaching in *Bhagavad-gītā* 9.4–5.

in nature and thus it constituted Kṛṣṇa's mercy upon him after Kṛṣṇa had witnessed Brahmā's bewilderment. However, it was a further bewilderment to end all bewilderment and make clear to Brahmā the position of his God and *guru*. Brahmā saw the calves and cowherds but they paid no attention to him, despite the fact that he was from the celestial world and his appearance in their midst was uncommon. Brahmā is described as "unborn" or "firstborn" (*aja*). The Sanskrit word *aja*, however, also means "goat," and the calves and cowherds treated him as such by ignoring him, a billy goat among them. At the same time, by ignoring him they implied that by his intelligence as the creator he wanted to bewilder them, but in fact he did not even know who they were, and thus they showed him that which he could not ascertain on his own. Although these calves and cowherd boys were Kṛṣṇa himself and they revealed this, Kṛṣṇa's calves and friends were also one with him, inasmuch as love for Kṛṣṇa and Kṛṣṇa are one and different. In fact, what Brahmā saw was that the expansions of Kṛṣṇa in the form of the calves and cowherds were Kṛṣṇa himself. Moreover, they were decorated with the love of his devotees in the form of garlands and *tulasī*. Thus the two—Kṛṣṇa and love of Kṛṣṇa—were inseparably intertwined. The Viṣṇu *mūrtis*' reddish eyes were symptoms of their intoxicated state brought about by their love of their devotees, and their smiles were indicators of their approval of the devotees' spiritual desires. Brahmā also saw how each of the universes emanating from the Viṣṇu *mūrtis* worshiped the *mūrti* they emanated from, as the personifications of each elemental aspect of the universal ingredients (earth, water, air, fire, etc.) offered prayers in unison with all the personified mystic *siddhis*. This vision stunned Brahmā, rendering him immobile and unable to speak.

Then as suddenly as these majestic Viṣṇu *mūrtis* appeared, they disappeared along with their *aiśvarya*, and Brahmā found himself in the beautiful bucolic setting of Vraja, where he sat, having fallen from his swan carrier.[23] As he touched down in Vraja, his mental picture of his own universe—"his world"—faded away. It is said that the celestial gods never touch the earth. The fact that Brahmā did implies that his celestial ego as a *deva* dissolved. And as his spiritual identity as a *sakhā* of Kṛṣṇa began to bud,

23. Brahmā's swan represents the power of discrimination—intelligence—and the ability to extract that which is essential, leaving the rest behind. As an example of this, swans are thought to be able to discriminate between milk and water and extract only the milk from a mixture of the two. But here, having exercised spiritual discrimination, Brahmā is leaving his intelligence behind and following his love-laden heart into the domain of *jñāna-śūnyā-bhakti*.

he developed some feeling for the sacred setting of Vraja, a realm apart from the multiverse and unto itself in the *paravyoma*, even as both of these worlds are contained within it.

What exactly did Brahmā feel? Śukadeva invokes the word *samā-priyam.*[24] He (*sa*), Brahmā, began to experience the dear (*priya*) influence, *hlādinī*, of Rādhā (*mā*), who presides over Vṛndāvana—Bhakti-devī herself presiding over all that is dear to Kṛṣṇa—*rādhā vṛndāvane vane.*[25] Vṛndāvana is that place where everything is alive in love for Kṛṣṇa and living harmoniously and where everyone is also dear to one another—*samā-priyam*. In Vraja, Lakṣmī's reverence for Nārāyaṇa is absent in Rādhā's love for Kṛṣṇa, and the distance between the object of worship and the worshiper is bridged as worship and self-sacrifice turn into love and self-forgetfulness. Friendly feelings, to be sure. Indeed, therein the mongoose and the cobra are friends, and animals and people are not afraid of one another, nor does anyone thirst or suffer from hunger. Blessed is Brahmā, through whose example Kṛṣṇa has shown us the way to his world! *Jaya* Rādhe!

As Kṛṣṇa withdrew his majesty, Brahmā found himself alone in the forest before Gopāla-deva. He had now entered the original *līlā-prakāśa* in which Kṛṣṇa in his original form had remained during the entire year. Kṛṣṇa was on his way to retrieve the calves as the cowherds continued their picnic in eager anticipation of his return. It was, that is, as if nothing had happened. A year on earth had passed elsewhere, but within this particular earthly *līlā-prakāśa*, no time whatsoever had passed. However, now Kṛṣṇa made time for Brahmā to express his love for him before Kṛṣṇa retrieved the calves and returned to the circle of his friends.

Kṛṣṇa stood before Brahmā with the yogurt rice and fruit in his left hand that he had taken from his friend Sukhada's plate. Stunned by Kṛṣṇa's beauty and charm, speechless, Brahmā prostrated himself at Gopāla's lotus feet, bathing them with the tears pouring from his two eyes facing Kṛṣṇa. However, to Brahmā's frustration, he could not respectfully face all of his four heads down at the same time, and try as he did, one head continually looked upward. And this upward-facing head and pair of eyes caused an upsurge of spiritual greed that in turn drew him upward to gaze anew upon Kṛṣṇa's beauty. Thus, he rose again and then fell again—again and

24. *Śrīmad Bhāgavatam* 10.13.59.

25. *Matsya Purāṇa* 13.38. Commenting on *Śrīmad Bhāgavatam* 10.13.59, Jīva Goswāmī writes that this phrase is also found in the *Padma Purāṇa*. While this particular *līlā* does not involve *mādhurya-rasa*, this does not preclude her influence—*hlādinī-śakti*—which pervades Vraja.

again—Kṛṣṇa's feet representing his majesty, his face his sweetness. As Brahmā rose, he gazed at Kṛṣṇa's lotus face with one pair of eyes, clearing the tears from them momentarily with his hands, while his other three pairs of eyes wept incessantly. Each time he rose, he faced Kṛṣṇa with a different head in order to behold his beauty with all eight of his eyes.

Overcome with love, his entire body trembling, only gradually could he begin to speak. When he finally did so, he spoke with natural humility. Slowly at first and gradually picking up speed, he uttered numerous spontaneously composed prayers, perfect in terms of *tattva* and filled with *bhāva*. As he uttered a prayer from one mouth, his other three heads pondered what Kṛṣṇa might be thinking in response, and having thought that out with three heads, he then uttered another prayer with a second mouth as if in response to what he imagined Kṛṣṇa's mental response had been.

The heart of all of Brahmā's prayers was this:

> Praising those with *rāgātmikā-sakhya-prema* and glorifying Vraja—the cowherd kingdom of Nanda—as the domain of *sakhyam*, Brahmā clearly stated that eternal (*sanātanam*) friendship (*mitram*) is the highest bliss (*paramānandam*). At the same time, he explained that Kṛṣṇa, as the complete expression of Brahman (*pūrṇaṁ brahma*), is also himself the highest bliss personified as one's eternal friend. Then praising the residents of Vraja in general and the cowherd boys in particular, he expressed his longing in *sambandhānugā-bhakti* to reside in Vraja by means of taking shelter of their lotus feet. He did not pray directly for Kṛṣṇa to bless him to become a cowherd boy but rather to attain the dust from the feet of the residents of Vraja (*yad gokule 'pi katamāṅghri-rajo-'bhiṣekam*)—their grace. Brahmā wanted the grace of the cowherd boys in particular, who were right there (*iha aṭavyāṁ*) in that very forest in the midst of Kṛṣṇa's cowherding that serves as portal to eternal friendship. Brahmā knew that the good fortune (*bhūri-bhāgyam*) of *rāga-bhakti* is attained only by the grace of such devotees. Thus Brahmā showed his skill in *bhajana* as he longed for *bhāva-bhakti* and then concluded his prayers with *nāma-saṅkīrtana*—*śrī-kṛṣṇa vṛṣṇi-kula*...[26]

But was Brahmā successful? Śrī Jīva Goswāmī writes in his *Gopāla-virudāvalī* 15 that Gopāla Kṛṣṇa blessed Brahmā with Vraja *bhakti*—*dadad vraja-bhaktiṁ tasmiṁs*.

26. *Śrīmad Bhāgavatam* 10.14.32, 10.14.34, 10.14.40.

Kṛṣṇa remained silent throughout Brahmā's recitation, but by the power of his veiled omniscience, he accepted all of Brahmā's prayers and blessed him. However, steeped in the *bhāva* of a very young village cowherd, Kṛṣṇa found this highly uncommon scene—a reddish-golden being with four crowned heads weeping and praying to God in the middle of the forest—somewhat bewildering. Then Brahmā circumambulated his deity and departed. Śrī Jīva Goswāmī comments, "Going over this story from beginning to end and back again, my mind is astonished."

Following Brahmā's departure, Kṛṣṇa retrieved the nearby calves and returned to the circle of his friends. Together they collected themselves and marched homeward, recalling the events of the day and their encounter with Aghāsura in particular.

> Summoning the calves, Kṛṣṇa entered the cow compound
> accompanied by the rambunctious, festive clamor of
> horns and bamboo flutes.
> His limbs were painted with minerals from the forest
> and decorated with flowers and peacock feathers.
> His glories, which purify those who hear them,
> were celebrated in songs spontaneously composed by his *sakhās*,
> his figure a feast for the eyes of the elderly *gopīs*.[27]

That is, while entering the village the cowherds composed songs and chanted in *līlā-kīrtana* about Kṛṣṇa's exploits. The calves were in front prancing and raising their tails, and the cowherds themselves were dancing all the way, causing the earth to tremble and the heavens above to open in amazement. Arms raised, buffalo horns and flutes resounding, the cowherds surrounded Nanda's son as they emerged with him from a cloud of cow dust at the junction of the jungle and village. Observing this scene, the sun set, out of deference to the brilliance of Kṛṣṇa's sapphire-like effulgence. Words cannot describe this spectacle, and they fail miserably to do justice to the feelings it stirs in the hearts of *sakhya-rati-upāsakas*.

This, then, is one sweet song they sang:

27. *Śrīmad Bhāgavatam* 10.14.47. Jīva Goswāmī says this verse demonstrates that Kṛṣṇa's friendship with these boys of Vraja is deeper than that which he expressed for those who were manifestations of himself. Thus, he emphasizes the festive nature of the scene. Sanātana Goswāmī allows that the words *gopī-dṛg-utsava-dṛśiḥ* may refer to *gopīs* such as Rādhā as well as elders such as Yaśodā with motherly love, but Viśvanātha Cakravartī identifies them only as elder *gopīs* with maternal affection. The latter seems more appropriate, given that at this time Kṛṣṇa is just ending his *kumāra-līlā*.

Today, Nanda and Yaśodā's son slayed a snake
and saved us from cessation.
The serpent's lips were like banks of clouds,
its teeth like mountain peaks.
Its heated breath bellowed like the wind from raging forest flames;
its split tongue invited us to explore its secret pathways.
Some of us in jest compared the serpent to a cave,
laughing as we marched into his mountain trap.
Others saw a snake alone, imagining its mood,
but all of us passed into his gaping jaws and fainted once within,
while other beings fainted outside as Kṛṣṇa entered too.
Then, glancing with affection, he brought us back to life
and glorified the forest as we picnicked in delight.[28]

Here, for the pleasure of his parents, the cowherds sang joyfully of the *ānanda* of Yaśodā and Nanda. Their princely cowherd son had returned as promised, victorious and protected by his royal assembly of *sakhās*, who, sporting dazzling dress and decorated with forest ornaments, were boundless in their enthusiasm. Those boys associated with Nanda's family praised Kṛṣṇa in relation to Nanda, and those associated with Yaśodā's family praised him in relation to Yaśodā. Then upon arriving home, Kṛṣṇa solaced Balarāma for his having missed such a sportive adventure, while the elders were amused but not surprised by the exaggerated tales the cowherds told. After all, boys will be boys.

28. Adapted from *Gopāla-campū* 1.11.53 (v33).

9

Gopāṣṭamī

The liberation of Aghāsura as well as Brahmā's bewilderment and subsequent *bhāva* occurred within the forest not far from the village. During Kṛṣṇa's late childhood, he and his friends herded calves close to the village and returned home not too late in the day. However, from the day of Agha's good fortune, and for one year up to and including Kṛṣṇa's acceptance of Brahmā's prayers, Kṛṣṇa and his comrades returned later and later, day by day, a pattern that did not go unnoticed by his parents. His childhood was nearing its end, his boyhood just beginning.

Grantha-rāja Śrīmad Bhāgavatam begins its description of Kṛṣṇa's *paugaṇḍa-līlā* with a reference to Gopāṣṭamī—*babhūvatus tau paśu-pāla-sammatau*—the day on which Rāma and Kṛṣṇa graduated from calf-herding and became fully initiated cow-herders. The eighth lunar day of the waxing moon in the month of Kārtika—Rādhā's month—is known by the learned as Gopāṣṭamī. From this day onward, Kṛṣṇa served as a cow-herder, whereas previously he had tended only calves. Kṛṣṇa's sweet, tender feet, praised by Brahmā, now bore the weight of his boyhood body, and thus they left lotus-like imprints wherever he traversed, blessing Mother Earth with his footprints, showing the way to *sakhya-rati*—*padair vṛndāvanaṁ puṇyam atīva cakratuḥ*. During Kṛṣṇa's boyhood *līlās*, Balarāma's prominence increased, even while Kṛṣṇa's romantic adolescent sensibilities began to manifest.[1]

1. See *Śrīmad Bhāgavatam* 10.15. This chapter is an overview of the *paugaṇḍa-līlā* and the beginning of Kṛṣṇa's adolescence—his *kiśora-līlā*. *Bhakti-rasāmṛta-sindhu* 3.3.71 states that in the middle of his boyhood, Kṛṣṇa's adolescence begins to manifest. In his comments on this verse, Jīva Goswāmī concurs. However, in his comments on *Śrīmad Bhāgavatam* 10.15.7, he explains that Rāma's *gopīs* manifest romantic feelings for him "at the very beginning of

Śrī Jīva Goswāmī describes Rāma and Kṛṣṇa's *paugaṇḍa* thus:

> As Kṛṣṇa and Balarāma reached *paugaṇḍa*, their intelligence increased. The luster of their black and white complexions defeated that of their *kumāra* period. Their chests expanded, their eyes elongated (toward their ears), and their limbs also became longer. Their hairdos and manner of dressing became more elaborate. They became skillful at learning new varieties of play, and their overall affection increased. So soft is their boyhood as it first emerges. I feel a great longing to see them.[2]

Kṛṣṇa's *kumāra-līlās* are enacted from his place of birth, Mahāvana; his *paugaṇḍa-līlās* from his home, Vṛndāvana; and his *kiśora-līlās* from Nandagrāma. Just how long his *paugaṇḍa*, or boyhood, lasts is a matter of opinion, as commentators answer this question differently.[3] For our purposes, Kṛṣṇa's boyhood begins with Gopāṣṭamī and ends just prior to his *rāsa-līlā* with Rādhā. However, his boyhood is essentially shortened with the early dawning of adolescence while he lives with his friends and subsequently becomes acquainted with Śrīdāmā's sister and those of his other friends.[4] *Līlās* characteristic of the *paugaṇḍa* age include Balarāma's prowess defeating Dhenuka, Kṛṣṇa's chastising of Kāliya, the cowherds protected from Kaṁsa's forest fire, as well as Kṛṣṇa's *pūrva-rāga līlās*—youthful, unacknowledged, romantic love in the separation of anticipation.

The days leading to the Gopāṣṭamī celebration caused further tension between *sakhya-* and *vātsalya-rasas*, tension that was gradually mitigated by factors such as the assistance of Kṛṣṇa's uncles, the confidence that Balarāma instilled, the eagerness of the cows to go out with Kṛṣṇa, and

---

their *paugaṇḍa*," and the same would apply to Kṛṣṇa's *gopīs*, because "a portion of *kiśora* manifests in *paugaṇḍa*." And of course, such feelings are mutual because were they one-sided the effect would be *rasābhāsā*, as explained in *Bhakti-rasāmṛta-sindhu* 4.9.13.

2. *Gopāla-campū* 1.12.4 (v2).

3. In *Gopāla-campū* Jīva Goswāmī gives *paugaṇḍa* only two years, whereas in his *Laghu-toṣaṇī* he extends it up to but not including the *rāsa-līlā*, which makes it three years long (5–8). In *Vaiṣṇava-toṣaṇī*, Sanātana Goswāmī also finds Kṛṣṇa entering adolescence at the outset of the *rāsa-līlā* in his eighth year. In *Muktā-carita*, Raghunātha dāsa also places Kṛṣṇa in adolescence after the Govardhana *līlā*, which occurs during his seventh year. However, Viśvanātha Cakravartī ends Kṛṣṇa's *paugaṇḍa* at six years, eight months, thus beginning his *kiśora-līlā* before the Govardhana *līlā*. In his *Ānanda-vṛndāvana-campū*, Kavi-karṇapūra more or less merges Kṛṣṇa's *paugaṇḍa-līlā* and *kiśora-līlā* together.

4. The idea here is that Kṛṣṇa's *paugaṇḍa* is shortened *in spirit* due to the influence of early adolescence.

astrological calculation. Thus, that which was unthinkable for Yaśodā turned into a mother's pride for her highly accomplished son.

When Abhinanda's wife arrived early one morning and, surprised upon not seeing Kṛṣṇa, wondered as to his whereabouts, Yaśodā opened up to her friend about what she perceived as a departure from Kṛṣṇa's normal behavior. While up until this point she had daily bathed and dressed her son, now he insisted upon attending to these rituals himself, expressing a measure of embarrassment before her and quickly heading to the cow pens after briefly showing respect to his parents. They were amused by his choice of attire but challenged by his brevity with them. Rāma acted similarly—both boys were now beyond their mothers' control, both wanted more than anything else to herd cows. This Yaśodā could surmise, but she remained in denial of it to the amusement of her friends and relatives.

Nanda Rāja began to notice a certain delight among his younger brothers, which they attempted to conceal as he approached. It became apparent to him that Kṛṣṇa was suddenly fond of spending more time with his uncles than with him. This was obviously the cause of their delight, but the reason behind it remained unclear to Nanda. If Kṛṣṇa was among them when his father approached, the flame of their enthusiastic conversation was quickly extinguished just before Nanda arrived. Among themselves they spoke of cowherding, sharing their own maturation to manhood as herdsmen and thus nourishing Kṛṣṇa's eagerness for accepting this responsibility.

After some days, Nandana and Sunanda, Nanda's younger brothers, began to reveal everything to him. They did so skillfully by initially broaching the subject indirectly, speaking of elderly Nanda's growing need to be relieved from his herdsman responsibilities. As Nanda ever so slightly acknowledged their concerns for him, this in turn opened the door for them to state the obvious. The glory of his son would be realized only as he took this responsibility upon himself. Indeed, from their perspective, Kṛṣṇa now desired to become a herdsman for this very reason. Furthermore, it was apparent that as a result of Nanda's penance in pursuit of conceiving his child, Nārāyaṇa had showered him with his blessing in the form of a skillful son. Kṛṣṇa was in fact what Nanda wanted him to be. Thus, he had no recourse now but to let him be who he was destined to be. In this way, Nanda Rāja's thoughts began to change from thinking about Kṛṣṇa as a young child to thinking about his future: a glorious boyhood as a herdsman.

Then a most auspicious day arrived unbeknown to everyone but nonetheless evident in the spirit of Kṛṣṇa's friends. When they arrived at

Nandagrāma as usual, there was a spontaneous determination in the air among them: today they would herd cows with Rāma and Kṛṣṇa. Balarāma, who had been awake with anticipation long before dawn, approved of this shared ambition. By now Rāma had attained a definite sense of leadership among the young *gopas* that had begun to manifest as a result of contemplating all that had occurred in his absence, starting from the liberation of Agha and ending with the epiphany and prayers of Brahmā. He developed, that is, a sense of responsibility for all of them and for Kṛṣṇa in particular that peaked on this day, at this very hour—the break of dawn.

The young sun, now rising from its bed of the eastern horizon to the chirping of birds, was about to begin wandering with its rays through the sky, illuminating the cowherd kingdom. Similarly, Kṛṣṇa, the uncaused cause behind nature, rose from his bed to the clamor of his friends, who called upon him to wander with cows throughout the forests of Vraja, shedding a light of certainty on the perpetuity of the clan of cowherds and their *dharma* of *go-sevā*. Today Kṛṣṇa would become a cow-herder!

> O dear friend, wake up, wake up! O moon of Gokula.
> The moon with faults, ashamed of your beauty, has departed.
> And as the morning birds sing,
> "Victory to the dawn, heralder of the sun,"
> victory, too, to you, O son of Nanda. The cows await you.

Indeed, on this day the cows curiously refused to let down their milk, much less budge from their pens to their pasture. Somehow it became clear that without the lead of Gopāla Kṛṣṇa, they would do neither. This was brought to Nanda Rāja's attention, who hurried to the cow pens as if hightailing like a herd bull, energized as he was by this news and his newfound joy in the conviction that the time had come for Kṛṣṇa to herd his cows.

Meanwhile, Kṛṣṇa's *priya-sakhās*, themselves eager to herd, insisted that they forgo their morning exercise and athletics in the courtyard and proceed with speed to the milking shed. Once there, Kṛṣṇa approached a seasoned and steady white cow and proceeded to milk her just as he had seen his elders do. Placing the pail between his legs after allowing her calf to drink, he milked her as though he had performed this *sevā* every day of his life. Lost at sea in a milk ocean of ecstasy, he and his friends milked out the entire herd and sent them out into a corralled pasture. They then discussed the still-unresolved concerns of Rohiṇī and Yaśodā and spoke excitedly among one another about exploring much deeper into Vraja's forests than they had to date, determined to prove their competence and thus dispel their mothers' concerns.

However, upon arriving back home, Kṛṣṇa, dispensing with any and all preplanned tact, simply blurted out with great emotion, "Mother, today I will herd the cows throughout the forests of Vraja." She replied, "Son, your father owns more than nine hundred thousand cows, and under his expert management, many assistants are engaged and well paid. You are the only son of a king, not an ordinary cow-herder, and thus there is no need for you to take up such laborious duties, glorious as they may be, what to speak of wandering throughout the deep, dark, and dangerous forests of Vraja!"

As if Kṛṣṇa was Prince Siddhartha, Yaśodārāṇī desired to keep her son within the confines of her cowherd palace and curtail even his calf-herding, lest he opt, as now seemed ever more likely, for a life in the forest. What would that lead to? *Nirvāṇa* is nowhere! But while Kṛṣṇa had no interest in *nirvāṇa*, he could not live without (*nir*) the forest (*vana*) of Vṛndāvana. Oh, if only Buddha with all of his wisdom had become a cowherd!

As she spoke, Kṛṣṇa's friends—Śrīdāmā, Dāmā, Vasudāmā, Kiṅkiṇi, Stokakṛṣṇa, Ujjvala, Subala, Atibala, Suniṣṭha, and others—stood at the door within earshot, dressed and ready to herd. Startled by their appearance, she called them, her voice full of affection: "O *gopas*, why do you stand at the door? Don't be afraid of me. Come over here. I want to ask you about something."

Led by Śrīdāmā and Sudāmā, the boys cautiously approached. They held flutes and herding sticks and were wrapped in beautifully dyed, variously colored cloths tied close to their waists with decorative belts, each boy's hair tied in a topknot. And on their faces they wore suspicious, barely discernable smiles, which they further concealed by lowering their heads, unsure of the outcome ahead.

Looking at them as they stood sheepishly before her, Yaśodā spoke to all of them by addressing their leader, Śrīdāmā: "O son of Vṛṣabhānu, what do you have to tell me regarding the rumors I'm hearing about all of you boys? O my dear child, in Vraja-maṇḍala you are an abode of *prema* and as praiseworthy as Hari himself. How is it that you have come to my house with the intention of taking my child deep into the forests of Vraja, herding full-grown cows? What is the value of taking the wealth of our lives, the cows, who so love the pasture grass we provide, into the dense, dark forests?"

Śrīdāmā replied, "Cows are by nature curious. This is not our fault. If their appetite for curiosity and exploration is not fed, they will be restless and difficult to control. I have learned this from my elders. If it were not for this, surely, we would all be content to remain at home." Then, casting a sidelong glance upon Kṛṣṇa as a signal for help, Sudāmā interjected, speaking to Śrīdāmā: "Śrīdāmā, Hari is now in his own home with his mother. Let him play here. But we are sons of cowherd men and have no purpose here as the day moves forward. Let us go and take care of the cows, who consider the forest an abode of happiness."

Understanding his cue, Kṛṣṇa made subtle gestures to his comrades, indicating that he would take it from here. "Mother, the family of Vṛṣabhānu is as wealthy and prestigious as ours. But despite our wealth and cowherd royalty, I am still a cowherd boy like Śrīdāmā. Our *ābhīra dharma* is protecting the cows, who are our wealth, just as reciting the Vedas is the *dharma* of the *brāhmaṇas*.[5] Do *brāhmaṇa* boys themselves recite, or do they have their assistants do it? And because we are cow-herders, like the cows we too are curious. How can one's nature be ignored?"

Astonished, Yaśodā thought to herself, "This son of mine is very expertly instructing about *dharma*, speaking like an ancient sage although only a child!" Śrīdāmā then took advantage of Yaśodā's amazement and spoke boldly to her in *vīra-rasa*, playfully emboldened by Kṛṣṇa's nod and glance.

> Is Hari only the object of *your* affection and not that of others such as ourselves? We do not consider him to be separate from our own *prāṇa*. He is the object of our *sakhya praṇaya*. And when he is with us, we also become *his* life airs. How can there be any danger in such an abode of friendship?
>
> And in our herding, Rāma will lead us. Who among the evil-minded are not afraid of him—Rohiṇī-nandana? What brought him here in Rohiṇī's womb on a dark mare in the night? Surely not fear of Kaṁsa, but rather his love for your dark son—Śyāmasundara. Do you not remember how Rāma was as if lame, deaf, dumb, blind, and practically unconscious in his infancy until he was placed on your lap and close to the love of his life within your holy womb? Who loves Kṛṣṇa more than Balarāma does, and what is the strength of his arms?

5. Kṛṣṇa is a member of the *ābhīra* caste, which is a mixture of the *brāhmaṇa* and *vaiśya* castes. Kṛṣṇa's grandfather Parjanya was the son of an *ābhīra* woman. Brahmā also kidnapped an *ābhīra* woman from Vraja—Gāyatrī—and married her, as related in the *Padma Purāṇa*. As a result of this *gāndharva* marriage, Viṣṇu promised to incarnate in the *vaiśya* community of Vraja.

> And who will dare to challenge us in the presence of our friend Maṇḍalībhadra, wielding as he does his bright, rounded sword? Indeed, thousands of such cowherds will surround the moon of Gokula like the brightest of stars in the sky of Vṛndāvana, which gives only happiness—Sukhadavana. Fear not, O queen of Vraja!
>
> In Vṛndāvana, there are no trees that do not bear flowers, if not fruits, and the flowers' fragrance is carried throughout the day by the forest's cool breezes, while at night Vṛndāvana's aromatic jasmine blooms. Vṛndāvana's fruits drip with nectar as they fall from the trees, as if offering themselves to Vraja-pati's prince, while the birds perched on the trees' limbs create a symphony of melodious sounds to which herds of various colored deer dance. I swear that going there, one never thinks of returning.

Then suddenly, as if summoned by Śrīdāmā's love, the *suhṛt* son of Rohiṇī, ruby earring dangling from one ear, the other decorated with a blossoming *karṇikāra* flower, entered the room bearing his buffalo horn, beautiful Rohiṇī behind him. He swayed into the room like an intoxicated elephant whose footsteps shook the earth beneath them, causing Yaśodā to think that should he approve Kṛṣṇa's desire for cowherding, how would it be possible to refuse?

At this age, Balavīra began taking himself seriously in his role as the *maryādā-puruṣa* in Kṛṣṇa's life, a role largely foisted upon him by Yaśodā. After all, he was Kṛṣṇa's elder brother by only eight days. And was he actually stronger? If so, to date he had not really proved it. Where was he when Bakāsura, Vatsāsura, and Aghāsura all attempted to slay Rāmānuja? Thus, to date his prowess as the protector of Hari was more the projection of Yaśodā than anything else. And now her own projection that gave him authority in her mind and his came to haunt her.

At the same time, her projection proved accurate, for in the *Bhāgavata*, Śukadeva has said as much and more about Baladeva as his boyhood matured:

> The whole of the universe rests on Rāma as a woven cloth rests on its warp and weft.[6]

Rāma bowed before his mothers and then stood next to Kṛṣṇa, with their cowherd friends flanking them on one side, Rohiṇī and Yaśodā on the

6. *Śrīmad Bhāgavatam* 10.15.35.

other. Then he solemnly announced, "Mother, today Kṛṣṇa should go to the forest with me and herd cows. Do not be afraid for him. Who can possibly harm him in my presence? From the distant stars in the sky to the ground beneath our feet, and from the eastern sunrise to the western sunset and every direction in between, there is no one who can defeat me." Hearing this, the chorus of cowherd boys raised their arms above their heads and spontaneously chanted "Rāma Rāma *mahā-bāho*!" with such force and feeling that any remaining opposition to their desire to herd cows with Kṛṣṇa resembled only the final moments of a sporting event whose outcome has already been decided.

Then, stunned and barely able to collect herself in the face of such insurmountable odds, the best of mothers multiplied by millions replied, "O mighty Balabhadra—Father—what you wish will certainly come to pass." But once she had appropriately addressed the elder brother as "father," her own husband came to mind. As if now prepared to assist in dispensing with any remaining obstruction, she added, "Still, we would be remiss not to ask for the consent of Śrī Vraja-pati. Let us wait for him to arrive."

Meanwhile, Vraja-pati Nanda was on his way back from the milking parlor along with other elder *gopas*. Their conversation centered on the temperament of the cows—their unwillingness to milk or move without Kṛṣṇa's direct involvement—and how Kṛṣṇa himself and his friends under his direction had risen to the occasion by milking and pasturing the lactating cows. He thus approached with amazement and also pride in his son's abilities.

Earrings swung from his ears, and his forehead was adorned with vertical *tilaka*. In the morning sun, his complexion appeared to vacillate in color between that of a pinkish conch shell and a darker shade of sandalwood paste. His protuberant belly indicated a long and satisfying life, as did his salt-and-pepper beard. Wrapped in silk, in his hand he held a goad, and on his feet he sported fragrant fine-grained sandalwood shoes.

As he arrived, he offered a blessing, causing some commotion: "May Kṛṣṇa bless you!" Smiles immediately spread across the faces of the young *gopas*, some of whom nudged one another, finding Nanda's blessing humorous. Noticing this, Nanda schooled them all. "Boys—Śrīdāmā, Sudāmā, Subala, Aṁśu, Stoka, Suvākya, and all of you gathered here—I have invoked the blessings of him after whom my son is named. Do you not know the virtue of naming one's son after Bhagavān?"[7] As the boys sobered, ready

7. "Kṛṣṇa" is also the name of one of the *vaibhava-vilāsa* expansions of Nārāyaṇa and is thus a name of God. See *Caitanya-caritāmṛta* 2.20.208–209.

to be schooled, Nanda, drawing upon the Purāṇic lore, told them at length about the amazing story of an ancient *brāhmaṇa*—Ajāmila—who named his son "Nārāyaṇa." Although Ajāmila was impious and involved with a prostitute, having called out his son's name at the time of death he was delivered by the messengers of Viṣṇu. Thus Nanda extolled the virtues of *śrī nāma*, fascinating while also edifying the young *gopas*. Then, as soon as Gopa-rāja Nanda finished the narrative, the boys spontaneously began to chant, "*Jaya* Rāma! *Jaya* Kṛṣṇa!" dancing as they did so. And then, along with Rāma and Kṛṣṇa, they bowed before Nanda Bābā, some saying affectionately, "By your mercy we are extremely happy," while others simply nodded in affirmation, all of them waiting now for Nanda's final approval of their plans.

Thus the scene slowly returned to normal yet remained surcharged from the Purāṇic wisdom and subsequent *nāma-kīrtana*. Yaśodā then ventured to focus her husband on the pressing concern of the hour. "These cowherd boys assembled in the courtyard want to take Hari to the forest for herding cows, and he desires the same. Their enthusiasm appears uncheckable, and to my astonishment they have also reasoned well in support of their desire. Furthermore, Rāma has given his consent. O Vraja-pati, I place this matter at your feet. What is your opinion?"

Gopa-rāja Nanda replied, "O Goṣṭharāṇī, we have discussed this earlier in private with no resolution, but in consultation with my brothers and in consideration of the latest development with our herd, I have reached a conclusion. Now even the cows are calling for this. Such is their love for our son! Furthermore, while Govinda is still very young, I am quite old. Nārāyaṇa blessed us with a son in our latter years. Thus, his youth corresponds with my age such that it mandates he take responsibility for the herd at an otherwise early age as I move toward retirement. And for that matter, it appears that his friends similar in age have already received permission from their fathers to herd cows. Thus, it appears now to be the norm in our cowherd community, and my mind has turned from fearful for his sake to proud of his boyhood maturity. If he is capable of relieving the burden of his aging father, then that is something to rejoice in. My birth has now attained its fruit. This is my conclusion."

Then, placing Hari on his lap, his hand on his son's back, Nanda asked him, "Govinda, are you capable of herding the cows in the very frightful forest?"

> Govinda: Father, I am capable if I am accompanied by my elder brother Balarāma.

Nanda Bābā: But some will say that you have not yet reached the appropriate age.

Govinda: Then how is it that the boys my age from well-to-do families, Śrīdāmā and others, have been granted permission to herd?

Nanda Bābā: Well said, son. What remains now is only to call an astrologer and determine the auspicious moment to celebrate and proceed.

Thus, Nanda called for a wise astrologer who could ascertain the past, present, and future, being adept not only in reading his child's natal chart—subject to any number of interpretations—but also in meditation and spiritual practice. And within moments, the very short, old, shaking, and disheveled Sarvajña arrived, wearing a thick sacred thread under loosely wrapped cloth, his face smiling pleasantly. His complexion was dark yet lustrous, and his forehead was adorned with thickly applied *tilaka* from the mud of the Yamunā, as were his arms and torso. He was talkative, while appearing to be residing in the heavens above. And speaking from there, he offered his blessing to the cowherd king: "May the Sun expand your power and health; the Moon your beauty and mental serenity; Mars your prosperity; Mercury your mercantile intelligence; Jupiter your spiritual knowledge of the scriptures; Venus the incomparable ability to compose poetry; and may Saturn, Rāhu, and Ketu continually effect the harm of your enemies. All glories to the king! What is your order?"

Śrī Nanda replied, "O Cakravartin, today Kṛṣṇa wants to go to the forest for herding cows. Therefore, please tell us if this eighth day of the bright fortnight of Kārtika aligns with his desire." However, Sarvajña replied as if he had not heard the king's request, which the king then placed before him once again, only to realize in due course that the *jyotiṣa* was hard of hearing. Indeed, the king next asked him if he was deaf, to which Sarvajña replied, "What? Please speak loudly." Nanda asked again, almost shouting, but to no avail. Thus, he turned the task over to the assembled cowherd boys, who in unison asked him the same question simultaneously in both of the astrologer's ears. However, Sarvajña only asked them to please speak louder. Thus, they moved closer to his ears as if to whisper and widened his ears' openings with their hands while shouting out the same question.

"Ah, understood. You are asking about the day of Baladeva's marriage, because on the marriage of the elder there is then the chance of marriage of the younger," Sarvajña replied. This in turn greatly frustrated Balarāma, who sounded out the same question with volume comparable to that of the deafening thunder following a nearby lightning strike. With this, he finally got through, and the eccentric *jyotiṣa* replied, "Ah, you want to know an auspicious day for the king's son to begin herding cows." With his response, the assembly of cowherds was overjoyed with relief that quickly turned to apprehension as to what reading he would arrive at.

However, as if he knew all along, he replied immediately and directly to the king with praise for this very day itself: "O virtuous king of Vraja, what can I say about the glory of this day—the lunar day of the waxing moon in the Kārtika month during the *śravaṇa* constellation on a Wednesday? On hearing of this day, the wise derive pleasure with regard to herding. The stars are auspicious, the day of the week and the date are auspicious, the *yoga* with the *karaṇa* is auspicious in the *lagna*, and all the planets speak to us of their pleasure concerning the proposed journey your son desires to embark upon. Furthermore, O king, long life span, destruction of enemies, fame, eloquence, and intellect all come to one who travels on this day. Indeed, it would be difficult to find a more auspicious day."

With this, Sarvajña then smiled brightly, his wise eyes twinkling like stars lighting the night sky of his otherwise concealed meditative mind, as he motioned for Kṛṣṇa to come near. Then he spoke ever so softly into Hari's right ear: "Above all, on this journey today, you with a complexion bearing resemblance to the effulgence of a dark sapphire (*nīlamaṇi*) will also glimpse the brightest (*ujjvala*) form of the Goddess who will become the lady of your life.[8] The beauty of all the women in all the worlds combined—earthly, heavenly, and even that of the great Goddess of good fortune herself—cannot compare to even the reflection of the rays emanating from her toenails." Kṛṣṇa, blushing, his heart beating rapidly, replied, "What did you say?" as the cowherds raucously celebrated Sarvajña's response to the king. Only Subala heard the beat of Hari's heart, muffled by the closure of his lotus eyes.

Thus, Nanda Mahārāja called for a festival, and word quickly spread to all corners of Vraja, heralded as it was with kettledrums and callers. Resident sages, *brāhmaṇas*, singers, dancers, and other artisans all assembled, as did men, women, and children from all sections of society. On Nanda Rāja's order, bards composed and recited the history of all that led to this event.

8. Just ahead in our narrative of Gopāṣṭamī, we find Kṛṣṇa formally introduced to Rādhā through Subala for the first time, as described by Dvārakānātha Ṭhākura in his *Govinda-vallabha-nāṭaka*. Other first meetings between Rādhā and Kṛṣṇa are also described by various *rasika* poets. Thus, we are concerned more with the feeling of the meeting than with the chronology.

Singers sang songs of their own composition in praise of herds, herdsmen, and Hari, as dancers danced in time, depicting herding and satisfied cows through their steps. Somehow the festival that followed lasted forever, while not delaying Kṛṣṇa and his cowherd friends from departing at the auspicious moment.

Elder *gopīs* blessed Yaśodā's son with a long life as they sprinkled grains and *dūrvā* grass on Hari's head and kissed his lotus face. Highly qualified sages wearing *tulasī* buds strung together in garlands bore waterpots containing water from all of the sacred rivers of Bhārata and sang hymns from the *Sāma Veda.*[9] Thus they looked as brilliant as the sun, their hair woven together in matted locks turned golden from its rays. The sages' concern was to shed light on Gopāla—Gopāla *tāpanī*—who was the only object of their inner life and whose dark complexion, shrouded in mystery, resembled the nourishing prospect of the dark rain cloud. Seeing the object of their meditation before them, they wept rivers of tears, only to lose sight of him, resorting then again to their minds' eyes.

And the *brāhmaṇas* chanted, "Victory to Nanda and his *nandana*! Victory to Gokula and its beloved Gokulānanda!" In response, Nanda and Yaśodā rose and then bowed to the *brāhmaṇas*, placing the dust from the *brāhmaṇas*' feet on Kṛṣṇa's head. Then the elder and younger *gopas* along with their family members offered respects to the king of Gokula and chanted, "May your Kṛṣṇa live long!" After this, drums resounded and wind instruments were played by experts, pleasing everyone.

When the music stopped, the *jyotiṣa* announced, "O King, the *lagna* for the journey has arrived." Then Rāma blew his horn, the sound of which reverberated throughout the universe. Following Rāma's lead, the young *gopas* responded with a symphony of their own. They blew horns and played various drums and other types of percussion instruments, such as small cup-shaped hand cymbals (*mañjīra*). Some played single-stringed mouth harps (*murchunga*), while others made musical sounds by cupping their hands to their mouths to create wind instruments. Others played various flutes, such as the very short six-holed *veṇu*, the very long four-holed *muralī* with an open end, and the mid-sized nine-holed *vaṁśī*, all of which were made from either bamboo or stone. Still others played stringed instruments such as the *tambura* and *vīṇā*, and all of this in an array of melodic structures with musical motifs—*rāgas*—capable of coloring the mind and influencing the

9. In *Tattva Sandarbha* 21, Jīva Goswāmī cites the *Garuḍa Purāṇa*'s statement that the *Bhāgavatam* is the *Sāma Veda* of the Purāṇas. He references Madhva's *Bhāgavata-tātparya* 1.1.1.

emotions of the audience with the *gopas'* own *rati*. Enthused by the tumult, the *gopas* danced to their music-making along with Bala and Kṛṣṇa.

> The *sakhās* were decorated in stunning fashion with a variety of peacock feathers, necklaces, swinging jeweled earrings, and beautiful jeweled ankle bracelets bearing small tinkling bells. Beautiful also were the locks of hair falling on their foreheads, their topknots towering upward like trees bound at the base with flower wreaths, and their long streams of hair cascading over their well-structured bones—the riverbed of their backs. Their forms were breathtakingly beautiful and dressed in a manner capable of captivating the universal mind. If that weren't enough, their dancing, music, and merrymaking were accompanied by the unparalleled singing of the *gopīs* sitting wide-eyed nearby. Repeatedly the *gopīs* ululated, bringing attention to the scene that none could escape, nor would anyone want to. Even the birds flying overhead were stunned, and their frozen formation appeared like flowers growing from the ground of the sky, the world turned upside down. The gods gave charity and the sun forgot to move ahead, as all moving and nonmoving beings traded positions. O residents of Vraja, how the sight of these mysterious boys must delight! A soothing ointment for the eyes, to see them. When will that day be mine?

Thus, Gopa-rāja Nanda and Yaśodārāṇī blessed Kṛṣṇa to begin herding cows. Śrī Jīva Goswāmī comments,

> If each and every speaker's mouth became ten thousand mouths and their lives lasted a thousand years, they could at best describe but one day of Kṛṣṇa's herding.[10]

After all, there is considerable mystery surrounding cows, as *Go-sūkta* states:

> Sacrifices take place because of cows. The *devas* appear because of cows. The Vedas, with their six *aṅgas*, appear because of cows.[11]

10. *Gopāla-campū* 1.12.32 (v4).

11. The *Go-sūkta* is from the *Ṛg Veda*. Baladeva Vidyābhūṣaṇa in his commentary on *Laghu-bhāgavatāmṛta* and Jīva Goswāmī in his commentary on *Brahma Saṁhitā* cite the following verse, which they attribute to *Go-sūkta*: *gobhyo yajñāḥ pravartante gobhyo devāḥ samuthitāḥ gobhir vedāḥ samudgīrṇāḥ sa-ṣaḍaṅga-pada-kramāḥ*. However, this verse is not found in any edition of the *Ṛg Veda's Go-sūkta* I could find.

Equipped with jewel-studded herding sticks, Rāma and Kṛṣṇa, their foreheads decorated with *tilaka*, set out to herd their father's cows. Although some tension between their parents' love and their friends' love remained, it was eased in Nanda's mind by his cows, whose parental love would accompany the boys. Nevertheless, Yaśodā ordered Kṛṣṇa's friends to surround him in a protective *maṇḍala* that serves *sādhakas* as a *yogapīṭha*, or central meditative altar, out of which Kṛṣṇa's *sakhya-rati-līlās* unfold.

> Imagine an eight-petal lotus within a hexagon that has four perimeter gates where four different desire trees stand. In the center, facing east, stands Kṛṣṇa with Balarāma on his right, both of them arising out of the *mantric kāma-bīja—klīṁ*—which fulfills all spiritual desires, *sva-sādhya*. Yaśodā told Śrīdāmā to stand in front (west) of her sons, Sudāmā to their right (north), Vasudāmā behind them (east), and Kiṅkiṇi to their left (south). Upon the eight meditative petals, she placed Stokakṛṣṇa, Aṁśuka, Bhadrasena, Arjuna, Subala, Vilāsa, Mahābala, and Vṛṣabha. These boys were then further surrounded by millions of *sakhās*, who in turn were surrounded by hundreds of millions of cows. May the *sakhya-rati-upāsakas' mantra-mayī-upāsanā* take on a life of its own, as the deep lake of their fixed meditation begins to spontaneously flow—*svārasikī*—like a river of herding *līlās* in all directions.[12]

Then, offering foot wash and *arghya* to the cows, feeding them sweet chickpeas, respecting them with *praṇāmas* and circumambulating them, Rāma and Kṛṣṇa began to herd the cows. However, with Kṛṣṇa behind them, the cows refused to go forward. Instead, they turned around to face him. Thus he reversed course and again went behind them, calling for them to proceed. But they again turned to face him. This circular motion continued for some time until Kṛṣṇa led them into the forest, gradually moving backward into the herd and surrounded by it and eventually ending up behind it. From there, he continued to herd them forward. Then the cows, secure in their understanding that Kṛṣṇa was among them, appearing to them as if he were in front, behind, and on all sides of them at once, raised their tails and began to dance and prance, kicking their hind legs high toward the sky while also mooing in ecstasy.

12. Nayanānanda Ṭhākura cites *Krama-dīpikā* and *Varāha Purāṇa* as sources for his description of the *sakhya-rati yogapīṭha*. At the four gates stand spiritual forms of the four well-known heavenly desire trees (*kalpa-vṛkṣa*): *mandāra*, *santāna*, *pārijāta*, and *haricandana*.

As they proceeded in the direction of Mount Govardhana, the *gopas* herded their cows by uttering unique sounds and never using their sticks to prod them. It was as if the boys and cows spoke the same language. And Kṛṣṇa increased the cows' bliss by composing cowherd songs, which is a trait particular to *gopas* such as himself.[13] To the *devas* it appeared that when the cows were happy, Kṛṣṇa was happy. When the cows were satisfied, Kṛṣṇa was satisfied, and when they were hungry, he experienced hunger. He brought them close to his chest, smelled them, embraced them, searched for them, collected them together, fed them, and protected them. Kṛṣṇa considered the cows to be as dear as his life, and without him they became disheartened and motionless like two-dimensional paintings. When they came close to Kṛṣṇa, they experienced bliss on smelling, seeing, hearing, tasting, and touching him. Thus, it is no wonder that *go-sevā* is an *aṅga* of *bhakti*![14]

Gradually the herd and young herdsmen disappeared from the sight of the villagers, who had climbed up onto their rooftops in the hope of keeping Kṛṣṇa in view. Then Śrīdāmā-sakhā placed a respectful request before Śrī Kṛṣṇa:

> None of those led by your mother were able to keep you from going to the forest, even as they called from their rooftops, "O son of Gokula's Nanda, O lotus of our community." O friend, if you accept, then let me make a suggestion. Although it is some distance from here, *my* mother also desires to see you in our house. Indeed, she only gave me permission to herd cows in the hopes that at some point as we wander throughout the forests of Vraja I would bring you, Rāma, and our friends to Vṛṣabhānu-pura. Let us go all the way to Vṛṣabhānu-pura and extend our play there. Please consider this request.

In the above description adapted from *Govinda-vallabha-nāṭaka*, the drama's author, Dvārakānātha Ṭhākura, envisions himself as a *sakhā* and resident of Vṛṣabhānu-pura. As he writes, he desires to invite Kṛṣṇa to his village and does so through the voice of Śrīdāmā. However, his pen reveals an element of respect within his budding *sakhya-rati*, as Śrīdāmā respectfully requests Kṛṣṇa to "please consider this request." Then, from within the Ṭhākura's heart, assuring him of the intimacy central to *sakhya-rati*, and

13. *Bhakti-rasāmṛta-sindhu* 2.1.87. Jīva Goswāmī comments that the word *pārāvatī* refers to particular songs composed by cowherds.

14. *Bhakti-rasāmṛta-sindhu* 1.2.110.

dispensing with any hesitancy or respect that would create distance and cause Dvārakānātha's *sakhya-rati* to contract, Kṛṣṇa says to Śrīdāmā:

> O friend, know that I have the same strong constant love for all of you that you have for me. Because of your words, I disregarded even my mother's instruction earlier today and went off to the forest. I am like a boat, and all of you, dear one, are like the best of boatmen. Wherever you wish to take me, I will go there without hesitation. It is not appropriate for you to speak to me with respect. We are equals. We will go. Let us go. Let's definitely go to your village.

Then Baladeva interjected and asked what Śrīdāmā had requested of Kṛṣṇa and where they were taking the *sakhās* and their cows. In reply, Śrīdāmā told Rāma that they would now go to Vṛṣabhānu-pura. And to secure his willingness as well, he suggested that once there, his mother, Kīrtidā, might give Rāma the delightful and intoxicating *mādhvī* beverage. Given Rāma's penchant for such beverages, this piqued his curiosity.

As the boys approached Vṛṣabhānu-pura, from a distance they could see its skyline beautified by large houses made of crystal and other similar stone, demarked by various colorful flags resting on the roofs. They saw rows of large ponds ornamented by groups of lotus flowers—yellow, red, white, pink, and blue—encircled by swarms of swirling honeybees, their pleasant buzzing accompanied by the sounds of the sporting swans and other waterfowl. The town was also beautified by gardens overflowing with a wide variety of blooming flowers. Śrīdāmā then told Sudāmā to go ahead of the others, bearing the news of their imminent arrival with Rāma and Kṛṣṇa.

His sudden arrival surprised Kīrtidā, who was not expecting her nephew Sudāmā to return so early in the day. Thus she remarked, "O son, I see that you have come hurriedly, the lotus of your face fully blossomed, but you are without Śrīdāmā and have returned so soon from the house of Nanda. Please come; sit. Tell me of the celebration at Nanda's residence. Its sounds reverberated throughout the Vraja-maṇḍala."

Sudāmā replied, "O mother, this is the joyful news of today that you alluded to earlier! By the permission of Yaśodā, my dear friend is going to the forest along with Balarāma and our other friends for herding the cows. And just now he is happily coming with his friends to Vṛṣabhānu-pura. Śrīdāmā sent me in advance to inform you so that auspicious preparations for Rāma and Kṛṣṇa's arrival can be arranged."

Thus, the kingdom of Vṛṣabhānu was elaborately decorated to honor the arrival of Rāma and Kṛṣṇa. Śrī Nayanānanda Ṭhākura envisions Vṛṣabhānupura in the shape of a thousand-petal lotus flower, extending sixteen miles in circumference. It is dotted with countless cowherd dwellings made of bricks and beautified by various clusters of trees and gardens. The *gopas'* houses are beautified by flags of different colors—white, yellow, red, and blue—arranged in sequence and fluttering in the breeze. The four external walls of each house are draped with forest flower garlands celebrating the four directions. Numerous species of flowers are always in full bloom therein, and there are rows upon rows of *campaka* flowers and varieties of jasmine, hovered over by maddened honeybees whose sound is very pleasing to the ear. The cooling breeze, bearing the fragrance of the flowers, blows very gently in all directions. Large lakes and placid ponds remain still, resplendent with many species of lotus flowers. From these lakes and ponds waterfowl sing, while on their shores peacocks dance. The bases of the banyan, fig, and mango are encircled by jewel-studded platforms. Various types of birds such as parrots move about, and some sit among these trees, and there are storks in the tall grasses, where crickets and other insects sing of their own good fortune. In the center of the town stands the palace of Rāja Vṛṣabhānu, surrounded by a moat.

With Rāma and Kṛṣṇa soon arriving, Kīrtidā stood at the door, *ārati* paraphernalia in her hands, surrounded by young *gopīs* bearing pitchers of drinking water. The girls' eyes were fixed ahead on the path on which the boys would soon appear. Within the palace, Rādhā's handmaiden Rūpamañjarī, who is the personification of Rādhikā's beauty (*rūpa*), informed her of the approaching herd of cowherds and their cows, headed by Nanda's famous son: "O Rādhā, the moon of Gokula is going to ornament the village now! Behold Hari, dressed as a dancer, his left hand in the hand of brother Śrīdāmā. Hari destroys the *dharma* of Vraja's damsels. His hair is decorated with strings of *campaka* flowers. His chest displays a pearl necklace. An enchanting flute is tucked in his belt, and the sandalwood paste on his blackish body is beautified by his extraordinary luster. In his hand he holds an excellent stick. He is led by Rāma, who is like a mountain of snow, and he is surrounded on all sides by his dear friends. The scene, of which he is the cynosure, looks like a lightning-clad monsoon cloud in the light of the rising moon surrounded by a rainbow."

Following Śrī Rūpa's lead, Rādhā peeped through an air hole in the wall intended to provide a cooling breeze, and there she saw Kṛṣṇa and his *sakhās*, a sight that made her heart melt. Overheated, Rādhā shyly beheld Hari, wrapped in silk that resembled lightning, his contrasting complexion like a dark monsoon rain cloud. As her heart thundered, torrential rains poured from her eyes and teardrops glistened on the cheeks of her lotus face. His eyes too were lotus-like, his face the best of moons. His palms and the soles of his feet were reddish. The nails on his hands and feet were like rows of stars illuminating his body by their soothing rays. Infinitely deep was the impression his appearance made on her lovesick heart, even now at the very beginning of Rādhā and Kṛṣṇa's *paugaṇḍa-līlā*, long before the consummation of their desires.

As Rāma and Kṛṣṇa arrived, Kīrtidā, Suśīlā, and other mothers welcomed them, "O sons, O Rāma and Mukunda, please come, please come." Their voices were barely audible over a chorus of "*Jaya! Jaya!*" that resounded from the mouths of the girls of the community, who sprinkled scented water on the ground before the blessed brothers. Immersed in an ocean of bliss, the mothers repeatedly cried out "May you live long" while kissing the boys' cheeks. Suśīlā then offered *ārati* to Rāma and Kṛṣṇa, who were circled on three sides by *sakhās* Śrīdāmā, Sudāmā, and Kiṅkiṇi, behind whom the multitude of cowherds sang *rasika* songs of their own composition in celebration, glorifying cows and the two cowherds Rāma and Govinda. Thus, the home of Kīrtidā and all of Vṛṣabhānu-pura was blessed on this eighth day of the waxing moon in the month of Kārtika.

Once inside, Śrīdāmā requested his mother to offer the intoxicating *mādhvī* beverage to Bala, explaining that earlier on the path he had secured his visit on the promise of such refreshment. He was confident that this alone would satisfy Rāma and that other delicacies, such as *śikhariṇī*, should be offered to Kṛṣṇa and his comrades. Balarāma was delighted with Śrīdāmā's words. As Kīrtidā gave Rāma a pot of *madhu*, he glanced playfully at Hari and told him, "Hari, my life, I know that you also desire to enjoy this beverage, but you are too young for that," and greedily consumed the pot of *madhu* in front of the assembled cowherds. Kṛṣṇa restrained Kīrtidā with hand gestures from giving him seconds, and at that Rāma retorted, "Enough delay, dear friends! I fear that the cows will stray from the path." But wishing to restrain the boys longer, Kīrtidā pulled Kṛṣṇa aside and said, "O dearmost son of Yaśodā, birth in Vraja, by which your association is attained, is rare, but to have you in my home under the control of Śrīdāmā's love is exceptionally rare. Today we are experiencing that for the first time. If you please pause long enough to eat something along with your friends, my life will be fulfilled." Kṛṣṇa replied, "Mother, please consider me as much your son as you do Śrīdāmā. He and I are equals." Thus Kṛṣṇa and his friends lunched playfully and laughed among themselves to the delight of their many mothers.

Kīrtidā then asked Rādhā's handmaidens where her doe-eyed daughter was on this happy occasion. But try as they did to make excuses for their mistress, Kīrtidā insisted on her presence. Being so informed, Rādhikā spoke aloud, "I have been called by my mother. Hari, Hari! Even if I remain unseen and in hiding, I am not able to stay composed. If I am to go as called for and if he boldly approaches me, surely, I will lose my self-control before that best of cowherd boys in front of all the elders."

To these wise yet shy words, Rādhā's *dāsī* Rūpa-mañjarī replied, "Do not fear, dear one. We handmaidens will surround you. And with you protected thus, how will Kṛṣṇa untie himself from the bond of friendship tied by your brother Śrīdāmā and others to act inappropriately before them and their elders? Surely among his closest friends there are some such as Subala who understand the ways of love, offer wise advice, and will thus restrain him. What's more, if you do not take advantage of this rare opportunity to see him up close, your loss will be inestimable, and regret will color your youth and, by extension, the rest of your long, painful life. Hesitation in the face of auspicious opportunity brings only misfortune. The time is always right to do what is right. Besides, what is supposed to happen will happen. Here, carry these betel leaves and nuts and go quickly surrounded by us, as the cowherds' lunch is almost over. Once Śrī Balabhadra resounds his horn of thunder, in a flash of lightning this auspicious scene will suddenly end and with it your good fortune."

Her mind changed by these words of wisdom, Rādhikā, surrounded by her *kiṅkarīs*, brought the pan wrapped in betel leaves on a golden dish. Then, as she beheld the lotus face of Śyāma Hari, he too gazed unblinkingly into her longing eyes as Subala, understanding the situation, gestured and introduced his friend to Rādhā with a whisper: "This matchless beauty standing before you is Śrīdāmā's sister, born at midday with the blessing of the sun—Mitra, the universal friend—and thus named Rādhā. With the melting of your heart upon seeing her, your complexion is beginning to turn a different shade of *śyāma*. Surely, she is the girl Sarvajña predicted you would meet today, the love of your life. Fortunately, others will think that your ecstatic symptoms are due to the heat generated by such a large indoor assembly. Hold my hand and dam the tide of the oceanic feelings of love you are experiencing for her in the presence of our elders." In this way, Subala assisted Kṛṣṇa and Rādhā in their hour of need, following up on his words with hand gestures, eye movements, and humming sounds that only Kṛṣṇa could understand.

Then, seeing Hari perspiring profusely, trembling, and appearing helpless—lovestruck in his boyhood by the *darśana* of the lotus of Śrī Rādhā's face—Sudāmā thought his condition to be the result of too much heat in the house due to so many people crowded inside. Thus, he started affectionately fanning his friend with the ends of his cloth, saying, "Alas!" Subala intervened. "O brother, not like that. Come, let's take everyone outside. Kṛṣṇa's body is very delicate, and he is feeling exhaustion from herding and overcrowding. Let us clear the room, give him some air, and let some delicate young lady whose nature and touch is as soft as dew gently fan him."

At the same time, Rādhā's *kiṅkarīs* also began to usher her out of the room, leaving Sudāmā's sister, Rūpa, to fan Śyāma as instructed by Subala. Then from outside Balarāma's horn thundered loudly, bringing Kṛṣṇa to his senses. Rāma then engaged his friends in attending to their cows in various ways as Subala escorted Kṛṣṇa back into the circle of his friends. As the young cowherds eagerly prepared to depart, Kīrtidā and Suśīlā implored Rāma to protect their sons, Śrīdāmā and Sudāmā, just as he protects Hari. Balarāma pridefully replied that he would do so. Then he and Kṛṣṇa led their friends into the forest, where the cows simultaneously rushed from all directions, jumping playfully, constantly swirling their tails up high and filling heaven and earth with their mooing. Then, with great force, the cows stampeded toward Kṛṣṇa, stopping suddenly in front of him and then surrounding him, some licking him. Observing this scene, Śrīdāmā spoke thus to Kṛṣṇa: "Dear brother, the cows had become anxious in their brief separation from you." On hearing these words of Śrīdāmā, Kṛṣṇa smiled charmingly as his herding *līlā* resumed, led now by Balarāma.

Jaya Rāma! *Jaya* Hari! *Jaya* Rādhe!

10

Tribute to Rāma

Following Gopāṣṭamī, Balarāma's prominence began to emerge and Kṛṣṇa took great pleasure in fostering it himself, sometimes in jest, in which there is often an element of truth. One day, as the young herdsmen, steeped in *sakhya-rasa*, entered the forest with their cows in front of them, Mādhava began to glorify his older brother in *hāsya-rasa*,[1] pointing out the forest residents' deep respect for him. The *Bhāgavata*'s fifteenth chapter of canto ten describes this day in a manner that highlights Balarāma's prominence during the brothers' *paugaṇḍa-līlā* while simultaneously speaking of Kṛṣṇa's *kiśora-līlā*. For this reason, the *Bhāgavata* refers to Kṛṣṇa at this chapter's outset as "Mādhava," indicating that the sweetness of Kṛṣṇa's romantic *līlās* is also at play.

As Kṛṣṇa gazed at the beauty of the forest, he smiled slightly and described the trees laden with reddish-brown fruits—*aruṇa*, the color of *sakhya-rasa*—as bending down out of respect for his older brother, Balarāma;[2] the bees as buzzing to broadcast Balarāma's auspicious qualities;[3]

1. *Hāsya-rasa* is indicated in *Śrīmad Bhāgavatam* 10.15.4 with the words *mudā smayann iva*, "with joy, almost laughing."

2. Implied here is the idea that while birth as a tree is a result of *tamas*—extreme ignorance resulting in an immobile and dimly conscious life—to be born as a tree in Vraja is not so. Indeed, such a birth is an upgrade over the ideal of *brahma-sāyujya*. Some *jñānīs* observing vows of silence and desirous of *brahma-sāyujya* become attracted to Kṛṣṇa's Vraja *līlā*, and thus he may bless them with birth as immobile trees in his *līlā*. These trees are described as *sumanaḥ* (good-natured), and they are depicted as having feelings of affection for Kṛṣṇa. Thus they are worshiped by the *devas* along with the feet of Balarāma, which the trees of Vraja strive to touch by extending themselves downward, rather than reaching their branches upward to attain heaven.

3. Here the bees are depicted as constantly buzzing and accompanying Rāma wherever

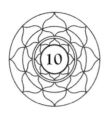

the peacocks as dancing for Rāma's pleasure; the deer as glancing lovingly at Rāma with eyes like those of young *gopīs*; the cuckoos as singing songs of the *Sāma Veda* in praise of Balarāma; the earth as blessed by the touch of his lotus feet as never before, despite the previous descent of numerous *avatāras* of Nārāyaṇa;[4] and the vines and bushes as blessed when Rāma picks their leaves and flowers to further adorn himself and Kṛṣṇa. Again, such glorification was done in jest—*hāsya-rati*. As we shall see ahead, Kṛṣṇa's jest is more apparent in his final praise of Rāma, in which he appears to emphasize the good fortune of the *gopīs*, whom he characterizes as especially blessed to be embraced by Balarāma, a blessing that even Lakṣmī is not afforded.

Balarāma is the presiding deity of *hāsya-rati*. Thus Kṛṣṇa's praise of him in this mood is poetically befitting. All that Kṛṣṇa said about Rāma was true and even more so of himself, but with a hint of humor and humility he avoided praising himself directly. Rāma responded to Kṛṣṇa's humor by looking away and smiling shyly, while the other boys heard the truth in Kṛṣṇa's jest with great joy. *Jaya* Rāma! *Jaya* Kṛṣṇa!

Although Kṛṣṇa relished *hāsya-rati* as he spoke, this *gauṇa-rasa* rested on his *mukhya sakhya-rasa*. In other words, here Kṛṣṇa related to Rāma purely as a friend and equal rather than in consideration of the fact that Rāma was his elder. Thus Kṛṣṇa subtly and with the help of humor emphasized the equality between himself and Balarāma that is central to *sakhya-rati-upāsakas*. And in praise of the two brothers, their friends expressed the same by responding with praise, sometimes referring to the two as "Kṛṣṇa and Balarāma" and sometimes as "Balarāma and Kṛṣṇa." In more philosophical language Śrī Jīva Goswāmī describes the two brothers as "ontologically equal"—*sama-prakāśatvam*.[5]

---

he goes, and thus they also indicate that constant chanting of the glories of Rāma and Kṛṣṇa affords one access to all the secrets of their *līlās*. In this way, the buzzing of the bees and the flourishing and variety in nature that they ensure implies the superiority of *hari-kathā* over a vow of silence in pursuit of indeterminate Brahman.

4. Here the *Bhāgavatam* says that only today (*adya*) in Vraja—during the *pauganḍa-līlā* of Balarāma—has the earth become fortunate. This is so because during this *līlā*, Rāma began to wander throughout Vraja, exploring its every corner. Where he did not personally step, his *sakhās*—extensions of himself—did. And the earth's fortune (*dhanya*) is its wealth of *dharma*, which at this time reached the height of *prema-dharma* not achieved previously despite the descent of numerous *avatāras*. Here Bhūmi lost her chastity to Varāha!

5. *Kṛṣṇa Sandarbha* 84.

We also find support for the oneness of Kṛṣṇa and Balarāma in *Bhagavad-gītā* 10.37, where Kṛṣṇa speaks of *vibhūtis*, or manifestations of his might. Therein he states, *vṛṣṇīnāṁ vāsudevo 'smi*: "Among the Vṛṣṇis, I am Vāsudeva." Jīva Goswāmī explains in *Kṛṣṇa Sandarbha* 81 that in the above *Gītā* verse, Kṛṣṇa is actually identifying himself with Balarāma, for a *vibhūti* of Kṛṣṇa cannot be Kṛṣṇa. Balarāma is also "the son of Vasudeva" like Mathureśa Kṛṣṇa and is thus referred to as "Vāsudeva." Moreover, like Kṛṣṇa, Balarāma is not an *avatāra* of Nārāyaṇa, and when *avatārī* Kṛṣṇa appears in the world as an *avatāra*, he is accompanied by Balarāma. They are "the Kṛṣṇa-Balarāma *avatāra*," as related in the *Bhāgavata*.[6] Thus the two are a pair, and Nayanānanda Ṭhākura repeatedly refers to them as the *yugala* of *sakhya-rati*, whereas Rādhā and Kṛṣṇa are the *yugala* of *mañjarī-bhāva*.

Furthermore, Balarāma is not a mere *āveśa-avatāra*—an empowered *jīva*—as some Vaiṣṇava theologians and texts suggest.[7] In *Kṛṣṇa Sandarbha* 84, Jīva Goswāmī explains that those who consider Baladeva to be an *āveśa-avatāra* are incorrect. Śrī Jīva supports his position by citing verses from the *Bhāgavatam* that describe the two brothers as virtual twins by way of repeatedly referring to them as an inseparable pair, invoking the dual case.[8] Our *tattva-ācārya* also refers to the *Vāsudeva-māhātmya* of the *Hari-vaṁśa Purāṇa*, wherein Balarāma and Kṛṣṇa are described as the sun and moon. Inspired by this metaphor, Jīva Goswāmī reasons that in common parlance the sun and moon are considered a pair, whereas this is not the case with Venus or any other planet in relation to the sun. Thus Kṛṣṇa and Balarāma are one pair, which Jīva Goswāmī further demonstrates with a *Bhāgavata* verse confirming the markings on the soles of their feet to be identical.

6. *Śrīmad Bhāgavatam* 1.3.23.

7. For example, "The greatly powerful Balarāma is a part of Śeṣa-nāga" (*Mahābhārata* 1.67.152).

8. *Śrīmad Bhāgavatam* 10.8.22, 10.23.38, 10.38.28, and 10.43.19. In his commentary on *Kṛṣṇa Sandarbha* 84, Satyanarayana Dasa explains, "The fact that Kṛṣṇa and Balarāma are spoken of as a pair is indicated in this verse [10.8.22] by repeated use of the dual case, beginning with the pronoun *tau*, 'those two.' The dual case is also employed in this verse in the words *saṁsṛpantau* (while these two crawled), *tan-nāda-hṛṣṭa-manasāu* (the minds of these two were delighted by those sounds), *upeyatuḥ* (these two returned), and *mātroḥ* (to their two mothers). The dual case is also used for Kṛṣṇa and Balarāma throughout the three other verses cited by Jīva Goswāmī. In fact, it is only in *Śrīmad Bhāgavatam* 10.38.28 that they are mentioned directly by name. Otherwise, they are simply referred to as a pair by way of the dual case."

> The two great beings [Kṛṣṇa and Balarāma], with their gracious smiling and glances of benediction, beautified the land of Vraja by their feet, which bore the marks of a flag, thunderbolt, goad, and a lotus.[9]

Such marks are not attributed to any other forms of the Godhead.[10]

Although Rāma is *sakhya-rasa* personified, he is Viṣṇu *tattva*, not *śakti-tattva*. The two, Rāma and Kṛṣṇa, are respectively *sevaka-* and *sevya-bhagavān*—God as servant and God as served. Let us take a moment to praise *sevaka-bhagavān*:

> Balarāma's beauty knows no bounds. His feet are soft like lotuses. The hands of his long, strong arms reach his knees. His broad chest is garlanded with a *guñjā-mālā*, and his dark hair is tied in a topknot circled with a bounty of forest flowers. His complexion is clear and white like reflective moonlight. He is Bhagavān of a friendly frame of mind: he sometimes serves, while at other times he is concerned with how his younger brother behaves. Sages call him Baladeva. Mighty, witty, wise, and well dressed in midnight blue, he wears a *tilaka* made of musk, dark in hue. His single earring kisses his cheek, and a lotus circled by bees decorates his ear. O Balarāma of voice deep in tone, when will I hear your call to serve—the sound of your buffalo horn?

Rāma represents the perfection of fraternal love for Kṛṣṇa but is also the object of fraternal love along with Kṛṣṇa. Here in his humorous praise of Rāma, Kṛṣṇa seeks to make the role of Rāma clear as the object of fraternal love, and although in doing so he speaks to all of his friends, the point is especially directed at his younger *sakhās* and his *suhṛt-sakhās*. This brings us to the second subtle level of his philosophical humor that is understood only by Kṛṣṇa's *priya-narma-sakhās*, who are influenced by *mādhurya-rasa*.

While Kṛṣṇa and Balarāma are one in *tattva*, they are also emotionally one only within their friendship with one another. Just prior to Kṛṣṇa's praise of Balarāma, Śukadeva refers to the two brothers with the dual case—*babhūvatus tau*—to emphasize the equality of the two resulting from the profuse affection in fraternal love they feel for one another. It is only from

9. *Śrīmad Bhāgavatam* 10.38.30.

10. In this section, we are reminded of the parallel between Gaura and Kṛṣṇa *līlā*: just as Kṛṣṇa made an effort to point out the ontological position of Balarāma, Caitanya Mahāprabhu made a concerted effort to point out the ontological position of Nityānanda Rāma.

the vantage point of *mādhurya-rasa* that an emotional difference between them is also understood, a difference that Kṛṣṇa concealed when speaking to the entire group of *sakhās*, even as he spoke covertly of it to his *narma-sakhās* at the end of his tribute.

Thus equality among friends gave way to Kṛṣṇa's romantic thoughts, to which the *narma-sakhās* are sympathetic, and this brought out an emotional difference between Kṛṣṇa and Balarāma. As Kṛṣṇa glorified the forest, its beauty began to remind him of Rādhā, and his mind turned in her direction. Thus, while glorifying Balarāma and focusing his friends on fraternal love for him, Kṛṣṇa also planned to leave the greater group of his friends in the care of Balarāma. As he and his confidential friends departed on the pretext of other engagements, his *narma-sakhās* assisted him in his rendezvous with Rādhā and the other *gopīs* at Rādhā-kuṇḍa. Thus the *narma-sakhās* found a second level of humor where the other *sakhās* did not. They smiled within, that is, with the insight that Kṛṣṇa glorified Balarāma to encourage the assembly of *sakhās* to focus their love on his twin, making it easier for Kṛṣṇa to slip away accompanied by *narma-sakhā-bhāva*.

The fact that Kṛṣṇa's mind is drifting toward his own desire for romantic love is apparent in the closing verse of his tribute, where he speaks of Rāma's embracing young *gopīs* to his chest, a fortune for the *gopīs* that exceeds that of Lakṣmī. However, although Balarāma has his own *gopīs*, Lakṣmī did not express a desire to be embraced by Balarāma. Thus, in the final verse of his tribute, Kṛṣṇa more clearly refers to himself and to his own romantic life—a reference noted in particular by his most intimate friends. Commenting on this verse as it is cited by Rūpa Goswāmī in his *Laghu-bhāgavatāmṛta*, Śrī Baladeva Vidyābhūṣaṇa explains that it speaks of the budding love of Rāma's *gopīs*, who are attracted to the potential of his heroism such as the slaying of Dhenuka and Pralambāsura.[11] But more so this verse speaks of Kṛṣṇa, who has already performed a number of heroic acts and who is also already aware of the enchanting excellence of Rādhā among the Vraja *gopīs*. Thus, in the verse of the *Bhāgavata* immediately following Kṛṣṇa's praise of Balarāma (ŚB 10.15.9), we find the following embedded in the text, as explained by Viśvanātha Cakravartī Ṭhākura:

> As Kṛṣṇa's romanticism was inflamed by Cupid following his own utterance "*gopyo 'ntareṇa bhujayor*" ("the *gopīs*, between both arms"—in 10.15.8), Kṛṣṇa, fully satisfying his elder brother, put the cows and

11. *Laghu-bhāgavatāmṛta* 5.344.

> the *sakhās* in one group and exclaimed, "Venerable brother, Subala and I will relax on the slope of a cave of Govardhana for a while and then return. In the meantime, you can sport on the banks of the Kālindī just ahead." After Kṛṣṇa said this they split up, and Śuka mentions in this verse (10.15.9) that Kṛṣṇa enjoyed in a secret place with the *gopīs* because of the appearance of *kiśora* even in *paugaṇḍa*.
> "After praising the elder brother in this way, Kṛṣṇa enjoyed on the banks of Mānasī Gaṅgā, a river at the base of Govardhana, while sending the cows to Vṛndāvana herded by Balarāma."[12]

In his own *Bhāgavatam* commentary on this same verse, Baladeva Vidyābhūṣaṇa concurs: "Kṛṣṇa, accompanied by the followers of Śrīmatī, enjoyed on the banks of a river at the base of a mountain."

In his *Kṛṣṇa-bhāvanāmṛta*, Viśvanātha Cakravartī Ṭhākura reveals a typical explanation conjured up by one of Kṛṣṇa's confidential friends as to why Kṛṣṇa and his *priya-narma-sakhās* need to separate from the assembly of their friends, leaving them with Balarāma.

> Madhumaṅgala, knowing Kṛṣṇa's mind as if he himself were a god, spoke to Kṛṣṇa thus: "O you who are adorned with a peacock feather, I have something to do and thus I am on my way. Earlier today I went to Bhāguri Muni to learn astrology because I had a great doubt that I asked him to dispel. However, he could not dispel it. Fortunately, Garga Muni, who is praised by all the *munis*, is just now bathing at Sūrya-kuṇḍa, and I am confident that he alone can clear my doubts."
>
> Kṛṣṇa, the killer of Keśī, replied, "O friend, my mind is also very eager to see Garga Muni, but it would not be polite to visit him with so many friends."
>
> Madhumaṅgala replied, "If you think it's not polite to go with so many boys, then let just the two of us go! The swan-like sun is swimming to the middle of the sky's lake. It's close to midday! The cows are resting in the cool *kadamba* forest, and our friends also want to take rest. Don't strain them unnecessarily with any more playful games!"

12. *Śrīmad Bhāgavatam* 10.15.9. Viśvanātha Cakravartī's insight into this hidden—*rahasya*—meaning of the verse plays off the previous verse, 10.15.8, in which Kṛṣṇa's mind drifts toward romanticism. Thus, in these verses we realize exactly what Kṛṣṇa's praise of Balarāma is really all about: a clever diversion from his intention to leave the larger group of *gopas* behind and, along with his *narma-sakhās*, to meet with Rādhā and her *sakhīs*.

> Hearing Madhumaṅgala's adventurous words, the *sakhās* said, "O friends, you two go together." Thus Kṛṣṇa and Madhumaṅgala blissfully went to Rādhā-kuṇḍa, swiftly passing through Pramodavana.[13]

Kṛṣṇadāsa Kavirāja similarly describes Kṛṣṇa's excuse for leaving the greater balance of the cowherd assembly with Balarāma at midday in pursuit of romantic love with Rādhā:

> Kṛṣṇa called his *surabhi* cows, who had been wandering here and there, with his flute. He and his friends then took the cows to the shore of the Mānasa-gaṅgā to drink. After the *surabhi* cows drank, the cowherd boys also refreshed themselves with its water, which was cool, delicious, and pure. They bathed in the river and played for a long time. Then Kṛṣṇa sat on the shore, surrounded by his friends. His jokes made them all smile and laugh as they enjoyed together eating a variety of preparations, such as spiced curd mixed with mangoes and other fruits. Kṛṣṇa then said to his friends, "All of you, please take care of the saintly *surabhi* cows with Balarāma for a few minutes while my friends Subala and Madhumaṅgala walk with me to see the beauty of Vṛndāvana forest.[14]

As we have learned earlier, Kṛṣṇa's *parakīya* romanticism plays a significant role in the *bhakti* of his *priya-narma-sakhās* that Balarāma does not participate in. Thus only these boys are aware of another level of humor within Kṛṣṇa's tribute to Balarāma. They know that on the pretext of glorifying Balarāma, Kṛṣṇa said what he needed to in order to shift the focus of the larger group of friends from himself to Balarāma and thus gradually separate from them with the view to rendezvous with Rādhā. Here Madhumaṅgala and Subala represent the *bhāva* of the entire group of *priya-narma-sakhās*, whose special and mysterious *sthāyi-bhāva* and corresponding *līlās* are thus foreshadowed here in canto ten of *Śrīmad Bhāgavatam*'s fifteenth chapter.[15]

In his *Preyo-bhakti-rasārṇava*, Nayanānanda Ṭhākura shares his insight into Balarāma's typical *līlās* with the greater balance of the cowherd boys

13. *Kṛṣṇa-bhāvanāmṛta* 8.62–67.

14. *Govinda-līlāmṛta* 6.38–39.

15. Here again we are reminded of the correspondence between Gaura and Kṛṣṇa *līlā*: Gaura sent Nityānanda Rāma back to Bengal from Purī and told him to remain there for uplifting others. Gaura instructed Nitāi to do so as their *antya-līlā* ensued and Gaura Hari turned from a public figure to his private life. Furthermore, Kṛṣṇadāsa Kavirāja depicts Rāmānanda serving Gaurasundara in his *antya-līlā* just as *narma-sakhā* Subala served Kṛṣṇa in his separation from Rādhā.

on any given day as Kṛṣṇa and his *priya-narma-sakhās* sport elsewhere. What follows is my own paraphrased rendering of the Ṭhākura's internal vision.

> At that time, Haladhara takes charge of all the cowherd boys, headed by Śrīdāmā, as they head to Śrīvana,[16] in search of stray cows. Along the way, they pick flowers, climb trees, and taste tree-ripened fruits. They dance, sing, clap, and cup their hands under their armpits, turning them into wind chambers serving as natural musical instruments, while other boys sound their flutes and buffalo-horn bugles. Jumping here and there, they shout out to their cows while herding them, as if speaking their language. Beholding the beauty of the forest, they decorate their bodies with red clay pigments, and with a gait resembling maddened elephants they flail their limbs as they run. Thus, the cowherd boys play in the company of Rāma and wander throughout this forest of Śrīvana into the early afternoon.
>
> From there, Balabhadra, Śrīdāmā, Sudāmā, and the others proceed south for some distance until they reach Kumudavana, where various blossoming flowers sweeten the breeze, bees sing, and peacocks dance. The *śuka* and *śārī* parrots debate and the cuckoos sing melodiously, while the forest birds all chirp and male herons snap their beaks and let out their explosive *sekow* call distinctive of the wetlands.[17] Therein Haladhara arm-wrestles, testing his strength against that of his challengers, and also engages in stick fighting along with Subhadra, Maṇḍalībhadra, and other older boys, tasting *yuddha-vīra-rasa*. Eventually he is encircled by the greater assembly of young herdsmen holding hands and imploring Haladhara to dance in the center of their circle, increasing the assembly's own dancing ecstasy and making Śrī Rāma's face flush with color.
>
> As the afternoon proceeds into its hottest hours, these fast friends proceed north all the way back to Bhadravana and from there to

16. Śrīvana is another name for Belvana because it is in this forest that Śrī (Lakṣmī) underwent austerity in an effort to become eligible to enter the *rāsa-līlā*. Nayanānanda Ṭhākura then envisions Balarāma and his *sakhās* traveling from the more central Śrīvana on the eastern side of the Yamunā, which lies directly across from Vṛndāvana, all the way to the southernmost forest of Vraja, Kumudavana. And from there he envisions the cowherd assembly returning and reaching the northernmost forest along the banks of the Yamunā, Bhadravana, only to then go west of Vṛndāvana and south of Śyāma-kuṇḍa, to Śrīdāmā's grove. Such a journey involves crossing the Yamunā three times.

17. The heron's call is thought to be the origin of the "fourth note" on the Indian scale.

> the west and just south of Śyāma-kuṇḍa, where they rest briefly at the base of a well-known *tamāla* tree as the songs of cuckoos and bees steal their minds and ears. To the south of Śyāma-kuṇḍa is the grove of Śrīdāmā, consisting of hundreds of internal divisions and thus known as Śata-varga. In that grove is Nāṭya-kuñja, a particular division designated for the dancing of Śrīdāmā-gopa. That enchanting Nāṭya-kuñja glows with a pinkish-sandalwood color. On the eastern side of Śata-varga is a wonderful banyan tree that has hundreds and hundreds of thousands of branches and subbranches. And under the cooling shade of that tree is a golden platform whose placement is such that it constitutes a place so blissful that no discord could possibly exist. Entering there, Balarāma rests briefly upon that platform, as the followers of Śrīdāmā are afforded the opportunity to prepare fruits and offer them to Rāma. Then proceeding onward, Balarāma visits the grove of Sudāmā-candra—Raṅga-kuñja—and those of other *priya-sakhās*, who are also blessed therein with the opportunity to serve him personally.[18]

Thus in the opening verses of the fifteenth chapter of the *Bhāgavata*'s tenth canto, Śukadeva relates the spirit of the *pauganḍa-līlā* with regard to Balarāma's prominence and gives a glimpse into Kṛṣṇa's midday pastimes more relevant to his *kiśora-līlā*. Following these introductory verses, the chapter focuses on the slaying of Dhenukāsura and then gives an introduction to the *līlā* in which Kṛṣṇa chastises Kāliya, both of which Balarāma plays a significant role in.

Here the *Bhāgavatam*'s speaker, Śukavaka, narrates the *līlā* out of chronological order due to ecstasy, for the chastising of Kāliya introduced at the end of the chapter chronologically precedes the slaying of Dhenukāsura. We know this because *Hari-vaṁśa Purāṇa* 2.13.1—devoid of the ecstasy of Śukavaka and the apparent confusion it can cause—lists these *līlās* in chronological order, with Kāliya *mardana* preceding the slaying of Dhenuka. Thus, in our narrative we shall continue first with the chastising of Kāliya.

18. In *Śyāma-kuṇḍāṣṭakam* 8, Raghunātha dāsa Goswāmī says that Rādhikā and her *sakhīs* created *kuñjas* in and around Śyāma-kuṇḍa for Subala, Madhumaṅgala, and other principal friends of Kṛṣṇa—*subala-baṭu-mukhebhyo rādhikādyaiḥ pradattam*. Rūpa Goswāmī, Kṛṣṇadāsa Kavirāja, and Viśvanātha Cakravartī all mention these *kuñjas* but only those awarded to Kṛṣṇa's *priya-narma-sakhās* and associated also with particular *yūtheśvarīs*. Here Nayanānanda speaks of similar groves south of Śyāma-kuṇḍa associated with *priya-sakhās*, who are not associated with particular *yūtheśvarīs*.

11

Converting Kāliya

Kṛṣṇa's cowherd friends were accustomed to his heroic exploits and welcomed them with confidence of their own. However, to the ears of everyone else in Vraja, these exploits, such as the liberation of Agha, were only adventure stories from the mouths of young boys, who in their elders' minds were prone to exaggeration. Thus, the Vraja elders took the stories with a grain of salt, but to the young cowherd boys they were factual in all the fascinating details the boys related and a cause of pride and further self-confidence, given their identification as equals of Rāma and Kṛṣṇa. For the young *gopīs*, on the other hand, these stories described the romantic hero of their dreams. The events surrounding Kṛṣṇa's chastisement of Kāliya had an overwhelming effect even on his cowherd friends—a veritable near-death experience—so one can imagine the trauma it caused to the elders, what to speak of the *kumārīs*. Both the elders and the *gopīs* experienced Kṛṣṇa's heroics firsthand for the first time during this *līlā*, which was particularly traumatic in that Kṛṣṇa's victory appeared for some time to be in question.

Thus, Śukadeva did not desire to retell this *līlā* to Rāja Parīkṣit and avoided doing so. But as his conclusion to the *pauganda* narrative arrived, he also felt conflicted out of a sense of not doing justice to Kṛṣṇa's boyhood because of not including this significant *paugaṇḍa-līlā*. Thus, in the midst of such conflicting emotions, Śukadeva related a very abbreviated form of the *līlā*. However, his abbreviation gave rise to a number of questions on the part of the *rāja*, and Śukadeva ultimately gave in to his student's spiritual curiosity and with trepidation filled in the details to the story. Here we will discuss this *līlā* in chronological order, placing it before the slaying of Dhenukāsura.

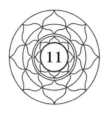

Śukadeva's narrative, consisting of two chapters of the *Bhāgavata* (10.16–17), includes the history of Garuḍa's role in Kāliya's presence in Vraja. From the Hindu mytho-historical record, we learn that the great bird Garuḍa was harassed in his childhood by the *nāga* sons of Kadrū, who was Garuḍa's maternal aunt. This childhood trauma served to color much of his adult Vaiṣṇava life, during which, with the blessing of Viṣṇu, snakes became his principal diet.

The name Garuḍa is derived from the Sanskrit verbal root *gṛ*, "to speak." Thus, in the Vedas he is constituted of Vedic *mantras* and serves as a metaphor for rhythms, sounds, sacrifices, and the *ātmā* itself, which is to be placed on the sacrificial altar. Later in the Purāṇas, Garuḍa more literally represents the pure individual self, inseparable from the Supreme Self, Viṣṇu. In the *Bhāgavata*, he is the powerful Vaiṣṇava zoomorphic carrier of Dvārakeśa Kṛṣṇa, whose insignia decorates Dvārakeśa Kṛṣṇa's battle flag. In his *Paramātmā Sandarbha*, Jīva Goswāmī identifies Garuḍa as a *nitya-mukta taṭastha-jīva*, exemplifying the possibility that the *taṭastha-jīva* has the capacity to reside on the spiritual side of the matter/spirit divide.[1] Śrī Rūpa Goswāmī places him in *dāsya-rasa* bundled together with *sakhya* (*saṅkula-rati*).[2] And Rūpa and Sanātana Goswāmīs both connect Śrīdāmā-gopa of Vraja with Garuḍa: in Vraja, Kṛṣṇa is often defeated in mock fighting by Śrīdāmā and as a result he must carry Śrīdāmā on his shoulders, whereas in Dvārakā Śrīdāmā merges with Garuḍa and carries Kṛṣṇa on his shoulders.[3]

Before becoming Kṛṣṇa's bird carrier in his Dvārakā *līlā*, Garuḍa is also associated with Vraja and its river Yamunā, from which he acquired fish to supplement his *nāga* diet, following the Vaiṣṇava principle of forgoing excessive violence.[4] At that time, out of material compassion the sage associated with the *nāgas*, Saubhari Muni, cursed Garuḍa to die should he harm another fish or snake living in the Yamunā. In this way, Saubhari

1. *Paramātmā Sandarbha* 46.
2. *Bhakti-rasāmṛta-sindhu* 3.4.83.
3. *Laghu-bhāgavatāmṛta* 1.5.374 and *Bṛhad-bhāgavatāmṛta* 2.6.202–203.
4. Jīva Goswāmī explained this principle in *Bhakti Sandarbha* 106, citing *Śrīmad Bhāgavatam* 3.29.15. Therein, excessive violence (*nātihiṁsreṇa*) is prohibited, qualifying the stricter *ahiṁsā* of the Jains for Vaiṣṇavas. Viśvanātha Cakravartī gives an example: "There is no harm in destroying leaves, roots, fruit, and small living entities that are hard to avoid or to see, in preparing various foods for the deity, cleaning the temple, and applying decorations while on the ground." This principle applies to Garuḍa, a Vaiṣṇava in the form of a man/eagle.

committed a Vaiṣṇava *aparādha*. Overwhelmed by his *sattvic prārabdha-karma* in the form of material compassion, he cursed a Vaiṣṇava observing the principle of avoiding excessive violence, and as a result, not only did the *muni* fall from his practice of underwater meditation within the depths of the Yamunā but all of the fish in this area of the Yamunā died. They died because Kāliya-nāga, who had also offended Garuḍa at Ramaṇaka near the ocean, went to the Yamunā to escape the wrath of Garuḍa, thinking that therein he would be safe from Garuḍa on the strength of Saubhari's curse. And where Kāliya went, his Vaiṣṇava envy went with him, taking physical shape in the form of poison that wreaked havoc in the Yamunā. Śrī Kavi-karṇapūra describes the scene thus in his *Ānanda-vṛndāvana-campū*:

> The burning venom of the great black serpent Kāliya constantly heated and even boiled the waters of the Yamunā. Goddess Yamunā felt as though she had a fiery black ball within her belly. Indeed, the poisonous vapors polluted the air and even caused birds flying overhead to fall down into the water. The entire atmosphere was contaminated by the inauspicious presence of Kāliya, who continually harassed the inhabitants of Vṛndāvana. The forceful exhalation of fiery poison from Kāliya's nostrils illuminated the Yamunā's otherwise dark waves with a crimson-gold radiance. The beauty of this scene [were it not for the calamity at hand] resembled the waves of the salt ocean glittering under the moonlight. The dense black smoke lingering above the Yamunā indicated the presence of a raging fire within. Due to the calamitous situation caused by the burning poison of that crooked serpent, nothing could live in the Yamunā except Kāliya's wives and sons. As one takes shelter under an umbrella, Kāliya stayed safely in a deep lake within the Yamunā.[5]

By the time Rāma and Kṛṣṇa had entered their *paugaṇḍa-līlā*, this ancient story was well known. For a very long time—*yugas*—Kāliya had ruled over a section of the Yamunā to the south that served almost like a lake unto itself, being so wide as to affect the flow of the current. No one could go to this section and return safely. Garuḍa, although not fearing Saubhari's curse, had long ago ceased from visiting the area himself, knowing that in the future his object of love would appear in Vraja and rectify the situation.

5. *Ānanda-vṛndāvana-campū* 3.9.

And before moving onward himself, he dropped celestial nectar on one large *kadamba* tree towering over Kāliya's lake within the Yamunā. During Kṛṣṇa's *pauganḍa-līlā*, this tree was the only form of life left standing on the shore of the lake. As we shall see, this *kadamba* tree—a tropical evergreen with scented orange flowers in dense globe-shaped clusters[6]—facilitated Kṛṣṇa's *līlā* of chastising and converting Kāliya, fulfilling the desire residing in Garuḍa's compassionate Vaiṣṇava heart.[7]

As Rāma and Kṛṣṇa learned of the ancient history related above, it piqued their boyhood curiosity, especially that of the more mischievous Kṛṣṇa. And to be sure, Yaśodā-māyī's repeated warnings to avoid this area of the Yamunā were only counterproductive. Not a day went by on which Kṛṣṇa did not contemplate observing this area firsthand and heroically restoring the Yamunā to her original pristine condition, appropriately dealing with Kāliya-nāga. However, in Kṛṣṇa's mind, the pious wives of Kāliya complicated the situation. Nor would Balarāma permit him to go there. Not only was Balarāma his appointed protector, but he also had a deep relationship with the *nāga* community. Indeed, Rāma eventually married a sector of Vraja *gopīs* who were previously from the *nāga* community,[8] and he himself serves Viṣṇu in a *nāga* form as Ananta Śeṣa. Moreover, in her previous life, Balarāma's mother, Rohiṇī, was Kadrū, the mother of Kāliya and Ananta![9] Thus, without Balarāma's blessing, Kṛṣṇa waited in anticipation for an opening.

In the *Bhāgavata* the Yamunā is also known as Kālindī, and in *Gopāla-tāpanī śruti* she is referred to as "the great daughter of the sun"—*bṛhad-bhānavyā*—and further identified therein with *svāhā* of the great eighteen-syllable Gopāla *mantra*. The *Bhāgavata* also refers to her as *kṛṣṇam* because

6. *Neolamarckia cadamba*, commonly known in English as the burflower tree or Leichhardt pine.

7. *Varāha Purāṇa* describes this tree as one that can be seen even today with eyes of devotion: "O large-eyed woman! The wise see something very astonishing there. In front of the lake of Kāliya, there is a huge, pure *kadamba* tree with hundreds of branches and sweet fragrance. All year, attractive and cool, it continues to flower. All the directions are illuminated by this tree." A *kadamba* also plays a significant role in Kṛṣṇa's *līlā* of stealing the young *gopīs*' clothes. It is also thought that the Theravada Buddhist Sumedha Buddha attained enlightenment under a *kadamba* tree.

8. There are also human communities associated with *nāgas* who are referred to by the same name. *Garga Saṁhitā* describes Balarāma's wives in Vraja as *nāgas*.

9. This is a Purāṇic perspective on the position of Rohiṇī, while *Śrīmad Bhāgavatam*'s perspective is more theologically profound: the motherhood of Rohiṇī—her *vātsalya-rasa*—is eternal. From this vantage point, Kadrū is a partial expansion of Rohiṇī.

of her dark color and her dearness to Kṛṣṇa. Poets describe her as the ecstatic perspiration pouring from Kṛṣṇa's dark complexion, and from an environmental perspective she is the main artery of the body of the Vraja community, its source of fresh underground water and a great channel for its commerce. If Vraja is the expansion of Kṛṣṇa's own body, the Yamunā is the central pathway of his *prāṇa*. More specifically, she is his *suṣumṇā-nāḍī*, the *nāḍī* through which *muktas* pass from their mortal body into the *paravyoma*, a course traversed by *rāga-bhaktas* simply by bathing in her waters. We see this in the case of Gopa-kumāra, for whom the Yamunā served as a portal from the Vraja-maṇḍala of this world to the *aprakaṭa-līlā*:

> That chief of charming heroes [Kṛṣṇa] sounded his *muralī* in his own playful manner and then escaped behind me, suddenly stepping into a grove. Alas! Though I ran after and looked everywhere for him, he had disappeared. Losing sight of him, I fainted and fell into the swift current of the Yamunā. As her forceful current carried me away, I regained awareness, although still disoriented, my fainting and reawakening both a product of *prema*. Looking about, I saw myself transported to another realm along a wonderful path in a vehicle flying faster than the speed of the mind and higher than one's imagination could reach. Collecting my wits, I was amazed to see myself passing through Vaikuṇṭha, the delightful Ayodhyā, and other realms, arriving at Goloka—the shining world above all others—which I had aspired for so long to attain. Everything there appeared the same as in this divine Mathurā-maṇḍala (on earth).[10]

Śrī Rūpa glorifies this most sacred river thus in his *Yamunāṣṭakam*: "Being witness to many of Śrī Mukunda's wonderful pastimes, she manifests these pastimes in the hearts of those who take shelter of her." The central nervous system of Kṛṣṇa is wired for receiving sacrifice and thus identified with sacrifice itself. The most complete form of sacrifice is *mahābhāva-svarūpiṇī* Rādhā, and Kālindī, the Yamunā personified, is her expansion.[11] And as

10. *Bṛhad-bhāgavatāmṛta* 2.6.10–14.

11. Rādhā's father's name is Vṛṣabhānu, which means "great light." The sun is the presiding deity of their family, worshipped by Rādhā. Rādhā is known as Vṛṣabhānu-nandinī, "she who gives joy to Vṛṣabhānu." *Bhānu* indicates the sun, and *vṛṣa* means "the greatest" or "best of its kind." But Brahman is the greatest light/sun, and thus Rādhā is the joy of the brightest sun (Brahman/Kṛṣṇa). *Vṛṣa* also means "bull." Rādhā was born under the influence of the sun in the sign of Taurus. The bull is the symbol of *dharma* (righteousness). Thus, Rādhā is the joy (*hlādinī-śakti*) of the brightest *dharma*—the *prema-dharma* of Śrī Caitanya.

we shall see ahead, Kṛṣṇa's punishment and conversion of Kāliya serves only as a subtext to his budding love for Rādhā, as he ultimately displays his artful dancing before her as a prelude to their romantic rendezvous and *mahā-rasa* yet to unfold.

Fortunately, Kṛṣṇa did not have to wait long for the desired opening to make its appearance. On the day that Balarāma's birth constellation arrived, Rāma was kept in the house to observe the auspicious bathing ritual. Śrī Rūpa Goswāmī cites Balarāma speaking to Subala:

> Today is my birth *tithi*. Therefore, my affectionate mother has kept me at home in order to bathe me. Subala! Tell Kṛṣṇa that I said that he should by no means go to Kāliya's lake today.[12]

Jīva Goswāmī explains that this was not Rāma's annual birthday, but only the day of the month that the moon entered his birth constellation—a minor celebration. However, Rāma's message did not reach Kṛṣṇa in time, and Rāma's absence provided Kṛṣṇa with a window of opportunity, through which he took no time to pass.

Taking advantage of Balarāma's absence, boy after boy surrounded Kṛṣṇa at arm's length, as if to make up for Rāma's absence and protect him, when in fact they were simply eager to gaze upon Kṛṣṇa's beautiful form without obstruction. However, only Balarāma knew that Kṛṣṇa desired to graze the pregnant cows on grasses near Kāliya's lake that had been growing undisturbed for some time and were thus thought to be exceedingly nourishing. Kṛṣṇa was not, however, permitted to enter the lake itself or even get too close to it. But this is not to say that had the boys known, they would not have gone with Kṛṣṇa, for like him they too were fearless in his company. Indeed, an adventure was at hand and thus there was no time for hesitation.

Upon grazing the cows and relaxing with his friends, Kṛṣṇa could not resist going ahead without them to view the legendary lake from its shore. It was eight miles wide and very deep as well. The water was black and bubbled with heat, and the air carried droplets of the boiling water onto the shore and scorched the land underfoot such that nothing could grow there. The heroism within Kṛṣṇa desired to call out Kāliya, but the thought of Kāliya's wives caused a wave of shyness to hold him back. As he was caught between these conflicting emotions, cries from the nearby cowherds and mooing of the cows captured his attention, distracting him from his contemplated heroics. In his momentary absence, the pregnant cows had wandered forward

12. *Bhakti-rasāmṛta-sindhu* 3.3.29.

and drunk contaminated water, and mooing pitifully they passed out as if dead. Seeing this, the cowherds drank the same water themselves, thinking that without the cows, their lives were meaningless. Crying out for Kṛṣṇa, they too passed out, as if having taken their own lives. Seeing their condition and commitment to cowherding—to *dharma*—Kṛṣṇa condemned his curiosity and considered his sense of heroism to have been no more than a rationalization of his impulsive nature that had now resulted in disaster. How would he explain himself to the elders? How could he continue his own life without his friends and cows, for what is a cowherd without cows? What is a friend without friends? Can there be *śaktimān* without *śakti*?

Understanding the situation, Kṛṣṇa's *aiśvarya-śakti* took advantage of the opportunity to enter his intimate *līlā* and play a significant role. Thus Kṛṣṇa manifested as many forms as there were fallen cowherds and embraced and picked up each and every one of them, bringing them back to life with his loving gaze. Because each boy experienced Kṛṣṇa personally reviving him, none of them were aware of the *aiśvarya* at hand, and thus they experienced only the most intimate sweetness in the arms of their beloved friend. However, although each boy experienced Kṛṣṇa's sweet, undivided loving attention, each boy also pondered the fact that Kṛṣṇa had resurrected him. They ultimately attributed this power to the well-known blessing of Gargācārya, who had predicted that Nārāyaṇa would perform miraculous acts through this boy. Coming back to life, as it were, the cowherds implicitly understood that Kṛṣṇa was the source of their own consciousness.

Then Kṛṣṇa also attended to each and every cow. Embracing their necks, scratching them, and whispering in their ears, Kṛṣṇa revived them, and they began to protectively lick Kṛṣṇa with great affection as if he were their unborn calves appearing before them. And their actual calves kicked from within their mothers' wombs, expressing their desire to have the *darśana* of Kṛṣṇa. However, once revived, the cows and boys remained somewhat disoriented. Tears flooding their eyes, they remained dazed. Kṛṣṇa then told them to move back farther from the lake to safety and proceeded with conviction and anger to the lone *kadamba* tree still standing on the lake's shore.

Climbing the *kadamba* tree, he surveyed the lake. Being a meticulous dresser—*suveśa*—he tightened his belt and tied his hair back. Seeing this from a distance, his friends drew near despite his previous words of caution. They were attracted to this quality of his and his heroism—both *uddīpanas* of *sakhya-rati*—and they also identified with his heroism themselves. Thus they came forward, their cows in front of them. And it seemed as though by closely following the exact path of Kṛṣṇa himself, they were immune to the previous poisonous effects in that area.

Then Kṛṣṇa, the source of all *avatāras*, suddenly dove from the treetop into the black waters below, wherein he swam underwater invoking Matsya within himself. Just imagine the beauty of Kṛṣṇa swimming with the ability of the Matsya *avatāra*! Kṛṣṇa's swimming made a pleasing music-like sound underwater, a vibration that Kāliya was able to tune in to. Snakes have no visible ears, and thus they do not hear sounds as humans do. But they are very sensitive to vibrations due to sensory nerves on their skin. However, *nāgas* are depicted as half serpent/half human, and thus Kāliya-nāga actually heard the vibrations emanating from Kṛṣṇa, which seemed to put him on notice within his own home.

Meanwhile, on the surface of the lake, large waves ensued. No longer seeing Kṛṣṇa, the cows also entered the lake, but because of Kṛṣṇa's purifying presence within the water, they were not adversely affected as before, although they were dismayed at his being out of sight and they mooed hauntingly. However, Kṛṣṇa's *sakhās* fainted into one another's arms—some fainting, others catching those who fainted—not from the effects of Kāliya's poison but from the thought of losing Kṛṣṇa. Had they not fainted, they would have dived in after him, which would have been worse. Thus they were saved by their *sāttvika-bhāvas*.

Then just as suddenly as Kṛṣṇa had submerged himself within the water, he emerged, but now immobilized within the coils of Kāliya, causing the *sañcāri-bhāva trāsa* (terror) and subsequent *sāttvika-bhāvas*—trembling, losing color, stuttering, and fainting—in the bodies of his cowherd friends.[13]

> When his dear *ābhīra* friends saw him wrapped and motionless within the *nāga*'s coils, they became very disturbed. They had given up everything for Kṛṣṇa—their families, wealth, wives, and associated pleasures—indeed, their very selves. Now, their intelligence overcome by terror, suffering, and sorrow, they fell to the ground.[14]

13. Here their fear is a *sañcāri-bhāva* and not the *gauṇa-rati* of *bhayānaka*, which involves fear arising out of contemplation of circumstances. The *sakhās*' terror in this situation is sudden and momentary by contrast. Nor is it fear *of* Kṛṣṇa, which does not arise in *sakhya-rati* but rather a sudden fear *for* Kṛṣṇa. See Jīva Goswāmī's explanation of *Bhakti-rasāmṛta-sindhu* 3.2.71 and 3.3.100.

14. *Śrīmad Bhāgavatam* 10.16.10. Here we are reminded of similar statements concerning the *gopīs*' sacrificial love for Kṛṣṇa. In this verse the word *kalatra* (wives) refers only to the cowherds' prospect of marriage. The spirit of the text is that all of these things were of no concern to them in comparison to their friendship with Govinda.

The cows, shedding tears and crying out as if uttering human words, stood motionless, stunned by intense grief. Not only the cattle but also the buffalo, deer, and other animals at some distance from the scene followed suit and acted similarly. Thus all of the firsthand witnesses of what appeared to be a tragic event were rendered incapable of informing others of the situation. If only Rāma had been there! Thinking thus, the *devas*—the underlying intellect of the natural surrounding environment—sent signals to him and the balance of the Vraja-loka in the form of inauspicious omens, macrocosmically manifesting as earthquakes and falling meteors, and microcosmically as the quivering of the left or right hand, eye, and thigh of the bodies of Vraja's inhabitants. These omens served to alert them and also to conceal Kṛṣṇa's powers from them for the sake of increasing the bittersweetness of the *līlā*. These villagers became like animals driven only by raw emotion upon seeing their offspring in imminent danger. Their bodies trembling, the earth quaking, and small meteors falling from the sky, they intuitively understood that danger was indeed afoot, and each and every one of them thought only of and for Kṛṣṇa's safety, as if it were synonymous with their own. Thus they turned to Balarāma for shelter with questioning minds, seeking both solace and a solution. And Rāma stood among them during the day's celebrations centered on himself like a pillar of confident support, the omens unable to dislodge his omniscience, and offered subsequent assurance as to Kṛṣṇa's safety.[15]

Pained by the Vraja *vāsīs*' pain of separation from Kṛṣṇa, while at the same time aware through his omniscience that Kṛṣṇa could not be in any real danger, Rāma resorted merely to smiling—*bhagavān mādhavo balaḥ*. Here Śukadeva describes Balarāma as "very intelligent," referring to his omniscience, but in the sage's budding *gopī-bhāva* he also expresses some initial loving anger toward Balarāma. How could he laugh in the face of the Vraja *vāsīs*' distress? Was he drunk, as he was known to be at times? Here the words *mādhavo balaḥ*, with which Śukadeva describes Rāma, imply both of these perspectives. The syllable *mā* means "knowledge," and *dhava* refers to the bearer of that knowledge, but *mādhavaḥ* also refers to Rāma's penchant for *madhu*, or intoxication. Furthermore, the epithet Mādhava refers to the fact that Balarāma was a descendant of the *kṣatriya* Madhu

15. This is described in *Śrīmad Bhāgavatam* 10.16.13–15. Verse 14 states that from the omens, the Vraja-loka thought Kṛṣṇa had died. However, the word *nidhanaṁ* can also mean "great treasure." Thus, they thought of Kṛṣṇa as the greatest treasure and not about his majesty (*atad-vidaḥ*) by which he himself could easily defeat Kāliya-nāga—*nidhanaṁ matvā prāptam atad-vidaḥ*.

dynasty of warriors, whose hearts are harder than those of simple cowherds. "How could Rāma have let something happen to Kṛṣṇa?" Śukadeva implies. In contrast, a *sakhya-rati-gopa* does not think like this, but he can certainly understand it.

Nonetheless, seeing Rāma's smile, everyone placed themselves in his hands, experiencing in the immediate some measure of relief and sufficient resolve to search sensibly for Kṛṣṇa's whereabouts. Balarāma had wanted to accomplish this, but was he thinking anything else? Yes, indeed. Rāma was amused that Kṛṣṇa was playing in the water with Kāliya-nāga, because this reminded him of how he, too, in his form of Śeṣa-nāga plays with and holds Kṛṣṇa/Viṣṇu while in the causal ocean. Furthermore, he knew that in his form of Śeṣa he was the brother of Kāliya, and thus Kāliya, also the half-brother of Garuḍa, was different from other menaces that Kṛṣṇa encountered. Surely Kṛṣṇa would deal with Kāliya differently than he had with Kaṁsa's henchmen, and this aroused curiosity in the mind of Balarāma.

By this time, it was already late in the afternoon, and Kṛṣṇa should have returned by now. Where was he, and what did the omens portend? Knowing the answer to these otherwise perplexing questions, Rāma led the villagers in the direction of Kāliya's lake, following Kṛṣṇa's distinct footprints. We learned earlier that Kṛṣṇa herded his cows barefoot, but how was it that his footprints remained undisturbed after so many hours? We are reminded that Kṛṣṇa's auspicious bodily characteristics, which include the markings on his feet, are *uddīpana-vibhāvas* for *sakhya-rati*. Although Kṛṣṇa moved amid millions of cowherd friends and cows, the cowherds were so stimulated in love for him by the markings on the soles of his feet that they were always careful not to step on his footprints or to allow the cows to do so. The rest of the forest residents along with the wind, rain, and sun all followed the cowherds' example through the course of the day, unless it was useful to cover or erase them in consideration of his romantic intrigues. Thus the villagers accompanied by Balarāma fixed their minds on following Kṛṣṇa's footprints without distraction. Just like calves fixated on their mothers' udders, they pursued the cream of the Upaniṣads—*śruti-sāram*—Kṛṣṇa and his ever-unfolding exploits.

Then from a distance, they saw the lake and Kṛṣṇa wrapped in the coils of Kāliya. As they neared the lake, they saw the cowherd boys—incapacitated now as Kṛṣṇa had been in Kāliya's coils for at least one *muhūrta*—and many kinds of weeping animals. They called out to the boys with questions as to what had happened but heard only silence in response. Then they called out to the animals, thinking they had confused the boys with the animals, given that the boys appeared inanimate while the animals were crying humanlike tears. Finally understanding their own confusion and the pitiful condition of the boys, they were plunged into desperation.

> Yaśodā's upper cloth became wet with hot tears. She reached a state in which all her senses ceased to function. What a calamity! Seeing Kṛṣṇa wrapped in the coils of Kāliya, Yaśodā experienced the *sañcāri-bhāva* of temporary insanity (*unmāda*). Thinking the animals had special powers derived from *mantras*, she pleaded with them with folded hands to destroy Kāliya. Thinking the trees were doctors [bearing medicinal leaves and bark], she asked them for medicine to counteract the poison.[16]

The young *gopīs*, however, did not experience the same grief of their elders, but rather grief combined with an intense love, which as of yet they did not understand.[17]

The elders, headed by Nanda, were first frozen in shock, but then they melted and began to flow unchecked into the water, their *vātsalya-rati* being suppressed and *karuṇa-rasa* taking precedence.[18] Alarmed by this, yet completely confident in Kṛṣṇa's ability, Balarāma, through his knowing glance, assuring smile, and, in some cases, long arms, checked their forward progress like a dam.[19] This is what he told the elders leading the charge:

> Wait! Garga Muni has said that according to Kṛṣṇa's birth chart he will save Vraja from all kinds of obstacles. Therefore, don't you think he himself will be saved from this apparent danger? Be patient. Furthermore, if you all jump and drown in the river and meanwhile Kṛṣṇa frees himself, who will raise my little brother? You will then be guilty of neglecting Garga's order to take care of this precious boy.

This was Balarāma's charming reasoning—asserting the elders' need to protect the child who was prophesized to protect them. Thus Kṛṣṇa's *aiśvarya*

16. *Bhakti-rasāmṛta-sindhu* 2.4.82 and 4.4.9.

17. In his commentary on *Ujjvala-nīlamaṇi* 15.184, Viśvanātha Cakravartī describes as a particular kind of *pravāsa* (sometimes termed *karuṇā*) the separation (*vipralambha*) arising in the minds of the young *gopīs* when they saw Kṛṣṇa in Kāliya's lake.

18. *Bhakti-rasāmṛta-sindhu* 4.4.7 explains that when *rati* transforms into lamentation in the heart by one's perception of another person's misfortune, it is called *śoka-rati*, the *sthāyi-bhāva* of *karuṇa-rasa*, which is particularly compatible with *vātsalya*.

19. *Śrīmad Bhāgavatam* 10.16.22.

was wrapped in *mādhurya*, nourishing the kind of reasoning by which the *līlā* goes round, all of which made perfect sense to the elders.

Kṛṣṇa, of course, noted Balarāma's conflicting feelings of confidence and distress: due to his omniscience, Rāma was confident of Kṛṣṇa's prowess, while at the same time he felt distress when seeing the distress of others, who lacked his omniscience and were thus unsure what the outcome might be. And, of course, Kṛṣṇa also felt the plight of his devotees. Thus, he felt the need to free himself from the coils of Kāliya. But why then did Kṛṣṇa wait so long to free himself, which resulted in all of this? Rāma knew the answer to this question, and thus he was not upset at Kṛṣṇa for prolonging his chastisement of Kāliya. Let us now explore this confidential topic as we proceed to the conclusion of this *līlā*.

As mentioned earlier, Kāliya was the son of Kadrū, sister of Vinatā. Thus his half-brother was the great Vaiṣṇava Garuḍa. He was also the full brother of Ananta Śeṣa, and his wives were all Vaiṣṇavas. Thus, he was influenced by *bhakti-saṁskāras*, and his wives in particular pointed out to him the virtues of Nārāyaṇa, planting the seed of *bhakti* in his heart. Although he did not cultivate that seed and in fact committed offenses, the spiritual well-wishing of his wives was the underlying cause for Kṛṣṇa's interest in him. Wherever *bhakti* goes, Kṛṣṇa follows. Despite Kāliya's arrogance and offenses to others, he was nonetheless kind to his own family. Thus, despite his wives' frustration with him, he still had a place in their hearts and consequently they always tried to turn him toward *bhakti*.

Given Kāliya's relationship with devotees, Kṛṣṇa's chastisement of him differs from how Kṛṣṇa dealt with the servants of Kaṁsa. It is said that the slaying of Kaṁsa's henchmen was done by the Viṣṇu within Kṛṣṇa, but notably it was Kṛṣṇa himself who chastised Kāliya. This is evident from the fact that after freeing himself from the embrace of Kāliya, which gradually turned into a loving one, not only did Kṛṣṇa chastise the snake with the soles of his feet, but he also danced on Kāliya's heads with a view to demonstrate his artistic talent to the young *gopīs* standing on the shore—a foreshadowing of their *rāsa-līlā* yet to come. Seen from the *mādhurya-rati* perspective, this was the motivating force of the entire *līlā*. Thus Kṛṣṇa remained in the coils of Kāliya, waiting until the young *gopīs* arrived so that he could display his dancing ability before them. But the broader point here is that Nārāyaṇa does not participate in such intimate *līlās*; and Lakṣmī, although desiring to, could not!

The beautiful sight of Kṛṣṇa swimming underwater served as an epiphany for Kāliya—a beginning to his reformation. The sound vibration coming from Kṛṣṇa was both challenging and inviting, as is the truth of Vedānta. Thus, Kāliya embraced Kṛṣṇa but also held him too tightly, just as novice devotees make mistakes in their efforts to serve until their faith is firm and scripturally well informed. Once Kṛṣṇa freed himself, Kāliya's awkward attempts to kiss him were more like biting him. This is how Kṛṣṇa experienced the struggle.[20] Then as Kṛṣṇa mounted Kāliya's many hoods and danced stunningly upon them to the sound of heavenly music, Kāliya simply surrendered to the loving chastisement of his *guru*. His lack of skill in *bhakti-sādhana* was made up for by his *śaraṇāgati*, at which point his wives also spoke up on his behalf.

The *nāga-patnīs* emerged along with their children and crawled onto the island within the lake, placing their children before Kṛṣṇa. They then prayed in three distinct stages, consisting of acceptance of Kṛṣṇa's chastisement as appropriate, veneration of Rāma and Kṛṣṇa in *aiśvarya-bhāva*, and a petition on behalf of Kāliya. And Kṛṣṇa gracefully accepted their petition.

In the end, Kāliya, assuming the *añjali-mudrā*, professed his remorse and commitment to *bhakti*:

> O Murāri! Before you, I am but a vile snake. Do not become angry with the most fallen and miserable. I have committed a great offense, not understanding who you were. Being the greatest fool, I have no protector. You should therefore protect me. Be pleased with me.[21]

The wives of Kāliya then presented Kṛṣṇa with the Kaustubha-maṇi, representing all *jīvas*, that Kṛṣṇa keeps on his chest.[22] *Nāgas*, being underworld guardians of the earth's treasures—minerals, gemstones, and other riches—are always associated with jewels. In the context of the developing *prakaṭa-līlā*, this eternal ornament of Kṛṣṇa was given to him by the *nāgas*, who are also thought to safeguard certain esoteric texts.[23]

20. This perspective is implied in the *Vaiṣṇava-toṣaṇī* of Sanātana Goswāmī.

21. In *Bhakti-rasāmṛta-sindhu* 4.6.5, Kāliya's petition is described as an example of *bhayānaka-rasa* (fear) on the part of one thinking he has offended Kṛṣṇa. Thus at this point Kāliya is considered to be a devotee, and in this *rasa* and this particular type of fear, the devotee becomes both the *āśraya-ālambana-vibhāva* and *viṣaya-ālambana-vibhāva*. *Śrīmad Bhāgavatam* 11.12.8 states that Kāliya attained unalloyed (*kevala*) *bhakti*. Viśvanātha Cakravartī comments that he attained *dāsya-rasa*. Rūpa Goswāmī lists four types of *dāsas*: *adhikṛta*, *āśrita*, *pāriṣada*, and *anuga* (*Bhakti-rasāmṛta-sindhu* 3.2.18). Among the *āśrita-dāsas*, he lists three divisions: *śāraṇya*, *jñāni-cara*, and *sevā-niṣṭhā* (*Bhakti-rasāmṛta-sindhu* 3.2.21). Rūpa Goswāmī describes Kāliya as a *śāraṇya* (*Bhakti-rasāmṛta-sindhu* 3.2.23–24).

22. This is mentioned in *Rādhā-kṛṣṇa-gaṇoddeśa-dīpikā* 2.129.

23. In the Buddhist tradition, Gautama was a *nāga* in his previous life. Thus, he had an

Kṛṣṇa then sent Kāliya back to Ramaṇaka, his original home near the ocean, as his *bhāva* imbibed in seed from his wives was not suitable for residing in Vraja. Kṛṣṇa also assured him that the scars on his heads incurred from his dancing would serve as Kāliya's Vaiṣṇava *tilaka*, seeing which Garuḍa would not harm him.[24] In parting, Kāliya also submitted that, should Garuḍa not be available in any instance, he himself would be pleased to become Kṛṣṇa's carrier. Thus, in some *kalpas* Kṛṣṇa ties together cloth supplied by the *nāga-patnīs*, harnesses Kāliya, and triumphantly rides him like a horse. How extraordinary is the victory of Kāliya Kṛṣṇa![25]

With Kāliya's departure, Kṛṣṇa left the island in the lake. To avoid getting wet, he walked on the heads of other *nāgas* to the shore. Prior to going to the lake, he had dressed himself in consideration of the possibility of entering it, but he left dressed anew in garments and jewelry supplied by the beautiful and well-dressed *nāga-patnīs*. His cowherd friends, spread across the eastern, western, and southern banks of the lake, were the first to greet him. Overall, it was as if they were unconscious and Kṛṣṇa was their consciousness, and thus with his return they again became animated, although clumsy at first. Śrīdāmā wanted to embrace him immediately, but his thick arms became paralyzed by the *sāttvika-bhāva stambha*, and he was unable to lift them. Other friends also lost control of their bodies, yet in the *sañcāri-bhāva harṣa* they experienced joy, even as they could not stand on their feet or speak coherently.[26] Their speech impeded, they could not convey their intimate feelings or even say, "O friend, it's me!" So intense were their multiple *sāttvika-bhāvas* that these ecstasies caused concern for Kṛṣṇa. Only after they—who had experienced this *līlā* from beginning to end—began to normalize did Kṛṣṇa proceed to address the elders, who

---

extremely good relationship with the *nāgas* and had asked them to keep the *Prajñāpāramitā-sūtra* text safe until humanity was ready to receive it. It was the great second-century Indian Buddhist master and philosopher Nāgārjuna who is thought to have received this text from them.

24. In *Bhakti-rasāmṛta-sindhu* 2.1.177, Rūpa Goswāmī cites Kṛṣṇa's marking Kāliya's heads with his feet as an example of his independence (*svatantra*) within his quality of being the controlling deity (*īśvara*). Although Kāliya offended Kṛṣṇa, Kṛṣṇa touched him with his feet and thus blessed him, whereas although Brahmā praised Kṛṣṇa after attempting to hide his friends and calves, Kṛṣṇa said nothing to him in response and appeared to ignore him. Thus, as an *īśvara* Kṛṣṇa acts as he chooses and is not obliged like other lesser *īśvaras* to respond in a particular manner.

25. *Bṛhad-bhāgavatāmṛta* 2.6.246–248. Here Sarūpa-gopa experiences this in the *aprakaṭa-līlā*.

26. See *Bhakti-rasāmṛta-sindhu* 3.3.97 and 3.3.104.

seeing the boys revived also began to return to normal. The young *gopīs*, however, did not normalize and Kṛṣṇa could not find the words to talk to them. When Kṛṣṇa emerged from the lake, they lost consciousness but saw him internally and then remained in a state of fainting and recovering for several days. When Kṛṣṇa saw the *gopīs*, he experienced new and explosive emotions internally that he was nonetheless able to control, while exhibiting different emotions externally. Finally, the trees, the animals, the birds, and others all normalized, and the water of the Yamunā itself became pure and crystal clear, its darkness now only a reflection of Kṛṣṇa's complexion.

Then Kṛṣṇa approached Rāma respectfully, and Rāma mildly admonished him with his glance. Although he was a pillar of strength throughout the entire ordeal—bearing the weight of the community's emotion—Rāma was withered within at the experience of the others' plight, even as he smiled slightly before his younger brother. Then all-knowing Kṛṣṇa embraced him, and before everyone the pair remained locked in one another's arms for what could have been a *yuga*, as everyone looked on lovingly. Their friends had a similar fraternal feeling and others had sympathy for the boys' fraternal love for one another. Let the poets try to capture this scene of Vraja and convey even a shadow of its emotions. Words fail woefully. *Jaya* Rāma! *Jaya* Kṛṣṇa!

With the return of his son to safety, Nanda Rāja gave charitably to the *brāhmaṇas*, who reminded him that Kṛṣṇa's ongoing well-being was tied to Nanda's piety. As people heard the news of Hari's exploits with Kāliya, they came from near and far to gaze upon Rāma and Kṛṣṇa. They made the connection between the inauspicious omens and Kṛṣṇa's hours of apparent danger and his subsequent victory. Talking about the details of the event, family members and extended family pressed the young *gopas* for more details and discussed their implications.

By now, the godly day-maker—Divākara—himself prepared to retire and rest in the west from the day's stressful events. How emotionally and physically exhausted, then, were the Vraja *vāsīs*, who were much closer to Kṛṣṇa than the *devas*? They wisely decided to spend the night camping in the forest rather than make the trek in the dark back to the village. However, they made their provisional camp some distance from the Yamunā for fear that residues of Kāliya's previous poisonous influence might still linger in the Yamunā's immediate vicinity.

Although they were hungry and had left Balarāma's *jayantī* feast behind untouched, they feasted on Kṛṣṇa's close company in the intimacy of their campout. They milked the cows but did not offer the milk to Kṛṣṇa or drink it themselves out of fear that it might be contaminated. As the light of the night's campfire dwindled, they retired, comforted by the fact that Kṛṣṇa now lay safely on Yaśodā's affectionate and protective lap.

Meanwhile, Kaṁsa's spies sent news of the day's events to Kaṁsa in Mathurā. He was livid to learn that not only had Kāliya been defeated but, worse yet, he had become a devotee of Kṛṣṇa! Thus, Kaṁsa sent his brother, an arsonist, with a plan to surround Nanda's camp with a forest fire. He reasoned that because they had not camped along the banks of the Yamunā, they would have no escape from the fire's flames.

Balarāma was the first to be awakened by the roaring blaze, and he quickly roused the other *gopas*. In desperation, the other villagers called out to Rāma and Kṛṣṇa out of fear for the boys' safety, unable to tolerate the thought of losing their company as a result of the fire.

> When the blazing forest fire, who was actually the brother of Kaṁsa, surrounded Kṛṣṇa like a cloud bank in the sky, a frown of anger appeared on Balarāma's forehead. Seeing the forest fire spread through the dry reeds, Kṛṣṇa's friends, not considering their own bodies, surrounded him on all sides. Thinking only of Kṛṣṇa's protection and of their attachment to him, they wept enough tears to extinguish the fire themselves. To others it appeared that Kṛṣṇa actually swallowed the fire, even as they reasoned that in fact he must have somehow blown it out, if it had occurred at all.[27]

To be sure, forest fires never occur in Vraja of their own accord. There are no arsonists living there. Lightning never strikes, and bamboo shoots rub together only to produce a melodious music-like sound, identifying themselves as family members of Kṛṣṇa's fortunate bamboo flute. Thus, as explained above, the fire was initiated by an outside force, but even then it couldn't damage the environment or its inhabitants. It could not take the lives of small animals and birds or those of the wish-fulfilling trees

27. See *Bhakti-rasāmṛta-sindhu* 2.5.66, an example of Balarāma experiencing *raudra-rasa*, and 3.3.101, an example of *aśru*, the *sāttvika-bhāva* of tears. The idea that Kṛṣṇa swallowed the fire is expressed in the *Bhāgavatam*. Jīva Goswāmī, in his *Gopāla-campū* rendering of this *līlā*, considers this poetic exaggeration of Śukadeva. Viśvanātha Cakravartī, elaborating on the words *ananta-śakti-dhṛk* in *Śrīmad Bhāgavatam* 10.17.25, writes that Kṛṣṇa's *saṁhārikā-śakti* (power of devastation), and not Kṛṣṇa himself, swallowed the fire. The intention of these Gauḍīya *ācāryas* is to emphasize that Kṛṣṇa himself is fully situated in *mādhurya* without majesty.

of Vraja so dear to Kṛṣṇa. Thus, by the power of Kṛṣṇa's desire, with the extinguishing of the fire, all that was burned returned unharmed, and no sign of fire remained. This in turn put the minds of the Vraja *vāsīs* at ease, thinking they had experienced some kind of group dream that tied them all together in their love for Kṛṣṇa. Thus they had no trouble going back to sleep, and with the break of day they happily prepared to head homeward.

However, confident that Kāliya's lake was now pure, as day broke Balarāma returned to the Yamunā with Kṛṣṇa in tow, followed by all of their *gopa* friends. Then, as if reenacting Kṛṣṇa's sporting with Kāliya, Balarāma pulled Kṛṣṇa into the lake, wrestling all the way and within its waters. While remaining in *sakhya-bhāva*, he was thinking of his serpent expansion Ananta Śeṣa.[28] The *sakhās* also jumped in the lake, engaging in water sports under the curious eyes of their cows, who appeared to be reflecting on the inner significance of what had taken place the day before between Kṛṣṇa and Ananta's brother. Only after playing for quite some time in this way did Rāma give everyone permission to return home, he himself leading the way.

> Accompanied by musical instruments, song, and dance,
> and the reciting of auspicious Vedic *mantras*
> in a monsoon shower of flowers falling
> from heaven to earth and thrown up again,
> chanting "*Jaya! Jaya!*" and shouting joyfully,
> the boys placed Kṛṣṇa in their midst, and danced,
> propelled by their inner uninhibited happiness,
> and entered the village encampment
> like stars entering the night sky.[29]

Kṛṣṇa heard from his intimate friends about the fainting spells of the young *gopīs*. Affected by their feelings, he played sweetly on his flute, which helped him to recover. Understanding his feelings through the sound of his flute, his intimate friends resolved to facilitate his meeting with these *gopīs* going forward.

The *gopas* herded their cows to their pens, led by Kṛṣṇa and his elder brother Rāma. They then all feasted on the remnants of Rāma's celebration from the day before. Although the numerous and sumptuous preparations were a day old and had been left suddenly and unprotected, they remained

28. Ananta Śeṣa serves Viṣṇu in *dāsya-bhāva*.
29. *Gopāla-campū* 1.13.64 (v53).

fresh, preserved by the power of the special ghee they had been cooked in, and thus they tasted as if they had just been prepared. Surely young Rādhā must have had a hand in the cooking. *Jaya* Rāma! *Jaya* Kṛṣṇa! *Jaya* Rādhe!

12

Rāma's Prowess

During their *pauganḍa-līlā*, Hari and Hali were for the most part inseparable[1]—that is, until their *kiśora* sensibilities began to manifest in earnest in the midst of their boyhood. As earlier in their late childhood, they played carefreely but less curiously, as the forest setting had become more familiar to them. Their curiosity was not lost altogether by any means, but now they employed their budding intelligence in inventing various games and challenges with their friends, and their minds were more active and at play. By now they were both also *vividhādbhuta-bhāṣā-vit*—fluent in the languages of all the nonhuman forest residents. This is the spirit of Śukadeva's description of them:

> Given the overwhelming abundance of fruits and flowers throughout the forest of Vraja, honeybees blinded by intoxication buzzed sweetly everywhere in song and the two brothers sang along with them, increasing the bees' inebriation. The two sang as if they were one, and their friends spontaneously composed and sang songs of their own, glorifying the brothers' unique qualities. Although the bees sang only in one note in unison, Rāma and Kṛṣṇa sang musical *rāgas* in accordance with that note, and their friends sang responsively in the same *rāgas*, filled with *rati* for the beloved brothers. Kṛṣṇa honked along with the swans, spoke with various other birds, and danced in imitation of the peacocks, who took him as their dance instructor. All of this gave rise to laughter among his friends and

1. *Hali* is short for *halin* (plow boy) and is sometimes invoked by Rādhā.

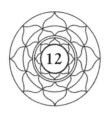

amazement on the part of the many types of birds, who felt that Rāma and Kṛṣṇa spoke their own languages better than they did.

When the cows wandered too far, they did not think that they were doing so, because they felt the *sphūrti* of Kṛṣṇa just behind them. Then he would call them each by name—"Haṁsī, Dhavalī, Gaṅgā, Yamunā"—in a deep, thunder-like voice (one of his auspicious bodily characteristics). Suddenly realizing the distance between themselves and Kṛṣṇa, they would run to him. Kṛṣṇa also imitated the roaring of lions and tigers, scaring himself and his friends, even though in their experience these otherwise ferocious beasts never harmed anyone in Vraja.

Sometimes the two brothers would sit together holding hands and evaluate their friends' talent and offer praise as they danced, sang, and wrestled before them: "Your singing and dancing defeat the denizens of heaven, and your wrestling defeats the all-pervasive fear throughout the three worlds." And what they said was not an exaggeration. Such are the *sakhās* of Vraja!

Then when Rāma was tired, one of his friends would turn his own lap into a pillow, and Kṛṣṇa would personally massage his older brother's feet, bring him refreshing water from the Yamunā to drink, and fan him. And anticipating Kṛṣṇa's fatigue from play-fighting with his friends, whose strength was equal to his as evidenced by the beads of perspiration on Kṛṣṇa's brow, these intimate friends would fashion beds out of new shoots and soft flower petals. Each group of boys made such beds, unaware of the other groups' efforts. And out of *prema* and with the assistance of his *acintya-śakti*, Kṛṣṇa rested in each bed simultaneously, each group thinking he lay in their bed alone. The boys also made pillows, but Kṛṣṇa rejected them and in their stead chose to lay his head on the laps of his *suhṛt-sakhās*. As Kṛṣṇa laid his head on such pillows, four other boys would massage his feet and fan him. Thus, they were so fortunate—*mahātmānaḥ*—that to say they were free from impiety would be an insult. Indeed, they were *hata-pāpmānaḥ*—free from any obstruction to their *sevā*—so intimate it was. Other equally fortunate boys gathered and sang softly and sweetly in a way that was supremely pleasing to the mind and appropriate for the occasion. Their hearts were melting with affection and pouring out through their eyes in the form of tears. These singers were all *priya-narma-sakhās*, who sang covertly about the *gopīs*, fostering the early manifestation of Kṛṣṇa's *kiśora* sensibilities. In this way, Kṛṣṇa, whose lotus feet as Nārāyaṇa in Vaikuṇṭha are served singularly by Lakṣmī, now heard songs about his countless Vraja Lakṣmīs sung by those friends, who were not tainted with a trace of veneration for him.[2]

These celebrated *sakhās* of Vraja were equal in prowess with Rāma and Kṛṣṇa. It is said, *gopaiḥ samāna-guṇa-śīla-vayo-vilāsa-veśaiḥ*: "These boys were similar [to Kṛṣṇa] in their qualities, character, age, actions, and dress." However, we see that they had no inclination to kill demons themselves because Kṛṣṇa's *līlā-śakti* repressed their tendency to do so and reposed it entirely in Kṛṣṇa. What about Rāma? one might ask.

Indeed, one day during the monsoon season, while the young cowherds were grazing their cows on the northeastern side of beneficent Mount Govardhana near what would later become Govinda-kuṇḍa, they were overwhelmed by the east wind carrying the redolence of the ripe *tāla* fruits from the palmyra orchard of Tālavana.[3] The Purāṇas tell us that the land in Tālavana is "even, smooth, and very expansive; the earth is black, densely covered with *kuśa/darbha* grass, and devoid of stones and pebbles." Tālavana borders the western shore of the Yamunā about eight miles southwest of Mathurā, midway between the metropolis and Mount Govardhana, and is a very pleasant and desirable place.

These *tāla* fruits already had a reputation for their succulence, but their scent in this season was beyond anything the cowherds had previously experienced. However, enjoying them presented a challenge that for the *sakhās* took precedence over their desire to taste the *tāla*: this *tāla* palm orchard was the residence of Dhenukāsura and his demonic associates, who did not allow anyone to enter and taste its *tāla* fruits, even though they themselves had no desire to taste them. Thus, the young cowherds feigned hunger in *prema* with a desire to see the heroics of Rāma, who to

2. *Śrīmad Bhāgavatam* 10.15.10–19.

3. *Borassus flabellifer* is a robust tree that can reach a height of ninety-eight feet. The trunk is gray and ringed with leaf scars; old leaves remain attached to the trunk for several years before falling. The leaves are fan-shaped and three meters long, with black teeth on the petiole margins. The fruits are black to brown with sweet, fibrous pulp, and each seed is enclosed within a woody endocarp. Palmpedia; "Borassus flabellifer"; https://www.palmpedia.net/wiki/Borassus_flabellifer.

date had yet to demonstrate his heroism in the field of demon slaying that his younger brother was already so adept at. And by now they were all well into the sixth year of their *pauganḍa-līlā.*

Thus Śrīdāmā, Subala, Stokakṛṣṇa, and others—Aṁśu, Arjuna, Viśāla, Vṛṣabha, Ojasvī, Devaprastha, Varūthapa, and Bhadrasena—all equal in strength with Rāma and Kṛṣṇa and thus uniquely qualified for companionship with them, lovingly pinched the nerve of Balarāma's heroic ego in an effort to egg him on and experience his heroism, which served as an *uddīpana-vibhāva* for their *sakhya-rati.* They praised playful, pleasing Rāma, whose long, mighty arms extended down to his knees—*rāma rāma mahā-bāho*; but at the same time they glorified Kṛṣṇa for the many heroic deeds the younger brother had already performed—*kṛṣṇa duṣṭa-nibarhaṇa.* In other words, they told Balarāma that although he had long arms and great strength, they had not been put to good use thus far. To emphasize this point and excite Rāma by presenting an opportunity for him to show his valor, and with a desire to increase his fame, some of the boys referred to him as greatly courageous—*mahā-sattva.*[4] Rāma could defeat Kṛṣṇa in wrestling and thus appeared the stronger, and for this reason the boys addressed him first, while at the same time presenting Balarāma a subtle loving challenge in the spirit of *vīra-rasa,* as they then described the situation in Tālavana in more detail:

> Therein so many fruits have already fallen on the ground—so ripe is the orchard—and many more fruits are falling by the day. But alas! They are guarded by that *durātmā*, Dhenuka. O Balarāma! O Kṛṣṇa! This *asura* is an ass, but a very strong one surrounded by many kinsmen all equal in strength.[5]

Hearing this, Kṛṣṇa laughed at his friends' *vaiśya* humor, noting that the boys were not afraid of Dhenuka, while Balarāma expressed righteous *kṣatriya* anger as the boys continued:

> Boys: No one goes to Tālavana, neither humans nor herds of cows, being terrified by this man-eating mule. Indeed, even birds avoid him overhead. Yes, such fragrant fruits never before eaten are found there! Their sweet smell is so strong it overwhelms us even here at

4. Sanātana Goswāmī notes that *mahā-sattva* is found in some editions, as opposed to *mahā-bāho*.

5. *Śrīmad Bhāgavatam* 10.15.22–23.

this very moment. O Kṛṣṇa! Get those fruits for us. Our minds are disturbed by their scent. O Balarāma! Our desire is great, and surely Kṛṣṇa will be pleased if you lead the way. Let's all go there.

Kṛṣṇa (laughing): From where have you gotten such greed?

Śrīdāmā: By association with a greedy butter thief.

Rāma: Well, greedy fellows—my friends—you are our equals, for sometimes you display your valor by moving your eyebrows, challenging us to a fight, and then you defeat us. Surely you don't need us to fend for you?

Śrīdāmā: Ah! But you two are princes: Kṛṣṇa, the son of the cowherd king and you a *kṣatriya* in our midst. Still, you graciously treat us as equals and we act as such among ourselves. But despite our internal sportive play, as a group we are one—a unit moving through the forest together—and in this respect, you are our leaders. Surely we shall go to Tāḷavana, but should you not be pleased to lead us?

Kṛṣṇa (laughing): Alright then, I have already destroyed many *asuras*, but Balarāma has not dealt with even one. He should lead the way, as you say, and slay Dhenuka, who because he is only a mule is not much of a challenge anyway.

Rāma: Well, my dear brother, you have been blessed with a way of saying things by which those things are accomplished. But let us leave the cows behind.

Thus, sharing laughter, Kṛṣṇa, dark as the all-consuming night sky, followed the moon-like Balarāma along with the multitude of shooting-star-like *sakhās*, who leapt and cried out, making sounds like threatening meteors, announcing their descent on Tālavana.

Along the way, Balarāma had time to reflect on the denigrating comments of the boys and how Kṛṣṇa had even added to them. Said with immense affection in jest, these barbs spurred him on to deal effectively with Dhenuka and his associates. Thus, he arrived at Tālavana eager to exhibit his strength. With his long, powerful arms, he announced the cowherds' arrival by shaking the largest palm and then subsequent palms one after another, fruits falling everywhere. Seeing his own strength, he laughed, and Kṛṣṇa and the cowherds, energized by his valor, laughed along with him.

Meanwhile, Dhenukāsura responded to the invasion by striking the broad chest of Balarāma with his hind legs, but Balarāma only laughed in response. And when the *asura* tried to kick him again, Rāma caught hold of his hind legs and threw him on top of the tallest palm tree, causing his demise. That tree fell onto another, and one after another, tree after tree fell. Thus, Balarāma exhibited tremendous strength for the pleasure of his friends, but not enough to distance them from him with reverence, as killing Dhenuka was but a small feat for one who holds the world together, Rāma being its warp and weft. He exhibited only the measure of strength required to deal with his opponent, thus remaining humanlike in the eyes of his friends. Nonetheless, considering Rāja Parīkṣit's reverential *dāsya-rati*, and balancing between majesty and intimacy, Śukadeva described Balarāma as God (*bhagavati*) of unlimited (*anante*) prowess.

Then Kṛṣṇa, out of love for his older brother, placed himself between Rāma and Dhenukāsura's enraged associates, who stampeded toward the brothers, the earth trembling under their hooves. Following the example of Balarāma, Kṛṣṇa caught the first of them by the hind legs and hurled him onto the top of a palm tree. And one after another, Rāma and Kṛṣṇa dispensed with them in this manner, creating a scene in the end that, despite death and damage, appeared beautiful because the heroism behind it was so pleasing to Rāma's friends, who lost interest in the fruits and left them for others. What could be more beautiful than *vaiṣṇava-toṣaṇī* and Rāma pleased to share his strength with his *sakhās*?[6] May he strengthen my resolve to enter his circle of friends.

6. A reference to the "pleasure of the devotees" and the so-named *Bhāgavata* commentary of Sanātana Goswāmī, wherein he describes this as a "shining scene." The later commentator Viśvanātha Cakravartī has followed his lead, comparing the beauty of the scene to that of red clouds (blood) and the dark-blue sky (the dark palm tree forest) at sunset.

13

Pūrva-rāga

After the liberation of Dhenukāsura, the cowherds turned homeward in celebration.[1] And they celebrated not only Rama's triumph but also the triumph of Kṛṣṇa's budding adolescence. By the time Dhenukāsura was delivered, Kṛṣṇa had entered into the *sandhyā* between *paugaṇḍa* and *kiśora*. This youthful blossoming of *kiśora* Kṛṣṇa stunned his friends as they also, along with Rāma, began to experience their own adolescence. And along with Kṛṣṇa's ever-fresh youthful appearance, his *narma-sakhās* were also well aware of his thoughts as they turned toward Rādhā. And as Kṛṣṇa and his friends began to experience adolescence during this *sandhyā*, so too did the *gopīs*.

As Śukadeva described Kṛṣṇa's *pūrva-rāga*, he was also stunned by Kṛṣṇa's adolescence. Sanātana Goswāmī comments that while relating Kṛṣṇa's *pūrva-rāga*, Śukadeva "developed that vision that he himself was a Vraja *vāsī*," and thus he attained *svarūpa-siddhi* in the midst of his Hari *kīrtana*.[2] In his *Bṛhad-bhāgavatāmṛta* commentary, Sanātana Goswāmī casts Śukadeva as a developing *sādhana-siddha* in *gopī-bhāva*.[3]

1. In his *Kṛṣṇa Sandarbha*, Jīva Goswāmī makes the point that only the demons killed by Kṛṣṇa attain liberation, not those killed by any of his *avatāras*. This insight is part of his effort to establish from scripture that Kṛṣṇa is the *avatārī*. However, Balarāma, who is Kṛṣṇa's other self, has this same power. Although the liberation of Dhenukāsura is not mentioned in the *Bhāgavatam*'s chapter describing Rāma's dispensing with him, *Śrīmad Bhāgavatam* 2.7.34–35 mentions that Dhenukāsura attained either *sāyujya-mukti* or status in Vaikuṇṭha. Alternatively, and in Balarāma's mind, Dhenukāsura's demise is attributed to Kṛṣṇa, from whom Rāma derived the power to slay him. This holds true for Rāma's slaying of Pralamba as well.
2. *Śrīmad Bhāgavatam* 10.15.41.
3. *Bṛhad-bhāgavatāmṛta* 1.7.158 and 2.7.151.

Rūpa Goswāmī refers to this period as *vayaḥ-sandhi*, "the joining of *paugaṇḍa* and *kiśora*."[4] With the dawning of Kṛṣṇa's adolescence, Balarāma's presence becomes less pronounced, and as we have seen, Kṛṣṇa finds reasons at midday to separate from the greater group of cowherds and meet with the *gopīs* along with his intimate friends before returning to the group and heading homeward. But such midday romanticism has not yet manifested. Kṛṣṇa and company return home following the slaying of Dhenukāsura, and Kṛṣṇa's lotus eyes meet those of the *gopīs* in the spot where the forest meets the pasture and the village begins. Thus, it is during this period that the feelings of separation in *pūrva-rāga* between Rādhā and Kṛṣṇa begin to manifest in earnest and their *parakīya-līlā* emerges from within like a smoldering volcano spewing lava that destroys everything in its path. Here we find the beginning of both Rādhā's rebellion and Kṛṣṇa's domestication. And we also find the fruit of Śukadeva's *kīrtana* narrative, as he himself follows the divine couple into *gopī-bhava*.

We have described the psychophysical characteristic of *kiśora* Kṛṣṇa earlier. But there is no end to the description of his beauty at this age. His face developed full cheeks and his hair turned from dark brown to deep black. His eyes became flirtatious and red on the edges while widening in size. His chest broadened. His arms thickened. His waist thinned, and his hips widened, while the legs supporting him solidified. His complexion remained dark but he appeared golden within. Seeing this contradiction, his two playful eyes—amazed—stretched themselves to his ears, both of which listened attentively to the deafening sound of Kṛṣṇa's newfound periods of silence. When he did speak, he often gave answers when silence was appropriate, and he was silent when answers were appropriate. He sometimes laughed at subjects worthy of lamentation and frowned at his friends' jokes. When his friends talked about the women of Vraja, he often blushed. When he did speak coherently, he took great pleasure in wordplay and intimate conversation with his *narma-sakhās*, often praising the forms of the young girls of Gokula in front of these friends. And the *narma-sakhās*, whose hearts were one with his, pointed out what they and Kṛṣṇa both knew, as Kṛṣṇa began to engage them in delivering messages to the *gopīs*:[5]

4. *Ujjvala-nīlamaṇi* 10.10. The stages of Kṛṣṇa's manifest adolescence, beginning in his boyhood, are termed *vayaḥ-sandhi*, *navya* (new youth), *vyakta* (manifest youth), and *pūrṇa* (full youth).

5. *Ujjvala-nīlamaṇi* 15.62.

> Since you are cunning and capable of understanding the heart, I will whisper into your ear about the unparalleled wealth of attraction possessed by the young milkmaidens—and also, my dear friend, of five or six in particular among them who are studded with splendor. Cupid, who conquers the world with his five arrows, has become blissful (knowing his work will be accomplished) by placing his weapons in their hands.[6]

But enough about *kiśora* Kṛṣṇa. What about Kiśorī's tender youth? Let us first relate Kṛṣṇa's subjective experience of Rādhā's *vayaḥ-sandhi*—not for the faint at heart—as Subala describes it to Hari.

> Subala to Kṛṣṇa: As royal spring-like youth enters the realm of Rādhā, her graceful hips appear to dance to the melodic tinkling of her sash's bells, inviting you with their musical charm. Her well-adorned yet slim waist, fearing itself to be lacking, delicately coils, apprehensive of your touch. Her chest's twin ripened fruits are gifts befitting the sovereign of youth that you are. Thus Rādhā, radiating an aura of elegance and charm, embraces adolescence, adorning herself with refined garments and ornaments.[7]

Rādhā and her friends also developed early symptoms of adolescence during their *paugaṇḍa* period, although they were slightly younger than Kṛṣṇa.[8] From external symptoms, something about their internal emotional life could be discerned, but these symptoms only hinted at that which remained hidden within. Physically they manifested the typical characteristics of young girls reaching puberty, day by day maturing like the waxing moon. But because along with this development their eternal internal love for Kṛṣṇa also manifested, their beauty was indescribable.

Rādhā's luster put gold to shame, even while she radiated a dark hue from deep within her *ātmā* in all directions. Because the monsoon cloud of Kṛṣṇa had manifested within her heart, her eyes for no apparent reason rained in sudden forceful showers, while her soft, delicate bodily hair stood on end. She sometimes stared blankly, shivered, or appeared stunned. It was as if the outstanding features of the natural world had combined together

6. See *Bhakti-rasāmṛta-sindhu* 3.3.77.

7. See *Ujjvala-nīlamaṇi* 10.13. Jīva Goswāmī attributes this verse to a friend speaking to Kṛṣṇa. Viśvanātha Cakravartī mentions Subala in his commentary. I have attributed it to Subala.

8. Rādhā is approximately one year younger than Kṛṣṇa.

and entered her physique, diminishing their own status in comparison. The moon weakened as Rādhā shone brilliantly; blossoms withered as their flowers appeared to erupt on her body; the deep-red color of the *bimba* paled, taking shelter of her lips.

At times Rādhā and the others all felt doomed, as their thoughts were fixated on that which would destroy their *dharma*—embracing Śyāmasundara's chest to their breasts. Thus, they condemned their birth with the purest *prema*. Rādhā thought,

> Although Kṛṣṇa's beauty is cool and refreshing to everyone, he only burns my heart. May the creator of my body reside in hell! What has contaminated my heart? Thinking of him constantly, I find myself full of shame. My father is famous among the famed. My mother is chastity among the chaste. Why does my heart seek to destroy their reputation?[9]

And all of the above and more manifested in Rādhā and the *gopīs* even before they got to know Kṛṣṇa!

Pūrva-rāga manifests in the context of lovers hearing about one another, hearing one another's names, hearing about one another's qualities, seeing a painting of one another, dreaming about one another, seeing one another indirectly from afar, seeing one another directly up close, and so on. In each case, actually meeting as desired is not possible, though longed for. In the *Bhāgavata* narrative we are following, the *gopīs' pūrva-rāga* is driven by hearing Kṛṣṇa's flute, hearing his qualities as sung by his *gopa* friends, seeing him first at a distance, and ultimately seeing him up close and exchanging glances with him.

On the homeward march of the cowherds after the slaying of Dhenukāsura, the *gopas* praised the qualities of Rāma and Kṛṣṇa in song accompanied by Kṛṣṇa's flute. Knowing that Dhenukāsura and his miscreant odd-toed ungulates had been destroyed, the rambunctious cows rejoiced, raising an extraordinary amount of precious Vraja *raja*, from which the hour of "cow dust" gets its name. This, then, is what the *gopīs* heard and saw from a distance: the description of Kṛṣṇa's qualities in song, the sound of his *muralī*, and copious cow dust covering the sun, which was embarrassed by Kṛṣṇa's brilliance. And at an elevation high enough for her to see him from a distance, Rādhā spoke to her friends as follows:

9. Adapted from *Gopāla-campū* 1.15.107–108.

> How beautiful is the gait of Kṛṣṇa returning from the forest! Subala is on his left, Hali on his right. Keeping the cows in front of them, the sons of the cowherds dance, clap, and sing about Kṛṣṇa's qualities.[10]

As the young herdsmen and their cows neared, Balarāma found an excuse to drift to the rear of the procession to facilitate the mutual expression of *pūrva-rāga* between Rādhā and Kṛṣṇa. Meanwhile, the natural shyness of Rādhā did not hold her back, because she and her friends and associate milkmaidens all moved to the front row in unison—strength being found in numbers—as if driven by a force beyond themselves. Standing there, first in line to greet Kṛṣṇa, they did so with stares from unblinking, wide-open eyes, like lotus flowers reacting to the warmth and light of new sun—Kṛṣṇa-*sūrya*. Nor was anyone looking at them, for all eyes were on Mukunda from the vantage point of different *bhāvas*, free from any distraction. But when he stared back, the *gopīs*' bashfulness returned, and they smiled coyly and covered their mouths with one hand, drawing their veils over their eyes with the other, even as they continued to see him through their thin, longed-to-be-bridal veils. In this way, *kiśora* Kṛṣṇa became aware of the sweetness of his *kiśorīs*' love for him, as they did of his love for them. He accepted their dazzling gaze as an offering, their eyes circling in *ārati* the length and breadth of his incomparable form again and again, fueled by the oil of *pūrva-rāga* in their hearts. And none of this went unnoticed by his *narma-sakhās*, whose hearts were one with both Kiśora and Kiśorī.

Subala's pair of eyes were dedicated thus: one eye was given to Rāma, the other to Kṛṣṇa, while the two together were given to Rādhā, following the lead of Kṛṣṇa! In other words, Kṛṣṇa's closest friend also considered himself Rādhā's *kiṅkara*,[11] the mere sight of whom serves as an *uddīpana-vibhāva* for Rādhā's *mādhurya-rasa*.[12] As we have seen earlier, he is so identified with her that his physical features closely resemble hers—*subala-nyasta-sārūpyā*.

This was indeed a glorious moment in Vraja, for even before Rādhā and Kṛṣṇa's *pūrva-rāga* for one another began to manifest, it was a forgone conclusion that they were meant for one another. For Rādhā, no other boy would do. For Rasarāja, Rādhā alone corresponds with his perfection as love's all-attractive object. With the outset of Rādhā's puberty, it was now time for their parents to plan and announce their engagement, already

10. Adapted from Phakīramohana Dāsa, "A Study of *Gopāla Krishna Padyāvali*," chap. 3 in *Bhakta Kavi Gopāla Krishna* (New Delhi: Sahitya Akademi, 2002), 44.

11. *Rādhā-kṛṣṇa-gaṇoddeśa-dīpikā* 2.198.

12. *Ujjvala-nīlamaṇi* 10.85.

written in the stars. However, that is not all that the stars had to say on the topic. Yes, they were a perfect match. But Kṛṣṇa, it would seem, also had a destined date with *dharma* that would make marriage in Vraja implausible for him.[13]

It was already known, at least by Nanda's family priest, *jyotiṣa* Garga Ṛṣi, that Kṛṣṇa was destined to kill Kaṁsa even before receiving the sacred thread—a prerequisite for marriage. With the killing of Kaṁsa, Kṛṣṇa would be further saddled for many years to come with establishing *dharma* in the world. Thus, all-knowing Gargācārya, who had previously presided over the *nāma-karaṇa* of Rāma and Kṛṣṇa and informed Nanda that Nārāyaṇa would do wonderful things through Kṛṣṇa, reappeared in Vraja, making his way to Paurṇamāsī's *bhajana-kuṭīra* along the Yamunā. His task: to inform her that in consideration of the finer details of Kṛṣṇa's natal astrological chart, Rādhā and Kṛṣṇa should not be betrothed. From this, Paurṇamāsī surmised that while Kṛṣṇa had a cosmopolitan destiny, Rādhā was village-bound in nature and would not flourish elsewhere. So strongly was she rooted in Vraja that even Kṛṣṇa would be only partially present elsewhere in pursuit of *dharma* because he is controlled by Rādhā's love. Thus, despite the fact that marriage in Vraja at this time was not possible, Kṛṣṇa would be theologically more present in Rādhā's love for him in Vraja than he was present even in his physical presence elsewhere. However, this esoteric truth was not something simple village girls could be preoccupied with, nor had this truth been revealed to them. Meanwhile, on the ground, the unpalatable talk of the need to marry Rādhā and her friends to someone other than Kṛṣṇa gradually sunk into the minds of the elders, and although there was a great wall of resistance at first, they eventually caved in to the *dharmic* perspective, at least externally, and arrangements to find other husbands were initiated. However, internally their sense that the *gopīs* and Kṛṣṇa belonged to one another remained in place, as the elders unwittingly created the conditions for *parakīya-bhāva*, which would bridge the inner desire of Rādhā and Kṛṣṇa with the outer reality.

When the news of the *gopīs*' marriage to others reached Kṛṣṇa, he appeared to take it in stride and even expressed happiness for the *gopīs*. However, to his closest friends, the smile on his face looked out of place,

13. From this point until the end of the chapter, our narrative follows *Gopāla-campū* 1.15, an original chapter of Jīva Goswāmī's that plays out the details of that which is embedded in the *Bhāgavatam*. At the end of this chapter, he portrays those listening to the bards' recital as having lost their discrimination because of *prema* and thus wondering, "Was this a recitation? Was it a drama? Was it a real pastime of Kṛṣṇa's?"

and looking closer they perceived the tracks of his tears, which told another story. Seeing Kṛṣṇa's inner feelings, they committed themselves to the role of accomplices in *bhāva* to building a *parakīya* bridge between the *sakhīs* and their *sakhā*.

However, when the girls were informed of such arrangements, they each decided on drastic measures that turned out to be the same. Thus, they found themselves at what was previously Kāliya's lake within the Yamunā, where the water was deepest and darkest. Realizing that they each had the same thing in mind, and with Rādhā as their leader, they clasped hands with one another and waded into the night waters, as Rādhā uttered the following:

> O Yamunā! May Nanda and Yaśodā be my in-laws and may Kṛṣṇa be my husband. May we always play in Vṛndāvana. May all those holding my hand out of affection and entering the water with me become happy. With this in mind, we take shelter of you.[14]

As they waded into waist-high water, they heard a voice apparently from the sky tell them not to be rash and say that they would never be enjoyed by anyone other than Kṛṣṇa. They were stunned by this and looked at one another for an explanation, when another miracle occurred. The waves of the Yamunā personified into a beautiful goddess who ushered them back to shore, where Vṛndā-devī had brought Paurṇamāsī and Madhumaṅgala, the latter jester now notably more sober than he ever had been or would be. Together Yamunā, Paurṇamāsī, and Vṛndā-devī consoled the girls, and Paurṇamāsī educated them by explaining in some detail the implication of what the sky had said, as Madhumaṅgala listened with rapt attention. It is not clear how well the *gopīs* were able to digest the depth of Paurṇamāsī's *parakīya-tattva-śikṣā*, but her own firm faith and affectionate assurances carried the day. In the end, she told them that she, Vṛndā, and Madhumaṅgala would always be there for them. Thus, it is at this point that Madhumaṅgala began to identify himself as Rādhā's *kiṅkara*, an identification that would

14. *Gopāla-campū* 1.15.120 (v48). To say that Kṛṣṇa was the desired husband of all the *gopīs* is not to advocate polygamy but rather to state a theological necessity. Note that the virtue of Rāmacandra's monogamous *eka-patnī-vrata* is extolled in scripture. Theologically speaking, Rādhā is the only *gopī* Kṛṣṇa desires, and it is only for the sake of relishing Rādhikā's different moods—such as *māna* (jealous anger), *khaṇḍita* (disappointment), *kalahāntaritā* (remorse after making a quarrel), and so on—that Kṛṣṇa appears to desire another girl, such as Candrāvalī. Thus, when it seems that Kṛṣṇa desires Candrāvalī, it is actually an aspect of Rādhā that he desires, and Candrāvalī and the other *gopīs* are all expansions of Rādhā that constitute particular moods of Rādhā for the sake of *rasa*.

eventually win him the special favor of Rādhā's fast friend and *parama-preṣṭha-sakhī* Lalitā. Paurṇamāsī then took Madhumaṅgala and Vṛndā to meet Kṛṣṇa, who was meditating elsewhere by moonlight.

> Kṛṣṇa sat in solitude on a slab of moonstone, one-minded in his meditation, with a view to attain the hand of Rādhā. Stealthily approaching, intent upon tending to Kṛṣṇa's *pūrva-rāga*, Paurṇamāsī asked, sounding like an oracle, "Is it so difficult to attain that upon which you meditate? After all, you have attained persons such as ourselves." Indeed, Paurṇamāsī, Madhumaṅgala, and Vṛndā were most uncommon, as they were manifestations of Vraja's *līlā-śakti* moving behind the scenes in anticipation of Kṛṣṇa's every desire.

Then, as Kṛṣṇa turned and opened his eyes, still trying to conceal his budding Rādhā *prema*, Paurṇamāsī placed Madhumaṅgala's hand in his and in effect handed Madhumaṅgala over to Kṛṣṇa to serve as his constant companion. Kṛṣṇa, understanding what this new companion would mean to him in his *līlās* of love and friendship, accepted Paurṇamāsī's gracious gift, and the two embraced in the intimacy of fraternal love, their hair standing on end, tears pouring from their eyes.

Paurṇamāsī then introduced Kṛṣṇa to Vṛndā-devī, and the two ladies departed, leaving Kṛṣṇa alone with Madhumaṅgala, who related in brief the preceding events that had taken place along the banks of the Yamunā. Kṛṣṇa was eager to introduce Madhumaṅgala to his friends, but his eagerness to do so was hindered by questions that lingered in his mind regarding the *gopīs*' attempted suicide. As Madhumaṅgala and Kṛṣṇa walked arm in arm, the latter taking support from the former, Kṛṣṇa also wondered aloud as to why he became choked up and short of breath in trying to talk about the implications of what had transpired. Kṛṣṇa thus sought further emotional support from his newfound friend.

Without knowing exactly what Paurṇamāsī had said to the *gopīs*, Kṛṣṇa asked Madhu how they had responded to Paurṇamāsī's *śikṣā*, whatever it was.

"They bowed their heads. Their breasts became moistened by their shower of tears, which in turn caused the *tamāla* trees to wither," replied Madhumaṅgala, as if to say that Kṛṣṇa, whose complexion resembles the *tamāla* tree, would have withered had he seen them.

"Do you know what was on their mind as they entered the Yamunā?" asked Kṛṣṇa.

"Yes," replied Madhumaṅgala.

"How do you know?" asked Kṛṣṇa.

"They constantly look at the *tamāla* tree, which has a color similar to yours."

Kṛṣṇa replied, "Please say more about this."

Madhumaṅgala said, "I know because of what the river goddess said. She lamented when the *gopīs* entered the river, and she related their intentions to us afterward. Rādhā entered the river saying, 'May Nanda and Yaśodā be my in-laws, and may Kṛṣṇa be my husband.' "

In a choked voice, Kṛṣṇa then said, "Come, let us go to meet with my friends."[15]

Thus, the *brāhmaṇa* boy Madhumaṅgala moved in with Kṛṣṇa and became his constant companion. His entry into Kṛṣṇa's life, coinciding with Hari's adolescence and *pūrva-rāga*, serves to illustrate Śyāma's need for such *narma-sakhā* friends from the very dawn of his never-ending romantic love life.

15. See *Gopāla-campū* 1.15.142–165.

14

Endless Summer

As the summer season ensued, it served the cowherds well by providing them with an opportunity for a wide range of sports, and water sports in particular, allowing them to take advantage of the many lakes and ponds, what to speak of the Yamunā. Furthermore, despite Vraja's proximity to what is now known as the Rajasthani desert, the heat did not become oppressive. Thus, the *Bhāgavata* informs us that summer appeared in name only—*grīṣmo nāmartur abhavan*.

In Vraja, there are six seasons annually, with each season being two months long. The new year begins in *hemanta* (prewinter), followed by *śiśira* (winter), *vasanta* (spring), *grīṣma* (summer), *varṣa* (monsoon), and then *śarada* (autumn). The lives of Vraja's residents revolve around these seasons, which structure their lives. The seasons are celebrated through rituals that correspond with each particular season, or *ṛtu*—a Sanskrit word that denotes the appropriate astrological time for Vedic *yajñas*. The term derives from the word *ṛta*, meaning "the order or course of things," which implies the teleological, or purposeful, nature of nature.

Nature provides and also speaks to us through symbols and signs, and ritual is the symbolic language through which we reply to nature, expressing our gratitude and love for her. If you love someone, they will tell you all their secrets. Accordingly, nature shares her deepest secret with those of us who adore her, revealing to such worshipers that the hidden soul of nature is the *ātmā*. If we listen to her carefully, she points us in the direction of ourselves—inward—and to the source we share with her, the *śaktimān* we are both different *śaktis* of. Thus she serves our shared compassionate source.

However, Vraja is a special place on earth—the *dhāma*—and therein Rāma and Kṛṣṇa sport eternally. Thus, in Vraja the divinity behind nature has the opportunity to serve her source directly, and the virtue of any particular season may appear during any other season for the sake of such *sevā*. In Vraja, nature herself is *alaukika*, or supernatural, and as such she surpasses the limits of the natural world—her shadow—in terms of its limited capacity to serve. Material nature may point us, or perhaps prod us, toward the *ātmā* and its likeness with the Absolute, but the *alaukika* nature of Vraja reaches much higher, bestowing *prema* and providing a most enchanting playground for adolescent Rāma and Kṛṣṇa along with their *sakhās* and *sakhīs*.

Thus, the *Bhāgavata* describes that it was as if only the best qualities of summer manifested, while those of the spring season stayed on to render further *sevā* to Mādhava, following the example of Balabhadra. Where did the excessive heat of the summer go? Madhumaṅgala privately suggested to Mādhava in jest that it had taken shelter of the boulder fortress on Rādhā's chest, as he pointed to a *tamāla* tree embraced by a jasmine vine, comparing the creeper's flowers to Rādhā's smiling face. Overall, the lush summer forest appeared as if the midnight blue of Śyāma's complexion mixed with his thoughts of the golden luster of Rādhā had turned the landscape emerald green.

During the summer months the days grew longer, and with the lengthening of the days, the cowherds' play was also further facilitated. They played different versions of hide-and-seek, such as *humbri*, as well as tag and contact sports.

> They played on the banks of the Yamunā and even played at fighting with sticks. And they danced, bending their feet to the sound of Kṛṣṇa's enchanting flute. Rāma and Kṛṣṇa were so much one with their buddies that these *sakhās* never hesitated even to slap the brothers' bottoms when playing tag or contact sports. But *humbri* was hard to play, for wherever they hid, they felt Kṛṣṇa's presence, as if there were nowhere to hide from him. And while they sought him, he also seemed to be everywhere at once. Thus, they wrestled instead and won and wiped Kṛṣṇa's runny nose, picked him up and held him close, and called him names such as "weakling who is competent only to fight with his nurse (Pūtanā)." They said, "My sister can subdue you—so true!" Then they sang songs celebrating their victory. And they also complained: "Our legs are breaking

tending to your cows. They run after anything green—the combination of *śyāma* and *gaura*—as if it were the most nourishing grass, while you sit under a tree and eat our lunches. What kind of friend are you?" Hearing this, some wholeheartedly agreed but then sang songs in praise of Kṛṣṇa's qualities, while others accompanied their singing with self-made musical instruments. And everyone danced, forgetting about eating, as the cows looked on approvingly with great curiosity. They then all refreshed themselves by bathing in the Yamunā along with their cows.

Afterward, Kṛṣṇa engaged in wordplay with *dvija-rāja* Madhumaṅgala:

Madhumaṅgala: Friend, you think you're such a *rasika*, so today I will debate you. Tell me, what is *rasa*? Let the *dvijas* (birds/*brāhmaṇas*) witness our discussion. I make my belly an ocean of flavor by filling it up with the juice of mangoes and jackfruit, but still, you consider *me* to be tasteless? O friend, your Vṛndāvana is full of varieties of fruit that are rarely available within the three worlds, and you are fond of rambling about therein with no interest in the flavors arising from the forest, your mind on something else! O friend, you are an *arasika*. The *gopīs* can purchase your heart merely by the movements of their eyes, but still, you call yourself the greatest *rasika* and so do others, because the masses tend to consider a worthless person most qualified.

Kṛṣṇa: O *brāhmaṇa* boy, I don't wander in the forest as an *arasika*! I wander around only because the cold water pleases my tongue on the summer days; the touch of the lotus flower pleases my skin; the fragrance of the sweet jasmine flowers pleases my nose; the fresh, orange-red *palāśa* flowers—the flame of the forest[1]—please my eyes; and the sweet cooing of the pigeons pleases my ears. Thus, all five of my senses experience bliss!

Madhumaṅgala: Kānu, these ripe summer mangoes *alone* please all my senses at once. They give joy to my eyes with their golden splendor. Their juice pleases my tongue. Their fragrance gives bliss

1. The *Butea monosperma*, or flame of the forest, produces scentless, bright orange-red flowers in racemes up to fifteen centimeters long, each flower consisting of five petals that comprise one standard, two smaller wings, and a curved beak-shaped keel. Its back-curving petals are covered with fine silky hair which, when seen at particular angles, change their color from orange red to a silvery salmon-pink.

> to my nostrils. Their softness pleases my skin, and the sound of their name—mango—pleases my ears! In this way, I can draw more *rasa* from one variety of fruit than you can from the entire forest! How can one taste *rasa* if one's mind is not one-pointed?[2]

Day after day, the cowherds played and played, sometimes resorting to well-known sports or games and at other times spontaneously making up games of their own, replete with rewards such as walking sticks and handmade flutes for the winners. They spun themselves around until they were dizzy and then clasped the hands of their friends and swung them and themselves, letting their friends go and sending them flying. They played with balls and threw fruits such as *bilva*, *kumbha*, and *āmalakī* at each other.[3] They threw these fruits into the air and then tried to hit them, throwing other fruits at them. Mindless mindfulness appeared to be their practice, one-pointed in their pointless play of *prema*. Overall, these boys were boastful and brash, free and fearless, and daring in the face of danger, with no thought of the future, living fully in the present moment of their eternal youthfulness.

During this period, *Hari-vaṁśa Purāṇa* describes Rāma and Kṛṣṇa thus:

> They looked splendid, milking ropes strapped over their shoulders, garlands on their chests. They were like young bull yearlings with budding horns—Rāma and Kṛṣṇa dressed in blue and gold cloth, respectively, each looking like the other. They resembled black and white clouds arrayed in rainbows. With captivating *kuśa* flowers ornamenting their ears, dressed in forest attire, the two traversed the forest trails.[4]

2. Adapted from *Kṛṣṇa-bhāvanāmṛta* 14.2–7.

3. *Bilva*, more commonly known as *bael* (*Aegle marmelos*), is a member of the Rutaceae (citrus) family. The tree is identified with Śiva, its three-lobed leaves employed in his worship. The *bilva* fruit is round and encased in a thin, hard shell measuring two to eight inches in diameter. Its medicinal qualities are praised in Āyurveda. *Kumbha* (*Careya arborea*) is a deciduous tree whose leaves turn red in the cold season. Its flowers are yellow or white, its fruit large green berries. *Āmalakī* (*Phyllanthus emblica/myrobalan*) is also a deciduous tree. Its round fruit is light green in color with a smooth, hard surface adorned by vertical stripes. It is also used widely in Āyurvedic medicine. The *āmalakī* fruit was the final gift to the Buddhist *saṅga* given by the great Indian emperor Aśoka. In the Theravada tradition, the *āmalakī* is also thought to have been the tree under which the twenty-first Buddha, Phussa, achieved enlightenment. Although all three of these trees/fruits are regarded highly, they surely attain their utmost glory in the playful hands of Kṛṣṇa's cowherds.

4. Cited in *Vaiṣṇava-toṣaṇī* 10.18.16.

As we learned earlier, one of the prominent *uddīpanas* of *sakhya-rati* is imitating kings and gods—*rāja-devāvatārādi-ceṣṭānukaraṇādayaḥ*. Such play is also indicated in the *Bhāgavata*'s description of the cowherds' summer pastimes—*karhicin nṛpa-ceṣṭayā*.[5] Sitting on a throne-like rock on Mount Govardhana, Kṛṣṇa would proclaim himself king of the forest and representative of Emperor Kāmadeva. Then he would appoint ministers and establish his royal assembly of cowherds, their herding sticks in hand.

Prabhu Sanātana's *Vaiṣṇava-toṣaṇī* suggests that it is at this time of the year and amid such play of imitating kings that the *dāna-keli*, or toll *līlā*, involving the *gopīs* occurs. There are a number of iterations of this *līlā*, some preceding the formation of the Gauḍīya *sampradāya* and two arising out of it—Śrī Rūpa's *Dāna-keli-kaumudī* and Raghunātha dāsa Goswāmī's *Dāna-keli-cintāmaṇi*. At this point in the *Bhāgavata*'s *prakaṭa-līlā* narrative Kṛṣṇa is enjoying the first summer of his adolescence, and thus the *Dāna-keli-līlā*, being a *pūrva-rāga-līlā*, is embedded in the text. Such is the vision of Sanātana Goswāmī.

Relative to *sakhya-rati*, one of the unique features of the Goswāmī's *dāna-keli* edition is the participation of Kṛṣṇa's *narma-sakhās*, who are most definitely showcased far more in the Goswāmī *līlā-granthas* overall than in any other *sampradāya* or related texts. Therein Subala, Madhumaṅgala, Ujjvala, Vasanta, Kokila, and Arjuna, among others, are present and prominent. *Dāna-keli* is said to be a great treasure for Kṛṣṇa's *narma-sakhās*.[6] Thus in this *līlā* we can glimpse the nature of the *rāgātmika narma-sakhās*' love for Śyāma and also for Rādhā, whose *anurāga* leading to *mahābhāva* is showcased by her *anubhāva* of competing emotions—*kila-kiñcita*. How amazing! Rādhā's love, while all-pervading, tends to increase at every moment; while important, it is devoid of pride; while pure, it is beset with duplicity.[7]

5. *Śrīmad Bhāgavatam* 10.18.15.

6. *Dāna-keli-kaumudī* 10.

7. Śrī Rūpa's *Dāna-keli-kaumudī* begins thus: "May the bouquet-like sight of Rādhā's *kila-kiñcita* bring good fortune. When Kṛṣṇa blocked Rādhā's path, laughter appeared in her heart. Her eyes brightened and tears flowed, reddening them. Her sweet relationship with Kṛṣṇa made her eyes enthusiastic, and her crying subsided, making her even more beautiful." Kṛṣṇadāsa Kavirāja describes Rādhārāṇī's *kila-kiñcita* in *Śrī Caitanya-caritāmṛta* 2.14.169–179. Following Śrī Rūpa's lead, Kavirāja explains that *kila-kiñcita* consists of seven ingredients that appear simultaneously with, and serve to augment and embellish, the dominant *sañcāri-bhāva* of jubilation (*harṣa*). These seven ingredients appearing together and also serving as symptoms of *kila-kiñcita* are pride, desire, tears, smiling, envy, fear, and anger. Kavirāja Goswāmī compares these seven ingredients to a delicious drink of jubilation consisting of yogurt, sugar, ghee, honey, pepper, camphor, and cardamom. It is of interest to

At midday Kṛṣṇa was informed by a parrot that Rādhā and her friends were in the vicinity, bearing ghee en route to a sacrifice.[8] Thus, while Baladeva and the other cowherds napped, Śyāma and his *narma-sakhā* ministers set up a makeshift tollbooth, ultimately to extract the toll of Rādhā's love for Śyāma in the early stages of their mutual *pūrva-rāga.*[9]

Kṛṣṇa appointed Madhumaṅgala as his accountant, Subala as his ambassador and scout, Ujjvala as his secretary, with Vasanta, Arjuna, Kokila, and others at his every disposal. Ahead of the other young herdsmen, Subala ascended Mount Govardhana, where he met Vṛndā-devī. As Subala and Vṛndā consulted with one another, Rādhā and her friends appeared in the distance, approaching the narrow pass stretching between the two sides of the mountain. Shaped like a peacock overall, this pass is conceived of as Girirāja's neck, his eyes the two *kuṇḍas* Rādhā and Śyāma, his face Kusuma-sarovara.

Subala ventured forth and met with Vṛndā-devī, with whom he discussed the impending *dāna-līlā*, much to her approval, knowing how much it meant to him and his friend. As they proceeded to Mānasa-gaṅgā, Subala saw Rādhā from a distance, and wonderstruck he questioned why such a Goddess among the *gopīs* should be burdened with such a petty and laborious task as carrying ghee for such a distance. Vṛndā-devī, staring at Subala's face, which looked exactly like Rādhā's, explained that there was a special benediction for those who brought ghee to the sacrifice that the girls were en route to: all their desires would be fulfilled. Then Subala, struck by Rādhā's beauty, tried to put it into words: "Ah, the rising and falling aura of her curved eyebrows defeats the beauty of the rainbow, and her *sakhīs* accompanying her move in time with her like choreographed flashes of lightning." But Vṛndā took exception to his praise, questioning if it was

---

note further that when Kṛṣṇa experiences Rādhā's *kila-kiñcita*, this ecstatic condition gives him more pleasure than his desired union with Rādhā that these symptoms get in the way of.

8. *Dāna-keli-cintāmaṇi* employs the green parrot, which happens to be Kāmadeva's carrier. The reason for the parrot's role as Kāmadeva's carrier is that parrots are particularly known for their humanlike lovemaking habits and monogamous commitment, which often leads to death from loneliness after the demise of a partner. The parrot carrier of Kāmadeva thus also implies the virtue of monogamy. As mentioned earlier, Kṛṣṇa ostensibly has many lovers, but in reality the principal *gopīs* are all manifestations of Rādhā for the sake of *rasa.* Such is her love for Kṛṣṇa.

9. In briefly retelling the *dāna-keli-līlā* in the following paragraphs, I have drawn various details from either Śrī Rūpa or Raghunātha dāsa, and that with my own emphasis on *sakhya-rasa*. Here *dāna-keli* is just one example of an instance in which Kṛṣṇa plays the role of a king, his friends play his ministers, and so on.

even possible to put Rādhā's beauty into words, stating that comparing her face to a lake of lotuses or a host of moons would be an understatement, for the beauty and effulgence of her face surpassed them even from a distance. Thus she glorified Rādhā by stating what she is not, as is often done when describing Brahman. Hearing this, Subala put his head in his hand, in embarrassment.[10] Then, with Rādhā now in view and knowing her desire, Vṛndā-devī sent Subala to bring peacock-feathered Kṛṣṇa to what would become the scene of the crime.

As Rādhā approached with her friends, she expressed her love for the forest environment at Govardhana, every aspect of which reminded her of Kṛṣṇa, even though as far as she could recall she had seen him only two or three times. Rādhā was reminded of Kṛṣṇa by his footprints that marked the path. The bamboo reeds reminded her of his flute and its good fortune of having unimpeded access to Hari's lotus lips. Would he suddenly appear and block their path? Was this the wonderful thing that Paurṇamāsī had predicted they would see today?

Then, suddenly, Vṛndā-devī magically appeared as if the forest had personified and pointed out to the *gopīs* that Mount Govardhana was already behind them and that in their sharing of hearts with one another they had veered off course. Thus, they changed directions, taking the southern path that led to the sacrifice.

As they turned, Girirāja was now on their right. With his many peaks glistening, he appeared in the *gopīs'* eyes more exalted than Ananta Śeṣa—the many-hooded serpent support of Viṣṇu—serving as a playground on which Kṛṣṇa enjoys himself with his friends.[11] Rādhā then expressed how charming the humming of the bees was among the blossoming lotus flowers at Mānasa-gaṅgā. And Vṛndā, expressing empathy, also took the opportunity to drop a hint of what was to come:

> Your head, a resting place of jasmine flowers, should not suffer. Why do you, who are soft and delicate, carry a pot of butter? Be kind and place the heavy pot on my head. Oh, look at that dark, passionately

10. Moons and lotuses refer to the inferiority of Candrāvalī (moon) and the brilliance and beauty of her *sakhī* Padmā (lotus). Subala's face looks the same as Rādhā's, hence his embarrassment.

11. Here we find support for the notion of some devotees that Govardhana can also be seen as a manifestation of Balarāma. Such devotees worship a pair of dark and light stones from Govardhana as Kṛṣṇa and Balarāma, respectively. In the *dāna-keli* of Rūpa Goswāmī, Vṛndā-devī speaks this verse glorifying Govardhana, describing him as similar to Ananta in appearance and service but more exalted and intimate with Kṛṣṇa.

> buzzing male bee, waist yellow with pollen. Shaking his head, buzzing loudly, he plays among the lady bees, blocking their path.

Then Rādhā, explaining that her burden was not the pot of ghee, suddenly saw Śyāma, and her body, trembling, revealed the burden of her budding love.

> Rādhā: Look! A person appearing like a dark yet full and radiant mind-stealing moon now stands before us dressed in dashing yellow garments atop Mount Govardhana!
>
> Vṛndā: O Rādhā, he waves his arms, which have the power to fulfill every desire of every doe-eyed girl in every direction. His broad chest has vowed to make every saintly *gopī* fall passionately in love with him. Rasika-śekhara has manifested before us.
>
> Rādhā (filled with wonder): Kṛṣṇa has traversed the path of my eyes previously, but I never saw such sweetness as I see in him today. O friend, my eyes have no power to capture even a single drop of the splendid handsomeness that shines on one of his limbs alone.
>
> Vṛndā: Whenever you see him, you say he is a wonder you have never seen before. Is Kṛṣṇa really a new person every time you see him, or do your eyes, made wild by love, forget that you have seen him before?[12]

As Kṛṣṇa approached, he confided in his friends his appreciation for the beauty of Śrī Rādhā, and his amorous feelings for her.

> Ah! This is Śrīdāmā's beautiful and pious younger sister, a flood of glittering moonlight that delights the lotus flowers of her dearest friends, and a charming roof under which the dancing peacock of my life's breath performs.

It was as if Kāmadeva himself and his associate Gandharvas—personifications of the possibilities of romanticism—had all descended at once to capture Rādhā's love for their king, the transcendental Cupid.[13] However,

12. As explained earlier, this is a symptom of *anurāga*. It causes Kṛṣṇa to appear ever fresh, as if one is seeing him for the first time again and again.

13. Gandharvas are thought to act as messengers between humans and the gods and are also associated with romantic love. The Vedic *gāndharva* marriage is one based on nothing other than mutual consent. *Mahābhārata* considers it the only viable form of Vedic marriage in Kali *yuga*. As we shall see in the next chapter, Kṛṣṇa considers the *gāndharva* rite "the highest *dharma*" with regard to marriage.

they did so for the most part acting ostensibly contrarian. And the *gopīs* for their part acted contrarian as well, attempting to ignore the imaginary king and his cabinet. It was Madhumaṅgala who then broke the ice.

> Madhumaṅgala: Intoxicated by her own internal battle with youth and womanhood, Rādhā is rendered a weak and confused woman at best as she now approaches you. O sober and compassionate king, you should check her false pride before she places her pedestrian hands on Your Highness, pushing you away as she ignores your tollbooth!
>
> Kṛṣṇa: Our *brāhmaṇa* advisor speaks the truth. These wicked girls are ignoring my toll and proudly going on their way. Such arrogance! My friends, I will now force them to pay the toll. Sound your flutes and buffalo-horn bugles! Stop these girls! And as your leader, with my own arms I will personally stop Rādhā, the leader of these crooked-hearted girls! Subala, grab Viśākhā! Ujjvala, stop Citrā! Vasanta, stop both Campakalatā and Tuṅgavidyā! Kokila, stop Lalitā!

Speaking proud, arrogant words that were in fact many-layered and laden with a special love, the *gopas* surrounded Rādhā and her friends, playfully placing them under arrest. Although overjoyed within at this development, Rādhā outwardly assailed Kṛṣṇa with the double-edged sword of her own sharp words of covert praise. And as Kṛṣṇa feigned anger, he told proud Rādhā,

> My dear proud thief, being the king of these parts, staffed by my excellent ministers and spies, I am well aware of the fact that you regularly traverse these forest paths selling dairy products on the black market for an inflated price. Now you must pay the price, not only for the products you bear today but for your previous crimes as well. Furthermore, since you are attempting as your defense to pass off this habitual criminal behavior in my court as something attributed to youthful innocence and not an actual crime, your cunning only compounds your crime, the price for which shall be nothing short of your youthfulness itself!

Subala then commanded that Rādhā and her *sakhīs* bow their heads to the ground before the land's sovereign king, but Lalitā replied that Paurṇamāsī had instructed them to bow only before *brāhmaṇas*. Arjuna replied that their king was nonetheless worthy of such homage on the strength of the words of *brāhmaṇas* themselves, to which the *brāhmaṇa* Madhumaṅgala readily attested.

Rādhā, charmed by Kṛṣṇa's verdict, nonetheless appeared outraged and indignant at his minister's command. Thus, she brought into question the entire tax, the tollbooth, and the so-called king and his ministers. And her *sakhīs* supported her, suggesting that the so-called king himself be reported to his mother and then to Kaṁsa, to whom local taxes were paid. Lalitā-sakhī, growing impatient, asserted that it was getting late and that it was more than time to move on from this farce of taxation to reach the sacrifice on time.

Subala then acknowledged that perhaps he and others had acted inappropriately and thanked Lalitā for being the instrument through which God had pointed this out to him. That being said, he then suggested that they all come together and consider an appropriate measure of taxation. Kṛṣṇa smiled at Subala's words and then suggested that were *he* in Rādhā's position, he would gladly give her his greatest wealth, which he demonstrated by embracing Subala—Rādhā's look-alike—hinting that he would like to embrace her. Rādhā understood Kṛṣṇa's intention, and her fine body hair stood erect. Losing sight of the dispute at hand, she spoke mentally to Subala in trance, longing to be in his position, realizing the advantage of *sakhya-rasa*:

> Even in front of his elders, Kṛṣṇa holds you on his lap, embracing you, causing the hairs of your body to stand erect in ecstasy. Then he rests his snake-like arm on your shoulder. O Subala! How many austerities did you perform in your previous life, if not over many lives, to attain this good fortune? And in what holy place?[14]

Taking advantage of Rādhā's ecstasy, Kṛṣṇa pretended to hear something in the distance and sent Subala to find out what it was. Subala returned and reported that his king's army had apprehended the greater balance of *gopīs* in the surrounding area, leaving only these few girls to deal with. Kṛṣṇa then called Ujjvala and asked him to give him the letter from the emperor Kāmadeva, under whom he reigned as king of this area. Ujjvala somehow

14. It is no wonder that Śrī Rūpa describes this *līlā* as particularly dear to Subala. Indeed, in many ways, Rādhā's thoughts correspond with Subala himself, who embodies the *sakhya-rasa* she desires to experience. Typically, such desire on the part of one in *mādhurya-rasa* to taste the compatible *sakhya-rasa* results in *sakhya-rasa* becoming a subordinate *aṅga-rasa* of the devotee's *mādhurya-rasa* (see *Bhakti-rasāmṛta-sindhu* 4.8). Here we find the reversal of the *narma-sakhā*'s desire to taste *mādhurya-rasa*.

supplied the letter, describing it as orders from the emperor giving Kṛṣṇa the duty of establishing the tollbooth. Then Kṛṣṇa read it aloud:

> Some cunning and arrogant girls with beautiful eyebrows cleverly avoid paying the proper tolls. Catch them, and if they try to cheat further, charge them a penalty a hundred times the amount of the toll. Cowherds are expert at accounting because of their daily practice of counting cows, and thus I have complete confidence in your ability to prevail and not be cheated by any sleight of hand on the part of these wily milkmaidens, who are able to deceive based on their womanly charm and unparalleled beauty alone, especially that of their leader, Rādhā.

Thus negotiations ensued, all of which were extremely unreasonable on Kṛṣṇa's part. However, the exorbitant tax he sought to extract—however high—was of no value to him in comparison to the youth of Rādhā that he was after, which he was unable to attain in full at this time. While there was little hope of compromise from either camp, both the *sakhās* and *sakhīs* in fact directly and indirectly supported the shared love in *pūrva-rāga* that played itself out to the limits of such budding love in separation. After considerable haggling, *dāna-keli* concluded with a promise to continue the debate, the *gopīs* pledging to pay on a future day, as they scurried off to the sacrifice thrilled by all that had transpired, leaving Kṛṣṇa longing for that day to arrive and fully supported in that longing by his friends.

When Kṛṣṇa returned to Rāma and the greater circle of cowherds, he who is the abode of happiness—*sukha-nidhi*—sat comfortably resting his left foot on his right thigh in *sukhāsana* beneath the large wish-fulfilling banyan tree, after which the Bhāṇḍīravana forest was named. As Hari sat casually, Śrīdāmā and Sudāmā engaged their followers in decorating their beloved friend with forest flowers. Some boys picked flowers; some strung them into garlands; others made flower earrings, armlets, and flower anklets. Expert in the art of decoration, some boys made other unique forest ornaments, as Sudāmā-sakhā personally decorated Kṛṣṇa under the admiring eye of Balarāma.

However, observing such adoration, Madhumaṅgala objected that in the presence of a *brāhmaṇa* such as himself among mere cowherds, such worshipful attention should have been directed to him, insisting that he now be decorated better than Hari. Sudāmā, smiling within, reverently agreed and turned his attention to Madhu. He brought the *dvija-rāja* to a separate grove and began to ornament him, making him look like a clown at best, unbeknown to the *brāhmaṇa* boy himself. When the ornamentation was completed, Madhu anxiously asked how his appearance compared to that of Hari, and Sudāmā assured him his handsomeness exceeded that of Nanda's son. Delighted, he walked hand in hand with Sudāmā into the midst of the *gopas*, who surrounded him dancing, hooting, howling, and laughing at him. Perplexed at their reaction, he did not know what to make of it until he saw his reflection in the clear water of the Yamunā. Outraged, he chased Sudāmā, who ran and hid behind Kṛṣṇa.

Sudāmā taunted Madhumaṅgala, "Ah! Such a beautiful result you have attained for your misdeeds!" And Madhu in turn vowed to make Sudāmā look like he had made him look. In this way, they exchanged insults and boasted until a wrestling match broke out. Arms and legs flew, bodies rolled in the dust, and cries of anguish and victory erupted from both sides, until finally pudgy Madhumaṅgala had enough and broke loose, taking shelter behind Hari. Despite his apparent defeat, he reasoned otherwise to his own satisfaction, preserving his self-dignity, proclaiming his prowess and protesting that *brāhmaṇas* such as himself should be protected by King Nanda's son from such unruly cowherds, who owing to their *vaiśya* temperament were prone to cheating. Thus Kṛṣṇa promised to protect him and challenged Sudāmā himself, taking the excitement to another level. Then Śrīdāmā stepped forward and asserted that given Sudāmā's exhaustion and to make it a fair fight, he should take Sudāmā's place.

The assembly of cowherds quickly took sides, rooting for either Kṛṣṇa or Śrīdāmā. Seeing their enthusiasm for the match, Kṛṣṇa suggested that action speaks louder than words and challenged each boy on both sides to join the match themselves, facing off with one another. Then Kṛṣṇa announced that those who lost would be bound to carry their victors on their shoulders. He then elected himself as the leader of one side and Rāma as the leader of the other. Rising to the occasion without a second thought, the boys paired off in the game of *hariṇākrīḍanaṁ* and simultaneously attacked their respective rivals.[15]

Subhadra fought against Gobhaṭa, Yakṣendra against Vīrabhadra, Bhaṭa against Mahāguṇa, Vijaya against Bhadrāṅga, Bhadrabhūṣaṇa against Bhadravardhana, Dāmā against Vasudāmā, Stokakṛṣṇa against Kiṅkiṇi, Bhadrasena against Vṛṣabha, Viṭaṅka against Puṇḍarīka, Kalaviṅka against Aṁśumāna, Varūthapa against Sucandra, Devaprastha against Maranda,

15. *Viṣṇu Purāṇa* 5.9.12.

Arjuna against Gandharva, and so on. Although the boys loved Rāma and Kṛṣṇa equally, some generally followed Rāma and others generally followed Kṛṣṇa. Jīva Goswāmī comments that to increase the measure of *sakhya-rasa*, Kṛṣṇa put his followers on Rāma's side and took Rāma's followers on his side.

The large limbs of the great banyan would assist the winners in mounting the shoulders of the losers. Bhāṇḍīra would also further assist their play by providing shade from the summer sun. The Purāṇa describes it thus:

> Bhāṇḍīra was so large as to appear like a mountain covering half the sky. Many varieties of birds of blue and various other colors frequented that great tree, whose profuse foliage made it appear like a cloud accompanied by a rainbow, or like a house decoratively overgrown with vines and flowers. It spread its broad roots downward and carried upon itself the sanctified clouds above. That banyan tree was like the lordly master of all other trees in the vicinity, as it performed the auspicious service of warding off the rain and the heat of the sun. Such was the appearance of that banyan tree, which seemed just like the peak of a great mountain.[16]

However, amid all of this *mādhurya*, Kṛṣṇa's *aiśvarya-śakti* gave rise to his omniscience, and thus she was partially involved in his suggestion that two sides should be formed and the winners rewarded by the privilege of making their opponents their palanquins. How so? Among the boys and disguised as one of them lurked Kaṁsa's henchman Pralamba, intent on doing his master's dirty work. Calling Rāma to his side, Kṛṣṇa pointed him out.

Earlier in the text of the *Bhāgavata*, Śukadeva points out that Pralamba, among others, was a formidable foe of the Yadu dynasty, with whom Balarāma was directly connected, being the son of Vasudeva. Thus, Kṛṣṇa desired to honor Rāma and make him famous for vanquishing Pralamba. While the boys chose sides and matched themselves with one another, Pralamba, disguised as a cowherd, and being socially awkward as an unknown among friends, was not sure which side to affiliate himself with and whom to face off with. However, he was able to understand how affectionate Balarāma was toward Kṛṣṇa and also that Kṛṣṇa was a worthy opponent. Thus, he reasoned it best to kill Rāma first, whom he considered to be the weaker of the two brothers, and in doing so weaken Kṛṣṇa's resolve and then kill him as well. Understanding Pralamba's mind and desiring to

16. *Hari-vaṁśa Purāṇa*, *Viṣṇu-parva* 11.18–22.

broadcast Rāma's glories, Kṛṣṇa quickly chose him to be on his side and matched him against him whom Pralamba considered merely "the son of Rohiṇī," lacking the prowess of Yaśodā's son, Kṛṣṇa.

When Rāma's side won, Kṛṣṇa carried Śrīdāmā, and Rāma mounted the shoulders of Pralamba. The game involved carrying one's victor to the great banyan tree, but Pralamba ran in the opposite direction while clinging to Rāma because he knew that Kṛṣṇa would protect Rāma if Pralamba tried to kill him in Kṛṣṇa's presence. Meanwhile, Kṛṣṇa once again sought to set the record straight as to his older brother's equality with him in prowess by allowing Rāma to slay this foremost among the demons—*dānava-puṅgavaḥ*.

Although Kṛṣṇa had informed Balarāma that Pralamba was a demon in disguise, Rāma was so absorbed in the competition that he treated Pralamba in terms of his cowherd dress—as a cowherd friend. However, Pralamba began to struggle with the weight of Balarāma as he ran away with him on his shoulders. While any cowherd boy of Vraja could carry Balarāma on the strength of his love for him, a demon like Pralamba could not bear Rāma's weight. Thus, Pralamba quickly tired, and in an effort to compensate for the gravity of the situation he now found himself in, he expanded his form, his cowherd dress falling to the ground, his actual appearance manifesting. In Vraja there is only beauty. Thus, even the dark demonic form of Pralamba clad in gold armor appeared beautiful like a dark cloud casting lightning while carrying the moon. At first Balarāma appeared concerned, as his *mādhurya* and *aiśvarya* vacillated between one another, producing a mixture of feelings. However, his concern was never for his own safety but rather that there might be other demons in cowherd dress that he should protect Kṛṣṇa from. Thus Balarāma dispensed with Pralamba and returned to the cowherd assembly at the base of the banyan, where Kṛṣṇa had arrived out of breath from carrying Śrīdāmā on his shoulders. Śrīdāmā's love was indeed quite weighty, and the fact that it left Kṛṣṇa breathless amazed Śukamuni, as expressed in the text of the *Bhāgavata*.[17]

Śukadeva in his *kīrtana* narrative describes Balarāma as *bala-śālinā*, "he who has special powers," or more specifically in relation to Rāma's mood in this particular *līlā*, "he who has the quality of praising Kṛṣṇa's strength." In other words, Balarāma felt, "I have killed this demon because of the power Kṛṣṇa has blessed me with." Understanding Rāma's love for Kṛṣṇa, the

17. *Śrīmad Bhāgavatam* 10.18.23. Sanātana Goswāmī says in his *Vaiṣṇava-toṣaṇī* commentary on this verse, " 'O King!' Śukadeva cries out in astonishment at how the Lord is controlled by his devotees."

other *sakhās* were awed by Rāma's *sakhya-rati*. They celebrated his triumph and praised him—*sādhu sādhu*—while also expressing their amazement at how Pralamba had disguised himself as one of them. The phenomenon of demons in the dress of devotees never ceases to amaze the devoted.

Then the assembly of cowherds, steeped in the *prema* of *preyo-bhakti*, surrounded and profusely blessed Balarāma, "May you forever play affectionately with your younger brother in Vraja and in so doing protect us as well." In response, Rāma praised Kṛṣṇa's prowess. *Jaya* Rāma! *Jaya* Kṛṣṇa! *Jaya* Gopa-vṛnda-pāla!

Subāhu then suggested, "Let Nanda remain the king of the cowherd village, but we shall crown Kṛṣṇa king of the forest so dear to us, a king Kaṁsa will live in constant fear of!" His suggestion was met with a roar of approval and the sound of drums, cymbals, horns, and other wind instruments accompanied by the affectionate mooing of each and every cow. The assembly quickly arranged their new king's throne at the base of the banyan, which they considered celestial—*surataru*. Kṛṣṇa humbly accepted their coronation as he was crowned with the tail of a male peacock—a symbol of the third eye of beauty/love and wisdom, which would characterize his reign. Then in his first act as the forest king, he appointed Balarāma as his prime minister, a decision met with unanimous and resounding approval. Śrīdāmā raised a royal umbrella over his *rāja*'s head, as he and the mighty Subala, Sudāmā, and others were appointed courtiers. *Rasarāja* Kṛṣṇa appointed Madhumaṅgala as his *śāstric* advisor and conferred on others the posts of gatekeeper and treasurer. He then formed an army of soldiers and gave dignified positions to the trees, birds, and deer as his woodland ambassadors.

Subāhu then garlanded the ever-enchanting *rāja*—king of the country of *rasa*—with a wreath of never-wilting forest flowers, carefully picked and woven together by Sukhada, which served as the Vraja version of Vaikuṇṭha's Vaijayantī garland of victory. Abhaya fanned his beloved king and appointed Suvākya to lead in song to a melody chosen by Suniṣṭha, as the assembly of *sakhās* in response chanted their king's names and sang of his glorious qualities and auspicious *līlās*, their voices choking in ecstasy. So tender was the cowherds' love for their king, so real was their play. The surrounding stones appeared to melt, but under scrutiny it was clear that they merely wept as they watched. The gods could only bow in silence from above, not only to the king but also to the cowherds' *praṇaya*. May this scene capture your heart, as it has mine.

Afterward, the royal priest, Madhumaṅgala, praised the king, taking his own esteemed seat.

> O Vṛndāvana-purandara, who is Indra compared to you! The Gaṅgā of your glorious deeds rises up from this forest like a great geyser to the top of the Himalayas and upward still to the heavens, where it bathes and purifies the head of Bṛhaspati. I, your priest, always wish you well. By my blessings have you obtained this kingdom. Now please fulfill my request. I have harbored for so long the desire to have a horse. Please give me one.[18]

As fate would have it, just then a large Vraja *nīlagāya* resembling a small horse approached, having been attracted by the music of the cowherds. Smiling, Kṛṣṇa suggested that Madhumaṅgala make this deer his horse but cautioned him not to ride the deer, noting that he was not a horseman to begin with and knew nothing about horseback riding.

> Madhumaṅgala: O Indra of Vṛndāvana! O crest jewel of the earthly kings! You mock me with your speech. Am I bound by my birth caste never to ride like a *kṣatriya*? Have you never heard the story of Viśvāmitra?[19] You know only of my birth but not of my qualities, by which I should be judged. Furthermore, what is impossible for a *brāhmaṇa* with powers attained by *yoga*?
>
> Hari: You speak boldly and we will certainly not thwart your desire. But wanting a horse is one thing, while riding one is quite another. By my edict you have attained a horse. What you do with him is up to you. I take no responsibility. Thus, it will not be my fault if you fall from the back of this horse.
>
> Madhumaṅgala: Very good! Please have your minions hold my horse as I mount him.

Thus, Madhumaṅgala climbed clumsily onto the deer's back, while his friends not only held the deer but also, and with greater difficulty, held their laughter within their hearts.

18. I have adapted this *līlā* from *Govinda-vallabha-nāṭaka*, act 5. I then return to the narration of the *Bhāgavata*, in which Kṛṣṇa delivers his friends and cows from a forest fire.

19. Here Madhumaṅgala refers to the famous scriptural account of Viśvāmitra, a *kṣatriya* by birth, being accepted as a *brāhmaṇa* based upon his character.

Following Madhu's instruction, they then bound his ankles together with a rope underneath the stomach of the deer to saddle him in. Then, stepping back, they could no longer contain themselves, and their laughter sent the already restless deer galloping, frightening Madhumaṅgala, his hair standing on end. With no end in sight and no way to dismount, Madhu cried out to Kṛṣṇa, questioning his king's commitment to protecting *brāhmaṇas*. To everyone's amazement, Kṛṣṇa then called the deer close with his flute, and the cowherds helped the *brāhmaṇa* dismount.

> Madhumaṅgala: O King! This horse is slower than an ass and therefore is not suitable for me. He could barely carry me and thus I have no use for him. Therefore, I am returning him to you.
>
> Śyāma (smiling and looking toward the cows for a feisty bull): Would you like to try another horse?

However, Kṛṣṇa's humor soon faded when he realized that during the commotion the cows had wandered off, perhaps in protest. Where had they gone when the cowherds' watchful eyes had been focused elsewhere? While ostensibly longing for sweeter and greener grasses—being cows—the herd was actually an unwitting instrument of Kṛṣṇa's *līlā-śakti*, who employed them in her arrangement to flush out a friend of Pralamba's hiding with evil intentions in a patch of nearby cane.

Rāma and Kṛṣṇa led the assembly of young herdsmen following the cows' footprints, broken branches, and bent grass along the *go-pada*—cow path—in search of their wealth. Up ahead, the cows had wandered into a cane patch that appeared scorched from the sun and parched for lack of rain. Therein the cows too felt the heat and became overwhelmed with thirst while still some distance from the Yamunā. The heat they felt, however, was not as much due to the summer itself as to the intention of another of Kaṁsa's agents making plans to engulf them and Rāma and Kṛṣṇa in a raging forest fire.

As the cows mooed pitifully, Kṛṣṇa responded by calling out to them in general and to some by name. His tone was thunderous while also reassuring, and the cows felt immediate relief on hearing it. Thus, soon the herd and herdsmen were again united, but only to find themselves surrounded by fire, crying out to Rāma and Kṛṣṇa.

All eyes stared lovingly at Kṛṣṇa—the more resourceful of the two brothers—the boys fearing they might lose his company. This was their only thought. Kṛṣṇa told the boys to close their eyes, which took some convincing. How would that help? And if they were to die on the spot, let it be with their eyes fixed on Kṛṣṇa.

Thus he thought,

> These boys, filled with affection for me, live without concern for their own safety. In their *śaraṇāgati* they see me alone as their protector, with whom they identify in *praṇaya* as their very self. If they see me swallow the fire, they will enter that fire to protect *me*, just as ordinary persons, without thinking, spontaneously protect themselves in times of sudden danger. Therefore, I must get them to close their eyes.

Such thoughts arising from his love-suppressed omniscience were of course thoughts he could not express, given the circumstances. Thus, Hari's *mādhurya-śakti* inspired the wise Subala to weigh in with special wisdom of his own:

> Friends! Kṛṣṇa has deep insight into the mystical powers of *mantras* and jewels and how to employ them to counteract the effects of fire. But invoking their power is not possible in public. Thus, we must close our eyes, that he will be alone and able to elicit their mysterious power. That is why he is telling us to close our eyes.

Subala's insight made perfect sense to them, and thus the cowherds closed their eyes and Kṛṣṇa swallowed the fire on the strength of his *acintya-śakti*. When he told the boys to open their eyes, they found themselves back at the base of the great banyan, their cows along with them. While the *sakhās* were confident of the power of jewels and *mantras*, Kṛṣṇa's ability to invoke such power astounded them! Thus, in their minds they began to consider that Kṛṣṇa must be some kind of *deva*, and as this thought played itself out, they happily reached the conclusion that since they were equals, so too were they!

As the sun prepared to retire in the distant mountains, Rāma and Kṛṣṇa rounded up the cows and headed homeward in the serenity of the late afternoon of the long summer day. *Go-dhūli*, the hour of cow dust, had once again arrived and preoccupied every man, woman, and child of the village, many of whom waited with watchful eyes fixed on the cow trail from their rooftops. Millions and millions of honeybees swarmed above the herd like a cloud providing shade, so attracted to Kṛṣṇa's scent as he departed that they left every other flower in the forest. Deer and birds of all variety assembled at the edge of the forest, attracted by the sound of Kṛṣṇa's *muralī*. The deer drank the notes from the cups of their ears, listening in trance, as the birds responded to the deep, haunting sound in their native tongues, augmenting the afternoon *rāga* of Śyāma's *rati*.

Hari's *rati* now turned toward the *gopīs* perched in their *candraśālikās*, small rooftop moon towers providing panoramic views. Balarāma raced ahead with his friends, eager to tell of his extraordinary exploits, while Kṛṣṇa drifted to the rear, surrounded by his intimate friends. As he exchanged glances with the *gopīs*, their faces turned a soothing reddish color, like moons lighted by the *rāga* of the setting Kṛṣṇa sun. And as the setting afternoon sun met the evening and the two merged into the starlit night, the *gopīs*' eyes met Kṛṣṇa's and they mentally merged with him in romantic love. The night sky of Kṛṣṇa contained and consumed everything while highlighting the star-like brilliance of Rādhā's *anurāga*, which was underscored by Subala as he pointed her out in the crowd. The *narma-sakhās*' general sympathetic consensus was as follows:

> O dear friend! For many days prior to and even into *paugaṇḍa*, we have not seen anything as amazing as what we now see as your adolescence begins to manifest. When you disappear in the morning into the forest like the sun sinking into the ocean, the *gopīs* in their *candraśālikās* look like lotuses growing in the sky, trying to sustain their lives soaking in the waters of love in separation. And when you reappear in the evening like the moon casting its soothing rays on the earth, these *gopīs* blossom in delight like night-blooming lotuses. There is nothing more amazing anywhere on the earth or anywhere in Brahmā's creation![20]

Once home, Kṛṣṇa was affectionately whisked away by Yaśodā to his room, her breasts overflowing with milk. Therein he was cared for by house servants Raktaka and Patraka, who offered him *pān* to relieve him of the fatigue from the day's heat. As Kṛṣṇa relaxed and chewed on the betel nuts scented with camphor, it appeared as if the *pān* were highly intoxicating. In actuality, Hari had lost himself in thoughts of the *gopas*' love-laden hearts in *sakhya-rati* that he had tasted throughout the day.[21] His servants began

20. Adapted from *Ānanda-vṛndāvana-campū*, *Kiśora-līlā*, chapter 11.

21. The word *pān* is derived from Sanskrit *parṇa*, meaning "leaf." *Pān* consists of the betel leaf and the areca nut. It is chewed for its psychoactive effect as a mild stimulant, causing a warming sensation in the body and slightly heightened alertness. It also freshens one's breath. Only much later through Western influence did it come to be combined with tobacco.

to prepare his bath, but given the long summer day, he checked them and requested permission from his mother to swim instead with some friends at nearby Pāvana-sarovara before milking the cows.

Yaśodā gave her permission and sent some servants along to carry his evening meal and fresh clothes. At that time Rādhā also went to Pāvana-sarovara with her handmaidens on the pretext of taking her evening bath there. In fact, though, she was hoping that Kṛṣṇa too would bathe there, and she desired to touch the water that had touched his body. Thus, they met at Pāvana-sarovara, although the *gopīs* and *gopas* were at opposite shores and some distance apart.

As the boys swam, Kṛṣṇa proposed a contest to see who among them could hold their breath the longest. With something else in mind, Kṛṣṇa won, taking the underwater opportunity to swim to the opposite side of the pond and pull Rādhā by her feet under the water and embrace her before quickly swimming back and surfacing among his friends. Then, after bathing and dressing there, Kṛṣṇa ate, drank, and rested before going to the barn to milk the cows. Such were his summer days.

15

Monsoon, Autumn, and Early Winter

With the passing of the summer heat, the cooling monsoon season ensued. The *rāja* of the summer sun had for the past eight months extracted a tax of moisture from the earth, and now in a torrent of reciprocation he spent that tax in the form of monsoon rain, dressing the barren, naked earth with emerald greenery and filling her with vital fluids, her lakes and rivers overflowing. During the monsoon season, the sky is often filled with dark rain clouds resembling Kṛṣṇa's *śyāma* complexion, and given this sense of equality between the two, the clouds and Kṛṣṇa share a friendship. Thus, the rain clouds of Vraja are themselves manifestations of *sakhya-rasa*.[1]

In the *Bhāgavata*, Śukadeva poetically depicts the monsoon and autumn seasons of Vraja to set the scene for the *līlās* occurring during these periods—a preface that serves, Śrī Jīva comments, as an "*uddīpana* for intense *ānanda*" that such *līlās* are filled with. In eight verses, Śukamuni depicts the typical daily cowherd *līlās* as the monsoon turns to the harvest season.

> When the Vṛndāvana forest was flourishing thus, filled with dates and blackberries, Hari, surrounded by his *go* and *gopālas* and accompanied by Balarāma, entered that forest for the sole purpose of playing. The cows, weighed down by their milk-filled udders, moved slowly. But when Bhagavān called them, they ran to him, milk dripping out of affection. Kṛṣṇa took note of the joyful female forest dwellers, the trees dripping with honey, and the caves, streams, and

1. See *Sārārtha-darśinī* and *Vaiṣṇava-toṣaṇī* 10.21.16. The *gopīs* glorify the fortune of those in *sakhya-rasa* such as the clouds, who are of the same complexion as Kṛṣṇa and give their bodies to him, forming an umbrella to shade him from the sun. Through the eye of their own *bhāva*, they see *sakhya-rasa* in the clouds.

> waterfalls that seemed nearby from the sound of the water echoing on Mount Govardhana. When it rained, sometimes Kṛṣṇa would take shelter of the hollow of a tree or a mountain cave and eat roots and fruits. Along with Saṅkarṣaṇa and together with the other boys, all equal to him in stature, he ate his lunch—yogurt rice brought from home—on a large makeshift stone table on the riverbank. Kṛṣṇa watched the contented bulls, cows, and calves grazing on green grasses and then sitting, eyes closed, chewing their cud, the cows tired from the burden of their heavy milk bags. Observing the overall beauty of the scene, a perennial source of joy, he offered his respect to the monsoon season itself, a manifestation of his *ātmā-śakti*. In this way, Rāma and Keśava resided in Vraja during the monsoon season, as autumn arrived with its cloudless sky, clear water, and gentle breezes.[2]

The boys surrounded Citta-hari for the purpose of sheltering him from the rain with makeshift umbrellas, greedy to relish the beauty of his smiling face as it reacted to the beauty of the forest during the monsoon season.

Characteristic of this season is the abundance of dates and *jambu* fruit.[3] And because of the rains, the grass was plentiful and fresh, which in turn caused the *kāmadhenus*' udders to swell. The monsoon season is thus also characterized by an abundance of milk. Here the *Bhāgavata* describes a *sāttvika-bhāva* exclusive to *vātsalya-rasa*: the cows' udders were wet with milk in loving response to hearing Kṛṣṇa affectionately call the cows' names. Driven by their *sthāyi-bhāva* in parental love, they desired to give their milk to Kṛṣṇa rather than to their calves.

Kṛṣṇa glanced mercifully upon the aboriginal women residing in the forest. He tasted tender roots and sweet fruits along with his friends, gathering together in the hollow of large trees and within the caves of Mount Govardhana, sometimes mystically accepting the competing invitations of

2. *Śrīmad Bhāgavatam* 10.20.25–32.

3. *Syzygium cumini*. In Sanskrit, *jambu phalinda* or *jambu*. In English, the "Indian blackberry." One of the few trees indigenous to India, it is perhaps more like a sweet olive, often served with a *masālā* topping. It is said that Śrī Rāmacandra lived on the *jambu* for years after his exile from Ayodhyā. His skin is often compared to the slick texture of the fruit, and temples constructed in his honor invariably host at least one *jambu* tree. Megha-deva—god of the clouds—is said to have descended onto earth in the form of the *jambu*, which is why the color of the fruit is like that of a dark rain cloud, a color that arguably identifies the *jambu* with *sakhya-rasa*. The Purāṇas describe the division of the cosmos into seven concentric island continents, at the center of which is Jambūdvīpa, "the island of *jambu* trees."

both trees and caves at the same time. From such natural shelters that openly embraced and lovingly hosted him and his friends, they looked out in awe as the thundering rains quenched the thirsty forest. They were comfortable while waiting for the rain to subside, exploring in conversation any number of interesting topics. But at times the rains reached such a torrential pitch, pouring forth from the heavens above, that the boys could not even hear one another speak, awed by nature as they sat intimately huddled with the source of her power. At such times, none of them—neither Rāma, Kṛṣṇa, nor any of their friends—had the slightest desire to depart. When you love someone, the hollow of a tree will suffice as a home for your love-laden heart.

As the time for lunch arrived, Saṅkarṣaṇa gathered together the multitude of boys as a single unit around a stone sufficient in size to serve as plate, table, and seat for all of the *sakhās*. That stone was situated on the bank of a beautiful *kuṇḍa*. As the boys unpacked their lunches, they first offered them to Kṛṣṇa, who honored the spirit of their love. But instead of eating first, Kṛṣṇa placed Rāma in the center and served every one of them. Only then did he eat lunch himself. Thus, *rasa-rasika* Kṛṣṇa and his friends were equally love and object of love for one another.[4]

Meanwhile, the *gopīs* had burned through the summer in separation from Kṛṣṇa but assumed that the monsoon season would give them relief from the heat. However, this was not the case. Like a monsoon cloud, Kṛṣṇa remained in their hearts. And from their lotus eyes, tears streamed such that the monsoon season itself took notice as the *gopīs* drowned in an ocean of love in separation. Subala detected that his friend's face was drenched not only by rain but also from the tears that expressed his *pūrva-rāga* for Rādhā, as the monsoon rain—assisted by the *gopīs*' tears—poured down so heavily that it arrested the minds of both the *gopas* and the *gopīs*, leaving them dependent on their hearts alone.

Fortunately, the harvest season that follows the monsoon is a season of plenty, and as such it is a time for considerable celebration, including the beginning of the new year and renewed hope. The harvest moon, which occurs around the time of the autumn equinox, is also an *uddīpana* for *śṛṅgāra-rasa* the world over. For several evenings, this moonrise comes soon

4. When we say Kṛṣṇa is *rasa*, we refer to him as the object—*viṣaya*—of *sakhya-rasa*. However, he is also a *rasika*, or one who tastes *rasa*. Thus, he is the object of love for his friends, but he is also a *rasika* who experiences his friends as the object of *his* love, rendering *him* the personification/shelter—*āśraya*—of *sakhya-rasa* (see *Bhakti-rasāmṛta-sindhu* 4.8.85). Also, in *Bhakti-rasāmṛta-sindhu* 2.1.16, Jīva Goswāmī comments that some opine that for the most intimate among the intimate associates, there is no distinction of *āśraya* and *viṣaya*.

after sunset and results in an abundance of bright moonlight early in the evening that serves as an aid to farmers harvesting their crops. But in the poetry of the *Bhāgavata*, it is described that while the gentle, jasmine-scented autumn breeze comforted everyone, being neither too hot nor too cold, it did not cool down the *gopīs*' passion. In the following year, however, it was indeed the autumn season that ultimately served as the setting for the consummation of their romantic love. During the present autumn season, the *gopīs* expressed their love for Kṛṣṇa to one another under the influence of his charming flute, as he set out to capture them through its haunting *rāgas*.

At first Kṛṣṇa began to perfect his flute playing only in the company of Balarāma, who was impressed by his younger brother's talent. Then he tried to affect his cows, who drank with their ears the ambrosia of the flute sound—which is synonymous with Kṛṣṇa himself. Although this ambrosia rendered any other taste bland, their milk yield increased even without their eating any grass or grain, and they did not need their calves' affection to let down their milk. It flowed spontaneously to the magical sound of Kṛṣṇa's *muralī*.

Kṛṣṇa then turned his attention to the birds and wild animals, who responded as if caged by the sound of his flute. The peacocks danced, while the other birds became silent like sages, intent only on listening to the haunting sound that tamed them along with other creatures of the forest. Indeed, the wild became civilized, while the civilized became wild.

When Kṛṣṇa turned his attention to inanimate nature, he caused rivers to cease flowing as if they were land and caused land to move like river currents. The unconscious became conscious, and the conscious became unconscious. *Mallāra-rāga*, capable of drawing rain from the clouds, caused the friendly clouds to weep upon hearing Kṛṣṇa's *vaṁśī* and vow to shade Kṛṣṇa from the sun in the spirit of *suhṛt-sakhās*.[5]

With his earthly success, Kṛṣṇa turned his attention to the heavens. There he captivated and stunned the celestial goddesses. However, all of this wonder heralded on heaven and earth caused only anguish in the hearts of the cowherd girls of Vraja. While deprecating their own position in remaining bereft of their lover's company, they praised the good fortune

5. This *rāga* is typically associated with the monsoon season—often referred to as *megha-mallāra* (*megha* means "cloud")—and is thought to be capable of producing rain. Graphically it is depicted as a sage walking in the rain. It is cited in Sanātana Goswāmī's commentary on *Bṛhad-bhāgavatāmṛta* 2.6.46 as that which Gopa-kumāra heard for the first time in Goloka as Kṛṣṇa returned from cowherding. It caused the trees to ooze sap, the breasts of the elderly *gopīs* to flow with milk, and everyone to weep.

of others affected by his flute in ways that enabled them to take advantage of his person. They also praised Kṛṣṇa's flute itself and its good fortune, a mere bamboo reed allowed to freely taste his lips. What was the good fortune of this bamboo flute's mother, who nursed him in his youth? That river, upon hearing her son's sound emanating from Kṛṣṇa's lips, erupted in ecstasy with goose bumps in the form of lotus flowers. Indeed, Rādhā prayed to take birth as a bamboo shoot turned into a flute. As such, she considered that in such a birth she would lose consciousness of who she was but Kṛṣṇa would know of her sacrifice in pursuit of his company.

But above all, the *gopīs* praised the cowherds' good fortune, as these boys frolicked openly with the two brothers Rāma and Kṛṣṇa amid their cows entering the forest at Mount Govardhana. This sight is truly the height of the beatific vision sages earnestly seek for *yugas*. The *gopīs* thought Kṛṣṇa was particularly charming in such company, and especially that of his elder brother.

> O friends! The perfection of sight is to see the beautiful faces of the sons of Vraja *rāja* Nanda—Rāma and Kṛṣṇa—as they enter the forest, surrounded by their friends and herding their cows ahead of them. As they depart for the forest, they hold their flutes to their mouths and glance back lovingly upon the Vraja *vāsīs*. Those who experience this scene are truly blessed.
>
> These two are charmingly dressed in a variety of fine cloth upon which forest-flower wreaths rest, and their hair is decorated with the feathers of peacocks entwined with clusters of mango sprouts and other flower buds. Water lilies are tucked behind their ears, and they hold lotus flowers in their hands. Kṛṣṇa and Balarāma stand out stunningly amid their cowherd friends like the best of stage performers, dancing and sometimes singing as well.[6]

Oh, not only to see them but to hear their songs! As they tire from dancing, they sing, and sometimes their *sakhās* spontaneously sing about them in songs of their own composition. Or the boys set up a competition: "Between the two of you, who is the best singer? Let the best one sing." Such is the

6. *Śrīmad Bhāgavatam* 10.21.7–8. Sanātana Goswāmī comments that mentioning Balarāma adds special beauty because of how he assists Kṛṣṇa at this time. Also, to conceal their romantic attraction to Kṛṣṇa or out of shyness, the *gopīs* mention Balarāma along with Kṛṣṇa.

sweetness of their song, the charm of their appearance, and the nature of their play. But let us catch our breath and continue the narrative.

Blessed, too, Rādhā exclaimed, was Mount Govardhana, referring to him as the very best of Hari's devotees and citing the many ways in which he serves Kṛṣṇa in *sakhya-rasa*. Rādhā's statement shows both her humility and the extent of Govardhana's glory. He is Kṛṣṇa and he is Kṛṣṇa's best friend. As we learned in the previous chapter, the *gopīs* considered Ananta Śeṣa merely his expansion, thus implicitly identifying Govardhana with Balarāma.[7]

Let us briefly discuss the Govardhana *līlā*, which also occurs in autumn. Its theological implications aside for the moment, psychologically speaking, young Kṛṣṇa's anger with Indra that led to the Govardhana *līlā* stems from his early childhood. The Vraja *vāsīs* traditionally worshiped Indra—the heavenly rain god—annually in autumn with a view to ensure sufficient rain for their crops and, more so, being primarily cow-herders, grasses for their cows.

The *Bhāgavata* informs us that one year during preparation for this Indra *yajña*, all of the household assistants in Nanda's house were engaged, leaving Yaśodārāṇī home alone with her mischievous child. Earlier the same year, during his mid-*kumāra-līlā*, Kṛṣṇa had often stolen butter from Nanda's neighbors, feeding it to monkeys and creating a disturbance with other young children his age. Thus, Yaśodā had questioned Nanda's animal husbandry. Why was her child stealing butter and yogurt from others' homes? Was Nanda's milk not sweet enough? With no sense of the allure of forbidden fruit to children, she had blamed her husband, who in turn had prepared special grasses for a select group of cows to remedy the situation.

On this day during the preparations for Indra's sacrifice, Yaśodā was home alone with her child, nursing him while at the same time boiling milk derived from Nanda's select group of cows to make milk sweets for her son. However, as Yaśodā was nursing Bala Kṛṣṇa, the milk on the stove began

7. Here I refer to Vṛndā-devī's comment in *Dāna-keli-kaumudī* cited in the previous chapter. In his *Vraja-rīti-cintāmaṇi* (3.10–11), Viśvanātha Cakravartī Ṭhākura also depicts Rādhā envisioning crystal-colored rocks on the mount as representations of Balarāma and dark, sapphire-like stones as representations of Kṛṣṇa. That Kṛṣṇa himself is Govardhana is well known and was revealed by him in the *Bhāgavata*'s Govardhana *līlā*. Indeed, his entire *dhāma* is nondifferent from himself as a manifestation of his *sandhinī-śakti*, presided over by Balarāma. That Govardhana as devotee serves in *sakhya-rasa* is mentioned in the *Sārārtha-darśinī* commentary on *Śrīmad Bhāgavatam* 11.12.8. Rādhā's glorification of Govardhana is found in *Śrīmad Bhāgavatam* 10.21.18.

to boil over. With no one there to assist her, she had to choose between suddenly setting Kṛṣṇa down and tending to the milk or letting the milk boil over and continuing to nurse baby Kṛṣṇa. Using her spiritual intelligence, she chose to tend to that which was being prepared for Kṛṣṇa from special grasses and special cows with special attention from Nanda and herself rather than to tend directly to Kṛṣṇa himself, at least for the moment. But despite all that went into her decision, Kṛṣṇa objected and accidentally broke a butter pot in the process. Then, fearing her rebuke, he ran away as she chased him out of fear of losing him altogether. Catching him, she then tied him to a grinding mortar. This in turn traumatized the child, and now in his seventh year, he realized that his childhood trauma was in part caused by Indra with his sacrificial demands. This, together with theological concerns regarding the value of the Indra *yajña* in the face of *uttama-bhakti* directed toward himself, the God of gods, caused him to take exception to this year's preparations for the celestial sacrifice. Thus, he recommended that the entire community's energy be diverted from the worship of Indra to the worship of Mount Govardhana, who readily supplied the cows', and thereby the cowherds', needs.

Convincing Nanda primarily with his charm and secondarily with his philosophical acumen, Kṛṣṇa directed that Govardhana *pūjā* be performed with considerable pomp and festivity. However, Indra's pride got the best of him and he showered Vraja with torrential rains, to which Kṛṣṇa responded by lifting the mountain with the smallest finger on his left hand, creating a huge umbrella under which all of the residents of Vraja took shelter. And in the midst of this, Hari showed Mount Govardhana to be nondifferent from himself.

Although the supremacy of Kṛṣṇa is central to this *līlā*, the reaction of the Vraja *vāsīs*, especially that of Kṛṣṇa's cowherd friends, is more important to those of fine theistic intelligence. The *Bhāgavata* employs majestic descriptions of Kṛṣṇa in Vraja primarily for the purpose of showcasing how his devotees react to such majesty, for their reaction shows the measure of their *prema*. For example, the *Bhāgavata* describes how Kṛṣṇa lifted Mount Govardhana, yet this majestic description serves essentially as a background to illustrate the intimate love of his friends, who felt he required their help to lift the mountain. Seeing themselves as his equals, Kṛṣṇa's friends hoisted up their herding sticks to assist Kṛṣṇa in holding the king of mountains. Śrī Rūpa cites the following verse as an example of the cowherd boys' affection for Govinda during the Govardhana *līlā*:

> You have endured seven nights on your feet without sleep, holding the hill. Surely you are tired. Our minds are disturbed seeing you in this condition. Dear friend, toss the mountain to Śrīdāmā, or at least place it in your right hand. Then we can massage your left hand.[8]

Thus, Kṛṣṇa's display of majesty was no match for his friends' *sakhya-prema*, and from this it is clear that the *Bhāgavata*, properly understood, is not about the power of God but rather his weakness in the face of love. In this *līlā*, Kṛṣṇa's power could not interfere with his friends' sense of intimacy and equality with him. Indeed, it only furthered their sense of intimacy, and this was only more evident after Indra came to his senses and apologized.

When Indra realized his offense, he approached Brahmā for advice on how to proceed. Brahmā suggested that he approach Surabhi, the celestial cow, and let her take the lead in a procession of Indra and other gods bearing gifts. They arrived after Mount Govardhana was returned to his natural setting and life in Gokula had more or less returned to normal. In the late afternoon, Kṛṣṇa was herding with his friends. At some distance from them, the gods and goddesses appeared, and Kṛṣṇa excused himself from his circle of friends, asking them to wait for him as he set out to meet the *devas*.

Surabhi spoke first, requesting Kṛṣṇa's blessing, and then Indra expressed his remorse. With Kṛṣṇa's permission, the gods performed a sacred bath consisting of Surabhi's milk and celestial water from the Gaṅgā brought down by the trunk of Indra's elephant carrier, Airāvata. As they bathed Kṛṣṇa, he too bathed them in return with his love-laden lotus-like glance of grace. The gods then dressed Kṛṣṇa in heavenly attire, and from the sky the name "Govinda" vibrated, as Kṛṣṇa was crowned God of the gods and the gods all offered him their gifts.

Indra presented Govinda with a parasol; the sun god gave him golden ornaments; Brahmā gave him a blue lotus; Śiva gave him a flute that he had made himself; and other *devas* gave various gifts that became all the more remarkable in Kṛṣṇa's possession. At that time, a throne appeared and Kṛṣṇa sat upon the throne as he was fanned with *cāmaras*. Goddess Aditi performed a mother's duties, Pārvatī those of a sister, and Garuḍa those of a servant, all in ecstasy.

8. *Bhakti-rasāmṛta-sindhu* 3.3.18. This is an example of *sneha* generated by the thought of Kṛṣṇa as an equal.

From a distance, Kṛṣṇa's friends witnessed all of this, motionless with unblinking eyes, as the *devas*, tears in their eyes, departed. With the gods' departure, the boys approached, filled with curiosity. Pleased with them, Kṛṣṇa decorated his friends with the heavenly garments and ornaments given to him and then worshiped his friends as gods, to their amusement and delight, dismissing the ceremony they had witnessed from a distance as something of little consequence in comparison to his friendship with them. Witnessing this exchange, the gods were stunned. In trance, they realized that these intimate friends of Govinda—one with him in form, qualities, and nature—were reaping the results of *sakhya-prema* itself, as no other benediction could afford them such power and influence over Bhagavān.

As the sun began to set on the mountain, Kṛṣṇa and company all headed home, showered by flowers falling from heaven. On the way, the boys imitated the gods and worshiped Kṛṣṇa: re-dressing him, ornamenting him, holding Indra's umbrella over his head, and fanning him with white *cāmara* whisks. Thus, Kṛṣṇa was bedecked with godly ornaments and attire, and his friends' bodies erupted, ornamented in *sāttvika-bhāvas*. As they neared the village, Balarāma pulled Kṛṣṇa aside and asked for a detailed explanation of all that had transpired between himself and the *devas*. Then, satisfied with Kṛṣṇa's explanation, he removed all of Kṛṣṇa's divine ornaments brought from the heavens, not wanting the elders to see him beset with majesty. Only then did he bring Kṛṣṇa to Vraja.

However, taking permission from Kṛṣṇa upon arrival, the boys ornamented themselves again, and Śrīdāmā began to worship Nanda with the celestial *cāmara* and other godly paraphernalia, creating quite a scene. Thus, Nanda sought an explanation as to what had taken place in the pasture. Śrīdāmā spoke first, saying that he and the others had been at some distance and distracted due to herding cows but that the heavenly items suggested that something divine had taken place. Kṛṣṇa himself shyly looked down, avoiding eye contact with his inquisitive elders, while the other boys confirmed Śrīdāmā's explanation. Then Madhumaṅgala boldly elaborated:

> O Nanda! Please listen. First a cow [Surabhi] spoke. Then someone covered with eyes [Indra] offered respects. A white elephant [Airāvata] took water from heaven and sprinkled it. Someone with four heads [Brahmā] and then a five-headed person [Śiva] began reciting praises, and many people bathed your son festively.

Then a voice from the sky gave direction to the stunned elders:

> O Nanda! Just as we gathered and crowned your son "Govinda"—chief of the cowherds—you should gather together, ornament your son, and install him as the prince of Vraja.

Filled with joy and pride by these sweet yet deeply profound words, the elders began considering among themselves their implications. Then they began a festival and honored Kṛṣṇa as the prince of Vraja, heir to the throne of Nanda Bābā.

However, Kṛṣṇa wasn't focused on his own accomplishments. He retired that night filled with thoughts of Rādhā, whose glance during the festival had pierced his heart. To express his suffering to her, he played the *kedāra-rāga*, appropriate for the first three hours of the night—one *prahara*—on the flute Śiva had given him. This *rāga* is highly nonlinear, and in its ascent (*ārohaṇa*) only six notes are used, while its descent (*avarohaṇa*) employs all seven notes of the scale. It is identified with Śiva and considered the best *rāga* for expressing romantic *bhakti-rasa*. The word *kedāra* also means "field," and thus Govinda created a musical field, in which the *gopīs* sowed the seeds of their desire for his company, acknowledging their attraction to him. However, unlike the other *gopīs*, Rādhā, for whom the melody was primarily intended, was unable to respond due to having lost consciousness altogether upon hearing it.

The day that Indra crowned Kṛṣṇa was the eleventh day of the waxing moon—Ekādaśī. On every Ekādaśī, Nanda Mahārāja dutifully worshiped Nārāyaṇa and observed the appropriate religious vows. However, this particular Ekādaśī was short, lasting only eighteen hours. This left six hours before sunrise, all of which were part of the Dvādaśī, or twelfth lunar day, on which the Ekādaśī fast is to be broken. The proper time for breaking the fast was prior to sunrise, and Nanda typically bathed before breaking his fast and completing his Ekādaśī *vrata*. Thus, he bathed in the Yamunā and began meditating on Nārāyaṇa.

However, bathing at this time was otherwise inauspicious, and thus a servant of Varuṇa (the water god) not well acquainted with *prema-dharma* inappropriately apprehended Nanda and took him to Varuṇa's underwater chamber. When Nanda disappeared, his assistants cried out for Kṛṣṇa and Rāma, who awoke and ran to the scene. Kṛṣṇa told Rāma to stay on the shore and care for Yaśodā, while he dove into the river to rescue his father. When Kṛṣṇa arrived, Varuṇa apologized on behalf of his assistant and brought Kṛṣṇa before Nanda, who was seated on a throne, still absorbed in meditation upon his deity. Then Kṛṣṇa touched Nanda's feet, and his meditation on Nārāyaṇa broke, Kṛṣṇa standing before him. Varuṇa then glorified Kṛṣṇa, and Nanda returned home with his son, trying to wrap his head around what had just happened. Especially perplexing to Nanda was Varuṇa's worship of his son! Nanda Rāja had learned of a heavenly encounter in the pasture and heard an oracle that evening that crowned Kṛṣṇa "Govinda," and then he had presided over the festival of anointing Govinda as his successor. Now Varuṇa had worshiped Kṛṣṇa in front of him as his meditation on Nārāyaṇa broke. To top it off, Nanda now had to explain to the other elders everything that had happened, the import of which he himself was still unclear about.

Theologizing together as best they could—remembering Gargācārya's words concerning Kṛṣṇa's likeness to Nārāyaṇa—the elders were reminded once again that Kṛṣṇa was no ordinary human, which in turn made them reconsider their own relationship with him. If he was a *deva* or an *avatāra*, where was he from? Did he have his own abode, and would they be with him in the afterlife? The elders put their questions before Kṛṣṇa, who then showed them Goloka, where the Vedas bowed in worship of him. But this too was confusing, and thus they preferred paying full attention to their present good fortune to be with him in such an intimate setting, enhanced as it was by the autumn season, which was coming to a close.

With the end of autumn and the Kārtika month, which is identified with Rādhā, the prewinter season, *hemanta*, begins with the month identified with Kṛṣṇa—Mārgaśīrṣa. *Hemanta* is cooler, its days shorter, and its moonlit nights longer. At the beginning of this season, during Kṛṣṇa's seventh year, the young girls—*kumārīs*—yet to be spoken for in marriage developed a desire to marry Kṛṣṇa.[9] The *Hari-vaṁśa Purāṇa* distinguishes them from older girls such as Rādhā and Candrāvalī, whose marriage had already been planned by their elders and whose sentiments were described earlier in the *Bhāgavata*'s *Veṇu-gītā* (10.21).

Among candidates for marriage, Kṛṣṇa was not suitable, because his astrological chart placed him outside of Vraja as a princely public figure shortly after attaining adolescence. In other words, he had a fateful date with *dharma*. Of course, this apparent obstacle to Rādhā's love for him in turn facilitated the couple's *parakīya-bhāva*, with all of its theological nuance,

9. In his *Laghu-toṣaṇī* 10.24.1, Jīva Goswāmī gives the following chronology of events: worshiping Govardhana (autumn), going to Varuṇa's abode, stealing the *gopīs*' clothing (winter), begging food from the *brāhmaṇas*' wives (summer), and then the *rāsa-līlā* (the following autumn).

which among other things assures us that Kṛṣṇa is not only the actual and only husband of the *gopīs*, he is for that matter also the husband of the *gopīs*' so-called husbands. He is the *puruṣa* and all others are *prakṛti*—*śaktimān* and its *śaktis*.[10] But all of this aside, the *kumārīs*, simple at heart, desired to marry Kṛṣṇa. They shared their feelings among one another, and with the help of Vṛndā-devī came up with a plan to attain their desired goal.

Vṛndā-devī gave the girls a *mantra*, and with her instructions they formed a deity of goddess Kātyāyanī out of clay.[11] With their *mantra* and deity in heart and hand, they embraced a month-long vow that included eating simply once daily and bathing daily at dawn in the cold water of the Yamunā.[12] Together they expressed the following *saṅkalpa*:

> O Kātyāyanī—goddess—O *mahā-śakti*, *mahā-yoginī*, *mahā-īśvarī*, *praṇāma* to you. Please make Nanda-suta my husband.[13]

Thus they worshiped like *sādhakas* enduring great austerity, becoming objects of worship themselves! They underwent great difficulty and the pain of austerity with great pleasure. Thus, properly understood, their *vrata* was actually driven by their *rāga*, in which affection for the beloved converts suffering into happiness.

10. The older *gopīs*' husbands are considered illusory or—as in the case of Rādhā's husband, Abhimanyu—a partial manifestation of Kṛṣṇa himself. These "husbands," or the sense that some of the *gopīs* are married, manifest only for the purpose of facilitating a particular type of *parakīya-bhāva*. The *kumārīs* under discussion also experience *parakīya-bhāva* but of a slightly different variety. The *Sāhitya-darpaṇa* and *Ujjvala-nīlamaṇi* specify that heroines in *parakīya-bhāva* are of two basic types: *paroḍhā*, the wife of another man, and *kanyakā*, a young unmarried woman still under the guardianship of her parents. Like the *paroḍhā* heroines, the *kanyakās*/*kumārīs*, being overcome by intense feelings of longing (*anurāga*), also cast aside all considerations of moral and social propriety (*dharma*) to meet with their beloved. Viśvanātha Cakravartī envisions the *kumārīs* of this *Bhāgavata līlā* as *nitya-siddhas* led by Dhyāna-kumārī. Sanātana Goswāmī comments that by their beauty they derided (*ku*) Cupid (*māra*). However, *Padma Purāṇa* as cited by Sanātana Goswāmī says that in their previous birth these girls had been the sages of Daṇḍakāraṇya, which would render them *sādhana-siddhas*.

11. Jīva Goswāmī describes this goddess as "Vaiṣṇavī *śakti*." She is also the *śakti* that presides over the Gopāla *mantra* chanted by the sages of Daṇḍakāraṇya, and she is represented in the *mantra* by the word *svāhā*. Here in the *prakaṭa-līlā*, the perfected sages appearing as *kumārīs* are given a new *mantra* that corresponds with their practitioners' ideal, represented in the Gopāla *mantra* by the words *gopījana-vallabhāya svāhā*.

12. In chapter 22 of *Kṛṣṇa, the Supreme Personality of Godhead*, Śrī Bhaktivedanta Swami Prabhupāda comments that these *kumārīs* "ate *haviṣyānna*...prepared by boiling together mung *dāl* and rice without any spices.... According to Vedic injunction, this kind of food is recommended to purify the body before one enacts a ritualistic ceremony."

13. *Śrīmad Bhāgavatam* 10.22.4.

Then, on the last day of Mārgaśīrṣa—the *pūrṇimā*—the *kumārīs*' *vrata* culminated in *avabhṛtha-snāna*, the ceremonial bath taken upon the completion of a Vedic sacrifice.[14] During their final bath—playful in nature and filled with discussion leading to songs about Śyāmasundara—the success of their *vrata* began to manifest as Kṛṣṇa-candra appeared on the scene out of nowhere. His sudden presence became known to the girls from the sound of his laughter emanating from the branches of a nearby *kadamba* tree. How had he gotten there?

Understanding the intent of the *kumārīs* within his heart, Kṛṣṇa had separated himself from the greater group of his friends. Accompanied by four of his closest *priya-sakhās*, who are personifications of his *antaḥ-karaṇa*, he approached the *kumārīs*' place of worship while they were bathing, their clothes on the shore.

As cited earlier in chapter 4, *Gautamīya Tantra* reveals:

> Famous are Dāmā, Sudāmā, Vasudāmā, and Kiṅkiṇi, personifications of Kṛṣṇa's *antaḥ-karaṇa*. Nondifferent from his very self, they should be worshiped like Kṛṣṇa with flowers and sandalwood.

Nayanānanda Ṭhākura comments:

> These four *sakhās* are nondifferent in form from Kṛṣṇa. Their dress and ornaments are impossible to do justice to within the limits of the written word. The personification of Kṛṣṇa's *buddhi* is the *gopa* named Śrīdāmā; the personification of Kṛṣṇa's *ahaṅkāra* is Sudāmā; the personification of Kṛṣṇa's *citta* is Vasudāmā; and the personification of Kṛṣṇa's *manas* is Kiṅkiṇi. There is not a single confidential *līlā* that Kṛṣṇa-candra secretly performs in Vraja that these four *gopas* are not witnesses to. Surely one is never abandoned by one's own intelligence, ego, heart, and mind. In all of one's actions, these accompany one, while always remaining in the background. None of Kṛṣṇa's *līlās* performed in Vraja throughout his three different ages are ever enacted without these particular boys. There is not a single thing about Kṛṣṇa that they are unaware of, from his parental relationships up to and including his amorous affairs.[15]

14. Viśvanātha Cakravartī alone envisions the *kumārīs* inviting Rādhā and other older girls, who were already betrothed, to join them on this day.

15. *Preyo-bhakti-rasārṇava*, chapter 2. Here again, Nayanānanda Ṭhākura opines that the cowherd Dāmā mentioned in the Tantra is actually Śrīdāmā-gopa.

Rūpa Goswāmī classifies these four boys as *priya-sakhās*, but Jīva Goswāmī in his comment to Śrī Rūpa's verse classifies them also as *priya-narma-sakhās*, in light of the *Gautamīya Tantra* verse cited above.[16] In other words, like the *priya-narma-sakhās*, they are aware of and at least invisibly participate in Kṛṣṇa's romantic affairs as much as his *antaḥ-karaṇa* does. However, as an exception to the norm, in this particular *līlā* they are *visibly* present and actively participate to a limited extent. Here it should be noted that although these *priya-sakhās* were the same age as Kṛṣṇa—seven—they were not as mature for their age as he was, and thus they were more innocent with regard to associating with girls.

As Kṛṣṇa and company neared the *kumārīs*, he hushed his four joking friends. And then, moving stealthily, he stole the young girls' clothes and quickly climbed up into a nearby *kadamba* tree, his friends following his lead. From the tree, he hung the *kumārīs*' clothes on its branches and then laughed amid joking about his theft with his four friends. This, again, was the beginning of the fulfillment of the *kumārīs*' desire to marry Kṛṣṇa—albeit a type of *gāndharva* marriage starting to unfold there in the forest.

The very sweet banter between Kṛṣṇa and the *kumārīs* that ensued has great power to captivate the *sādhaka*'s heart. Kṛṣṇa began by instructing the *kumārīs* through the medium of his friends, telling them what to say. But when he told them to pull the girls out of the water, the girls frightened them by claiming to possess the *śakti* of the goddess as a result of their impressive *vrata* and threatened to pull all four of them into the water along with the mastermind of the crime they were now accomplices to.

In his *Sārārtha-darśinī*, Śrī Viśvanātha Cakravartī characterizes the initial volley between the *kumārīs* and Kṛṣṇa, in which Kṛṣṇa denied any wrongdoing:

> Kṛṣṇa: O young girls of Vraja! Do you know who has hung these clothes on this *kadamba* tree? I was herding the cows from afar and I saw them and thought, "Today the *kadamba* tree is very colorful with flowers and fruit." To see this astonishing spectacle, I ran here and climbed this tree.
>
> *Kumārīs*: Those are our clothes.
>
> Kṛṣṇa: That cannot be. If they were yours, how did they end up in this tree?

16. *Bhakti-rasāmṛta-sindhu* 3.3.36–37.

Kumārīs: You have stolen them and put them there.

Kṛṣṇa: Are you blaming me? I am the son of King Nanda. Am I a thief? Perhaps you want to complain to Kaṁsa in Mathurā?

Kumārīs: Don't get angry. Just look closely at the clothing and see if they are women's or men's clothing.

Kṛṣṇa: According to my intelligence, because these are so colorful, they must be women's clothing. But so what? In this universe, you are not the only women. Are there no other women?

Kumārīs: True, but who other than us comes to this isolated forest?

Kṛṣṇa: O girls who like to wander in lonely places, are you the only women that wander in lonely places and play secretly?

Kumārīs: O fool, we did not come here to play. We came to worship the goddess, the very deity of this *kadamba* tree.

Kṛṣṇa: Are you the only young women worshipping the goddess? Are there no others?

Kumārīs: There are no others.

Kṛṣṇa: O foolish ones, every night the *deva* women come on celestial vehicles and perform worship of the goddess here.

Kumārīs: Even if they did perform worship here, why would they leave their clothing here and go away?

Kṛṣṇa: O young girls, you do not know anything. Tonight they will come again and perform worship. After bathing, they will don these clothes. That is why they set them aside here.

Kumārīs: You do not know the truth. Today we will perform worship. The deity of the forest has placed those clothes high up in the tree for us to wear after bathing.

Kṛṣṇa: If these clothes are really yours, then come here if you like and claim your own clothes. Take them after paying me one small fee each to satisfy me after you have insulted me. You must come each individually, not all at once or two or three together, because out of greed for the cloth, one woman will take more than one cloth.

Kumārīs: We cannot go.

Kṛṣṇa (laughing): O girls! Because of your intense austerities, you have become weak and cannot come here.

Kumārīs: No, we do not trust your cheating words.

Kṛṣṇa: I am speaking the truth to you. I am not joking. I have never told any lies. From birth till now, I have not had any occasion to lie. What is the proof? These young boys are the witnesses. They are reliable as witnesses because they naturally report whatever they see.

By claiming to be truthful (*satyam*), Kṛṣṇa implied that he was actually vowing to the *kumārīs* (*satyam*) to reciprocate in kind with the vows they had made. Thus the *gāndharva* marriage began in earnest, as Kṛṣṇa inserted his friends into the wedding in progress as witnesses—his "best men."

Kumārīs: From far off, please throw the clothes to us in the water, or have the young boys bring them here.

Kṛṣṇa: How am I to know whose clothing is whose? Furthermore, I am very religious, and as such I don't touch others' things even with my fingernail. You must each come here and claim your own clothes. I do not take, give, or even touch others' things. That is my rule.

At this point the *kumārīs* began to internally acknowledge that a *gāndharva* marriage was in fact in progress and thus their desire was being fulfilled. Still, they hesitated.

Kumārīs: Because you are so impudent, you may disgrace us as we come out of the water. In fear of this and being respectable women, we will not go near you.

Kṛṣṇa: Let one of the young girls among you come forward. If I do not disgrace her, then others can come one by one.

And thus they came out of the water, but they came together. Within the water, their faces, which were all that Kṛṣṇa could see, appeared more beautiful than lotuses, which do not grow in the *hemanta* season. But as they emerged from the river, he saw their heads and their long dark hair, with which they covered their breasts, their hands covering the lower part of their beautiful bodies—embodiments they were of the highest *prema*. Then Kṛṣṇa told them to fold their hands in prayer above their heads to overcome what he described as their offense to the river for bathing naked. With the younger girls in front, the older girls shouted to Kṛṣṇa's friends,

"What was that?" as if they had heard something in the bushes. Thus, the boys momentarily turned their attention elsewhere as the girls folded their hands in prayer above their heads. When Kṛṣṇa saw the *kumārīs* naked, their *gāndharva* marriage with him was confirmed. And Kṛṣṇa explained as much, promising to consummate their union in the coming months. *Gopāla-campū* cites Kṛṣṇa thus:

> Mutual acceptance between bride and groom is what the *gāndharva* marriage consists of. And this mutual acceptance is the highest *dharma*, manifesting naturally as it does between lovers. Having attained the fruit of your *vrata* by this *gāndharva* rite, please return to Vraja. Soon, on a forthcoming night, we will meet again.[17]

Thus, Hari stole the *kumārīs*' hearts and their clothes but returned only their clothes, keeping their hearts for himself. He married them on the last day of Mārgaśīrṣa and thus it became his favorite month.[18] However, for various reasons, the reunion that Kṛṣṇa promised would soon arrive, at which time the marriage would be consummated, did not manifest until the autumn moon of the following year. Meanwhile, *Gopāla-campū* relates the following episode that occurred prior to that autumn evening.

Throughout the remainder of *hemanta* and through the entire winter—*śiśira*—Kṛṣṇa did not meet again with the *gopīs*. Despite the playful *gāndharva* rite, Kṛṣṇa was despondent because Rādhā's hand had been promised in marriage to another, owing to circumstance beyond his and her control. Her plight was his plight, and thus he spent his nights playing his flute aimlessly into the early spring—*vasanta*.

Then, one spring day, a green parrot trained by Vṛndā spoke to Kṛṣṇa of Rādhā's condition, and shortly thereafter Vṛndā-devī brought him a note written by Rādhā with her fingernail on a budding June magnolia *campaka* flower, golden in color such that it resembled Rādhā's own complexion. This is what the message said:

> In Vṛndāvana, you are a dark *tamāla* tree and I am a golden *campaka* flower. Vṛndā-devī alone can arrange our meeting because left to ourselves we are in a state of suspended animation. No one else can do this.[19]

17. *Gopāla-campū* 1.21.85 (v39).
18. Sanātana Goswāmī explains that this is why Kṛṣṇa, in his *gītā-śikṣā*, identifies himself among months with Mārgaśīrṣa.
19. *Gopāla-campū* 1.21.108 (v55).

Hearing Rādhā's message, Kṛṣṇa was filled with new enthusiasm. Entering the forest on that full-moon night, he played his flute with the intention of attracting the *gopīs*' hearts, assuming that Rādhā would come along with them. And the *gopīs* came, all of them. They came alone, they came in groups of two and three, and they came from all over Vraja. However, Rādhā alone—attended by her *mañjarīs*—was not among them. Hearing his flute, Rādhā had fainted and remained comatose. Unaware of Rādhā's condition but at a loss without her despite the presence of all the other *gopīs*, Kṛṣṇa sent the other *gopīs* home, pacifying them to some extent with his words.

Meanwhile, Rādhā's condition continued on into the morning and thus was of great concern to both Vṛndā-devī and Paurṇamāsī. The elderly mystic had Rādhā's maidservants bring their dearmost to her thatched hut deep within the forest. Then she called for Madhumaṅgala and sent him to bring Kṛṣṇa to Rādhā's bedside.

Madhumaṅgala found his friend dismayed at his inability to attract Rādhā's attention the night before with his otherwise very effective musical talent. What kind of flautist was he if he could not attract Rādhā? Such was Kṛṣṇa's condition when his *brāhmaṇa* friend came to fetch him bearing ominous news that at the same time explained Kṛṣṇa's apparent failure. Hearing the name of Rādhā animated him. Hearing of her condition heartened, concerned, and all but suspended him. Collecting himself, he took the outstretched hand of Madhu and proceeded without delay to the thatched hut of Paurṇamāsī.

Upon his arrival, Paurṇamāsī explained the situation and reasoned that because Kṛṣṇa was the cause of Rādhā's condition, he must also be the cure. She gave him a place to sit and asked him plainly but sternly, smiling ever so slightly, "What should we do?"

Embarrassed, Kṛṣṇa replied, "Oh! What happened?" Paurṇamāsī informed him of Rādhā's comatose condition and suggested that by his touch alone could she be revived. However, to the ire of Madhumaṅgala, Kṛṣṇa merely replied, "Who, her?" Madhumaṅgala then spoke in riddles, his anger mixed with affection for his friend, while praising Rādhā's love for him: "If the cloud does not acknowledge the lightning that resides within it, that lightning will not fully manifest." Madhu's words pleased Paurṇamāsī, who glanced lovingly at his face. Clearly, he empathized with Rādhā's plight and expected Kṛṣṇa to acknowledge her condition to be a manifestation of her love for him, that it might flourish that much more. But Kṛṣṇa dismissed his words as prattle, causing Vṛndā-devī to take exception to Kṛṣṇa's apparent hard-heartedness. Thus she urged him to reach out and bless Rādhā with his lotus hand. After all, Rādhā had been unconscious for hours.

Ostensibly, Kṛṣṇa's apparent hard-heartedness arose from a concern for *dharma*. How could a *brahmacārī* such as himself touch a married woman? However, internally the stirring of *sāttvika-bhāvas* had begun, as Rādhā lay before him in an ecstatic swoon. Soon they would manifest all over his body. Softening, he asked that he be requested to act in some other way that would not bring him in conflict with *dharma*. Madhumaṅgala then took Kṛṣṇa's hand and pulled him close to Rādhā, asking Paurṇamāsī to step outside. He then stationed Vṛndā-devī between the two lovers and exited himself. Outside the cottage he stood motionless, while keeping the interior scene clearly in view. In his own mind, he took the role of an instructor, should further advice be required. In doing so, he actually followed Rādhā's own teaching inscribed on the flora she had sent to Kṛṣṇa earlier, in which she had underscored the role of the forest goddess—Vṛndā—in uniting the *campaka* flower with the *tamāla* tree.

Vṛndā then praised the beauty of Kṛṣṇa's face and told him to bring it before the mirror of Rādhā's face, with the expectation that by looking into her eyes he would see his own face from her perspective and understand the feelings she had for him and how she held him alone in her heart. But tears gushed from Kṛṣṇa's eyes, and his body hair stood on end. Trembling and with a choked voice, all he could say was, "Whaaaat should I do?" To which Vṛndā replied,

> O prince of Vraja! Rādhā has the highest *prema* for you. O Kṛṣṇa! Rādhā, the form of *rasa*, corresponds with the period of your youth. Intuiting your desire for union as well as your pain of separation, and accepting your pain as her own, she constantly gives up her own happiness. Knowing this, you play the flute for her.[20]

With Kṛṣṇa stunned and as such appearing to hesitate, Vṛndā grabbed his hand and placed it over Rādhā's heart. Then Rādhā's swoon broke. And the two, hand and heart together, gazed into the depth of each other's souls for an eternal moment. However, Kṛṣṇa quickly became embarrassed in the presence of Vṛndā, and covering his head he staggered out of the cottage into the open arms of Madhumaṅgala, who stabilized him and slowly, making light, brought a smile to his friend's face, readying him to reenter the circle of their friends.

20. *Gopāla-campū* 1.21.143–144.

Rādhā, who had awoken as if from a dream, was unsure what had actually taken place and what was imagined. Thus Vṛndā lovingly consoled her. Still recovering, Rādhā offered respects to Paurṇamāsī. Then she returned to the welcoming arms of her maidservants and friends. However, she kept her happiness within herself, not telling others all that had transpired. Śrī Jīva Goswāmī asks, "Which poet can even slightly describe the joyful condition of Rādhā and Kṛṣṇa when they met?" And if some *kavi* could, to describe it is one thing, but to empathetically experience it is another. *Praṇāma* to Vṛndā-devī. *Daṇḍavat praṇāma* to Madhumaṅgala.

16

Yajña-patnīs and Sakhya-viraha-bhāva

In the following year on a hot summer day just a month or two before his eighth birthday, Kṛṣṇa turned to his friends and began to glorify the trees of Vraja. The *Bhāgavata* begins this narration referring to Kṛṣṇa as Devakī-suta, the son of Devakī. In doing so, it indicates that on this day, Rāma, Kṛṣṇa, and their friends had wandered far from Vṛndāvana—*vṛndāvanād gato dūram*—and in fact were close to metropolitan Mathurā, where Kṛṣṇa's secondary mother, Devakī, resided. Indeed, as we shall see ahead, Kṛṣṇa did so for the hidden purpose of teaching the difference between egos arising out of caste and those derived from *bhakti*, reciprocating in love with the latter. He chose to teach this lesson through the *yajña-patnīs*, wives of ritualistic *brāhmaṇas*, whose husbands had lost sight of the true purpose of Vedic sacrifice. The wives were devotees of Kṛṣṇa who longed for his *darśana*, having heard about his charming nature, form, qualities, and *līlās* from Vraja garland makers and traders.

Appreciating the umbrella of shade the *aśoka* trees provided from the summer sun, Kṛṣṇa addressed his friends as follows:

> O Stokakṛṣṇa and Aṁśu, O Śrīdāmā, Subala, and Arjuna! O Viśāla, Vṛṣabha, Ojasvī, Devaprastha, and Varūthapa! Look at these most fortunate trees, who live their lives for the sake of others. Tolerating wind, rain, heat, and snow, they provide us cover.[1]

Here Kṛṣṇa mentions the ten boys that immediately surrounded him, protecting him from all directions—north, south, east, west, northwest,

1. *Śrīmad Bhāgavatam* 10.22.31–32.

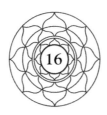

northeast, southwest, southeast, up, and down. Stokakṛṣṇa, Aṁśu, Śrīdāmā, and Subala were to the east, south, west, and north of Kṛṣṇa, respectively. Arjuna, Viśāla, Vṛṣabha, and Ojasvī were in the southeast, southwest, northwest, and northeast, respectively. Devaprastha protected Kṛṣṇa from above by holding a parasol over his head, and Varūthapa protected him from below by sweeping the path ahead of him. These protectors were a mix of *sakhās*, *priya-sakhās*, and *priya-narma-sakhās* chosen by Yaśodā on this particular day. And this entire *maṇḍala* of protection was further overseen and choreographed by Bhadrasena, a leading *priya-sakhā* who was also Balarāma's attendant. Glorifying the resident *aśoka* trees, Kṛṣṇa extended the circle of his humanlike friends/protectors to include these deeply rooted providers. *Śoka* means "sorrow," and thus these trees—*aśoka*—relieved the suffering and sorrow of others, as friends should do for one another. Although Kṛṣṇa asked Suvākya to say something in glorification of the trees, this *sakhā* deferred to Kṛṣṇa's own eloquence—clever and pleasing to the ear, sweet in its diction, composition, and tone—suggesting he accept that honor himself. Thus, Kṛṣṇa spoke in glorification of the trees, and all that he said about them applied equally to his friends:

> *Aho!* As is the case with *sādhus*, trees will never neglect those who are in need. Trees live for others, providing leaves, flowers, fruits, shade, bark, wood, and roots, as well as their scent, sap, ashes, pulp, and shoots. Their example should be followed: one's birth is successful if it ends in sacrifice for others—doing so with one's breath, wealth, thoughts, and words—*prāṇair arthair dhiyā vācā*.[2]

Here Kṛṣṇa glorifies trees in general for the purpose of distinguishing them from some humans, who despite thinking themselves superior are not, as evidenced by their self-centeredness. If even trees can be magnanimous, certainly humans can and should be. As we shall see ahead, such self-centered humans can also be wrapped in religious garb, and Kṛṣṇa thought of such persons as he glorified the trees. He also thought of the sacred trees of Vraja, said to be *kalpa-vṛkṣas* and *alaukika* in nature, about which there is considerable ancient and modern lore as to their generosity and supernatural nature. Thus Kṛṣṇa schooled his friends on different levels.

Then, as the boys moved on with sobering, magnanimous thoughts in mind, they passed through the forest and turned south toward the Yamunā to water their cows. They first let the cows drink, and only after the cows

2. *Śrīmad Bhāgavatam* 10.22.33–35.

were satisfied did the boys drink, that being the decorum of a cowherd. Just as a king's first priority must be the satisfaction of his constituents, the first priority of cowherds is their cows. After the cows drank, Kṛṣṇa and the boys cupped their hands and drank from the same river. They did not use cups, which was customary for others. Again, they used their hands since the custom of using cups did not apply to cowherds and would have distanced them somewhat from the cows they served. As far as possible, the cowherds should do as cows do.

The boys then leisurely herded their cows as the day passed. But when hunger struck them, it was late and they were far from Vṛndāvana. This was the unseen arrangement of Kṛṣṇa, who had a hidden purpose in mind that the boys were unaware of. Thus some boys nudged others to approach Rāma and Kṛṣṇa and mention their hunger, which they did with some embarrassment for apparently thinking only of themselves after Kṛṣṇa's lesson on selflessness. However, this too was Kṛṣṇa's arrangement. Actually, the boys thought that if they were hungry, Rāma and Kṛṣṇa must also be hungry. Such was their identification with the two brothers, revealing as it did the boys' actual motive for broaching the topic. As the boys approached the two brothers while engaging in Rāma-Kṛṣṇa *kīrtana*, their mood turned playful yet filled with theological insight.

> Rāma! Rāma! Your arms are so long and strong. O Kṛṣṇa, who worsts the wicked, we suffer from hunger—the greatest enemy of all. Please appease our appetite. Show us your favor.[3]

The boys first called out to Rāma because when he is respected, Kṛṣṇa is pleased. Thus, they followed the proper etiquette. Repeatedly chanting his name, they underscored their hunger. Although they referred to his prowess—his mighty arms—they also implied that his name indicates that he lives only for the pleasure of Kṛṣṇa, and being Kṛṣṇa's friends, he should please them as well. And they chanted Kṛṣṇa's name, stressing his prowess but also implying that because his name means the "highest bliss," he should make them blissful and alleviate their hunger—the greatest enemy of all. In this *līlā*, the *Bhāgavata* informs us through the *gopas* that Rāma *nāma* has the power to end world hunger.

Charmed by his friends' appeal, Kṛṣṇa began to reveal his hidden purpose in wandering so far from Vṛndāvana on this particular day. Thus, he told his friends to approach the nearby Vedic *brāhmaṇas* engaged in ritual and ask

3. *Śrīmad Bhāgavatam* 10.23.1.

them for food on behalf of Rāma and himself. Referring to them as desirous of material acquisition—*svarga-kāmyayā*—he indicated the *brāhmaṇas*' selfishness, ignorance, and lack of insight into the purpose of the Vedas.

Kṛṣṇa told his friends to ask for rice on behalf of himself and Rāma and thus to chant their names while begging. But he also suggested that they invoke the name Saṅkarṣaṇa first, an epithet for his older brother that speaks of his power and divinity. Rāma, he reasoned, is also more clearly from a *kṣatriya* lineage, and thus persons absorbed in caste consciousness at the cost of essential spirituality might pay more attention to a request on his behalf.

Thus, the boys followed Kṛṣṇa's instructions. They approached prayerfully with folded palms and bowed humbly before the *brāhmaṇas*. However, the brilliance of the boys' forms and spotless character far outshone those before whom they bowed, as the holy names of Rāma and Kṛṣṇa danced on their tongues and *sāttvika-bhāvas* decorated their limbs. They had all intention of bowing to the *brāhmaṇas*, but ultimately they had no choice but to fall before them in the ecstasy of their *nāma-kīrtana* and the humility that accompanies it.

Although Kṛṣṇa had told them to mention that they had come on behalf of Balarāma and to thus mention his name first, out of their special affection for Kṛṣṇa they spontaneously mentioned his name first. Intending to invoke Rāma *nāma* first, they thought of him, and his love for Kṛṣṇa came to mind, and thus Kṛṣṇa *nāma* issued forth from their mouths instead. In essence they nonetheless followed Kṛṣṇa's instruction by explaining that they had come on the order of Balarāma. But the *brāhmaṇas*, a virtual mountain of pride, could not recognize the volcano of *sakhya-prema* before them with its lava capable of turning them and their ritualistic perspective into rubble. Thus, they showed the beautiful boys no respect and in fact ignored them altogether.

These boys were all simple at heart and straightforward. They were also humble, but they were not fools. Thus, while at first they considered that they may have been at fault for the *brāhmaṇas*' lack of response to their request on behalf of Rāma and Kṛṣṇa, they quickly understood the minds of the priests and spoke further in words layered with lessons the *brāhmaṇas* would have done well to heed, words prefaced by a blessing—*bhadraṁ vo*—that marked the beginning of the *brāhmaṇas*' deliverance.

> Rāma and Acyuta, tending their cows, are hungry now. They want cooked rice from you. Among those who know *dharma*'s essence,

surely you are all the best. Thus, if you have faith in these two, please give them the rice they request.[4]

Rāma and Acyuta are described as being hungry because of the labor of herding cows. Furthermore, *go-sevā* never ends. Thus they were too busy to come themselves and ask for rice. In this way, the cowherds explained the reason for the brothers' request.

Here the cowherds refer to Kṛṣṇa by his epithet Acyuta, "infallible." This is the status of his *gotra*, his lineage—Acyuta-gotra. Unlike in *varṇāśrama-dharma* of the *karma-mārga*, governed by *rajas*, in which gains are lost in due course, in *nirguṇa prema-dharma* there is never any loss. Effort spent in *bhakti* results in an irrevocable gain.

Furthermore, Gauḍīya Vaiṣṇavas often identify themselves as members of the Acyuta-gotra in reply to those asking about their family lineage or caste. Having taken exclusive shelter of Kṛṣṇa, as a result of their Vaiṣṇava birth through *mantra-dīkṣā* they are no longer bound by birth or caste considerations. Those who are actually *dharma-vittamāḥ*—who know the essence of *dharma*—understand this and the place of *bhakti* in relation to *varṇāśrama-dharma*. Thus, it was with a trace of sarcasm that the cowherds referred to the *brāhmaṇas* as "the best among those who know *dharma*."

What they actually said was that those who have exclusive faith in Kṛṣṇa have fully understood *dharma*, as explained in the *Gītā*—*sarva-dharmān parityajya mām ekaṁ śaraṇaṁ vraja*.[5] In this concluding *Gītā* verse, Kṛṣṇa says that those who surrender to him alone—*śaraṇāgatas*—transcend *varṇāśrama-dharma*. *Śaraṇāgati* is the outward expression of *śraddhā*, or divine faith, which constitutes *adhikāra* for treading the *bhakti-mārga*. Unfortunately, the *yajñic brāhmaṇas* had no such *śraddhā*.

Then again, *prema-bhakti* is difficult to understand. Thus the *brāhmaṇas* thought, among other things, "If Kṛṣṇa *is* God, how can he be hungry?" In this way, they rationalized their refusal to even acknowledge the presence of the boys or their request and demonstrated their lack of acquaintance with the essence of *dharma*: it is measured by the extent to which Hari is pleased, *saṁsiddhir hari-toṣaṇam*.[6] They had not looked into the heart of an

4. *Śrīmad Bhāgavatam* 10.23.7. The blessing referenced above is found in 10.23.6. Here the idea is that, intuiting the *brāhmaṇas*' lack of respect for Rāma and Kṛṣṇa, the *gopas* compassionately said more or less, "May God have mercy on you." As a result of this blessing and through further association with the *brāhmaṇas*' wives, in due course he did.

5. *Bhagavad-gītā* 18.66.

6. *Śrīmad Bhāgavatam* 1.2.13.

actual *mahājana—dharmasya tattvaṁ nihitaṁ guhāyāṁ mahājano yena gataḥ sa panthāḥ*[7]—nor could they recognize the pure hearts that these *sakhās* wore on their sleeves.

Within the tenth canto *līlā* narrative of the *Bhāgavata*, the chapter under discussion begins to address the difference between *varṇāśrama-dharma* and *prema-dharma* for the first time, although it has been philosophically addressed throughout the book. This important difference is introduced in this chapter as a prelude to the treatment it receives in the following Govardhana *līlā* and the five chapters that follow it chronologically—*rāsa-pañcādhyāya*.[8] In these five chapters, this point is driven home in no uncertain terms, as the Vraja *gopīs* radically forgo *varṇāśrama* law to elope in love with Kṛṣṇa.

Where there is law, there is no love, and where there is love, there is no law. However, those who love also respect the law as much as it applies to those requiring its rule. They follow the law to set an example for such persons; that is, they follow the moral law as much as it does not conflict with love of God. They know the rules well enough to know when to break them and thus better than those who know them but do not know that rules are made to be broken.

In this chapter, Kṛṣṇa's friends set out on his order, amid *kīrtana* of his holy name, to beg food from Vedic *brāhmaṇas* engaged in a particular type of sacrifice. Although they were transcendental to the rules governing Vedic ritual, they demonstrated that they were inherently familiar with such rules; they knew it was not prohibited to accept food from this particular type of sacrifice at the time they asked—unlike the *brāhmaṇas*, who implicitly refused their request. The *gopas* also knew the Vedic injunction *annasya kṣuditaṁ pātram*, "Anyone who is hungry is a fit candidate for receiving food in charity," whereas the priests had lost the plot. Thus, as *ananya-bhaktas*, the *gopas*, not the *brāhmaṇas*, were actually *dharma-vittamāḥ* (knowers of *dharma*).

While *dharma* begets virtuousness, *ananya-bhakti* accomplishes that and much more. Thus, we find *varṇāśrama-dharma* represented within the *līlā* as well, even as its limitations are made clear. *Brāhmaṇas* are to be

7. *Mahābhārata*, *Vana-parva* 313.117.

8. The actual chronology of the *prakaṭa-līlās* is explained by Jīva Goswāmī in *Gopāla-campū*. Therein we find that Kṛṣṇa steals the *kumārīs*' clothes during the *hemanta* season of his seventh year after performing the Govardhana *līlā*. Then Kṛṣṇa blesses the *yajña-patnīs*, and this chapter is followed by the *rāsa-līlā*. However, in the *Bhāgavata* itself, which follows the order of Śukadeva's ecstasy, the Govardhana *līlā* occurs after Kṛṣṇa blesses the *yajña-patnīs*.

respected, as we find in the *līlā*, but the very prominent farcical *brāhmaṇa* of Vraja—Madhumaṅgala—also speaks loudly to the fact that caste consciousness and pride among *brāhmaṇas*, common in Kali *yuga*, is humorous at best in comparison to Kṛṣṇa consciousness. In this *līlā*, we find the *dharmic brāhmaṇas* proud of their pennies and as such unable to recognize the wealth of *prema* before them.

Thus the boys returned to Kṛṣṇa empty-handed. They approached Kṛṣṇa first, for fear that Balarāma would be enraged at the *brāhmaṇas'* disrespect for his younger brother's request and also because it was Kṛṣṇa who had sent them. However, when Kṛṣṇa heard their report, he simply laughed and suggested they approach the *brāhmaṇas'* wives. By laughing, Kṛṣṇa taught that when devotees beg on his behalf they may encounter opposition but they should not be discouraged, for the loss lies only with those who do not give. Why be angry with those who are the losers? Still, Rāma's potential anger derived not from self-pride but from love of Kṛṣṇa because in his mind Kṛṣṇa was offended, his request having been ignored. Sanātana Goswāmī comments that Kṛṣṇa also taught his friends that in this world, women tend be more inclined to love God than men.

Over and above everything else that Kṛṣṇa taught by orchestrating this entire *līlā* was the glory of the love that the *brāhmaṇas'* wives had for him. This was the driving force behind all that had transpired. Occurrences such as the *sakhās'* wandering a great distance from Vṛndāvana, the glorification of the trees that turned out to be more virtuous than the *brāhmaṇas*, the boys' hunger and consequent begging, and the *brāhmaṇas'* ritual and refusal to honor Kṛṣṇa's request were all ultimately orchestrated for the purpose of showcasing and reciprocating with the *yajña-patnīs'* love.

As mentioned earlier, these *brāhmaṇīs* had heard about Kṛṣṇa from garland makers and traders and were struck with love for him. They spent their time primarily hearing and chanting about him, and their love for him had drawn him to them. Indeed, out of love for them Kṛṣṇa forgot to eat. God may not need to eat, as their husbands had concluded, but he lives on the love of his devotees. Feeding him is, then, one of the ways by which they naturally show their love for him. If you love someone, you feed them—to love is to serve. And at this point, the *brāhmaṇīs'* love in separation warranted the reciprocation of initial union. Thus, Kṛṣṇa felt confident to instruct his friends to inform them that he and Saṅkarṣaṇa were nearby.

Kṛṣṇa did not tell the boys to inform the ladies that he and Rāma were hungry, because he felt that this would cause them some distress. He also knew that just hearing his name and seeing his friends would make the hearts of the *brāhmaṇīs* leap. Unlike their husbands, they would not ignore the boys. And seeing the boys—their dress, their gestures, the way they carried themselves in fraternal love for Kṛṣṇa—would serve as an *uddīpana-vibhāva* for the *brāhmaṇīs'* own budding *mādhurya-bhāva* for Kṛṣṇa. However, Kṛṣṇa described something about the measure of the *brāhmaṇīs'* love for him—their austerities in service to him, their detachment from their non-devotee families, their preoccupation with hearing and chanting about him—which astounded the boys and made them eager to meet the *yajña-patnīs*. Thus, the cowherds fell over one another in their effort to meet such like-minded devotees, despite the difference in their *bhāva* for Kṛṣṇa—*sakhya* and *mādhurya*, respectively.

The *brāhmaṇīs'* hearts had already melted from hearing about Kṛṣṇa and from the faint sounds of his distant flute's melodious *rāgas* inviting them to love him. And now they saw his friends standing before them:

> The boys' flutes were tucked in their attractive belts, their herding sticks were in hand, their endearing dress and uncommon decorations were drawn from the forest, they were painted with red oxide from Mount Govardhana, their broad foreheads adorned with *kastūrī tilaka*. They placed fragrant flowers over their ears, they were garlanded with wreaths of jasmine buds, they had their hair tied in topknots and pinned with peacock feathers, and they were chanting Rāma Kṛṣṇa, Kṛṣṇa Rāma . . .

The ladies' love for Hari ascended on high. In their *sādhaka-dehas* as Mathurā *brāhmaṇīs*, they experienced the Vraja *siddha-dehas* of Kṛṣṇa's *sakhās*. Seeing the boys, who reminded them of the cowherd they had seen in their meditation and heard about from the simple-hearted lady merchants of Vraja, the *yajña-patnīs* fainted. Shocked and now nervous, the boys tried to revive them, all the while chanting in *nāma-kīrtana*. But all the ladies heard was "Rāma" and "Kṛṣṇa," which caused them to gain and lose consciousness repeatedly. However, when they eventually stabilized, they spontaneously desired to serve these boys and assumed they were hungry. Although Kṛṣṇa did not directly instruct the boys to speak of his hunger to the *yajña-patnīs*, the *brāhmaṇīs* intuited that the young boys, so far from home and herding for hours, must be hungry, and the *gopas* said as much. Thus, they gathered all the food prepared for their husbands' sacrifice. And bearing it in vessels upon their heads, tears falling from their eyes, they followed Kṛṣṇa's friends to the *aśoka* grove where he awaited them in anticipation. Upon arrival, their *śoka*—misery—arising from love in separation was mitigated. Praise to Mādhava, his *brāhmaṇīs*, and his *mitraṁ sanātanam*.

There, along the banks of the Yamunā in a grove of *aśoka* trees, the object of their meditation appeared before them. At last, they saw with their eyes the object of their love for the first time.

> His *śyāma*-colored body was wrapped in a golden garment reminiscent of dawn's early light, which dissipated the dark night of the *brāhmaṇīs'* separation. His form radiated a romantic effulgence that captured the *yajña-patnīs* within its embrace and aroused their amorous sentiments. He was dressed like an artiste from a drama set to music. Shoots of different-colored fresh grass and flower buds adorned his body, and it appeared as if the goddesses of all flowering plants surrounded him and were further beautified by him. Natural mineral dyes were painted in different patterns on his limbs and face. He was garlanded with forest flowers from head to toe. And his hair, tied in a topknot, was pinned with the plume of a peacock. He rested his left hand affectionately on the shoulder of Subala-sakhā, and in his right hand he playfully twirled a fragrant lotus flower, indicating that his heart was spinning in response to the *bhakti* of the *brāhmaṇīs*. Smiling broadly, his face was framed with locks of curling jet-black hair dancing playfully on his cheeks, contrasting with white water lilies placed over his ears.[9]

As they approached, the burden of the vessels they bore on their heads weighed heavily on Kṛṣṇa's heart, and thus he welcomed them and invited them to sit with him. In the course of their discussion, Kṛṣṇa instructed them to return home, assuring them that their husbands would now be favorable to their spiritual pursuit. At first, the *brāhmaṇīs* resisted and suggested they would be prepared to live in the forest—homeless—to have his

9. *Śrīmad Bhāgavatam* 10.23.22. This is one of three *Bhāgavata* verses thought to most perfectly describe Śrī Kṛṣṇa. The other two are 10.21.5 and 10.14.1. Some argue from the *mādhurya-rasa* perspective that they are perfect (10.14.1), more perfect (10.23.22), and most perfect (10.21.5), the latter having been spoken by the Vraja *gopīs*. However, 10.14.1 is spoken in Brahmā's budding *sakhya-rasa*, and the other two both depict Kṛṣṇa along with his *sakhās*, in whose presence he shines that much brighter. And 10.23.22 depicts him with his left arm very affectionately draped over the shoulder of Subala-sakhā, arguably implying that he longs to embrace the *brāhmaṇīs*, while also overtly expressing his deep fraternal love for his friends. Thus some may rank 10.23.22 as the most perfect and underscore the presence of *sakhya-rasa* in all three.

company, but Kṛṣṇa explained the nature of his Vraja *līlā*, instructing them that through further meditation in separation they would attain their ideal in *siddha-dehas* as Vraja *gopīs*, not in their present *brāhmaṇī sādhaka-dehas*.

Here, for the sake of preserving the nature and the particular social structure of his humanlike *līlā*, Kṛṣṇa's *līlā-śakti* prevailed over both his and the *brāhmaṇīs*' desire—*satya-saṅkalpa*—to unite with one another then and there. If Kṛṣṇa were to elope with the *brāhmaṇīs* in this *līlā*, how would they fit into his love life with his *gopīs*? How could they live in the forest?

Thus, following his instruction driven by the wisdom of his *līlā-śakti* they returned home. And as Kṛṣṇa had promised, their husbands were now miraculously favorable to their wives' spiritual pursuit, having realized and repented for their mistake. Indeed, in a reversal of roles, the *brāhmaṇas* accepted their wives as their *gurus*, and imbibing their wives' mood as followers of the Vraja *gopīs*, they offered prayers like this to Kṛṣṇa's milkmaidens, following the example of their wives:

> The *gopīs*, who are the crest jewels among all the maidens of the world and have spent many lives engaged in *prema-dharma*, have learned well the art of amorous intrigues from the *guru* of their own adolescence. And it is Kṛṣṇa, to whom they have given the fruits of their learning, who in turn has given them a passing grade after a thorough examination. To them I offer myself.[10]

The *gopas* were mystified by all of this, but it was not their place or the right time to inquire further about the fortune of the *yajña-patnīs*. Indeed, it was well past time to eat. Thus, Kṛṣṇa sat all of his friends down and served each of them what turned out to be a meal well worth waiting for. He tasted the *yajña-patnīs*' offering as well, smiling approvingly to the delight of all of his friends. The meal included all four types of foods (that which is licked, chewed, drunk, and sucked) and all five tastes (salty, sweet, sour, bitter, and pungent). *Jalebīs* shaped like peacock feathers were the highlight of the meal. These in particular Madhumaṅgala never forgot, often reminding Kṛṣṇa of the delicacies with intense longing.[11]

In Madhumaṅgala's expert opinion, these saintly women cooked so nicely that if even one particle of the food fell on the ground and was thus covered with dust, it should be retrieved and consumed at all costs. He suggested

10. *Ujjvala-nīlamaṇi* 3.2. Viśvanātha Cakravartī attributes this prayer to "the women of Mathurā."

11. See *Lalita-mādhava* 9.38.

that these women be locked up in a forest cottage and engaged solely in cooking for Kṛṣṇa, Balarāma, and himself. Kṛṣṇa responded by calling him a glutton driven to the point of insanity at the cost of proper decorum. Laughing, the other boys suggested that Madhumaṅgala confine *himself* to a hut next to the *brāhmaṇīs* and worship them to satisfy his appetite. Then this farcical *brāhmaṇa* accused the others of gluttony, for after all it was they who had begged for food from the *yajña-patnīs*, and not a self-controlled *brāhmaṇa* such as himself, who was doing his friends a service by honoring the offering in their lowly midst.

Thus they carried on in their merrymaking and then rounded up their cows, as Kṛṣṇa chanted the names of the leaders of each of his 108 groups of cows on a *mālā* of 108 jewels. This jewel *mālā* represents the twenty-five subdivisions of the four basic colors of Nanda's cows—white, red, black, and yellow—that together make up one hundred groups of cows along with eight other groups, defined by characteristics other than their dominant colors: speckles, *tilaka*, other special markings, and variously-shaped heads, such as *mṛdaṅgas*, lions, and so on. With the cows readied and Kṛṣṇa's arm resting on Subala's shoulder, the cowherds joyfully headed homeward following his lead. However, when they arrived, they uncharacteristically kept the events of the day concerning the *yajña-patnīs* to themselves. Thus, what appeared to the village elders as a comparatively uneventful day for their sons was in fact extraordinary.

In this way, the summer passed. Under the following autumn harvest moon, Kṛṣṇa consummated his relationship with Rādhā and also with the *kumārīs*, as he had promised to do previously after stealing their clothes. This is described in the five chapters of the *Bhāgavata* centered exclusively on *mādhurya-rasa*—*rāsa-pañcādhyāya*. These five chapters of the *Bhāgavata* are the apex of its *līlā* narrative.

Following the *rāsa-līlā*, the *Bhāgavata* relates Rāma and Kṛṣṇa's celebration of Holī as well as Nanda and his constituents' visit to Ambikā. Kṛṣṇa's encounter with Kaṁsa's henchman Ariṣṭa follows, which, although not described in the *Bhāgavata* itself, led to the formation of the legendary Rādhā-kuṇḍa and Śyāma-kuṇḍa, which are so prominent in the Gauḍīya focus on Kṛṣṇa's midday *līlās*. Then Kṛṣṇa killed Keśī and Vyomāsura, after which Akrūra arrived in Vraja bearing Kaṁsa's invitation for Rāma and Kṛṣṇa to participate in a wrestling match in Mathurā.

Kṛṣṇa's departure for Mathurā was heartbreaking to the Vraja *gopīs*, young and old alike, none of whom could accompany him. He boarded

Akrūra's chariot along with Balarāma, and his closest friends followed. He was also chaperoned by his father, Nanda Bābā, riding separately with Kṛṣṇa's *sakhās* on a bullock cart.

Akrūra, though, raced ahead of Nanda and his friends and took an alternate route. However, Nanda and company arrived at the gate to the capital before Akrūra, where they waited in anticipation. They had departed later but arrived earlier, ahead of Akrūra's faster horse-driven chariot. Where were Rāma and Kṛṣṇa? This is an interesting theological question.

Akrūra had stopped at the famous Ananta Tīrtha along the Yamunā at midday and asked the brothers' permission to bathe and recite his *mantra*. Although he kept this to himself, he felt that he had offended the Vraja *vāsīs*, and the *gopīs* in particular, by taking Kṛṣṇa away from them. He hoped that he could purify himself and be relieved of any adverse reaction by bathing at a sacred *tīrtha*. Understanding his mind, the brothers obliged him.

However, after he had seated Rāma and Kṛṣṇa comfortably on his chariot, shading them from the midday sun, he bathed and recited his *mantra*, only to see Kṛṣṇa and Balarāma before him in the water as his *mantra* meditation broke! Bewildered, he returned to his chariot, where Rāma and Kṛṣṇa sat unmoved. Thus, he returned to the river, and there he saw the brothers manifest themselves as Ananta Śeṣa and Viṣṇu, respectively, blessing him with *darśana* of Vaikuṇṭha!

Thus it is here, at what later became known as Akrūra-ghāṭa, that *svayaṁ* Bhagavān and his Vraja *līlā vaibhava-prakāśa*—Balarāma—manifested themselves as Vāsudeva and Mūla-saṅkarṣaṇa, forms that correspond with the *prema* of their devotees of Mathurā. Where then did the original Rāma and Kṛṣṇa go? They remained in the hearts of their Vraja *līlā* devotees. However, as Vāsudeva and Saṅkarṣaṇa approached the gates of Mathurā, where Nanda and the *gopas* waited in anticipation, who did Nanda and the *gopas* see? Where were *their* Rāma and Kṛṣṇa? The answer to this theological question is that in Mathurā Nanda and the *gopas* alone saw Rāma and Kṛṣṇa, by the force of their *prema*, while the residents of Mathurā saw Vāsudeva and Saṅkarṣaṇa, just as Śrī Caitanya saw Jagannātha Swāmī holding a flute and sporting a peacock's plume as his crown while others saw him as majestic Jagadīśvara. Rāma and Kṛṣṇa's beauty lies in the eyes of their beholders!

In Mathurā, Kṛṣṇa and his friends explored the town prior to the wrestling match that Kṛṣṇa and Balarāma were invited to participate in,[12] much

12. *Śrīmad Bhāgavatam* 10.41.19, 10.41.24, 10.41.39. See also *Gopāla-campū* 2.4.9.

like they had previously explored the forest of Vraja day after eternal day, following Kṛṣṇa's lead. His *sakhās* witnessed Kṛṣṇa's dealing with King Kaṁsa's unsubmissive servant—the laundry man—and enjoyed the king's vestments along with Kṛṣṇa and Balarāma. They witnessed the devotion of the tailor/weaver and how Kṛṣṇa gave him a *gopa-svarūpa* corresponding with his meditation.[13] They also met the florist Sudāmā, who used to go to Vṛndāvana and collect flowers. There he sometimes saw Kṛṣṇa in his rustic dress and experienced fraternal feelings for Hari. Kṛṣṇa also bonded with this florist because he had the same name as his *priya-sakhā* comrade Sudāmā, brother of Rādhā's handmaiden Rūpa-mañjarī.[14] Thus, while in Mathurā, Kṛṣṇa sought this florist out, and in the company of his friends Kṛṣṇa blessed him with *sakhya-rasa.*

Kṛṣṇa's friends also tasted *hāsya-rasa* during his interaction with Kubjā, to whom he gave *mādhurya-rasa* while astonishing others with *adbhuta-rasa* as he stepped on her toes and, grasping her ears, pulled her up and straightened out her hunchback, showcasing her otherwise beautiful features to everyone. Was Kubjā actually an expansion of Satyabhāmā, whom the earth is an external manifestation of, Kubjā's hunchback representing the burden of the earth resulting from *adharma*, personified as Kaṁsa? As Kubjā offered the essence of the earth element in the form of the scented oils she had prepared to Kṛṣṇa rather than Kaṁsa and now stood erect, she appeared in her upright position with her natural beauty revealed to predict the outcome of Kṛṣṇa's visit to Mathurā—*dharma* would be reestablished and earth unburdened and beautified thereby. Notably, Kṛṣṇa's romantic feelings for the earth—Kubjā—date back to his Varāha *avatāra.*[15]

His friends then praised him as he broke the sacrificial bow but cautioned him with regard to the mad elephant Kuvalayāpīḍa, whom he nonetheless defeated. And they watched with confidence and delight as Rāma and Kṛṣṇa

13. *Gopāla-campū* 2.4.24. See also the commentaries on *Śrīmad Bhāgavatam* 10.41.42 of Jīva Goswāmī and Viśvanātha Cakravartī.

14. This account of Sudāmā's sister differs from that of *Rādhā-kṛṣṇa-gaṇoddeśa-dīpikā*. It is the opinion of *Preyo-bhakti-rasārṇava*. The difference is discussed further in chapter 5, note 32.

15. Aside from my comment concerning Varāha *avatāra*, Viśvanātha Cakravartī cites this perspective, attributing it to some unnamed commentators. Otherwise, Kubjā's *mādhurya-rasa* is considered to be *sādhāraṇī*, or ordinary, in that it involves a personal spiritual desire on her part to relish conjugal love with Kṛṣṇa rather than the desire for romantic union with him solely for his pleasure, as in the case of the *samartha-rati* of the Vraja *gopī nāyikās*. The two are similar in appearance while quite different in essence, although sometimes both are referred to as *sambhogecchā-mayī*—"filled with the desire for union."

defeated the wrestlers in the public arena and Kṛṣṇa then at last defeated King Kaṁsa in the climax of his heroism, which served as an overwhelming *uddīpana* for their fraternal love. While it was then time for Kṛṣṇa to return to Vṛndāvana, extenuating circumstances arose that prevented his immediate return. It is at this point that his *sakhās*' separation from him began, first with talk of mediating the separation of those steeped in parental and romantic love and then, in the context of doing so, while feeling the full face of separation themselves.

Kṛṣṇa's friends could be relied upon to console those steeped in parental and romantic love, for while parental and romantic love are characterized by longing and doubt, fraternal love is characterized by familiarity and confidence.[16] Kṛṣṇa's friends were convinced that he would return, and in private they talked about this among themselves. Thus they did not require consolation and were expected to console others. Indeed, consoling his friends would have the opposite effect of creating doubt. As we shall see ahead, in Kṛṣṇa's apparent absence from Vraja, at times he mystically appeared before his devotees as if a hallucination—*sphūrti*. During such mystical appearances, Kṛṣṇa's friends and his cows think that Kṛṣṇa is fully present, being unable to distinguish between his personal presence and his *sphūrti*. However, those whose love in separation is characterized by longing and doubt—those in *vātsalya* and *mādhurya*—cannot even trust that Kṛṣṇa's direct presence is something they can count on, what to speak of trusting in a mystical vision of him.[17] Thus in Mathurā Kṛṣṇa turns to his friends and their own impending separation with the expectation that they can assist him in consoling his parents and lovers.

> Although not pleased with Kṛṣṇa's logic for remaining in Mathurā for an extended period, Nanda Bābā nonetheless knew that it was well reasoned and with concern for the well-being of everyone in Vṛndāvana in mind. After all, Kṛṣṇa had just rid the earth of the evil and very powerful King Kaṁsa, and those seeking revenge could wreak havoc in Vṛndāvana should he immediately return there. Thus, Nanda Bābā could understand that it would be safer for Kṛṣṇa to stay in Mathurā, where he could surely defeat such persons and protect the village from any collateral damage. Nonetheless,

16. To console the Vraja *vāsīs* in other *rasas*, Kṛṣṇa notably sends his best friend, Balarāma, and also Uddhava, whose *dāsya-bhāva* is bundled with *sakhya*, which thus affords him *praṇaya*.

17. See Jīva Goswāmī's commentary on *Śrīmad Bhāgavatam* 10.46.6.

all Nanda could do and say in response was beat his forehead and tearfully blurt out, "Your mother will be opposed. How will I make her understand?"

Kṛṣṇa told his father that he would write to her himself. Sitting down, he wrote her a letter on the spot and gave it to his dear friend Śrīdāmā to deliver. Śrīdāmā, his voice choked up, then read the letter aloud, in which Kṛṣṇa explained that he was still present in Vṛndāvana and that Yaśodā's experience of him in dreams was actual. Indeed, he said that he was eating her cooking daily. And to convince her, he related the preparations she had been making, although with no appetite to eat them herself. He told her to eat or he himself would fast.

This in turn caused Nanda to ask about Kṛṣṇa's friends: "But how will your friends, who also depend on your love, maintain *their* lives?"

Kṛṣṇa replied, "Like my mother, all my dear friends can also experience my presence through *sphūrtis* of me. But unlike my mother, who will see me only in dreams, my *sakhās*, because of their *praṇaya*, will experience me while they are awake."

"What about your cows?" Nanda continued. "Like your friends, will the cows be able to directly experience you?"

Kṛṣṇa replied, "I will use another method to give them the experience of my ongoing presence. Cows operate more by smell and sound than they do sight, although they also discern by form. Stokakṛṣṇa should wrap himself in my cloth laden with my fragrance and play the flute. Subala should dress in Balarāma's blue cloth and take his horn. Then they should sit among the cows."

With a display of affection, he gave Stokakṛṣṇa and Subala, who were endowed with his own qualities, his clothing filled with the scent of his limbs and decorated them properly with his own ornaments.

Then, pulling Subala aside, he also gave him a message to deliver to the *gopīs*. He told them that only a shadowlike form of himself plays in Mathurā, while his actual form plays in Vraja. A person is present in that place in which he is mentally absorbed, while that person's physical presence is but a shadow of himself appearing elsewhere. In his private message to the young Vraja *gopīs*, he also reassured

> them of this truth by revealing that he was aware in detail of what took place when they each individually experienced *sphūrtis* of him in his apparent absence since coming to Mathurā.
>
> Kṛṣṇa then turned to Madhumaṅgala with affection and said, "Oh! You also go as my representative. Since I have unexpectedly left, serve Paurṇamāsī to ensure auspiciousness for me and make everyone happy as before."
>
> Then, looking at the servants and the young boys lacking discriminating power, all of whom stood in silence with lowered heads alongside Nanda, Kṛṣṇa tearfully said, "Since they are all affectionate like my friends and my father, these servants and young boys should follow Nanda and my *sakhās*."
>
> Then Nanda departed as Kṛṣṇa, overwhelmed by feelings of impending separation, turned toward the city, while Balarāma followed Nanda and the others as far as he could, bidding farewell before returning to the capital with the sagacious encouragement of Nanda Bābā to follow and care for his younger brother. Fearing that his separation from Kṛṣṇa would be a cause of further suffering, Balarāma took leave of everyone with determination and on meeting his brother sought out a solitary spot. There they embraced each other and wept together. What more can be described?

Śrī Jīva Goswāmī writes, "Remembering Kṛṣṇa, Balarāma, Nanda, the cowherds, Śrīdāmā, and his friends, . . . my mind now gives up everything because of the pain, fearing further separation."[18] As Shelley says, sweetest tales tell of saddest times.[19] Read and weep. O Gopa-vṛnda-pāla! O beloved *sakhās*! Your story of mutual love in both union and separation burns a deep impression on my heart and thus assures me I will one day attain the *sakhya-prema* you share.

18. This *līlā* narrative has been adapted from *Gopāla-campū* 2.4.

19. Shelley's actual stanza from "To a Skylark" is as follows: "We look before and after, / And pine for what is not: / Our sincerest laughter / With some pain is fraught; / Our sweetest songs are those that tell of saddest thought." Here he refers to the inherent dichotomy of life: to know joy, we need to know pain. And in Gauḍīya terminology, union is enhanced by separation.

PART 3

Center

Aprakaṭa-Līlā

17

The Aprakaṭa-līlā

Our focus within the radius of this circle of friends has been the *prakaṭa-līlā* and its progression from Rāma and Kṛṣṇa's *śeṣa-kumāra* to their *kiśora-līlā*. We ended our description of the *prakaṭa-līlā* with Kṛṣṇa attempting to mitigate the separation of his devotees whom he leaves behind as his princely *līlā* of Mathurā commences. Here in the center of our circle, we will focus on the *aprakaṭa-līlā*. The section or *prakāśa* of Kṛṣṇa's *aprakaṭa-līlā* that our Gauḍīya *ācāryas* have brought to our attention is Kṛṣṇa's adolescent pastoral *līlā*.

If we were to take Kṛṣṇa's adolescent pastoral *līlā* and stop it from proceeding to Mathurā and then focus our attention on his typical teenage day in Vṛndāvana, we would find ourselves in a *prakāśa* that is fully developed into the ideal setting for *sakhya-* and *mādhurya-rasas*. In this setting, Kaṁsa's supply of assassins has been exhausted, and he himself remains as a distant background feature. All of the principal *līlā-sthalīs* have been established and now serve as favorite haunts to revisit and endearing memories for the *gopas* and *gopīs* to recall. And above all, Rāma-Kṛṣṇa and their friends have attained the ideal age of adolescence. Kṛṣṇa at eleven and a half behaves like he is sweet sixteen.

Thus, from the life of Kṛṣṇa depicted in the *Bhāgavata*'s *prakaṭa-līlā*, we turn to an eternal day in the life of *kiśora* Kṛṣṇa's *aprakaṭa-līlā*. We also turn from the more general *līlā-smaraṇam* consisting of reciting and listening to the *sakhya-rasa-līlās* of the *Bhāgavata* to the prospect of deeper *līlā-smaraṇam* in the form of *mānasī-sevā*, or mentally serving Kṛṣṇa-Balarāma and Rādhā-Kṛṣṇa throughout the twenty-four hours of the day in one's internal *siddha-deha*.

In such *mānasī-sevā* of *narma-sakhā-bhāva*, the spiritually advanced *sādhaka* follows the *bhāva* of a *narma-sakhā* such as Subala. Under his direction and that of the *sādhaka*'s *guru* also serving in *sakhya-rasa*, he or she serves Kṛṣṇa-Balarāma. Throughout his description of the daily *aprakaṭa-līlā* of Kṛṣṇa and Balarāma, Nayanānanda Ṭhākura explains that the *sādhaka*'s internal *līlā-sevā* follows the lead of one of Kṛṣṇa's *rāgātmika-sakhās* and the lead of one's *guru* in the form of a *sakhā* (*guru-rūpa-sakhā*). Similarly, in *Jaiva Dharma*, Ṭhākura Bhaktivinoda gives the following example of Vrajanātha, having been asked by his *guru* about his budding *ruci*, expressing his desire to serve under the direction of Subala:

> Vrajanātha: Prabhu, whenever I meditate on Śrī Kṛṣṇa's pastimes, a desire to serve him by following in the footsteps of Subala arises in my heart.
>
> Bābājī: Which service do you like?
>
> Vrajanātha: When the cows wander far off to graze and Kṛṣṇa sits somewhere to play his flute, with Subala's permission I would very much like to water the cows and bring them back to Kṛṣṇa-bhāi. This is my heart's desire.
>
> Bābājī: I bless you that you will attain Kṛṣṇa's service as a follower of Subala. You are eligible to cultivate *sakhya-rasa*.[1]

Readers will recall from chapter 5 of this text that *narma-sakhās* have both a *sakhya-rasa yūtheśvara* such as Subala and, in the realm of *mādhurya-rasa*, a *yūtheśvarī* such as Viśākhā. *Sādhana-siddhas* serve under the direction of such group leaders and their *guru* in his *sakhya-rasa-svarūpa*. They serve Kṛṣṇa-Balarāma and Rādhā-Kṛṣṇa relative to the unfolding of the daily *līlā*, and they also serve their group leaders and their *guru*, often rendering personal service at appropriate times of the day.

Broadly speaking, we see this example in the *mānasī-sevā* of Kṛṣṇadāsa Kavirāja Goswāmī, out of which *Govinda-līlāmṛta* arises. For example, in his *Caitanya-caritāmṛta*, Kṛṣṇadāsa Kavirāja identifies his *guru* as Raghunātha dāsa Goswāmī,[2] who in his Kṛṣṇa *līlā-svarūpa* is Tulasī-mañjarī. Then in his *Govinda-līlāmṛta*, Śrī Kṛṣṇadāsa projects himself into his own *aprakaṭa-līlā*

1. *Jaiva Dharma*, chapter 21.
2. *Caitanya-caritāmṛta* 3.20.145.

narrative, referring to himself therein as Kastūrī-mañjarī, who is often found following along with Tulasī-mañjarī, assisting her in her *sevā*.[3]

Caitanya Mahāprabhu also instructed Raghunātha dāsa Goswāmī to engage himself in this *mānasī-sevā*:

> Do not listen to or speak gossip. Do not eat tasty food or be fashion conscious. Do not expect honor, yet honor others. Constantly chant Kṛṣṇa *nāma*, and mentally serve Rādhā-Kṛṣṇa in Vraja (*mānasī-sevā*). These, in brief, are my instructions; from Svarūpa you will get specifics.[4]

Thus, it should be clear that *mānasī-sevā*, or mentally serving Rādhā and Kṛṣṇa throughout the twenty-four hours of the day, is a form of *smaraṇam* suitable for contemplatives who have renounced the world. The descriptions of Kṛṣṇa's *aprakaṭa-līlā* differ from the *Bhāgavata*'s broader *prakaṭa-līlā* narrative in that they are primarily intended to be meditative tools suitable for fostering complete absorption in the *līlā*, in which the spiritually advanced *sādhaka* ultimately finds himself or herself a participant in a meditative *gopa* or *gopī* identity that has been developing over the course of the *sādhaka*'s entire practicing life.[5] This development typically turns from one that the *sādhaka* is relatively unaware of to a focused pursuit in its maturity. This ripened fruit, of course, grows from the seed of *śraddhā*, the *bhakti-saṁskāras* one has received, and the subsequent *sādhana* that the *sādhaka* participates in. Thus, descriptions of the divisions of Kṛṣṇa's *aprakaṭa-līlā* day are a meditative tool that best serves spiritually advanced *sādhakas*. However, this does not mean that those lacking such qualification cannot acquaint themselves with the Gauḍīya descriptions of Kṛṣṇa's typical day in his *aprakaṭa-līlā* setting. Such descriptions show the spiritually advanced *sādhaka* what *sevā* opportunities are available throughout the course of Kṛṣṇa's typical day. Books are written to be read, even while it

3. The Gauḍīya community has identified Kṛṣṇadāsa Kavirāja with Kastūrī-mañjarī. This understanding appears to have arisen in the hearts of *sādhakas* using his text as a tool to aid their own practice. He is not mentioned in *Gaura-gaṇoddeśa-dīpikā*, which predates both *Govinda-līlāmṛta* and *Caitanya-caritāmṛta*.

4. *Caitanya-caritāmṛta* 3.6.236–237.

5. Gauḍīya *ācāryas* differ in their descriptions of the *aprakaṭa-līlā*'s nature. Here I am taking the *aṣṭakāla-līlā-granthas* as descriptions of a particular window of the *aprakaṭa-līlā* drama into which Gauḍīya *sādhakas* desire to enter.

may require repeated readings and a highly qualified teacher to draw out the full measure of their implications.

Thus, we shall proceed at this point and freeze our *līlā* lens and focus on the abovementioned frame of the *līlā* alone. In doing so, we follow the lead of our Gauḍīya *pūrvācāryas* who have set in poetry their vision and experience of this particular section of the divine drama, describing a typical day in the life of Rādhā and Kṛṣṇa's *kiśora-līlā*, its twenty-four hours divided into eight sections. Here, again, the vision is one that turns from the *prakaṭa-līlā* on earth to the *aprakaṭa-līlā* of Goloka.

The scriptural seed for this setting is found in the *Sanat-kumāra Saṁhitā*,[6] a subsection of the *Śiva Purāṇa*, and it is significant that Sanātana Goswāmī is identified in part with Sanat-kumāra.[7] Śrī Sanātana is of course the elder brother and *śikṣā-guru* of Rūpa Goswāmī, who penned eleven verses—*Śrī Śrī Rādhā-kṛṣṇayor-aṣṭakālīya-līlā-smaraṇa-maṅgala-stotram*—following the lead of the *Saṁhitā* that Kṛṣṇadāsa Kavirāja in turn rendered into longhand in the form of his tome *Govinda-līlāmṛta*. Viśvanātha Cakravartī later did the same, authoring *Kṛṣṇa-bhāvanāmṛta*, and other Gauḍīya saints have also contributed texts of their own, most notably Kavi-karṇapūra's *Kṛṣṇāhnika-kaumudī* and the later *Bhāvanāsāra-saṅgraha* of Siddha Kṛṣṇadāsa Tātapāda. Thus, this basic framework of a typical eightfold day in Kṛṣṇa's eternal adolescent life in Vraja serves as a wellspring from which unlimited streams of *līlās* flow in all directions.

The eight meditative divisions of Kṛṣṇa's day are as follows:

Niśānta (predawn): 3:36 a.m. to 6:00 a.m.

Prātaḥ (morning): 6:00 a.m. to 8:24 a.m.

Pūrvāhna (forenoon): 8:24 a.m. to 10:48 a.m.

Madhyāhna (midday): 10:48 a.m. to 3:36 p.m.

Aparāhna (afternoon): 3:36 p.m. to 6:00 p.m.

Sāyāhna (dusk): 6:00 p.m. to 8:24 p.m.

Pradoṣa (evening): 8:24 p.m. to 10:48 p.m.

Niśa (night): 10:48 p.m. to 3:36 a.m.

6. *Sanat-kumāra Saṁhitā* 197–285.
7. *Gaura-gaṇoddeśa-dīpikā* 181.

Although Kṛṣṇadāsa Kavirāja's *Govinda-līlāmṛta* does showcase *sakhya-rasa* to some extent, previous *ācāryas* have mostly written about the eightfold daily *līlās* from the foundation of romantic love, thus providing a visualization of the *līlās* for *sādhakas* in pursuit of this ideal—*mādhurya-rasa*. The principal *līlā-granthas* mentioned above are also written in Sanskrit poetry and thus layered with meaning that requires a knowledge of the language and its surrounding culture to uncover all the texts' implications.

Nayanānanda Ṭhākura's *Preyo-bhakti-rasārṇava* is of course an exception. But while he has written descriptively in Bengali prose about this same *līlā* section from the foundation of fraternal love, his work is very brief in comparison. His focus is on the ideal of *priya-sakhā-bhāva*, or *kevala-sakhya-rasa*. From the *kevala-sakhya-rasa* perspective, Nayanānanda Ṭhākura divides the day similarly but excludes the *niśānta-* and *niśa-līlās*, during which the *sakhās* are asleep, dreaming of daytime *līlās* that they participate in during their waking hours. His rendering also differs in that it does not describe Rādhā's corresponding day, as do the earlier *mādhurya-rasa aṣṭakāla-līlā-granthas*. Furthermore, it excludes any discussion of Kṛṣṇa's midday romantic *līlās* that his *priya-narma-sakhās* readily participate in and are essential to.

Thus, here in the center of our circle we shall explore the divisions of Kṛṣṇa's day briefly in English, from the perspective of the *priya-narma-sakhā*. This *bhāva*, as we have seen, is a mixture of *sakhya* and *mādhurya* in which the latter nourishes the former, taking it to new heights and thereby leaving no *sevā* too intimate to preclude such *sakhās*' participation in the corresponding *līlā*.

Unlike Nayanānanda Ṭhākura's rendering, our description of the divisions of Kṛṣṇa's day will include the romanticism of the *madhyāhna-līlā*, as this *līlā* includes the participation of Kṛṣṇa's most intimate friends. Insight into this section of the midday *līlā* is one of the unique contributions of the Gauḍīya *sampradāya*.

But how shall we deal with the *niśānta-* and *niśa-līlās*, in which the *narma-sakhās*' participation is limited at best? We learned earlier from Rūpa Goswāmī's citing of the qualifications of Subala that it is not for lack of qualification that the *narma-sakhās* do not actively participate in any particular intimate romantic *līlā*.[8] We also learned from Raghunātha dāsa Goswāmī's *Prema-pūrābhidha-stotram* that friends like Subala-sakhā

8. *Rādhā-kṛṣṇa-gaṇoddeśa-dīpikā* 2.42 also states that there are no confidential topics whatsoever about which these *priya-narma-sakhās* are unaware.

are known to participate in Rādhā and Kṛṣṇa's *niśa-līlā*. Furthermore, the *narma-sakhās' sevā* during Kṛṣṇa's waking hours of the *prātaḥ-līlā* (6:00 a.m. to 8:24 a.m.) indicates their acquaintance with Rādhā and Kṛṣṇa's late-night lovemaking extending into the *niśānta-līlā*. Seeing the love marks on his body, his attire in disarray, and his lack of sleep, they readily connect the dots in a manner that Yaśodā's *vātsalya-bhāva* cannot, and in doing so they provide further cover for Kṛṣṇa with their wit to conceal his late-night and predawn romantic dalliances before the questioning eyes of the elders. Thus, *narma-sakhā-upāsakas* should be acquainted with these two *līlā* divisions. In the least, these late-night and predawn *līlās* are part of the *narma-sakhās'* spiritual imagination.

But there is also another sense in which participation in the *niśa-* and *niśānta-līlās* pertains to *narma-sakhā-upāsakas*. As we learned from the circumference of this circle of friends, the opportunity to serve within the Vraja *līlā* in *sakhya-rasa* comes to us through Gaura *līlā* and the grace of Nityānanda Rāma. In this *līlā*, eternal associates of Kṛṣṇa serve in perfected *sādhaka-dehas*. Again, they are *siddhas* in the role of *sādhakas*.

For example, Śrī Rūpa, who is Rūpa-mañjarī in the Vraja *līlā*, serves in Gaura *līlā* as a *kiśora brāhmaṇa* boy in *dāsya-rasa*. Similarly, the *dvādaśa-gopālas* externally serve Gaura and Nityānanda in *dāsya-rati* in a *guru-śiṣya* relationship, while internally participating in *sakhya-rasa* in the Vraja *līlā*, where they see their deities of Gaura and Nityānanda turn into Kṛṣṇa and Balarāma. The general rule is "worship in Nadīyā; live in Vraja." Gaura *līlā* is the way to Kṛṣṇa *līlā*. However, the former is also the natural extension of the latter, and thus arguably Gaura *līlā* itself—being the ramification of the most introspective moment in Kṛṣṇa's life and *līlā*—has its own eternal *aprakaṭa* expression. Thus, the two *līlās*, which are inseparable from the Gauḍīya perspective, afford the humble Gauḍīya Vaiṣṇava the opportunity to participate in both of them in two different identities that are themselves inseparable and complementary. Just as the *śiṣya* serves his or her *guru*, who is the microcosmic representation of *guru-tattva* (*vyaṣṭi-guru*), the *śiṣya* similarly serves the macrocosmic (*samaṣṭi-guru*) representation of *guru-tattva*—Gaura and Nityānanda—in a servant-preceptor relationship. And such service transports one into the *aprakaṭa* Gaura *līlā* in *dāsya-rasa* as a *brāhmaṇa* boy, a type of *dāsya-bhakti* akin to that of Vraja that is touched by *sakhya-rasa*.[9] Thus, *narma-sakhā-upāsakas* will participate in

9. *Bhakti-rasāmṛta-sindhu* 3.2.91 explains that the *dāsya-bhaktas* of Vraja, whom Rūpa Goswāmī refers to as *anugas*, attain the stages of *prema*, *sneha*, and *rāga*. And when the stage

Gaura's *niśānta-* and *niśa-līlās*, which correspond with these same divisions in Kṛṣṇa *līlā*. While in one's internal *narma-sakhā* identity one may not typically participate in Rādhā and Kṛṣṇa's predawn and late-night *līlās*, in one's Gaura *līlā* identity one will participate in Gaura's *niśānta-* and *niśa-līlās*.[10] One does so by being present and, for example, participating in the *līlā-kīrtana* led by Svarūpa Dāmodara.

The eightfold divisions of Gaura *līlā* are the same as those of Kṛṣṇa *līlā*. However, comparatively little has been written about these divisions. The earliest mention of them is found in the *paddhati* of Gopāla-guru Goswāmī, Gaura Kṛṣṇa's young yet very close associate.[11] Both Gopāla-guru Goswāmī and his disciple Dhyānacandra Goswāmī composed handbooks to assist *sādhakas* in the *mānasī-sevā-smaraṇam* of the *rāga-mārga* in pursuit of *mañjarī-bhāva* along with the attainment of *dāsya-bhāva* in Gaura *līlā*. We find the following four verses in Dhyānacandra Goswāmī's handbook describing the eightfold divisions of Śrīmān Gaurasundara's daily *līlā*:

> During the predawn hours (*niśānta*), the *sādhaka* shall meditate on Prabhu sleeping in his own home. In the early morning hours (*prātaḥ-kāle*), Prabhu rises from bed, bathes, and dines. In the forenoon hours, Prabhu becomes absorbed in Kṛṣṇa *līlā-smaraṇa* and experiences intense feelings of separation. In the midday hours, Prabhu performs astonishing pastimes on the bank of the Gaṅgā. The *sādhaka* shall meditate on Gaura in this way. In the afternoon hours, Prabhu joyfully roams about Navadvīpa-dhāma. In the early evening hours, he returns home, displaying his enchanting beauty. In the late evening hours, he meets with his close associates at the home of Śrīvāsa Ṭhākura, where they participate in a *mahā-saṅkīrtana*

---

of *rāga* manifests, their *dāsya* is touched by *sakhya*. He cites the well-known Raktaka as an example.

10. In Gaura *līlā* we find all types of devotees participating in these *līlās*. However, the extent to which they follow Gaura internally as he enters into the romanticism of the Vraja *līlā* depends upon their own internal *bhāva*. For example, when Nityānanda Rāma experienced Gaura entering Rādhā *bhāva*, he bowed from a distance owing to the parameters of his own *bhāva*. *Dāsya-bhaktas* in Gaura *līlā* who have *sakhya-rasa* identities in Kṛṣṇa *līlā* do not manifest *gopī* identities when Gaura enters into the Vraja *rāsa-līlā* at Śrīvāsa Aṅgana any more than *dāsya-bhaktas* of Gaura *līlā* with *gopī* identities in Vraja manifest *gopa* identities when Gaura enters into his *gopa-svarūpa* and cowherding *līlās*.

11. From the oral tradition, we learn that "Gopāla-guru" is a nickname given to the young son of Murāri Paṇḍita by Gaura Kṛṣṇa himself. He is otherwise known as Makaradhvaja Paṇḍita.

festival far into the night. In this way the *sādhaka* shall meditate in *ānanda* on Śrīmān Gaura-candra.[12]

Dhyānacandra Goswāmī explains that the *sādhaka* should meditate on himself as a *sādhaka* in Gaura *līlā*, wearing white cloth, decorated with *tilaka*, a fragrant garland around his neck. On this *sādhaka*'s chest the holy names are written in sandalwood paste. His mood will be *guru sevotsukāṁ*.[13] This is very clearly an advocacy of meditative *dāsya-bhakti* for Gaura Kṛṣṇa in the *aprakaṭa* Navadvīpa, within which a corresponding Kṛṣṇa *līlā-svarūpa* in *mādhurya-* or *sakhya-rasa* arises—meditation within meditation, if you will. And we see this in the perfected *sādhaka-dehas* of the Vṛndāvana Goswāmīs and also the *dvādaśa-gopālas*.

Today these two early Goswāmī *paddhatis* are often combined with the nineteenth-century handbook of Siddha Kṛṣṇadāsa, and together the three are sometimes referred to collectively as *paddhati-traya*, the three *bhajana-paddhatis* of the Gauḍīya *sampradāya*. In between the two early *paddhatis* and the later one, we also find Viśvanātha Cakravartī Ṭhākura's seventeenth-century Sanskrit *stotram*, encapsulating the eightfold divisions of Gaura Kṛṣṇa's day, a *stotram* comparable to Śrī Rūpa's *Śrī Śrī Rādhā-kṛṣṇayor-aṣṭakālīya-līlā-smaraṇa-maṅgala-stotram*. Cakravartī Ṭhākura's eleven verses are found in his *Stavāmṛta-laharī*, a collection of twenty-three *stotrams*. This particular *stotram* is entitled *Śrīmān-mahāprabhor-aṣṭakālīya-līlā-smaraṇa-maṅgala-stotram*. A devotee named Kṛṣṇadāsa who appears to have been a disciple of the Ṭhākura also composed a Bengali rendering of Cakravartī Ṭhākura's Sanskrit *stotram* and elaborated on it with his own meditative Bengali commentary, *Śrī Gaurāṅga-līlāmṛta*.

The Vṛndāvana *aṣṭakāla-līlā-granthas* mentioned above do not include Kṛṣṇa's departure for Mathurā. Similarly, the *granthas* that provide a window into the eightfold daily *līlā* of Nimāi Paṇḍita focus on young Nimāi's householder life in Navadvīpa, with no hint of his embracing *sannyāsa* and departing as he does in the *prakaṭa-līlā*. In this section of the *līlā*, Gaura is a householder devotee of Rādhā and Kṛṣṇa. As such, his Vaiṣṇavism is in full display, his student life finished, while he remains forever young—Gaura-kiśora. He worships at home and engages in *nāma-saṅkīrtana* throughout the

12. *Śrī Gaura-govindārcana-smaraṇa-paddhati* 74–77.

13. Here the Goswāmī's description of the Gaura *līlā-svarūpa* is a generic prototype, as is his description of the *mañjarī-svarūpa* drawn from the *Sanat-kumāra Saṁhitā*, although the latter description is more specific in that he elaborates on its eleven features (*ekādaśa-bhāva*).

nine islands of Navadvīpa, locating his nocturnal *kīrtana-rasa* headquarters in the courtyard of Śrīvāsa Ṭhākura.

To the spiritual eye, Navadvīpa appears as a nine-petal lotus arising in the Gaṅgā delta, each island representing one of the ninefold *aṅgas* of *bhakti* enunciated by Prahlāda in *Śrīmad Bhāgavatam*. Vyāsa spoke the *Bhāgavata* to Śukadeva high in the Himalayas, where the Gaṅgā begins its earthly current. In Nadīyā, where the Gaṅgā reaches its culmination and enters the ocean at the Bay of Bengal, Gaura *līlā* appears as the culmination of the *Bhāgavata* narrative—*Caitanya-bhāgavata*. Earthly Navadvīpa is a particular manifestation of the *aprakaṭa* Navadvīpa. Dhyānacandra Goswāmī offers the following *dhyāna* of this latter Nadīyā *nitya-līlā*:

> On the beautiful bank of the Gaṅgā lies Śrī Navadvīpa-dhāma. Decorated with delightful groves and gardens, it is shaped like a tortoise shell. There, row upon row of palatial buildings resound with *prema-saṅkīrtana*. I pray to that Navadvīpa-dhāma, nondifferent from Śrī Vṛndāvana-dhāma and unequaled in the three worlds.
>
> The banks of the Gaṅgā are adorned with beautiful blossoming trees and vines and cooled by a gentle breeze arising from her waves. Swarms of black bees play happily amid four varieties of lotus flowers, while swans, *cakravākas*, and other birds play within the water. The bathing *ghāṭas* on her banks are made of precious gems. She exhibits a variety of ecstasies, purified and colored by the dust of Gaura's lotus feet.
>
> The soil of this sacred land along the banks of the Gaṅgā is a beautiful golden color. This most auspicious Navadvīpa has been inundated by a flood of Kṛṣṇa *prema* and is worshiped by a great number of devotees. There are various kinds of fruits and flowers in the trees and creepers. Groups of multicolored birds lost in *prema* sing sweet sounds that steal away the hearts and ears of everyone.
>
> The opulence of Navadvīpa-dhāma is extraordinary within transcendence. There are trees there with emerald trunks, branches of gold, delicate sapphire and ruby leaves, buds of coral, diamond flowers, and *vaidūrya*-like fruits. These indescribable trees are eternally self-effulgent.
>
> Within that great ever-existing city lives a group of mild-natured *brāhmaṇas*. Their houses are surrounded by pleasant courtyards,

> beautiful pleasure groves, and gardens. Here and there among the groves are sporting areas with platforms for sitting. There, effulgent devotees are always engaged in great festivals and celebrations, because in each of their houses a *mūrti* of Śrī Kṛṣṇa resides.[14]

Notable in such descriptions, be they of Nadīyā's *nitya-vihāra* or of Goloka's Gokula, is an element of majesty that is not present in the *prakaṭa-līlā*, at least not to the naked eye. Houses are envisioned to be constructed of valuable minerals, gates and pillars of precious and semiprecious stones, and so on. Indeed, the settings are extremely opulent even while bucolic, the natural environment sporting coral and emerald trees with branches of gold. But such poetic descriptions do not represent the actual wealth of these sacred domains, and thus they arguably have a secondary purpose in mind. On the one hand, they employ overwhelming material value in an effort to try to do justice in word to the actual wealth that lies beyond the counterfeit value of anything from within our space-time continuum, and perhaps on the other hand they serve the purpose of attracting the attention of those who covet such material opulence. But the actual wealth of these *dhāmas* is their *prema*—the intimacy they afford the devotee in loving rapport with the Godhead. That this *prema* is sometimes depicted as taking place in houses constructed out of gold, rubies, emeralds, and the like suggests that therein precious stones are used as mere construction materials. And despite such opulence, the temperament of the residents remains simple and humble with no air of the pride common among the privileged. Here our prince is a prince of the cowherds, Kṛṣṇa, and a *brāhmaṇa* boy, Gaura.

The temperament of the Gaura and Kṛṣṇa *līlā rāgātmikas* and their wealth of *prema* is our ideal. Among friends we have no interest in diamonds *or* rust. Let our interest be in gathering dust from the feet of Gaura's servants and Kṛṣṇa's friends!

Before discussing the typical *līlās* of Gaura and Kṛṣṇa as they manifest during the eight divisions of the day from the vantage point of a *narma-sakhā*, let us first elaborate briefly on Goloka's *aprākṛta* setting set forth in various sacred texts:

> Therein, the highest abode or setting of the *aprakaṭa-līlā*, sustained by a portion of the spiritual energy of Baladeva—Ananta—is termed Gokula, the center of Goloka. It is described by Jīva Goswāmī as

14. *Śrī Gaura-govindārcana-smaraṇa-paddhati* 11–14.

"the abode of cows and *gopas*," *go-gopa-vāsa-rūpa*. Gokula is envisioned as a lotus consisting of a thousand petals. The pericarp of the lotus— the protrusion surrounding the seed—is Kṛṣṇa's *dhāma*, the *yogapīṭha* wherein he himself resides. This pericarp is also geometrically depicted as a great hexagonal *yantra*, providing six distinct sections centered around a diamond pivot that is presided over by both *puruṣa* and *prakṛti* and further overlaid with and sonically represented by the luminous eighteen-syllable Gopāla *mantra*. Here, *prakṛti* refers to Kṛṣṇa as the cause of the *mantra*, and *puruṣa* refers to Kṛṣṇa as the deity presiding over it.[15] The *mantra*'s six sounds correspond with the six sections of the hexagon, while the *mantra*'s seed corresponds with the center of the *yantra*. The pericarp is said to be flush with the bliss of *rasa* derived from *prema*.

Moving outward from the pericarp, the filaments of the lotus represent Kṛṣṇa's *gopas*, referred to as his *aṁśas*, or parts, implying their likeness to him in appearance and their sense of equality with him in love. The petals of the lotus represent his *gopīs* and the forests of Vraja, over which Śrī Rādhā presides. Furthermore, the entire *yantra* is encompassed by a quadrangle known as Śvetadvīpa,[16] whose four corners represent the fourfold *vyūha* expansions of Kṛṣṇa—Vāsudeva, Saṅkarṣaṇa, Pradyumna, and Aniruddha. It is endowed with the four goals of human endeavor—*dharma*, *artha*, *kāma*, and *mokṣa*—the eight treasures of liberated life, and the eight *yogic siddhis*. Guardians in their *mantra* forms are posted in all ten surrounding directions, that are themselves surrounded by the four Vedas. And finally, it is resplendent overall with astonishing *śaktis*.[17]

15. *Prakṛti* is present as the abode of the *mantra*. That *prakṛti* is also Śrī Kṛṣṇa in person. He has been called *prakṛti* in this context because he is the cause of *prakṛti*.

16. In his commentary on *Brahma Saṁhitā* 5.5, Jīva Goswāmī explains that the square representing Śvetadvīpa includes both the inside and outside of the inner circle of Gokula. Outside this circle Kṛṣṇa's *līlā* is majestic, whereas the *līlā* inside the circle is intimate. As explained by Bhaktivinoda Ṭhākura in his commentary on this verse, the *aprakaṭa* Gaura *līlā* is included within this inner circle. In his *Gopāla-campū* 1.1.22, Jīva Goswāmī refers to this inner section of Śvetadvīpa as "Para-śvetadvīpa." And referring to this realm in *Caitanya-bhāgavata* 2.23.290, Vṛndāvana dāsa Ṭhākura informs us that ongoing revelation will reveal that the inner realm known as Śvetadvīpa also refers to Navadvīpa—*śvetadvīpa-nāma, navadvīpa-grama, vede prakāśiba pāche*.

17. Śrī Jīva Goswāmī has penned an extensive commentary on the *Brahma Saṁhitā*, the first five verses of which poetically, geometrically, and sonically describe the *aprakaṭa* realm of Goloka as a lotus *maṇḍala* that is superimposed with a *yantra*, creating spaces that

Jīva Goswāmī quotes such passages to establish that there is a supreme spiritual abode that corresponds with the fountainhead of divinity—Gopāla Kṛṣṇa. However, in his *Gopāla-campū*, where he also dwells on the *aprakaṭa-līlā*, we find less cryptic and much more poetic descriptions of this realm, written with a different purpose in mind: to entice others to go there. Thus, let us also cite Jīva Goswāmī's description of the *aprakaṭa-līlā* in which his longing to attain it is found, for when such *sādhus* reveal the longing of their hearts, it is considered a great blessing for *sādhakas* to take advantage of—*guhyam ākhyāti pṛcchati*.

Despite all that has been said over the centuries about the *aprakaṭa-līlā*, in the opening section of *Gopāla-campū*, where the *aprakaṭa-dhāma* and its *līlā* are extensively glorified as an introduction to the narrative, Śrī Jīva repeatedly expresses his inability and the limits of language to do justice to this fascinating *aprakaṭa-līlā* and its *dhāma* that he longs to attain:

> Moreover, there the water is like nectar. What, then, of real nectar? There, the speech, which is song, is a sweet beverage for the ears. How much sweeter, then, are the songs therein! There, walking is the height of artful dancing. How much more must the dancing there be respected!... What is its power? How amazing! What skill in dancing! What place is this? Has the *prema* described by Śukadeva taken a body?...
>
> In Goloka, Kṛṣṇa resides with his prominent friends. My heart has become inundated by their sweetness and has become attracted to them at every moment. Oh! What shall I do? I have hastily begun this description, but I do not know how to continue.... I can honestly say that I do not hanker after objects that give pleasure, nor do I disdain them. But I have developed a desire to see the eternal planet of Kṛṣṇa, which produces affection for Kṛṣṇa and for which Kṛṣṇa has affection....
>
> In Goloka, there is absorption in Kṛṣṇa's beauty and appropriate pastimes: First he calls the cows from the sheds for taking them to the pasture. Then he plays with his friends. The cows wander away. He goes searching for them. He calls for them and then goes far away to fetch them. He tells his friends to go and bring the cows.

---

are then invested with the sounds of the eighteen-syllable Gopāla *mantra*. These two paragraphs are a paraphrasing of this section and Śrī Jīva's insight into its significance found in both this *Brahma Saṁhitā* commentary and his *Kṛṣṇa Sandarbha*.

Then he plays again with his friends. Remembering these pastimes, I become excited. Sometimes Kṛṣṇa and Balarāma hold hands, laugh, and make others laugh. This agitates my heart. The sound of the flute may make the trees blossom and may suddenly liquefy mountains. It may make the water stop flowing or make the river flow to the west instead of the east.... When Kṛṣṇa wanders about for his pastimes in various places, while the trees blossom in bliss, there are no questions and no speaker required to answer them. There is nothing to ask and nothing to explain....

While herding the cows, the boys, with tears in their eyes, sing songs with sweet melodies. Remembering the past events from Kṛṣṇa's birth, they immediately begin to faint. How should the mind be controlled, since those cowsheds make my mind desirous of seeing them? The trees, like the abodes of the cowherds, are surrounded by powdered cow dung, fragrant and shining like excellent musk. The cowsheds give rise to hundreds of memories of the trees, the young calves, and the cows, who surpass *surabhi* cows and are present there at night. In the dawn and dusk as well, memories arise: "Let the calves free. Milk the cows. Collect the milk buckets. Gather the cows. Go to the house. Put Kṛṣṇa in front. Sing the pastimes of Kṛṣṇa. Shed tears while your hairs stand on end!" The blissful daily actions of the cowherds overcome my heart!

It is worth noting that while Śrī Jīva Goswāmī has been identified with *mañjarī-bhāva*—Vilāsa-mañjarī—in his childhood he worshiped the *mūrtis* of Kṛṣṇa and Balarāma. He was also especially blessed and instructed by Śrīmān Nityānanda, and more than any of the other *sampradāya*'s founding *ācāryas* he has at times expressed his affinity for the *sakhya-rasa-līlās* of Kṛṣṇa and his *sakhās*, as we see in the above passage. And aside from his affinity, he also underscores the exalted state of *sakhya-rasa* from the *tattva* vantage point. In his *Prīti Sandarbha* 100, Jīva Goswāmī asserts that all of Vraja's kinsmen (*bāndhavas*) are touched by friendship (*mitratā*) but among them Kṛṣṇa's *sakhās* are the most exalted. "They alone," he writes, "are endowed priorly with heaps of merit (*kṛta-puṇya-puñjāḥ*) indicating that among all those who strive for the pleasure of Kṛṣṇa, these *sakhās* are *parama-śreṣtha*—preeminent."

Furthermore, unlike Rūpa Goswāmī, whose preferred name for Kṛṣṇa is Mādhava, Śrī Jīva's preferred name is Gopāla, and it is only out of deference to Śrī Rūpa that he entitled the earliest of his *līlā-granthas*, dedicated to his *guru*, *Mādhava-mahotsava*. And in his *Prīti Sandarbha*, Śrī Jīva describes the Vraja *sakhīs'* love for Kṛṣṇa to be "*mādhurya* mixed with *sakhya-rasa*."[18] Surely this *mañjarī gopī*—a handmaiden of Rādhā—will be pleased to bless *sādhakas* longing for *sakhya-rati* to attain *their* ideal and enter the *aprakaṭa-līlā*, never to return. Oh! With such a blessing, it is enough to be on one's way! Seeking such a blessing while citing Śrī Jīva's desire to attain that *līlā*, let us now turn our attention to the *aṣṭakāla-līlā* as viewed from the perspective of *narma-sakhā-bhāva*. *Jaya* Kṛṣṇa! *Jaya* Gaura! *Jaya* Rāma! *Jaya* Rādhe!

18. *Prīti Sandarbha* 82. Śrī Jīva writes that the queens in Dvārakā have *kānta-bhāva* mixed with *dāsya* (*dāsya-miśra kānta-bhāva*) whereas the *gopīs* of Vraja have *kānta-bhāva* mixed with *sakhya* (*sakhya-miśra*). See chapter 31 for more insight on Śrī Jīva's perspective.

18

Predawn

Niśānta-līlā

Gaurasundara awakens at approximately 3:30 in the morning. Some *rasikas* place him in the extended outdoor area of Śrīvāsa Ṭhākura's courtyard, while others envision him already at home, having returned in the wee hours of the morning from his *niśa-līlā saṅkīrtana* to his own bedroom.[1] Siddha Kṛṣṇadāsa's *Guṭikā* finds Gaura, Nityānanda, and Advaita-candra in the outlying area of Śrīvāsa Ṭhākura's courtyard, asleep on jeweled beds in their own separate pavilions, surrounded by their principal associates. There Gaura is serenaded by the Rādhā-Kṛṣṇa *niśānta-līlā-kīrtana* of Svarūpa Dāmodara as he wakes from what little sleep he was able to catch during the night to the sounds of peacocks, parrots, and other feathered friends.

However, Gaura is unsure of his identity and location in his early waking hours, being mentally absorbed in Rādhā and Kṛṣṇa's *niśānta-līlā*. In their predawn *līlā*, Rādhā and Kṛṣṇa also awaken deep within the forest to the sounds and advice of various talking birds orchestrated by Vṛndā-devī and also to the service of Rādhā's friends and maidservants, who have risen before the two lovers with a view to prepare fresh garlands, cosmetics, and other items as they relish the predawn *darśana* of the divine couple.

The sound of the peacocks is perhaps most well known at this hour and difficult to sleep through. In the minds of Rādhā's maidservants, the peacocks' *ke-kā* clearly asks the rhetorical questions, "Who (*ke*) other than Śyāma can subdue the romantic pride of Rādhā, and what (*kā*) woman other

1. Dhyānacandra Goswāmī and Viśvanātha Cakravartī place him at home, while the later Siddha Kṛṣṇadāsa places him in Śrīvāsa Ṭhākura's extended courtyard.

than Rādhā can control the mad elephant of Kṛṣṇa's love?" The cuckoos sound the unalterable romantic fifth note,[2] and as Rādhā and Kṛṣṇa awaken and begin to get their bearings, talking birds offer them salient advice about their dawning *parakīya* problem: the rising sun.

Just as the learned twice-born *brāhmaṇas* chant the *Puruṣa-sūkta* hymns to awaken Viṣṇu, Vraja's various parrots and myna birds, who are also twice-born (once within the egg and once again when the egg hatches), chant to awaken Rādhā and Kṛṣṇa. However, while Viṣṇu's twice-born openly proclaim his glories, the Vraja twice-born seek to conceal the glory of Rādhā and Kṛṣṇa's intimate love for one another—the open secret of the Vraja-maṇḍala. Just as the Vedas mandate a measure of eligibility to be heard, similarly the intimate secrets of Rādhā and Kṛṣṇa's predawn love are not for everyone's ears. What, then, is the qualification of Kṛṣṇa's *narma-sakhās* headed by Subala, to whom these talking twice-born relate these secrets later during the *prātaḥ-līlā*, as these *gopas* sport in Nandagrāma at Kṛṣṇa's *raṅga-sthala* (sports arena)?

As the moon faints and falls from the sky and the stars fade from sight, the prospect of the "long night of the day" arises for Rādhā. Surely Kṛṣṇa had her in mind when in the *Gītā* he told Arjuna, "For she who has harnessed her passions with her intelligence (*saṁyamī*) by fixing it on her soul (me), that which is day for everyone else is her night—the long night of separation from her soul."[3] However, the earliest tint of *aruṇa* on the eastern horizon—the color of *sakhya-rasa*—also reminds Bhāskaropāsikā Rādhā that she does have friends, including Kṛṣṇa's *narma-sakhās*, to help her find her way into his association even under the watchful eye of the sun, whom she worships in the hope that this god will keep the secret of her paramour affair.[4]

2. The first (*sa*) and fifth (*pa*) notes on the Indian musical scale are considered anchors that are unalterable. The "perfect fifth" is comparatively constant, or stable. In Indian aesthetics it is associated with the humors of *mādhurya* and *hāsya*. The fifth note issuing from Kṛṣṇa's *muralī* plays a significant role in the Vraja *līlā* drama, which in an overarching sense can be construed as a romantic (*mādhurya*) comedy (*hāsya*). Cuckoos have played a role in human culture for thousands of years. In Europe, the cuckoo is associated with spring and with an adulteress deceiving her husband. In Japan, the cuckoo symbolizes unrequited love. In India, cuckoos are sacred to Kāmadeva, the god of romantic desire and longing.

3. *Bhagavad-gītā* 2.69.

4. Raghunātha dāsa Goswāmī includes the epithet Bhāskaropāsikā (she who worships the sun) in his *Śrī Śrī Rādhikā-aṣṭottara-śata-nāma-stotram*. *Mitra* in the masculine means "sun," and in the neuter gender it means "friend." Rādhā worships the sun because Jaṭilā,

Rādhā and Kṛṣṇa must hurry home, but separating is easier said than done. As the natural environment concertedly cautions them not to remain in their flower bower a moment longer lest they be found out, they rise yet fall again in love's embrace, incapable of letting one another go. And it is only when the shrieking she-monkey Kakkhaṭī warns them of Jaṭilā's admonishing approach that the two bodies with the same soul come to their senses, each heading homeward, stumbling along their separate paths and, in the confusion arising out of their union, wearing pieces of each other's clothing. Hearing Kakkhaṭī's white lie and believing it, Rādhā cannot tolerate the possibility that her lover's reputation might be spoiled, and thus she seeks to hasten the pace of her vehicle that is the limbs and minds of her *mañjarīs*. However, her *mañjarīs* know that although it is of paramount importance that Rādhā hurry homeward, her mother-in-law is still at home preoccupied more with thoughts as to why her son—Rādhā's husband—sleeps in the cowshed, unaware of Abhimanyu's well-kept secret of his emasculated status as a eunuch.[5]

But who will help Kṛṣṇa as *he* stumbles lovestruck along the path, his lotus eyes crossed, one looking toward the path Jaṭilā would take, the other following the distant outline of Rādhā as she scurries in the opposite direction down another path?[6] That is *sevā* his *narma-sakhās* can only dream about, although even in this world dreams can come true.

Such is the preoccupation of Gaurasundara, a breathtaking sight to behold as he lies on milky-white silk bedsheets, his head raised slightly on a puffy cream-like pillow. Above his head is a canopy, his shoes await his lotus feet, and his torso shines with an effulgent *upanayana*, all expansions of Nityānanda Rāma assisting him from head to toe.

---

her mother-in-law, tells her to and also because of how sun worship figures astrologically into her natal chart. Jaṭilā thinks that if Rādhā performs the appropriate *pūjā*, her husband, Jaṭilā's son, will be blessed with more cows, the wealth of cowherds—*dharma* brings *artha*. But on the pretext of worshiping the sun god, Rādhā meets with Kṛṣṇa at midday, making only a show of worship. Thus, the sun acts as a friend and shields her paramour affair. He does so in great measure at his brightest hour, midday, as Rādhā worships him.

5. This is the implication of *Govinda-līlāmṛta* 3.29.

6. Rādhā divides her time between Yāvaṭa and Varṣāṇā, her married and her parental homes, respectively, both of which are quite a distance from her *niśānta-līlā* flower bed, as is Kṛṣṇa's home in Nandagrāma. However, these various *līlā-sthalīs* are compared to petals of the lotus that is Vraja. When Rādhā and Kṛṣṇa travel what would otherwise be a long distance, that lotus all but closes, enabling them to quickly step from one petal to the next before it opens again. Just imagine.

In Gaura *līlā mānasī-sevā*, the *sādhaka* awakens at the feet of *śrī guru*, washes his own hands and face, wakes his *gurudeva*, and then prepares various items for the worship and service of Gaura under his *guru*'s guidance. He strings garlands, grinds sandalwood, prepares the *ārati* paraphernalia, decorates the *mṛdaṅgas* and *karatālas* as he has been trained to do, and so on. Then, hearing the *līlā-kīrtana* of Svarūpa Dāmodara describing the predawn *ārati* of Rādhā and Kṛṣṇa performed by Lalitā-sakhī, Gaura roars like a lion in ecstasy, and the assembled devotees offer *ārati* to him. Then Gaurasundara and the assembled devotees return to their homes. However, out of love for Gaura Kṛṣṇa, Nityānanda and his associates as well as the Goswāmīs and their followers remain with him at his house and therein render various services, as does the *sādhaka* before returning to his or her own residence.

19

Morning

Prātaḥ-līlā

Jagannātha Miśra's grounds surround an opulent thirty-room house on the bank of the Ganges, where the best of each of the six seasons are all simultaneously manifest and nature appears eager to serve Gaurasundara. As the sun rises, devotees following the lead of Nityānanda Rāma begin to arrive from their own cottages, assembling in the courtyard outside of Gaura's quarters in the southern section of the main structure. They have come to awaken him and let the day in his service begin.

Śacī, Mālinī, and Sītā Ṭhākurāṇī are the first to enter Gaura's bedroom, where his parrot Vicakṣaṇa is already glorifying him. Śacī is aghast at what appear to be bruises on his beautiful body, ostensibly a result of his falling during his *niśa-līlā saṅkīrtana-rasa*. In truth, they serve only to beautify his body and covertly represent his internal absorption in *mādhurya-rasa*, being comparable to the mascara, *kuṅkuma*, and other love marks that Yaśodā detects on Kṛṣṇa's body in the morning. As Gaura wakes, he reveals his dreams, and Svarūpa Dāmodara is inspired to portray them in *līlā-kīrtana*. Gaura then bathes in the Gaṅgā, listens to the *Bhāgavata* recital of Gadādhara, attends the *ārati* of the household deity, and joyfully honors breakfast *prasāda* with his associates.

At this hour in Vraja, our attention goes first to the houses of Rāma and Kṛṣṇa's comrades—to Vṛṣabhānu-pura and its surrounding area as well as to the outlying area surrounding Nandagrāma. For the most part, Kṛṣṇa's *sakhās* hail from these two areas.

Nayanānanda Ṭhākura envisions Nandagrāma as a lotus with a circumference of sixteen miles. Within this area there are countless beautifully constructed cowsheds and human dwellings amid manicured gardens that host celestial plants and wish-fulfilling tress. Therein, the best of each of the six seasons is always manifest, and thus trees are constantly blossoming and bearing fruit. A wide variety of birds and animals live there without fear.

Nanda's palace is in the center of the compound, surrounded by a large wall that is covered by a thatched roof and decorated with colorful flags and white *cāmara* whisks. Within this palace, Balarāma's quarters are to the south and Kṛṣṇa's quarters are to the north. Within the perimeter wall of the compound, there are also many other residences, including those of Nanda's four brothers—Upananda, Abhinanda, Sananda, and Nandana—which surround his house on four sides.

Many *suhṛt-sakhās* are members of Nanda Bābā's extended family, and thus they are more prominent in the Nandagrāma area. Subhadra, Kuṇḍala, Daṇḍī, Maṇḍala, Sunanda, Nandī, and Ānandī in particular are Kṛṣṇa's paternal cousins. Other prominent *suhṛt-sakhās* from this area include Śubhada, Maṇḍalībhadra, Bhadravardhana, Gobhaṭa, Yakṣendra, Bhaṭa, Bhadrāṅga, Vīrabhadra, Mahāguṇa, Kulavīra, Mahābhīma, Divyaśakti, Suraprabha, and Raṇasthira. Among them, Vijayākṣa, the son of Kṛṣṇa's wet nurse Ambikā, is the leader of all the *suhṛt-sakhās*. All of these *sakhās* have been appointed by Nanda to protect Kṛṣṇa.

Many prominent *priya-sakhās* and *narma-sakhās* are members of the extended family of Vṛṣabhānu Rāja, and thus they reside in the Vṛṣabhānu-pura area. Among them, Śrīdāmā, Sudāmā, Vidagdha, Ujjvala, Subāhu, and the mysterious Subala are to be remembered.[1]

Nayanānanda Ṭhākura also envisions Vṛṣabhānu-pura in the shape of a thousand-petal lotus flower extending sixteen miles in circumference.[2]

1. The oral tradition identifies Subala with Vṛṣabhānu-pura, while *Garga Saṁhitā* identifies him as a member of Nanda's family. However, the latter identification is suspect in that the same verse of the *Saṁhitā* also includes Śrīdāmā, who is Rādhā's brother, in Nanda's family. Then again, in *Rādhā-kṛṣṇa-gaṇoddeśa-dīpikā*, Rūpa Goswāmī describes Kaṇḍava and Daṇḍava, two sons of Kṛṣṇa's paternal uncle Upananda, as "staying in the company of Subala," which implies that Subala resides in Nandagrāma. Some Vaiṣṇavas differing from Rūpa Goswāmī envision Subala as a twin brother of Rādhā. For our purpose, we have simply referred with feeling to Raghunātha dāsa Goswāmī's epithet for Rādhā *subala-nyasta-sārūpyā* and underscored the mystery of his person.

2. In Nayanānanda's meditation, both Nandagrāma and Vṛṣabhānu-pura appear to be the same size and in the shape of lotuses. His text describes Nandagrāma as a lotus with "a circumference of sixteen miles" and Vṛṣabhānu-pura as a lotus "extending sixteen miles."

Countless cowherd dwellings made of bricks and beautified by various clusters of trees and gardens dot the land. Flags of different colors—white, yellow, blue, and red—arranged in sequence and fluttering in the breeze beautify the *gopas'* houses. Forest flower garlands drape the four external walls of each house, celebrating the four directions. Numerous species of flowers are always in full bloom, and rows upon rows of *campaka* flowers and varieties of jasmine attract maddened honeybees whose sound is very pleasing to the ear. The cooling breeze, bearing the fragrance of the flowers, blows gently in all directions. Large lakes and placid ponds flow and simultaneously remain still, resplendent with many species of lotus flowers. From these lakes and ponds, waterfowl sing, while peacocks dance on the shore. Jewel-studded platforms encircle the bases of the banyan, fig, white lily, and mango. Various types of birds such as parrots move about, some sitting among these trees, and storks inhabit the tall grasses, where crickets and other insects sing of their own good fortune.

In the center of the town stands the palace of Rāja Vṛṣabhānu, surrounded by a moat. The homes of Vṛṣabhānu Rāja's brothers are nearby. To the east is the residence of Ratnabhānu; to the south is the residence of Subhānu; to the west is the residence of Bhānu. About Vṛṣabhānu-pura, Nayanānanda Ṭhākura concludes, "I have never seen a place anywhere in all these three worlds that could be compared to this realm."

From these two realms, all the boys mentioned above and innumerable others all rise at six in the morning with meeting Rāma and Kṛṣṇa in mind. Along with them rise the *narma-sakhās* Gandharva, Arjuna, Vasanta, Kokila, and Sanandana; *priya-sakhās* Kiṅkiṇi, Stokakṛṣṇa, Vasudāmā, Bhadrasena, Vilāsi, Puṇḍarīka, Viṭaṅkākṣa, Kalaviṅka, and Priyaṅkara; *sakhās* Ojasvī, Viśāla, Vṛṣabha, Devaprastha, Varūthapa, Mandāra, Kusumāpīḍa, Maṇibandha, Karandhama, Candana, Kunda, Kalinda, and Kulika. They all wake to the sound of Rāma's horn but are checked by their mothers' affection from immediately heading to Nanda's residence. Patience is not a virtue in the minds of young boys, and they have little if any patience as their mothers attempt to make them presentable before they march off to Nanda's estate. Leaders of their respective groups are met first in their own homes by their *sakhā* followers (*upa-sakhās*), who assist them in readying themselves, performing parentally mandated duties, and gaining release. Then all of them in the trillions and more—*sakhās* and their *upa-sakhās*—merge into one steady stream and flow into Nanda's courtyard like rivers into the ocean of Balarāma's affectionate embrace.

Upon arrival, they stamp their feet in unison and dance to the very pleasing sound of the churning of butter throughout the village as they chant the glories of Rāma and Kṛṣṇa in *līlā-kīrtana* of their own spontaneous composition. This veritable churning of the *nirguṇa* ocean of milk gives rise to their song, which constitutes "another creation" altogether—*tad-vāg-visargo*—another day in the life of *svayaṁ* Bhagavān.[3] That which the cowherds sing about and imagine, layered as it is with many implications, serves as a forecast for the day ahead. Whatever they say, whatever they feel, all comes to pass in one form or another. And as the cowherds sing, they also cry out to Kṛṣṇa, "Get up, Kānāi! Get up and come with us to the cowshed!"

Kṛṣṇa's sleep at this hour is deep, but his adopted housemate and the family *pūjārī* Madhumaṅgala, already late for the *pūjā* of *śālagrāma* Narasiṁha, awakens at the sound of the *sakhās* and greets them from the balcony. Following his lead, *narma-sakhās* ascend and assist in waking Kṛṣṇa while keeping Yaśodā in the dark as to his previous night's romantic exploits. Love marks that look like bruises and scratches—such as smears of Rādhā's dark mascara and red *kuṅkuma*, lipstick from her rose-like lips, and marks from the tips of her fingernails—send shock waves through the maternal mind of Yaśodā. And why is he wearing a blue garment instead of his saffron-yellow shawl?

> Yaśodā to Paurṇamāsī: Is Kṛṣṇa wearing Balarāma's shawl? Have his friends somehow wrestled with him in the night, wounding him?

With the help of the wise, elderly Paurṇamāsī, whose parental love is bundled with fraternal love and who is the most respected person in all of Vraja, these *narma-sakhās* find clever excuses to hide the effects of Kṛṣṇa's secret romantic interludes from Yaśodārāṇī. However, typically they do not do so without humor at Kṛṣṇa's expense. Madhumaṅgala's play on words serves as an example:

> O Mother, what you say is true. Although I try to forbid them, Kṛṣṇa's frolicsome boyfriends/passionate girlfriends ignore me and always play roughly with him![4]

3. One of the *Bhāgavata*'s creation stories involves the churning of the material ocean of milk. But the *Bhāgavata* (1.5.11) describes *itself* as "another [transcendental] creation" arising out of its poetry. And here we find milk, butter, and yogurt droplets on the ground below with Acyuta lying in rest above, the cowherds' song making waves.

4. *Govinda-līlāmṛta* 2.19. Here the word *vayasyālī* can mean "boys" or "girls."

Of course, Kṛṣṇa takes Madhumaṅgala's word usage to mean (as it could and as was secretly and humorously intended) "passionate girlfriends" and smiles at his friend, even as he is also somewhat angry with him for putting him at risk. But Yaśodā understands Madhumaṅgala to be speaking about his *sakhās* and concludes, "Alas, boys will be boys." Then, Paurṇamāsī, her parental affection suppressed and giving way to fraternal love, quickly changes the subject, reminding Kṛṣṇa that the calves will not drink their mothers' milk without first seeing him and that Rāma and all of the two brothers' friends are clamoring below for him to proceed to the cowshed for milking. Thus, Govinda rises from bed and, with the assistance of the family servants, washes his face and brushes his teeth.

Yaśodā then instructs Balarāma to make sure that Kṛṣṇa does not delay after milking and that he returns in a timely manner for breakfast. But Kṛṣṇa takes exception to this instruction:

> Mother! Don't you have faith in me? Why are you speaking about me to Balarāma without saying anything to me? And if I were not the most well behaved among the boys, why would I agree to be controlled by Balarāma?[5]

However, Yaśodā is well aware of his misbehavior, and she reminds him that during his childhood the village ladies repeatedly witnessed and reported it to her. Thus, she prods him to proceed to the cowsheds under the watchful eye of Balarāma.

Kṛṣṇa then enters the courtyard below, where the chanting of his *sakhās* has reached a fever pitch. In his left hand he holds the right hand of one of his *narma-sakhās*, and in his right hand he holds his flute. Behind him, Paurṇamāsī follows closely. Seeing him, the already wide eyes of his friends bloom broader like bounteous lotus flowers and shower benedictions through their tears. As Hari tucks his flute in his belt, one boy quickly reaches out and holds his right hand, while others clutch the ends of his cloth or try to touch his effulgent form. And this scene lasts as if forever—that is, until interrupted by Yaśodā's shout from the balcony:

> O child! Go to the meadows and milk. Take this gold bucket and this rope. Then return home for breakfast without delay.

Meanwhile in Yāvaṭa, where Rādhā resides in proximity to her in-laws, Mukharā, her maternal grandmother who is favorably disposed toward

5. *Kṛṣṇa-bhāvanāmṛta* 3.48.

Rādhā's love for Hari, wakes her, admonishing her for sleeping late on the day she is scheduled to worship the sun. Then she notices Kṛṣṇa's yellow *cādara* on Rādhā's chest. Outwardly she expresses concern, which is immediately dismissed by Viśākhā, who explains as she whisks the cloth away that the elderly Mukharā has mistaken the color of the cloth under the influence of the morning sun.

And as Rādhā rises, she and her dearest associates engage in *hari-kathā* when the *gopī* messenger Madhurikā relates what she has just witnessed during Kṛṣṇa's waking at Nandagrāma. What nectar she fills Rādhā's ears with! *Kṛṣṇa-bhāvanāmṛta* relates,

> In the midst of his *narma-sakhās*, he looked especially brilliant and beautiful! O Mistress! What can I say about the smile on *rasajña* Kṛṣṇa's lotus-like face as he relished the soft words his friends whispered in his ears at every step? How can I know the meaning of those words? May your bee-like mind search out [the honey of] that meaning![6]

Such descriptions overwhelm Śrī Rādhā. But as her *mañjarīs* gradually bring her to her senses, they assist her in bathing and dressing, which sometimes takes place at Kiśorī-kuṇḍa on the eastern side of Yāvaṭa. In the surrounding garden of this area there is a jeweled temple with a tall steeple, a moon tower for gazing into the heavens as well as out into the distance below. From this tower, Rādhā and company can observe Kṛṣṇa heading toward his father's herd of cows.

Narma-sakhās are well aware of this moon tower and also of other *gopīs* in the immediate vicinity who have scurried to their rooftops to gaze upon the scene below. Thus, they whisper about them into Śyāma's ears, conveying messages from their *yūtheśvarīs* as they make their way to the cowshed. In jest, Madhumaṅgala plays with words that while poetically describing the heavens at dawn—the fading stars in the face of the rising sun—when read between his lines speak of the star-like *gopīs* shyly hiding themselves as the sun-like face of Kṛṣṇa looks upward toward them. *Narma-sakhās* know that Kṛṣṇa has noticed these Vraja *sundarīs* but is trying to keep his head down in an inner battle with his lotus eyes, owing to the oversight of Balarāma. Such jesting, so fine-tuned to his inner thoughts, brings a smile to Hari's face that he must cover with his hand, his head down, lest he break out into laughter. But then all of Hari's friends themselves

6. *Kṛṣṇa-bhāvanāmṛta* 3.54–55.

burst into laughter at Madhumaṅgala's poetic efforts, some knowing its inner meaning, others not.

From the barn, a concert of mooing calves and cows, grounded in the baritone of the bulls, captures everyone's attention, bringing Kṛṣṇa down to earth to focus on the task at hand. As he approaches the cowsheds, Śyāma calls out the names of his cows: "*Hihī* Gaṅgā, Godāvarī, Śavalī, Kālindī, Dhavalā, Dhumrā, Tuṅgī, Bhramarī, Yamunā, Haṁsī, Kamalā, Rambhā, Campā, Kariṇī, Hariṇī!"

Then, placing the golden pail between his legs, Kṛṣṇa begins milking as Rāma also milks nearby. At first the boys watch, and then at Kṛṣṇa's command they each begin milking, looking back and forth at what they are doing and at Kṛṣṇa. As the boys continue to milk, Kṛṣṇa passes his own milking on to another *gopa* so that he himself can oversee the entire event. Moving from cow to cow, he scratches their necks and feeds them fresh fodder from his hand, whispering sweet words into their ears. When Mahārāja Nanda sees his son's responsible behavior, his heart swells with pride.

It should not be lost on *sādhakas* that Gopāla is the protector of cows. One should try to understand the extent to which he himself is identified with them. In his opinion there is no one more fortunate in this world than cowherds because they always protect cows, bathe in the river of dust from the feet of cows, touch cows, chant the holy names of cows, and have *darśana* of cows throughout the day and into the night. And the Tantra says,

> One should scratch the cows, feed them, and circumambulate them. Gopāla is happy if the cows are always happy.[7]

But once the cows are milked, the *sakhās*' labor of love turns to play, and among themselves they begin to dance, sing, and carry on whimsically. However, as their play delays Rāma and Kṛṣṇa from returning home for breakfast, Yaśodā comes to fetch them bearing cheese and butter out of concern for their apparent lack of hunger. If young boys are not hungry, something is wrong! Then, coaxing her son with delicious and nutritious delights—grabbing him by the tongue—Nandarāṇī makes Kṛṣṇa dance if he is to taste her butter. Envisioning this scene, Gokula-candra dāsa sings in the *bhāva* of a *priya-sakhā*:

7. *Gautamīya Tantra*, cited in *Bhakti-rasāmṛta-sindhu* 1.2.110.

> Holding his mother's hand, the best of dancers dances, greedy for *dadhi*, *dugdha*, *sara*, and *nanī*. Particles of kicked-up cow dust stick to beautiful Śyāma's body, splendorous like drops of water clinging to a cloud. Filled with *ānanda*, Yaśodārāṇī gazes upon the face of Hari and exclaims, "You dance very nicely, my jewel among the Yadus! O Nanda, come see how much bliss is flowing here! Behold the dancing of your own son! Everyone is filled with joy to see his moon-conquering face! Over and over, they say, 'Dance more! Dance more!' " Then Nanda comes and kisses Kṛṣṇa again and again, drowning in a shower of *sukha*. The hearts of all the elderly *gopas* and *gopīs* surrounding this scene attain *ānanda* beholding this dancing. Gokula-candra says, "Listen, O Nandarāṇī! This dancing is but the external expression of every *gopa*'s and *gopī*'s *prāṇa*!"

Then Yaśodā embraces Kṛṣṇa and offers him his choice of the abovementioned variety of milk products—yogurt, milk, butter, and cream—and with Nanda's blessing she takes him and his brother home, but not before telling his friends that without them her sons have no appetite. Thus, she invites them to join Rāma and Kṛṣṇa for breakfast after first going home and bathing and dressing for the day while her sons do the same. In anticipation of returning, all the *sakhās* and *upa-sakhās* return to their homes singing in praise of Rāma and Kṛṣṇa along the way. Arriving first at the homes of their *yūtheśvaras*, the *upa-sakhās* assist them in milking their family cows. Then they render personal service to their group leaders, who bathe, dress, delight in refreshments, and rest. Finally, all the *upa-sakhās* return to their own homes, perform their morning duties, rest, and prepare themselves to return to Nanda's house for breakfast.

Meanwhile at Nanda's, cooking has already begun at the urging of Yaśodā, who places Rohiṇī in charge before going to fetch her sons. But upon returning home, her thoughts go to Rādhā and the blessing Rādhikā received from Durvāsā: "Rādhe! Whatever you cook will taste like nectar. But moreover, whoever tastes it will be blessed with a long life, beauty, and fame that will increase day by day." Kṛṣṇa is God weakened by love. Surely any strength that he has is derived from Rādhā's cooking!

In response to Yaśodā's desire, Kṛṣṇa's *līlā-śakti* brings Kundalatā into the scene. She is the wife of Upananda's son Subhadra, and she is Kṛṣṇa's dear informer throughout his romantic *līlās*. Upon seeing her, Yaśodā asks her to bring Rādhā to cook for Kṛṣṇa, and this is a request that Rādhā's mother-in-law, Jaṭilā, cannot refuse, given the instruction she received from the wise Paurṇamāsī to never disobey the instructions of Yaśodā, queen of the cowherds.[8]

Internally Rādhikā receives the invitation to cook for Kṛṣṇa with joy, but externally she expresses caution. She does this for two reasons: Kundalatā is Kṛṣṇa's trusted informer, and at least on the surface Rādhā does not entirely trust the knave-like son of Nanda. Furthermore, she seeks to gain the trust of her mother-in-law and retire any of her suspicions as to her marital chastity. And this in turn causes Jaṭilā to insist that Rādhā go with Kundalatā, whom Jaṭilā assumes is trustworthy, which of course she is but not in the way that Jaṭilā assumes. Mission accomplished, and Rādhā is on her way to Nandagrāma.

As she approaches, who stands at the main gate but Kṛṣṇa, his arm resting on Subala's shoulder. By now he is dressed for dining, having been assisted in bathing and choosing the color of his cloth and ornaments by family servants such as Raktaka and Patraka—an elaborate daily ritual. Kundalatā sees Kṛṣṇa first and describes what she sees, pouring the nectar of his sight that she drinks with her eyes onto her tongue and into the ears of Rādhikā. At the same time, Subala sees Rādhā first and points her out to Kṛṣṇa, describing sixteen features of her stunning appearance:

> Her body is freshly bathed. She wears a pearl shining at the tip of her nose, a dark-blue cloth, and a sash around her waist. Her hair is tied up in a braid. Attractive earrings hang from her ears. Her body is anointed with a mixture of *kastūrī*, *candana*, *kuṅkuma*, and camphor. She wears flowers in her hair, a *kusuma* flower *mālā* around her neck, and she holds a lotus in her hand. In her mouth she chews *pān*. On her chin is a dot of *kastūrī*, and her eyes are anointed with *kajjala*. Playful patterns are drawn on her cheeks, a covert version of the *kāma-yantra* serves as her *tilaka*, and the bottoms of her feet are painted with red *alta*.

Subala's description is saturated with his overwhelming admiration. Then, as Rādhā faints at the sight of her lover, her *mañjarīs* hold her up and revive her[9] such that with their help and that of her *sakhīs*, she is able to understand the sign language of a *narma-sakhā* who at that moment places a golden

8. See the "*Vaidya-veśa-milana*" of Viśvanātha Cakravartī Ṭhākura's *Camatkāra-candrikā* for a charming description of how Jaṭilā once decided not to allow Rādhā to go to Nandagrāma and how that decision backfired on her.

9. In his *Vilāpa-kusumāñjali*, Raghunātha dāsa Goswāmī prays for this *sevā*.

campaka flower garland around Kṛṣṇa's neck. In doing so he symbolically assures both Rādhā and Kṛṣṇa that although now is not the time, with the dedicated help of Kṛṣṇa's *narma-sakhās* the couple will be able to unite with one another even in broad daylight as the day proceeds.[10] Such is the commitment of Subala and the assembly of *narma-sakhās*.

Then, shining ever brighter amid her *sakhīs* and *mañjarīs*, Rādhā comes before her lover's mother and bows at her feet. Nandarāṇī quickly raises her up and embraces her as if Rādhā were her own daughter and bathes her with tears of love. This in turn fills Rādhā's maidservants with both pride and timidity at once, as they also bow before the mother of all mothers and receive her loving embrace.

The motherhood of Yaśodā is boundless. If anyone refers to her as "Mother," she loves that person as her child. She sees all the young *gopīs* and *gopas* as her children, who in her mind never grow up and always appear undernourished. Thus, she is forever lactating—one of *vātsalya*'s *sāttvika-bhāvas*—and she does not hesitate to gather any child into her arms and onto her lap, from where she proceeds to nurse them. And she knows the favorite dishes of every young *gopa* and *gopī*. And regardless of the time of day, as soon as she sees a child, she thinks of feeding her darling son or daughter: "O Lālā, at least you must eat something. I will prepare the dishes that you like most and feed you." Although she oversees and engages others in cooking for everyone living in and visiting her home, she herself insists on boiling and churning all the milk.

After she greets the young *gopīs*, led by Rādhā, the cooking proceeds in earnest and Nandagrāma becomes a beehive of activity, with more of Kṛṣṇa's friends arriving one by one and in groups of three or more. In the midst of such commotion, there is sufficient time for *narma-sakhās* to meet here and there with their *yūtheśvarīs* and receive any pertinent messages.

Gradually all the boys assemble together with Rāma and Kṛṣṇa in the center. They joke with one another, they discuss thoughtful subjects with what appears to be keen insight, and *narma-sakhās* whisper among themselves. On this particular morning, Nandarāṇī cut their playing short by coming to the milking area bearing sweets and sending the boys home early to bathe and dress. Thus, at Balarāma's welcome suggestion they then all proceed to the *raṅga-sthala* to wrestle and sport with one another while the

10. Here the golden *campaka* vine represents Rādhā, and Kṛṣṇa represents the dark *tamāla* tree around which the *campaka* vine grows.

morning cooking continues, despite the fact that Rāma, Kṛṣṇa, and all their friends have already bathed and dressed for breakfast.

Nayanānanda Ṭhākura locates this *raṅga-sthala* in one of the many courtyards in Nanda's compound. The Ṭhākura describes it as an athletic arena with a circular formation constructed to facilitate Rāma and Kṛṣṇa's penchant for sports in a park-like setting. Here the boys pair off and wrestle with one another, locking arm in arm, displaying their individual strength and admiring the strength of their opponents. In wrestling, gymnastics, and any variety of other sports, these boys exhibit amazing skill, daring, and confidence. Among them, none is better at handling a ball than Balarāma, whatever the sport may be. The hands of his long arms are adept at handling any size ball.

All around the *raṅga-sthala* nature abounds, and many parrots, male (*śuka*) and female (*śārī*), gather at this hour. It is here and from these parrots that the *narma-sakhās* learn about relevant details of the predawn pastimes of Rādhā-Mādhava. As the boys take a break from their play and wander in admiration of nature, they converse with the parrots and myna birds. Surely to hear these birds speak is to taste the cream of the Vedic milk—*śruti-sāram ekam*.

However, amid their play, Hari seeks to assuage his sudden feelings of separation from Rādhā by hearing and chanting her name, a time-tested method—Rādhā *nāma-kīrtana*—he learned from Subala. However, given the circumstance, which includes the presence of Balarāma, he must do so covertly. Thus, in his cleverness, he invites a newborn parrot to sit on his arm and asks him if he can recite a religious poem:

> *dhārādhara nindi jara sundara varaṇa*
> *sei nārāyaṇa sad āmarā śaraṇa*
>
> Let us take shelter of Nārāyaṇa, whose beautiful bodily effulgence resembles a fresh rain cloud.

However, the young parrot cannot learn and recite so much at once. Thus, Kṛṣṇa coaxes him, feeding him pomegranate seeds, and suggests that he learn just the first line of the verse. But when he cannot do this either, Kṛṣṇa suggests he chant just the first word of the verse—*dhārādhara*. Then the young parrot successfully chants *dhārā dhārā dhārā*, which through repetition transforms to the ear into "Rādhā Rādhā Rādhā," to the sound of which Hari dances and delights his *narma-sakhās* with his cleverness.

As Kṛṣṇa is then surrounded by all his friends, he turns to boast of his athletic prowess:

> Our wrestling match today was world class! Have you ever before seen such skill? And what about my gymnastic skills and acrobatics? Did you see how I hoisted my friends up while I was lying down and then lowered them down again? Friend, Madhumaṅgala, where were you? You didn't wrestle with us today! Among us there are many expert in wrestling and gymnastics, but who is as expert as I am? I can high jump; I can lift other boys and let them down again while holding them with my thighs, knees, and shanks!

Madhumaṅgala, who has been sitting idly on the sidelines the whole time, replies.

> Madhumaṅgala: *He sakhā*! What do you know about wrestling? You were too busy with that young parrot to see my wrestling ability! But you would be even more amazed to know what I was studying earlier today.
>
> Kṛṣṇa: What were you studying?
>
> Madhumaṅgala: Astrology.
>
> Kṛṣṇa: From whom?
>
> Madhumaṅgala: From Śrī Bhāguri Muni.
>
> Kṛṣṇa: What is the result?
>
> Madhumaṅgala: Omniscience!
>
> Kṛṣṇa: Oh, can you tell me what I'm thinking?
>
> Madhumaṅgala: Just wait! In a few moments, I'll reveal everything!
>
> Kṛṣṇa: How is that possible?
>
> Madhumaṅgala: By calculating the rising astrological sign.

Thus, Baṭu begins counting on his fingers and drawing lines on the ground, pretending to think deeply. Then he looks up into the sky and moves his head back and forth. Grinning confidently, he then replies.

> Madhumaṅgala: *He priya-sakhā*! Kṛṣṇa-candra! Listen, there is a beautiful valley with two enchanting lakes at the foot of a large mountain. Within these clear lakes swims a golden female swan. And at this very moment you are anxiously pondering how to capture

her. However, you cannot capture her because she is protected by her entourage. Still, you are trying to find—by any means—a way to attain her for yourself. Hey, my friend! This is the enlightened insight I have acquired from my brilliant astrological calculation!

Kṛṣṇa: O Paṇḍitjī! You've read my mind! But will I be able to catch this swan today? Please calculate further and see.

Madhumaṅgala then becomes silent and again pretends to calculate. As his so-called meditation breaks, he replies.

Madhumaṅgala: *He* Kṛṣṇa! I've just realized how you can capture that swan! You must hide behind and take shelter of the trunk of a colorless tree [*vivarṇāgrā śākhā*: Viśākhā-gopī]. And then if you enchant that beautiful *haṁsinī* with your *mohana vaṁśī*, you can catch her in a secluded place and fully enjoy her company! After all, your melodious flute can allure all types of birds and animals! But now I am quite fatigued from my efforts and have overtaxed my brain! Therefore, please present me with suitable remuneration for my service!

Kṛṣṇa: O *rāja* of soothsayers! Please take your reward of pomegranate seeds.

Madhumaṅgala: *He sakhā*! Why do you honor a learned *brāhmaṇa* like me as if I were a young parrot? Is that befitting of someone with your good judgment?

Kṛṣṇa: *He* friend! This *dvija* recited Nārāyaṇa's [Rādhā's] name. You are also a *dvija* by whose mercy Nārāyaṇa [Rādhā] can be attained. Thus, you are both equally venerable! However, because you are more learned, I will give you the whole pomegranate!

Madhumaṅgala (pleased): *He priya-sakhā*! Because you have fed an honest, highly qualified *brāhmaṇa* a whole pomegranate, today two pomegranates will come into your hands, and your ambition to embrace the chest of that *haṁsinī* will be fulfilled.[11]

However, one pomegranate is not enough to fill the belly of Baṭu *dvija-rāja*, and given the morning sports, the entire assembly is also more than ready for breakfast. Coinciding with their hunger, Nandarāṇī calls Madhumaṅgala

11. Adapted from *Kṛṣṇa-bhāvanāmṛta* 6.8–6.23.

to come and make the offering to Narasiṁha-deva as she also invites the entire assembly of *sakhās* to be seated.

The seating in Nanda's *bhajana-mandira* is somewhat formal. The dining room is perfumed with incense. The dining area is covered with fresh cloth and set with golden water pitchers, with seats assigned for each and every cowherd. Śrīdāmā and Subala sit on Kṛṣṇa's left, Balarāma sits on his right, and both Kṛṣṇa's left and right are further flanked by other cowherds. Madhumaṅgala sits across from and facing Kṛṣṇa and is flanked on his left and right by many other cowherds. Nanda Rāja presides over the assembly. Rohiṇī serves the cowherds innumerable dishes and delights, and Yaśodā encourages each *gopī* to personally serve the dishes she has prepared. Despite the somewhat formal nature of the typical daily breakfast, the setting is nonetheless intimate and ripe for *hāsya-rasa*:

> Madhumaṅgala suddenly blurts out, "Kṛṣṇa has no appetite, Balarāma eats only a little rice and yogurt, Śrīdāmā is a small eater by nature, and Subala has become weak from eating too little and thus cannot speak up for himself.[12] Alas! Shameful are those who lack the skill to eat sumptuously. And this is especially so with this food cooked by Rādhikā, its taste defeating the nectar of immortality!
>
> "Alas, in the company of prosaic people, poetic composition is wasted! Nonetheless, I must say something concerning the opportunity at hand. These four categories of foodstuffs before us—that which is licked, chewed, drunk, or sucked—are actually the four fruits of all human pursuits taking shape, and to enjoy them is the fifth, *prema*. But how lamentable it is that only I am eligible for such *prema*!"
>
> Śrīdāmā replies, "Quickly eat these oblations that are your everything! Fill up your belly with those things by which you attained your ill-conceived status as a *brāhmaṇa*, rather than by actual religiousness, what to speak of knowledge of Brahman, O Madhumaṅgala."
>
> Madhumaṅgala responds, taking the high ground, "Ah, Śrīdāmā, you are but a cowherd! Do not speak of Brahman when I am about

12. In Sanskrit dramatic literature, the hero is typically accompanied by a companion known as the *narma-saciva* or *narma-suhṛt*, who acts as a kind of minister to his recreation. Subala is particularly well spoken, as the chief minister of Kṛṣṇa's diversions.

to relish *rasa*, of which you know nothing. Go to the forest and attend to your duty of herding the cows.

"I've studied all the Vedas and their supplements, and despite what others have said, my keen insight tells me there are six *rasas*. Through our six senses—touch, taste, smell, sight, sound, and thought—we experience and thus relish six *rasas*. We touch the softness of this food, taste its savor, smell its fragrance, behold its form, hear its sound while we eat it, and mentally feel blissful having done so. Thus, this sixfold *rasa* of food can be relished through our six senses in the worship of food, by which we are all maintained, whereas those who give up *sabjī*, rice, and *dāl* for some so-called spiritual *rasa* are like those who leave an oasis to run after a mirage."

Balarāma then inquires, "How do you experience the taste of these mellows?"

In reply, Madhumaṅgala explains his *sāttvika-bhāvas*: "I weep profusely if I don't get my curries, and my body is studded with horripilation when I do get my meal. Look! My bodily hue becomes smooth after eating and the color of my complexion changes. I also lose my voice when eating and I become immobile after eating sufficiently."

Śrīdāmā then retorts, "Baṭo! You are a *brāhmaṇa* from the forest. You should eat only leaves, fruits, and roots! You are not supposed to enjoy all this. Go and perform your penances!"

Madhumaṅgala says, "O clever cowherd Śrīdāmā, you are correct! However, I performed penances in my last life, eating only fruits, roots, and leaves. And now in this birth they have transformed into curries! The residents of the material heavens, who are clearly visible to me every day, know that my enjoyment is not possible for those who did not perform penance. How else can it be? While tending your cows, you came in contact with the slight breeze carrying the scent of my body as I walked by you, and thus you became purified by the power of my penances. Therefore, today you can share my enjoyment. Thus, I have showed you how I remember my last birth. Now, as a reward, you must give me sweet rice!"

Vrajeśvarī then tells Rohiṇī, "*Sakhī*, Madhumaṅgala has grown tired of remembering his previous birth and speaking about it. Give this

> ascetic lots of sweet rice!" But as soon as smiling Rohiṇī goes to give him his sweet rice, Subala forbids her, saying, "First, you must feed the monkeys! They are also tired of speaking and they are also ascetics. They tolerate cold and heat. They eat only fruits, flowers, and leaves, and aren't they learned and aware of their previous births?"
>
> Kṛṣṇa says, "Friend Subala! *Brāhmaṇas* are meditating on Brahman, and monkeys are interested only in filling their bellies with bananas. There is a great difference between them!"
>
> Subala says, "Hari, I cannot see any difference between *brāhmaṇas* and monkeys! There is not even any difference between their names—*nara* [man] and *vānara* [monkey]. And Madhumaṅgala has interpreted the word 'Brahman' to refer to his belly, taking it to be unlimited and everlasting. He sits down three times a day to meditate on how to fill up his belly, and for this he is fixed in celibacy. Sometimes he is so absorbed in grabbing huge amounts of cooked food that he eats with two hands, just like a monkey!"
>
> Hearing Subala's joking words, everyone, including Madhumaṅgala, laughs. Madhu then chokes a bit and coughs loudly, his face turning red. Yaśodā says, "Baṭo! Don't laugh while you eat! Wait and calm down! O boys, don't laugh and joke with Madhumaṅgala while he eats."[13]

Kṛṣṇadāsa Kavirāja appears well acquainted with the culinary arts. In *Govinda-līlāmṛta*, as well as in other books, he lists page after page of mouthwatering preparations and their respective cooks along with Rādhikā and Rohiṇī. And all the *sakhās* eat to their full satisfaction, leaving only Yaśodā dissatisfied. What is the cause of her dissatisfaction? It is not with the cooking, the serving, or the *sakhās*: she does not think Kṛṣṇa has eaten enough! And there is some truth to this, for his mind has been vacillating between honoring the meal and the honorable *gopī* who cooked it—Rādhā. Thus, Hari eats to Yaśodā's satisfaction, concerned that his mother might understand his mind and coaxed by Rohiṇī, who reminds him of the trouble Rādhā has taken to cook.

After breakfast, host Nanda Bābā arranges beds for the boys to recline upon and rest. Meanwhile, Yaśodā sits Rādhā and her friends down for breakfast. Yaśodā admires Rādhā, secretly desiring that she marry her son.

13. Adapted from *Kṛṣṇa-bhāvanāmṛta* 6.45–6.87.

Thus, she often gives Rādhā a gift, such as a box of ornaments she has collected that are just suitable for a bride, implying her desire to see Rādhā marry Kṛṣṇa.

Then, after waking from their post-breakfast nap, the cowherds are eager to depart for herding. Among themselves they rearrange their attire in consideration of the adventure ahead, and Kṛṣṇa's *narma-sakhās* separate from the group to wake him. Their own bodies erupting in ecstasy, they shower Madana Gopāla with their tears of *ānanda* and light up his life with their bright, smiling flower-like faces full of dedication and ecstatic anticipation of the *goṣṭha-vihāra* ahead.

Narma-sakhā group leaders engage their followers in assisting them as they dress Hari for herding. They offer scents, fresh cloth, ornaments, and a garland foretelling victory, consisting of five types of forest flowers. They make *tilaka* from musk and grind fragrant sandalwood mixed with their tears into a thick paste and then apply the *tilaka* with their fingers. Then they apply the sandal paste and different-colored mineral dyes in decorative patterns on his face and arms. They place rings on his fingers, some of which have his names engraved on them, and they decorate his ears with shark-shaped earrings that swing and kiss his cheeks. And unable to check their jealousy, they kiss his cheeks themselves! They adorn their dear friend with a jeweled necklace, the centerpiece of which is his Kaustubha-maṇi, and they complement this necklace with a *guñjā-mālā*, which gives his dress and ornamentation an attractive rustic appearance.

Before Subala slips away to meet Viśākhā and exchange Rādhā's cloth for Kṛṣṇa's cloth, he asks one privileged *narma-sakhā* to place a reflective pearl necklace around Hari's neck. This mirror-like necklace allows Kṛṣṇa to see Rādhikā's reflection when he looks down as if to look away. Such is the intimate *sevā* of Śyāma's *narma-sakhās*.

Their Gopāla Kṛṣṇa wears a belt, bracelets, armlets, anklets, and ankle bells. His friends hang his horn on his left side and tuck his jeweled flute into his belt on his right side. In his left hand he holds a stick, and in his right hand he holds a lotus. His crown is a crest of rainbow-like peacock feathers, and in their hands Gopāla himself is the exciting, elusive, priceless prospect said to lie somewhere beyond the sky.

How good does he look? About as good as his friends, who, like him, are also endowed with flutes, horns, ornaments, and *gopa-veśa*, serving more or less as mirrors before him. With similar gestures and gait, their faces bright, they head out to herd with Kṛṣṇa in the center of the assembly, enchanting the minds of the *gopīs*—*kata bane chuṭāchuṭi bane khāi luṭāpuṭi sei dina kabe habe mor*.

20

Forenoon

Pūrvāhna-līlā

During his midmorning *līlā*, Gaurasundara leaves his own house accompanied by his friends, singing and dancing in Śrī Kṛṣṇa *saṅkīrtana*. In the pastures of Godruma along the Gaṅgā delta, Gaura sees charming young cowherds herding beautiful cows of various colors. The cowherds call out to him:

> Brother, you are Gopāla. The form of a *brāhmaṇa* does not suit you. Come! We will carry you on our shoulders, herd cows, and bring you to your mother in Māyāpura. . . . O brother! Come to my house every day. You may be the God of the *brāhmaṇas*, but you are the life of the *gopas*. . . . Look there! Seeing you, all the cows moo and leave aside their grass and calves.[1]

The beautiful forest is filled with exotic birds, and the trees beckon and bow, offering their fruits and flowers to Nimāi Paṇḍita. Amid this scene, the best of the twice-born is transported into his *ābhīra goṣṭha-līlā* of Vraja. Nitāi and others who are internally situated in Vraja's *sakhya-rasa* are transported along with Gaurasundara, donning their *gopa-svarūpas*. Others are transported into their *gopī-svarūpas*, in which they experience the perfection of their lotus eyes—to see Kṛṣṇa accompanied by Rāma and his friends and cows entering the forest.

1. See *Navadvīpa-bhāva-taraṅga* 44–50.

Steeped in fraternal love, Gaura and Nitāi visit the homes of Śrīdhara and other *nitya-siddhas* from the Vraja *līlā* who are also absorbed in *sakhya-rasa*. There, they recall Rāma and Kṛṣṇa's *pūrvāhna-līlā*.

In Vraja, surrounded by countless *sakhās*, Rāma and Kṛṣṇa herd their cows through the main gate and into the fields leading to the forest. Their cows are both grazers and browsers, who thus nibble on both the grass below and the flowering tree branches above. As soon as the cows graze the grass and move forward, new shoots of fresh grass sprout immediately. As the cows nibble on the leaves of the trees, these trees also sprout new leaves.

Even Lakṣmī, who appeared from the ocean of milk, is astonished by the waves of Kṛṣṇa's milk cows, who shake their tails with no need to brush off flies but rather only to increase the splendor of the scene. Here and there, individual cows will kick up their hind legs and tails and "hightail" it toward him at full speed and then come to a complete stop right before him. Then he will speak something sweet into their ears and send them back to the herd. The ears of both the bulls and the cows also long to hear his flute, their snouts to smell the fragrance of his body, their eyes to see his lotus face, their tongues to taste him and vibrate as they call to him. Meanwhile, Kṛṣṇa's friends compose songs and sing in praise of the cows and their comrades, Hali and Hari.

Coming from near and far and passing through Nanda's gate atop Nandīśvara hill, the young *gopas* are stunned by the hill's glories.

> ...filled with the bellowing of cows, the shouts of the cow-herders, and the songs of bards and artisans, shining with love, and dearer to the prince of Vraja than even Mount Govardhana, such is Nandīśvara...which has been created to increase the opulence of the cows...[2]

The sound of the *gopas'* flutes and horns, accompanied by the percussion of the cows' hooves, supports the song and dance of the most extraordinary cowherd boys, gathered in groups denoted by either their ages or their measure of maturity. They hold sticks for herding and some bear sticks for mock fighting. Some *suhṛt-sakhās* bear bows and blunt-tipped arrows, swords, or spears that never harm a hair on any creature's head but that

2. See Raghunātha dāsa Goswāmī's *Vilāpa-kusumāñjali* 60 and *Vraja-vilāsa-stava* 8.

are nonetheless brandished about by cowherds touting their prowess and imagining the possibility of encountering danger and demons deep within Vṛndāvana.

Assembled *brāhmaṇas* chant, "May the two brothers live long!" And as the *sakhās* depart, they discuss their previous group conquests as if the individual cowherds were all one, while distinguishing the glories of Rāma and Kṛṣṇa. Thus, this hour is filled with the joy of the excitement and anticipation that the *sakhās* share with Rāma and Kṛṣṇa, as well as with the welcoming forest just ahead.

However, those left behind feel differently. The tension between *vātsalya-* and *sakhya-rasas* is palpable, while *mādhurya-rasa* makes plans in *parakīya*—*sakhīs* sending secret messages, speaking with longing lotus eyes to Kṛṣṇa's *narma-sakhās* and to Hari himself. Somehow, they will meet under the sun, though the details are still to be determined.

Nanda and Yaśodā, along with other elders, follow Kṛṣṇa as far as they possibly can. And Kṛṣṇa, although facing forward, sees them from the corners of his long lotus eyes, which afford him such cow-like range of vision. Thus, he turns to send the elders back.

Yaśodā then orders and organizes his friends around him, he the central whorl of the lotus of her heart, his friends the surrounding petals. She cares for every inch of Kṛṣṇa, from the topknot and peacock feather that crown his head to the soles of his lotus feet. Thus she bears a parasol and shoes. Kṛṣṇa, however, refuses to accept them, and this impresses his parents with his sense of *dharma*—*gopālanaṁ sva-dharmo*—his oneness with his father's herd:

> Herding the cows is my *dharma*. Just as cows have no shoes and parasols to protect them from the sun, cowherds also go without them—*yathā gāvas tathā gopās*. *Śāstra* states that such is faultless conduct. If one follows *śāstra*, one is protected from both above and below.[3]

Their pride and surprise at their young son's wisdom and religious sensibilities momentarily mitigates their anguish at the thought of his separation. But the scriptures also mandate that one serve Bhagavān and, by extension in her mind, one who bears his name—Kṛṣṇa. Hence Yaśodā passes her parasol to Vijaya-sakhā, who carries it with him for such *sevā*.

Yaśodā then ties a protective amulet consisting of a powerful Narasiṁha *mantra* around her son's wrist and chants the names of Nārāyaṇa presiding

3. *Govinda-līlāmṛta* 5.28–29.

over different parts of his delicate body, weeping because of both her *harināma* and the stunning sight of her son. And before her powerful display of parental affection, Kṛṣṇa cannot but fall at her feet and beg her and Nanda for their permission to proceed, which at last they grant. Śrī Kṛṣṇadāsa Kavirāja writes that they feel as much affection for Balarāma as they feel for Kṛṣṇa.

As Kṛṣṇa moves forward with his hungry herd looking back at him, Yaśodā-nandana turns once more to speak to his parents. Giving Yaśodā a reason to live, he asks her to send someone with sweetened and spiced cheese—*rasālā*—for his lunch, even though all the cowherd boys have packed lunches. Animated, she responds that she will send all his favorite preparations, and she urges him not to wander too far or return too late. Kṛṣṇa replies that he will eat what she sends and return home only if he is assured that she and Nanda will eat something themselves in his absence and be there to receive him.

While his parents and other elders thus remain behind, the *gopīs* do so as well, but only physically, for he takes their minds with him through his enchanting and assuring glance. He speaks to Rādhā through the movements of his eyes, conveying in part his *parakīya* strategy:

> O Sumukhī! Don't lament. Close your eyes and let the sun move toward midday. Then we will meet in the forest at your *kuṇḍa*.[4]

Kavirāja Goswāmī informs us:

> The arrows of Rādhā and Kṛṣṇa's gazes pass one another in midair and then pierce each other's hearts, filling their minds with *ānanda*, despite their pending separation. The current of *prema* takes its own course. Who can understand it? Going to the forest, Kṛṣṇa catches the fish of Rādhā's heart in the net of his beauty and takes it with him, while Rādhā traps the swan of Kṛṣṇa's yearning heart in the cage of her contracted glance![5]

Because Kṛṣṇa takes the *gopīs*' minds with him in this way, their bodies are sure to follow in due course. But for now, the *yūtheśvarīs* all faint in the arms of their maidservants.

In contrast to the condition of those left behind, who go through the motions of their daily duties with their minds elsewhere like those of

4. *Govinda-līlāmṛta* 5.40.
5. *Govinda-līlāmṛta* 5.43.

jīvan-muktas, the immobile forest flora begin to dance, while the fauna take on the complexity of humanlike characteristics. As he touches the border between the pasture and the forest, Kṛṣṇa finds himself in the middle of these two opposite emotional reactions. Thus, he turns to his friends and completely absorbs himself in his *sakhya-rasa goṣṭha-vihāra*, carefree and independent, as the forest, awakened by Vṛndā-devī and decorated with his arrival, explodes into all variety of *sāttvika-bhāvas*.

Vṛndā-devī is the presiding deity of the forests, and thus all the forest flora and fauna are under her jurisdiction. Furthermore, having received a special *siddha-mantra* from *tapasvinī* Paurṇamāsī, she is able to perform what would otherwise be impossible. For example, she can cause a forest to display the specialty of any particular season at any desired moment, or she can make all the seasons manifest anywhere at once. By her service to Kṛṣṇa, it is not surprising to see a fruit tree with one branch bearing new leaves, another branch buds, another flowers, another unripened fruit, another ripe fruit, and another leaves about to fall. Thus, as Kṛṣṇa enters the forest, the following happens under Vṛndā-devī's magical direction:

> The forest gave pleasure to all of Kṛṣṇa's senses: bees by sweetly buzzing, birds by joyfully chirping, fruit by oozing sweet juice in jubilation, and the gentle breeze by acting as a dancing master for the flowering creepers and by flirting with the fully blooming lotuses. Seeing Kṛṣṇa approach, the trees smiled, blossoming with clusters of flowers; they sang with swarms of bees; they danced, fluttering their leaves; they offered drinks in the form of honey, and food in the form of their fruit. The creepers began to serve him by dancing, with secretly smiling faces in the form of their flowers, covered by veils in the form of their leaves, while being kissed by the singing bees.[6]

There are twelve forests—*dvādaśa-vana*—in the Vraja-maṇḍala, all magical, and Rāma and Kṛṣṇa wander at will throughout them with their cows and friends. From north to south, there are five forests on the eastern side of the river Yamunā: Bhadravana, Bhāṇḍīravana, Bilvavana, Lohavana, and Mahāvana. From north to the south on the western side lie Khadiravana, Kāmyavana, Vṛndāvana, Bahulāvana, Madhuvana, Tālavana, and Kumudavana. Aside from these twelve principal forests mentioned in the Purāṇas, Nayanānanda Ṭhākura notes that there are twenty-two

6. *Govinda-līlāmṛta* 6.17–19, translation by Bhanu Swami.

subforests—*upavanas*—beginning with Kadamba-khaṇḍī. Together these forests and Mount Govardhana serve as the primary playground for Kṛṣṇa's *goṣṭha-vihāra*.

Upon entering the forest and being freed from the shackles of parental oversight, all the *sakhās* start to sing and dance. They joke and laugh, bumping into one another and tumbling playfully onto the forest floor. Some friends imitate Kṛṣṇa's attachment to his parents and their attachment to him, while some *narma-sakhās* imitate the *gopīs'* lotus-eyed longing while hiding as if timid behind trees. They cover their heads and peek at Kṛṣṇa, smiling shyly and making fun of him. Others imitate the cows, who while moving forward look backward to see the lotus face of Kṛṣṇa. And when Kṛṣṇa raises a particular point worthy of discussion, sometimes one of his friends questions his premise and refutes him. In this way, they celebrate their intimate hours alone with him who is the attraction of everyone as if he were their equal, while also entertaining him with their athletic skills, stick fighting, and dancing, as others render menial service to him and his older brother.

Like Rāma and Kṛṣṇa's attire, the dress and ornamentation of his friends is astounding! Sometimes they wear colorful headbands or stylish simply tied turbans. They wear earth-toned, finely woven silk-and-cotton cloths of different colors covering their hips and elegant shawls over their shoulders. Overall, they arrange their garments like dramatic performers and connoisseurs of the arts. They stand lavishly decorated from head to toe yet in a manner perfectly suitable for herding and frolicking in the forest. In their hands they hold flutes, the dear friend of the cowherds—*vaṁśī priya-sakhī*—and herding sticks, and around their necks hang garlands of various forest flowers and different-colored pearl necklaces.

Kṛṣṇa's friends appear almost as if they have attained *sārūpya-mukti*, except that only some of them bear the same *śyāma*-colored complexion as Kṛṣṇa.[7] Others bear complexions that are the same whitish color as Balarāma. Still others have pigmentation that varies between golden, reddish, bronze, yellow, blue, and other colors. Some even have multicolored complexions.

7. *Sārūpya-mukti* refers to attaining a form like that of Nārāyaṇa. It is one of four types of *mukti* in Vaikuṇṭha. Here the *sakhās* have attained forms like Kṛṣṇa. However, the *prema* of Goloka exceeds the bliss of *sārūpya-mukti*, which technically speaking does not pertain to Vraja, where Kṛṣṇa is not thought to be God.

Nayanānanda Ṭhākura envisions the young herdsmen heading straight for the base of the great banyan tree after which Bhāṇḍīravana is named, some blowing flutes and horns, others fashioning wind instruments with their hands and leaves, and still others imitating the calls of their mooing cows. The trek from Vṛndāvana to Bhāṇḍīravana is a long one and involves crossing the Yamunā. Some boys swim across with their cows, while others climb across on the long limbs of the majestic banyan that straddles the entire river. At the base of the celestial tree is a solid-gold platform that surrounds it. When they arrive, arrangements are made for Rāma and Kṛṣṇa to rest briefly on this platform for one *daṇḍa* (twenty-four minutes). And the *guru-rūpa-sakhās* guide their followers in rendering various personal services to Rāma and Kṛṣṇa suitable to the circumstances, each boy following in the *bhāva* of their *rāgātmika* role model. Some boys make a bed of fresh leaves. One offers his lap as a pillow, while others massage Kṛṣṇa's lotus feet. Some boys collect ripe fruits and affectionately feed Kṛṣṇa. At the same time, another group of friends similarly serves Balarāma. Then the two groups also exchange services, and thus all the *sakhās* have the opportunity to serve both brothers.

After the brothers rest and refresh themselves with fresh water and forest fruits, amid dancing, singing, and joking, games begin. The favorite of such games in proximity to Śrī Bhāṇḍīra is some form of fighting challenge—tasting *yuddha-vīra-rasa* and the consequences of winning and losing, assisted by the limbs of the tree. Nayanānanda Ṭhākura sings in earnest of this scene, blessing his readers:

> In the company of his cowherds, Hari plays.
> They dance and sing, and then they sit and rest.
> Afterward, they drink cool, refreshing water,
> eat sweet fruits, and wash their hands and mouths.
>
> They chew on betel nuts scented with camphor,
> as Sucandra and others massage the brothers' limbs.
> Kṛṣṇa sweetly speaks *narma-kathā* with Subala
> and other dear ones, smiling, joking, laughing.
>
> Rāma-Kṛṣṇa taste *yuddha-vīra* with their *priya-sakhās*—
> arm wrestling, stick fighting, combat clubs in hand.
> They play *vāhaka-krīḍā*, a game in which
> the losers carry the winners on their shoulders.

Sometimes Rāma's group wins,
and Kānāi carries Śrīdāmā on *his* shoulders.
Other times, Bhagavān climbs on Śrīdāmā's shoulders.
Whoever believes these things will surely behold them.[8]

At any time, any one of the boys can conquer any other!

The *jāta-ruci-sādhaka*, following the lead of his *yūtheśvara* and his *guru-rūpa-sakhā*, who stands beside him, renders service in Bhāṇḍīravana at this time, in accordance with his *ruci*.

Kavi-karṇapūra then envisions Kṛṣṇa turning his attention from his friends to his cows, who he understands are thirsty. Sounding his flute, Śyāma directs the *sakhās* to lead the cows to water. Śrīdāmā takes charge of the cows and bulls and leads them to drink from a nearby pond with a jewel-studded bank. And after they quench their thirst, Śrīdāmā personally feeds them tender shoots from the *śallakī* tree until they are fully satisfied.[9] Then the boys drink, using their hands as cups, splash one another, dive in, and swim. After swimming, they bathe in the sun, dress again, and render personal service to Rāma and Kṛṣṇa, assisting them in the same. Some boys bring flowers. Others paint Kṛṣṇa with colorful clays and mud from the banks of the pond, decorating themselves similarly. *Upa-sakhās* decorate Kṛṣṇa's hair with flowers and place flowers over his ears, while those in *narma-sakhā-bhāva* whisper into his ears, imparting messages from their *yūtheśvarīs*. Some boys climb trees and pick fruits such as mangoes and jackfruit. Some make fans out of the fallen feathers of peacocks and fan the objects of their love.

Beautiful, placid ponds can be found in all the forests of Vraja. They are still and peaceful like the minds of self-realized sages. However, when the cowherds swim in them, the waves they create are miraculously all concentric, owing to the boys being centered only on pleasing Kṛṣṇa. These waves, all in concentric circles, bring beauty and movement to the ponds, a beauty that adds to rather than takes away from the ponds' stillness—turning peace into love.

Nayanānanda Ṭhākura highlights Bhāṇḍīravana, Kāmyavana, Bahulāvana, and Madhuvana in his description of the *pūrvāhna-līlā*. The cowherds

8. See *Preyo-bhakti-rasārṇava*, chapter 8. This Bengali song is to be sung in *toḍi-rāga*, appropriate for late morning. *Toḍi* is depicted graphically as a gentle, beautiful woman anointed with saffron and camphor, holding a *vīṇā* and standing surrounded by deer in a lovely green forest, where she fosters fun and frolicking.

9. *Śallakī* (*Boswellia serrata*) is a plant that produces Indian frankincense.

visit these forests and others freely, according to their will. The multitude of *sakhās* move as if one, each boy's mind focused differently but only on Rāma and Kṛṣṇa. And regardless of whether close to the two brothers or at some apparent distance, all the boys feel the same measure of affection from them. They are all different and one; all close, never far.

As mentioned earlier, no one can compare with Balarāma at playing ball. Such is the insight of Nayanānanda Ṭhākura. And among the *sakhās*, the variety of games involving balls is unlimited. Newer and newer ball-centered games are created by the day, and they occupy a good portion of the *pūrvāhna-līlā*. One such game spontaneously created by Balarāma in Madhuvana involves any round fruit that has fallen to the forest floor. In this game, the *sakhās* collect whatever round fruits they can find and throw these balls at one another. Anyone who is hit by a ball is eliminated, and in the end, one winner is left standing. Although this is a typical *pūrvāhna-līlā* game, let us reflect on the first time it was played at Madhuvana.

Although Balarāma is best at ballhandling, this does not mean he is best at avoiding being hit by a ball, especially when teamed up on, which is within the rules of play. Thus, he argues that in this ball game, despite his advantage in ballhandling, the field of play is leveled because others can hit him with a ball. However, Hari proves difficult to hit, owing to his speed and exceptional athleticism.

As Hari eludes everyone's effort to hit him with a ball, all the boys team up to defeat him, while Balarāma observes, now taking the role of referee. According to their plan, four *sakhās* hide in the brush surrounding a large wish-fulfilling tree, while all the other *sakhās* throw their balls *at* Kṛṣṇa but purposely over his head toward the tree. Seeing this and confident of his speed and dexterity, Kṛṣṇa runs to the base of the tree to collect the balls with the intention of hitting each of his friends as they approach, eliminating them all. But as he reaches the tree and before he can collect even one ball, the four friends emerge from hiding and bombard him with balls!

However, as the boys celebrate their victory over Kṛṣṇa, he raises an objection, claiming that because he is the son of the king of the cowherds, he should receive deferential treatment. This is met with absolute outrage, and Balarāma calls foul. Thus, not only is Kṛṣṇa eliminated from the game but also his friends tie him to the tree and ignore him for the better part of the hour as they invent new games and play on without him, leaving Kṛṣṇa weeping and wailing, his tears flooding the roots of the tree towering over him in fraternal love.

But why does he weep? Why does he not resist when they begin to tie him to the tree? Why does he not argue further or call on Balarāma's sense of fairness, claiming that elimination is one thing but tying him to the tree is also out of bounds, and thus make the case that the two fouls canceled one another out? The skillful *sakhya-rati-sādhaka* knows that Kānāi-lālā weeps not out of dismay or any sense of unfairness. Bhagavān weeps uncontrollably in ecstasy, relishing the extent to which he is being treated as an equal among friends and experiencing that he himself has attained *sakhya-rasa*!

After playing such games, Kṛṣṇa leads his friends and cows to the foot of Mount Govardhana. Here the cows drink from Mānasa-gaṅgā, and the *sakhās* once again relish *jala-keli*, swimming along with their cows. However, at this time the lady-like forest begins to remind Kṛṣṇa of his lady lover, Śrī Rādhā.

Seeing the vines embrace the trees, he is reminded of her embrace. The golden color of the *campaka-latā* reminds him of her lustrous complexion. The wide eyes of the deer attracted to his beauty remind him of Rādhā's affectionate gaze. The chirping of various birds reminds him of Rādhā's ankle bells and the bells around her waist, and the blooming lotuses remind him of her beautiful face. Indeed, the entire forest becomes an *uddīpana* for his *prema-mādhurya*, reminding him of her *rūpa-mādhurī*. Thus, he hungers for her embrace while he simultaneously becomes concerned for the hunger of his friends as midday approaches.

Suddenly Dhaniṣṭhā appears as a godsend and answer to Kṛṣṇa's two conflicting concerns. She is a *gopī* maidservant of Yaśodā who resides in Nandagrāma. Her love for Rādhā and Kṛṣṇa is extraordinary, but she favors Kṛṣṇa over Rādhā, and thus she is one of his confidantes in his romantic pursuits. She and several maidservants bear refreshments for Kṛṣṇa and his young *gopālas*. She also appeases his hunger for Rādhā because Kṛṣṇa sees her as an ideal person through whom he can deliver a message to Rādhā, given that Jaṭilā is not suspicious of her. However, now Kṛṣṇa is also met with the challenge of separating himself from his *sakhās*, *suhṛt-sakhās*, and *priya-sakhās*, and he does so with the help of his *narma-sakhās*, who are tied to his romantic heart.

Madhumaṅgala, despite his voracious tongue and never-ending appetite, prefers to tend to Kṛṣṇa's hunger for Rādhikā. Thus, he uncharacteristically excuses himself from the meal early, explaining that he has a prior appointment at Sūrya-kuṇḍa with a famous astrologer. It is as if Kṛṣṇa's heart has a mind in the form of his *narma-sakhā*, leading him to his heart's desire. When he hears Madhumaṅgala's fabricated excuse for departing, his heart floods with love for both his *narma-sakhā* and Rādhā, and he expresses a keen interest in accompanying Madhumaṅgala with a small number of like-minded friends. Every day some similar excuse arises from Kṛṣṇa or one of his *narma-sakhās*, which sets the stage for their midday departure and Śyāma's rendezvous with Rādhā.

Kṛṣṇa assures the other boys that he will return shortly, while simultaneously glorifying Balarāma and inspiring the greater balance of the infinite number of *sakhās* to remain with and serve him exclusively until he returns. The oneness of Kṛṣṇa and Balarāma in terms of *tattva* is underscored in this *līlā*, as is the emotional difference between them as well. The rest of the boys are content to remain with Rāma because the two brothers are nondifferent, while the *narma-sakhās* are particularly tuned in to the emotional difference between the two brothers and are thus carried with Kṛṣṇa into his romanticism.

Then Dhaniṣṭhā tells her assistants to return to Nandagrāma while she remains to pick some flowers for the *pūjā* of Bhagavān Narasiṁha, the household deity of Nanda Rāja. This is her excuse for remaining in the forest and making herself available to assist Kṛṣṇa in his effort to meet with Rādhā in broad daylight. Because from an astrological perspective it is thought that excursions begun when the moon is in Dhaniṣṭhā *nakṣatra* will be most successful, Dhaniṣṭhā's presence helps to assure Kṛṣṇa that he will be successful in his midday excursion. Here we find Dhaniṣṭhā in the *sevā* of Śrī Kṛṣṇa-candra![10]

When Kṛṣṇa separates from the greater group of *sakhās*, he is accompanied by Madhumaṅgala and Subala, who represent *narma-sakhā-bhāva*. Typically his *līlā-śakti* personified, Vṛndā-devī, also appears on the scene and places *campaka* flowers—symbolic of Rādhā—in Kṛṣṇa's hands. In this way, Vṛndā subtly assures Kṛṣṇa that he will be successful in his pursuit of a midday *milana* (meeting) with Rādhā, which causes him to tremble.[11]

10. In Hindu astrology a *nakṣatra* denotes a lunar mansion, and in Indian astronomy a *nakṣatra* is one of twenty-eight sectors along the ecliptic. Dhaniṣṭhā is the twenty-third. In Hindu scriptures the personified *nakṣatras* are the daughters of Dakṣa and wives of the moon god, Candra. In Vraja it was customary to name one's daughter after the *nakṣatra* related to the time of her birth.

11. Here we are following the depiction of a typical yet particular day described in *Govinda-līlāmṛta*. The spirit of this section of the *pūrvāhna-līlā* is that with the help of the *narma-sakhās*, Vṛndā, and others, Rādhā and Kṛṣṇa overcome various hurdles relative to their *parakīya-bhāva*, thus assuring the youthful couple's midday *milana*. Thus, this portion of the *līlā* is filled with intrigue played out in a wide variety of pastimes.

Madhumaṅgala then takes the flowers from Kṛṣṇa's hand and places them over his friend's ears, indicating further that Kṛṣṇa will soon be ornamented by Rādhā's love. And as the magnolias decorate Kṛṣṇa's *rūpa-mādhurya*, they too become more beautiful.

In the company of his *narma-sakhās*, Dhaniṣṭhā, and Vṛndā, Kṛṣṇa gains confidence, seeing them as skilled generals in his effort to conquer the kingdom of love that Rādhā embodies. Kṛṣṇadāsa Kavirāja describes Kṛṣṇa's generals as highly skilled in the arts of conquering and ruling. Thus, Kṛṣṇa tightly grasps Madhumaṅgala's right hand with his left hand and heads toward Kusuma-sarovara, halfway between Govardhana and Rādhā-kuṇḍa, along with Dhaniṣṭhā, Vṛndā, and Subala, plotting along the way.

Meanwhile, Rādhā has returned to Yāvaṭa, escorted by Kundalatā, who expertly puts Jaṭilā at ease by declaring that she guarded Rādhā so closely that she did not touch even the shadow of Kṛṣṇa. She also explains the new ornaments in Rādhā's possession to be a gift from Yaśodā, indicating her satisfaction with Rādhā's cooking and behavior. Jaṭilā then tells Kundalatā and Rādhā's feisty supporter Lalitā to accompany her daughter-in-law to Sūrya-kuṇḍa, where Rādhā will worship the sun god to increase the prosperity of her son and strengthen Rādhā's marriage vow. Jaṭilā tells her to collect the following items required for the worship of the sun god, also known as Mitra—the patron divinity of friendship:[12] a reddish copper pot; milk, yogurt, and ghee from an *aruṇa*-colored cow; various items cooked in that same ghee; molasses, red hibiscus flowers, saffron, red sandalwood, and a lotus garland.

Jaṭilā of course has been duped, as the proposed pilgrimage to Sūrya-kuṇḍa serves as Rādhā's opportunity to meet Kṛṣṇa. Thus, Rādhā and her friends, intoxicated by this prospect, support one another as they stagger to Rādhā's quarters. Therein Rādhā reclines. And her *mañjarīs* Rūpa and Rati, in intimate *sevā* that borders on friendship, climb onto her bed with her to massage her lotus feet.

Meanwhile, Vṛndā has sent a variety of forest flowers to Rādhā from which to make a garland for Kṛṣṇa. Thus, Rādhikā sews her love into the wreath and also prepares *pān* for her lover. Then she gives these gifts to Tulasī-mañjarī and Kastūrī-mañjarī to bring to Kṛṣṇa and tells them to find out from Subala

12. "Mitra" also implies that which brings about an alliance, friendship being central to bonding. The reddish items appropriate for the worship of the sun correspond with his color at sunrise—*aruṇa*—the color of *sakhya-rasa*. Mitra is also known as *padma-bandhu*, the "friend of the lotus," which opens its petals and reveals its beauty through his association. Thus, lotus flowers are also included in Sūrya *pūjā*.

and Vṛndā details concerning her planned rendezvous with Kṛṣṇa on this particular day. Rādhā then goes to her kitchen, ostensibly to prepare sweets for Sūrya *pūjā* but with the intention of offering them to Kṛṣṇa.

Upon his arrival at Kusuma-sarovara, Kṛṣṇa relishes the serene setting, but his mind is occupied with strategies on how to proceed. If he signals Rādhā by playing his flute, many other *gopīs* will also come. If he sends Vṛndā, Subala, or Madhumaṅgala, they will arouse Jaṭilā's suspicion, given their well-known allegiance to him. Thus, he concludes that sending a message with Dhaniṣṭhā to Kundalatā, who favors him and has Jaṭilā's implicit trust, is the best course to take. But Vṛndā, while agreeing, adds that patience is a virtue and it is quite possible that one of Rādhā's handmaidens could be in the area picking flowers. And if they have the advantage of meeting one of them before proceeding, they will be better informed about Rādhā's present situation and thus in a better position to make a well-thought-out plan of action.

As fate would have it, Tulasī-mañjarī arrives on the scene at that exact moment. She is delighted to find Kṛṣṇa discussing the means to attain Rādhā with his admirable associates, all of whom are well aware of Tulasī's intimacy with Rādhā. Thus, they all joyfully marvel at this sudden turn of events and the insight of Vṛndā. Kṛṣṇa then concludes that because Tulasī-mañjarī, also known as Rati, is never far from Rādhā, surely she is nearby as well, and his otherwise restless eyes focus on the forest pathway. Tulasī then gives the garland sewn by Rādhā to Madhumaṅgala and the betel she prepared to Subala. Madhu garlands Kṛṣṇa, who in turn gives his red *guñjā-mālā* to Tulasī, expressing his *anurāga* for Rādhā.

Rādhā and her *mañjarīs* go hand in hand. Without her *mañjarīs*, there will be no union between Rādhā and Kṛṣṇa. And Kṛṣṇa knows this very well. Kṛṣṇadāsa Kavirāja depicts Tulasī-mañjarī pretending that Rādhā has been restrained by Jaṭilā, sending Kṛṣṇa into the depths of despair, only to bring him out of it by telling him she was only joking. Thus, she has him in her hands. And everyone present is delighted to see her bring out his love for Rādhā. Thus, to the delight of Kṛṣṇa, it is determined that Rādhā will meet Kṛṣṇa at Rādhā-kuṇḍa, and Tulasī and Vṛndā prepare to go there to make prior arrangements. More precisely, on this day they will meet at the bower of Viśākhā named Madana-sukhada-kuñja, just northeast of Rādhā-kuṇḍa.

Tulasī/Rati-mañjarī serves within the *gaṇa* of Viśākhā, a subgroup within the *yūtha* of Rādhā. Thus, she plays a prominent role in the *Govinda-līlāmṛta* of Kṛṣṇadāsa Kavirāja Goswāmī, who, as we learned earlier, in his *mañjarī-svarūpa* as Kasturi-mañjarī is a follower of his guru, Raghunātha dāsa Goswāmī/Rati-mañjarī. And for our purposes, Viśākhā is an ideal *yūtheśvarī* for *narma-sakhā-bhāva*. Like Rādhā, her heart is very soft.

Who could be more dear to Rādhā than Viśākhā? She was born on the same day and at the same time as Rādhikā, and because "Viśākhā" and "Rādhā" are two different names for the same *nakṣatra*, these two maidens bear the same name. Moreover, they are similar to one another in conduct, qualities, and resolve. Arguably, Viśākhā is Rādhā's best friend.

Viśākhā's father, Pāvana, is a scholar. And following in his footsteps his daughter is also very learned and a teacher of the arts—especially singing. She also excels in clever and humorous speech, defeating even Saraswatī in eloquence. Her grove, selected for today's tryst, is compared to a rain-cloud. It is illumined by Viśākhā's *bhāva* and her complexion that is more brilliant than lightning. In contrast to that brilliance, her dress is like the night sky speckled with stars. Thus the grove serves Kṛṣṇa's purpose well. According to the plan, he will wait there along with his *narma-sakhās* for Rādhā's arrival.

However, the intrigue leading to Rādhā and Kṛṣṇa's *milana* would not be complete without the complications arising from Candrāvalī's parallel effort to meet Kṛṣṇa. Here the expertise of Tulasī's *mañjarī-bhāva* in navigating the obstacle course of *parakīya* is notable and comparable to that of Kṛṣṇa's *narma-sakhās*, who on any given day may be burdened with a similar task. Candrāvalī must be pacified and Rādhā must be victorious. After all, the light of the moon is but a reflection of the sun's shine.[13]

Candrāvalī is of course a particular *bhāva* personified. In the broadest sense, Rādhā is a *vāmā-nāyikā* and Candrāvalī is a *dakṣiṇā-nāyikā*. Here *vāmā* (left) and *dakṣiṇā* (right) refer to dominant and submissive heroines (*nāyikās*), respectively.[14] Śrī Rūpa has written two verses, one in which

13. Candrāvalī (many moons), a personified aspect of Rādhā (astrologically related to the sun), is a very important character in this transcendental romantic comedy. However, her role is for the most part that of a foil, and as such she is often the butt of jokes and derision on the part of Rādhā's supporters. She is dramatically employed to bring out from Rādhā that which so enchants Kṛṣṇa. But given her nature, she is satisfied in this role. She could never deal with Kṛṣṇa as Rādhā does, nor does she think that Rādhā should.

14. Rādhā is the source of all the different romantic *bhāvas* we find individually manifest as different *gopīs*. Nonetheless, she has her dominant nature, which is most attractive to Kṛṣṇa. Although rarely, she does at times express the *dakṣiṇā-bhāva* for Kṛṣṇa's pleasure. We find an example of this in the *madhyāhna-līlā* narrative of Kavi-karṇapūra's *Kṛṣṇāhnika-kaumudī*.

Rādhā speaks and the other in which Candrāvalī speaks, wherein they each criticize the other and in so doing describe the other's mood.

Rādhā speaking to a friend:

> Candrāvalī has an ambiguous attitude; she tries to cover all bases; her approach to love is simpleminded; I think she is naturally dumb. She makes the lotus of expertise in pleasing a man wither up and die, and what is more, she delights in these flaws. And yet, somehow, she is being engaged in trying to bring life to Kṛṣṇa's hopes! *Sakhī*, on seeing this, is there anyone on earth who can stand for it?

Candrāvalī speaking to a friend:

> Stop trying to persuade me to be meaner to Kṛṣṇa! And don't even mention the name of that other *gopī*, what to speak of comparing her to the full moon with all its sixteen phases. Her wicked behavior would enrage even a tranquil-hearted monk. Fie on her! The prince of Gokula, the most virtuous of the virtuous, who is worshiped by all the people of Vraja, falls down at her feet, and yet she does not even move her eyebrows to acknowledge his presence![15]

Returning to our narrative, Candrāvalī's *sakhī* Śaibyā comes to bring Kṛṣṇa to Candrāvalī. But seeing Rādhā's *mañjarī*, she attempts to hide her purpose and claims that she is on a mission to invite Rādhā to Candrāvalī's festival involving the worship of Durgā.[16] Tulasī, of course, sees through Śaibyā's deception and outwits her, claiming that she is there for the purpose of picking flowers and bringing Vṛndā to a prior engagement of Rādhā's with Śyāmalā at Rādhā's request. In other words, her presence there has absolutely nothing to do with Kṛṣṇa, whom she ignores as if he is not even present, and then she quickly departs with Vṛndā and Dhaniṣṭhā.

Then Kṛṣṇa feigns interest in meeting with Candrāvalī but suggests a distant meeting place—Gaurī-tīrtha—and begs for her patience given his present cowherding responsibilities. And playing along, Madhumaṅgala pretends to remind Kṛṣṇa of an important message from Nanda delivered by Dhaniṣṭhā. Thus, assisted by Madhu and employing his own expertise at improvising, Kṛṣṇa strengthens his case for Candrāvalī's patience, buying himself time.

15. *Ujjvala-nīlamaṇi* 9.48–49, translation by Jagadānanda dāsa.

16. Just as Rādhā worships Sūrya, Candrāvalī worships Durgā. Each *gopī*'s deity is determined astrologically.

> O Madhu, yes! Overwhelmed with joyful thoughts of meeting with Candrāvalī, I almost forgot. What would I do without your keen memory?
>
> Dear Śaibyā, Vasudeva told my father that Kaṁsa has sent rustlers to Vṛndāvana today to steal our cows, and my father sent this warning to us through Dhaniṣṭhā. Thus, Madhu and I are scouting in this area and are about to return to herding. Therefore, if I'm tardy today it is in consideration of extenuating circumstances. But I will come as soon as possible.[17]

Thus, Kṛṣṇa deceives Candrāvalī's *sakhī* and pretends to return to cowherding, while Śaibyā, confident she has been successful in arranging a meeting between Kṛṣṇa and Candrāvalī, returns to her mistress. But as she departs, Kṛṣṇa heads to Rādhā-kuṇḍa and Śyāma-kuṇḍa with Subala and Madhumaṅgala.

The entire area of Rādhā-kuṇḍa/Śyāma-kuṇḍa is filled with a great variety of forest bowers, presided over by *sakhīs* and *narma-sakhās* and dedicated to the service of Rādhā and Kṛṣṇa. All of Rādhā's eight closest friends—Lalitā, Viśākhā, Citrā, Indulekhā, Campakalatā, Raṅga-devī, Tuṅgavidyā, and Sudevī—preside over bowers surrounding Rādhā-kuṇḍa, and there are also eight bowers surrounding Śyāma-kuṇḍa presided over by Kṛṣṇa's *narma-sakhās*, who have dedicated their *kuñjas* to the service of their *yūtheśvarīs*.

To the northwest lies Subala's *kuñja*, dedicated to Rādhā; to the north lies Madhumaṅgala's *kuñja*, dedicated to Lalitā; to the northeast lies Ujjvala's *kuñja*, dedicated to Viśākhā; to the east lies Arjuna's *kuñja*, dedicated to Citrā; to the southeast lies Gandharva's *kuñja*, dedicated to Indulekhā; to the south lies Vidagdha's *kuñja*, dedicated to Campakalatā; to the southwest lies Bhṛṅga's *kuñja*, dedicated to Raṅga-devī; and to the west lies Kokila's *kuñja*, dedicated to Sudevī.

Candrāvalī cannot come to this area dedicated solely to Rādhā. Here Vṛndā employs hundreds of forest *devīs*, who pick fruits and collect flowers and other items for Rādhā-Kṛṣṇa's *sevā*, storing them in jeweled cottages that also surround Rādhā-kuṇḍa. Throughout the area are numerous crystal pathways and celestial trees, at whose bases are jeweled platforms of different shapes and sizes that, among other things, act as dramatic stages upon which Rādhā and Kṛṣṇa, their *sakhīs*, and Kṛṣṇa's *narma-sakhās* enact pleasure pastimes.

17. See *Govinda-līlāmṛta* 6.83–85.

In his *Govinda-līlāmṛta*, Kṛṣṇadāsa Kavirāja describes his mystical vision of this area in considerable detail over many, many verses. Indeed, this area, in which Rādhā-kuṇḍa and Śyāma-kuṇḍa are imagined to be the eyes of the peacock-shaped Mount Govardhana, is central to Gauḍīya Vaiṣṇava *nitya-līlā-sevā*. Kavirāja Goswāmī encourages his readers to believe in his mystical vision and to see it themselves.

> These two *kuṇḍas* appear in their actual form—*svarūpa*—in the hearts of *siddhas* and also in the hearts of *sādhakas* who develop the appropriate *bhāva*. But to materialistic people they appear mundane.[18]

When Kṛṣṇa arrives there, he is greeted by Dhaniṣṭhā and Vṛndā, and as Vṛndā shows him her elaborate arrangements, she reminds him of Rādhā. Thus, he sends Dhaniṣṭhā to hasten her arrival. He also instructs Vṛndā to post two *sakhīs*—one on the cow path, the other on the path leading to Gaurī-tīrtha—to deceive and turn away any possible wayward cowherd friend on the cow path and any *sakhī* of Candrāvalī on the other path who might be looking for him as he waits impatiently in the company of his *narma-sakhās* for Rādhikā's arrival.

18. *Govinda-līlāmṛta* 7.119.

21

Midday

Madhyāhna-līlā

On the bank of the Ganges within a beautiful forest filled with the scent and sight of colorful flowers, Gaurasundara tastes Rādhā-Mādhava's midday Śyāma-kuṇḍa and Rādhā-kuṇḍa *līlās*. Revelation of these *līlās* and the exalted status of Rādhā-kuṇḍa are unique contributions of the Gauḍīya *sampradāya* to the religious world. They are great treasures that would have otherwise remain sealed.[1]

In Viśvanātha Cakravartī Ṭhākura's vision, the flower garden in which Gaura tastes these *līlās* is hidden from the general public. Groups of tall *kadamba* trees surround it in all four directions, and at the base of these trees, dense thornbushes grow. These thornbushes discourage others from going there. The love life of Rādhā-Kṛṣṇa is sweeter than roses, but we will have to pass through the sharp thorns of renunciation to appreciate its scent.

Love is not realized without risk. The meeting of Rādhā-Govinda at midday is risky, and their devotees go to great lengths to bring it about. During these pastimes, both the *gopīs* and the *priya-narma-gopas* are prepared to give their lives for the union of Rādhā-Mādana Gopāla. They cannot bear the pain of Rādhā's separation from Kṛṣṇa or Kṛṣṇa's separation from Priyājī, yet for them to meet under the midday sun is next to impossible without some kind of intrigue. Thus, we pray at midday following the

1. The *Padma Purāṇa* does equate Rādhā with her *kuṇḍa*; it also points out the virtue of bathing in her lake and narrates the *līlā* within which Rādhā-kuṇḍa appears. But the Gauḍīya founding *ācāryas* have underscored the glory of Rādhā-kuṇḍa and disclosed far more than anyone else concerning Rādhā and Kṛṣṇa's midday romance at Rādhā-kuṇḍa.

footsteps of Subala, *yugala-milana sukhera kāraṇa jīvana chāḍite pāri*: "To bring about the union of Rādhā-Kṛṣṇa, I am prepared to give up my life."[2]

Siddha Kṛṣṇadāsa envisions Gaura's midday *līlā* taking place along the bank of the Ganges. In his vision, Gaurasundara experiences the six seasons of Nadīyā corresponding with those of Vraja. As Svarūpa Dāmodara leads *līlā-kīrtana* of Kṛṣṇa's *madhyāhna-līlā*, Gaura Kṛṣṇa and his devotees experience the various midday *līlās* at Rādhā-kuṇḍa and other parts of Vraja. Siddha Kṛṣṇadāsa depicts Gaura's enactment of Holī, the springtime "festival of colors," in particular. This *līlā* begins with Gaurīdāsa Paṇḍita in the mood of Subala covering Gadādhara with colors as an intense battle ensues. At the end, Gaurīdāsa emerges declaring victory for Gaura's side.

In his *Śrī Śrī Gaura-tattvāmṛta*, Śrī Gauralāla Goswāmī envisions Gopāla in the midst of the midday Holī Vraja *līlā*. Battle-worn and exhausted from his skirmish with the *gopīs*, Śyāma has his pride at risk. But Subala-sakhā intervenes and saves his friend's dignity with his brilliant play on words. Śrī Goswāmījī then concludes, "Therefore, since that Subala has appeared today in Śrī Gaura *līlā* as Śrī Gaurīdāsa Paṇḍita Ṭhākura, just by taking the shelter of his lotus feet one can attain the great fortune of seeing even the most confidential *līlā* of *nidhū-nikuñja*. What doubt is there about it?"

In his *madhyāhna-līlā*, sometimes Gaura steps aside from his associates in a moment of introspection. The poet Rādhā-mohana sings,

> "O brother, you know my heart, so why do you delay? Please bring her! Show me Rādhā or I will die!" Taking Prabhu with him, Gaurīdāsa steps into the water. Showing Gaura his reflection, Gaurīdāsa says, "There is your Rādhā!" Gaura then takes the reflection of his own face to be that of Rādhā. Tears of love flow, and his heart becomes happy. Rādhā-mohana says, "But for Gaurīdāsa, who else knows the depths of Prabhu's heart?"

Rūpa Goswāmī describes the *madhyāhna-līlā* as consisting of a multitude of pastimes, all of which decorate Rādhā and Kṛṣṇa with a variety of ecstatic emotions. Prominent among these *līlās* is Rādhikā's Sūrya *pūjā*. This *līlā*

2. This phrase is from *Siddhi-lālasā* 10 of Bhaktivinoda's *Gītā-mālā*. It is spoken in his *mañjarī-bhāva*, but as we shall see at the conclusion of this chapter, it also applies to *narma-sakhās*, as exemplified by Subala.

takes place on Sunday, the day designated for worship of the sun god.[3] *Govinda-līlāmṛta* centers its *madhyāhna-līlā* narrative on this *pūjā* pastime. It occurs on a typical Sunday during the months of the year that Rādhā resides at Yāvaṭa, where she is more restricted by proximity to her in-laws.

Kṛṣṇadāsa Kavirāja takes his readers on a long and winding road to Sūrya *pūjā* by veering left and right along the way, following *mahābhāva-svarūpiṇī* Rādhā's various moods. He also shows how these *bhāvas* affect *dhīra-lalita* Kṛṣṇa. It becomes abundantly clear that Gauḍīya Vaiṣṇavism is about Rādhā's love for Kṛṣṇa, a love—*hlādinī*—of which there is a little in every devotee.

The *madhyāhna-līlā* is optimal in terms of the opportunity it presents Kṛṣṇa's *narma-sakhās* to relish their highest reach in the realm of *rasa*—*rūḍha-mahābhāva*. In our narrative, we find Kṛṣṇa at Rādhā-kuṇḍa along with his *narma-sakhās*, and Tulasī-mañjarī bringing Rādhā the *guñjā-mālā* of Kṛṣṇa and the magnolias that previously decorated his ears. As Tulasī arrives, she offers these gifts to Rādhā, who is further reminded of him whom she is already fully absorbed in thought of. Her *mahābhāva* is so deep that her associates are fully occupied in attending to it at every step. She vacillates between pretending to be uninterested in Kṛṣṇa and outwardly longing for his embrace. She laments out loud about her fate, surrounded as she is by a husband who speaks harshly, an envious cousin, a sister-in-law who hates her, and a treacherous, busybody mother-in-law—all of whom are obstacles to the pursuit of her heart's passion, who is the love of every other girl's life.

Coming to Rādhā's emotional rescue, Dhaniṣṭhā arrives and brings the news that Kṛṣṇa is longing for Rādhā while waiting for his beloved at her *kuṇḍa*. Rādhā is uplifted from her ocean of ecstatic despair, and our Goddess departs, flanked by Lalitā and Viśākhā and followed by Tulasī and Rūpa. A host of their followers also depart, bearing items for their maiden's service and the paraphernalia required for Sūrya *pūjā* collected previously by Kundalatā. As Rādhā enters the forest, its splendor reminds her of Kṛṣṇa. Simultaneously, the same forest reminds Kṛṣṇa of Rādhā.

Seeing a buck running with a herd of does, Rādhā is reminded of Kṛṣṇa's flirtatious nature and the fact that many *yūtheśvarīs* roam the forest in hope of meeting with him. Suddenly, she sees a dark *tamāla* tree encircled by a golden vine and with a peacock perched upon it, the composite of which she mistakes for Kṛṣṇa crowned with the plume of a peacock and embraced by a *gopī* glowing with a golden countenance. And when her associates try

3. *Govinda-līlāmṛta* 2.49.

to tell her otherwise, she turns against them, assuming they are defending Kṛṣṇa rather than supporting her. Then, realizing her mistake with their help, embarrassed, she laughs at herself along with them. Such are the effects of her *mahābhāva*.

Meanwhile, Kṛṣṇa's condition at Rādhā-kuṇḍa is critical. There in Viśākhā's bower, after Subala garlands him with a wreath of golden *campaka* flowers, the color of which reminds him of Rādhā's complexion and intensifies his longing for her, he lies in a faint attended by his *narma-sakhās*. On such occasions, Subala's followers also have the opportunity to render intimate *sevā* to Rādhā's *nāgara*. *Narma-sakhās* fan him and sing appropriate songs recounting his love life in melodies suitable for midday, their voices more beautiful than the birdsong of the Asian koel. Indeed, the birds gather in silence to listen to the singing of the *narma-sakhās*. One can never say enough about their songs and the sound of their voices, which affect even Kṛṣṇa's dreaming as he lies in trance. Such *līlā-kīrtana* gives Kṛṣṇa internal visions that are as real as those of his waking experience, or even more real. Through *kīrtana*, *sādhana-siddha sakhās* have entered this meditative supersubjective realm, and then from within this realm they again engage in Hari *kīrtana*! *Kīrtana* leads to a kind of meditation that leads to another level of *kīrtana* altogether. Surely many *narma-sakhās* have honed the art of such singing under the tutelage of their *yūtheśvarī* Viśākhā here in her grove.

To the sound of his *sakhās*' song, Kṛṣṇa comes to his senses, and the scent of Rādhā's body also reaches him from the forest. Hearing detailed descriptions of her beauty and charm in the *kīrtana* of his *narma-sakhās*, Kṛṣṇa begins to hallucinate, mistaking features of the forest to be Rādhā approaching. As he rises to approach her, Subala supports and steadies him, bringing him to his senses. Then, remembering something about Rādhā that he previously experienced along with Subala, Kṛṣṇa tries to put his feelings into words. The following gleaned from the heart of Caṇḍīdāsa serves as a typical example of such an effort:

> Dear friend, Subala! Please tell me, where is that blessed girl we just saw the other day bathing at the Yamunā? Tender in age, that *navīna-kiśorī* had a brilliant golden complexion. She was sitting partially immersed in the water with one leg crossed over another while cleansing her beautiful body. As she came out of the river, the tresses of her dark hair fell upon the curve of her golden hips. She was using her *sāri* as a ground cover to sit upon, and her braid was untied and disheveled.

A golden necklace was swaying near the base of her breasts, which were more shapely than Mount Sumeru. Dazzling were her two conch-shell bangles, like two slender phases of the moon, that made me forget everything.

She was wending her way while wringing out her wet blue *sāri*, and along with it my very life! Since the day of that *darśana*, Subala, my heart has been restless, overcome with a feverish pitch of passionate *prema*.[4]

And Subala replies along these lines:

O Nāgara-cāṅda, sweetest moon of lovers, you refer to the daughter of Rāja Vṛṣabhānu—Vinodinī Rādhā. She is coming to meet you, overcoming all obstacles, which serve only to strengthen her resolve.

Fortunately, Vṛndā arrives and pacifies Kṛṣṇa further, volunteering to find Rādhā in the distant forest and hasten her arrival. Subala then removes from over Kṛṣṇa's ears two blue lotus buds that have been sweetened by his maddening musk-like bodily aroma and hands them to Vṛndā to give to Rādhā.

Vṛndā departs just as the Vraja *sundarīs* arrive at Sūrya-deva's temple and pay their respects to Mitra. Therein, Rādhā prays that she may attain Govinda's lotus feet and turns toward her *kuṇḍa*, intending to bathe before engaging in worship. But to her surprise, Vṛndā appears on the scene.

Rādhā: O Vṛndā, where have you come from?

Vṛndā: I have come from the base of Kṛṣṇa's feet.

Rādhā: Where is he?

Vṛndā: He is in a grove on the bank of your *kuṇḍa*.

Rādhā: What is he doing?

Vṛndā: He is learning to dance.

4. Here I am paraphrasing Caṇḍīdāsa's description of Kṛṣṇa's first *darśana* of Rādhā, in which Kṛṣṇa marvels at Rādhā's appearance, sharing his feelings with Subala in confidence. As we learned earlier from *Subala Maṅgala*, Subala is thought to have appeared in another incarnation prior to Śrī Caitanya in the person and poetry of Caṇḍīdāsa, whose poetry was very dear to Gaura Kṛṣṇa in his *antya-līlā*. At that time Rāmānanda cites in the spirit of Subala the poetry of Caṇḍīdāsa to pacify and embellish the moods of Mahāprabhu.

Rādhā: Who is his teacher?

Vṛndā: Your form has appeared everywhere in the trees and creepers as the best dancer, and they are teaching him to dance, following in your footsteps.[5]

This is surely good news! However, Rādhā hesitates to react to it as such and questions the veracity of Vṛndā's poetry. Is she merely exaggerating and perhaps covering for Kṛṣṇa, who is known to be unreliable? But Vṛndā assures her of Kṛṣṇa's actual condition while suggesting that if Rādhā wants to avoid him, perhaps she should bathe at Śyāma-kuṇḍa instead.

In any case, the Sūrya *pūjā* must be performed, and thus Vṛndā engages her *vana-devīs* in making further arrangements for the worship. And as Rādhā departs, now believing in the implications of Vṛndā's verse, Vṛndā-devī sends two parrots to serve as lookouts and messengers, one to Yāvaṭa and the other to Sakhī-sthalī, to spy on Jaṭilā and Candrāvalī, respectively. Then, anticipating all the pastimes that might occur as the midday *līlā* proceeds, she engages her *vana-devīs* in advance. They gather the appropriate paraphernalia from the jeweled storehouses at Rādhā-kuṇḍa and arrange them in the various bowers around Rādhā-kuṇḍa. She also informs the forest fauna and flora to ready themselves for Rādhā and Kṛṣṇa's arrival at any particular bower. Then, eager to witness the imminent *yugala-milana*, Vṛndā hides in a nearby bower, where she is joined by Madhumaṅgala's *brāhmaṇī* sister, Nāndīmukhī, one of Kṛṣṇa's talented female messengers.

Meanwhile, despite Rādhā's feigning disinterest in Kṛṣṇa, Rādhā's group proceeds to her lake. Rādhā has had so many previous hallucinations of Kṛṣṇa that when her lotus eyes catch the actual *darśana* of Śyāmasundara through a row of *bakula* trees, she doubts that the *mohana-rūpa* before her is really her beloved. Her doubt is then fortified as his peacock plume falls from his head and his flute from his hand upon seeing her! Is that her Vaṁśī-dhārī, her *śikhi-puccha-cūḍā-manohara*?[6]

But there he stands—stunned and shaken—in all his transcendental beauty, further decorated by *sāttvika-bhāvas*. His *narma-sakhās* stand on either side and behind him. As Rādhā was doubtful, Kṛṣṇa is also unsure whether the love of his life is actually there standing before him in the distance, and Subala assures his friend that what he sees is not merely a

5. *Govinda-līlāmṛta* 8.77.

6. Vaṁśī-dhārī means "holder of a flute," and *śikhi-puccha-cūḍā-manohara* is "he who captivates the minds of all, wearing a peacock-feather crown."

sphūrti. Subala-sakhā then proceeds to describe Rādhā's beauty in compelling detail. Her appearance enters Kṛṣṇa's eyes, and her scent and sound enter his corresponding senses. Then, this sight, scent, and sound take shelter of the chamber of his sympathetic heart, only to rise up and dance upon his tongue in the form of words.

Kṛṣṇa praises the beauty of Rādhā before his *narma-sakhās*, seeking to clarify the vision before him. Similarly, Rādhā speaks in the midst of her *sakhīs* of Kṛṣṇa's beauty, also seeking confirmation that indeed the son of Nanda himself is standing before her. Both groups of friends eagerly confirm that indeed Kṛṣṇa and Rādhā are before each other and encourage them each to move toward one another.

Although Rādhā is as eager to embrace Kṛṣṇa as Kṛṣṇa is to embrace her, she is at the same time affected by other emotions—*sañcāri-bhāvas*—some of which are contradictory. Her eagerness (*autsukya*) pulls her forward, while her shyness (*lajjā*) in the presence of her friends and Kṛṣṇa's *narma-sakhās* holds her back. At the same time, her prideful contrariness (*vāmatā*) tries to drag her homeward, as if to spite her friends, who have created this awkward situation. Thus, she is practically paralyzed, only to then be overpowered and driven by the *sañcāri-bhāva* of concealment (*avahitthā*), which wins the day and causes her to pretend to be uninterested in Kṛṣṇa and concerned only with picking flowers for Sūrya *pūjā*.

Flower picking on the part of the *gopīs* is a *līlā* that plays itself out over and over again in a variety of midday settings. Many Gauḍīya *mahājanas* have shared their hearts with us in their poems and songs as to their experiences of the delightful interactions between Kṛṣṇa and the flower-picking *gopīs*. Kṛṣṇa, supported by his friends, claims ownership of the landscape and thus alleges that it is illegal for the *gopīs* to pick flowers. Such claims on the part of Kṛṣṇa make him out to be king of the forest under the rule of Emperor Kāmadeva—the god of love—who in Sanskrit is conveniently named Anaṅga ("without a body," or, in other words, invisible).[7] Kṛṣṇa, as

7. The *Śiva Purāṇa* explains that on behalf of the *devas*, Kāmadeva tried to distract Śiva from his meditation so that he would marry Pārvatī and beget a son, for only such a son could slay the demon Tārakāsura. However, Śiva responded to Kāmadeva's efforts with an angry glace that burned the body of Kāmadeva, making him invisible, which only made him more dangerous. And despite Śiva's initial reaction, Kāmadeva was successful in attracting him to Pārvatī. From the *bhakti* perspective, the implication here is that the *jñāna-mārga* unto itself is not effective in destroying lust. Instead, it serves only as suppression of sensual desire, leading to frustration, whereas *bhakti* is effective even for those unqualified for contemplative life. Indeed, Kṛṣṇa's *rāsa-līlā* is also referred to as *kāma-vijaya*, victory over lust, because simply hearing and reciting it retires lust by attracting the *sādhaka*

the emperor's forest king, of course has ministers and soldiers of his own, his *narma-sakhās*, who seamlessly shift into various roles as the *līlā* necessitates. However, Rādhā's own claim to royalty, supported by her friends and maidservants, brings Kṛṣṇa's into question and ultimately rules the day. Here we will follow the lead of *Govinda-līlāmṛta*'s version of this *līlā*.

As Rādhā turns from Kṛṣṇa to pick flowers, Kṛṣṇa begins to address her and suggests that in her haste her attire and ornamentation are out of place (*vibhrama*), and he says that he would be happy to assist her in rearranging her attire.[8] But as he reaches out to touch her, she withdraws, manifesting *kila-kiñcita-bhāva*—pride, ambition, weeping, smiling, envy, fear, and anger in the midst of jubilant shrinking away—which is said to be just one example of how such emotions exhibited prior to union are millions of times more pleasing than the union they culminate in.[9]

Then Rādhā turns to pick a *punnāga* flower from a tree that has not yet blossomed.[10] But as she reaches out to find at least one bud, the entire tree flowers in response to her touch, and Kṛṣṇa's body also erupts in flowers of ecstatic horripilation when he sees this.

Well versed in the logic of love and youthfulness, Rādhā and Kṛṣṇa, both being the best students of Tāruṇya Bhaṭṭa (venerable youthfulness), then begin to debate.

> Kṛṣṇa: Who's picking my flowers?
>
> Rādhā: No one.
>
> Kṛṣṇa: Who are you?
>
> Rādhā: Don't you know?
>
> Kṛṣṇa: No.
>
> Rādhā: Then leave.
>
> Kṛṣṇa: I am a honeybee. Where should I go?
>
> Rādhā: Go to your lady bee.

---

to Madana-mohana—Kṛṣṇa, who bewilders (*mohana*) Madana/Kāmadeva.

8. *Vibhrama* is the *anubhāva* of confusion, which causes *gopīs* to sometimes mis-dress in their excitement to meet Kṛṣṇa.

9. *Caitanya-caritāmṛta* 2.14.174.

10. *Calophyllum inophyllum*, known as the Indian laurel and *nāga-campaka*, is an evergreen tree bearing fragrant flowers with white petals and yellow stamens. It is associated with the worship of Viṣṇu.

> Kṛṣṇa: Oh hey! You are my lady bee.
>
> Rādhā: How is that possible?
>
> Kṛṣṇa: Because your heart craves the flower, certainly you're a honeybee![11]

And if Rādhā is not a honeybee, then surely she is a thief! Thus, Kṛṣṇa asks her why she is stealing flowers, with a play on words that also asks why she is trying to steal his mind, noting that she will not be successful regarding the latter because he is a *brahmacārī* and he has the support of his friends. Furthermore, Kṛṣṇa asserts that he knows that she and her accomplices wander freely in the forest of Vraja stealing flowers in the name of worship, although he has not seen her do so because he is busy attending to his *dharma* of cowherding. Thus, on the order of Kāmadeva, he is there at Rādhā-kuṇḍa only for the purpose of catching her red-handed.

Kṛṣṇa tells Rādhā that the forest inhabitants themselves have also complained to him, and Madhumaṅgala also points out that the forest has been left penniless after Rādhā robbed it of its beauty and sweetness, appropriating it for her own bodily luster. Following up on Madhu's point, Kṛṣṇa proceeds to convincingly make his case. The most charming friend of Subala-sakhā explains how the beauty of the forest is all present in Rādhā's body, as if she has stolen it. In other words, in jest Kṛṣṇa seeks to convict her, while he actually praises her beauty by comparing her body to all of the forest's beauty combined. And what appears as his effort to embrace her, he claims, is actually his need to arrest her, and thus it in no way conflicts with his vow of celibacy. Although Rādhā is certainly charmed by her lover's clever words, she replies that while some women will entertain the wordplay of men seeking to conceal their lust, she sees through it and is going elsewhere! Kṛṣṇa then grabs her *sāri* as she pulls away, and she replies further in jest,

> "Hey, Kṛṣṇa! You're calling *us* thieves, as if *you* are a saint? With your beautiful body, you steal the beauty of everything, both material and spiritual! Indeed, the *kumārīs* whose clothes you stole are surely a testament to your *dharma-niṣṭhā*! By the way, why did they have to fold their hands above their heads in prayer to *you*? There are many young girls of marriageable age in Vraja, but no one wants to marry you, because although you claim to be the dashing *rāja-putra* of the cowherds who has forgone marriage out of a preference for celibacy,

11. See *Govinda-līlāmṛta* 9.20.

> you are a womanizer unfit for marriage. It is only out of frustration that you wear the saffron cloth, while your mind is always as restless as a stallion in the presence of a mare.
>
> You have not planted a single sapling or flower in this forest, yet you claim to be its caretaker! What kind of caretaker are you when you let your cows uproot the grass, flowers, vines, and everything else growing here? It is *my sakhī* Vṛndā who maintains this forest, and thus it is known as Vṛndāvana. However, she gave her kingdom to me, and I was crowned "Vṛndāvaneśvarī." My throne is hidden away in Lalitā's bower. Therein I preside where no male can enter. Such is my royal status, and thus I suggest that you and your *gopas* get on with your actual caste's animal husbandry and stop impersonating nobility.[12]

Kṛṣṇa is exceedingly charmed by Rādhā's words and gestures, and to her delight he grasps her hand as she looks at him with one eye of consent and to Lalitā with the other in desperation. Then Lalitā physically comes to her rescue, scolding Kṛṣṇa in no uncertain terms and standing between him and his beloved. But Viśākhā intervenes and suggests that the couple perform the *kandarpa-yajña*, a religious name for lovemaking ideally within marriage. Thus, she ties the two together with their cloth, as is the custom in Hindu marriage ceremonies.

Here we see the two sides of the *parama-preṣṭha-gopī* friends of Rādhā. They have equal affection (*sama-snehādhikā*) for Rādhā and Kṛṣṇa, unlike her *mañjarīs*, who have slightly more affection for Rādhā (*rādhā-snehādhikā*) than they do for Kṛṣṇa. While Lalitā favors Rādhā at the moment, Viśākhā now favors Kṛṣṇa. And Kundalatā separately also chimes in on Kṛṣṇa's side. She suggests that the two lovers unite under the guise of various religious rituals, such as *pañca-devatā-pūjā* and *nava-graha-pūjā*, rituals she says she learned from Nāndīmukhī. In Kundalatā's mind, the five *devatās* and nine sacred stones/planets somehow become parts of Rādhikā's body that Kṛṣṇa must touch.[13] However, Kundalatā's efforts are only partially successful, and eventually the poetic banter turns physical, as Kṛṣṇa grabs at one *gopī* after another.

12. See *Govinda-līlāmṛta* 9 for the extended conversation.

13. In Kundalatā's humor, the five *devatās*—Gaṇeśa, Śiva, Caṇḍī, Viṣṇu, and Sūrya—become Rādhā's left and right breasts, and her forehead, mouth, and lips, respectively. The nine planets become Rādhā's two lips, two eyes, two cheeks, two breasts, forehead, and face.

Such is the divine love play of these religious adolescent boys and girls, which pushes the envelope from obligatory religion to lawless love. In these affairs, the *gopīs* and *narma-sakhās* desire only the pleasure of Rādhā and Kṛṣṇa, by which they themselves become spiritually nourished. They are all transcendentalists. Their minds and bodies are designed only for Kṛṣṇa's pleasure! The *gopīs* in particular are expansions of Śrī Rādhikā's *hlādinī-śakti*, the essence of which is *prema*. This *prema* is personified as the vine of Rādhā, while her friends and maidservants are its leaves, blossoms, and flowers. When this love vine is sprinkled with the nectar of Kṛṣṇa's love *līlās*, they become happier than if they were watered themselves.

In these affairs, Kṛṣṇa's flute holds a special place. As we have seen earlier, it sometimes falls from his hands. Rādhā catches it effortlessly without Kṛṣṇa's realizing it and then passes it among her friends, who deny Kṛṣṇa's accusation that they have stolen it. At other times, the *gopīs* make plans in advance to steal it, given that it practically renders them helpless to maintain their religious vows, if not driven to break them.

The stealing of Kṛṣṇa's flute is a very popular *līlā*, and thus there are many expressions of it. Within the Gauḍīya tradition itself, there are three distinct flute-stealing narratives. In Rūpa Goswāmī's *Vidagdha-mādhava* drama, we find the earliest version and what is perhaps the most theologically significant, and this with regard to Subala's love for Rādhā in particular. However, because this pastime occurs during the night—*niśa-līlā*—we will look at it in greater depth in our description of the entire *niśa-līlā* ahead.

Kavi-karṇapūra's flute-stealing *līlā* occurs during the springtime Holī celebrations. This *līlā* extends throughout the day and into the night. The first outbreak of Holī occurs in the early morning as Rādhā and her *sakhīs* walk to Nandagrāma to cook for Kṛṣṇa. Along the path, Kṛṣṇa and his *sakhās* attack the *gopīs*, throwing colored dye over them and creating a red cloud. Kṛṣṇa takes advantage of this cloud and secretly embraces Rādhā before reappearing amid his friends, all of whom are bent on further mischief. Later that same day, Madhumaṅgala plays a prominent role with regard to the theft of Kṛṣṇa's flute. Unlike in Śrī Rūpa's drama, in which Rādhā accidentally ends up with Kṛṣṇa's flute, in *Ānanda-vṛndāvana-campū* the *gopīs* make a plan to steal it.

However, the *gopīs*' plan is overheard by Madhumaṅgala,[14] who advises Kṛṣṇa and ultimately convinces him to let *him* hold the flute and protect it with his priestly powers. As could be expected, Madhumaṅgala accidentally

14. Kavi-karṇapūra refers to Madhumaṅgala by the name Kusumāsava.

drops the flute while declaring victory for Kṛṣṇa in a singing competition Madhu has organized between his friend and Lalitā. His victory is of course disputed, but the flute is now in the *gopīs*' hands.

The flute is passed from one *gopī* to another, and Kṛṣṇa searches the *gopīs* to his satisfaction. Ultimately, the flute ends up in Rādhā's hand and falls from her dress as Kṛṣṇa searches her. Kṛṣṇa retrieves the flute, and Madhu celebrates. Kavi-karṇapūra comments that Kṛṣṇa derives more pleasure from boldly attacking the *gopīs* while searching for his flute than he does from uniting individually with them.

In Kṛṣṇadāsa Kavirāja's *Govinda-līlāmṛta*, Kṛṣṇa's flute ends up in Rādhā's hands when it falls from his waist as he tries to embrace her amid her friends and handmaidens as they wind their way toward their prescribed Sūrya *pūjā*. When Kṛṣṇa realizes his flute is missing, he searches the *sakhīs* and *mañjarīs*, while Rādhikā exits into a forest bower without the flute, which is now in Vṛndā's blouse. As Kṛṣṇa approaches the bower, Rādhā tries to escape but is unsuccessful, and therein the divine couple perform the so-called *kandarpa-yajña*, giving pleasure to everyone involved in the *līlā*, all of whom desire to see them unite.

Thus far in Kṛṣṇadāsa Kavirāja's narrative leading up to the flute theft, Kṛṣṇa's *narma-sakhās* have not been participants. However, *narma-sakhās* are most certainly eligible to participate, as we know from Śrī Rūpa's *veṇu-haraṇa-līlā*. And should Rādhā on another day escape from her bower and delay uniting with Kṛṣṇa despite all of the engineering of her *sakhīs* to unite her with him, we know from Rūpa Goswāmī that Subala-sakhā is the perfect person to bring her back and even render further *sevā* therein having done so:

> What *sevā* is Śrīmān Subala not eligible for! When a lover's quarrel arises between the enemy of Agha and his beloved, Subala pacifies the heart of Kṛṣṇa's darling with endearing words, thus convincing her to return to her lover. He prepares a bed fit for their erotic exploits, and when Kṛṣṇa perspires in his lovemaking and lies fatigued on his beloved's breast, Subala resorts to fanning him.[15]

Although Rādhā and Kṛṣṇa are together again at this point in *Govinda-līlāmṛta*'s midday *līlā* narrative, Kṛṣṇa's flute has not been returned. Madhumaṅgala implies that Rādhā is the thief by reminding Kṛṣṇa of her criminal record—how she has stolen the beauty of the forest. As he tries to

15. *Ujjvala-nīlamaṇi* 2.14.

stir things up again, Nāndīmukhī arrives with a message from Paurṇamāsī. Having heard about rough dealings surrounding the theft of Kṛṣṇa's flute, her message is that Rādhā and Kṛṣṇa should stop quarreling and jointly rule over the forest kingdom, nurturing their love for one another. But her message goes on to say that should another quarrel arise, Nāndīmukhī should consult with Vṛndā, determine the guilty party, and report back to her. This in turn starts the playful quarreling all over again, as Kṛṣṇa claims that Nāndīmukhī knows very well how Rādhā has stolen the forest's beauty along with his flute.

Earlier during their *rati-keli* within the forest bower, when Rādhā wasn't looking, Kṛṣṇa wrote a message on a white lotus petal using red *kuṅkuma* and tucked it in his turban. Now he produces the message as evidence supporting his claim, pretending that the mythical emperor sent it to him. Kṛṣṇa gives it to Nāndīmukhī to read:

> Greetings! Kāmadeva, the all-powerful lord of love, hereby announces to Nāndīmukhī, Kundalatā, Vṛndā, and all the assembled *sakhīs* that Rādhā stole the forest's beauty! This wealth of beauty must be returned. And then all of you should settle Rādhā and Mādhava's dispute over the flute.[16]

However, Kṛṣṇa's evidence is suspect. He has been in Rādhā's presence and then alone with her, but Rādhā did not see anyone deliver such a message. Lalitā replies further:

> If Kandarpa Rāja has eyes, all he needs to do is open them to see that the forest derives its splendor from Rādhā. And what is all this about stealing a flute that was designed to steal the chastity of the young girls of Vraja?[17]

Desiring to relish the beauty of the forest and demonstrate her claims, Lalitā pushes Rādhā forward, and the assembly begins an extensive tour of the subforests, each forest manifesting one of the six seasons. As the tour begins, it becomes apparent that Rādhā's beauty nourishes the forest, but Kṛṣṇa cries foul.

Kṛṣṇa claims that while it is true that the forest appears nourished by Rādhā's presence, when she goes home she magically takes its beauty with her. Then, suddenly, everyone hears the sound of the flute, as it captures a

16. *Govinda-līlāmṛta* 12.20.
17. See *Govinda-līlāmṛta* 12.22–25.

breeze despite being hidden within Vṛndā's blouse. Rādhā then claims to have been exonerated, and Vṛndā makes up a story on the spot.

Lalitā had previously suggested that perhaps Kṛṣṇa dropped his flute at Kusuma-sarovara and Śaibyā picked it up. Agreeing with Lalitā's tale, Vṛndā adds to it. When she saw Śaibyā steal the flute, she sent the she-monkey Kakkhaṭī to steal it back, which she did, giving it to Vṛndā for safekeeping. Thus, Vṛndā hands the flute back to Kṛṣṇa with no explanation as to why she held it so long and allowed the controversy to continue. But upon getting his *vaṁśī* back, Kṛṣṇa does not pursue the issue and instead begins to play it, as if to see if it still works. And it does, exhibiting its miraculous powers before everyone. Following this, the group, guided by Vṛndā with Rādhā and Kṛṣṇa together at the head, tours the forest as it manifests all six seasons. Subala and Madhumaṅgala point out to the tour group many features of the seasons and forests in terms of their readiness to serve Rādhā and Kṛṣṇa.

After any number of *līlās*—such as swinging, sporting in the water, listening to parrots glorify Rādhā and Kṛṣṇa, and so on—Kṛṣṇa and his friends sit for lunch. Readers will recall that Kṛṣṇa departed from lunch early with his *narma-sakhās* as his *madhyāhna-līlā* began. Thus, he and his *narma-sakhās* are hungry after touring the various forests and experiencing the different seasons. In *Govinda-līlāmṛta*, they enter Raṅga-devī's bower on the southern end of Rādhā-kuṇḍa. Within this bower lies a *padma-mandira* (lotus temple), and the *bhojana-vedi* (altar for food offerings) is located on its northern side. Here Kṛṣṇa sits on a flower *āsana* covered by a white cloth. Subala sits on his left and Madhumaṅgala on his right, while Rādhā and her associates serve lunch consisting mostly of uncooked items gathered from the forest by Vṛndā and her *vana-devīs*.

The meal includes four different kinds of coconuts and a wide variety of mangoes with different tastes and textures. Some mangoes are seedless, some have edible thin skins, some are chewed, and others are sucked on after one makes a hole on one end. Kavirāja Goswāmī mentions wild guavas, grapes, dates, palm fruits, wood apples, raspberries, monkey jackfruits, bananas, Indian plums, coffee plums, palm seeds, cucumbers, pears, grapefruits, oranges, currants, pomegranates, watermelons, sour plums, and various other berries and fruits.

Rādhikā also serves dishes cooked at home earlier in the day that in pretense were prepared for Mitra-deva but were actually intended for the best of friends and his friends. As each item is served, Madhumaṅgala weighs in on it, making the *sakhīs* laugh. This is a very intimate setting among friends that provides ample opportunity for *jāta-rati-sādhakas* to serve in *narma-sakhā-bhāva*. Following the meal, they assist Vṛndā in making a flower bed for Kṛṣṇa to rest on. Rādhā's *mañjarīs* then have the opportunity to massage Kṛṣṇa, while those serving in the wake of *narma-sakhā-bhāva* follow their *yūtheśvaras* and arrange flower beds for them and render personal service to them and their *guru-rūpa-sakhā* before taking rest themselves. While Kṛṣṇa and his friends rest, Rādhā and her associates relish their remnants and then take rest themselves, Rādhā together with Kṛṣṇa.

After resting, all these friends typically play a game of dice or some similar competitive game of chance. However, amid such games, suddenly the parrot that Vṛndā sent to spy on Jaṭilā arrives and informs the group that she is in fact on her way, suspicious and wondering what is taking so long. Alarmed, they regroup halfway between Rādhā-kuṇḍa and Sūrya-kuṇḍa, where they make plans to effectively deal with Jaṭilā's rightfully suspicious mind. According to the plan, Kundalatā takes Rādhā to Sūrya-kuṇḍa, where they meet Jaṭilā. When Jaṭilā asks what is going on, Kundalatā tells her that they have been looking all day for a suitable *brāhmaṇa* to conduct the *pūjā* but all of them have been engaged elsewhere. However, she says further that while they did find one qualified *brāhmaṇa* from Mathurā, who for that matter is well known for his expertise in Sūrya *pūjā*, he has been hesitant to assist them. His name is Viśvaśarma, and he is the student of Gargācārya. Today he was all the way out in Kāmyavana, where he met Kṛṣṇa cowherding. Then, out of respect for him, Madhumaṅgala brought him all the way to Ariṣṭa-kuṇḍa to take his midday bath. But when Kundalatā asked him to preside over the *pūjā*, Madhumaṅgala cautioned him, saying he may have to encounter Jaṭilā's harsh character.

"Ariṣṭa-kuṇḍa" is an alternate name for Śyāma-kuṇḍa. Kundalatā uses it to keep Śyāmasundara off Jaṭilā's mind. And for the same reason, she tells Jaṭilā that Śyāma has been far away today on the outskirts of Vraja at Kāmyavana. She also portrays Madhumaṅgala as very considerate but through him raises the complaint that Jaṭilā is unnecessarily harsh in her dealings with Rādhā, who has been innocently looking for a suitable *brāhmaṇa* all day. All of this throws Jaṭilā off balance, questioning her own suspicion and now concerned that the *pūjā* may not be performed, which would be inauspicious for her son.

Thus, Jaṭilā pleads with Kundalatā to try and find that *brāhmaṇa*, pacify him, and convince him to return. Kundalatā then increases Jaṭilā's anxiety by expressing her doubt that the *brāhmaṇa* boy, if he can even be found again, will agree to return. She urges Jaṭilā to be extremely hospitable and on her very best behavior. Desperate, Jaṭilā goes so far as to suggest that Kundalatā take Dhaniṣṭhā with her to find Madhumaṅgala, which should be relatively easy. She tells Kundalatā to then invite Madhumaṅgala and promise him a reward in her name if he can bring Viśvaśarma, whom she will also reward handsomely.

The *brāhmaṇa* boy—Viśvaśarma—is, of course, Kiśora Kṛṣṇa in disguise. And although Kundalatā and Dhaniṣṭhā are in on the plan, they are nonetheless astonished to see Kṛṣṇa in his *brāhmaṇa* disguise, the Vedas personified before them. He who is worshiped by the *brāhmaṇas*—*namo brahmaṇya-devāya*—appears before everyone as a *brāhmaṇa* himself. And all of them find him to be everything a *brāhmaṇa* should be and more.

As he arrives at Sūrya-kuṇḍa, he blesses Jaṭilā's son that he may be wealthy with cows, and he also blesses her son's wife. Then, as is customary before starting the *pūjā*, he asks Jaṭilā the name of her son's wife. When Jaṭilā utters "Rādhā," Kṛṣṇa in disguise appears surprised and tells Jaṭilā that she is truly blessed to have this girl as her daughter-in-law. Then he explains that jewel-like Rādhā is famous throughout Mathurā for her chastity. Thus, he himself is now honored to make her acquaintance.

Kṛṣṇa then instructs Rādhā to repeat after him as he guides her through the *pūjā*. But all his made-up *mantras* have double meanings. Externally, they appear appropriate to Jaṭilā, who thinks her daughter-in-law is further dedicating herself to her husband. However, the hidden meaning within the *mantras* is that by repeating the *mantras* Rādhā is committing herself further to Kṛṣṇa. Rādhā and company follow the inner meaning with delight. Then Madhumaṅgala, who has been chanting Vedic *mantras* to create auspiciousness, tells Rādhā that to complete the *pūjā* she must engage in *go-sevā* by giving the best cow from her husband's herd to the priest as *dakṣiṇā*, the inner meaning of his words being that to complete the *yajña* of love play at hand, she must offer her senses—*go*—to Kṛṣṇa.

However, Jaṭilā is a bit stingy, and the thought of offering her son's best cow to the priest does not sit well with her. Thus, she interrupts and, taking two gold rings from Rādhā's fingers, places them on a plate along with various sweets and offers it to the priest. But Kṛṣṇa responds by telling her that he never accepts gifts in return for his services, which include astrological readings and readings derived from physiognomy, and furthermore that he has learned from Gargācārya that the real wealth lies in pleasing the

Vraja *vāsīs*. Here he subtly implies that the wealth of his life is the pleasure of Rādhā, who by now is finding it difficult to contain her love for Kṛṣṇa, given his charm. Meanwhile Madhumaṅgala insists that Kṛṣṇa accept a gift to complete the ritual and then accepts one of Rādhā's rings for himself and one on Kṛṣṇa's behalf. Then he ties both rings and a sweet from the offering in his cloth and dances in delight, even as Kṛṣṇa discourages his less-than-dignified behavior.

Kṛṣṇa then gets his desired reaction from Jaṭilā, who asks Kundalatā to ask him to read Rādhā's palm. Although he first states that he never touches women, being a *brahmacārī*, he then relents and says that he will make an exception because of Kundalatā's affection for him by reading Rādhā's upraised palm from a distance. But as he comes closer to her, he too finds it difficult to contain his love for her.

His reading is, of course, an auspicious one, comparing Rādhā to Lakṣmī herself. Then Kṛṣṇa asks Jaṭilā her son's name and, upon hearing it, pretends to intuit his nature. He tells Jaṭilā that her son's life will be beset with obstacles but that by the auspicious influence of his wife he will pass over them. Jaṭilā is thus awed that Rādhā is part of her family. Here Kṛṣṇa manages to fool Jaṭilā with his dress and words while simultaneously amusing Rādhā and expressing his love for her. He also removes Jaṭilā's doubt concerning Rādhā's chastity, at least for the moment. Thus he proves himself to be expert in accomplishing many tasks at once, and he does so in the most charming manner, to the delight of his friends and lovers. It is no wonder that even Nārāyaṇa finds Kṛṣṇa attractive and thus has no reason to object to Lakṣmī's desire to join him in such *līlās*! There is really no one like him other than his intimate friends.

Meanwhile, Subala in hiding has been observing the pretense of the Sūrya *pūjā*, and at this point he sees that both Rādhā and Kṛṣṇa are about to break out into ecstatic symptoms. Concerned that their inability to contain their love for one another will take over the scene and spoil the thus far well-executed plan, he comes out of hiding. As if just arriving from cowherding at Kāmyavana, as a representative of the young herdsmen he invites Viśvaśarma and Madhumaṅgala to come and accept an offering of fruit and milk from them.

Kṛṣṇa comes to his senses and understands that Subala is playing his part and telling him that it is time to go. It is also true that Kṛṣṇa's friends are missing him and by now they are possibly nearby in search of him. However, Kṛṣṇa replies by telling Subala that he has a prior lunch engagement with Gargācārya's daughter and her husband, Bhāguri Muni, and suggests that Madhumaṅgala take his place and accept the cowherds' fruit and milk offering on his behalf.

The idea here is that Kṛṣṇa now realizes that he must separate from Rādhā and reunite with his friends. But rather than pretend to follow Subala in the direction of Kāmyavana, he desires to spend as much time as he can with Rādhā, even if that means following Rādhā for only a short distance and observing her from behind. For this reason, pretending to follow Subala west in the direction of Kāmyavana will not do. Instead, Viśvaśarma/Kṛṣṇa pretends that he has been invited to lunch at Gārgī's residence, which is to the north in the same direction as Yāvaṭa. Subala understands how Kṛṣṇa has edited the plan on the fly, driven by his emotions, and arrangements are made for everyone to depart accordingly: Rādhā and her *sakhīs* follow Jaṭilā to Yāvaṭa, with Lalitā in the rear. Vṛndā remains in the forest. Subala and Madhumaṅgala offer to escort Viśvaśarma/Kṛṣṇa to Gārgī's house before returning to herding. Thus they follow somewhat behind Rādhā's group, tending to Kṛṣṇa as his romantic love in separation sets in. Lalitā has placed herself behind Rādhā and started a conversation, giving Rādhā an excuse to look back from time to time and see Kṛṣṇa, as *her* romantic love in separation also sets in.

Such is a typical midday portion of Kṛṣṇa's *aprakaṭa-līlā* on a Sunday. Other days are similar in terms of the measure of romantic intrigue and humor, and there are a wide variety of pretenses by which Rādhā is allowed to enter the forest day after day. Sometimes she goes with permission to pick flowers; sometimes Kṛṣṇa imitates the sounds of birds in a manner so compelling that Jaṭilā gives the *gopīs* permission to go and see them; sometimes the *gopīs* go to the forest for the purpose of bringing milk to participate in a religious sacrifice, and so on. However, sometimes Rādhā is held back. And it will be appropriate, given the angle from which we are viewing the *aṣṭakāla-līlā*, to conclude this discussion of the *madhyāhna-līlā* by citing a well-known example from the oral tradition of the latter in which Subala plays a significant role—*subala-milana*.

On this day, as morning turns to afternoon in the midst of their *vinoda-vilāsa*, Kṛṣṇa pulls Subala-sakhā aside from the rest of his friends. Walking arm in arm with his most intimate friend, Kṛṣṇa speaks:

> Subala, please come close. I want to tell you something from my heart. I have no more intimate friend than you, but seeing your face reminds me of another face that I cannot get out of my mind. Thus,

> I do not feel happy here anymore. Let the two of us go to the bank of that Rādhā-kuṇḍa and sit there. When we arrive, I will open my heart to you.

Arriving at Rādhā's lake and beholding the beauty of the forest, Śyāma tells Subala that upon seeing such beauty, his mind cannot rest. He must meet with Rādhā. However, on this day, no prior arrangement has been made, and Rādhā is held hostage in her household. As the poet Govinda dāsa relates, then Vṛndā arrives with a golden *campaka* flower wreath, and she garlands Subala for the pleasure of Kṛṣṇa. Subala in turn removes the garland from his neck and lovingly places it around Kṛṣṇa's neck. But as Subala does so, Kṛṣṇa falls into a faint. Govinda dāsa says, "Out of love, Śyāma looks up. His eyes are red. His entire body is weak and slack. Holding the hands of Subala, Śyāma falls unconscious." Thus, Subala calls out, "O *bhāi*, Kānāi, say something! Without you, I have no one else in all of Vṛndāvana. What has happened to you? Was there a snake coiled within the flower wreath? If so, why did it not bite me first?"

Then, of course, Subala understands that the golden garland on Śyāma's chest has served as yet another *uddīpana* and thus Kṛṣṇa has fallen into the *sāttvika-bhāva* of *pralaya* in a fever of love for Rādhā. Thus Subala dips the edge of his cloth in the *kuṇḍa* and freshens Kṛṣṇa's face with it, reviving him.

> Subala: O Kānāi, now I understand why you have fallen into this faint. But how can I bring Rādhā here at midday? She is not a fruit or a forest flower that I can just pick for you. And she is guarded by her mother- and sister-in-law.
>
> Govinda: Whatever you say, Subala, I cannot live without Rādhā.
>
> Subala: You are asking for something supernatural. Then again, some people say you are God, and sometimes you seem to accept their assessment. Thus, you must give me the power to accomplish this task. Only then will it be possible.
>
> Govinda: So be it.
>
> Subala: Brother, by your grace I will bring her.

Thus, Subala finds Kṛṣṇa in emotionally troubled romantic waters and assures him that as his friend he is sailing right behind and prepared to lay his body down like a bridge to bring him to shore and ease his mind. Indeed, Kṛṣṇa is desperate, in that his longing for Rādhā has overwhelmed him and it has not been possible for Rādhā's *sakhīs* to free her from the confines of her household. Thus, Kṛṣṇa appeals to Subala to somehow bring Rādhā to her *kuṇḍa*. Despite the formidable challenge this presents to Subala, he has no alternative other than to miraculously make this happen.

Here, the tenderness of Kṛṣṇa's love for Subala is palpable, as Kṛṣṇa reveals his mind to him in confidence. The significance of Subala's role in Rādhā and Kṛṣṇa's romanticism is also underscored, for here Kṛṣṇa burdens him with a task that Rādhā and all her *sakhīs* together cannot accomplish, despite Rādhā's extreme condition being comparable to Kṛṣṇa's intense longing for her.

As Subala heads to Yāvaṭa, he takes shelter of *nāma-kīrtana*, singing his favorite names of Kṛṣṇa. He thinks that if Kṛṣṇa *is* God, there is more power in his name than in him, even while the two are one. Thus, by the power of *harināma*, he thinks he will be successful, when in fact Kṛṣṇa's necessity is the mother of Subala's invention.

First of all, he requires an excuse for showing up at Yāvaṭa. For this, he first returns to the herd and collects Kṛṣṇa's favorite among the newborn calves before departing for Yāvaṭa. This red heifer is young enough to walk on her own yet small enough to carry as well. Showing the young heifer affection, Subala picks her up and tells her his mission as he proceeds to Yāvaṭa. Then, nearing the gate of Jaṭilā's compound but still out of sight, he tells the calf to pass through the gate ahead, sets her down, and twists her tail to get her going. With a burst of speed, the heifer races ahead and passes through the gate, where Jaṭilā is sitting making cow-dung patties.

Then, as Subala nears the gate himself, Jaṭilā hears his singing. Despite her apparent dislike for Kṛṣṇa, she finds some charm in Subala's fraternal love for him, even while thinking he could have made a better choice of friends. In Kṛṣṇa *līlā*, everyone without exception loves Subala. When Jaṭilā sees him, she affectionately asks what he is doing there. But her presence does not make things easier for Subala, who by now has come up with a plan of action that involves getting by Jaṭilā and into her compound, where Rādhā's residence is also located, without raising suspicion.

Thus, Subala replies that he is looking for a particularly spunky calf, dear to his friend, that got separated from the herd, and at the same time he expresses his fatigue and thirst as a result of his effort to retrieve the heifer. Jaṭilā has of course seen the calf pass through the gate, and she tells Subala that she will bring him a glass of fresh, cool water, which is not what Subala wants to hear. Subala then tells Jaṭilā that recently he was afflicted with a serious illness and as a remedy he must worship the goddess Durgā, from whom he received the cure, which includes vowing not to accept water from the hand of a widow. Here, Subala's mind shifts from thinking only of Kṛṣṇa to thinking only of Rādhā in his effort to unite them. Durgā is the world goddess *from* whom it is difficult (*dur*) to go (*gā*). But "Durgā" is also a name for Goddess Rādhā, whom it is difficult to go *to*. Subala's serious disease is of course the partial influence of Kṛṣṇa's contagious fever for Rādhā.

"Alas," Jaṭilā replies, "the calf is within the compound." Then, with suspicion, "But I have never heard of such a vow. And you have become a devotee of the goddess? Can you sing a song in praise of her?" Jaṭilā's unexpected request catches Subala off guard. Thinking of Goddess Rādhā as his only shelter, he manages to spontaneously compose and recite thus:

> O Goddess, I know only Kānu, his *veṇu*, and his *dhenu*. What can I know about you? Yet tears from my eyes pour forth for you like the *jala* of the Yamunā. My heart is your temple. Please reside there.

Hearing Subala's prayer and poetry, Jaṭilā is impressed! Thus, she tells him that he can get a glass of water inside from her daughter-in-law, who is in her quarters, suggesting that he avoid not only herself but also her daughter, Kuṭilā, as a measure of extra caution in consideration of his vow. Jaṭilā also suggests that Subala rest a bit before collecting the calf, who by now is most likely suckling the teats of Rādhā's nurse cow Bahulā and bonding with Rādhā's calf Tuṅgī, and she then closes the gate. Now one third of Subala's mission has been accomplished.

When Rādhā sees Subala, she is overjoyed. The poet Dīna Bandhu dāsa describes their meeting and exchange of words.

> Rādhā: My dear Subala! What a surprise to see you! Tell me, what is your *prāṇa-sakhā* doing? Hearing his flute and his *sakhās*' buffalo bugles, I become stunned thinking of the hardships he faces in the forest. Godforsaken, I can't go there! Thus, I cry but light a fire to pretend my tears come from the kitchen smoke. If only I had the fortune to be a *sakhā*! To attain such a blessing, I would drown myself in the ocean, for then I could always see Kṛṣṇa.

> Subala: Listen, Vinodinī! I've come to take you to Kṛṣṇa, who has fallen unconscious at your lake in thought of you! Here, put on my clothes and give me yours. Then go there and I will wear your clothes and stay here. Seeing you, our Śyāmasundara will regain his life!

Thus, the two look-alikes change clothing. Rādhā puts her jewelry on Subala, and Subala ties her hair in a topknot, while Rādhā in turn ties Subala's hair in a braid.

However, Rādhā presents a problem: her breasts give her away. But Subala has already thought of a solution to this problem in advance and tells Rādhā to collect Kṛṣṇa's calf in her arms and in this way hide her breasts. Rādhā is amazed at how clever and well thought out Subala is. Calf in her arms, she prepares to depart, her left foot forward. But Subala stops her and informs her that cowherds always depart leading with their right foot. Unquestioning at this point, she steps into her role and heads for the gate, her head down looking at the calf and the ground below. Just ahead stands Jaṭilā, who is fooled by Rādhā's disguise. Thinking she is Subala, Jaṭilā wishes him a safe journey returning to the herd.

Rādhā then dances her way into the forest. She is overjoyed at the prospect of meeting Śyāma at her lake, as she also amuses herself pretending to be a *gopa*, something she has wished for previously on more than one occasion. However, seeing her dressed as Subala, Kṛṣṇa thinks his friend has returned without her. Just see how well she plays her role and how much the two—Rādhā and Subala—resemble one another! Here, B. R. Śrīdhara Deva Goswāmī envisions Rādhā-Govinda's conversation.

> Kṛṣṇa: Oh, Subala, you have come back without Rādhārāṇī! Couldn't you bring her?
>
> Rādhārāṇī (joking): No, it was impossible for me to bring her in the daytime.
>
> Kṛṣṇa: Then what am I to do? I can't tolerate my life any longer.
>
> Rādhārāṇī: If you say so, I can go to Candrāvalī and bring her.
>
> Kṛṣṇa: No, no. Curd cannot satisfy the thirst for milk. It is not possible!
>
> Rādhārāṇī (embracing Kṛṣṇa): Can't you recognize your maidservant? You failed to recognize me![18]

18. Swami B. R. Sridhar, "The Service of Sri Radha," chap. 9, in *Loving Search for the Lost Servant* (Soquel, CA: Ananta Printing and Publishing, 2007), 101.

Thus, two thirds of Subala's mission—its centerpiece—is completed. Rādhā and Kṛṣṇa are united in broad daylight. Jñāna dāsa relishes this scene in his song along with the assembled devotees:

> On the left of the adolescent boy stands the fresh teenage girl. Jñāna dāsa begs for the shelter of their feet. From all sides, the Vaiṣṇavas clap their hands. Seeing the couple Rādhā-Kṛṣṇa, they chant, "Hari Hari."

Then Rādhā explains to her somewhat confused lover how she got there and why she is dressed as Subala. Hearing her explanation, Kṛṣṇa's heart swells in fraternal love for Subala, but he also expresses concern for him. How will Subala escape, and how will Rādhā return?

At Yāvaṭa, in great risk to himself, Subala busies himself performing the duties of Rādhā—lighting the fire, cooking, cleaning the floors with cow dung, and so on—just as if he were Rādhā himself. And he is very convincing. Jaṭilā is not the least bit suspicious. Thus, when Subala asks her permission to take a jug and retrieve water from the Yamunā, Jaṭilā grants it. Deceiving Jaṭilā in this way, Subala makes a beeline for the forest, his eyes roaming cautiously in all directions. Dīna Bandhu dāsa says, "Oh, when will I receive the dust of Subala's feet as he completes his mission?"

Subala arrives at Rādhā's *kuṇḍa* dressed in her attire and smiling, bearing a water jug on his hip. Seeing him, Kṛṣṇa also smiles broadly, and Rādhā shyly lowers her head. Kṛṣṇa then listens attentively and with great amusement to Subala's description of his mission, amazed at Subala's cleverness and devotion. But time is of the essence, and Jaṭilā will become suspicious should Rādhā not return soon. Well aware of this, Subala tells Rādhā to change clothes with him again. Then, Rādhā takes water from her lake and returns to Yāvaṭa. How privileged we are to learn of this secret, intimate *līlā* from the hearts of the *rasika-bhaktas*!

As we have seen, the intimate union of Rādhā and Kṛṣṇa is central to the *madhyāhna-līlā*, and Kṛṣṇa's *narma-sakhās* play a significant role in helping to bring this union about, despite various obstacles and even at great personal risk—*yugala-milana sukhera kāraṇa jīvana chāḍite pāri*. Having done so, along with Kṛṣṇa they turn their attention once again to cowherding as they reunite with Balarāma and the rest of their friends, who at this point are longing for Kṛṣṇa's return.

22

Afternoon

Aparāhna-līlā

At the prompting of his intimate devotees, Nimāi, flanked on either side by Nitāi and Gadādhara, begins his homeward march, drawn by the love of Śacī and others who have waited the entire day for his return. At this time, Gaurasundara tours the town of Navadvīpa, filling it with the sound of *nāma-saṅkīrtana*.

Śrī Vṛndāvana dāsa says, *navadvīpa je heno mathurā rāja-dhānī*: "This Navadvīpa is just like the opulent capital of Mathurā."[1] No one can describe its beauty and the nature of its inhabitants, all of whom are absorbed in love of Gaurāṅga-sundara. They sing of his dancing, golden form as if he belongs to them—*āmāra gaurāṅga sundara nāce, āmāra gaurāṅga sundara nāce*—following him through the streets of Nadīyā. The same cowherd Kṛṣṇa who leads his cows homeward at the hour of cow dust—*go-dhūli*—now sings, swoons, dances, and falls down in the ecstasy of *nāma-saṅkīrtana*. The same Rāma and Kṛṣṇa who paraded themselves boldly through the town of Mathurā accompanied by their *sakhās* en route to kill the demonic Kaṁsa now walk fearlessly through the streets of Navadvīpa. The cynosure of all, even the blind, they enter each and every house, offer their *praṇāma* to each and every deity, and in this way capture each and every heart.

At *go-dhūli*, Rāma and Kṛṣṇa call their cows, driving them home from Govardhana. They bugle, play their flutes, and sing. As the cows head homeward, the cowherds form a circle behind them with Rāma and Keśava dancing in the center to the sound of the cowherds singing madly, "Hare

1. *Caitanya-bhāgavata* 3.5.521.

Kṛṣṇa Hare Kṛṣṇa, Kṛṣṇa Kṛṣṇa Hare Hare, Hare Rāma Hare Rāma, Rāma Rāma Hare Hare." Similarly, arriving at the bank of the Gaṅgā, the cows and cowherds of Gauḍa-maṇḍala-bhūmi express their joy upon having Gaura and Nityānanda's *darśana*, and they follow them as they cross the sacred Ganges.

In Māyāpura, Śacī-devī eagerly waits for Gaura and Nitāi to arrive along with Advaita and the assembly of devotees. She greets them affectionately as they bow before her. After the reception, various arrangements are made for Gaura and his guests. Then, sitting in the balcony, the devotees participate in Kṛṣṇa *līlā-kīrtana*, retelling Kṛṣṇa's *aparāhna-līlā* in song, led by Svarūpa Dāmodara.

In the Vraja *līlā*, Nayanānanda Ṭhākura finds Balarāma and the greater balance of *sakhās* just south of Śyāma-kuṇḍa in Śrīdāmā-sakhā's bower of Śata-varga (one hundred divisions). Therein, Rāma is sitting upon a golden throne at the base of an expansive banyan tree, located within the grove's division known as Nāṭya-kuñja (dancing grove), which lies in the eastern corner of Śrīdāmā's bower. He is served by many *sakhās* following Śrīdāmā's directives.

From this bower, Balarāma leads the *sakhās* a short distance to the east, where they enter Sudāmā's grove, which is called Raṅga-kuñja (enchanting sportive bower). From there they proceed to Sucandra-sakhā's headquarters, Rasālaya-kuñja (abode of *rasa*), where suddenly Kṛṣṇa and his *narma-sakhās* rejoin them.

Kṛṣṇa daily reunites with Rāma, his *sakhās*, and his herd in one such grove, much to the delight of the assembly, which has begun to long for his company. Thus, Rasarāja is drawn from *mādhurya-rasa* to *sakhya-rasa*. The present prospect for *mādhurya* has passed. Rādhā has returned to Yāvaṭa, filled with longing for Kṛṣṇa. But then, by way of *vātsalya-prema*, the opportunity for reuniting with Kṛṣṇa presents itself, as Yaśodā sends a *sakhī* requesting Rādhā to prepare some sweets for her son and bring them to Nandagrāma as the hour of cow dust—*go-dhūli*—approaches and with it Kṛṣṇa's return.

Meanwhile, before gathering the cows and heading home, Kṛṣṇa submerges himself in an ocean of *sakhya-rasa*. Although his *sakhās* have been focused on Balarāma, as Rāma begins to internally long for Kṛṣṇa's return so too do his *sakhās*. Although he has been gone for hours, his absence feels like a long minute to his friends. The *sakhās*' preoccupation with Balarāma makes it possible for them to be separated from Kṛṣṇa in the height of their play for several hours without realizing how long he has been gone. But as their attention is once again focused on him, their long minute of separation becomes unbearable.

Thus, Kṛṣṇa reappears, and as he does, he is bombarded with amusing chatter, including punditry, praise, questions, derision, rhymes, and riddles. Although some of this chatter is incoherent, it is nonetheless saturated with fraternal love and thus well understood and deeply felt by Rāma and Govinda.

Observing the sun wheel of time—*kāla-cakra*—the *sakhās* realize that Kṛṣṇa has been gone for more than a minute. Thus, their most pressing questions are about where he has been and what he has been doing. He answers relative to the day and his prior excuse for separating from the group.

When asked on a typical Sunday, "*Bhāi*, why did you leave us for so long?" Kṛṣṇa blames his *narma-sakhās* and answers with a half-truth.

> Kṛṣṇa: I was distracted and kept captive by Subala and Madhumaṅgala.
>
> *Sakhās*: Where did you go?
>
> Kṛṣṇa: They dragged me to see the beauty of the forest, but I was delayed from returning because of Madhumaṅgala's voracious appetite. Wherever we went, he stopped to eat!
>
> *Sakhās*: Didn't Madhu share his wealth with you?
>
> Kṛṣṇa: Yes, of course. But after eating, I fell asleep. And when I woke up, I became enchanted by the beauty of Rādhā-kuṇḍa. So we played in the groves there for some time, napped some more, and then listened to parrots and other talking birds.
>
> *Sakhās*: So you're saying that you forgot about us?
>
> Kṛṣṇa: No! I was more than ready to return, but Madhumaṅgala insisted that I watch him perform Sūrya *pūjā*. Hence, I am late.

Some boys are satisfied with such explanations, while others are not. Thus, a wide range of fraternal feelings are expressed, and those unable to say anything chime in by blowing their antelope horns, flutes, and wind instruments made from leaves or by blowing into their cupped hands. And a host of percussion and stringed instruments can also be heard as the *sakhās* surround Rāma and Govinda, rendering *sevā* arising out of *sakhya-rasa* and celebrating Kṛṣṇa's return.

As the chatter dies down, Kṛṣṇa and Balarāma sit together on a platform at the base of a large tree. Relative to whose grove they are in on any particular day, that *rāgātmika-sakhā*'s followers serve the two brothers under his direction. One *sakhā* weaves a flower garland together with pearls and coral, and another places it around Kṛṣṇa's or Rāma's neck. Another boy rubs *kuṅkuma* into dark *aguru* wood, mixes this paste with camphor, and rubs it on the limbs of Kṛṣṇa and Balarāma. Another *sakhā* waves a white *cāmara* whisk, while another boy blissfully offers them fresh betel nuts. One *sakhā* brings water, and another holds an umbrella made of fresh twigs and leaves. Some boys massage the brothers' limbs, while others massage their lotus feet. Nayanānanda Ṭhākura says,

> What can I say about the magnificence of Balarāma sitting on the same seat with Kṛṣṇa? The effulgence of their two beautiful bodies makes it appear as if the sun and moon have arisen together. These youthful brothers—*yugala-kiśora*—agitate the mind with their sheer beauty of refreshing adolescence. In the association of one's *guru* in the form of a *sakhā*, one realizes one's *siddha-deha* and thereby participates in this scene.[2]

Continuing his description of a typical Sunday, Kṛṣṇadāsa Kavirāja next envisions Balarāma noticing that Madhumaṅgala has something wrapped up in his cloth, as if hiding it from everyone. He suspects that it is a delicacy. Indeed, it was cooked by Rādhā, who offered it to Sūrya-deva with Kṛṣṇa in disguise as the head priest. In fact, the vows and offering she made to Sūrya were secretly offered to Kṛṣṇa. No wonder Madhu is hiding and hoarding the *prasāda*! Just see his greed for *bhakti*.

When Rāma asks Madhu what he is hiding, Madhu replies that it is the *prasāda* of the sun god that Vraja *vāsīs* typically prepare and offer on Sundays. In this way, he exhibits his knowledge of religious practice, as if speaking to an ignorant cowherd. Madhu hopes that his response will end the conversation, as he wanted to keep the delicacies to himself. In fact,

2. This and earlier sections of this chapter adapted from Nayanānanda Ṭhākura's *Preyo-bhakti-rasārṇava* appear at the very end of the *madhyāhna-līlā* rather than at the beginning of the *aparāhna-līlā*. Such events more or less appear at the *sandhyā* between the two periods of the day.

he had been contemplating the taste for hours, pondering when and where to eat them without others noticing.

However, Balarāma persists, insisting that Madhu open his stash and share it with everyone. As Madhumaṅgala's worst nightmare begins to unfold, he tries desperately to ward off his friends by asserting that as a saintly *brāhmaṇa* he cannot be a party to the greed of the surrounding cowherd boys. Nor is it time to eat, he asserts, faulting the religiously ignorant cowherd caste that much more.

Balarāma in return warns Madhumaṅgala that the boys, being as greedy as they are, might take his delicacies by force and thus he would be better off offering some of the *prasāda* to them in advance. But Madhumaṅgala takes Rāma's advice as a veiled threat and warns of his mystic powers derived from his vow of *brahmacarya* and overall priestly status. He then dismisses the strength of the cowherds altogether, including that of Balarāma, comparing it to nothing more than a blade of grass that bends to the wind.

Taking their signal from Balarāma, several *sakhās* surround Madhumaṅgala. At first they politely beg for his mercy and some morsels of the *prasāda*, fully knowing that he will never agree. Thus, on the pretense of begging, they position themselves to take Madhu by surprise and steal all the delicacies.

From behind, one *sakhā* reaches around and covers Madhu's eyes, while another grabs the *prasāda*, runs, and distributes it to the others, who eat it in front of Madhumaṅgala while taunting him. Along with the delicacies, they find the two gold rings from Rādhā's fingers that Jaṭilā gave to Madhumaṅgala in haste. However, Subala, knowing their source, snatches the rings with a plan of his own in mind.

Then one boy pulls the rear tail of Madhu's *dhotī* out from his waist, and as he turns to address this assault, another boy unravels his *dhotī* from the front. Another *sakhā* knocks his turban off, and yet another undoes his hair, while others steal his flute and stick, humiliating the so-called *brāhmaṇa*.

Madhumaṅgala's reaction to all of this begins with laughing and ends with cursing. He laughs at what he proudly claims the reaction for the cowherds' abuse will be, such as being chased by a tiger. Growling, he scolds and curses his friends and then steals Kṛṣṇa's herding stick and chases them. At first, the attackers disperse, but eventually they stand their ground, and a match of skilled stick fighting commences, serving as entertainment for Kṛṣṇa, who eventually intervenes, stops the fight, and brings Madhumaṅgala within his loving embrace.

Kṛṣṇa kindly returns Madhumaṅgala's shawl, turban, flute, and stick and suggests that everyone embrace. However, when Madhu realizes that his *dakṣiṇā* of gold rings has been plundered, he becomes furious. He then labels the other cowherds as great offenders so impure that he refuses to touch them lest he become contaminated himself. He stands back and shouts out, "Don't touch me!"

Turning to Balarāma, Madhu does not spare him. Showing him no deference, he points his finger at Rāma, blaming him for instigating and encouraging the sin of stealing from a *brāhmaṇa*, and he refuses to speak with him until he atones. Eventually, Subala will explain with good reasoning why he took the rings, and in due course Madhu's tongue and belly will be served to his satisfaction. May Subala share his secret with *sakhya-rasa-upāsakas*, perhaps giving them the opportunity to assist him in returning Rādhā's rings.

Meanwhile, Kṛṣṇa suggests a game of *hādu-gudu*, and everyone enthusiastically participates. This is a game played between two teams of seven players, the object of which is for a single player on offense—the raider—to run into the opposing team's half of the court, tag out as many of their defenders as possible, and return to his own half of the court in a single breath without being tackled by the defenders. Points are scored for each player successfully tagged by the raider, while the opposing team on defense earns a point for tackling the raider. Players are taken out of the game if they are successfully tagged or tackled, but they can be "revived" for each point scored by their team from a tag or tackle.[3]

But how among cowherds can one be sure that a raider has held his breath while on the opposing team's side of the field, especially if that raider is a thief like Hari? The answer is that one cannot be sure. Thus, as they play, an argument between Hari and Śrīdāmā ensues. The game is interrupted, as Śrīdāmā and Kṛṣṇa challenge one another and members of each team support their teammate, Hari or Śrīdāmā, by boasting and hurling insults.

> Śrīdāmā insults Hari:
>
> I, Śrīdāmā, well known for my strength, have always been and will always be victorious. For evidence, one need look no further than

3. *Hādu-gudu*, also known as *hutu* and *kabaḍḍī*, is an ancient game of Indian origin. The seventeenth-century Vaiṣṇava saint and poet Tukārāma describes Kṛṣṇa playing *kabaḍḍī* in his childhood. The game is also mentioned in Buddhist literature. It is said that Gautama Buddha played *kabaḍḍī* with peers for recreation. Tibetan monks are also known to play the game, considering it an important tool for breath control, meditation, and physical strength.

> the history of your shoulders.[4] Without thinking things through, you angrily make proud claims that lead only to your infamy. You take credit for having slain *asuras*, but that pride is not well reasoned. The *brāhmaṇas* killed Pūtanā with their *mantras*, not you. Who will take Bakāsura seriously? And did you enter Agha's mouth alone? You claim you lifted Mount Govardhana, but I say that being pleased with our *pūjā*, the mystic mountain levitated in bliss. Tell me, why are you so proud?[5]

Thus, team sport is abandoned, and a wrestling match takes its place, as the large circle of friends forms the ropes of the makeshift wrestling arena.

Who wins? That depends upon which side one is on! After some time, Śrīdāmā pins Kṛṣṇa's shoulders to the ground and declares victory, which is echoed by a chorus of cheering from Śrīdāmā's side. Hari's team is silent until, upon getting up from the ground, Hari declares victory. How so? Hari points out that during the match it was his nose that continued to point upward, while in the end it was Śrīdāmā's nose that faced the ground! One can only imagine how loud Hari's team cheered in response.

In this way, Govinda plays with his *sakhās* under every tree and beside every vine, giving *ānanda* to every animal and every feathered creature—indeed, to every entity, be they moving or nonmoving. However, now it is late in the afternoon, and as the sun begins to set on blessed Vraja, Kṛṣṇa feels the *vātsalya-prema* of his elders and begins to turn his friends homeward. In turn, the forest residents begin to feel Govinda's pending separation with his every step forward. Thus, Hari turns to call and collect the cows, a domesticated form of forest inhabitant with a sense of *vātsalya*.

As mentioned earlier in the radius of this text, the herd of Hari consists of 108 groups of cows. Twenty-five subdivisions of the four basic colors—white, red, black, and yellow—together make up one hundred groups of cows along with eight other groups defined by characteristics other than their dominant colors: speckles, *tilaka*, other special markings, and particular-shaped heads resembling *mṛdaṅgas*, lion heads, and so on. Each group also has its natural leader. Wherever she leads, the rest of her group follows. Thus, Hari calls out the names of the leaders of the different groups. He does so either by chanting their individual names aloud on a *mālā* of 108

4. The "history of your shoulders" refers to the fact that Śrīdāmā has defeated Hari many times and consequently with each defeat Hari had to carry Śrīdāmā on his shoulders.

5. *Kṛṣṇa-bhāvanāmṛta* 16.6–7.

jewels or by somehow calling out their names through the notes of his flute. Kṛṣṇa's friends find the mystery of this musical artistry most fascinating.

A number of the leading ladies' names are mentioned in the sacred texts: Dhavalī, Śavalī, Padmā, Hariṇī, Raṅgiṇī, Kañjagandhā, Rambhā, Camarī, Khañjanī, Kajjālākśī, Śaṇḍā, Bhramarikā, Sunadā, Sunandā, Dhūmrā, Saralī, Kālī, Marālī, Pālī, Gaṅgā, Tuṅgī, Piśaṅgī, Kālindī, Vaṁśī-priyā, Śyāmā, Haṁsī, Kuraṅgī, Kapilā, Godāvarī, Indu-prabhā, Śonī, Śyenī, Triveṇī, Yamunā, Candrālikā, Narmadā, Vilohinī, Bodhiṇī, Dhūmalā, and Suśīlā. Among all of them, Dhavalī and Śavalī are prominent.

These cows had been grazing and trusting that Kṛṣṇa was behind them. They felt Rāma's presence but not Kṛṣṇa's absence. Hearing their names, they gallop toward Kṛṣṇa, tails high in the sky, kicking their hind legs up, their udders overflowing with milk. With grass still between their teeth, they lift their snouts and smell Kṛṣṇa's scent, which along with his sight causes them to affectionately moo softly. Surrounding Hari, they lick his beautiful body, tasting and in effect cleansing it from head to toe with motherly affection before he returns home. And Hari returns their affection by scratching their necks, stroking their backs, and whispering into their long ears, reminding them of their hungry calves, with whom they will soon share their wealth.

As the rest of the cows follow and Rāma and Hari lead the herd homeward, Mother Earth in conjunction with the cows' hooves raises her dust—*dhenu-reṇu*—re-dressing and decorating Kṛṣṇa's form, as if turning her whole body into dust to wrap Kṛṣṇa in her embrace, and as if on behalf of all the forest residents, who also desire to hold him to their hearts. Oh, how charming Rāma and Hari appear, covered with cow dust, as do their friends and the cows themselves, being also embraced by the earth's dust! Indeed, clouds of dust rise into the sky to announce Rāma and Hari's return to the impatient elders and the longing adolescent Vraja *sundarīs*. Thus, the sun in Vraja sets out of embarrassment, and the clouds in the sky disappear at this hour, being replaced by the self-effulgent brilliance of Kṛṣṇa dressed and decorated in clouds of *go-dhūli*.

Not only the sun but also all the gods in Goloka offer praise to Rāma and Hari as they proceed. Although the gods are accurate in their majestic praise of Kṛṣṇa, such praise is the butt of jokes among Kṛṣṇa's *sakhās*. They think that the gods do not realize that it is Nārāyaṇa that exhibits power through Kṛṣṇa, not Kṛṣṇa himself. Thus, they mock the gods' praise, laugh, and make fun of the gods themselves. At this time, there is no road to the village that is not decorated by *sakhās*, no *sakhā* that does not play, no play without humor, and no humor that does not give happiness to Kṛṣṇa.

> Picture a festive parade consisting of multicolored cows draped in silk, their horns and hooves plated in gold and silver, bells around their necks. Among them are black buffalo too. Behind them yet leading the way, running and frolicking as they herd, are the multitude of *sakhās*, festively dressed and decorated, dancing and playing various musical instruments. Some older boys bearing bows and blunted arrows[6] run and then stand in protective postures, and all of them together fix their long lotus-like eyes on Rāma and Kṛṣṇa, the best of brothers.
>
> The road ahead from the forest to the village is like a rope in a game of tug-of-war, held on either end by the *prema* of those, on one hand, who wish to prolong staying in Kṛṣṇa's company and, on the other hand, those who desire to reunite with him at the end of the road. Below, the earthen floor is softened for the tender soles of Hari and Hali by the prancing hooves of the cows and then swept smooth by their tails. Above, the sky has turned its gaze away from the so-called opulence of heaven and leans over the earth to witness the procession, longing for a role in this *sakhya-rasa-līlā*. The entire scene is surrounded by and covered in the upraised dust—*go-dhūli*—as Mother Bhūmi powders Hari, Hali, their friends, and their animals in her loving embrace.

Meanwhile, in Yāvaṭa, Rādhā has prepared a variety of sweets for Kṛṣṇa, including some of his favorite dishes, such as *amṛta-keli*, *karpūra-keli*, and *pīyuṣa-granthi-pālikā*, all famous in Vraja.[7] Rādhā's handmaidens have dressed and decorated her, and together they ascend to the top of the moon tower,

6. *Bhakti-rasāmṛta-sindhu* 4.3.8 says that the *sakhās*' arrows have leather tips and that during mock fighting they sometimes shoot them at one another. It cites the example of Śrīdāmā showered with arrows shot by his friends and deftly intercepting them with the whirling of his stick to the astonishment of Kṛṣṇa.

7. *Amṛta-keli* consists of ripe bananas, wheat flour, *dāl* flour, coconut, pepper, condensed milk, cardamom, cloves, nutmeg, cinnamon, and camphor, fried in ghee and then soaked in sugar water. *Karpūra-keli* consists of chickpea flour, yogurt, pepper, sugar, coconut powder, nutmeg, cardamom, cloves, bananas, and particles of fried mung batter, fried in ghee and soaked in honey, camphor, and condensed milk. *Pīyuṣa-granthi-pālikā* consists of knotted shapes of the abovementioned ingredients, fried and then soaked in a mixture of *pañcāmṛta*—yogurt, milk, ghee, honey, and sugar.

seeking the *darśana* of Śyāma, who is now approaching, as understood from the rising cloud of dust kicked up by the cows.

Yāvaṭa sits three kilometers to the northeast of Nandagrāma, and during the months that Rādhā resides there, Kṛṣṇa makes his way home through her in-laws' village. Similarly, Vṛṣabhānu-pura, also known as Varṣāṇā, sits to the southwest of Nandagrāma at a similar distance, and during the months that Rādhā resides at her father's village, Kṛṣṇa changes his course and passes through Varṣāṇā on his way home. As one would expect, the road home goes through Rādhā!

As the herd approaches the urban area, the cows' familiarity with the surroundings makes them more anxious to reunite with their calves, and thus they rush ahead. Balarāma, Śrīdāmā, Sudāmā, and others rise to the occasion. Keeping up with the herd, they display their expertise at herding in such trying circumstances.

However, this turn of events gives Kṛṣṇa the opportunity to lag behind with Subala, Ujjvala, and other *narma-sakhās*, who assist him as his lovestruck lotus eyes search out Rādhā's whereabouts. Suddenly seeing her in the distant moon tower, Kṛṣṇa is astonished. He has seen Rādhā previously in the forest groves where she reigns supreme as the queen of Vṛndāvana, but now he is seeing what appears to be another Goddess in the moon tower, and she is affecting him as much if not more. Thus, he calls out to his friends in desperation,

> Bho Śrīdāmā, Subala, Vṛṣabha, Stokakṛṣṇa, Arjuna, and others! Did you see that? Although she is not the Goddess of the groves, here some other startled Goddess, who inundates all the worlds with the flood of her elegance, has stolen everything from your dear friend![8]

And having seen him at a distance from the moon tower, Rādhā's friends take her to the bushes along the roadside, keeping her in hiding to get a closer look at her love as he passes by. Then Kṛṣṇa senses her presence, when suddenly her friends, unable to control themselves, out her with a push! And there the two, stunned by each other's *darśana*, stand motionless, staring at one another and thus desperately in need of help, given the paramour nature of their love. After all, they are on the roadside near the gate of her

8. *Rādhā-rasa-suddhā-nidhi* 228. Here although friends like Śrīdāmā, who do not directly participate in Kṛṣṇa's romantic life, are up ahead, in his lovestruck confusion Kṛṣṇa mentions their names nonetheless. Had Śrīdāmā, Rādhā's older brother, heard Kṛṣṇa's passionate cry, he would have blushed. See *Vidagdha-mādhava* 1.76, where it is implied that Śrīdāmā is embarrassed to hear his friend suddenly express passion for Rādhā.

in-laws' estate. Thus, Rādhā's *mañjarīs* pull her back and escort her into the house, where they tend to her. And Kṛṣṇa's *narma-sakhās* are afforded a similar Kṛṣṇa *sevā* opportunity. Following the lead of Subala-sakhā, they revive Hari, steady him, and help him homeward, while assuring him that he will meet again with Rādhā after-hours. Similarly, Rādhā's maidservants pacify her with the same assurance.

By now, Tulasī-mañjarī has delivered the dishes Rādhā prepared into the hands of Yaśodā. And Kṛṣṇa, with the help of his friends, catches up to Balarāma at the outskirts of Nandagrāma. Yaśodā has engaged Rohiṇī in cooking the main meal of rice, *dāl*, and vegetables from her personal garden. At Yaśodā's request, Atulā, the wife of Nanda's younger brother Nandana, assists Rohiṇī in cooking. Then, as Rāma and Kṛṣṇa approach, everyone heads to the gate.

In his *Bṛhad-bhāgavatāmṛta*, Sanātana Goswāmī depicts one special afternoon that captures the scene at the edge of the forest where the villagers gather at this time. The special feature of this particular day is that we learn about it from the lips of a *sādhana-siddha narma-sakhā*—Sarūpa—who describes this scene as he enters the *nitya-līlā* for the first time.

Sarūpa enters the *aprakaṭa* realm as its afternoon *līlā* nears completion. He finds himself in Gokula, the center of the lotus of Goloka. He is amazed that everything there looks like the rural setting along the Yamunā of North India's Mathurā district. It is very similar but not the same. There is an undeniable sense of transcendence to it, even as it appears to function as things do on earth. For example, he sees that the sun is setting. It is as if the earthly Vraja from where he has come is a partial or worldly representation of this original, transcendental, humanlike realm. Full of wonder, he tries to understand where he is and begins to ask around. However, the people there appear despondent and at a loss for words. At the same time, they are filled with an extraordinary love. The mere sight of this love transmits it to Sarūpa-gopa as if it were contagious. Eventually, someone replies to him and tells him that he is in Nanda Rāja's cowherd kingdom.

> Walking, overwhelmed with joy yet trying to control myself, I met an elderly gentleman who was sitting, sobbing profusely, and incessantly chanting, "Kṛṣṇa! Kṛṣṇa!" With some tact and effort, I got him to speak and heard him say in a choked voice that this town belonged to Nanda, the king of the cowherds, Śrī Kṛṣṇa's father. Hearing these words, I fainted on the spot, overcome with delight. After a moment, that compassionate old man revived me, and I

> ran ahead and sat in front of the town gate. There I saw hundreds of thousands upon tens of millions of wonders unseen, unheard of, and unimaginable by anyone of this world. . . .
>
> Then an elderly lady came by, and I bowed and asked her plaintively where Śrī Nanda-nandana was playing today. She replied, "This morning, the life force of the Vraja *vāsīs* went into the dense forest to play with his revered brother and his young friends, herding his cows. As evening approaches, surely he will return. Otherwise, we will not survive. All the Vraja *vāsīs* are waiting here on the bank of the Yamunā, their eyes transfixed on the road ahead. Even these trees stand with leaves upraised, eager to see him. Surely he will come along this path."
>
> Feeling as though I had been anointed with a downpour of the purest nectar, I then fixed my eyes on the path that she pointed to. My thighs paralyzed by *paramānanda*, I somehow proceeded forward until I heard a distant yet distinct sound: Kṛṣṇa's *mohana-muralī* in *megha-mallāra-rāga* mixed with the mooing of his cows. It was like nothing I had ever heard before, and by its enchanting power, it immediately overwhelmed everyone in the village.[9]
>
> By the power of that sound, sap poured forth from the trees lining the path, a flood of tears fell from the eyes of every embodied being in the cowherd village, milk rained from the breasts of all of Kṛṣṇa's mothers, and the rapid currents of the Yamunā reversed and the river then stood still. I did not know whether that flute poured out venom or *rasāmṛta*, whether its sound was as hard as thunder or as soft as water, whether it was hotter than fire or cooler than the moon. But that sound drove all the Vraja *vāsīs* crazy.[10]

Sarūpa saw women running from their homes bearing items to greet Kṛṣṇa, with some carrying food on their heads. They ran as Sarūpa did toward the sound of the magical *muralī* and the mooing of the cows. Not yet seeing the flute bearer or his herd, the women stumbled along the path, ornaments in disarray. As they ran, they sang Hari's names and sang of his *līlās*. Other

9. *Megha-mallāra-rāga* is a monsoon *rāga* calling for the first rains to quench the thirst of the earth after the long, hot summer. Similarly, Kṛṣṇa sounds this *rāga* on his flute to quench the thirst of the villagers, who are withering and dying of thirst in his extended absence.

10. *Bṛhad-bhāgavatāmṛta* 2.6.35–48.

women stayed in their homes stunned and unable to walk, or they fell into a faint. Some carried others who were themselves unable to walk. All of them diverse in complexion and adorned with various ornaments, their beauty shamed that of Goddess Lakṣmī.

> Then suddenly I saw him from a distance, his shining *madhura-muralī* in hand. Running quickly toward me from within his group of friends and animals, he spoke sweetly to Śrīdāmā, "Look, here is my dear friend Sarūpa, the sun who shines on the lotus of your family!"
>
> Kṛṣṇa wore rustic dress appropriate for the forest, which, along with his earrings, peacock-feather crown, and garland of *kadamba* flowers, swayed to and fro. His fragrance perfumed all directions, and his beautiful lotus face blossomed with a playful smile. His lotus eyes beamed with a glance of benediction, and the variety of his beautiful features combined to form his singular, unmatched beauty. With the fingers of his lotus hand, he repeatedly pushed back the long locks of his hair adorned with *go-dhūli*.... His beauty, which captured the hearts of the ever-dear devotees of Vraja, was an ocean abounding with countless excellences.
>
> As he leapt forward and came close to me, compelled by the affection of his helpless devotee, I fainted in *prema*. He caught hold of me, his arm beneath my neck, and then suddenly he too fainted and fell to the ground... moistening the path with his tears.[11]

Thus, at this particular hour of cow dust, Gopa-kumāra/Sarūpa attained *vastu-siddhi*.[12] Needless to say, when Kṛṣṇa regained consciousness and everyone understood that *nitya-siddha sakhya-prema* had just manifested itself in yet another form for the pleasure of Kṛṣṇa, Sarūpa was welcomed, well received, and treated just as if he had been there all along.

Thus, every afternoon at this hour, the villagers regain their life air. First they see the cloud of cow dust. Then they hear the mooing of the *dhenu*, and then the sound of Kṛṣṇa's flute. Finally, they see him! By now, Kṛṣṇa has decorated his friends with flower ornaments from the forest, just as they have also decorated Kṛṣṇa and Balarāma. Some boys wear flower crowns;

11. *Bṛhad-bhāgavatāmṛta* 2.6.55–61.

12. Bhaktivinoda Ṭhākura invokes the term *vastu-siddhi* to refer to the second (final) stage of spiritual perfection; he refers to the first (penultimate) stage as *svarūpa-siddhi*. In *svarūpa-siddhi*, one typically enters the *līlā* in meditation and is thus qualified to take birth in the *prakaṭa-līlā* and from this portal enter the *aprakaṭa-līlā*, attaining *vastu-siddhi*.

others wear flower garlands; still others sport flower armlets and bracelets; while Rāma and Kṛṣṇa are adorned with all such flower ornamentation and more.

As the boys approach with the village in sight, they stop and congratulate one another for their achievements during the day—their wrestling victories, their speed in sport, their wit, recalling their jokes, and so on. Then Kṛṣṇa turns and tells them all in earnest how happy they have made him, filling him with a joy that only he and they can know—their secret of secrets among so many secrets. And with this, he smiles at his *narma-sakhās* and lowers his head, blessing them and expressing eternal gratitude for their special love.

Dutiful in terms of his *dharma*, Kṛṣṇa counts the cows again before making the final march home. Every one of them is thus accounted for before proceeding. And if any mother is missing, Kṛṣṇa calls her again with his flute and waits for her to arrive. There is not a single star-like cow in Nanda's herd or the herds of Śyāma's *sakhās* that exists outside of the sky of Kṛṣṇa's mind.

Then, as if a choreographed act, they all proceed in unison, so one with one another that it is as if they are a single entity dancing to its feelings of fraternal love. Every boy blows his horn or flute, and the cows all moo in response and move forward, their hooves thundering down the road ahead. It is as if a military parade of limitless victorious troops has arrived on the scene of citizens previously devastated by the foreign occupation of separation. And among the troops are the fatherland's princes, liberating those previously occupied and banishing any other thought than that of the joy of union now at hand. *Jaya* Rāma! *Jaya* Kṛṣṇa!

At last, Nanda and Yaśodā again embrace their sons at the edge of the forest as they did earlier in the day. However, in this *aparāhna-līlā* they have no fear of impending separation as they do in the morning at the time of Kṛṣṇa's departure. At this hour, *vātsalya-prema* knows no bounds, as elder *gopas* and *gopīs*, after having spent the entire day with concern for the boys' well-being, once again have Rāma and Kṛṣṇa in their midst safe and sound. Withered and wilted from their daytime *viraha*, like flowers in desperate need of water that have been battered by the wind on a sunny day, they are revived by the nectar of Kṛṣṇa's return as he flows into their arms. And his assurances steady them as their senses come to life like the petals of a thirsty flower opening to the downpour of his raincloud-hued brilliance.

With her own *sāri*, Yaśodā wipes the cow dust from Śyāma's face and limbs as she experiences the *sāttvika-bhāva* exclusive to her *vātsalya-rasa*—milk flowing profusely from her breasts. Nanda embraces his sons and smells their heads, and then he and other elder *gopas* walk with Kṛṣṇa and Balarāma to the cow pens, both boys determined to dutifully attend to the evening milking.

Arriving at the cow pens, Gopala oversees the *sevā* of further separating the cows into groups of those with newborn calves, those who are nurse cows, those whose calves have been weaned, those within two months of calving who will not be milked, those who have been bred and are thus not yet lactating, and those who are heifers who have not been bred. He also separates the buffalo and bulls from the cows of Nanda's herd as well as from the cows of his *sakhās*' herds.

Despite Nanda's pride for his sons and the pleasure he takes in seeing their sense of responsibility, his heart concurs with the insistence of Yaśodā that they come inside, clean up, eat something, and relax after the long day and leave the majority of the later afternoon chores to others. Later, she insists, Kṛṣṇa can return to milking. When eating is mentioned, Madhumaṅgala defects to Nanda and Yaśodā's side of the argument, pulling Kṛṣṇa's arm. And the three, now outnumbering the two brothers, are victorious.

As Yaśodā takes Kṛṣṇa to the house, his friends follow him and depart for their own homes with their herds—some large, some small—only upon the insistence of Yaśodā. She expresses sympathy for their mothers, who follow her motherly lead and return to their homes with their sons. On such days, each group leader lovingly embraces Rāma and Kṛṣṇa as they exchange sweet words, their voices faltering, tears in their eyes. Thus, the *sakhās* return to their homes accompanied by their *upa-sakhās*. There, the leaders are assisted by their followers, who afterward return to their own homes. However, on other days some boys remain, dispatching some of their followers to attend to their cows. Who can say who among the *sakhās* departs and who remains on any given day? But all the *sakhās* return after some time and participate in the following *sāyāhna-līlā*.

23

Dusk

Sāyāhna-līlā

With the outset of the evening, Śacī-devī engages Viṣṇupriyā in preparing *bhoga* for her household deities Kṛṣṇa and Balarāma,[1] while Gaurasundara, assisted by servitors, bathes and dresses for the evening. After he has bathed and dressed, he offers *pūjā* to the Gaṅgā with a ghee lamp inside a clay cup, and his devotees follow his example. After the lamps are offered, they are placed in the river, augmenting its effulgence as they float downstream.

When the assembly of devotees returns to Śacī's home, she asks Gadādhara to offer *ārati* to Rāma and Kṛṣṇa, and sometimes Gaura himself offers the *bhoga*, to her delight. Seeing him engaged in Viṣṇu *bhakti*, Śacīmātā is very pleased with her son's *dharmic* nature, and she looks lovingly at his lotus face, just as Yaśodā-māyī looks upon Vrajendra-nandana after being reunited with him at the end of the day. During the *ārati*, all the devotees engage in *kīrtana*.

However, Nimāi is not content to remain at home, and suddenly, steeped in Rādhā *bhāva*, he becomes obsessed with the desire to go to Śrīvāsa Ṭhākura's house. Thoughts of meeting with Śrī Rādhā arise in Śrī Kṛṣṇa's mind at this time of day, and thus initial arrangements are made during the *sāyāhna-līlā* for Kṛṣṇa to meet with her. As similar thoughts overtake Śrī Gaurāṅga, the *dhāma-vāsīs* light the path with brilliant lamps and make music while Gaurāṅga makes his way to the courtyard of Śrīvāsa, where he will taste *saṅkīrtana-rasa* into the night.

1. See *Caitanya-bhāgavata* 2.8.28–33. Śacī worshipped Kṛṣṇa-Balarāma *mūrtis*.

As the sun sets in Vraja, it becomes evident that its effulgence is merely a reflection of the brilliance of Kṛṣṇa. The sun appears to light the day, but it is actually Kṛṣṇa who lights the day in Vraja. The setting of the sun proves this point, since after it sets, Kṛṣṇa continues to light the night. And the sun only appears to light the outer world, while in fact Kṛṣṇa lights the inner world, dissipating the darkness of ignorance, and thus the outer world becomes bright.

The sunset appears to turn the western sky red, but in fact the goddess of the western direction turns red from her *anurāga* upon thinking that with Kṛṣṇa's westward movement from Yāvaṭa toward Nandagrāma he is coming to embrace her. And only out of embarrassment upon realizing this does the sun set. At this time, Mukunda enters Nanda's house and merges into the sweetness of his elders' ocean of parental affection—*vātsalya-rasa*—while the sun prepares to dive into the sea of separation, setting and then rising again with the dim hope of attaining him, the only bright spot in its life.

Yaśodā embraces her sons as streams of tears flow from her lotus eyes. Kṛṣṇa asks her why, if she loves him so much, is she crying instead of paying attention to him as he sits before her? Ignoring his query, Yaśodā holds him on her lap, and with the water of her tears and the corner of her *sāri*, she cleans the cow dust from his lotus face and undresses him, wrapping his loins in a handloomed cotton *gamchā* suitable for bathing. Rohiṇī then circles the bodies of the twins with a ghee lamp to dispel the darkness and help Yaśodā examine their precious forms, an act that also serves as a form of the sacred *ārati* ritual.

Seeing the love marks on Kṛṣṇa's body, Yaśodā expresses concern with how roughly Kṛṣṇa's friends have played with him during the day. She also asks him why he did not return sooner. Madhumaṅgala agrees with her and portrays himself as the only sensible, sober, and responsible boy among Kṛṣṇa's rowdy friends. Of course, he knows that the love marks Yaśodā discovers are a result of Kṛṣṇa's romantic interludes. And in agreeing with her as to the inappropriate behavior of Kṛṣṇa's friends, he refers to them as *vayasyālī*, which can be taken to mean either "girls" or "boys," causing Kṛṣṇa to smile slightly. Madhu then sticks up for Kṛṣṇa by explaining to his mother that in Kṛṣṇa's fraternal play, he forgets *himself*, so how can he be expected to remember *her*? It is only by the grace of the sensible Madhumaṅgala that he has returned home at all, something Madhumaṅgala should no doubt be rewarded for.

Then Yaśodā engages the household servants in bathing and dressing Rāma and Kṛṣṇa. Tulasī-mañjarī stands nearby, after having delivered the evening sweets prepared by Rādhā, and now has the opportunity to participate in Kṛṣṇa's bath. She does so by smearing scented oil on his limbs, a service opportunity arising out of Yaśodā's deep *vātsalya-rasa*, which precludes her from thinking that Kṛṣṇa or the *gopīs*, whom she has known since the *līlā* of their birth, are of age.

In *Bṛhad-bhāgavatāmṛta*, the *narma-sakhā* Sarūpa, who has just entered the *aprakaṭa-līlā* for the first time, looks on during this *sāyāhna-līlā* as a number of young *gopīs* bathe, dress, and ornament Kṛṣṇa, with Yaśodā's permission, while she tends to the evening cooking. When these *gopīs* try to take Kṛṣṇa's flute from his hand by force, however, he objects, knowing their feelings for his *muralī*. Indeed, they might throw it in the Yamunā! Thus, Hari tries to keep it out of their reach, and as this becomes impossible, he signals to Sarūpa with his eyebrows and tosses it into the open palm of his friend, who is standing nearby, looking on and admiring Śyāma's romanticism.

While Rāma and Kṛṣṇa, as well as Madhumaṅgala, are bathed and dressed, Yaśodā adds Rādhā's preparations to the meal Rohiṇī has been preparing. Then Nanda arranges for the meal to be offered to the household deity. Sometimes Madhu himself offers the meal, and at other times his young male *brāhmaṇa* assistants do so under his direction. After the offering, the three—Baṭu, Rāma, and Hari—all sit and snack, and other friends begin to return and relish the sweets along with them. Madhumaṅgala praises the *prasāda* and the preparations of Rādhā in particular:

> O Mother! If one is fortunate enough to smell these cakes, is it possible that he or she could still be attracted to Svarga or *apavarga*? Fie on the creator for not giving me a limitless belly! Moreover, in my well-reasoned opinion, anyone who utters "No, thank you" when offered more cakes is the worst offender.[2]

After relishing these refreshments, the boys proceed to the cow pens, where milking is already underway and is to be completed before the sun sets into the sea. Everywhere in Gokula, lamps are lit in anticipation of the night sky. At the same time, Dhaniṣṭhā collects Kṛṣṇa's remnants and gives them to a *sakhī* to bring to Rādhā. Upon arriving, this *sakhī* also pours nectar into Rādhā's ears by describing Kṛṣṇa's activities. And as Rādhā learns that Kṛṣṇa is now milking, she goes to Pāvana-sarovara and

2. *Kṛṣṇa-bhāvanāmṛta* 17.25.

climbs the moon tower there to watch her beloved carry out his *dharma* so attentively and with such dedication. Kṛṣṇa is, after all, a cowherd in the final analysis—the best cowherd—and thus his milking within the circle of his friends is a sight to behold! Indeed, Rādhā eagerly drinks this milking scene through her eyes and pours it into the pail of her heart, where it is churned into various *sañcāri-bhāvas*. And as much as she may long to taste *sakhya-rasa* on occasion, this *rasa* itself serves almost like a *sañcāri-bhāva* for her *mādhurya-rasa*. There is a compatible interplay of *aṅgī-* and *aṅga-rasas*—*mādhurya* and *sakhya*, respectively.

Prior to Kṛṣṇa's arrival at the *gośālā*, Nanda is overseeing the milking in progress, but he is distracted by his eyes, which cannot stop looking at the path on which Rāma and Kṛṣṇa will soon appear. Then Kṛṣṇa strides confidently onto the scene, his feet adorned with jeweled slippers. Different-colored cows whose udders have already been milked fill themselves with milk again at the prospect of being milked or even touched by him or his brother. Cows' udders yet to be milked overflow, moistening the ground with their milk. Just being in Hari's presence lifts their mooing to new heights. Calves moo, cows moo, and bulls moo too, accompanied by the sounds of milk gushing into golden milk pails and occasional shouts from cowherds.

As Rāma and Kṛṣṇa call out the names of their *dhenus*, these cows raise their ears and look lovingly in Rāma and Kṛṣṇa's direction, tears pouring from their eyes. The brothers scratch the necks of their cows, who raise their heads and lick the brothers' bodies. Finally, the boys sit down on stools. Placing golden pails between their legs, they milk one cow after another, their friends following suit, while servant boys carry flasks full of milk from the barn to the house and bring them back ready to be refilled. Inside the house, an ocean of milk is joyfully processed.

The entire scene appears like a colorful concert conducted by the words, gestures, and loving glances of Kṛṣṇa, accompanied by a dancing troupe of calves balancing on their front legs as they kick their hind legs high into the sky and butt heads with one another. These calves clear the way for baritone bulls to bellow and lock horns, drawing attention to themselves in their desire to be embraced by Hari, who looks on while resting his arm on the shoulder of Subala, captivated not as much by the scuffling bulls as by the beautiful sight of the adolescent yearlings. Oil lamps begin to light the night, accompanied by the *kīrtana* of the cows' mooing and birds' chirping as they settle safely into their nests. It appears as if *ārati* is being offered to Śyāma and Subala standing arm in arm, the reddish moon rising only for their *darśana*. What, then, can be said of all that Rādhā sees through *her* lotus eyes, her distance from the scene bridged by her love for Śyāma Gopāla?

After milking the cows, Rāma and Kṛṣṇa escort the calves and cows to their respective pens and then proceed to Nanda's household *mandira* accompanied by their friends and Nanda. They arrive in time to attend the evening *ārati*, which is performed either by Baṭu—*dvija-rāja*—himself or by one of the *brāhmaṇa* boy's young assistants. After the *ārati* and subsequent socializing, everyone sits down for their evening meal. Typically, Nanda entertains guests for dinner, which for the most part includes extended family members—his brothers, their wives, their sons and daughters, and other relatives. Nanda's nephews, who are close in age to Rāma and Kṛṣṇa, are almost always in attendance.

During the evening meal, Nanda Mahārāja seats his older brothers to his right and his younger brothers to his left. Rāma and Kṛṣṇa are seated across from him with their cousins to Kṛṣṇa's left and the young *brāhmaṇa* boys to Balarāma's right. During the milking, the women have been cooking, and now they serve the meal. Both the cooking and the serving are sublime and infused with affection. In serving, Yaśodā, the mother of all mothers, knows the favorite dishes of everyone seated as well as the measure of their individual appetites, and thus she directs the serving accordingly.

Given the presence of so many elders, the atmosphere of the evening meal is different from that of the morning meal, which precedes the day of herding. It is more formal in consideration of the guests, and thus the maternal sentiments of Yaśodā, Rohiṇī, and others are more subdued, as are the fraternal sentiments of Kṛṣṇa and his friends. The *brāhmaṇas* are served first, then the elder cowherd men, and finally Kṛṣṇa and his friends. After the elder and younger *gopas* have eaten, the elderly *gopīs* eat their meal together, being served by the younger *gopīs*.

Govinda-līlāmṛta explains:

> The evening meal is twice the morning meal. Madhumaṅgala's joking is more subdued before the elders, and Yaśodā's eagerness to serve her sons is concealed.[3]

That said, despite the more formal nature of the evening meal, it is even more pleasing to Kṛṣṇa's parents, who are hosting it. The obvious reason for this is that along with their own ecstasy, they also relish the bliss of their extended family members, who are delighted at the opportunity to

3. *Govinda-līlāmṛta* 20.51.

dine together with Rāma and Kṛṣṇa. Furthermore, Madhumaṅgala does manage to interject *some* humor into the setting:

> My understanding is that one is fortunate to be born in a good family. This we all share. More fortunate still is to take a second birth and receive the sacred thread. I—with my *brāhmaṇa* birth, of course—have that good fortune as well. And Nanda, being a *vaiśya*, is also qualified to receive the sacred thread as a "friend of the twice-born *brāhmaṇas*"—*dvija-bandhu*. Thus, he is now the ruler of his caste, king of the cowherds. Therefore, foods cooked in ghee in this household are fit for *brāhmaṇas* such as me. But there is a most auspicious third birth as well, and that is attained by eating the sweets cooked by the daughter of Rāja Vṛṣabhānu. This is known from the transformation experienced by the *brāhmaṇa* sage Durvāsā. Previously he had a bitter tongue from which curses issued forth even toward Vaiṣṇavas such as Ambarīṣa. This we have learned from Nanda Bābā's Purāṇic discourses. However, I have seen that after Durvāsā tasted the *pāyasa* prepared by Rādhā, his tongue became sweet and explained the esoteric significance of Kṛṣṇa's *brahmacarya*.[4] Thus, I long to take such a third Vaiṣṇava birth myself. However, Rādhā's sweets are highly coveted, and I have been seated too far down the line to know if there will be any left by the time I am served. Furthermore, those sweets may be stolen by the servers without being served at all or after being served only to the *vaiśyas* seated here, owing to the servers' bias and the limited supply of such sweets. Therefore, I should be served first![5]

It is also noteworthy here that despite the multitude of Kṛṣṇa's cowherd friends present on any such occasion, their presence unto itself does not inhibit anyone in the least. And while their presence may inhibit Rādhā and Kṛṣṇa's romanticism, the *narma-sakhās*' presence creates no such shyness.

However, not every evening meal is tempered with formality in consideration of invited guests. Nor is Rādhā absent from every evening setting at Nandagrāma. In *Bṛhad-bhāgavatāmṛta*, we find the description of a very special afternoon and subsequent *sāyāhna-līlā* and its evening meal. We have referred to this day in brief above. This is the day in eternity in which

4. This is a reference to *Gopāla-tāpanī Upaniṣad* 2.8–23.

5. *Gopāla-campū* 1.2.50. The three types of birth are *śaukra* (taking birth in a good family), *sāvitra* (receiving the sacred thread), and *daikṣa* (receiving Vaiṣṇava *mantra-dīkṣā*).

narma-sakhā Sarūpa attains *vastu-siddhi* in the *aprakaṭa-līlā*. Sarūpa describes the evening meal that he attended on this day to his disciple, Janaśarmā, as the "emperor of meals" in terms of its artistry, fragrance, color, taste, quantity, serving containers, and the affection with which it was served. Both Nanda and Yaśodā took turns feeding portions of it to Kṛṣṇa, which he playfully accepted. Sarūpa also describes the beginning, middle, and end of the meal in terms of the various dishes eaten, as well as the beauty of Kṛṣṇa's tongue as he opened his mouth and the beauty of his cheeks filled with mouthfuls of various delicacies—all of this beyond words. He mentions the presence of Rādhā and other *gopīs*, the sweets they prepared and served, and Kṛṣṇa's glorification of these dishes. Sarūpa continues:

> And with his own hand, Kṛṣṇa also fed some of those items to me. Then Rādhā brought mind-stealing (*manohara*) *laḍḍus*—both small round ones and large flat ones—and set them down on Kṛṣṇa's left. Kṛṣṇa picked one of them up with his fingernails and put it on the tip of his tongue. But then he made a facial expression of disgust as if they tasted like bitter neem. Kṛṣṇa's brother smiled, his mother became upset with Rādhikā, and his father expressed surprise. Rādhā's innocent girlfriends were pained, and her competitors were delighted.
>
> Since I was born in the family of Rādhā's brother, Kṛṣṇa threw all the *laḍḍus* onto my plate. Surprised to find them extremely tasty, I eagerly ate them all. Rādhā secretly looked at Kṛṣṇa and arched her eyebrows, and Kṛṣṇa, nodding his head, gratified her with a gentle smile and a sidelong glance. Then I understood: *vidagdha-śiromaṇi* Kṛṣṇa was only pretending in play for the delight of his devotees in an effort to please them and lighten the burden of their love for him. Then Kṛṣṇa washed his mouth and playfully chewed *pān*. Glancing at Rādhikā, he put the chewed *pān* in my mouth.[6]

Joking at the expense of Rādhikā, Kṛṣṇa emphasized to Sarūpa that which he had expressed earlier to Śrīdāmā upon first seeing Sarūpa in the pasture: upon departing from Nandagrāma that night, Sarūpa would go home to Varṣāṇā with Śrīdāmā as a member of Rādhā's family. And Kṛṣṇa, glancing at Rādhā as he placed the *pān* that she had prepared for him into Sarūpa's

6. *Bṛhad-bhāgavatāmṛta* 2.6.127–134.

mouth after he had chewed on it, facially expressed his love for both Rādhikā and Sarūpa at the same time.

However, as we have seen above, typically Rādhā is not present in Nandagrāma during the *sāyāhna-līlā*. She is at home in Yāvaṭa or Varṣāṇā, and from there Rādhikā sends one of her *mañjarīs* to bring the sweets she has prepared for the evening at Yaśodā's request. After the men and boys have finished their evening meal, this *mañjarī*, filled with *praṇaya* for Rādhā and Kṛṣṇa, has the opportunity to give or receive a message to or from Subala-sakhā regarding the secret meeting place chosen for that night. Sometimes this meeting place is selected by Rādhā and at other times by Kṛṣṇa.

At this time, the atmosphere at Nandagrāma is relaxed and social. Yaśodā dines casually with her friends while others begin to clean the kitchen, and evening entertainment is just ahead. In the evening, Nanda Bābā is the perfect host, and he has the opportunity to sit with the young *gopas* and inquire from them about their adventures in the forest. He advises them and shares his experience. He answers their questions; and when asked, he tells a tale.

No one knows how many tales Nanda knows. Practically speaking, there is no Purāṇic story that he has not committed to memory, and he always draws new meaning as he retells such tales. When he instructs the young *gopas*, they sit with undivided attention that often ends in astonishment. He loves every cowherd boy as if each one were his own son. And their love for him knows no bounds. To sit at his feet or on his lap, from which he allows any *gopa* so seated to pull on his beard as he showers Kṛṣṇa's circle of friends with affection, is to experience a perfect father.

At such times, every young *gopa* idolizes Nanda, and steeped in *suhṛt-rati*, they desire to be like him, the ideal herdsman. He never scolds anyone, but nonetheless he teaches by his example. He does not merely know. He knows what to do and does it. Should a bull become unruly, he circles such a bull and prays, "You are *dharma*. *Ahiṁsā* is *dharma*. Please bless us." What more can be said about Nanda Bābā! Let there be a *Nanda Purāṇa*!

After such heartwarming sessions, Kṛṣṇa relaxes in the company of his *narma-sakhās*. However, he is anxious at the same time, and he asks them about the beauty he experienced in the meadow that afternoon that destroyed his patience and enchanted him. Of course, he is speaking about Rādhikā but asking whether it was actually her that he saw or whether such a beautiful girl actually exists at all. Perhaps he mistook the beauty of the forest to be such a beauty. Such is his love-intoxicated condition that his *narma-sakhās* tend to. And in the context of assuring him that the object of his own love is real and that her love for him is at least as deep as his love for her, Subala delivers Rādhā's message to him on this moonlit night, and their meeting place is finalized.

Meanwhile, before Rādhā's *mañjarīs* return to her, Yaśodā asks the maidservants present to please sit and eat. However, Dhaniṣṭhā informs her that *mañjarīs* such as Tulasī and Kastūrī will not even drink water before Rādhā has eaten. Pleased with the measure of their devotion to Rādhā, Yaśodā arranges to send various dishes with them to bring to their Goddess. Dhaniṣṭhā makes sure that some of Kṛṣṇa's remnants are mixed in with the rest of the meal, and then she sends Rādhā's *mañjarīs* back to Yāvaṭa. There they dine playfully with Rādhā in a manner not unlike the playful dining of Kṛṣṇa and his *sakhās*. Jaṭilā insists that Rādhā subsist on the food remnants of her so-called husband, Abhimanyu, who has already eaten and gone to the cowshed to bed down for the night, but the *mañjarīs* assist Rādhā in skillfully avoiding his leftovers.

Then, just as Kṛṣṇa, assisted by his *narma-sakhās*, plans to meet with Rādhā, she, assisted by her *sakhīs*, makes plans to meet with Kṛṣṇa.

24

Evening

Pradoṣa-līlā

In his *Gaurāṅga-līlāmṛta*, Kṛṣṇadāsa, a disciple of Viśvanātha Cakravartī Ṭhākura, pens the following Bengali verse describing Gaura's *aprakaṭa pradoṣa-līlā*:

> *pradoṣe śrīvāsa-mandire praveśa adhika ullāsa hiyā*
> *tathā priya-gaṇa mana anurūpa koraye adbhuta kriyā*
>
> In the evening, Gaura goes to the house of Śrīvāsa, his heart blossoming in great delight. There he performs wonderful pastimes in accordance with the desires of his dear friends.

Kṛṣṇadāsa's Bengali verses and subsequent commentary follow the spirit of his *guru*'s Sanskrit verses from *Śrīmān-mahāprabhor-aṣṭakālīya-līlā-smaraṇa-maṅgala-stotram*.

In Kṛṣṇadāsa's commentary, as Gaura Hari arrives at Śrīvāsa Ṭhākura's residence his devotees also assemble there. Among them, *narma-sakhās* from the Vraja *līlā*, such as Subala and Madhumaṅgala, are present in their Gaura *līlā-svarūpas*. Thus they are blessed, for even in the *aprakaṭa-līlā* not every devotee can enter Śrīvāsa Ṭhākura's courtyard and Gaura's nocturnal *rasa-kīrtana*. The gate is locked and Gaurasundara holds the key. No one can enter without his permission, and once it is granted, no one leaves until Gaura does during the next morning's predawn *līlā*.

Significant in Kṛṣṇadāsa's verse above are the words "his heart blossoming in delight"—*adhika ullāsa hiyā*. As the verse explains, Gaura's heart delights in knowing his devotees' hearts, which are full of love for him. However, more significant than the fact of his omniscience is the fact that their hearts are laden with the wealth of love such that they completely purchase him and cause him to enact wonderful pastimes. Indeed, he manifests a unique form that perfectly corresponds with the heart and form of each of his devotees, who serve him in their own Gaura Kṛṣṇa–centered *līlā-prakāśa*.

The words *mana anurūpa* imply that Śrī Gaurasundara acts in ways that correspond with the hearts of his devotees. In Gaura's *prakaṭa-līlā*, this plays out when he reveals his devotees' Vraja *līlā-svarūpas* amid Gaura *ārati* accompanied by *nāma-saṅkīrtana*. In the *aprakaṭa pradoṣa-līlā* under discussion, Gaura's devotees also offer *ārati* to him and sing in *nāma-saṅkīrtana*. Purchased by their love, which serves as a portal to the *aprakaṭa* Vraja *līlā*, Gaura Kṛṣṇa and his devotees find themselves transported there. This is certainly wonderful!

Within Nanda's estate there is a great assembly hall suitable for entertainment. It plays a prominent role in Jīva Goswāmī's *Gopāla-campū*, where it is first mentioned. It is also mentioned in *Govinda-līlāmṛta* and in Nayanānanda Ṭhākura's *Preyo-bhakti-rasārṇava*. In Nayanānanda's text, it is described as a "garden temple" covered by a large awning.

At the outset of the *pradoṣa-līlā*, Vraja *vāsīs* fill Nanda's assembly hall, ostensibly to witness a wide variety of entertainment. Minstrels put the exploits of Rāma and Kṛṣṇa to music; poets recite; scholars lecture on the Purāṇas; and dancers, jugglers, clowns, and magicians all perform for the pleasure of the *rāja*. The underlying motivation of all the performers and the entire audience, however, is to have the *darśana* of Rāma and Kṛṣṇa. But as far as Nanda knows, Rāma is resting and Kṛṣṇa is about to do the same.

Nanda feels the growing anticipation of the assembly as well as Yaśodā's contrasting concern for her sons' need to rest after yet another very busy day. Thus, the *rāja* is perplexed as to how to proceed. However, without his knowledge, the *narma-sakhās* have dressed Rāma and Kṛṣṇa in royal attire. And surrounding them, they suddenly burst onto the scene, escorting the two cowherd princes to the raised platform reserved for them.

All eyes turn toward Kṛṣṇa:

> The guests' hearts swell like the ocean as the moonlike Hari rises on the *ghoṣa* mountain. Their *cakora*-like eyes feel delight in the sight of this Hari moon. Their hair stands on end like herbs nourished

by it. And in its soothing light, the lilies of their smiles unfurl like blooming lotuses of the night.[1]

In his meditative *antara-darśana*, the poet Rāya Śekhara envisions cowherd prince Kṛṣṇa at this time wearing a red-and-gold bandana around his head, the balance of his forehead decorated with sandalwood paste. Captivating earrings adorn his ears. A pearl hangs from his nose, a jewel necklace from his neck, and on his chest hangs a locket appropriate for this particular social occasion. The dashing sash around his waist holds a dagger. Holding hands with Balarāma, he enters the assembly.[2]

As Kṛṣṇa enters, he folds his hands before the priests and elders, showing them respect. He looks compassionately upon those who are junior to himself, and he sits among and playfully converses with his intimate friends. Rāma and Kṛṣṇa are seated among their friends but on an elevated platform. Kṛṣṇa is seated in the center, with Śrīdāmā and Sudāmā on his left and Balarāma on his right. Below and in front of Kṛṣṇa and Balarāma, the *narma-sakhās* are seated. Row after row of *sakhās* surround the cowherd princes, while servants bearing lamps light the night. All in all, the arena and its gathering of Nanda Rāja's subjects puts the celestial Amarāvatī hall of Indra and the denizens of heaven to shame.

At first, sages recite from the Vedas and extol the virtues of Kṛṣṇa's ancestors, and the entire audience stands and responds enthusiastically, creating considerable commotion. Then Nanda settles the crowd and orders the evening entertainment to commence.

Male and female dancers perform *tāṇḍava* and *lāsya*, respectively.[3] Actors dramatize the *līlās* of the *parāvastha-avatāras* Rāma and Narasiṁha.[4] Magicians perform astounding acts, such as causing a white dove to appear from underneath an empty woven basket turned upside down, upon seeing which

1. *Govinda-līlāmṛta* 21.6. The *cakora* is a type of partridge with a melodious voice. In Hindu poetry, it is thought to subsist on moonbeams and thus is always longing for and looking toward the distant moon.

2. *Aṣṭakāla-līlā-padāvalī* 97. Rāya Śekhara was a disciple of Raghunandana Goswāmī who was proficient in Vrajabuli poetry. When someone is wearing royal attire, a dagger typically represents compassion and the courage to defend all who are oppressed.

3. *Tāṇḍava* is a masculine form of dance associated with Śiva. It consists of a combination of difficult poses and limb movements. *Lāsya* is the feminine dance form related to the goddess Pārvatī that denotes happiness, grace, and beauty.

4. The term *parāvastha* is used by Rūpa Goswāmī in his *Laghu-bhāgavatāmṛta*. It refers to the three *avatāras*, Kṛṣṇa, Rāma, and Narasiṁha, who exhibit all six forms of opulence—wealth, strength, fame, beauty, wisdom, and renunciation—in varying degrees, descending in order beginning with Kṛṣṇa.

Kṛṣṇa desires that the dove have a companion. Thus, the same magician covers the dove and then lifts the basket again, revealing two doves, who fly off, ostensibly to where they have magically come from. Everyone present is amazed, especially the young cowherds. Jugglers juggle, and acrobats balance themselves on raised bamboo poles. Tantrics showcase their *yogic* abilities, such as pushing a string through one nostril and pulling it out the other. After the circus concludes, Nanda rewards the performers with gold, ornaments, and expensive clothing, which they formally appreciate, although they feel more blessed by the evening *darśana* of Rāma and Kṛṣṇa that they have just experienced. Concluding its description of the evening entertainment, *Govinda-līlāmṛta* muses:

> While the audience, with eyes akin to *cakora* birds, drinks the moonbeams of Kṛṣṇa's sweet smile, they paradoxically remain unfulfilled, for what they consume through their gaze trickles forth as tears. Such is the mystique of *prema*; who can fathom its depths?[5]

In the vision of Nayanānanda Ṭhākura, after the performers are rewarded and they disperse, Madhumaṅgala, not to be outdone by anyone, puts on a comedy of his own for the pleasure of all the *sakhās*. The heightened enthusiasm of the *sakhās* is, however, met with Yaśodā's concern for her sons' need to rest for the night. Thus, she sends the young household servant Raktaka to bring Kṛṣṇa and Balarāma to their separate bedrooms, at which time they must bid good night to all their friends except for Madhumaṅgala, who sleeps in Kṛṣṇa's bedroom.

Thus, Kṛṣṇa embraces Śrīdāmā and speaks sweetly to Subala and other *narma-sakhās* regarding confidential affairs. It is a scene that lasts as if forever, involving farewells and last-minute conversations recalling earlier events of the day and those just witnessed, while also suggesting adventures to be pursued in the days ahead. All of these previous and future events form lasting impressions that give rise to dreams throughout the night. Despite the confidence central to *sakhya-rasa*, the impending separation creates a heartrending scene.

As we learned earlier, some boys live in Nandagrāma and are for the most part related to Nanda Rāja's extended family. Others live in Vṛṣabhānupura as members of the extended family of Vṛṣabhānu Rāja. They all march homeward by torchlight in lighthearted conversation.

5. *Govinda-līlāmṛta* 21.16.

Central to Vṛṣabhānu-pura is the estate of Vṛṣabhānu Rāja and Kīrtidā, much like Nanda and Yaśodā's estate is central to Nandagrāma. Arriving there, all the boys from this vicinity first visit the *rāja*'s family estate. At this time, evening entertainment is also taking place within Vṛṣabhānu's compound. Indeed, the mood is festive and contagious, spreading itself throughout Varṣāṇā. Thus, the boys participate in the festivities at Śrīdāmā's house before proceeding to their own homes.

Meanwhile, as Rādhā's elder brother, Śrīdāmā-gopa, finally beds down, Rādhikā, who is now living in Yāvaṭa, secretly prepares to steal into the night and meet with Kṛṣṇa at their prearranged location. One of many such locations is highlighted in *Govinda-līlāmṛta*: Govinda-sthala, a tiny island within the dark and rushing waters of the Yamunā.

This sacred text shares a lengthy poetic description of the island, emphasizing its wide variety of flora and fauna. It is shaped like a lotus flower with a thousand petals, each petal a different bower. At the center of this lotus formation stands a jeweled cottage made out of precious stones and surrounded by golden-colored banana trees that resemble the stamens of a lotus.

Back at Nandagrāma, Kṛṣṇa endeavors to please his mother by retiring for the night. However, after the lights go out, so too does Hari. He heads to Govinda-sthala or any other prearranged meeting place, driven by the desire to experience Rādhā's love. He departs through the side door of his bedroom after locking the front door. Sometimes he goes alone, and sometimes he is assisted by *narma-sakhās* such as Subala.

On the particular night of Kṛṣṇadāsa Kavirāja Goswāmī's depiction of the *pradoṣa-līlā*, the moon is waxing. In consideration of the moonlight, certain measures are taken to help ensure that Rādhā is not seen as she steals into the night. The same holds true for the dark-moon night, when opposite measures are taken. During the full moon, Rādhā wears white garments, dons white pearl jewelry, places white flowers in her hair, and smears her limbs with a whitish unguent consisting of camphor and sandalwood paste. Dressed so, she is more illuminating and love intoxicating than the moon's shine, even as she aims to hide herself with her outfit. During the waning-moon nights, Rādhikā wears dark-blue garments, musk ointment, *kṛṣṇa-aguru-tilaka*, blue-lotus ear decorations, and blue sapphire ornaments.

We are reminded of Raghunātha dāsa Goswāmī's vision of a similar waxing-moon, if not full-moon, night during the spring season on which a meeting place had not been prearranged. We find this description in the first verse of the Goswāmī's *Prema-pūrābhidha-stotram*—"The Hymn Known as the Cream of *Prema*"—which we referenced earlier, in the circumference of this *sakhya-maṇḍala*.[6]

In this *bhāva*-infused poetry, Gaura's Raghu of Svarūpa, deeply absorbed in trance, is experiencing himself in his *bhāva-deha* as Tulasī-mañjarī. Therein, this vision comes to him, and then he loses sight of it and longs for it to return. What does he see? First, this is what he says:

> O Rādhe! Dressed in a white flower garment and anointed with ground camphor, on a sweet moonlit spring night you place your hand on the shoulder of one of your *dūtikās* as you follow Subala. For just one moment, may my eyes delight in this sight!

And again, what does he see? He glimpses a section of the final portion of Vraja's *pradoṣa-līlā*. On this moonlit spring night, he first sees Kṛṣṇa along with Subala, basking in the moonlight within a forest bower. The night is extremely beautiful and soothing. However, its beauty serves as an *uddīpana* that brings Śyāma's deep, tempestuous love for Rādhā to the surface, as the sights and sounds of the forest remind Kṛṣṇa of Rādhā's beauty, the sound of her ankle bells, and so on. Subala immediately understands Kṛṣṇa's condition. Thus, he takes it upon himself to find the *dūtikā* (messenger) Vṛndā and tell her to somehow bring Rādhā to him. Then Subala will escort the two of them and any *mañjarī* Rādhā chooses to the bower where Kṛṣṇa is longing for Rādhā's love.

Meanwhile, Rādhā is also affected by the enchanting atmosphere, which brings *her* love for Kṛṣṇa to the surface. Thus, she longs to meet him, as if in her *anurāga* she has never been able to do so thus far. As her heart swells, *dūtikā* Vṛndā, bearing the news concerning Śyāma's condition, appears on the scene.

As Subala waits midway between Yāvaṭa and the bower, Vṛndā arrives with Rādhā, who, burdened by the news of Kṛṣṇa's heartache, rests her hand on Vṛndā's shoulder, Rādhā's maidservant Tulasī following like her shadow behind her. Once they meet up with Subala, he leads them to Kṛṣṇa.

In his *Stavāvalī* commentary, Ananta dāsa Bābājī cites a Bengali verse from the *Gauḍīya Vaiṣṇava Padāvalī* restating the vision of Śrī Raghunātha dāsa's Sanskrit *śloka*. My English rendering follows:

> In the sweetness of spring, trees full of fragrant flowers glitter in the moonlight, filling the night with their redolence, as Rādhikā pursues

6. See chapter 5.

> her Hari *abhiṣāra* (rendezvous). She is dressed in a shining white, flower-like garment, and her limbs are also adorned with white ornaments. Accompanied by Subala-sakhā, she walks along coyly, her hand resting on Vṛndā's shoulder. She who is Hari *abhisāriṇī* is my *īśvarī ṭhākurāṇī*. May she quench my thirsty *cakora*-like eyes with *ānanda* for just one moment. Such is my mind's desire!

Thus, Dāsa Goswāmī sees Rādhikā for a split second in his meditation, and along with her he sees himself in his *mañjarī-svarūpāveśa* as Tulasī-mañjarī. Such is the result of his *bhāva*-infused imagination, grounded and deeply rooted in *rasa-tattva*: Rādhā *darśana*, a rare vision that even all-attractive Kṛṣṇa pines for. Dāsa Goswāmī sees this picture in meditation, and then it dissipates. Coming back to external consciousness from his spiritual trance, he then poeticizes about it, living only in longing to experience it again. His perspective is that of *mañjarī-bhāva*, from which we learn something significant about the *narma-sakhās*: the nature of Subala's occasional participation in the final portion of the *pradoṣa-līlā*, extending into the *niśa-līlā*, to which we now turn.

25

Night

Niśa-līlā

The *bhāva* in which Śrīmān Gaurasundara leaves his home and enters the courtyard of Śrīvāsa Ṭhākura is that of Rādhā stealing into the night to rendezvous with Śyāma. In Śrīvāsa Ṭhākura's courtyard, Svarūpa Dāmodara sings in *līlā-kīrtana* of Vraja's *niśa-līlās*, and Gaura is transported into that sacred realm. Then the *mahā-rasa-saṅkīrtana* is performed, and everyone experiences the *rāsa-līlā* from their Vraja *svarūpa* perspective.[1] Following the *saṅkīrtana*, the devotees assemble and enjoy refreshments. When Śrīvāsa hands Gaura a mango, he places it in the ground, and a mango tree full of fruit immediately sprouts. The devotees are all amazed, and they then feast on the miraculous mangoes. Following the refreshments, everyone bathes in the Gaṅgā before retiring for the night. Gaura either sleeps there in the compound of Śrīvāsa or returns home.

With the late-night *milana* of Rādhā and Kṛṣṇa, their *niśa-līlā* begins in earnest. Although it is centered on the meeting of Rādhā and Kṛṣṇa, all

1. Here the term *rāsa-līlā* means one of two things, relative to one's Kṛṣṇa *līlā-svarūpa*. For *gopī-bhāva* it refers to the *rāsa* dance *līlā* itself, a *līlā* that *narma-sakhās* may witness to some extent. For others, it refers simply to the height of *rasa* experienced in any *līlā* relative to their *svarūpa*. As Jīva Goswāmī explains, "The pastime that contains the greatest amount of *rasa* is called the *rāsa-līlā*." Here *rasa* refers to "relish," and when it is written with a long "a" as *rāsa-līlā*, it refers to the *līlā* that contains the most relish. Objectively, the *rāsa* dance is the *līlā* with the most *rasa*, while subjectively speaking that *līlā* with the most *rasa* is relative to one's *sthāyi-bhāva*.

the other Vraja *sundarīs* also meet their beloved Śyāmasundara at this time. *Govinda-līlāmṛta* cites Kṛṣṇa's thoughts at this hour, thoughts very similar to those depicted in the poetry of the *Bhāgavata* as that most sacred text begins its five-chapter *rāsa-līlā* narrative describing the climax of the *prakaṭa-līlā*.

> When Hari sees the moonlit night, the forest, the bank of the Yamunā, and his dearmost *gopīs*, the desire for *rāsa-vilāsa*—enjoyment of the *rāsa-līlā*—arises in his heart.[2]

Rūpa Goswāmī cites a verse in which a *sādhana-siddha gopī* enters this *rāsa-līlā* setting for the first time. As she does, Kṛṣṇa teases her and asks what she is doing there and what kind of boy she thinks he is. He does so in the presence of Subala:

> "O foolish girl! Go back to the village. Don't flutter your eyes at me. I am not the type of boy you think I am! Why are you talking so much?" When Kṛṣṇa speaks in a teasing manner with this new girlfriend, Subala's eyes widen with laughter as he gazes at Kṛṣṇa's face.[3]

Here, amid his fraternal love, Subala-sakhā experiences *hāsya-rasa* as an *aṅga* of his fraternal love along with *mādhurya-rasa*.[4] Thus, we find *narma-sakhā-bhāva* present once again during the *niśa-līlā*. We also found it in Raghunātha dāsa Goswāmī's *Prema-pūrābhidha-stotram*, cited in our description of the *pradoṣa-līlā*. Therein, Śrī Raghunātha dāsa refers to the *niśa-līlā* and its sweetness—*madhu madhura niśāyāṁ*...

We saw Subala bring Rādhā to Kṛṣṇa at the end of the *pradoṣa-līlā*. Thereafter, he does not return home as the *niśa-līlā* commences. Along with Vṛndā and Tulasī-mañjarī, Subala remains and relishes the transpsychological mood swing of Rādhā. As she approaches the gate to the bower and sees her beloved Śyāma within the gate, suddenly she turns to Subala without speaking to Kṛṣṇa and asks Subala with indignation why he has brought her to this particular bower. Ignoring Kṛṣṇa, she abruptly informs Subala that she is going home. Subala offers no answer as to why he has brought

2. *Govinda-līlāmṛta* 22.5. See *Śrīmad Bhāgavatam* 10.29.1 for the comparison.

3. *Bhakti-rasāmṛta-sindhu* 4.8.27. From the commentary of Bhaktivedanta Swami Prabhupāda in his summary study of *Bhakti-rasāmṛta-sindhu*—*The Nectar of Devotion*—we learn that this pastime takes place during the *niśa-līlā*.

4. Śrī Rūpa cites this verse as an example of *sakhya* as the *aṅgi-rasa* mixed with *hāsya* as the *aṅga-rasa*. Lest one mistakenly take this to indicate that *mādhurya* is not always present as an *aṅga-rasa* in the *narma-sakhā*'s *bhāva*, Jīva Goswāmī comments that *mādhurya-rasa* is also present in this *līlā* as an *aṅga-rasa* nourishing Subala's *sakhya-rasa* along with *hāsya-rasa*.

her there, nor is Rādhā really asking for one, and Subala and Vṛndā drown in their experience of Rādhā's *mahābhāva*. Here her *mahābhāva* expresses itself as outwardly angry but internally pleased—*kuṭṭamita-bhāva*.

Why is Rādhā angry and threatening to return to Yāvaṭa? She desires to see just how eager Kṛṣṇa really is to meet with her, and thus she pretends to be uninterested in him. After all, why would a girl from such a noble family be interested in this young knave? Because he is so charming, of course! Thus, Rādhā-vinodinī gives Hari the opportunity to display his charm and his strength, to the delight of Subala, Vṛndā, and Tulasī, as he picks Rādhā up and carries her back into the bower.

Of course, every night is different. And while on some nights all the *narma-sakhās* may be content to dream through the love play of the *niśa-līlā*, at other times they are active participants. Another example of their active participation is found in *Vidagdha-mādhava*'s *veṇu-haraṇa-līlā*. Readers will recall that this *līlā* is described in chapter 21. It is centered on the competitive love between Rādhā and Candrāvalī, and both Madhumaṅgala and Subala play significant roles in the *niśa-līlā* on this particular night.

Śrī Rūpa's *veṇu-haraṇa-līlā* begins as the moon rises and the cows are settled in for the night. Kṛṣṇa has skipped out on the evening milking and is standing on Mount Govardhana with his friend Subala. Subala asks Śyāma what his sudden eagerness is all about and what he expects to gain by forgoing the milking. Kṛṣṇa explains that someone had described a peacock using the word *candrakāvalīm* (a fan of feathers) to describe the bird's raised rainbow-like tail as it danced madly before him. Kṛṣṇa says that upon hearing this word he was reminded of Candrāvalī and now he longs to meet with her.

However, Kṛṣṇa's eagerness does not do much for Subala, who disinterestedly suggests that Kṛṣṇa beckon her with his flute. Following Subala's suggestion, Kṛṣṇa plays his flute and insists that Subala should support him in his effort to attract Candrāvalī, to which Subala merely replies, "Okay."

Meanwhile, Rādhā is in a hut within a bower of *karṇikāra* flowers close to Mukharā's house, near the northern pastures along the bank of the Yamunā. Candrāvalī, on the other hand, is in the vicinity of the southern pastures, where she is accustomed to staying. There she is lamenting that Kṛṣṇa seldom comes to this area, which is her way of saying that he loves Rādhā more than he loves her. However, Padmā, one of her *priya-sakhīs*, informs her that at this very moment Kṛṣṇa is on the slope of Mount Govardhana very near to Candrāvalī's village, Sakhī-sthalī. Candrāvalī replies in disbelief, only to hear the sound of Mādhava's *muralī*.

Thus, Kṛṣṇa and Candrāvalī meet and exchange words. However, the meeting goes south when Kṛṣṇa indirectly and accidentally expresses his love for Rādhā. While he intends to say that in the fire of his separation from Candrāvalī he seeks relief from a forest stream—*dhārā*—he mistakenly utters, "Rādhā." Candrāvalī of course picks up on it, as does her *sakhī* Padmā. And despite Kṛṣṇa's excuses and efforts to convince her that he was not referring to Rādhā, Candrāvalī is no fool. Expressing jealous anger at first and then hiding her face, she pretends otherwise. Given her overall nature, Candrāvalī, unlike Rādhā, is somewhat ashamed of her own jealous anger. Supported by Padmā's logic as to the fact of Kṛṣṇa's love for Rādhā, Candrāvalī turns homeward. Kṛṣṇa laments, but Subala tells him that she did not appear to be upset. Then Kṛṣṇa explains to Subala that from the signs on Candrāvalī's face she was angry with him at heart. However, Subala is Rādhikā's *kiṅkara*, and he looks for an opportunity to turn Kṛṣṇa toward her and away from Candrāvalī.

This opportunity presents itself when Kṛṣṇa decides to enter a nearby grove of *bakula* trees and strategize with Subala about how to proceed. Therein Kṛṣṇa admires the pleasant scenery, telling Subala, "This grove, with its abundance of water [*nīra adhika*], is very pleasant." Of course, the words *nīra adhika* can be read as *nīrādhikā*, meaning "without Rādhā." Subala takes it that way and sees it as an opportunity to express his conviction: "If Rādhā *were* here, *then* it would be very pleasant." Hearing this, Kṛṣṇa embraces his friend and concurs, telling him to relate this truth to Lalitā and thereby to Rādhā herself. Thus, in Śrī Rūpa's drama, Subala's dedication to Rādhā is underscored amid Kṛṣṇa's *niśa-līlā.*

Śrī Rūpa's *veṇu-haraṇa-līlā* continues well into the night. Further romantic intrigue involving Rādhā and Candrāvalī is assisted by Madhumaṅgala's blunders, which repeatedly put Kṛṣṇa in a jam before both milkmaidens. The "theft" of the flute occurs when Rādhikā extends her *sāri* to receive an offering of flowers from Kṛṣṇa, who, bewildered by her enchanting eyebrows accidentally hands her his flute along with the flowers. Thus, the *līlā* takes yet another turn as it extends itself through the *niśānta-līlā* and into the following day.

From Rādhā's hand, the flute is stolen by Jaṭilā, who catches Rādhā and Kṛṣṇa together in the predawn hours. Jaṭilā then loses the flute later that morning to the she-monkey Kakkhaṭī, who is working under Vṛndā's direction, and eventually Kakkhaṭī secretly gives it to Vṛndā. Meanwhile, Rādhā is held captive by Jaṭilā and her son.

Kṛṣṇa's condition is critical at this time, and Subala is determined to mitigate his pangs of love in separation. Thus, Subala, disguised as Rādhā and bearing Kṛṣṇa's flute, returns the *muralī* and partially mitigates Kṛṣṇa's pain of separation, letting him think that he is experiencing the *darśana* of Rādhā without getting too close to him. In disguise, Subala also serves as cover for Rādhā. As such, he manages to save her from the accusations of Jaṭilā. When Jaṭilā thinks Subala is Rādhā and brings the disguised Subala before the council of elderly women, claiming she has caught Rādhā red-handed with Kṛṣṇa the night before, Subala removes his disguise, to the embarrassment of Jaṭilā, and Rādhā's good name is preserved.

Thus, through Śrī Rūpa's *veṇu-haraṇa-līlā*, we find further evidence confirming that *narma-sakhā-bhāva* may on occasion also play a role in the *niśa-līlā* and, for that matter, the *niśānta-līlā* as well. Here it will be helpful to once again remember Rūpa Goswāmī's rhetorical question posed in his role as Rādhikā's handmaiden—Rūpa-mañjarī—with the intention of instilling love for Subala in the heart of one of her new friends: "What *sevā* is Śrīmān Subala not eligible for!"[5] Of course, there are particular services he does not render, given his role, but there is no *līlā* time frame that he is disqualified to participate in. However, to be clear, the *niśa-līlā* is not about *sakhya-rasa*, and it is even less so than the *madhyāhna-līlā*. The same holds true for the *niśānta-līlā*. But as we have seen, *narma-sakhā-bhāva* can sometimes participate in the *niśa-līlā* and *niśānta-līlā* time frames, and this fact serves as yet another example of how *sakhya-rasa*'s influence pervades Kṛṣṇa's Vraja *līlā*, albeit in a supporting role.

Because the *aṣṭakāla-līlā-granthas* of the Gauḍīya *sampradāya*, focused as they are on *mādhurya-rasa*, do not highlight any occasional supporting role of *narma-sakhā-bhāva* during the *niśa-līlā* beyond what has been related above, we will not explore this *līlā* in depth. But the typical *niśa-līlā* setting is, after all, one that *narma-sakhās* are at least eligible to dream about, and thus herein we shall describe it in brief.

Following the *aṣṭakāla-līlā* narratives, we find the *niśa-līlā* beginning with the meeting of Rādhā and Kṛṣṇa as Vṛndā and her *vana-devīs* worship the divine couple, drawing items for their worship from the opulence of the sacred forests. Rādhā and Mādhava again experience the six seasons as they pass through the forests of Vraja singing, dancing, and joking while they recite riddles. When Kṛṣṇa and the *gopīs* arrive at the bank of the Yamunā, the *gopīs* form a circle, which Rādhā and Kṛṣṇa stand in the center of. Thus,

5. *Ujjvala-nīlamaṇi* 2.14.

the great *rāsa-līlā* commences, and despite the moon's phase at the time, the moon eternally turns full every night during the *rāsa-līlā*. After the *rāsa* dance, Kṛṣṇa and the *gopīs* become intoxicated from drinking fermented honey, initially intended for relieving their fatigue. Their lotus eyes roll, and Rādhā-Mādhava fall asleep on a flower bed. Upon awakening, they bathe and play water sports in the Yamunā. After bathing, they enjoy sweets and forest fruits before they bed down for the night, assisted by *sakhīs* and *mañjarīs* fanning them and massaging their feet before they themselves also take rest.

This brings us to the conclusion of our *niśa-līlā* discussion, the final time frame of the *aṣṭakāla-līlā* viewed through the lens of *narma-sakhā-bhāva*. But as we conclude, surely readers will recall that at the outset of this *aṣṭakāla-līlā* narrative we suggested another way in which *narma-sakhā-upāsakas* may participate in the *niśa-līlā*: Such is the grace of Gaura and his Nadīyā *aprakaṭa-līlā*! Gaura's *niśa-līlā* takes place during the perpetual full moon shining down on the courtyard of Śrīvāsa Ṭhākura, the Nārada Muni of Gaura *līlā*. As we have seen, Nārada is an expansion of the Vraja *līlā*'s Madhumaṅgala.[6] Thus, Kṛṣṇadāsa Kavirāja also identifies Śrīvāsa with Madhumaṅgala, and arguably Vṛndāvana dāsa Ṭhākura does as well.[7] Surely Madhumaṅgala, a *narma-sakhā* and *kiṅkara* of Śrī Rādhā, has established a residence (*vāsa*) for Rādhikā (*śrī*) in the core of his heart—*śrīvāsa*. Thus, under the spiritual bias of *narma-sakhā-bhāva*, it is quite natural to assume that Gaura has chosen such a *narma-sakhā*'s heart, manifest as an eternal courtyard of *kīrtana*, as the most sacred place in which to experience the *rāsa-līlā* of Vraja in Rādhā *bhāva* and to share that experience with his devotees. After all, "The best friend is he who reminds one of his beloved"—*gāḍhopakārī smṛti-daḥ priyāṇām*.[8]

6. See chapter 2, footnote 32.

7. In *Caitanya-caritāmṛta* 2.14.229, Śrīvāsa expresses the spirit and *anubhāvas* of Madhumaṅgala. *Caitanya-bhāgavata* 2.2.270 also implies that Śrīvāsa internally identifies with *sakhya-rasa* of Vraja: When Mahāprabhu comes to see Śrīvāsa while he worships his Narasiṁha deity, he breaks Śrīvāsa's trance and tells him to recite prayers. Śrīvāsa cites the first of Brahmā's prayers, in which the object of love for those in *sakhya-rasa* is described. Similarly, in the Vraja *līlā*, Madhumaṅgala is also the *pūjārī* for the household Narasiṁha deity of Nanda Mahārāja. And after Gaurasundara embraced *sannyāsa*, Śrīvāsa moved to Kumārahaṭṭa and worshiped deities of Gaura-Nityānanda. He was also the lead singer in Nityānanda's *kīrtana* group during the Ratha-yātrā, and when he first met Nitāi, and Gaura asked Śrīvāsa to chant an appropriate *Bhāgavata* verse, he recited 10.21.5 describing Kṛṣṇa in rustic cowherd dress surrounded by his *sakhās* singing of his virtues.

8. *Bṛhad-bhāgavatāmṛta* 1.7.128.

PART 4

Tangents

Sakhya-Tattva-Śeṣa

26

Birth of Balarāma

The elderly mystic Paurṇamāsī, wrapped in saffron cloth and effulgent as the full moon after whom she is named,[1] arrived in Vraja accompanied by the farcical *brāhmaṇa* boy Madhumaṅgala, who was posing as the student of Nārada.[2] These two companions forever remain their present ages.

The timing of their arrival coincided with the yet unknown pregnancy of Yaśodā, an event that the entire cowherd community longed for in such measure that they became consumed by their *laulyam*—a longing like that experienced in the long dark night of the soul's separation from its source. Paurṇamāsī ended this darkness with a mystic insight that she readily shared with the cowherds: the male child that Nanda and Yaśodā longed for—an heir to the kingdom of the cowherds—was already within Yaśodā's womb!

At this time, an auspicious childbearing lady arrived stealthily on a black mare. Like a cow of plenty, this woman was named after the asterism Rohiṇī, which is depicted as a reddish (*aruṇa*) cow that brings tidings of a plentiful harvest.[3] This second mother, bearing him who would be the very best friend of Yaśodā's own child, met in bliss with Yaśodā. The camaraderie of the ladies would be excelled only by their sons' fraternal feelings for one another.

Rohiṇī's son appeared on the full moon of the Śrāvaṇa monsoon season, eight days before the birth of Yaśomatī's Nandana. What can be said about

1. In *Gopāla-campū*, Jīva Goswāmī dresses Paurṇamāsī in saffron despite the fact that she is named after the full moon and the fact that Rūpa Goswāmī drapes her in white in *Rādhā-kṛṣṇa-gaṇoddeśa-dīpikā*.

2. See footnote 32 in chapter 2.

3. *Aruṇa*—reddish brown/rust—is the color of *sakhya-rati*. The black mare mentioned in the previous sentence conceals Rohiṇī's nighttime escape from Mathurā to Vraja.

his appearance, when words fail even in capturing the fullness of ordinary events? Although words fail to do justice to him, we are not rendered silent. He himself was from far beyond meditative silence, from a realm about which one cannot say enough.[4] Crystal-like in complexion, like the sun's light reflected in the full moon, this boy was born to give joy to the son of Yaśodā, to reflect his light and make it approachable, just as the *guru* does in relation to God.

Perhaps the most astounding thing about his birth was that despite his beauty and other auspicious qualities, he seemed unconscious of the world around him. Only when Yaśodā took him on her lap and he could feel his brother within her womb would he come to life, and only after her son, Kṛṣṇa, was born did this peculiarity subside. His names are Rāma, Bala, and Saṅkarṣaṇa—Balarāma—and he is Kṛṣṇa's best friend and older brother. Although he is *sakhya-rasa* personified, he is Viṣṇu-tattva, not *śakti-tattva.* The two, Rāma and Kṛṣṇa, are respectively *sevaka-* and *sevya-bhagavān.*

Balarāma's beauty knows no bounds. His feet are soft like lotuses, the hands of his long, strong arms reach his knees, his broad chest is garlanded with a *guñjā-mālā*, and his dark hair is tied in a topknot circled with a bounty of forest flowers. His complexion is clear and white like reflective moonlight.

He is Bhagavān of a friendly frame of mind: he sometimes serves, while at other times he is concerned with how his younger brother behaves. Sages call him Baladeva. Mighty, witty, wise, and well dressed in midnight blue, he wears a *tilaka* made of musk, dark in hue. His single earring kisses his cheek, and a lotus circled by bees decorates his ear. O Balarāma of voice deep in tone, when will I hear your call to serve—the sound of your buffalo horn?

4. This is the implication of *Vedanta-sūtra* 1.1.5, *īkṣater nāśabdam*. Bhagavān and his abode cannot be captured by the limits of mind or speech, but this should not render us silent when it comes to him. Rather, about him we can speak forever. Such is his nature.

27

Baladeva tattva

In Rūpa Goswāmī's *Laghu-bhāgavatāmṛta*, Balarāma is categorized as a *vaibhava* form of Kṛṣṇa.[1] The two-armed, flute-bearing cowherd Gopāla Kṛṣṇa is *svayaṁ-rūpa*, the original form of the Godhead, in whom all other manifestations of himself are contained.[2] For the sake of his *līlā*, sometimes *svayaṁ-rūpa* Kṛṣṇa expands into replica forms of himself, such as when picnicking with his friends along the banks of the Yamunā. At that time, Kṛṣṇa expanded himself such that each cowherd thought that Kṛṣṇa was sitting across from him and placing food in his mouth alone. Similarly, in his *rāsa-līlā*, Kṛṣṇa expanded into as many forms as there were *gopīs* dancing with him. This type of expansion of *svayaṁ-rūpa* Kṛṣṇa, in which each form manifested is exactly the same as his *svayaṁ-rūpa* in both physicality and psychology, is termed *prābhava-prakāśa*. However, when *svayaṁ-rūpa* Kṛṣṇa expands himself for *līlās* that require different emotional content, such expansions are termed *vaibhava-prakāśa*, even while such forms are for the most part physically the same as his *svayaṁ-rūpa*. In the Vraja *līlā*, only these two kinds of expansions are required: forms of Kṛṣṇa with the same emotional makeup and forms with differing emotional makeup. While the *prābhava-prakāśa* forms are many—as many as there are *gopas* and *gopīs* for Kṛṣṇa to stand between—there is only one *vaibhava-prakāśa* in Vraja: Balarāmajī.

Following Śrī Rūpa's lead in *Laghu-bhāgavatāmṛta*, Kṛṣṇadāsa Kavirāja Goswāmī elaborates, explaining that the *vaibhava-prakāśa* forms of Kṛṣṇa differ from *svayaṁ-rūpa* Kṛṣṇa in emotional content.[3] Śrī Kṛṣṇadāsa goes on

1. *Laghu-bhāgavatāmṛta* 1.4.48–49.
2. *Laghu-bhāgavatāmṛta* 1.1.11–12.
3. *Caitanya-caritāmṛta* 2.20.171.

to say that other than the difference in their complexions, the two, Kṛṣṇa and Balarāma, are equal.[4] In *Hari-vaṁśa Purāṇa*, Kṛṣṇa speaks to Balarāma, stressing the brothers' oneness in *tattva*:

> That which I am, you are as well. That which you are, I am as well in eternity. We have become two, but we are certainly one in two bodies, a pair endowed with great power.[5]

The emphasis here is on the divinity of Balarāma, as well as on Kṛṣṇa and Balarāma as the combined object of love for those who idealize *sakhya-rati*. This is an important *tattva* perspective: Kṛṣṇa and Balarāma are both the Godhead. They appear in the world together, not separately. However, despite this oneness of Kṛṣṇa and Balarāma in *tattva*, there is a difference between the two, a difference in both complexion and emotion—*bhāva*.

Color and emotion are related. Thus, the difference in their complexions also speaks of their emotional difference from one another. Kṛṣṇa's complexion is *śyāma* (indigo), and in Indian aesthetic theory this color corresponds with the *rasa* over which he presides, *śṛṅgāra/mādhurya-rasa*.[6] Balarāma's color is *pāṇḍura* (whitish), like that of the moon or a crystal, and this is the color assigned to the comedic *rasa*—*hāsya*—over which Balarāma presides and which among the *rasas* is the best friend of *sakhya-rasa*.[7] Indeed, in the *Śrīmad Bhāgavatam*'s tenth canto, fifteenth chapter—the height of *sakhya-rasa* in the *Bhāgavatam*—we find that Kṛṣṇa's lengthy praise of Balarāma amid their friends is spoken in the rapture of *hāsya-rasa*.

Both the crystal and the moon are agents of reflection. The crystal expresses the color of that which is placed beside it, and the moon reflects the light of the sun. These two objects from the natural world, which are identified with Balarāma's complexion, also tell us something about his emotional makeup. Kṛṣṇa is *sevya-bhagavān* (served Bhagavān), and Balarāma

4. *Caitanya-caritāmṛta* 2.20.174.

5. *Hari-vaṁśa Purāṇa* 2.14.48.

6. Gauḍīya Vaiṣṇavas often refer to *śṛṅgāra-rasa* (romantic love) by the term *mādhurya*, which has an earlier precedent in Indian aesthetic theory. Gauḍīyas justify the use of this term by stating that it is appropriate because of *śṛṅgāra-rasa*'s sweetness (*mādhurya* means "sweetness"). However, *mādhurya* is also employed to refer to the intimacy of humanlike love we find in Vraja overall, as opposed to *aiśvarya-prema*, or majestic, more formal love for Kṛṣṇa's form of Nārāyaṇa found in Vaikuṇṭha.

7. While one might think that Balarāma presides over *sakhya-rasa* itself, this honor belongs to Vāmana/Upendra, the Viṣṇu *avatāra* and friend of Indra. Interestingly, when Indra apologized to Kṛṣṇa for the disturbance he caused in the Govardhana *līlā*, he anointed Kṛṣṇa the God of the gods, giving him the names Govinda and Upendra.

is *sevaka-bhagavān* (servitor Bhagavān). Balarāma causes us to thoughtfully reflect back upon Kṛṣṇa, the object of his *sevā*, from whom Rāma draws his light and life in ways that no other manifestation of the Godhead does.

In *tattva*, Balarāma is God himself, but emotionally he experiences himself primarily as Kṛṣṇa's friend.[8] His *sakhya-rati* is bundled with *dāsya-* and *vātsalya-rati*;[9] that is, within the context of his *sakhya-rati*, Balarāma sometimes expresses himself in service to Kṛṣṇa and at other times acts as Kṛṣṇa's well-wisher. In other words, Balarāma's *sakhya-rati* mediates between two otherwise incompatible emotions, *dāsya* and *vātsalya*. In Vraja his *sakhya* predominates, although examples of his *dāsya* and *vātsalya* are not lacking.[10] Outside of Vraja, in Mathurā and Dvārakā, his *dāsya* is more dominant,[11] and outside of Kṛṣṇa *līlā* itself his *dāsya* is that much more prominent in his *sevā* rendered to countless *avatāras* of the Godhead.

Although we are concerned only with Balarāma of Vraja, it may help us in understanding his role in the Vraja *līlā* to look beyond this pastoral realm to Rāma's role elsewhere. With the exceptions of the Nara Nārāyaṇa and Mohinī-mūrti *avatāras*, wherever Kṛṣṇa manifests, his consort does as well.[12] As Dvārakā Kṛṣṇa, he is accompanied by Rukmiṇī; as Nārāyaṇa, he is accompanied by Lakṣmī; and as all of his *līlā-avatāras*, he is accompanied by a corresponding Lakṣmī as well. However, wherever Kṛṣṇa manifests himself as Viṣṇu along with Lakṣmī, Balarāma in the form of Ananta Śeṣa accompanies him. Here, three is not a crowd. Balarāma is more concerned with Kṛṣṇa than he is with any consort of his own. Even in the expansions in which he *is* accompanied by a consort—Mūla-saṅkarṣaṇa, Mahā-saṅkarṣaṇa, Lakṣmaṇa, and Nityānanda—his relationship with his consort is secondary to his preoccupation with *sevā* to Kṛṣṇa, Nārāyaṇa, Rāmacandra, and Gaura Kṛṣṇa, respectively.[13]

8. In *sakhya-rasa* he also experiences himself as the object of his friends' love along with Kṛṣṇa. He is also the object of love for devotees in *dāsya-*, *vātsalya-*, and *mādhurya-rasa*. But he is not the object of romantic love for Kṛṣṇa's *gopīs*.

9. *Bhakti-rasāmṛta-sindhu* 3.4.81. This bundling of *rasas* is termed *saṅkula-rati*, the permanent combining of *rasas* in which one *rasa* predominates. Balarāma's *saṅkula-rati* is *sakhya-rasa* bundled together with lesser influences of *vātsalya* and *dāsya*. This teaching of Rūpa Goswāmī is discussed in greater detail in chapter 4.

10. See *Caitanya-caritāmṛta* 1.5.136–141.

11. In *Prīti Sandarbha* 82, Jīva Goswāmī explains that in Vraja Rāma's *dāsya* and *vātsalya* are situated within his *sakhya* whereas in Dvārakā his *sakhya* and *vātsalya* are situated within his *dāsya*.

12. Kṛṣṇa's Nara Nārāyaṇa *avatāra* is celibate, and Mohinī is female.

13. Notably, when Rāmacandra married Sītā, Lakṣmaṇa married her younger sister,

Aside from the exceptions mentioned above, every manifestation of Viṣṇu is accompanied by an expansion of Balarāma who serves him in all respects other than in the romanticism of Lakṣmī.[14] While Lakṣmī is *śakti-tattva*, Balarāma is Viṣṇu *tattva*. Nevertheless, he serves much like the *śakti-tattva* in *sakhya*, *dāsya*, and *vātsalya*. Kṛṣṇadāsa Kavirāja describes him as the root of the serving ego in all devotees—*bhakta-abhimāna mūla śrī-balarāme*.[15] Furthermore, Balarāma is the very fabric of existence—its warp and weft—presiding as he does over the *sandhinī-śakti*, or existential potency of the Godhead. From his serving ego, the realms for Kṛṣṇa's various *līlās*, those of both this world—*sṛṣṭi-līlā*—and the world beyond, are manifested.

While Nārāyaṇa and his *avatāras* are not separate from *svayaṁ* Bhagavān Śrī Kṛṣṇa, in that they are his partial manifestations, they are nonetheless emotionally complete. However, unlike them, Balarāma is not emotionally complete without Kṛṣṇa. He lives only for the service of Kṛṣṇa. In his commentary to *Śrīmad Bhāgavatam* 10.1.24, Jīva Goswāmī writes, "He shines only in connection with Kṛṣṇa, who is nondifferent from himself. Balarāma cannot stay anywhere without Kṛṣṇa." Similarly, in *Gopāla-campū* 2.20.32, Śrī Jīva explains, "Balarāma does not consider himself Balarāma without the presence of Kṛṣṇa."

In Vraja, Balarāma is Kṛṣṇa's best friend, but he is not directly involved in Kṛṣṇa's romantic life, and his own romantic life in Vraja is but an afterthought. Balarāma's being Kṛṣṇa's older brother precludes his being directly involved in the romanticism of Rādhā and Kṛṣṇa that is central to the Vṛndāvana *līlā*. His direct involvement or presence would inhibit the intimacy of Kṛṣṇa's romantic love for Rādhā. As Kṛṣṇa's elder brother, he is the *maryādā-puruṣa* in his younger brother's life, ably assisting Yaśodā in looking out for him and assuring Kṛṣṇa's *maryādā* (appropriate behavior). But though he will report to the elders on Kṛṣṇa's behavior, he does not report Kṛṣṇa's secret romantic rendezvous. Instead, he facilitates them during the day by occupying the friends of Kṛṣṇa not inclined to participate in these affairs. Thereby, he assures these friends' restful nights filled with dreams of fraternal sport, and at the same time he indirectly facilitates Kṛṣṇa's midday love sports in the company of his

---

Ūrmilā, but when Rāma was exiled, Lakṣmaṇa left Ūrmilā behind and entered the forest along with Rāma to serve his older brother.

14. Balarāma serves Kṛṣṇa/Viṣṇu in ten ways: as his shoes, clothes, bed, umbrella, seat, sacred thread, house, ornaments, pillow, and himself personally. By serving as his bed, he is thought to indirectly participate in Kṛṣṇa's romantic life.

15. *Caitanya-caritāmṛta* 1.6.88.

most intimate friends. Surely, if Balarāma does not report on Rādhā and Kṛṣṇa's romantic affairs, they are no more than rumors. This is what Rāma's elders make of his silence. Thus, in the drama of the Vraja *līlā*, Balarāma is an important supporting actor. His own romantic life is like that of the hero's best friend, who also has a wife, but in the drama the audience does not even know her name.

The first reference to Rāma's romantic life appears in the fifteenth chapter of the tenth canto of the *Bhāgavata Purāṇa*. As Kṛṣṇa concludes his tribute to Rāma, his humor heightens. While ostensibly glorifying Balarāma, in this line he humorously refers indirectly much more to himself:

> The *gopīs* are fortunate because you directly embrace them to your chest, which is desired even by Lakṣmī.[16]

Here, Kṛṣṇa's glorification of Balarāma refers more directly to himself because it is Kṛṣṇa's chest that Lakṣmī desires to embrace, not Balarāma's. However, there is truth in jest; Balarāma does have his own *gopīs* and romantic life. But as we shall see, romanticism is not central to his life as it is to Kṛṣṇa's *līlās*.

Balarāma's *gopīs* first appear in the *Bhāgavata*'s thirty-fourth chapter of the tenth canto. The setting is the eve of Holī, the "festival of colors" as it is popularly known around the world today. This gathering is categorically different from Kṛṣṇa's late-night secret rendezvous with his *gopīs*. For one thing, Holī is religious play that follows the observance of Śivarātri. Furthermore, it is publicly celebrated by young and old alike throughout Vraja.[17] In contrast, Kṛṣṇa's *rāsa-līlā* with his *gopīs* is a paramour tryst of longing and lovemaking. During Holī, both Kṛṣṇa and Balarāma frolic together with Vraja's young milkmaidens while notably also accompanied by many cowherd friends.[18] This *līlā* also involves the *aiśvarya* of slaying the lustful Śaṅkhacūḍa. Jīva Goswāmī writes about Balarāma in this *līlā* that "along with Balarāma, filled with the joy of *sakhya*, the group gathered together."[19] Thus, it is clear that although Balarāma has his own *gopīs*, his *mādhurya* in relation to them is overshadowed by his *sakhya-rasa* for Kṛṣṇa.

16. *Śrīmad Bhāgavatam* 10.15.8.

17. On the eve of Holī, fires are lit in memory of the burning of Hiraṇyakaśipu's sister, who unsuccessfully tried to burn Prahlāda to death.

18. *Śrīmad Bhāgavatam* 10.34.20. See Sanātana Goswāmī's commentary and Jīva Goswāmī's reference to *Bhaviṣya Purāṇa*. Furthermore, in his commentary to *Bhakti-rasāmṛta-sindhu* 3.5.23, Jīva Goswāmī depicts Balarāma during Holī with parental feelings for Rādhā.

19. *Prīti Sandarbha* 403.

However, the seed of intimate love is sometimes sown in such public settings.[20] And so, a particular group of young *gopīs* fell in love with Balarāma during Holī, and it is to this seed of their love that Balarāma eventually tends many years later, albeit with some measure of hesitation. As we shall see, he marries these *gopīs* only with prodding from others upon returning to Vraja from Dvārakā in the context of delivering Kṛṣṇa's message to Kṛṣṇa's *gopīs*. To better understand the secondary nature of Rāma's personal romantic life in comparison to his primary preoccupation with Kṛṣṇa's friendship—his *sakhya-rati*—it will be helpful to examine the essence of this *līlā*, *Śrīmad Bhāgavatam* 10.65, drawing upon the Gauḍīya commentaries and related texts.

Kṛṣṇa's longing to return to Vraja from Dvārakā was also shared by Balarāma. Rāma wanted to return to Vraja and wanted Kṛṣṇa to return along with him. However, day after day Kṛṣṇa made excuses for not returning, to the point that Rāma began to question his brother's love for Vraja—for their parents, friends, servants, cows, and for the young *gopīs* that had fallen in love with Kṛṣṇa. Thus, Rāma finally confronted Kṛṣṇa. Reassuring Rāma of his love for his devotees, Kṛṣṇa explained his dilemma: Nanda had instructed him to follow the orders of Vasudeva, who would not allow him to depart to Vraja. Thus, he suggested that Rāma return without him, bearing news of him and reassuring everyone in Vraja of his love for them. In particular, he gave Rāma a message to deliver to the *gopīs* who had risked their reputations for him. As an aside, Kṛṣṇa also told Balarāma to marry the young *gopīs* who had fallen in love with him during the Holī celebration—who had not really been on Balarāma's mind. Thus, Rāma departed for Vraja. As he approached the village, he changed his clothes into rustic attire to reunite with the *rāga-mārga* devotees there. Once there, he reassured them of Kṛṣṇa's love for them, and with further prodding he also married, following Kṛṣṇa's request.

Rāma met with his parents first and then his friends. It was abundantly clear to him that his friends and well-wishers were internally unhappy without Kṛṣṇa but went through the motions of caring for their cows in an effort to please him during his visit, and this in turn brought a constant flow of tears to his eyes. His friends said:

20. In his *Ānanda-vṛndāvana-campū*, Kavi-karṇapūra mentions a mutual attraction between Balarāma and his *gopīs* that arose during the Holī festival, comparing it to Kṛṣṇa's relationship with his *gopīs*. He does this even as he invokes Balarāma's majestic epithet Haladhara and ignores the fact that the love between Rāma and his *gopīs*, as seen through the lens of the Vṛndāvana Goswāmīs, is *svakīya* in nature rather than *parakīya*.

> O Bala, will you and Kānu soon play again together with us? Our lives and the cows' lives are now in a precarious position. Please revitalize us so that we can live and play as we did previously.[21]

Then, after two or three days, Balarāma made arrangements to meet with Kṛṣṇa's *gopīs*. This meeting is the very heart of his return. It is really what the chapter is all about: Rāma's ability to represent Kṛṣṇa before those *gopīs* who gave their lives to him.[22]

Viśvanātha Cakravartī comments on Śukamuni's description of Balarāma's meeting with Rādhā and her companions: The sage's words, *rāma-sandarśanādṛtāḥ*—honoring Rāma after having had his *darśana*—have a twofold meaning. They imply not only that the *gopīs* show deference to Rāma but also that Balarāma bows to the *mahābhāva* exhibited by Kṛṣṇa's *gopīs*.[23] In his rendering of this *līlā* in the *Gopāla-campū*, Śrī Jīva depicts Balarāma referring to Kṛṣṇa's *gopīs* "respectfully."[24] Śukadeva then invokes Balarāma's epithet Saṅkarṣaṇa, implying that Balarāma had the ability to represent and thus attract Kṛṣṇa, or draw (*karṣaṇa*) his attention and thus his presence, in such a way that Kṛṣṇa actually appeared there before the *gopīs* in the person of Balarāma. From the oral tradition, it is thought that this resulted in Rāma's assuming the dark complexion of Kṛṣṇa, even as he never thought of enjoying Kṛṣṇa's *gopīs* for himself. It was in the confidence (*viśrambha*) central to *sakhya-rasa* that Kṛṣṇa had entrusted Rāma with this task of pacifying the *gopīs* in ways that, previously, Uddhava was unable. Rāma did so by causing Kṛṣṇa's presence to be felt and then promising to go to Dvārakā and bring Kṛṣṇa there by force in a manner that Uddhava could not. This is an example of Balarāma's expertise in representing Kṛṣṇa. After this, only at Rādhā's compassionate request and not without permission from his elders, Balarāma separately met with the unnamed *gopīs* who were attracted to him in youth during the Holī celebration:[25]

21. *Gopāla-campū* 2.20.28.

22. In this *līlā*, Baladeva, as the elder brother, exhibits sympathy for and approval of Kṛṣṇa's romanticism with the *gopīs*.

23. *Śrīmad Bhāgavatam* 10.65.9.

24. *Gopāla-campū* 2.20.45.

25. Kavi-karṇapūra does mention a *gopī* named Pūrṇānandā, describing her only as "Balarāma's dear-most girlfriend," and he identifies this *gopī* in part with Gadādhara dāsa of Gaura *līlā*, whom he also identifies with Candrakāntī-gopī. See *Gaura-gaṇoddeśa-dīpikā* 155. *Garga Saṁhitā* 8.9.1 describes Balarāma's *gopīs* as "*nāga* girls." The text describes the worship by which these snake-girls attained Balarāma. This *upāsanā* is in the mood of *aiśvarya* and involves worshiping Balarāma along with his Dvārakā wife, Revatī.

> Rādhā said, "We accept your promise to bring Kṛṣṇa back. Now, if you will accept all of my associates who have preserved their youthful chastity all along for you alone, rejecting their own enjoyment and remaining in their homes, thin and as if infirmed, then I will keep these women close to me, while you go and bring your brother.
>
> To which Balarāma replied, "Although this is not the time for that, I shall do it somehow in order to console all of you. But still I must first receive the permission of the elders."[26]

The elders gave their permission. Indeed, they repeatedly requested him to do the needful, yet still Rāma hesitated to participate in a marriage celebration in the absence of Kṛṣṇa. As such, with some prodding Balarāma agreed to marry these anonymous *gopīs* by the *gāndharva* rite in a secluded area—Rāma-ghāṭa—just north of the great banyan tree at the base of which Rāma, Kṛṣṇa, and their *sakhās* often met together to sport and strategize. The marriage took place with no formal arrangement and no wedding guests, with Rāma intoxicated and amid majesty, chastising the river Yamunā and miraculously dragging her to him with his plow. While *Śrīmad Bhāgavatam* employs five lengthy chapters in describing Kṛṣṇa's *rāsa-līlā*—the centerpiece of the entire text—this Gauḍīya *grantha-rāja* employs only four verses to describe the *rāsa* dance of Balarāma at Rāma-ghāṭa (10.65.17–18 and 10.65.21–22), the last two of which do not appear in all manuscripts of the text.[27]

In the least, his *gopīs*' anonymity underscores the challenge of the *sādhaka* to follow their example, as is essential in *rāgānugā-bhakti*. Furthermore, Rāma's majestic display on this occasion is telling for the discerning devotee.[28] In his commentary on *Caitanya-bhāgavata*, Bhaktisiddhānta Saraswatī Ṭhākura writes that the difference between Rāma's rendezvous with his *gopīs*

26. *Gopāla-campū* 2.20.49.

27. That *Bhāgavata* verses 10.65.21–22 describing Rāma's romantic encounter with his *gopīs* are not found in all manuscripts is the opinion of Bhaktisiddhānta Saraswatī Ṭhākura, stated in his commentary on *Caitanya-bhāgavata* 1.1.28. He bases his opinion on the fact that Śrīdhara Swāmī, Sanātana Goswāmī, Jīva Goswāmī, and Viśvanātha Cakravartī have not commented on these verses, while Vīrarāghava Ācārya of the Rāmānuja sect and Vijayadhvaja Tīrtha of the Madhva *sampradāya* have. Thus, only two verses are dedicated to describing Rāma's *rāsa-līlā* in some manuscripts.

28. It is also notable that the romanticism of both the Holī festival and the *gāndharva* rite at Rāma-ghāṭa described in *Śrīmad Bhāgavatam*, unlike the text's chapter leading up to the *rāsa-līlā* of Kṛṣṇa, does not mention *sādhana-siddhas* entering these *līlās*.

at Rāma-ghāṭa and Kṛṣṇa's *rāsa-līlā* is one of *maryādā* as opposed to *rāga*.[29] In other words, the romantic affairs of Rāma are not an example of the *kāma-rūpa-bhakti* experienced between Rādhā and Kṛṣṇa but rather *bhakti* in the mood of *maryādā*. On the other hand, Rāma's fraternal love *is* an example of the *rāga-bhakti* referred to as *sambandha-rūpa*, which involves *dāsya*, *sakhya*, or *vātsalya-rati*. Thus, Balarāma's *rāsa-līlā*, as Vṛndāvana dāsa refers to his *gāndharva* marriage at Rāma-ghāṭa, is anticlimactic in the chapter it is described in.[30] Indeed, Gauḍīya theologians commenting on this *līlā* stress the fact that Rāma has his own *gopīs*; *he does not consort with Kṛṣṇa's gopīs*. And no *Bhāgavata* commentators detail a *sādhana* by which a *sādhaka* could become Rāma's lover.[31]

While some Gauḍīya Vaiṣṇavas identify Anaṅga-mañjarī as Balarāma's *śakti*, she is Rādhā's younger sister, and Balarāma does not have a romantic relationship with her. Anaṅga-mañjarī is in love with Kṛṣṇa, not Balarāma. Furthermore, the idea that she is the *śakti* of Balarāma is not embraced by any of the Six Goswāmīs nor by Vṛndāvana dāsa Ṭhākura, Kavi-karṇapūra, or Kṛṣṇadāsa Kavirāja. The idea that she is Rāma's *śakti* comes from the late sixteenth-century text *Anaṅga-mañjarī-sampuṭikā*, which posits a number of theological ideas that appear to contradict themselves in some cases and, furthermore, are in concert with neither the *siddhānta* of the Goswāmīs nor that of the *Śrīmad Bhāgavatam*, or any known scripture for that matter. Such

29. *Caitanya-bhāgavata* 1.1.22.

30. Vṛndāvana dāsa emphasizes Balarāma's *rāsa-līlā* only in the context of asserting that he too, like Kṛṣṇa, is God. In doing so, Vṛndāvana dāsa also conflates Balarāma's *gāndharva* marriage at Rāma-ghāṭa described in *Śrīmad Bhāgavatam* 10.65 and the text's description of Holī in 10.34. His basic argument is that while sages consider such romantic affairs between men and women a stumbling block to spiritual progress, Rāma's romanticism, like Kṛṣṇa's, is glorified in the *Bhāgavata*. He argues so in the context of building a case for the divinity of Nityānanda Rāma. Thus, Vṛndāvana dāsa also cites other verses from the *Bhāgavatam* in this section of *Caitanya-bhāgavata* to establish the divinity of Balarāma for his readers.

31. To be clear, it is not that Balarāma does not have a robust romantic life. He most certainly does. This side of Balarāma is the focus of his devotees at the Dauji Mandir in Baldeo within the Vraja-maṇḍala. There, he is the *kula-devatā* of the Ahivasi Gaur *brāhmaṇas*, and as such from their angle of vision, Balarāma displaces Kṛṣṇa and takes his place as the protagonist in the *līlā*. For these devotees, Daujī reigns supreme accompanied by Revatī-devī. From this angle of vision, Balarāma is a *kṣatriya* and older brother who is stronger and more righteous than Kṛṣṇa. In Baldeo, the virtues of Balarāma's *maryādā* are extolled over the capricious nature of Kṛṣṇa. At Dauji Mandir, one will not hear the Gauḍīya *tattva-sūtra* "*kṛṣṇas tu bhagavān svayam*." However, at Baldeo textual support for the centrality of Balarāma is lacking.

theological ideas, for example, include equating Balarāma and Nityānanda Rāma with Rādhā.[32]

If one nonetheless accepts Anaṅga-mañjarī to be the *śakti* of Rāma, leaving aside *Anaṅga-mañjarī-samputikā*'s other more questionable tenets, one must consider her one with Rāma only from the *tattva* perspective, for as *śakti-tattva* she would originate in Balarāma and only in this sense be nondifferent from him—as Rādhā is nondifferent from Kṛṣṇa. But Rādhā *is* at the same time *different* from Kṛṣṇa in her experience of *bhāva*, and thus her experience is not his. This difference is central to Gauḍīya Vaiṣṇavism. Indeed, Gaura *līlā* arises out of it. Similarly, Anaṅga-mañjarī conceived of as Balarāma's *śakti* would also be different from Balarāma in *bhāva*, and it is *bhāva*, not *tattva*, that makes the *līlā* go round. Thus, of course, it is in our interest to stress the *difference* between Rāma and Anaṅga-mañjarī, if indeed one accepts that they are related as *śaktimān* and *śakti* to begin with.

In the climax of the Vraja *līlā*, Kṛṣṇa is driven to ponder and pursue Rādhā's aesthetic rapture. There is no parallel to this between Balarāma and Anaṅga-mañjarī. Nor does Balarāma feel the necessity to experience Rādhā's love for Kṛṣṇa from Rādhā's vantage point, because he loves Kṛṣṇa from another vantage point, that of *sakhya-rasa*. Notably, a prominent tenet of Śrī Rūpa's *rasa-tattva* is that each and every *rasa* is spiritually complete for each individual devotee. For that matter, how could Balarāma desire to experience Anaṅga-mañjarī's romantic love for Rādhā and Kṛṣṇa and Anaṅga-mañjarī's *sambhoga* with Kṛṣṇa, the latter in particular being unthinkable for anyone constituted of *dāsya*, *sakhya*, or *vātsalya-rasa*?[33] Rāma has his own relationship with Kṛṣṇa in fraternal love, and the parental aspect of his *saṅkula-sakhya-rati* provides the emotion through which he also relates with Rādhā.[34] Furthermore, when one in *sakhya-rasa* is sympathetic to *mādhurya-rasa*, the *rasa* of romantic love serves as a subordinate influence to enhance one's fraternal love rather than manifesting a separate *gopī* identity. Thus, as Kṛṣṇa's desire to experience Rādhā's *bhāva* manifests,

32. See chapter 28 for a commentary on *Anaṅga-mañjarī-samputikā* and how its theology has influenced the tradition.

33. Purāṇic stories describing Śiva's unfulfilled desire to enter the *rāsa-līlā* or Pāṇḍava Arjuna's desire to understand more about the *gopīs* seek to extol the glories of *gopī-bhāva*. They do not speak of a person already absorbed in the Vraja *līlā* in a particular transpsychological identity that by its very nature precludes a desire for romanticism with Kṛṣṇa.

34. Raghunātha dāsa Goswāmī's *Śrī Rādhikā-aṣṭottara-śata-nāma-stotram* 9 describes Rādhā as "she who receives parental affection from Balarāma"—*vātsalyācyuta-purvajā*. Thus, Balarāma loves Rādhā as if she were his younger sister.

Balarāma—true to his relationship with Kṛṣṇa—is there as his best friend to assist Kṛṣṇa in this extraordinary pursuit that gives rise to the extension of Kṛṣṇa *līlā* known as Gaura *līlā*. Unlike the Vraja *līlā*, where Balarāma's participation in Kṛṣṇa's romanticism is significant but limited and indirect, in Gaura *līlā*, Rāma plays a much more overt role in its dissemination as Nityānanda Rāma, who spreads Gaura's gift of *śṛṅgāra-rasa* far and wide.

28

Anaṅga-mañjarī

Anaṅga-mañjarī: A Historical and Theological Perspective

Rūpa Goswāmī introduces the world to Śrī Rādhā's younger sister, Anaṅga-mañjarī, in his *Rādhā-kṛṣṇa-gaṇoddeśa-dīpikā* (1550 CE). There is no prior reference to this family insight in any other text, Gauḍīya or otherwise. Along with telling us her name, Śrī Rūpa divulges other significant information about Anaṅga—her age, temperament, complexion, dress, her husband's name, and the fact that she is dear to Lalitā and especially dear to Viśākhā.

> Anaṅga-mañjarī, Śrī Rādhā's younger sister, bears an enchanting complexion resembling a golden *ketakī* flower and wears clothes resembling a blue lotus. Her beauty and sweetness attract even Cupid.[1] Her husband is the proud and arrogant Durmada, the younger brother of Śrī Rādhā's husband. She is very dear to Lalitā-devī and more so to Viśākhā.[2]

Śrī Rūpa lists Anaṅga as a *vara-sakhī*, which he describes thus:

> In addition to the eight *variṣṭha-sakhīs*, there are eight other exalted *sakhīs*—*vara-sakhīs*. They are all twelve years old and have almost

1. Cupid is also known as "Anaṅga," which means "without limbs"—invisible. It is said that when Cupid tried to distract Śiva from his meditation, his *samādhi* broke, and in his anger, he incinerated the body of Cupid with his fiery glance. Thus, Cupid became invisible and that much more dangerous. The implication here is that *jñāna* is not as effective in conquering lust as *bhakti* is. Indeed, Cupid himself is attracted to Anaṅga-mañjarī and her *bhakti*.
2. *Rādhā-kṛṣṇa-gaṇoddeśa-dīpikā* 121–122.

> grown out of their childhood. They are Kalāvatī, Śubhāṅgadā, Hiraṇyāṅgī, Ratnalekhā, Śikhāvatī, Kandarpa-mañjarī, Phullakalikā, and Anaṅga-mañjarī.[3]

Although two of these *vara-sakhīs* bear the name *mañjarī*—Anaṅga and Kandarpa—in *Rādhā-kṛṣṇa-gaṇoddeśa-dīpikā*'s list of *mañjarīs* their names do not appear.[4] Thus, from Rūpa Goswāmī's perspective, these two are *mañjarīs* in name but not in function. They function instead as *vara-gopīs*, who, unlike *mañjarīs*, are not adamantly opposed to personal romantic invitations from Kṛṣṇa. *Mañjarī-bhāva* is characterized as being dedicated exclusively to the *bhāva* of Rādhā and thus to uniting her with Kṛṣṇa rather than uniting with him oneself. Indeed, unwillingness to succumb to Kṛṣṇa's occasional seduction is central to the underlying math of the *mañjarīs*' sacred aesthetic rapture (*rasa*): one pleases Kṛṣṇa more by serving and assisting Rādhā in her romantic desires than by romanticizing with Kṛṣṇa oneself, for no one can satisfy Kṛṣṇa in romantic love more than Rādhā can.[5]

Thus, although Anaṅga, like Rādhā's *mañjarīs*, is also dedicated to the personal service of her older sister, unlike with Rādhā's *mañjarīs* this is not at the cost of a romantic interlude with Kṛṣṇa should the opportunity arise, as it does. In his *Muktā-carita*, Raghunātha dāsa Goswāmī describes Kṛṣṇa's invitation to Anaṅga and how it delights her. Mentally she accepted his invitation "like a hymn of flowers decorating her ears, as she glanced at him in return," even though the public setting of this invitation and the levity behind Kṛṣṇa's words prevented her from following through on this particular occasion. That is to say, her reaction was not like that of a typical *mañjarī*.

The above references to Anaṅga-mañjarī, together with Raghunātha dāsa Goswāmī's epithet for Rādhā *anaṅga-mañjarī-jyeṣṭha* among 107 other

3. *Rādhā-kṛṣṇa-gaṇoddeśa-dīpikā* 97–98.

4. Some later editions of this text do include Anaṅga's name in Rūpa's list of *mañjarīs*, but her name was likely added by later devotees. The absence of Kandarpa-mañjarī's name in Śrī Rūpa's list of *mañjarīs* in any edition of the text serves as further evidence that some *gopīs* may be *mañjarīs* in name only. Thus, it is not unprecedented to describe Anaṅga-mañjarī as such. That she is a *mañjarī* in name only is also the position taken by the late Ananta dāsa Paṇḍita of Rādhā-kuṇḍa. However, Dhyānacandra Goswāmī lists her as a *mañjarī* in his *Gaura-govindārcana-smaraṇa-paddhati*. He also describes her as equal to the life force of Rādhā—*rādhikā-prāṇa-samām*—to say she is dear to her older sister Rādhā.

5. It is implied by Viśvanātha Cakravartī Ṭhākura in his *Kṛṣṇa-bhāvanāmṛta* that a *mañjarī* may, against her will, find Kṛṣṇa's advances unavoidable on rare occasion.

names for our Goddess, constitute the entirety of what the Six Goswāmīs have written about her. But is there anything else that can be said about her? Later theologians think so, and some of them have said much more. However, the focus here is to examine how such theologizing might enhance and add to the Goswāmīs' perspective, as well as how it might contradict their insight. Given the specifics of later theologians' position on Anaṅga-mañjarī, we will need to revisit the Goswāmīs' insight regarding the nature of Kṛṣṇa's older brother, Balarāma—understanding of which is central to this text's musing on the circle of Kṛṣṇa's friends. And to do that, we must turn to Gaura *līlā* and the illustrious consort of Nityānanda Rāma, Śrī Jāhnavā-devi.

Jāhnavā and her sister, Vasudhā, married Nitāi in their youth. They are naturally identified with Balarāma's eternal consorts, Revatī and Vāruṇī, respectively. No one has suggested that Nitāi's wives are incarnations of any of Balarāma's Vraja *gopīs*, who are practically unknown. Indeed, Rūpa Goswāmī does not mention any of them in his *Rādhā-kṛṣṇa-gaṇoddeśa-dīpikā*, a book intended to shed light on the Vraja *līlā pārṣadas*. That he does not mention any of them individually by name or even as a group underscores his emphasis on viewing Balarāma in Vraja exclusively through the lens of fraternal love.

With the passing of Nitāi that cast a prominent light on Jāhnavā, new theological conjectures arose as to her inner identity in Kṛṣṇa *līlā*. Such thinking arose in conjunction with the fact that Jāhnavā identified with the same ideal—*mañjarī-bhāva*—that the Goswāmīs highlighted in their newly published works. Thus, Jāhnavā's ideal did not match with the *aiśvarya-bhāva* of Revatī. What, then, is her Vraja *līlā* identity?

Jāhnavā took the long pilgrimage to Vraja at least twice, if not three times. During one of her visits, standing in the shade of one of Vraja's wish-fulfilling trees at Rādhā-kuṇḍa, Gopīnātha revealed himself to her. Shortly thereafter, the Vaiṣṇava community established a temple for Rādhā-Gopīnātha therein to commemorate Jāhnavā's vision. In Jāhnavā's mind, however, the deity of Rādhā standing next to Gopīnātha was too small. Thus, upon returning to Bengal, she had a larger deity of Rādhā carved and sent this deity to replace the smaller one. But rather than replacing the smaller deity altogether, the local priests designated her as Anaṅga, Rādhā's younger sister. Artistically speaking, it was common to depict younger siblings by making them smaller in size.[6]

6. Even today, when artisans make deities of Kṛṣṇa-Balarāma, they will make Kṛṣṇa

During her final pilgrimage to Vraja, Jāhnavā passed on, and it was at this time that some devotees began to feel they had an answer concerning Jāhnavā's Vraja *līlā* identity. They identified Jāhnavā with Anaṅga-mañjarī. Indeed, sacred lore of the time asserted that upon passing, she entered into the smaller deity of Anaṅga.

Sometime after Jāhnavā's passing, Kavi-karṇapūra published his *Gaura-gaṇoddeśa-dīpikā*. Therein he identifies Jāhnavā with Revatī, with the caveat that some devotees consider her Anaṅga-mañjarī. In his book, Kavi-karṇapūra includes various opinions on the Vraja *līlā* identities of the Gaura *līlā pārṣadas* and makes no effort to sort out which opinion is correct. For Kavi-karṇapūra, either there is more than one correct answer, or he merely leaves it to his readers to decide which opinion to embrace. This leaves us to wonder: Whose opinion was it that Jāhnavā is Anaṅga-mañjarī?

There is reason to believe that Jāhnavā's identification with Anaṅga was first promoted by her adopted son and disciple Rāmāi Ṭhākura, who accompanied her to Vraja.[7] Rāmāi Ṭhākura and Vīracandra, the son of Nityānanda and Vasudhā, both became disciples of Jāhnavā at a young age. Of the two, Vīracandra Goswāmī is the most celebrated; however, Rāmāi Ṭhākura was no doubt an influential devotee. Vīracandra Goswāmī and Rāmāi Ṭhākura appear to have differed theologically. To attribute the insight into Jāhnavā's Vraja *līlā* identification with Anaṅga-mañjarī to Rāmāi is to compliment him, for this insight, despite its peculiarity, was entertained as a distinct possibility by Kavi-karṇapūra and over time it has been for the most part accepted uncritically.

But let us critically examine this theological perspective. Perhaps what stands out most is the idea that since Jāhnavā is Nityānanda Rāma's principal consort, if in Vraja she is Anaṅga-mañjarī, then Anaṅga of Vraja is also Balarāma's principal *śakti*. However, in the drama of Vraja *līlā* there is no hint of this, and from the Gauḍīya perspective Balarāma's Vraja *śaktis*

---

smaller than Balarāma as a way of conveying that Kṛṣṇa is Rāma's younger brother.

7. In his biography of Rāmāi Ṭhākura—*Muralī-vilāsa*—Rājavallabha, Rāmāi Ṭhākura's nephew, cites a verse that he attributes to Rūpa Goswāmī. He describes it as one verse of an *aṣṭakam* composed by Śrī Rūpa and spoken to Rāmāi Ṭhākura in Vraja. The verse identifies Jāhnavā with Anaṅga-mañjarī. However, Rāmāi Ṭhākura himself has not cited this verse in his earlier *Anaṅga-mañjarī-sampuṭikā*, nor is the *aṣṭakam* available anywhere else. Scholars have also doubted that the verse was composed by Rūpa Goswāmī, given the grammatical problems with it. See Neal Delmonico's article "Vipinvihari Goswāmī and the Goswāmīs of Baghnapara" in *Journal of Vaishnava Studies* Vol. 28 No. 2/Spring 2020. Note that Delmonico mistakenly identifies *Muralī-vilāsa* with the sixteenth rather than the seventeenth century. He also mistakenly dates *Anaṅga-mañjarī-sampuṭikā* after *Muralī-vilāsa*.

are clearly a section of *gopīs* who are associated with the *nāga* community and whose names are unknown. Turning to the Ahivasi Gaur *brāhmaṇas* of the Dauji Mandir in Baldeo, we find that they enshrine Revatī as Rāma's principal consort with no mention of Anaṅga. Furthermore, from Rūpa Goswāmī's perspective Anaṅga is a *vara-gopī* who is romantically involved with Balarāma's younger brother, and she has no romantic relationship with Balarāma himself. How then could Rūpa Goswāmī have neglected to tell us this significant fact concerning Anaṅga in his *Rādhā-kṛṣṇa-gaṇoddeśa-dīpikā* dedicated to revealing such details?

In this way, the idea that Jāhnavā is Nityānanda Rāma's principal consort but has no such relationship with him in Vraja stands out. How can she be Balarāma's principal consort and have no *mādhurya* relationship with him, while having such a relationship with Kṛṣṇa? Historical accounts of Jāhnavā's pilgrimages to Vraja in texts such as *Bhakti-ratnākara* describe her visiting the haunts of Balarāma's pastimes with intense longing for him, a longing not found in Anaṅga-mañjarī. These theological concerns beg a resolution, and it appears this is what Rāmāi Ṭhākura set out to do in support of his initial insight.

Rāmāi Ṭhākura and Anaṅga-mañjarī-sampuṭikā

After Jāhnavā's passing, when she subsequently became identified with Anaṅga-mañjarī, Rāmāi Ṭhākura settled in Bengal at Baghnapara, a place named after its abundance of Bengali tigers. Vaiṣṇava lore informs us that Rāmāi Ṭhākura was able to tame a tiger with his chanting of *harināma*. Thus, he captured the faith of the locals by his compelling example of spiritual prowess. Once established there, Rāmāi started a school of thought based on the Goswāmī theology but departing from it at times, especially when it came to Baladeva *tattva* and Anaṅga-mañjarī/Jāhnavā. This departure is evident in Rāmāi's book *Anaṅga-mañjarī-sampuṭikā*. Although he is a notable devotee by example, his theological efforts arguably contradict the founding Gauḍīya *ācāryas* at times and leave something to be desired in comparison with the tightly knit, scripturally supported theology of the Goswāmīs that educated members of the *sampradāya* have come to expect.

Anaṅga-mañjarī-sampuṭikā is a Bengali text with Sanskrit quotations from obscure texts cited here and there to support some of its theological insights. *Dharaṇī-śeṣa-saṁvāda* is one such support that the book relies upon most in the name of scriptural *pramāṇa*. This *saṁvāda* is sometimes described as a section of the *Brahmāṇḍa Purāṇa*, a conversation between Earth and

Śeṣa. However, after scouring two editions of this Purāṇa, I found no such conversation.[8] Another work relied upon by Rāmāi Ṭhākura is *Bhajana-candrikā.* The author of this book is Vṛndāvana Candra dāsa, a member of the Nityānanda *parivāra.* Neither of these books has been cited in any core Gauḍīya text, and they reach conclusions that are not entertained by the founding *ācāryas* of the *sampradāya.* Indeed, in some instances they contradict the founders' conclusions.

The first wave (*lahari*) of Rāmāi's work focuses on *śakti-tattva* and is subtitled "*Śakti-tattva-vicāra*" (deliberation on the internal potency). The subsequent three waves are "*Rasa-kautuka*" (the play of *rasa*), "*Yūtha-vivaraṇa*" (description of Anaṅga's group), and a second "*Yūtha-vivaraṇa*" that includes "*Atha-samprārthanā*" (concluding prayers). The entire text consists of 184 verses and was written somewhere between 1590 and 1610, predating *Caitanya-caritāmṛta* (1615). Let us first examine its *śakti-tattva* section.

In Bengali verse, this wave starts out in traditional praise of the gurus: Śrī Caitanya, Nityānanda Rāma, Advaita, and Gadādhara. This is followed by praise of Nityānanda's wives, Jāhnavā and Vasudhā, and the son of Vasudhā and celebrated disciple of Jāhnavā, Vīracandra. Verses 1.10–11 are in Sanskrit, and the second line of verse 1.10 states the following, *namaḥ kṛṣṇa svarūpāya namāmyanaṅga mañjarīm*: "I offer my *praṇāma* to the *svarūpa* of Kṛṣṇa, Anaṅga-mañjarī." These Sanskrit verses are followed by Bengali verses asserting that Nityānanda has the form of Anaṅga-mañjarī (*sei tanu anaṅga mañjarī*) and that Anaṅga-mañjarī is the *śakti* of Balarāma (*rādhāra anujā yei, balarāma śakti sei*). Rāmāi Ṭhākura then supports the latter claim with a Sanskrit verse from *Bhajana-candrikā.*

In his own Bengali verse (1.18), Rāmāi Ṭhākura then emphatically states that Kṛṣṇa, Balarāma, and Rādhā are one—*rādhā-kṛṣṇa balarāma aikya vastu.* He adds to this that their *dhāma, aiśvarya, mādhurya,* and *prema* are all one and that one should not think otherwise. In verses 1.19–21 he identifies Rāma with *sat-śakti,* Kṛṣṇa with *cit-śakti,* and Rādhā with *ānanda-śakti.* He appears to say that the Absolute is *sad-cid-ānanda* and is personified as these three persons, who are one. Rāmāi supports this with a reference from the *Dharaṇī-śeṣa-saṁvāda,* the last line of which adds something controversial,

8. Dhyānacandra Goswāmī does refer to this conversation, attributing it to the *Brahmāṇḍa Purāṇa* and informing his readers that the *mantra* for the worship of Nityānanda Prabhu is found therein. However, if it is, it is most certainly an instance of interpolation. The actual text of this Purāṇa is not about Gauḍīya Vaiṣṇavism, which it predates by centuries.

sad ānandāṁśato rāmaḥ puṁ prakṛtyātmakaḥ paraḥ: "The *sat* aspect of Balarāma expresses itself as both *puruṣa* and *prakṛti* (male and female)."

Verse 1.29 is a citation from *Bhajana-candrikā* stating that there are two types of *līlās*, internal and external, both of which are eternal. The former appears in many forms, while the latter is said to be secret. Rāmāi takes this to mean that the external *līlās* refer to those that Balarāma manifests in his male form in *dāsya*, *sakhya*, and *vātsalya*. He goes on to explain something about Balarāma's *saṅkula-bhāva* without using this term, citing the prominent examples from the *Bhāgavatam* that illustrate Rāma's love in the moods of servant, friend, and parent. Before concluding the first wave, Rāmāi asserts that when the *sat* and *cit* features combine, Balarāma's male form and pastimes manifest. This is somewhat confusing because he has already said that Balarāma is the manifestation of *sat* unto itself. But perhaps he means to say that Balarāma presides over *sat* and the *sandhinī-śakti*, even as he is also constituted of *sad-cid-ānanda*.

Concluding this section, Rāmāi begins the second wave by saying that it is the *ānanda* feature of Balarāma from which his secret internal *līlās* are manifest, alluding to Balarāma's proposed female form. This topic is addressed in the text's second wave—*rasa-kautuka*.

Having listed and reflected briefly on the points highlighted above from the *sampuṭikā*'s first wave, let us now examine them in greater detail. The idea that Anaṅga-mañjarī is the *svarūpa* of Kṛṣṇa and that Nityānanda is also the form of Anaṅga-mañjarī constitutes a blurring of *tattvas*. The idea that Anaṅga-mañjarī is the *śakti* of Balarāma of course follows from the idea that she is Jāhnavā's Vraja *līlā-svarūpa*. This point is perhaps novel more than it is controversial.

Rāmāi's emphasis on the oneness of Rādhā, Kṛṣṇa, and Balarāma turns on a yellow light of caution, while the idea that Balarāma has male and female forms changes it to red. Regarding the yellow light, according to the Goswāmīs' theology Kṛṣṇa and Balarāma are one, and Kṛṣṇa and Rādhā are one. But this does not mean that because Kṛṣṇa and Balarāma are one and Kṛṣṇa and Rādhā are one, therefore Balarāma and Rādhā are non-different. Why not? Because the sense in which Kṛṣṇa and Balarāma are one is different from the way that Rādhā and Kṛṣṇa are one. Balarāma and Kṛṣṇa are both Viṣṇu *tattva*/*śaktimān*. Balarāma is Kṛṣṇa's *vaibhava-prakāśa*, whereas Rādhā is Kṛṣṇa's *śakti*, with whom he is one and different as *śakti* and *śaktimān*. And of course, Balarāma also has his *śakti* counter-whole with whom he is one and different.

As for the red light, the idea that Balarāma has male and female forms flashes as something unheard of in the Goswāmī theology, wherein Balarāma *tattva* is explained at length. When the text implies that the female, internal, so-called secret *līlās* of Balarāma are the preoccupation of the more *rasika* devotees, this does not help its claim. But to be fair, in this section Rāmāi demonstrates that he is acquainted with the mainline Gauḍīya perspective on Balarāma *tattva*, and in brief he represents it accurately. Without arguing against it or desiring to contradict it, he goes on to say further that there is another, inner side to Balarāma, which we can assume he has been chosen to reveal.[9] In developing this revelation, his notion that Balarāma in male form is a combination of his *sat* and *cit* features is peculiar, as is the idea that it is the *ānanda* feature of Balarāma from which his female feature manifests. This is especially so when he goes on to explain in the second wave that this female feature is a manifestation of Balarāma's *sat* combined with his *ānanda*. Indeed, in effect Rāmāi appears to have left male Balarāma without *ānanda*, and female Balarāma without *cit*. While it is hard to imagine that he intends to say this, in the least his presentation begs for more clarity.

The second wave introduces us to an example of Anaṅga-mañjarī's participation in *līlā*. However, this narrative is preceded by eighteen verses in which we learn the following:

1. It is the *sat* feature of Balarāma that has both a male and female expression (2.4 citing *Dharaṇī-śeṣa-saṁvāda*).
2. The syllable *ra* in Rāma is Rādhā and the syllable *ma* in his name is Madhusūdana/Kṛṣṇa (2.9 citing *Dharaṇī-śeṣa-saṁvāda*). This implies that Rāma is Rādhā and Kṛṣṇa.
3. From the union of *sat* and *ānanda*, Balarāma comes into being (2.12 citing *Dharaṇī-śeṣa-saṁvāda*).
4. In his *ānanda* feature, Balarāma assumes a yellow complexion in the mood of Rādhā (2.14).
5. Anaṅga-mañjarī is another form of Rādhā, nondifferent from her (2.15).
6. Balarāma assumes the form of Anaṅga-mañjarī to give pleasure to Kṛṣṇa (2.16).

9. In 4.22 Rāmāi asks rhetorically that if he does not reveal these *līlās* (presented in waves 3 and 4), who will know about them? It would seem that in his mind the same holds true with the *tattva* of his book.

7. In his *ānanda* feature, Balarāma is Rādhikā herself (2.17 citing *Rasa-kalpataru*[10]).

8. Through Balarāma, Rādhā in the form of Anaṅga-mañjarī appears. Hence Balarāma is Rādhā, who, again, is Anaṅga-mañjarī (2.18).

The *līlā* narrative of this wave is said to be an elaboration on a passage from *Bhajana-candrikā*. The narrative begins with a detailed description of Anaṅga-mañjarī's beauty and ornamentation. She is also described as a *yūtheśvarī* as she heads into the forest to meet Kṛṣṇa, accompanied by her own group. Here Kṛṣṇa says that *yūtheśvarī* Anaṅga is more glorious than other *yūtheśvarīs* and even more glorious than Rādhā herself. He is eager to make love to her, and he tells her so. Then other *yūtheśvarīs*, including Rādhā, arrive, and they all encourage Anaṅga to make love to Kṛṣṇa, which she does. This lovemaking is followed by maidservants of Anaṅga serving Rādhā and Kṛṣṇa.

Thus, in Rāmāi's second wave, Anaṅga is considered to be Bhagavān; Rādhā and Kṛṣṇa combined; Rādhā; a separate group leader from Rādhā with her own maidservants; and a *mañjarī* herself at least in name, while acting in a manner that is uncharacteristic of *mañjarī-bhāva*. In Rāmāi Ṭhākura's mind, all of this is included in Balarāma *tattva*. However, this theology is sorely lacking in terms of supportive scriptural evidence. The texts cited are obscure at best, and the reasoning presented from the evidence does not ring the conclusive bell of *siddhānta* that students of the Goswāmīs' theology are accustomed to hearing.

In the third and fourth waves, Rāmāi Ṭhākura describes and names various *sakhīs* in play during the *līlā* narrative found in wave 3. What stands out here is Rāmāi's assertion that the Goswāmīs in their *mañjarī-svarūpas* are the leaders within Anaṅga's group of *mañjarīs*. According to the Goswāmīs' theology, the Goswāmīs are the leading *mañjarīs* within Rādhā's *yūtha*. Drawing *rasika* implications from these waves, followers of Rāmāi's theology assert that what makes Anaṅga's group unique is that it provides the extra added attraction of direct union with Kṛṣṇa for those in *mañjarī-bhāva*.[11] However, such claims are suspect in that, as already mentioned, the Goswāmīs place themselves in Rādhā's group, not Anaṅga's. Within Rādhā's group, they are famously *rūpānugās*, followers of Rūpa-mañjarī, not *anaṅgānugas*. As we

10. This is another obscure, if not unknown, text.

11. This is the position adopted by Gadādhara-prāṇa dāsa, a contemporary member of the Bhagnapara lineage. In his unpublished articles, he makes the unsupported claim that this is also the position of Ṭhākura Bhaktivinoda.

know, their *mañjarī-bhāva* is characterized as being staunchly opposed to any romantic union between themselves and Kṛṣṇa, even if Kṛṣṇa should propose it. This is their extreme Rādhā *dāsyam*, which is more pleasing to Kṛṣṇa than union with any of them. Indeed, Kṛṣṇa suggests such union only to see and take pleasure in their Rādhā *dāsyam* expressed in their resistance.

Finally, at the end of his fourth wave, Rāmāi Ṭhākura prays with great eagerness and humility to enter the Vraja *līlā* in the group of Anaṅga-mañjarī. Here his genuineness is apparent.

Conclusion

How successful, then, is Rāmāi Ṭhākura's effort? The answer to this question depends on which measuring stick one uses. Rāmāi Ṭhākura and his text created a distinct school among the followers of Gaura-Nityānanda. His literary contribution was followed by two other works in his lineage, each a century apart. *Muralī-vilāsa* is an early seventeenth-century biography of Rāmāi Ṭhākura written by Rājavallabha Goswāmī. *Vaṁśī-śikṣā* is the work of Premadāsa Miśra, which was written approximately in 1716. Rāmāi Ṭhākura was successful in establishing a theology at the end of the sixteenth century, based upon the Goswāmī theology but with its own theological twist. And this school continues today. But Rāmāi was not successful in convincing mainstream Gauḍīya Vaiṣṇavism of the entirety of his Balarāma/Anaṅga *tattva*.[12] In a very limited sense, though, some of his theology was embraced by prominent members of the Gauḍīya lineage during his lifetime and made its way into core Gauḍīya texts.

As we have already seen, Kavi-karṇapūra accepted the idea that Jāhnavā has a Kṛṣṇa *līlā-svarūpa* as both Revatī (*aiśvarya-bhāva*) and Anaṅga-mañjarī (*mādhurya-bhāva*).[13] Although his *Gaura-gaṇoddeśa-dīpikā* precedes *Anaṅga-mañjarī-samputikā*, its core idea that Jāhnavā is Anaṅga certainly comes from the ranks of Rāmāi.

Kṛṣṇadāsa Kavirāja, so faithful to the Goswāmīs' theology, hints at the possibility that Anaṅga is identified with Ananta Śeṣa, Balarāma's

12. Some sects other than his own have also embraced Rāmāi Ṭhākura's identification of Nityānanda Rāma with Rādhā and also the idea that Balarāma ultimately relishes *mādhurya-rasa* with Kṛṣṇa as the object of his love. The outlier Gauḍīya following of Caraṇa dāsa Bābājī is an example. In his *Charita-sudhā*, this is implied.

13. In *Gaura-gaṇoddeśa-dīpikā* 184, Gopāla Bhaṭṭa Goswāmī is also identified with both Anaṅga-mañjarī and Guṇa-mañjarī. The Rādhā-ramaṇa Goswāmī families who follow Gopāla Bhaṭṭa Goswāmī refer to him as Guṇa-mañjarī (see *Gopāla-bhaṭṭa-śatakam* 71—*ya iha kuñja-gṛhe guṇa-mañjarī*).

expansion. He does this in his *Govinda-līlāmṛta*, which also precedes *Anaṅga-mañjarī-samputikā*. But as we see from Kavi-karṇapūra's text, Rāmāi Ṭhākura's insight was out and about before he put it to paper.

In *Govinda-līlāmṛta* during the midday pastimes, Kundalatā playfully informs Kṛṣṇa that the nine planets and ten directions must be worshiped before the sacrifice to Cupid (Rādhā and Kṛṣṇa's union) can proceed. In response, Kṛṣṇa asks the names and positions of those ruling over the ten directions. Then Kundalatā, in jest, winking at her friends, tells Kṛṣṇa that the gods of the directions have all come before him, eager to fulfill his desires. After identifying eight *gopīs* with eight different directions and their presiding gods, she concludes with the final two directions, up and down:

> Rūpa-mañjarī (up) here in front of you is Brahmā, and Anaṅga-mañjarī (down), skillful at creating bliss in *rasa*, is Śeṣa.[14]

Obviously Rūpa Goswāmī is not Brahmā in any real sense, but in his later work, *Caitanya-caritāmṛta*, Kṛṣṇadāsa does compare Rūpa Goswāmī to Brahmā. Just as Kṛṣṇa revealed the Vedic truths to Brahmā, Gaura Kṛṣṇa revealed them all to Rūpa Goswāmī. It is possible that by his identification of Anaṅga with Śeṣa, Kṛṣṇadāsa has something more than jest in the back of his mind, such as ontology.

A century later, Viśvanātha Cakravartī Ṭhākura in his *Gaura-gaṇa-svarūpa-tattva-candrikā* describes Śeṣa's manifesting as all of the couches on which Kṛṣṇa reclines, assisting him thus in his romanticism. He goes on to identify Śeṣa with Anaṅga-mañjarī and refers his readers to *Govinda-līlāmṛta* for support, citing Kundalatā's joking referenced above.[15] However, Viśvanātha Cakravartī Ṭhākura does not cite *Anaṅga-mañjarī-samputikā* in support of his position.

In *Caitanya-caritāmṛta*, which was published after *Anaṅga-mañjarī-samputikā*, Kṛṣṇadāsa Kavirāja Goswāmī does not mention any connection between Anaṅga and Balarāma, despite a lengthy explanation of Balarāma/Nityānanda *tattva*. This final work of Kṛṣṇadāsa was intended to be faithful to the Goswāmīs' theology and directly, or indirectly by omission, a dismissal of other theological perspectives.[16] Notably, *Caitanya-caritāmṛta* does not

14. *Govinda-līlāmṛta* 9.96–98.

15. *Gaurāṅga-gaṇa-svarūpa-tattva-candrikā* 34–38.

16. In *The Final Word: The "Caitanya Caritāmṛta" and the Grammar of Religious Tradition* (New York: Oxford University Press, 2010), Tony K. Stewart convincingly portrays *Caitanya-caritāmṛta* as the text that served to establish the orthodox understanding of Gauḍīya Vaiṣṇava theology at the dawn of the seventeenth century.

mention Jāhnavā at all, what to speak of Anaṅga. Neither does Vṛndāvana dāsa, author of the *Caitanya-bhāgavata*, which Kṛṣṇadāsa repeatedly defers to. Vṛndāvana dāsa is, of course, a *sakhya-rasa* devotee of Nityānanda Rāma.

Thus, during Rāmāi Ṭhākura's time and for quite some time afterward, his theology, although alive and well, remained a school unto itself rather than being fully integrated into the mainstream of orthodox Gauḍīya Vaiṣṇavism. Only the notions that Nitāi's Jāhnavā is Anaṅga and that Anaṅga is Balarāma's *śakti* have gained wider acceptance. It should be noted that even in Rāmāi Ṭhākura's own line, Premadāsa's *Vaṁśī-śikṣā* does not accept Rāmāi's identification of Jāhnavā with Anaṅga-mañjarī.[17]

In modern times, Bhaktivinoda Ṭhākura received *dīkṣā* in the line of Rāmāi Ṭhākura from Bipin Bihari Goswāmī.[18] Even so, in all of his voluminous writing, he never cites *Anaṅga-mañjarī-sampuṭikā*. His theology regarding Balarāma/Nityānanda *tattva* is chaste to that of the Goswāmīs. In his writing, he does not embrace the idea that Nityānanda Rāma is both Anaṅga and Balarāma combined in pursuit of *mādhurya-rasa*, nor does he embrace the identification of Nityānanda/Balarāma with Rādhā.[19] He

17. Amiya P. Sen, "Sources on the Life of Chaitanya," in *Chaitanya: A Life and Legacy* (New Delhi: Oxford University Press, 2019), 123. In *Vaṁśī-śikṣā* Vaṁśīvadana Ṭhākura, Rāmāi Ṭhākura's grandfather, rather than Jāhnavā, is identified with Anaṅga-mañjarī.

18. Bhaktivinoda Ṭhākura also accepted Jagannātha dāsa Bābājī as his *śikṣā-guru*. Notably, Bhaktivinoda's personal assistant for the last seven years of his life, Kṛṣṇa dāsa Bābājī, penned *Bhaktivinoda-carita*, in which only Jagannātha dāsa Bābājī of the Narottama *parivāra* is mentioned as the *guru* of Bhaktivinoda. Therein Kṛṣṇadāsa writes that "Attaining his mercy, Bhaktivinoda disseminated his teachings in the form of books." This emphasis appears related to the fact that while Jagannātha dāsa Bābājī accepted Bhaktivinoda's vision of Śrī Caitanya's birthplace, Bipin Bihari Goswāmī after some years of also acknowledging it, changed his opinion. In his book detailing the Baghnapara lineage, the grandson of Bipin Bihari, Kanan Bihari Goswāmī, states that Bipin Bihari Goswāmī declared Bhaktivinoda guilty of an "untruth" concerning the Māyāpura *janmasthāna* and thus rejected him. Thus, some followers of Bhaktivinoda feel that Jagannātha dāsa Bābājī was ultimately more influential in Bhaktivinoda's spiritual life, as it is not uncommon for one's *śikṣā-guru* to take precedence over one's *dīkṣā-guru*, while other followers of Bhaktivinoda simply ignore Bipin Bihari's rejection of Bhaktivinoda from the Baghnapara lineage.

19. Nor did Bhaktivinoda promote the Rasarāja theology of Vaṁśīvadana Ṭhākura (Rāmāi Ṭhākura's grandfather) that runs through the Baghnapara lineage. In his *Hindu Encounter with Modernity* (page 93), Śukavaka dāsa conflates *mānasī-sevā* with the Rasarāja doctrine and, based on this mistake, states that Bhaktivinoda embraced this doctrine, one that departs significantly from that of the Vṛndāvana Goswāmīs. And notably, the prominent lineages today of Hari Gopāla dāsa Bābājī, Nani Gopāla Adhikārī, and Bhakti Vilāsa Ṭhākura stemming from Bhaktivinoda and coming through Lalitā Prasāda Ṭhākura also do not promote this doctrine nor the other teachings of *Anaṅga-mañjarī-sampuṭikā* that constitute a departure from the Goswāmīs' perspective on Baladeva/Nityānanda *tattva*.

does identify Jāhnavā with Anaṅga and the natural extension of that in which Anaṅga-mañjarī is seen as Balarāma's *śakti*. He also aspires to enter Rūpa-mañjarī's group under Lalitā-sakhī as a *rūpānugā* with the blessing of Anaṅga-mañjarī, whom he also desires to serve.[20]

The oneness of Anaṅga and Balarāma as *śakti* and *śaktimān* does not place Balarāma/Nityānanda in *mādhurya-rasa*. They are one inasmuch as Rāma's *śakti* is his and not an independent entity. Despite the oneness in *tattva* of *śakti*/*śaktimān*, the two have their own separate identities and participation in the *līlā*: Rāma in *sakhya-rasa* and Anaṅga-mañjarī in *mādhurya-rasa*.

This teaching on the *bhedābheda* of *śakti*/*śaktimān* is what Rūpa Goswāmī himself teaches. However, he is silent on the notion that Nityānanda Rāma's Jāhnavā is Anaṅga-mañjarī in the Vraja *līlā* and is thus Balarāma's *śakti*. While his silence on this theological perspective may be deafening to some, if we leave aside the rest of *Anaṅga-mañjarī-samputikā*, we will find that unto itself this understanding need not be seen as a contradiction to Śrī Rūpa's teaching. Indeed, a number of staunch *rūpānuga* Vaiṣṇavas have embraced it. We have seen that Kṛṣṇadāsa Kavirāja implied its possibility and that Kavi-karṇapūra accepted it. Later, Viśvanātha Cakravartī and Ṭhākura Bhaktivinoda also accepted it. And it is also alive and well in the Bhaktivinoda *parivāra* following Bhaktisiddhānta Saraswatī Ṭhākura.

From the outset of this discussion, I have described this theological perspective as "peculiar"—the idea that Balarāma's primary *śakti* has no romantic relationship with him but instead has one with Kṛṣṇa. But perhaps "unique" in the world of God's consorts is a better way to describe it, and in this view she does after all have a relationship with him in his Gaura *līlā* appearance as Nityānanda Rāma. *Jaya* Rāma! *Jaya* Kṛṣṇa! *Jaya* Radhe!

20. It is also notable that Bhaktivinoda Ṭhākura's *dīkṣā-guru*, Bipin Bihari Goswāmī, took exception to portions of *Muralī-vilāsa* and *Vaṁśī-śikṣā*. In his *Daśa-mūla-rasa*, he refers to "repugnant philosophy" (*viruddha darśana*) present in *Vaṁśī-śikṣā*, which he attributes to interpolation and further labels "*sahaja vādīra* . . . *prakṣipta varṇana*" as "*sahajiyā*" interpretations. See Lucian Wong's article, "Against Vaiṣṇava Deviance: Brāhmaṇical and *Bhadralok* Alliance in Bengal." Wong, Lucian. 2018 *Religions* 9, no. 2: 57. https://doi.org/10.3390/rel9020057. However, Bipin Bihari Goswāmī does not directly address the issues raised in this chapter.

29

Brahmā-stuti

Bhaktivedanta Bhāvānuvāda

Brahmā begins his prayers by respectfully glorifying the form of Kṛṣṇa who appears before him. Brahmā expresses his desire to attain that *prema* of which this particular form is the object—the *viṣaya-ālambana-vibhāva* of *sakhya-rati*. First, he describes Kṛṣṇa's form in terms of its *śyāma* complexion—comparing it to a soothing rain cloud—his body wrapped in a golden cowherd dress that resembles lightning. Kṛṣṇa's form is of course further illumined by the *prema* of his eternal associates and as such is like a rain cloud of love showering down upon his thirsty earthly *sādhakas*.

However, since dark complexion and golden dress are also features of Nārāyaṇa, would not such praise be more appropriately offered directly to Nārāyaṇa? Are not Kṛṣṇa's complexion and dress, properly understood, those of Nārāyaṇa? To dispose of this doubt, Brahmā then seeks to distinguish Kṛṣṇa from Nārāyaṇa and assert the superiority of Kṛṣṇa's form by praising his forest ornaments—his *gunja*-berry earrings, his forest-flower garland, and the flowers in his hair and over his ears, placed there with the *prema* of his *sakhās*. Nārāyaṇa is not so ornamented with intimate fraternal love and as such lacks the sweetness of Kṛṣṇa. Nor is he crowned with Kṛṣṇa's peacock feather, which Brahmā also praises, a crown representing both head/knowledge (its eyes) and heart/love (its beauty). The feather's eyes are wise in that by love they are blinded to finding fault. Such is Kṛṣṇa, known more for mercy in this form than in any other form of himself.[1]

1. Although Kṛṣṇa's transcendental eroticism has not yet manifested in the pages of the *Bhāgavatam*, Kṛṣṇa's peacock feather also represents his romanticism, for as the peacock raises his colorful feathers, dancing in courtship as if looking in all directions for love, so

Brahmā also points out that while majestic Nārāyaṇa has four hands, Kṛṣṇa has two. Further, he asserts that this *dvibhuja* form of Gopāla Kṛṣṇa is more charming, affording his devotees a variety of love not available in Nārāyaṇa's abode. This point is indicated by the fact that Kṛṣṇa held in his left hand cowherd yogurt rice stolen from his friend's plate and in his right hand a herding stick. Brahmā thus praises Kṛṣṇa's hands and the items they hold as well as his soft, sweet feet, which due to insufficient body weight and underdeveloped markings on his soles during his *kumāra* age leave no distinct footprints in the forest. Brahmā also praises Kṛṣṇa's horn and flute and then distinguishes Gopāla Kṛṣṇa from Vāsudeva Kṛṣṇa of Mathurā by praising Kṛṣṇa as the cowherd son of Nanda—*paśupāṅgajāya*—with intense longing to attain his company as a cowherd friend (ŚB 10.14 1).

To underscore the theological implications of his praise of Kṛṣṇa's form, which on the surface appears to be no more than a description of the form of an ordinary cowherd boy, Brahmā then states that although he himself is well known as the creator and has an extraordinary and venerable four-headed form, unlike his form that consists of material ingredients, Kṛṣṇa's form is not made of material ingredients (*na tu bhūta-mayasya ko 'pi*).

Furthermore, although Brahmā is capable of turning his mind inward in deep introspection, he states that such contemplation unto itself cannot afford one the experience of Gopāla Kṛṣṇa's *dvibhuja-rūpa*. Thus, he implies that the *sattvic* disciplines of *jñāna* and *yoga* centered on arresting the restless mind and experiencing the *ātmā* afford one only an atomic experience of *ānanda*—*ātmānanda*. In comparison to that, what is the bliss of Kṛṣṇa's form, his *svarūpānanda*, and moreover what is the bliss Kṛṣṇa experiences within through his fraternal love with his friends—*svarūpa-śakti-ānanda*? In answer to these questions, Brahmā says that he cannot fathom the bliss of Kṛṣṇa's *sad-cid-ānanda-rūpa*, what to speak of the bliss Kṛṣṇa derives from interacting with his *svarūpa-śakti* in the form of his friends. Brahmā describes Kṛṣṇa's form as *sveccha-mayasya*, implying both that Kṛṣṇa's form is self-manifest and that it is manifest in his merciful response (*anugraha*) to the desires of his friends. His form and person are inextricably intertwined with his friends' love for him. His form arises out of their love and is at the same time the cause of their love. It is self-manifest in that Kṛṣṇa's self includes his internal *svarūpa-śakti* that *bhakti* is also constituted of. Love and its object are simultaneously one and different, interpenetrating one another. Like sugar, Kṛṣṇa's form is inherently sweet. However, his *svarūpa-śakti* tastes

---

too does Kṛṣṇa look in all directions for Rādhā and dance under her influence.

his sweetness in ways that he cannot, other than through this *śakti* manifest as his intimate friends. Thus, the *ānanda* of his *svarūpa-śakti* exceeds that of his *svarūpa*. Kṛṣṇa's form does not answer to the world of things or thoughts, and it also dances above and beyond the stillness of the quieted, introspective mind. It can be known only by his grace, the principal agents of which are Kṛṣṇa's devotees (ŚB 10.14.2).[2]

The notion that *bhakti* possesses greater salvific efficacy than *jñāna* is central to Brahmā's tribute. *Jñānīs* and *yogīs* often overtly appear more spiritual than devotees to the untrained eye, and this is particularly so when *jñānīs* and *yogīs* are compared to Kṛṣṇa's cowherd friends, who in many respects appear just like ordinary, uneducated cowherds, as does Kṛṣṇa himself. Thus, Brahmā feels the need to make his case for *bhakti* unequivocally, and for the extreme form of *bhakti* that Brahmā experienced in particular. After all, *Śvetāśvatara-śruti* 3.8 states, *tam eva viditvāti mṛtyum eti*: "Knowing Brahman one can surpass death." If this is so, then how can an apparently ignorant person attain liberation? Thus, Brahmā answers this question by making a clear case for the preeminent position of *jñāna-śūnyā bhakti*—*bhakti* unencumbered by knowledge[3]—that he witnesses in Kṛṣṇa's friends:

> Rejecting any endeavor for knowledge in an ascending, self-effort-based approach to knowing your indeterminate feature of Brahman and showing no interest in your majestic features, your friends feel at home here in your bucolic abode as cowherds with no ambition to go elsewhere.[4] From here they loudly sing about and listen to recitations of your glorious acts and qualities, endeavor to understand your witticisms and intentions, and touch you through service to you and through accepting service from you. Thus, they are preoccupied with you and those related to you through their words, thoughts, and deeds, and by this alone they conquer you

2. In this *līlā* we find that Kṛṣṇa manifested his *aiśvarya* more than in any other recorded instance. However, he was able to do this only in the absence of his *svarūpa-śakti* in the form of his friends' fraternal love. Arguably, in their presence he could not do so. Such is the power of their love.

3. *Caitanya-caritāmṛta* 2.8.66 employs this term—*jñāna-śūnyā-bhakti*—when discussing this verse. It refers to *bhakti* that is not in pursuit of either Brahman or knowledge of God's majesty.

4. Here the words *sthāne sthitāḥ* (remaining in one's position) can also refer to the fact that *bhakti* transcends *varṇāśrama*. Regardless of one's position in the socioreligious order, one can take to *bhakti* and achieve a goal that transcends that of *varṇāśrama*. As such, *varṇāśrama*—*karma-mārga*—cannot afford one realization of Gopāla Kṛṣṇa. Thus, the *sādhana* of *uttama-bhakti* is not covered by *jñāna* or *karma*.

> with such love—making you their equal—despite the fact that you are otherwise unattainable by ordinary verbal, mental, and physical efforts (ŚB 10.14.3).[5]

Brahmā then continues to speak very strongly yet indirectly in praise of *bhakti*, stating that those who reject *bhakti*, the path of the highest good (*śreyaḥ-sṛtiṁ*), in pursuit of spiritual monism (*kevala-bhodha labdhaye*) experience only the trouble they have undertaken—on paths such as *jñāna*—and not their desired goal. In contrast, the benefits of *bhakti* are many, both in this world in the stage of *sādhana* and in the next in the stages of *bhāva* and *prema*. Therefore, lesser gains such as realizing the extent to which the *ātmā* is one with its source—the aim of *jñānīs*—is also included within its scope (ŚB 10.14.4). Thus, Brahmā, speaking with emotion for *bhakti*, explains that by rejecting *jñāna* and embracing *bhakti*, regardless of one's socioreligious status and corresponding measure of karmic implication, one conquers Kṛṣṇa. Rejecting *bhakti*, even if one embraces *jñāna*, one follows a path that will bear no fruit whatsoever. Strong words.

But what about *yoga* unto itself? Brahmā asserts that there is a long history of *yogīs* hearing from devotees about Kṛṣṇa and then mixing their *yoga* with *bhakti*—offering the fruits of their desires and deeds to him—and thereby attaining him or liberation through *yoga* mixed with *bhakti*. Thus, rather than rejecting *bhakti*, those *yogīs* and *jñānīs* who even partially embrace *bhakti* attain their ideal. However, by mixed *bhakti* they do not attain the same experience of Kṛṣṇa's sweetness and charming qualities that his unalloyed devotees do. Typically, they attain Kṛṣṇa's aura of *nirviśeṣa* Brahman, while some may realize one of his qualities, such as his compassion. Kṛṣṇa manifests himself in this world out of compassion for his devotees. That quality of his is easily understood, but no one can understand the extent of his unlimited transcendental qualities, not even some computer genius capable of counting all the atoms of the earth, a blizzard's flakes of snow, or all the shining particles of sunlight (ŚB 10.14.5–7).[6]

5. What is said in this verse about the approach of Kṛṣṇa's friends is typically understood to refer to his devotees on the *rāga-mārga* in general. They attain him by remaining in the company of *sādhus* and hearing and chanting about him regardless of their social position, and in doing so they make no effort to attain *nirvikalpa samādhi*.

6. Saṅkarṣaṇa, the expansion of Balarāma, is said to have counted every atom, yet even his source, Balarāma, expressed, earlier in this *brahma-vimohana-līlā*, his inability to fully understand Kṛṣṇa.

Thus, Brahmā concludes this section of his tribute focused on the efficacy of *bhakti* with the obvious: Simply loving Kṛṣṇa is by far the best course of action. And it is comparatively easy to do, given his compassion for his devotees. One who serves him steadfastly as a way of life, accepting whatever happiness or distress one experiences as either that which one is due in consideration of one's diminishing *prārabdha-karma* or as Kṛṣṇa's arrangement to draw one closer to him, inherits the treasure of the shelter of his liberated lotus feet. His devotees spend their lives in this way, rather than performing severe austerities and penances with the great physical and mental effort required on other paths. They simply serve him instead, and that according to their means, endeavoring only for his grace (ŚB 10.14.8).

Having expounded both directly and indirectly upon the extraordinary efficacy of *bhakti*, Brahmā next underscores the only formidable obstacle to the *bhakti-mārga*: offense—*aparādha*—either to *bhakti* herself or to the object of *bhakti*, Bhagavān. Such offenses are sins of the soul rather than sins of the flesh arising out of material desire.

In explaining *bhakti*'s efficacy, Brahmā spoke of those who reject *bhakti* and how such rejection renders their efforts to attain transcendence ineffective. Such outright rejection of *bhakti* can constitute an offensive disposition toward her. However, Brahmā proceeds in his next verse by holding himself up as a glaring example of one who has offended the perfect object of love/*bhakti*, *svayaṁ* Bhagavān himself—Śrī Gopāla Kṛṣṇa.

How did Brahmā offend Kṛṣṇa? He wanted to test the power of Kṛṣṇa by exercising his own magical powers, and in doing this he sought to interfere with Kṛṣṇa's picnic lunch. Then, witnessing Kṛṣṇa's subsequent display of majesty, he realized his own insignificance in comparison to Kṛṣṇa, the Paramātmā, whose magic bewilders magicians. He realized in some measure the difference between power derived from Kṛṣṇa's *māyā-śakti* as opposed to that of his *svarūpa-śakti*. Thus, Brahmā compared himself to a mere flame in the fire of Kṛṣṇa (ŚB 10.14.9).

Then, having acknowledged his offense, Brahmā appeals to Kṛṣṇa's compassionate nature, begging for forgiveness. Speaking to *nirguṇa* Kṛṣṇa, he describes himself as the locus of *rajo-guṇa*, who in this instance is also influenced by the darkness of *tamo-guṇa*, giving rise to false pride. But despite his fallen position before him who is infallible—*acyuta*—Brahmā nonetheless asserts that in terms of his position as Brahmā he is Kṛṣṇa's servant, an *adhikṛta dāsa*, and thus worthy of Kṛṣṇa's compassion. By referring to Kṛṣṇa as Acyuta, Brahmā implies that Kṛṣṇa never fails to show compassion to his servitors (ŚB 10.14.10).

Here Brahmā begins to resort to his conventional ego as the god of the secondary creation—a Brahmā—referring to how Kṛṣṇa in his form as the Puruṣa fathered him at the dawn of creation. Thus, Brahmā makes it overwhelmingly clear that Kṛṣṇa is the fountainhead of divinity, the *avatārī*, of whom even Bhagavān Nārāyaṇa is an *avatāra*.

This philosophical point is, of course, central to Gauḍīya Vedānta.[7] Nārāyaṇa accepts only reverential love, whereas Kṛṣṇa can accept either reverential or intimate humanlike love. Were Kṛṣṇa an aspect of Nārāyaṇa, Nārāyaṇa's *avatāra* would be more aesthetically complete than himself. And because Kṛṣṇa himself is more aesthetically robust than he is in his majestic feature as Nārāyaṇa, he must have an abode where fraternal love of God eternally plays itself out. Thus, because Kṛṣṇa is the source of Nārāyaṇa, there is the possibility of fraternal love of God in a realm above and beyond Nārāyaṇa's majestic Vaikuṇṭha.

Brahmā now understands this important point of *tattva* out of which the *bhāva* of fraternal love can arise. Over the next eight verses, he speaks as if in conversation with Kṛṣṇa so as to make this point of *tattva* clear and in doing so invoke Kṛṣṇa's compassion. He speaks and thinks with his four heads what Kṛṣṇa might say in response and then speaks again as if answering Kṛṣṇa.

> Kṛṣṇa: What are you saying? You are God. No? Your body is the universe. Who am I to forgive you?
>
> Brahmā: What kind of god am I? If I use my hand stretched from my pinky to my thumb as a measuring instrument, my height is only seven such spans. I am a very small creature enclosed within a disposable clay pot–like universe, a cosmic egg composed of the basic material elements. And what is your glorious position in comparison? Unlimited universes emanate from the pores of your body. You are Mahāviṣṇu/Saṅkarṣaṇa, the first *puruṣa* and original *avatāra*—the compassion of Nārāyaṇa personified. Therefore, you should show me compassion.
>
> O Adhokṣaja,[8] you are also the second *puruṣa*, Garbhodakaśāyī/Pradyumna, presiding over this particular universe, from whom I

7. The ancient commentator Śrīdhara Swāmī, as well as Śrī Caitanya's contemporary Vallabhācārya, also embraces this perspective.

8. Adhokṣaja is a name that the Vraja *vāsīs* employed to refer to Kṛṣṇa's miracle of surviving the collapse of the cart—a form assumed by the demon Śakaṭāsura—under which

appeared in the world, born as it were from the lotus-like umbilical cord emanating from your navel. As such you are like my mother, and a mother does not take offense when her child kicks her within the womb.

Kṛṣṇa: But you are not within me like a fetus within the womb of its mother.

Brahmā: Actually, there is nothing outside of you. Such is the panentheistic nature of the world. You are my mother and my father. It is said in scripture that after the deluge when the upper, middle, and lower planetary systems are submerged in water, Nārāyaṇa/Garbhodakaśāyī lies down on that water and gradually a lotus flower grows from his navel. At that time, someone referred to as "the unborn"—*aja*—appears upon that lotus. Certainly, these words are not false. Am I not that unborn one?

Kṛṣṇa: If so, you are the son of Nārāyaṇa, not me.

Brahmā: Ah, but *you* are Nārāyaṇa, appearing as the first, second, and also the third *puruṣa*, who is the soul of every soul, the eternal witness of the world—*akhila-loka-sākṣī*. Nārāyaṇa is the shelter (*ayana*) of everyone (*nara*), even as he lies in the universal waters and by his *yogamāyā* appears delimited to the material eye. If you were limited by time and space, I could have seen you when I looked for my source at the dawn of creation. But I could not see you. Instead, I saw you within my heart in meditation only after I followed your oracle advising me to engage in *tapa* culminating in *bhakti*. It was as if you were playing hide and seek with me even then.

Again, you are that Nārāyaṇa. More clearly, Nārāyaṇa himself is a limb (*aṅga*) of your body—*nārāyaṇo 'ṅga*. This is what I saw in your extraordinary display of majesty at the culmination of your cowherding *līlā* with your friends after I tried to hide your friends and calves from you, foolishly thinking I could subject you to a game of hide and seek of my own design. You are Nārāyaṇa and you are at the same time not Nārāyaṇa, in that Nārāyaṇa properly understood is

---

he had been placed for his safety. Sanātana Goswāmī takes this epithet invoked by Brahmā as a subtle reference to Kṛṣṇa's mischievous childhood, for which his elders always forgave him. Thus, Brahmā employs it to strengthen his case for forgiveness, since he is but the mischievous child of the second *puruṣa*, who is one of Kṛṣṇa's *avatāras*.

only your *avatāra*,[9] and your *līlās* of hide and seek with your friends are sweeter than Nārāyaṇa's *līlās*.

Indeed, your mother claimed that she saw the universe inside you as she looked within your mouth,[10] and this is further evidence in support of my earlier point that the external illusory world is also within you, even when it appears to be outside of you. And it is not that the world appearing within you is merely a reflection of the outside world.

Kṛṣṇa: How is that possible?

Brahmā: Such is your *acintya-śakti*, your *yogamāyā*! Have you not just shown me that you yourself and everything within this creation are manifestations of your inconceivable potency—*māyātvam*? At first you appeared alone and then you manifested yourself as all of your calves and friends of Vraja—*vraja-suhṛd-vatsāḥ*. Then those calves and friends appeared as an equal number of four-handed Viṣṇu forms worshiped by all, including myself. And after that you appeared as an equal number of universes. Finally, you reappeared in your original form, demonstrating that you are the unmeasurable, nondual ultimate reality—Brahman (ŚB 10.14.11–18).

Next Brahmā states in four verses that Gopāla Kṛṣṇa standing before him in *gopa-veśa* is the root of both the *guṇa-* and *līlā-avatāras*. He is the source of the creation, its maintenance, and its destruction (*jamādy asya yataḥ*), and at the same time he appears within the manifest world in countless forms, *avatāras*, as an act of grace. He has no birth but appears to take birth, and in so doing he ends the birth and death of his devotees. Because of him there is no death for his devotees, and because of him *dharma* is protected and the unrighteous are righted. Nothing is impossible for him! Thus, Brahmā rightly concludes, "Who can understand the play—*yogamāyā*—of your innumerable *avatāras*? You are the infinite being, sixfold in opulence, and hidden within everyone—*ko vetti bhūman bhagavan parātman*! The dream-like illusory world appears real only because of your appearance within it, by which it can be understood in relation to its source (ŚB 10.14.19–22).

9. The epithet Nārāyaṇa can refer to Nārāyaṇa as the Lord of Vaikuṇṭha, as Mahā-saṅkarṣaṇa of Vaikuṇṭha, and also as any of the three *puruṣa-avatāras* appearing in this world.

10. Brahmā is able to cite this example by the power of his limited omniscience, as he endeavors to make the case for the position of Kṛṣṇa as the *avatārī*, whose compassion Brahmā is in pursuit of.

While emphasizing that Kṛṣṇa is *satya* (real), Brahmā distinguishes between the individual *ātmā*, who is also real, and Kṛṣṇa as the Paramātmā, who by contrast is the original person—*puruṣaḥ purāṇaḥ*—and thus the *ātmā*'s source, for it is he who "becomes many." He is self-effulgent like the *ātmā*, but unlike the *ātmā* he is infinite and primordial—*svayaṁ-jyotir ananta ādyaḥ*. Like the *ātmā*, he is eternal and imperishable, but unlike the *ātmā*, he is unimpeded in bliss and free from the influence of material contamination—*'kṣaro 'jasra-sukho nirañjanaḥ*. Kṛṣṇa is also complete in himself, nondual, and free from ignorance and mortality. But in a broader sense, here Brahmā is also saying that while the materially conditioned *jīva* can be seen by his limiting material form that has none of these attributes, Kṛṣṇa's form is different. It has these attributes, and one can only see Kṛṣṇa's form if he allows one to see it. His form is all-pervasive even when by his grace it appears before one as if delimited within space. In this sense, he is completely different from the materially bound *jīva*. And this, Brahmā continues, can be understood by one who learns to see the *ātmā* and the Paramātmā through the sun-like eyes of *śrī guru*, who teaches the Upaniṣads—*gurv-arka-labdhopaniṣat-sucakṣuṣā*—the result of which is crossing over the ocean of material existence. Such devotees who mix *jñāna* with *bhakti*, Brahmā says, attain the beatific vision of *śānta-rasa* (ŚB 10.14.23–24).

While it can be said that knowledge of the *ātmā* alone does away with *saṁsāra*, knowing the *ātmā* in full involves knowing it is rooted in Bhagavān, who presides over *māyā*. The *jīvātmā* that does not know Bhagavān, as he can be known only through *bhakti*, remains constrained by *māyā*. That is her *sevā* to Bhagavān. Such *jīvātmās* are turned away from God and as such are fearful. But that *jīvātmā* who knows itself to be rooted in Bhagavān is not under the constraint of *māyā* nor subject to ongoing transmigration (ŚB 10.14.25).

That said, the terms *bondage* and *liberation* refer only to the influence of *māyā*, for *avidyā* and *vidyā* are her potencies. Thus, just as for the sun there is no night or day, for the *ātmā* there is no bondage and no *mokṣa*. Here Brahmā minimizes the ideal of *mokṣa* by stating that the *ātmā* itself is always transcendental and *mokṣa* refers only to the absence of *māyā*. The absence of *māyā* is not an eternal ongoing event. It happens in time and as such cannot in and of itself be the eternal goal of life. Nor does *māyā* have the power to give *mokṣa*. She is constituted of the *guṇas*, and her *vidyā* potency within *sattva-guṇa* cannot give experience of the *nirguṇa* realm.

In contrast, *nirguṇa-bhakti* for Bhagavān removes *māyā* in the context of giving eternal love (ŚB 10.14.26).

With a sense of astonishment, Brahmā exclaims that those who have understood the difference between the *ātmā* and *māyā* but at the same time think that Kṛṣṇa is only an *ātmā* like themselves are utterly ignorant. They look only within their own *ātmā*, or they look to Kṛṣṇa's indeterminate feature—*nirviśeṣa* Brahman—for enlightenment. Brahmā says, "Such persons do not seek you—Kṛṣṇa—as you appear in your Vraja *līlā*, you who are the determinate Absolute and the support of Brahman. How astounding is the ignorance of those who consider themselves knowledgeable!" (ŚB 10.14.27).

However, *sādhus* seek Kṛṣṇa both within and without, for he is unbounded—*ananta*. They also distinguish the reality of the *ātmā* and Paramātmā from *māyā*'s illusion, rejecting that which is unreal. Brahmā gives an example to illustrate his point concerning their rejection: Just as a person, when reaching for a rope, first makes sure that it is not a snake, similarly, rejecting the unreal is required in order to embrace that which is real. Fixing the mind on Kṛṣṇa does not happen without rejecting illusory material life, nor does attaining Kṛṣṇa in Vraja happen without rejecting the effort-based, external paths of *yoga* and *jñāna*. By emphasizing on one hand the realness of the *ātmā* and distinguishing it from the illusion created by *māyā* and on the other distinguishing it from being absolutely identical with God, Brahmā also calls for the rejection of *vivarta-vāda* (ŚB 10.14.28).[11]

Having waxed philosophical over so many verses, Brahmā glorifies the playful nature of Kṛṣṇa in his *sakhya-rasa-līlā*, referring to him as such—*deva* (playful)—and asserts that, despite what he has said about Kṛṣṇa thus far, he can be known as such only by his grace. Indeed, no face of the Godhead can be known without his grace. Here Brahmā speaks of a fraction—*leśa*—of Kṛṣṇa's grace, and in so doing he emphasizes further that without some small measure of *bhakti*, those pursuing *brahma-sāyujya* will not be successful, regardless of how qualified they may be otherwise. Even if one desires to attain Kṛṣṇa's quality-less, indeterminate feature of *nirviśeṣa* Brahman, one requires his quality of compassion (ŚB 10.14.29).

11. Monistic *vivarta-vāda* posits, among other things, that the individuality of the *ātmā* is a false perception. Jīva Goswāmī likens the concept to the "piece of sky" contained in a clay pot. When the pot is broken, the sky within is understood to be one with the entirety of the sky (*pariccheda*). He also cites the analogy of a reflection (*pratibimba*), in which that which is reflected appears to be contained within that which it is reflected upon. In his commentary on this verse, Jīva Goswāmī explains how these analogies fail.

Brahmā began his *stuti* with a very sweet description and glorification of Kṛṣṇa's form, expressing his desire to attain it in *līlā-sevā*. Then gradually he spoke more philosophically and of the majesty of Kṛṣṇa. Now in this final section of his prayers he returns to sweetness. He does this in the context of expressing his own inner ambition more clearly, his budding *bhāva* arising out of the *tattva* enunciated above. Thus, he shifts from the perspective of his conventional ego as Brahmā to fixation on his ideal, his developing sense of his Vraja *līlā* ego. He does so first in a general way, very humbly expressing his ambition to always take birth as a devotee regardless of the species, thinking such a birth to be better than that of a non-devotee Brahmā. He also implies that before him in Vraja there are many species, but actually they are all great devotees dedicated to Kṛṣṇa's lotus-like feet. They are all Kṛṣṇa's people. Thus, Brahmā begs for Kṛṣṇa's grace, which is achieved by serving his devotees and by which Brahmā too can become such a devotee, and furthermore he expresses his desire to reside in Vraja among Kṛṣṇa's eternal associates (ŚB 10.14.30).

Given his experience in this *līlā*, Brahmā then glorifies two groups of devotees in particular, those who were seen to be most fortunate, as he himself seeks a similar good fortune. These devotees are Kṛṣṇa's *vātsalya-* and *sakhya-rasa* associates. Other than how they benefitted the most from this *līlā*, Brahmā emphatically praises them as the most fortunate for another reason as well. He is concerned about Kṛṣṇa's possibly suggesting that because Brahmā is very exalted in human society as well as among the gods, perhaps he should aspire to take birth among the royalty of the Yadu dynasty rather than within a lowly cowherd community. In response to this possible suggestion by which Kṛṣṇa might test his resolve, Brahmā first praises the mothers and cows of Vraja, astounded as he is by their good fortune.

Brahmā says that although Kṛṣṇa is full in himself, in this *līlā* he who is full is nonetheless nourished further by the breast milk of the mothers and cows of Vraja! How much so? Brahmā says more so than Kṛṣṇa had been nourished to date by the cumulative effect of all the sacrificial fires that had been offered to him. And furthermore, Kṛṣṇa could not get enough of the taste of these mothers' milk and thus he expanded into the forms of millions of calves and cowherd boys and drank it for a year! In saying this, Brahmā speaks with great conviction as to his own desire to enter the so-called lowly cowherd community. He will settle for nothing less. Śrī

Jīva Goswāmī says that in praising the cowherd people, Brahmā indicates his own inner longing to live among them. Although he is glorious as Aja for being "unborn" or having an uncommon birth, he now desires to have a mother and father in Vraja, taking an apparent ordinary birth in Kṛṣṇa's *prakaṭa-līlā*. He sees this as far superior to his majestic birth from the lotus stemming from Nārāyaṇa's navel (ŚB 10.14.31).

After expressing his astonishment at the good fortune of the mothers of Vraja, in intense bliss, Brahmā then emphasizes with even greater astonishment the good fortune of those friends of Kṛṣṇa (*yan-mitram*) steeped in *sakhya prema*—Śrīdāmā and the other young boys.[12] Glorifying Vraja—the cowherd kingdom of Nanda—as the domain of friendship, Brahmā clearly espouses his *niṣṭhā*: Eternal (*sanātanam*) friendship (*mitram*) is the highest bliss (*paramānandam*). Simultaneously, he states that Kṛṣṇa, as the complete expression of Brahman (*pūrṇaṁ brahma*), is himself the highest bliss, personified as one's eternal friend. Having praised the residents of Vraja in general and the cowherd boys in particular, he expresses his longing in *sambandhānugā-bhakti* to reside therein himself by means of taking shelter of the dust of the *gopas*' lotus feet. As seen above in his prayers, he does not pray directly for Kṛṣṇa to bless him to become a cowherd but rather prays to attain the dust from the feet of the residents of Vraja—their grace—and that of the cowherd boys in particular, who were right there in the midst of Kṛṣṇa's cowherding *līlā* that serves as portal to eternal friendship. He prays in this way, knowing that *rāga-bhakti* is only attained by the grace of such devotees. Thus, Brahmā shows his skill in *sādhana*, the spirit embedded in his praise being his longing in *sambandhānuga-bhakti* to attain the friendship he is astonished by (ŚB 10.14.32).[13]

Then, continuing to glorify the cowherd community, Brahmā states that at times, such as during the *prakaṭa-līlā* when Kṛṣṇa returns home from cowherding with his friends, the *devas* presiding over the senses taste something of the bliss of Vraja through the senses they preside over. In contrast, the cowherd boys taste the highest bliss with all of their senses at all times.

12. While the words *yan-mitram* in this central verse of Brahmā's prayers can be understood in a number of different ways (see chapter 30), here I have followed Viśvanātha Cakravartī's rendering—*śrīdāmādi bālakānāṁ sakhā*.

13. Any sense in which this verse might be construed to be less than full-blown advocacy of *sakhya-rasa* and a glorification of Kṛṣṇa's *sakhās* can be attributed to the fact that Brahmā also feels a measure of shame for having offended Kṛṣṇa's friends, which causes him to speak very humbly and with some restraint. See chapter 30 for a detailed explanation of this central verse of Brahmā's prayers.

Thus, Brahmā again prays to take birth in the cowherd community, where Mukunda is everyone's all in all, and be bathed—*abhiṣeka*—from head to toe in its cow dust. However, out of humility, Brahmā implies that should he not be qualified to attain his ideal of *sakhya-rasa*, may he at least attain some type of residence in Vraja. In this way, he extols the virtues of Vraja and any and all of its residents (ŚB 10.14.33–34).

Brahmā, his mind reeling at the staggering measure of the Vraja *vāsīs'* love for Kṛṣṇa, reaches the four-headed conclusion that as a result of their selflessness, in which everything they do and everything they are connected with is for his pleasure alone, Kṛṣṇa remains eternally in their debt. Yes, he has given himself—which is everything—in return, but he also gave that to Pūtanā, who merely dressed like a Vraja *vāsī*. What then does he have left to give to his Vraja *līlā bhaktas*? Thus, Brahmā accurately depicts Kṛṣṇa as an eternal debtor. Such is the wealth of Vraja *bhakti* (ŚB 10.14.35).

Then, because Vraja *bhakti* is difficult to understand, Brahmā offers the following comparison and explanation: "These Vraja *vāsīs* are not like *sannyāsīs* of the *jñāna-mārga*, who give everything up and at best come to you empty-handed, looking for peace. These cowherd people come to you with houses, families, friends, and so on, all of which are extensions of their own identity as your devotees and, as such, all of which are placed at your disposal. Love is a thief, a house is a prison, and infatuation is a ball and chain if they are not extensions of those who consider themselves to be yours. But these cowherd people go beyond that. Indeed, they think that *you also belong to them*, and they are correct" (ŚB 10.14.36).

But how can God be someone's son and intimate friend? How can he act just like people of the world whose identities as friends and sons are an illusion? Are not Kṛṣṇa's appearances as a son and friend also a type of illusion rather than eternal roles he plays in a drama, entrance into which is the highest goal of life? This is not a good argument, and it has already been answered when Brahmā explained that Kṛṣṇa's friendship with Śrīdāmā and the multitude of Vraja *sakhās* is eternal—*mitraṁ sanātanam*. Nonetheless, this argument surfaces again in Brahmā's heads. Admittedly, it is hard to understand with even one head. Brahmā answers his own mental query by stating that when appearing in this world, Kṛṣṇa increases the bliss of his devotees; that is, he brings about the end of their material life by becoming their friend, son, and so on. His friendship ends illusion, and thus it cannot be an illusion itself. His relationships with his devotees in

Vraja mimic material relationships even as they transcend them. Kṛṣṇa is really the son of Yaśodā and really the source of everything, and he showed both of these truths to her. Or it should be understood that the intimacy of Kṛṣṇa's relationship with his friends is itself the fullest expression of his majesty, his Godhood. Baladeva Vidyābhūṣaṇa comments that the Vraja *vāsīs* have an imprint on the back of their heads that says *aiśvarya*, but they do not see it. Should one ask further how could they not see it, one might reply that being "lowly cowherds," perhaps even if they could see it, they could not read it. Divine ignorance is truly bliss! (ŚB 10.14.37)[14]

Brahmā then once again deprecates *jñāna* and indirectly praises *bhakti* with a touch of sarcasm: "What more can be said? Those who think they know some indeterminate reality that lies beyond you and thus do not understand your appearance in this world, your friendships, and so on, should know this: O Prabhu! Your magnificence lies beyond the reach of mind, body, or speech. The glory of your mind and body are beyond me, even as I stand here before you. And so too is the magnificence of your speech, especially the wonder of the words you exchange with your friends, words that render the Vedas speechless!" (ŚB 10.14.38).

Then, humbled by all that has been revealed to him, Brahmā asks permission to depart. Although he longs for residence in Vraja, he knows that to attain a suitable form in which to reside there, he must engage in *bhajana* arising out of the *tattva* he has espoused. In his present four-headed form, he rightfully feels out of place. However, he steps decidedly in the right direction, away from his ego as a controlling, world-creating god. And referring to Kṛṣṇa as he who knows and sees all (*kṛṣṇa sarvaṁ tvam vetsi sarva-dṛk*) and as he who is the master of the universe (*jagatāṁ nātho*), Brahma offers the world to its actual proprietor (ŚB 10.14.39).

Driven now by humility and absence of any sense of false proprietorship, Brahmā concludes his praise as he departs by engaging in *nāma-saṅkīrtana*—*śrī-kṛṣṇa vṛṣṇi-kula*. In Brahmā's mind the name *vṛṣṇi-kula* refers primarily to Nanda's community, who are extended members of the Vṛṣṇi dynasty,

14. The idea that Kṛṣṇa exhibits greater *aiśvarya* in Vraja is also explained by Rūpa Goswāmī. Citing the *Brahmānanda Purāṇa* in 1.5.529 of his *Laghu-bhāgavatāmṛta*, Śrī Rūpa explains that Prince Kṛṣṇa of Dvārakā endeavored more to slay demons therein with the help of his *cakra* than young Kṛṣṇa of Vraja did in slaying the wicked, which he did while playing with his friends! And, of course, Brahmā himself has just witnessed the height of majesty here in Vraja. But moreover, the sweetness of Kṛṣṇa's Vraja *līlā* itself is arguably the be-all and end-all of majesty. Indeed, the fact that the Godhead makes himself so accessible is mind-boggling.

Nanda being the half-brother of Vasudeva. Thus, Brahmā sings first and foremost of cowherd Kṛṣṇa, the delighter of the lotus—*puṣkara-joṣa-dāyin*—of Nanda's clan (ŚB 10.14. 40).

From the Gauḍīya perspective, it is significant that Brahmā ends his *stuti* with *nāma-saṅkīrtana*. He offended the "named" and departed, but the "name" went with him, as described below. Kṛṣṇa is nondifferent from his name, but at the same time his name is said to be more merciful than his person. If one offends the form and person of Kṛṣṇa, Kṛṣṇa's name does not necessarily disregard such an offender and is known to remain with him or her as a means by which, through *saṅkīrtana* of Kṛṣṇa *nāma*, the offender can counteract the offense. And this is what happened to Brahmā.

Because of his offense of interrupting Kṛṣṇa's picnic with his intimate friends and questioning the divinity of cowherd Kṛṣṇa due to his unconventional behavior by Vedic standards, Brahmā was born on earth. He took birth in West Bengal as an outcaste in terms of Hindu caste considerations. However, he was born during the *prakaṭa* Gaura *līlā* and dubbed "Brahmā Haridāsa" by the orthodox *brāhmaṇa* Vaiṣṇava elder Advaita Ācārya.

Brahmā's birth in Gaura *līlā* is also predicted in the *Śrīmad Bhāgavatam* 11.5.33, as understood by Viśvanātha Cakravartī Ṭhākura. Therein, we find the phrase *śiva-viriñci-nutam*, a reference to Brahmā (*viriñci*) and Śiva both appearing in Gaura *līlā*. And Cakravartī Ṭhākura has taken it a step further by informing us that Śiva and Brahmā appeared therein as Advaita Ācārya and Haridāsa Ṭhākura, respectively.[15] Śrī Caitanya later in his *līlā* bestowed upon Haridāsa the title Nāmācārya. Thus, through the medium of *nāma-saṅkīrtana* leading to *līlā-smaraṇam*, Brahmā Haridāsa attained his ideal of *sakhya-rasa*.

15. In *Navadvīpa-dhāma-māhātmya*, Bhaktivinoda Ṭhākura makes the connection between Brahmā's offense in Vraja and his Muslim birth as Haridāsa, and in that text Brahmā laments that he was not born as a *gopa*. Such lamentation constitutes the early stages of his longing to attain such a cowherd birth. Īśāna Nāgara's *Advaita Prakāśa* also connects Brahmā with Haridāsa, as does Locana dāsa's *Caitanya-maṅgala*. *Advaita-maṅgala* identifies Haridāsa with Brahmā and describes Advaita Ācārya's *śikṣā* to him concerning the Hare Kṛṣṇa *mantra* to include the idea that this *nāma-mantra* represents the seventeen principal *gopīs* and fifteen principal *gopas* of Vraja that correspond with the *mantra*'s thirty-two syllables. However, the text does not identify the principal *gopas* or *gopīs* Advaita had in mind, who otherwise are thought to be twelve and eight in number, respectively, and whose identities are common knowledge.

Thus ends the *Bhaktivedanta Bhāvānuvāda* of *Śrīmad Bhāgavatam*'s *Brahmā-stuti*. Brahmā's prayers are a milk ocean of Gauḍīya *tattva*, the churning of which gives rise to the cream of *sakhya-rasa*. This *bhāvānuvāda* follows the lead of the Brahmā-Madhva-Gauḍīya commentaries as well as those of the Rudra *sampradāya*, both ancient and contemporary, that were respected by the founding Gauḍīya *ācāryas*. Those seeking further grammatical and commentarial support for its feeling can find it in the abovementioned commentaries.

30

Aho Bhāgyam!

The great Bhaktisiddhānta Saraswatī Ṭhākura composed a Bengali verse that represents the very spirit of his approach to the *rāga-mārga*. The occasion for its composition was the building of the famous Baghbazar Gauḍīya Maṭha, an opulent marble temple constructed in Calcutta (present-day Kolkata). His disciples, apparently like materialists, concerned themselves with raising funds and doing all the activities involved in constructing the temple. His *sannyāsī* disciples went door to door to raise money, which was thrown at the deities' feet in the context of building them a lavish temple. The deities were those of the *rāga-mārga*: Śrīmān Gaurasundara and Rādhā-Kṛṣṇa. The spirit of this *sevā* was reverential worship—however, not of Nārāyaṇa but rather of the *rāga-mārga* itself. The idea was that *sādhakas* giving proper respect to this highest of ideals would in turn cause the residents of that realm, the *rāgātmikas*, to take notice of them and give them entrance, by which they could cross over such reverence.

Below I cite the Ṭhākura's Bengali verse followed by a translation of the verse, which includes an explanation of its implications:

> *pūjala rāgapatha gaurava bhaṅge*
> *mātala harijana viṣaya raṅge*

> Devotees reveling in the intoxication of offering the desirable things of this world in glorification of and with reverence for the ideal of *rāga-mārga-bhajana* will thereby remove all worldliness from their hearts by such divine *sevā*, and in turn their reverence will be broken, as actual *rāga-mārga* participants (*rāgātmikas*), attracted by their attitude, will reach down and bring them within their fold.

After the Ṭhākura's passing, Bhakti Sundara Govinda Mahārāja suggested that the word *viṣaya* (material enjoyment) could be changed to *kīrtana*, a suggestion that met with the approval of his *guru*, the founder of Sri Chaitanya Saraswat Math, Bhakti Rakṣaka Śrīdhara Deva Goswāmī. The words *viṣaya raṅge* mean that those pursuing the *rāga-mārga* revel in the *līlās* (*raṅge*) of the perfect object of love (*viṣaya*). However, in this world the principal means of entering into such relish is reveling in *kīrtana* (*kīrtana raṅge*). As such, this version of the Ṭhākura's verse was engraved in stone over the Chaitanya Saraswat Math temple deities, Śrī Gāndharvikā-Giridhārī and Gaurāṅga-sundara. Here *kīrtana* also refers to the dynamic outreach of Bhaktisiddhānta Saraswatī, who in his glorification of the *rāga-mārga* mostly spoke about what it was not, given that this high ideal lends itself to being misunderstood.

Thus, Bhaktisiddhānta Saraswatī Ṭhākura taught his followers to glorify the example of the *rāgātmikas*, in whose hands the *pūrṇaṁ brahma* has become an intimate friend on equal terms. In doing so, his disciples humbly felt themselves lacking qualification to directly participate in higher aspects of *rāga-mārga-bhajana*. They instead appealed through their *kīrtana* to the *rāgātmikas* for their grace, which increased their eligibility to tread the *rāga-mārga*. Thus, the Saraswata lineage differentiated itself from those who felt that their (often imaginary) budding *lobha* qualified them to engage in the higher practices and, in doing so, sometimes set a morally compromised standard that cast a shadow on the precepts of Mahāprabhu, misrepresenting the high ideal of *rāga-mārga-bhajana*. However, Bhaktisiddhānta Saraswatī Ṭhākura stressed that his disciples were not to lose sight of the aim of their dynamic *kīrtana*—*rāga-mārga*—and become proud of their preaching accomplishments and offensive to other Vaiṣṇavas.

In consideration of the above, I have selected the central verse from Brahmā's prayers, which exemplifies such reverence of the *rāga-mārga* with the ideal of *sakhya-rati* in mind. It can be incorporated into one's *sakhya-rati-bhajana* in consideration of Bhaktisiddhānta Saraswatī Ṭhākura's Bengali verse and overall approach outlined above, which assures that one's eligibility will increase. I will first cite it, and then I will explain it in a number of ways, drawing on how it has been commented upon by our Gauḍīya *ācāryas*. My explanation will culminate in how its composition renders it an example of *rasollāsa*. This *rasollāsa* understanding makes the verse a suitable prayer in reverential glorification of *sambandha-rūpa sakhya-rasa* with the desire to attain this same ideal oneself.

First the general meaning of the verse:

> *aho bhāgyam aho bhāgyaṁ*
> *nanda-gopa-vrajaukasām*
> *yan-mitraṁ paramānandaṁ*
> *pūrṇaṁ brahma sanātanam*

> O how fortunate! O how fortunate are the people of Nanda Gopa's Vraja. He who is the *pūrnaṁ brahma*, the *paramānanda*, has become their eternal friend.

In this verse the word *paramānanda* speaks of Kṛṣṇa as the giver of friendship in *prema*. Because *paramānanda* follows the word *mitram*, it can be understood to qualify friendship as the highest bliss. Śrī Jīva explains in his *Krama Sandarbha*, "The word *paramānandam* [supreme bliss] is the explanation of the word *mitram* [friendship]. Thus, the meaning is that in friendship the highest bliss is attained."[1]

It is he who is the highest bliss himself—Gopāla Kṛṣṇa—and he alone who gives this kind of bliss. Other forms of the Godhead are also forms of bliss and give *prema*, but they are not the highest forms of bliss and as such cannot give the highest *prema* (the bliss of friendship that permeates Vraja). In his *Krama Sandarbha*, Śrī Jīva Goswāmī explains further:

Ānandam is in the neuter gender for metrical reasons. Otherwise, here *ānandam* concurs with the *śruti* passage *vijñānam ānandaṁ brahma*: he is knowledge and bliss (*Bṛhad-āraṇyaka Upaniṣad* 3.9.28). Other forms of Bhagavān are blissful, and as such they also give a type of *prema* for different reasons, relative to the measure of bliss they are constituted of. But Kṛṣṇa is bliss itself in full, and he gives the fullest measure of bliss, only out of the bliss that he is to the people of Vraja. This is to be known from the *śruti* alone.[2] *Parama* (in the highest degree) combined with *ānanda* (sweetness) indicates extraordinary sweetness, just like the sweetness of sugar candy, which represents the highest point in the progress of sugarcane from molasses. This is both good fortune and astonishing.

Furthermore, this *ānanda* is *sanātana*, *mitraṁ paramānandaṁ sanātanam*—the bliss of eternal friendship, not temporary bliss. Thus, it is worthy of attainment, unlike that happiness which only makes an appearance and

1. In his *Bhakti-rasāmṛta-sindhu* commentary, Jīva Goswāmī feels that this same verse can also be interpreted to serve as an example of the spirit of *sakhyam* as an *aṅga* of *sādhana* for spiritually advanced *sādhakas* (see 1.2.188–194).

2. Here it is likely that Śrī Jīva is referring to *Gopāla-tāpanī śruti*.

cannot be relied upon to endure. It is not like the illusory attainments of this world. There is oneness between Kṛṣṇa as *paramānanda* and the friendship he shares that is also *paramānanda*—oneness and simultaneous difference. Kṛṣṇa is the object of eternal fraternal love, and his existence as such depends upon the eternal existence of such love in the form of his friends—*nitya-siddha kṛṣṇa-prema 'sādhya' kabhu naya.*[3] Our goal, our ideal, must be eternal and faultless. Here Brahmā acknowledges that this is the case with *sakhya-rasa.*

The all-pervasive yet invisible Brahman is thus not *paramānanda*, but Kṛṣṇa as *pūrṇaṁ brahma* is. And the creator Brahmā is astounded at his good fortune to actually see Brahman manifesting in a charming form that is not less than Brahman itself but rather the most complete form of Brahman—*pūrṇaṁ brahma.* This Brahman—Kṛṣṇa—is full because in this form Brahman tastes and gives the highest bliss—*mitraṁ paramānandam.* Just as *mukti* with form is more blissful than formless *mukti*, a *mukta* whose object of love has a spiritual form experiences more bliss than one who worships formless Brahman. This is the general rule. However, the words *pūrṇaṁ brahma* indicate not only Brahman with form but moreover him who among the many forms of the Godhead has the most complete form, him alone who is *rūpa-mādhurya.*

Brahmā's astonishment, which is evident by his repetition—*aho bhāgyam! aho bhāgyam!*—shows that he is beginning to experience *preyo-bhakti-rasa.* In *Bhakti-rasāmṛta-sindhu*, Śrī Rūpa cites the example of Brahmā's praise to illustrate that there are *nitya-siddha* devotees—Kṛṣṇa's *sakhās.* Śrī Jīva comments that Brahmā's repetition here is not faulty, because it expresses transcendental wonder, and Viśvanātha Cakravartī describes Brahmā as full of bliss and wonder as he speaks this verse. The basis of *rasa* is a sense of wonder (*camatkāra*). *Camatkāra* is the expansion of the heart (*citta vistara*) and the supernatural artistic delight derived from contemplation of the beauty of Kṛṣṇa—his form, qualities, and *līlās.*

When we examine this verse in the context in which it appears in the *Bhāgavata*, we understand that while the verse speaks in a general way as to the good fortune of Nanda Gopa's cowherd kingdom, which is the very abode of intimate friendship not found elsewhere, it is more precisely a statement in which Brahmā expresses his own budding *sakhya-rati* in glorification of Kṛṣṇa's intimate friends. The friendship of Vraja extends down to touch *dāsya*, up in *saṅkula-rati* to also touch *vātsalya*, and ultimately further up to mingle with *mādhurya.*

3. *Caitanya-caritāmṛta* 2.22.107.

In his comments on Brahmā's prayers to Gopāla Kṛṣṇa, Viśvanātha Cakravartī Ṭhākura states that Brahmā, who was previously treading the *vaidhī-bhakti-mārga*, is now longing for *rāgānugā-bhakti*. He comments further, "After praising the Vraja *vāsīs* with *rāgātmikā-vātsalya-prema* [in the previous verse, ŚB 10.14.31], in this verse Brahmā praises those with *rāgātmikā-sakhya-prema* in particular and also all those relishing other intimate relationships with Bhagavān in general." In other words, this verse, while speaking in general about the fortune of all the residents of Vraja and how they are to one extent or another touched by *sakhya-prema*, more specifically glorifies *sakhya-prema* itself and the young cowherds who personify it.[4]

Sanātana Goswāmī comments, "Brahman is herein described as the friend of Śrīdāmā and the other cowherd boys." These cowherds are the *āśraya-ālambana-vibhāva* of *sakhya-rasa* that Brahmā witnessed playing in fraternal love with the *viṣaya-ālambana-vibhāva* of *sakhya-rasa*—Gopāla Kṛṣṇa—now standing before Brahmā. Thus, here Brahmā prays respectfully for that same *rasa*, the seed of which he received at the dawn of creation. Similarly, commenting on the *bhakti aṅga* of *sakhyam* described in *Bhakti-rasāmṛta-sindhu*, Jīva Goswāmī cites this verse as an example of a *sādhaka* identified with the *aṅga* of *sakhyam*. In this case the *sādhana* is *sambandhānuga*. Thus, Brahmā's verse praises *nitya-siddha-sakhās* of Vraja in the spirit of wishing to attain this ideal himself.

Finally, in his *Prīti Sandarbha* Jīva Goswāmī characterizes this verse as an example of *rasollāsa*, or the exultation of *sakhya-rasa* as the highest bliss by virtue of the cleverness of Śukadeva/Brahmā's use of words that at first glance appear to constitute an incompatible mixture (*ayogya saṅgati*) of reverence and *sakhya-rati*. Ordinarily such an incompatible combination would result in *rasābhāsā*. However, in this verse rather than the undesirable *rasābhāsā*, we find the most desirable *rasollāsa*.

Previously Śukadeva had been a *brahma-vādi*, and thus his *citta* was still slightly influenced by his previous *jñāna-bhakti-saṁskāras*, despite coming under the *Bhāgavata*'s influence of *rāga-bhakti*. Given this background, he uses the reverential Upaniṣadic words *pūrṇaṁ brahma* in glorification of *sakhya-rasa*. However, in this verse his clever use of such words (*bhaṅgī-viśeṣa*)

4. Steeped in *sakhya-rati* himself, Nayanānanda Ṭhākura explains ŚB 10.14.32 in his first chapter of *Śrī Preyo-bhakti-rasārṇava*: "Just see, these residents of Vraja—men, women, or anyone else living there—all desire to attain *sakhya-rati* with Kṛṣṇa. . . . With this in mind, Śrīla Vyāsadeva has described the Vraja *vāsīs* as *bhāgyam*—most fortunate."

leads to the experience of unprecedented wonder (*camatkāra*) in his heart, as it had led to in Brahmā's heart. In *Prīti Sandarbha* 192, Jīva Goswāmī writes, "By the cleverness of expression [*bhaṅgī-viśeṣa*] in pointing out the unique glory of the Vraja *vāsīs*' fortune, Brahmā demonstrates the excellence [*utkarṣa*] of fraternal love [*bandhu-bhāva*]. For this reason, this verse is an instance of *rasollāsa*."

It is indeed wonderful that the *pūrṇaṁ brahma* has become a friend on equal terms with the young *gopas* of Vraja. This amazing situation is due to the power of their *prema*. Therefore, we bow before them with the confidence that, given their very generous and benevolent nature, they will grant us access to their inner circle in due course. May the whole world know that such a possibility exists—*aho bhāgyam!*

31

Sakhya-miśra Kānta-bhāva

Rādhā pines for preyo-bhakti

śrīdāma sudāma saṅge jakhana vane jāo raṅge
takhana āmi duyāre dāṅdāye
mane kari saṅge yāi guru-janāra bhaya pai
āṅkhi rahe tuyā pāne ceye

When you go playfully on your way to the *vana* with Śrīdāmā and Sudāmā, standing at my door I long to join you. Yet here I fear the *vrajera guru jana*, and thus my gaze alone goes with you.

— *Prārthanā* of Narottama dāsa Ṭhākura, song 57

Although the *mādhurya-rasa* of Vraja is the primary focus within the Gauḍīya *sampradāya*, the extent to which this *rasa* is influenced by *sakhya* is considerable. Within the primary *rasas* of Vraja, only *sakhya-rasa* is compatible with *mādhurya-rasa*; that is, only *sakhya-rasa* can serve to nourish *mādhurya-rasa*, while *vātsalya-rasa* causes it to contract, and *dāsya-rasa* is neutral in its ability to affect this *rasa*.

Together these two divine sentiments—*sakhya* and *mādhurya*—come from Goloka to the world of our experience, most prominently through the dispensation of Śrī Caitanya and Nityānanda Rāma, as windows of opportunity though which one can enter the *līlā* of Vraja. And in Vraja Kṛṣṇa's male and female friends are dearer to him than his own life. As such, meaningful longing for *mādhurya-rasa* also includes within itself the kind of deep appreciation if not affinity for *sakhya-rasa* that we find in Śrī Jīva Goswāmī—Vilāsa-mañjarī—who in his childhood worshiped, slept, and played with *mūrtis* of Kṛṣṇa and Balarāma.[1] How could it be otherwise? Thus, it will be useful to explore fraternal love's role in support of the *mādhurya* of Vraja and to underscore in particular Śrī Jīva Goswāmī's perspective on the extent to which *sakhya-rasa* influences the Vraja *gopīs'* love. To begin, let us first turn to Rūpa Goswāmī and his treatise on *mādhurya-rasa*, *Ujjvala-nīlamaṇi*.

It is clear from the outset of *Ujjvala-nīlamaṇi* that *sakhya-rasa* is an indispensable ingredient of Rādhā and Kṛṣṇa's romantic life. In his second chapter Rūpa Goswāmī explains that in a drama centered on paramour love, the hero (*upapati-nāyaka*) requires a number of confidants. He then proceeds to list the various types of male friends who help facilitate the love life of Kṛṣṇa and his *gopīs*. Here Śrī Rūpa draws from Viśvanātha Kavirāja's classical treatise on Indian aesthetics, *Sāhitya-darpaṇa* (3.39–40), wherein four types of male companions of the hero are mentioned: *ceṭa*, *viṭa*, *vidūṣaka*, and *pīṭhamarda*, to which Rūpa Goswāmī adds the *priya-narma-sakhā*.[2] Except for the *pīṭhamarda*, all of these companions are devoid of male egos when they are involved in assisting Kṛṣṇa and the *gopīs* in their love life. The *pīṭhamarda*, on the other hand, is never devoid of his male ego, but he is not directly involved in his friend's romanticism. However, neither is he unaware of it, and at times he may indirectly participate in it.

In Vraja, Śrīdāmā is the *pīṭhamarda*, the friend who has qualities equal to Kṛṣṇa's. The often-cited example of Śrīdāmā's involvement in Kṛṣṇa's romantic life is the instance in which he stands up for Kṛṣṇa's reputation when Candrāvalī's husband, Govardhana-malla, questions it.[3] Śrīdāmā's rebuke implies that while covering for Kṛṣṇa he is aware of his friend's love for Candrāvalī and supportive of it. Viśvanātha Cakravartī Ṭhākura comments that when Śrīdāmā says that he is a friend of Kṛṣṇa and threatens Govardhana-malla, it is implied that he knows Kṛṣṇa's inner feeling of constant love for Candrāvalī.

It is also clear from Śrī Rūpa's *Vidagdha-mādhava* drama that Śrīdāmā is aware of Kṛṣṇa's love for his sister, Rādhā, and with some embarrassment approves of it. Therein we find the following conversation.

> Kṛṣṇa (stopping in his tracks): O friend Śrīdāmā! Have you ever seen the remarkable Rādhā? (Embarrassed, Śrīdāmā lowers his head.)

1. *Bhakti-ratnākara* 1.720.
2. *Ujjvala-nīlamaṇi* 2.1. As mentioned in the introduction to this book, the *priya-narma-sakhā-bhāva* is one of the unique insights of Rūpa Goswāmī.
3. *Ujjvala-nīlamaṇi* 2.11.

> Subala (commenting on Kṛṣṇa's love-crazy question): Why do you ask if Śrīdāmā has ever seen her? Rādhā is his sister!
>
> Kṛṣṇa: Come. Let us go to the edge of this *kadamba* forest for a moment where I will absorb my heart, agitated from pursuing Rādhā, in playing the flute.[4]

The *ceṭa* is a servant friend who according to *Nāṭyaśāstra* is garrulous and fond of quarrel. Rūpa Goswāmī describes this companion further as skillful at accomplishing the tasks expected of him and bold enough to be counted on in acts that require secrecy. In Gokula, Kṛṣṇa's principal *ceṭas* are Bhaṅgura and Bhṛṅgāra.[5]

To help us understand the role of such *ceṭas*, Rūpa Goswāmī cites a verse in which a servant friend informs Kṛṣṇa of how he spoke to Rādhā earlier, informing her of something astonishing laden with hidden meaning: A so-called *mādhavī* vine in a nearby bower was flowering in the present autumn season rather than waiting for the spring! "Hearing me tell her this," Kṛṣṇa's companion told him, "Rādhā entered the bower." Thus, the two of them, Mādhava and his *ceṭa*, proceeded to the bower.[6]

The *Nāṭyaśāstra* describes the *viṭa* as a "rogue companion." Śrī Rūpa adds that he is cunning, persuasive, and skillful at disguising himself. He also has a reputation, well deserved or not, for being well versed in Tantric arts, employing herbs and *mantras* by which one can bring women under one's control. Kaḍāra and Bhāratībandhu are the two principal *viṭas* of Gokula.

Rūpa Goswāmī cites an example of a *viṭa* speaking to Śyāmā-sakhī, introducing himself to her as a "friend of her friend." Exercising his persuasiveness further, he tells her in the midst of her *māna*, "Since the women of Vraja know my reputation with regard to my skills, none of them dares to disobey me. O Śyāmā! O friend! It is not proper for you to give up Kṛṣṇa, who destroys the chastity of all the young women by playing the soft, sweet sound of his flute."[7]

The *vidūṣaka* is a jester, a glutton, and the most common friend of the hero. Rūpa Goswāmī mentions two *vidūṣakas* by name, Vasanta and

4. *Vidagdha-mādhava* 1.76.

5. Also prominent among *ceṭas* are the well-known Raktaka, Patraka, and others like them, who are not necessarily garrulous or fond of quarrel but are nonetheless servants of Kṛṣṇa whose *dāsya-bhāva* is mixed with *sakhya*. See *Rādhā-kṛṣṇa-gaṇoddeśa-dīpikā* 2.74 and *Bhakti-rasāmṛta-sindhu* 3.2.91.

6. *Ujjvala-nīlamaṇi* 2.4.

7. *Ujjvala-nīlamaṇi* 2.6.

Madhumaṅgala, and informs his readers that there are other *vidūṣakas* as well. Madhumaṅgala is famous throughout the Goswāmī *līlā* narratives. He has been introduced earlier, and we have explored his nature and seen the considerable extent of his participation in Kṛṣṇa's romantic life.

Of course, Madhumaṅgala is also a *narma-sakhā*. However, although he is intimately involved in Kṛṣṇa's romantic life and is a *kiṅkara* of Rādhikā, his *vidūṣaka* disposition often causes him to say and do things that interfere with Kṛṣṇa's efforts to woo Rādhā, things that sometimes also embarrass Śyāmasundara. Thus, unlike other *narma-sakhās*, he sometimes lacks tact in delicate dealings between the two lovers and at times also before elders. He is nonetheless a prominent source of *hāsya-rasa* within the *līlā* drama that in many respects is a romantic comedy. Thus, in his role as *vidūṣaka*, he is an indispensable *sakhā* in the love life of Rādhā and Kṛṣṇa.

The *priya-narma-sakhās* are many, and their role in Kṛṣṇa's romantic life is significant. As we have seen, they are *kiṅkaras* of their *yūtheśvarī gopīs*, and the *gopīs*' mere sight of them serves as an *uddīpana-vibhāva* for *mādhurya-rasa*. Furthermore, the influence of *mādhurya* on the fraternal love of the *narma-sakhās* is, as we have seen, "sympathetic" love—*anumodana*—which Jīva Goswāmī refers to as "*sakhī-bhāva*." And without the influence of *sakhī-bhāva*, be it in the form of Kṛṣṇa's male friends or Rādhā's girlfriends, the romantic life of Rādhā and Kṛṣṇa is incomplete. As we have seen, among the *narma-sakhās* Subala is the most prominent.

In *Ujjvala-nīlamaṇi* we find an instance in which Rūpa-mañjarī seeks to arouse love for Subala in the heart of one her girlfriends, a newly arrived *sādhana-siddha mañjarī*. In doing so, Rūpa-mañjarī utters the famous verse in which the eligibility of Subala-sakhā for participation in Rādhā and Kṛṣṇa's romantic life is praised and underscored as limitless—*kva śrīmān adhikāritāṁ na subalaḥ sevā-vidhau vindati.*[8]

Regarding Rādhā's female friends, her *sakhīs*, a large part of Rādhā's love for Kṛṣṇa is intertwined with the friendly love she shares with them. This is her *sakhī-praṇaya*. Kṛṣṇadāsa Kavirāja compares this *sakhī-praṇaya* with Rādhā's soothing sandalwood paste that is smeared over her body.[9] Such is the nearness and soothing influence of her female friends.

While Rādhā is the principal heroine of the Vraja *līlā* and the best example of *kānta-bhāva*, her friends embody different types of *sakhī-bhāva*,

8. *Ujjvala-nīlamaṇi* 2.14. The background to this verse is Viśvanātha Cakravartī Ṭhākura's insight. Also see chapter 5 of this book for elaboration on this verse.

9. *Caitanya-caritāmṛta* 2.8.170.

without which her *kānta-bhāva* cannot be fully experienced. While this *sakhī-bhāva* is not *sakhya-rasa* for Kṛṣṇa, it nonetheless serves as an example of fraternity within *mādhurya-rasa* mutually exchanged between Rādhā and her *sakhīs*.[10]

From the side of her *sakhīs*, their love for Rādhā—their friend—serves as a *sañcāri-bhāva* that nourishes their *sthāyi-bhāva* for Kṛṣṇa. However, in the most extreme form of *sakhī-bhāva*—*mañjarī-bhāva*—the *mañjarīs'* platonic love for Kṛṣṇa serves in reverse as a *sañcāri-bhāva* nourishing their maidservant type of fraternal love for Rādhā![11] Here Rādhā becomes the primary object of the *mañjarīs'* love, and as such they love her slightly more than they love Kṛṣṇa. These *sakhī mañjarīs* see both Rādhā and Kṛṣṇa as the combined object of their love (their *sthāyi-bhāva*), and as a result of their maidservant type of fraternal love for Rādhā and their platonic love for Kṛṣṇa, both of whom they seek to unite, they also vicariously experience the height of the divine couple's romantic love for one another (its *sambhoga*). In other words, the *mañjarīs' sakhī-bhāva* with all of its nuance that underscores fraternal love includes within its scope all that one can experience in *kānta-bhāva*, albeit vicariously.[12] And for this reason, within the Gauḍīya *sampradāya* it is considered preferable to *kānta-bhāva*. To be clear, here the idea is that by serving Rādhā as one's maidservant/girlfriend one can come as close as one can to the fullness of her romantic experience, which exceeds that of any other heroine. Better to be Rādhā's maidservant than to be her competitor in *kānta-bhāva*. The math is simple, while the way in which it plays itself out is complicated. And with regard

10. Here *kānta-bhāva* refers to the mood of Rādhā and other heroines who exemplify *sambhogecchā-mayī mādhurya-rasa*. In this form of *mādhurya-rasa*, Kṛṣṇa's *rāgātmikā* heroines directly seek to personally fulfill Kṛṣṇa's desire for romantic intimacy. Here *sakhī-bhāva* refers to the different varieties of *tad-tad-bhāvecchātmika mādhurya-rasa*, also referred to as *tad-anumodana*, or sympathetic love for the heroine, by which the *sakhī* experiences the romantic life of Kṛṣṇa and his heroine vicariously. See *Bhakti-rasāmṛta-sindhu* 1.2.297–298.

11. In his *Vilāpa-kusumāñjali* 16, Raghunātha dāsa Goswāmī famously refers to the love of Rādhā's *sakhīs* for her as "*sakhya*," while referring to his own *mañjarī-bhāva* aspiration as a kind of servitude. Therein he bows to the friendship—*sakhyāya*—of Rādhā's *sakhīs*. But although Rādhā's *mañjarīs* are maidservants, they are also nonetheless her *sakhīs*, or friends—maidservant friends. The fact that their servitude is imbued with friendship is clear throughout the Goswāmīs' *līlā-granthas*.

12. However, this is not the case with the *priya-narma-sakhās' sakhī-bhāva*, because as pointed out in chapter 5, their sympathetic love arises in the context of their *sakhya-rasa* and is thus partial (*leśa*) rather than direct (*sākṣād*), as in the case of the *mañjarīs* who are situated in *mādhurya-rasa*.

to this dynamic, surprisingly we find that a form of fraternal love plays a prominent role.

Turning to *kānta-bhāva* itself, let us briefly consider its *praṇaya*. In chapter 4, we learned that *praṇaya* is central to *sakhya-rasa*. Indeed, *praṇaya* literally means "intimate friendship." Therein we also learned that *praṇaya*'s *taṭastha-lakṣaṇa* consists of the absence of any sense of reverence between friends, the presence of which would create a distance between them. This marginal characteristic of *praṇaya* implies a deep sense of intimacy—*viśrambha*—with the object of one's love, and this *viśrambha* of *praṇaya* is the *pradhāna* of *sakhya-rasa*, its primary feature. In his discourse on *mādhurya-rasa*, Rūpa Goswāmī also informs us that wise persons identify *praṇaya*'s *svarūpa-lakṣaṇa* as "*viśrambha*"—*svarūpaṁ praṇayasyāsya viśrambhaḥ kathito budhaiḥ*.[13]

While *praṇaya* is central to *sakhya-rasa*, it also plays a significant role in the *kānta-bhāva* of *mādhurya-rasa*, where its manyfold complexities and varieties arise. In contrast, *praṇaya* is absent in *dāsya-* and *vātsalya-rasas*, in which a sense of equality between love and its object is lacking.

Thus, we find the very primary feature of *sakhya-rasa*—*viśrambha/praṇaya*—present and prominently manifest within the *kānta-bhāva* of Vraja.[14] Therein this *praṇaya* expresses itself in a manner relative to *mādhurya-rasa*, but the common ground that *praṇaya* shares with *sakhya-* and *mādhurya-rasas* is no doubt something that Jīva Goswāmīpāda pondered along with the other influences of fraternal love impacting *mādhurya-rasa* that we have considered above. He pondered them and reached an astonishing conclusion, to which we shall now turn.

In his *Prīti Sandarbha* 84, Jīva Goswāmī explains the twofold effect of *prīti*: *Prīti* creates impressions in the devotee's heart for a particular *rasa*, and then as a result of these impressions, one's spiritual identity arises. He then proceeds to list the hierarchy of different *rasas*—*śānta*, *dāsya*, *vātsalya*, *sakhya*, and *mādhurya* in this order—placing *sakhya* above *vātsalya*, in contrast to the hierarchy given by Rūpa Goswāmī. Śrī Jīva then proceeds to give an overview of these different expressions of divine love.

After describing the different *rasas* in brief, Śrī Jīva also mentions that in some devotees we find a combination of *rasas*. Readers will recall that Rūpa Goswāmī refers to such combinations as "*saṅkula-bhāva*." Although Jīva

13. *Ujjvala-nīlamaṇi* 14.110. Here, by the word "*svarūpa*" Rūpa Goswāmī implies that *praṇaya* is a condition of friendship that arises out of *viśrambha*.

14. There is a subtle distinction between *viśrambha* and *praṇaya*. Thus, while *viśrambha* is present in *vātsalya*, *praṇaya* is not.

Goswāmī does not invoke this term, he cites most of the same examples that Śrī Rūpa cites: Uddhava, Yudhiṣṭhira, Bhīma, Arjuna, Balarāma, and so on.

As we have seen earlier, all of Rūpa Goswāmī's examples involve various combinations of *dāsya*, *vātsalya*, and *sakhya*, omitting combinations that would include *mādhurya*. From this, one is led to believe that *saṅkula-bhāva* does not include other *rasas* combined with *mādhurya-rasa*. However, while not citing any such examples, Śrī Rūpa does not explicitly rule out the possibility that some devotees may be constituted of a mixture of *mādhurya* and other *rasas*, while Jīva Goswāmī has affirmed this possibility, citing the Vraja *gopīs* as examples of *mādhurya* mixed with *sakhya* (*sakhya-miśra*) and the queens of Dvārakā as examples of *mādhurya* mixed with *dāsya* (*dāsya-miśra*).[15] To be clear, in Jīva Goswāmī's opinion the *kānta-bhāva* of Vraja, its *sthāyi-bhāva*, is constituted of a mixture (*miśra*) of *mādhurya* and *sakhya*, in which *mādhurya* predominates.[16]

It is difficult to argue against Vilāsa-mañjarī, who in her childhood *sādhaka-deha* as Jīva Goswāmī worshiped Kṛṣṇa and Balarāma. Childhood impressions can last a long time. But fortunately we do not have to argue here. There is room for more than one spiritually well-reasoned perspective on this topic. And while Jīva Goswāmī may appear alone in his opinion, that may not necessarily be the case. The extent to which his opinion may differ from those of others of his stature is another discussion. In *Prīti Sandarbha*, Jīva simply states his opinion, offering no further explanation. Not being one to shy away from supporting arguments, here it appears that he does not consider his opinion controversial. However, while he himself has said no more, the influence of *sakhya-rasa* on Vraja's *mādhurya-rasa* love cited above may serve as support for his perspective.

In concluding, let us turn to Śukadeva's famous *Bhāgavata* verse central to Brahmā's *stuti* (ŚB 10.14.32). Therein he has characterized Vraja as the very abode of friendship (*maitrī*) and thus the great fortune of those who reside therein, where the Para-brahman has become everyone's eternal friend. Of course, here we must take the idea that everyone in Vraja has a friendly relationship with Kṛṣṇa in a broad sense, for obviously not everyone

15. Here Jīva Goswāmī uses *miśra* (mixed) rather than *saṅkula* (combined).

16. Jīva Goswāmī concludes that when the combined *rasas* in *saṅkula-bhāva* are not compatible with one another, the devotees experience each of the sentiments at different times. See *Bhakti-rasāmṛta-sindhu* 4.8.81. He does not comment on how such *saṅkula-bhāva* plays out in cases where the *rasas* combined in a devotee are compatible with one another, but obviously the *rasa* by which one is defined (in this case *mādhurya*) would be nourished by a second favorable *rasa* (in this case *sakhya*).

in Vraja is defined even in part by the *sthāyi-bhāva* of *sakhya-rati.* But the Vraja *gopīs* are childhood friends of Kṛṣṇa and his male friends, girls who in their adolescence have fallen in love with Madana Gopāla. Even a cursory reading of any of the Goswāmīs' *līlā* narratives bears this vision out. But is there any direct evidence of the *gopīs*' tasting *sakhya-rasa* similar, for example, to the evidence cited to demonstrate that other devotees are emotionally constituted of more than one *rasa*?

To answer the question posed, let us turn to Raghunātha dāsa Goswāmī's *Vraja-vilāsa-stava* 93:

> *mallīkṛtya nijāḥ sakhīḥ priyatamā garveṇa sambhāvitā*
> *mallībhūya mad-īśvarī rasa-mayī mallatvam utkaṇṭhayā*
> *yasmin samyag-upeyūṣā baka-bhidā rādhā niyuddhaṁ mudā*
> *kurvāṇā madanasya toṣam atanod bhāṇḍīrakaṁ taṁ bhaje*
>
> I worship Bhāṇḍīravana, where *rasa-mayī* Rādhā, my *īśvarī*, the beloved of Hari, dressed herself as a wrestler along with her *sakhīs*, as did Hari. Proud and eager to play, she battled with Bakāri, resulting in *mādana-toṣaṇī.*

On a typical day in Bhāṇḍīravana, Rāma and Kṛṣṇa wrestle with their friends, competing with one another in the shade of the great banyan tree, after which this forest is named. They also stick fight, arm wrestle, and so on in the midst of the majesty of Bhāṇḍīra, the most magnanimous of all the wish-fulfilling trees of Vraja. Its base is surrounded by a golden platform, and in this setting, as referenced in the *Gautamīya Tantra* 10.153, we find a *yogapīṭha*, or meeting shrine for *sakhya-rasa.*

However, Rādhikā also sometimes meets with Kṛṣṇa under the Bhāṇḍīra, and on more than one occasion she does so in the dress of Subala.[17] Here Raghunātha dāsa Goswāmī references a *līlā* wherein Kṛṣṇa is alone at the base of Bhāṇḍīra. Gopāla plays his flute and in doing so signals his whereabouts, and Rādhā and her *sakhīs* respond by seeking him out. Arriving at the meeting place beneath the banyan, Rādhā asks Kṛṣṇa what he does here along with his friends, in meetings she is not privy to but eager to learn about. Kṛṣṇa then tells her tales of his wrestling prowess, with which no one can compare. He is charming even as he boasts, for it is known to Rādhā that in such matches he often loses to her elder brother, who relates such

17. This is the insight of Ananta dāsa Paṇḍita, cited in his commentary on *Vraja-vilāsa-stava* 93.

conquest with great *sakhya-rasa* pride. Charmed by Kṛṣṇa's descriptions of his *sakhya-rasa līlās*, Rādhā in the spirt of a *sakhā* then challenges him to a wrestling match.

Wrestling among friends is common. In Śrī Rūpa's vocabulary wrestling is an expression of *yuddha-vīra*, a secondary or *gauṇa-rasa*. This *rasa* is a dear friend of *sakhya-rasa*, but Rūpa Goswāmī informs us that there are different opinions as to whether or not *yuddha-vīra* is also compatible with *mādhurya-rasa*.[18] Is Rādhā about to taste *yuddha-vīra-rasa* as a compatible *rasa* with her *mādhurya*, or is she in the midst of tasting *sakhya-rasa*, as its friend *yuddha-vīra-rasa* serves as an *aṅga-rasa* to nourish that fraternal love? Given the ambiguity voiced by Rūpa Goswāmī concerning the influence of *yuddha-vīra* on *mādhurya-rasa*, it is safer to side with the latter in this instance. And this is further supported below.

In Dāsa Goswāmī's verse, Kṛṣṇa is referred to as Bakabhida. This is an epithet that takes us to Kṛṣṇa's *śeṣa-kumāra-līlā* in which he slayed and liberated Bakāsura. In my translation of this verse above, I have referred to Kṛṣṇa with a synonym, as Bakāri, the enemy of Bakāsura. The liberation of Bakāsura marks the first time in his *prakaṭa-līlā* that Kṛṣṇa in no uncertain terms personally slayed and liberated a great menace by exhibiting the kind of heroic prowess that is an *uddīpana* for *sakhya-rasa*.

Previously in Gokula Mahāvana, Kṛṣṇa liberated villains in ways that concealed that he made a concerted effort to slay them. For example, he merely sucked the breast of Pūtanā and weighed down Tṛṇāvarta. And so their demise could more readily be attributed to other factors. Then after the Vraja *vāsīs* crossed the Yamunā and relocated in Vṛndāvana, Rāma and Kṛṣṇa began herding calves with their friends. Shortly thereafter the villain Vatsāsura appeared amongst them in the form of a calf. And although Kṛṣṇa understood his intentions and brought about his demise and deliverance, he did so in a manner such that it was not entirely clear to his comrades that he was exhibiting heroic prowess. He simply grabbed Vatsāsura's tail as he stroked the so-called calf and then whirled around. But then, on the same day when he met with the evil intentions of Baka, he clearly exhibited the kind of heroic prowess that would come to characterize the days ahead in calf- and cowherding *līlās* with his friends.

18. *Bhakti-rasāmṛta-sindhu* 4.8.7. Jīva Goswāmī states that Rūpa Goswāmī believes *yuddha-vīra* is compatible with *mādhurya-rasa*. Śrī Jīva also acknowledges that others disagree. However, other than Raghunātha dāsa Goswāmī's verse under discussion, we find no examples of the *gopīs*' experiencing *yuddha-vīra-rasa*. And Kavi Karṇapūra is among those who do not think that *yuddha-vīra-rasa* is compatible with *mādhurya-rasa*.

By invoking the epithet Bakabidha, Dāsa Goswāmī transports his readers into *sakhya-rasa*. However, he has also invoked the epithet Madana, a clear reference to the erotic. Madana refers to Kāmadeva—Cupid—and to Kṛṣṇa as the transcendental cupid, in relation to whom the erotic experience of his *gopīs* is entirely selfless and free from mundane lust.

In this *līlā*, as Rādhā challenges Kṛṣṇa to a wrestling match, he replies by telling her that to wrestle one needs to dress for the occasion. Thus, Rādhā does so along with her friends, all of whom Kṛṣṇa tells her he can easily defeat. However, during the match Kṛṣṇa is defeated by Rādhā's beauty, even as the match itself turns out to be a tie. Thus, Rādhā in the dress of a wrestler gave erotic pleasure to Madana—*madanasya toṣam*.

From the two epithets invoked in this verse, the reader with feeling for the subject will detect two primary *rasas*, *sakhya* and *mādhurya*, and one secondary rasa, *yuddha-vīra*, which is clearly compatible with *sakhya-rasa*. Given the setting beneath the great Bhāṇḍīra and given Rādhā's inquiry into the nature of Kṛṣṇa's *sakhya-rasa līlās* there, she is expressing a desire to taste such *līlās* herself. And as she does, *sakhya* gradually gives way to *mādhurya*, as Kṛṣṇa is stunned by her beauty in wrestling attire and cannot defeat her. *Jaya* Radhe! May she and her friends be praised everywhere for their love and friendship.

Index

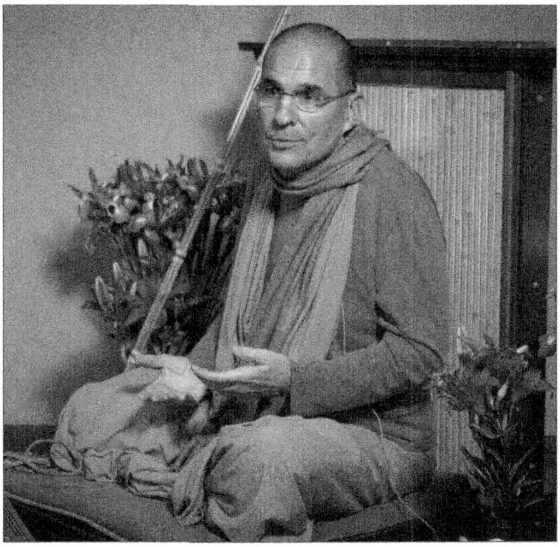

About the Author

Swāmī B. V. Tripurāri, a respected authority on devotional Vedānta, is widely recognized for his eloquence as a public speaker and writer. An ordained monk in the Caitanya Vaiṣṇava tradition for more than half a century, he distinguished himself under the guidance of his revered *guru*, the world-renowned Śrīla A. C. Bhaktivedanta Swami Prabhupāda, who considered Swāmījī to be a pillar of his mission and empowered with the *śakti* required for the wide dissemination of Gauḍīya Vaiṣṇava literature—*grantha prasāra avatāraḥ*.

Swāmījī also received further guidance and blessings from Śrīla Bhakti Rakṣaka Śrīdhara Deva Goswāmī, who told him, "You know everything. Your Guru Mahārāja has given you everything. Go and start a mission. I will be in the background assisting as needed."

Swāmī B. V. Tripurāri has embraced the instructions and ideals of his *gurus* as the cornerstone of his life. As a spiritual mentor, he has compassionately shared his wisdom and insights for over five decades. He is renowned for his deep immersion in the core Gauḍīya texts, coupled with his remarkable broadmindedness and adaptability to the changing world. He offers personal guidance at weekly *darśanas* and spiritual retreats throughout the year.

Printed in Great Britain
by Amazon

45208581R00300